Theatre Craft

John Caird is an Honorary Associate Director of the Royal Shakespeare Company, Principal Guest Director of the Royal Dramatic Theatre, Stockholm and a freelance theatre, opera and musical theatre director and librettist working regularly at the National Theatre in London, in the West End, on Broadway and all around the world.

As well as directing numerous productions of classic plays from Shakespeare and Jonson to Gorky, Strindberg and Brecht, he has directed the world premières of many new plays, operas and musicals. He has also directed, co-directed and adapted novels for the theatre and musical theatre, including renowned productions of *Les Misérables*, *Nicholas Nickleby*, *Hamlet*, *Candide* and *Peter Pan*.

THEATRE CRAFT

A Director's Practical Companion
from A *to* Z

JOHN CAIRD

faber and faber

Faber and Faber, Inc.
An affiliate of Farrar, Straus and Giroux
18 West 18th Street, New York 10011

Printed in the United States of America
Originally published in 2010 by Faber and Faber Limited, Great Britain
Published in the United States by Faber and Faber, Inc.
First American edition, 2010

Library of Congress Control Number: 2010283390
ISBN: 978-0-571-23737-1

www.fsgbooks.com

10 9 8 7 6 5 4 3 2

For young directors everywhere

Foreword

This book is addressed to you, the director, whatever your age or level of experience. You may be an aspiring director. You think, or know, or think you know that directing is the life for you, but you're not sure quite what it is you're aspiring to. You may be a beginner director, someone who has directed a play or two as a student or an amateur, and developed a taste for the job. You want to go further, but you don't know how to go about it. You may be an Assistant Director, already in the profession but apprenticed to an experienced director, spending your days in rehearsal watching your principal at work and itching to get your hands on a play of your own.

You may be an experienced director in your own right but suffering from the commonest of occupational complaints – artistic loneliness. All other theatre professionals – actors, designers, Stage Managers, administrators – work with a variety of directors. Only directors themselves are isolated, never getting a glimpse of one another's working process and only able to judge the work of others by the finished product. We who should know most about our peers and their work are often in the greatest ignorance. For you this book may provide a few companionable moments.

You may be a director or 'producer' of opera, conversant with the disciplines of imagining and staging a production in the opera house but nervous when faced with casting a play and working with actors and the spoken word.

You may not be a director at all. If this book proves useful to directors, it should also be useful to those who work with directors, as almost everyone else in the theatre is obliged to do.

Even if you have never worked in the theatre or aspired to do so, you may still be intrigued by the craft of theatre, how plays work, how they are mounted, how actors are cast and rehearsed, how directors and designers have imagined the productions you delight in attending.

I have tried to write a practical and instructive companion, so I have avoided the use of anecdotal material concerning my own career or anyone else's, only occasionally crediting a theory, innovation or idea where not to do so would seem ungrateful. The best companions in life are not generally those who agree with everything we do and say. If this work contains ideas with which you cannot concur, I hope it will provoke positive ideas of your own.

Directing is such a subjective craft and the methods of directors are so particularly formed by their subjective experience that a brief summary of my life in the theatre may help readers to put my thoughts into some sort of context.

I started acting at school. I was at an all-boys school so I acted male and female roles, most notably Desdemona in *Othello*, a performance that was happily not filmed for posterity. My parents took me and my siblings to the theatre, to opera, to concerts, as often as they could afford, but I had my most formative early experiences watching student performances of Shakespeare in Oxford college gardens. Subsequent school trips to Stratford to see Shakespeare 'done properly' sealed the deal. I was hooked for life.

I trained as an actor at the Bristol Old Vic Theatre School under the inspirational leadership of the late Nat Brenner, who put up with my impertinence and incompetence with the best of graces, though it must have been apparent to him, as to his colleagues, that my talents as an actor were limited to say the least. After a blessedly short career as an actor – blessedly for audiences and fellow actors alike – I worked for two or three years in a number of different theatre jobs: crewman, fly-man, sound technician, prop-master and in various stage managerial positions. These experiences supplied me with an all-round education in the allied crafts of theatre for which I have never ceased to be grateful. More importantly, they taught me never to take the work of anyone in the theatre for granted, whatever their function or level of experience.

From these toeholds on the cliff-face of theatre I applied for and didn't get various bursaries and grants. So instead I started to direct my own small lunchtime and late night shows using the actors I had got to know in my other capacities. I got my first proper directing job at Contact Theatre in Manchester, where I directed plays and wrote and directed projects for Theatre in Education programmes. After that I directed freelance for a year or two in theatres, colleges and drama schools in Britain and abroad before going to the Royal Shakespeare Company as an Assistant Director.

In a directorial career that spans thirty-five years and counting, I have spent twenty of them in or closely allied to permanent companies of one sort or another – the RSC, the National Theatre of Great Britain and the Royal Dramatic Theatre in Stockholm most notable amongst them. With these companies and others I have directed plays by Shakespeare, Jonson, Middleton, Farquhar, Gay, Bulwer-Lytton, Pinero, Shaw, Barrie, Strindberg, Chekhov, Gorky, Brecht, Anouilh and Beckett.

I have also had the great pleasure of directing the first productions of new plays by a wide variety of living authors whose companionship in the rehearsal room has provided me with some of my happiest insights.

In the company of many an august collaborator, I have adapted novels by Voltaire, Dickens, Hugo, Brontë, Teru Miyamoto and Jean Webster for the theatre or musical theatre.

In opera I have directed Verdi, Mozart and Puccini and in musical theatre I have co-written, adapted, directed or co-directed the premières of works by Lloyd-Webber, Boublil and Schönberg, Gordon, Schwartz and Previn.

In a career perhaps more remarkable for its variety, or its catholicity, than any other virtues it may have possessed, I have written and directed the very smallest shows and the very largest, everything from the absolute intimacy of a single actor surrounded by a string quartet to the preposterous grandiosity of a spectacular Las Vegas magic show. My productions have been performed in theatres of every possible configuration, from the smallest in-the-round chambers to vast arenas, in both subsidised and commercial theatres, in schools, colleges, sports centres, prisons and in dozens of different languages and countries. They have had long runs and short, been critically acclaimed and reviled – often at one and the same time – made money and lost money, been revived and revised with old casts and new, reproduced on radio and television, been fondly remembered, barely recalled or utterly forgotten.

Most people who work in the theatre do so because they love it. And they continue to love what they do without the spurs either of celebrity or financial reward. I learnt this simple fact about the theatre and its inhabitants before I had even considered becoming a director. If there is any true learning in this book it has been gained from the work I have done with a dearly beloved and ever-increasing band of actors, singers, authors, directors, designers, choreographers, stage management and administrators – my collaborators in half a lifetime of creative endeavour.

If I have shamefully stolen the ideas of any of these friends, I make no apology for it. That is what theatre is like. It is a community of shared experience. Whatever I know, I am quite happy for others to use or reject as they see fit. And if my dear colleagues see their original, or even not-so-original, thoughts reproduced here, they know my gratitude is implicit in the repetition.

Finally, I should perhaps say a few words about my terms of reference, geographical, social and literary.

For readers in America and Canada, I am aware that there are significantly different terms of professional reference on your side of the Atlantic just as there are in other parts of the English-speaking world, and I have done as much as I can to include mention of them.

Directors, playwrights, actors and administrators come in all sizes, shapes and ages and in both genders, but consistently describing their contributions in terms of 'he and she', or 'hers and his', creates a wearisome style of writing, so I have taken the conventional step of using masculine pronouns when referring to both male and female practitioners.

Throughout the book I refer to a wide variety of plays, plots and characters, and in doing so I have concentrated heavily on the works of Shakespeare with occasional mention of, amongst others, Ibsen, Chekhov, Jonson, Shaw and the odd Greek. This is not because of a narrowness or invidiousness of interest, but because those works represent the commonest ground for directors working in text-based theatre and therefore the most reliable and long-lasting exemplars. In any event, the plays of Shakespeare are not a bad touchstone for plays generally, ancient and modern, and if you haven't read them by now you should probably get started.

Acknowledgements

This book has been a long time in the making and I owe a great debt of gratitude to Dinah Wood at Faber and Faber for keeping my nose to the grindstone. Her patience, encouragement, and sweet-natured bullying have inspired me to forge ahead in the teeth of a very busy production schedule. To her and to all at the house of Faber, many thanks.

Thanks too to Max Webster for his wise and timely notes on the unfinished manuscript, to Paul Hecht for setting me right on American usage and terminology and to the learned Neil Titman for his help with the structural edit. They have all given me invaluable support and advice.

Above all, thanks to my wife Maoko for the space and the grace to let me work in peace, and to my dear children who have surrounded me with their necessary chaos and kept my playing fresh along with their own.

A

Abstraction

Abstraction, or the freedom from a representational depiction of reality, is easy enough to achieve in the visual arts but virtually impossible in the theatre. The minute you have a human figure in the shape of an actor walking onto the stage, that figure brings with it a representational style. The moment a series of words is spoken, however sensible or nonsensical, a meaning is evoked that represents a recognisably human experience to an audience. Abstract movement or abstracted ideas may be fundamental to the work of some modern directors, but unless the human figures conveying those abstractions are disguised beyond recognition, there will always be a realistic element in their appearance.

If pure abstraction is unachievable in the theatre, elements of the abstract are always present, in **theatrical conventions** of one sort or another and in the necessary imaginative flights an audience makes in order to complete the work of the author, director, actor or designer.

ABSTRACT DESIGN

Abstraction is commonly used in the design of sets, lighting and sound, but the word 'abstract' is rarely used in definition. More commonly used terms are 'conceptual', 'expressionistic' or 'impressionistic', all vague enough to mean what the user wishes them to mean, but all conveying the idea of an abstraction away from representation.

In practice, abstract design is usually mixed with some degree of **naturalism**. For instance, a **set design** may eschew naturalism in terms of its architecture but still provide a suitable environment for the placing of tables and chairs. A **lighting design** may concentrate on the abstract mood of a play while still making references to the time of day or night or to the weather, or a **sound design** may create a non-naturalistic soundscape that uses naturalistic sounds as a set of basic ingredients.

There are designers who aspire to pure abstraction in their work. They are the inheritors of the abstract movement in fine art and sometimes have such a pure aesthetic that they are genuinely offended by any attempt to pull their work towards representation or naturalism of any sort. If you work with such artists, you must be ready to share their aesthetic viewpoint. Productions where the director and actors are trying to work naturalistically on an abstract set, or where the set design is naturalistic and the sound or lighting design abstract, will always struggle for coherence. Before you agree to a form of abstract design in any department, be sure the actors can work in a sufficiently abstract style to match their surroundings.

Absurdism

Absurdism is the belief that the existence of humanity is inherently meaningless and that the actions of anyone striving against the truth of this proposition are therefore absurd.

THEATRE OF THE ABSURD

The Theatre of the Absurd was never a movement but rather a loose categorisation on philosophical and aesthetic grounds of a group of playwrights, mostly French, or writing in French, immediately after World War II. For Camus, who coined the term *absurdisme*, and for Beckett, Ionesco, Adamov and all their imitators, drama of the absurd seemed the only rational response to the horrifying and apparently meaningless events of the war and the global chaos that came after it.

In his authoritative book on the subject, Martin Esslin defines the Theatre of the Absurd as striving 'to express its sense of the senselessness of the human condition and the inadequacy of the rational approach by the open abandonment of rational devices and discursive thought'. Thus absurdist playwrights tend to eschew any sort of coherent story or consistent character motivation and they refuse to allow any didactic or moral conclusions to be drawn from their work. Instead they invite the spectator to escape for a brief time from the illusion of a structured society to enjoy a glimpse of the world as it truly exists – amoral, pointless and cruelly, laughably absurd.

As the years have gone by since these plays were written, the absurdist label has itself become increasingly meaningless, and we judge them more now on their inherent value as pieces of drama or literature. The plays of Beckett are great works of poetic drama whether absurd or not, and plays written centuries before the brief flourishing of the Theatre of the Absurd now seem to be the natural progenitors of it. If *Endgame* is an absurdist play, then so is *King Lear*.

Accent

The word 'accent' has two common, and confusing, usages in the theatre.

It is used as a synonym for **dialect**, the idiosyncratic pronunciation or idiomatic usage that different people use in speaking the English language, or indeed any language. Thus you will hear the layman refer to an actor having a poor American accent, or an actor 'putting on' an excellent Cockney accent, where most professional theatre people would use the word 'dialect'.

It is also used, incorrectly, as a synonym for **stress**, as in 'She's putting the accent on the wrong word', or 'He's accenting the right words, but he's still not making any sense'.

While accent and dialect have become more or less interchangeable terms, accent and stress are two different things and the distinction between them is useful. Accent denotes the way that a word is inflected in common parlance. Thus the words 'happy', 'father' and 'letter' are all accented on the first syllable, the words 'forget', 'abstain' and 'persuade' on the second. All English words of more than one syllable have an accent – or two or even more in longer words – and with the exception of a few words like 'controversy' or 'kilometre' there is usually only one correct way of accenting them. So it is with all inflected languages.

Accent

Stress, on the other hand, is the emphasis given to a word within a line of text. Thus in the prose line 'There was no possibility of taking a walk that day', the stressed words are 'possibility' and 'walk'. The word 'taking', pronounced with an accent on its first syllable, is unstressed.

The correct stress of a line is generally indicated by the author's intended meaning, especially in a poetic text, but even then it can be a matter of interpretation, whereas the accenting of a word is either correct or not.

In poetic texts you do get collisions between stress and accent, where the rules of prosody strongly suggest a stress that is at odds with the way a word is accented in common idiom. Thus in Act II Scene 7 of *As You Like It*, Duke Senior says to Orlando:

> *If that you were the good Sir Rowland's son,*
> *As you have whispered faithfully you were,*
> *And as mine eye doth his effigies witness*
> *Most truly limned and living in your face . . .*

In the third line the iambic **metre** demands that the word 'effigies' be accented on the second syllable, making its meaning incomprehensible to a modern audience. But if the actor accents the word on the first syllable, as modern idiom would prompt him to do, the line becomes metrically halting. Some directors 'fix' the line in performance by changing it to 'And as mine eye his effigies do witness', making the line both speakable and comprehensible. Though some regard altering Shakespeare in any way as heretical, directors of his plays, and other old texts, may perhaps be forgiven if they shift some unimportant words about in order to help a modern audience understand the author's intended meaning.

Accompaniment and Accompanists

In **opera** and **musical theatre,** the accompaniment is the musical support for the singers' voices. As written by the best composers, it can have a strong communicative power. Singers must learn to treat their accompaniments as reservoirs of feeling and meaning. The character's conscious thoughts are in the sung words, but the subconscious spirit of the character is in the accompaniment – the inner life that lies under the words, or too deep for the words to express.

The accompanist is the musician, usually a keyboard player, who accompanies the singers in musical theatre rehearsals and auditions, in opera known as the **répétiteur.** His musicianship should include a total ease with sight-reading, an ability to transpose music from one key into another at sight, an ability to dictate and then stick to a strict tempo, and a familiarity with all the common forms of musical composition, ancient and modern, classical and popular. The best accompanists are adaptable and sympathetic musicians with a natural talent for teaching and with more of an interest in the gifts of others than with the importance of their own expressiveness.

A useful technique in rehearsal is to spend just a few minutes requiring the singers to listen to the accompaniment unadorned by the melody. A good accompanist can communicate great feeling in the carpet of sound underlying the melody, and by listening to the accompaniment for its own sake singers are often surprised to find how much of a story it can tell. The best singers ride on their accompaniments with a natural ease and familiarity – creating an intimate duet of singer and sound. Inexperienced singers wrestle with their accompaniments and are thrown by them in the process.

In small musical theatre or opera companies the conductor or **Musical Director** may have to double as accompanist, but this should be avoided if possible. Singers need to practise following the conductor's beat, and they can't do that if his hands are always on the keyboard.

Nowhere are the skills of a good accompanist more in evidence than in a well-run audition room. An audition pianist must be able to take elaborate and idiosyncratic instructions from the most demanding of divas and play with absolute confidence from sheet music that is often faintly photocopied, boldly scrawled upon or ragged with overuse.

Accompanists often double as Assistant Conductors or Assistant Musical Directors, and in poorer companies the accompanist may well be the conductor or the Musical Director or both. In any event, a good accompanist should be able to lead a company of singers in their daily warm-up routines and basic vocal rehearsals.

Acoustics

The acoustics of a theatre are its auditory characteristics. These are defined by its interior architecture, the relationship between its stage and its auditorium, and the extent to which its empty spaces and the surfaces confining them are receptive to the actor's or singer's voice.

A good acoustic is one that carries the spoken or sung word from the stage to every part of the auditorium with resonance, clarity and uniformity.

A bad acoustic deadens the actor's voice with lack of resonance, resonates it too much producing an echo or boom effect, or produces an uneven variety of sound in different parts of the auditorium with 'deaf spots' or auditory black holes in some places and mini echo-chambers in others.

To make matters complicated, 'good' and 'bad' can be both relative and subjective judgements, depending on the preference of the performer, and largely because of this the language used to describe the acoustic qualities of a theatre is often imprecise and contradictory. Actors and directors stand on stages all over the world and clap their hands or declaim a few lines to test the acoustic and then pronounce it 'dead' or 'live', 'dull' or 'bright', 'dry' or 'wet', 'woofy', 'bouncy', 'ping-y', 'boomy', 'echo-y' and so on. The phrases used can become so colourful that you might be at a wine-tasting, as in 'a grateful acoustic with just a little too much brightness', or 'generous through the stalls but rather cavernous in the mezzanine'.

Perhaps the lack of a universal language of acoustics merely underlines what a complex science it is, and one that you have to be a real expert to understand. But you shouldn't let that deter you from learning the basic rules and how to apply them to the theatres in which you work, however you describe your judgements and preferences.

Theatres with perfect acoustics are rare indeed, if they exist at all, and most theatres have problems of one sort or another. The romantic notion that the Greeks got it right and all we need to do is copy their perfect theatres to solve all our problems is belied by the experience of actually sitting in one of them and straining to hear the actors as they bellow their lines across the often vast spaces on which they are built. Likewise with the Elizabethan theatres: the Globe, the Rose and the Swan no doubt had their acoustical problems together with their dissatisfied actors and audiences, and modern **replicas** have done nothing to persuade us otherwise. But it took the twentieth century to provide the world with the very worst theatre acoustics imaginable, largely owing to their architects' slavish preference for what must be the least sympathetic acoustical material ever invented – concrete. The most egregiously bad examples are found in the vast concrete culture palaces built all over the world in the 1960s, 70s and 80s.

Since then, the science of acoustics has come a long way and no new theatre is now designed without the advice of a qualified team of acousticians, but even the most expert advice can still prove to have been inadequate once the buildings are completed, so the acousticians work on, making their fine adjustments to the absorbent, resonant or reflective surfaces on the stage and in the auditorium.

Most theatre people believe that the most suitable acoustical material for the human voice is wood, and it is used in the construction of most of the best theatres. Wood has the capacity to absorb and reflect sound at the same time as reverberating with it and is deeply sympathetic to the harmonic complexity of the human voice. Many musical instruments work on the same principle. But some brick and plaster theatres are extraordinarily good acoustically, and very occasionally you will find yourself in a concrete theatre that isn't an absolute killer of the human voice.

Acoustics

Directors, of course, often have little choice where their productions are to be mounted, so whatever your preferences, you will at some point have to cope with the worst that the architects can throw at you. But there is still much you can do to alleviate acoustical problems wherever you meet them. Start by learning to spot them.

COMMON CAUSES OF BAD ACOUSTICS

1 Overlarge theatres

There is a limit to the range of the human voice. Seats furthest away from the stage in a large theatre will often be at the very edge of this range and in very large theatres they will be effectively beyond.

2 Overhangs

In tiered auditoria, any seats that are tucked back underneath an overhang are likely to suffer acoustical problems.

3 Side seats

Seats that are facing sideways to the stage and therefore not always in a direct line of contact with the actor's voice may receive their sound second-hand, after it has bounced off another surface. In a **thrust theatre**, or a **theatre-in-the-round**, this problem migrates around the auditorium as the actors move around the stage, but is always most noticeable in the seats to which an actor has turned his back.

4 'Deaf spots'

Anywhere in an auditorium there may be local pockets, sometimes only a few seats wide, sometimes larger, where the acoustics are inexplicably poor.

5 'Hot spots'

There may be one very small area on a stage that produces an extraordinarily resonant effect when an actor speaks from it. Many actors love to locate such spots, especially for the delivery of long and important speeches, but the easy resonance on stage

8

may be attended by a confusing echo effect in distant parts of the auditorium.

6 Soft fabrics

Old-fashioned theatres full of velvet drapes, or stage sets that are covered in curtains, carpets and hangings, can soak up sound like blotting paper soaks up ink.

7 Bare walls

Large expanses of unadorned surface can cause sound to bounce about an auditorium, resulting in a confused acoustic with some seats getting an echo effect and others a delay in receiving any sound at all.

8 Fly towers

Many large modern theatres have massive fly towers that yawn hungrily over the stage, gobbling up any sounds fed to them from below. This problem can be exacerbated in a production using a minimalist set. The fewer reflective surfaces there are on stage, the more the sound will sail blithely up the fly tower.

9 Technology

Most theatre machinery makes a noise, and the combined hum of all the electrically powered technology in a theatre can have a seriously negative effect on its acoustics. **Silence** in the theatre is golden but increasingly hard to achieve.

10 Air conditioning

Air conditioners can be extremely noisy machines, especially for anyone sitting near an outlet and a powerful system badly installed will set up strong currents of air in the theatre. Disturbed air is not a good conductor of the spoken word. A current of air blowing from the auditorium onto the stage will whisk the words from the actors' mouths and blow them up the fly tower or into the wings.

Acoustics

Most theatres are affected by some of these problems and the worst theatres by most of them. But don't despair, there is much you can do.

REMEDIES FOR BAD ACOUSTICS

1 Strong voices

Employ well-trained actors with good diction and strong, resonant voices. You can have the best acoustics in the world and still be sunk by inadequate vocal skill in your actors. Little voices or lazy voices are useless in the theatre, whatever the acoustics.

2 Acoustic awareness

Make your actors aware of the acoustical problems in the house. During **technical rehearsals,** have the actors sit in all parts of the auditorium listening to their colleagues on the stage. Find half an hour of quiet theatre time for the actors to speak their lines to one another from all over the auditorium and stage. Awareness of the problem is half the battle. Diligent actors hate being inaudible and will strive to be heard in the worst seats, but they must first know where those seats are. Talk to your actors about 'the intention to be heard', not just about raising their volume. Loudness in itself is rarely the answer to inaudibility. Distinctness can only be achieved by a combination of **projection** and **diction**.

3 Fluid staging

In thrust theatres and theatres-in-the-round, your actors must learn to pitch their voices all around them, being especially careful when they turn their backs on any part of the audience. You can help them do this by adopting a staging style that keeps them on the move.

4 Less fabric

If the sound is being soaked up by a lot of soft fabric in the house or on the stage, try removing bits of it. If the material is necessary for masking, try backing it with a hard, sound-reflective material or replace it altogether with a hard surface.

5 More fabric

If there's too much 'bounce' in the acoustic, try hanging soft fabric in the wings or on the auditorium walls, but be careful how you go. You don't want to deaden the sound altogether.

6 Intelligent design

You and your designer must consider the architecture and the acoustics of the theatre before you design the show. A stage design can radically affect the acoustic in the auditorium. A forestage thrusting into the auditorium can get your actors closer to the audience. Reflective surfaces on stage can act as sounding boards for the actors' or singers' voices, especially useful in opera. Raising the stage can put the actors more in touch with the upper tiers in an auditorium. Building a **rake** into the design can turn the surface of the stage itself into a sounding board. This is especially useful in neutralising the effect of a cavernous fly tower.

7 Silent technology

As far as possible, try to silence all noisy technology in the theatre. Have machinery regularly serviced, especially anything cooled by a noisy fan. If you can't silence the machines, put them in boxes or surround them with soft, sound-absorbent material. Close all doors around the stage and auditorium during the performance so that noise and air currents are locked out.

8 Silent air conditioning

If your air-conditioning system is noisy, servicing it often helps. If that doesn't work, try masking off the noisiest outlets with hard material. If that doesn't work, try turning it down to a very low level during the performance. If that doesn't work, turn it off completely. If the auditorium gets too hot during the show then turn it back on at the interval. Better for the audience to be hot than straining to hear.

Acoustics

9 Sound enhancement

In a very large theatre, or one with a horrible acoustic, you may be tempted to rely on mechanical help in the form of sound **amplification**. Indeed, some theatres are fully equipped with sound-enhancement systems and use them as a matter of course, but they are dangerous tools and should only be used when all other methods have failed. If you have to use sound enhancement, try using ambient microphones, in the form of float-mikes along the front of the stage or hanging-mikes over the stage. As an absolute last resort, you may have to put **radio-mikes** on the actors, but as they cost a lot of money, distort the natural tones of the actors' voices and delegate much of the artistic integrity of the show to the Sound Operator, they really should be a last resort.

EMPTY THEATRES AND FULL THEATRES

A theatre's acoustic will change when its seats have people in them, often quite significantly. Irrespective of how noisy or quiet an audience is being, its physical presence disturbs the way the patterns of sound move about the building, making it more or less receptive to sound in different areas. An audience's clothes will absorb more sound than will empty seats. An overhang or 'deaf spot' problem will be made worse by having a row of people sitting just in front of it.

Psychologically speaking, the presence in a large theatre of a thousand or more pairs of ears, provided they can hear reasonably well in the first place, will make the acoustic of a space seem much better than it did when it was empty. Conversely, if the audience is struggling to hear, the acoustic will seem to have worsened in their presence. This is why it is so important to talk to the actors about their 'intention to be heard'. The audience has certainly come intending to hear, so the minimum requirement from the actors is that they should complete the contract from their side of the footlights.

Acting

Acting is the art of pretending to be another person – or the craft that actors use to create and perform an imagined character. In text-based theatre actors derive these creations from a mixture of their own personalities and the character that has been written for them.

Most of your time in rehearsals will be spent appraising this mysterious alchemy and it must hold a real fascination for you. Your ability to help an actor find a character, blend that character's life with those of the other characters in the drama and then remove yourself from the equation will largely define your talent as a director.

Actors use a complex pattern of physical and vocal expression, thought and feeling to create their characters, and no definition of the process will ever be true for all actors. Definitions of acting are made all the more subjective for the director because no two directors have quite the same approach. A director who has been an actor will have a different view of the actor's craft than a director who has never appeared on a stage, the one being able to refer to an instinctive personal method and a natural empathy with actors' concerns, while the other must rely on an imaginatively drawn version of the same thing – the actor in his mind. Not that one sort of director is better equipped than the other. The subjective experience of the director who has acted can be a valuable tool but can also be an imaginative fetter as he struggles to release his actors from his own perception of how their parts should be played. Similarly the objective distance of the non-actor director can have its value in an ability to stand back and look at the structure of the whole drama irrespective of any one actor's part in it.

If the acting process is too complex to admit of a universal set of governing rules, it is still worthwhile trying to define. By doing so we may happen upon some useful truths and help to describe how a director can be an influence on his actors and their acting process.

The shallowest and therefore least demanding sort of acting is mimicry or **impersonation** – a trick that cannot really be called acting at all but often passes for it. The mimic catches a pattern of speech or movement from his subject and reproduces it, accurately or not depending on how good a mimic he is. What he misses is the pattern of thought that lies beneath the external physical life. To understand the thoughts of another person an actor must first understand the life that gives rise to those thoughts, and the best way of understanding another life is to empathise with it. The ability to empathise with a character is what separates the mimics from the true actors, those who impersonate from those who become.

THE ART OF BECOMING

This is a two-way process. It involves the actor making a journey away from himself towards the character, but also the character being obliged to make a journey towards the actor. This exchange of journeys can sometimes be uneven, with the character doing all the travelling and the actor scarcely moving from home, or the actor going so far away from himself that he disappears completely into the character. The best exchanges are characterised by balance and agreement, the actor and the character meeting at a place that neither the actor nor the author of the character could quite have foreseen. Part of your job as a director is to create an atmosphere in rehearsal conducive to these exchanges, to recognise them when they occur and to share with your actors your pleasure in their achievement.

There is a joint act of will at the heart of all acting. In capturing the essence of a character the actor must exert his will over the character but must in turn yield to the character's will. Some characters are more easily captured than others, some proving so elusive or mutable that they are never captured twice in quite the same way. Some come and go, actors capturing them only to lose them again.

Some characters so powerfully capture the actor that they never quite leave him, even after the play is long gone, the actor thereafter being able to fall into the character without a moment of consideration, as if he were remembering an old friend and bringing him back to life – the voice, the face, the body, the movement, all accurately and fondly recaptured.

GOOD ACTING AND BAD ACTING

If the acting process is hard to define, the difference between good acting and bad acting is also fraught with subjective judgement. Theatre-lovers as well as practitioners have their favourite actors and their least favourite, and no two people ever share quite the same preferences. Even actors that have achieved high distinction in their profession are still reviled by some. How may one account for this extreme divergence of taste? Leaving aside the obvious prejudices based on age, gender, sexuality and perception of **beauty** for which there is never any accounting, what is it that causes people to form such strong views on what constitutes a good or a bad actor? As a director you are bound to consider this question very carefully. Your work, dependent as it must be on good acting, will also be judged on other people's views of what constitutes good acting. But you can't please everybody and you can't base your casting choices or rehearsal decisions on other people's tastes. You can only rely on your own. You must therefore develop your own strong sense of what you think good acting is, personal to you while still being open to the consideration if not the influence of the tastes and prejudices of the profession at large.

Where to start? Try to define what it is that gives you pleasure when you enjoy an actor's work, what makes you smile or laugh, or what moves you. Ask yourself what it is the actor is doing to convince you that he has become the character. Does the actor truly believe what he is doing and do you believe along with him? Why do you believe? Does the actor's portrayal of the character accord with some personal experience of your own, or is the actor taking you into an imaginative world that is convincing for some other reason? Are you admiring the actor for some rare skill he possesses or because he seems to be drawing from a deep emotional well? Are you enjoying his enjoyment, his relish of the craft of acting? Does the actor resemble you in some way, or do you think or wish you resembled him? Does your admiration of him spring from personal identification? Can you tell from your seat in the auditorium whether you would like the actor personally in real life?

Acting

You must also examine your more negative reactions to actors. Don't just write them off as 'not your cup of tea'. Why does a particular actor irritate you, or why do you find him unconvincing? In what way is he insufficient? Is it his artistry you find wanting, or his personality? Is he trying too hard to please the audience, or not hard enough? Does he seem vain, or humourless or bombastic or lacking in intelligence? If so, do you think he would be the same way as a private person?

By looking critically at the actors you admire and the actors you don't much admire and what seems to make them tick on stage and off, you will build up a picture of the way you make your judgements about them and whether or not those judgements are fair, reasonable and objective.

Here are some judgements of my own to help you make yours.

GOOD ACTING – SEVEN CARDINAL VIRTUES

1 *Competence*

A good actor must have a good instrument and know how to use it. His voice must be resonant, his diction precise, his face mobile, his body supple, his memory accurate, his movement natural and his mind alive.

2 *Expressiveness*

An expressive artist must have access to true emotion and the ability to communicate it to an audience vividly and variously. His organs of expression, his face, voice and body, must be equal to the task of transmitting everything his artistry dreams up.

3 *Believability*

If an audience is to believe that an actor has become his character, he must believe in it himself. Good actors should empathise so deeply with their characters that the audience is unable to see where actor ends and character begins. Acting that doesn't look like acting must always be the goal.

4 *Humour*

Intelligence, education and knowledge are all useful attributes for an actor but not indispensable virtues. Indeed, a sense of humour can mitigate the absence of all three. Without humour, true wit is impossible and without wit comedy is hopeless.

5 *Courage*

Standing up in front of a thousand or so complete strangers and pretending to be someone you're not takes courage. Failure on this scale when it happens can be truly humiliating. Even rehearsals are fraught with potential embarrassment, and the committed actor must sometimes take a very deep breath before throwing himself into an emotional scene for the first time. The older and more successful the actor, the greater the possible fall and so the more courage required.

6 *Humility*

A good actor serves the play, his fellow actors and his audience. He may be confident to the point of boisterousness, but he should never be overbearing or insolent. His artistry must include an awareness of when enough is enough, when acting threatens to become overacting. In other words he must have taste, and taste is merely a refined form of humility. Even in a star – or perhaps especially in a star – humility is an essential virtue. Without it he runs the risk of believing in the importance of his own celebrity and ending up only being able to play himself, or with himself.

7 *Companionability*

With acting, company is everything. The best acting happens in the best acting companies and the best actors must therefore be companionable. Actors change their professional surroundings regularly. Their circle of colleagues and friends is in constant flux and the demands on their artistry never the same twice. If an actor is to survive this irregular routine with cheerfulness and discipline, he must derive genuine enjoyment from an endeavour that can only ever be mutually achieved.

Acting

BAD ACTING – SEVEN DEADLY SINS

1 *Incompetence*

Lack of technical competence in acting can express itself in many different ways, the most common being lack of vocal power, physical stiffness, woolly diction and shaky memory, and the most extreme involving speech impediment, tone deafness, nervous incapacity and total memory lapse.

2 *Dullness*

Monotony of vocal expression or flatness of characterisation is sometimes caused by a basic dullness of thought, but more often by an insufficiency in the organs of expression. The actor thinks he is being vivid and interesting, but his voice, face and body are not equal to transmitting his thoughts, however imaginative they might be.

3 *Shallowness*

If believability is the crucial test of an actor's commitment to a character, shallowness of thought will prevent him achieving it. Lazy thinking, second-hand ideas, copycat emotions, borrowed performances, mimicry, mugging and method are all symptoms of a fundamental lack of interest in the life of the character the actor is supposed to be playing. In its least obtrusive form, the shallow actor quietly flits across the surface of his character doing no discernible damage to the play. The shallow actor with the big ego is the real danger. He can destroy the believability of everything around him by treating his role as a licence for showing off when in truth he has little or nothing to show.

4 *Humourlessness*

Beware the actor who doesn't get the joke, or whose own jokes are crude, cruel or tasteless. Beware the actor who thinks he's a hoot but hasn't really a funny bone in his body. Beware the actor who solicits laughter with a flawless technique but never finds another actor funny. A sense of the absurd is a necessary part of a civilised mind. Rehearsal rooms without laughter are places of despair.

5 Fear

Fear is the enemy. Fear of failure, fear of others' success, artistic vertigo, jealousy, bitchiness, pusillanimity, superstition and prejudice must all be firmly booted out of an actor's life if he wants to be a proper artist. Even a great actor can be prone to little spells of faint-heartedness, but even in its mildest forms an actor must learn to manage his fears. Fear, like mediocrity, is catching, and if allowed free rein it can develop into full-blown paranoia. A single paranoid actor in an ensemble can act like a black hole in space, sucking all the good acting out of everyone else.

6 Vanity

An actor must take pride in his work, of course, but must never be vain of his appearance or performance. Narcissism is an occupational hazard in the theatre. If an adoring public constantly tells you you're beautiful and brilliant and enviable it takes a strong mind not to agree with their view. But you can't really submerge yourself in another person's life if you're inordinately fascinated by your own. Vanity struts the stage in many forms. It overacts, it pompously declaims, it smirks at its own cleverness, obsesses over its appearance and constantly compares itself with others.

7 Cynicism

If good company provides the essential atmosphere for good acting, cynicism can poison it. Watch out for the hardened pro who's seen it all before, the curl of the lip at the enthusiastically proposed idea, the condescending patronage of the junior actor, the unwarranted suspicion of someone else's professional motives. Disappointment is usually the cause. Disappointment breeds envy and envy breeds cynicism. But good acting requires belief and faith and trust in the good nature of others. To all cynics the message must be the same: come into the body of the church or put yourself out of your misery and give up acting.

Actioning

'Actioning' is a system of textual analysis for directors and actors in rehearsal. It splits each character's text up into little parcels of **motivation**, each one defined by an appropriate verb or verbs of action. Thus the action implied by a simple line such as 'I love you' might be 'to assure', or 'to confess' or 'to own' or 'to blackmail' and so on, including combinations of those actions in various admixtures.

There are directors who are so devoted to the system that they find it impossible to rehearse a play without first having thoroughly 'actioned' it, requiring all the actors in the company to analyse their characters' speeches using the prescribed method. But some actors take to actioning better than others. There are those who become addicted themselves and will privately 'action' their scripts even when a director doesn't demand it. There are those who put up with the discipline, drawing what good they can from it and rejecting what they find invasive of their private acting method. And there are those who can't abide it, finding it an irrelevant and rigid form of analysis foreign to their more instinctive way of looking at the world and the people in it.

The system undoubtedly has its strengths. Based as it is in the work of **Stanislavsky**, it can be a fine defence against woolly thinking in actors, obliging them to be more thorough in their search for motive and character than perhaps they might otherwise choose to be. It can give directors unused to considering the complexities of human behaviour a system of character analysis that teaches them something of the range of choices available to the actor in rehearsal. And it can always be used sparingly and therefore unsystematically, only deployed by a director when there is a textual crux that cannot be resolved by normal discussion between actor and director – a little dose of actioning to clear up an irritating local complaint.

Like all systems it is only as strong as the person using it, and it can become an arbitrary and pointless tool in the hands of an unimaginative or dogmatic user. Actors who are forced against their will or natural inclination to use the system may easily show signs of mental fatigue in rehearsal, their brains working overtime to make all their 'actions' fit the director's expectations of them. The avid devotee of actioning would see this as a sign that the system was working, but might be disappointed to hear what the actors are saying outside rehearsal.

Some directors of a controlling nature, unhappy with the way that the actors grow up and leave the rehearsal nest to manage on their own in performance, can be guilty of using actioning as a sort of leash or tether well into the run of the play. They may not mean to do it, but their obsession with the system makes them think that a variation from it or, worse, a rejection of it will invalidate their work. The most fanatic actioners turn the system into a religion, something to be believed in, without any sense of its true usefulness or complexity. The directors who gain most from the system are the least dogmatic, able to adapt it to their own style and accommodate different levels of enthusiasm and proficiency in others.

If actioning works for you and if your actor colleagues genuinely find it valuable, then it can be a useful tool, but the more experienced you get the more likely you are to grow out of it.

In any event, by the middle of a good rehearsal period any systems should start to fall away and be replaced by the actors 'becoming' their characters in defiance of any forms of analysis, exploring aspects of the emotional and the spiritual that can never be entirely prepared for, and discovering new and unexpected 'actions' in the living relationships between the characters.

Actors

Actors are your most important collaborators. Indeed, the fact that they are ultimately much more important to the art of theatre than you are should be a constant touchstone in your career.

The skill and artistry of actors is defined by their necessarily complex personalities, so working with them requires a similarly complex response from you. When you rehearse with actors you must be ready to engage with them as private people, exchange ideas with them as intellects, rely on their physical and vocal and imaginative powers and draw on the inner world of their emotions and memories. If you want to be a successful director you must love actors and acting, or learn to love them.

Actors are social creatures. Even the loners amongst them rely on a social context for their work, a society that includes other actors, writers, stage management, **Casting Directors**, administrators and, of course, audiences. You represent only one element in their social milieu, and an element that is not constantly present in their daily working lives. When you are present you may not always be regarded with trust or affection. This is because you are, directly or indirectly, an employer of actors. By casting them, calling them to rehearsal and then controlling them you put yourself in the position of a parent rather than a friend, but a parent whose usefulness has largely been outlived once rehearsals are over. Thus though you may have many actor friends, some of them intimate friends, you will always remain on the outskirts of their fraternity.

Actors are bound together not by who they are but by what they do.

There are good actors and bad, intelligent and dim, instinctive and considered, wise and foolish, broad-minded and mean-spirited, highly educated and scarcely literate and every possible shade in between. Never be guilty of treating actors as a tribe, of patronising them or underestimating them. If you do you will be cutting yourself off from the richest source of your own inspiration.

To grow as a director, you must study to understand your actors, to mine their talents, cherish their strengths, work round their weaknesses, enjoy their complications and forgive them their trespasses. But understanding requires more than sympathy for the actor. It also requires analysis of the actor's instrument and studious judgement concerning its application.

THE ACTOR'S INSTRUMENT

As a violinist plays the fiddle or a pianist the piano, a singer's instrument is the voice and an actor's the whole person. A musician, however talented or skilful, makes a sound only as good as the quality of his instrument and so it is with an actor.

The actor's instrument is comprised of four elements – body, face, voice and mind – and is exploited by two further attributes, talent and skill. Your awareness of the way in which each of these elements manifests itself in a particular actor and is exploited by his talent and his skill will let you assess whether he should be cast in a particular role and, if cast, how best you can exploit his strengths and disguise or ignore his weaknesses.

The best actors work with a fine balance of these elements, each one supporting and complementing the other. But not all actors are so gifted or so balanced. Some have a natural physical grace but are weak vocally. Some have fine intellects but seemingly unexplorable emotions. Some have conventional minds and thrilling voices. And so on. No actor is perfect and no two actors are the same.

Most experienced actors have found a way of exploiting their gifts by relying on what is strong and disguising what is weak. In doing so, they develop over time an instinctive personal method that you could describe as their acting personality. Less experienced actors will have less defined acting personalities, so their strengths and weaknesses will be easier to spot. Whether your actors are old hands or young, you must deal with them as they come to you and develop your own skills of support and judgement.

The more experienced you are yourself, the better you will know how to respond to a particular actor's talent. But be very careful before you try to make any change in an actor's professional per-sonality or dismantle any part of it for the sake of another actor or for your own directorial ends. Unless you have first underpinned an actor's perceived flaw with appreciation of some other strength that he possesses, your insight alone will not be enough to change him for the better, and if you end up damaging his confidence for no discernible return, you won't be easily forgiven.

One of your first tasks, then, when embarking on a rehearsal process is to make a dispassionate assessment of the acting person-ality of each of the actors in your company based on the elements and attributes that make up the whole instrument. Once you get a bit of experience you will learn to do this without much calculation, your assessments occurring to you only when a particular actor's strengths or weaknesses need to be emphasised, disguised or balanced within the ensemble.

THE ACTOR'S BODY

Actors come in all shapes and sizes, but an actor's physical shape is rarely the defining aspect of his performance. If you and the actor are both happy that he is playing the part then his shape becomes the shape of the character and that's the end of it.

Difficulties arise when an actor feels he is physically inadequate or wrong for the part. Audiences will believe almost anything if clearly instructed to do so, and an actor who believes in his own suitability will be best able to take advantage of that fact, but there are occasions when an audience's willingness to believe is not enough and the actor's lack of confidence serves to make things worse.

When this happens, most actors will come clean about their fears and ask you for help without being prompted. Others more used to living in denial will dream up ways of disguising their inadequacies, hiding their shapes inside their everyday clothes or favouring a particular sort of cut in their costume designs. This most commonly occurs with actors unhappy about their fatness or unfitness, but you will also come across short actors who insist on wearing lifts in their shoes, or tall actors with habitual stoops or bald actors with preposterous toupees that they refuse to acknowledge they are wearing. Whatever the disguise, these symptoms always point to the same failing – a lack of confidence in the actor's natural shape.

Some actors are incurably out of love with their own bodies, but most of these are easy enough to help. The best tactic is to ignore the supposed weakness and concentrate instead on the actual strength. The better an actor feels about his instrument as a whole, his voice, his face, his intelligence and his wit, the less self-conscious he will be about his body and the happier he will be to abandon his disguise and notice that the actors around him are just as imperfect as he is.

Most actors live very happily with their own bodies and positively enjoy the exploitation of any peculiarity they might have. If there is a natural modesty in an actor it usually conflicts with an equally natural and childlike urge to perform unashamedly. In comedy especially, it's impossible to play the fool and hold on to a disguise at the same time, so the disguise is usually discarded in favour of the laughter.

The abandonment of personal disguise is a necessary stage in a successful rehearsal period, especially when actors are required to change their appearances in order to realise their characters. An actor can't adopt the physical attributes of a new character if he can't let go of his private physical self-image. In the end it is always the actors who are most comfortable in their own skins who are most able to transform themselves by their acting alone.

Whatever an actor's physical shape, it is the way the body moves on stage that most defines an audience's appreciation of it. Some actors move easily, with a natural physical grace that never leaves them whatever they are required to do. Others, locked inside their intellects or bound by their private feelings, find physical movement embarrassing. This difference in ease and proficiency of movement tends to iron out actual or perceived differences in the physique of different actors. Strength or speed of movement can create a semblance of real physical power or agility on stage, whereas a locked-up actor with the body of an athlete can come across as physically weak. A fat actor can be fleet of foot and appear lighter than he really is. An older actor with a dancer's grace or a gymnast's suppleness can shed years in a single movement across the stage.

The one thing that is undisguisable when an actor moves on stage is any self-consciousness he might be feeling. The resulting stiffness or awkwardness is the failing in actors that is most evident to audiences, but actors displaying such symptoms may not be suffering from any fundamental lack of physical ease or training. No actor can be physically relaxed, for instance, if he is questioning his rightness for the part or harbouring other negative thoughts about his performance. An actor happy with his performance in every other way, happy to be cast, well versed in the text and the thoughts behind the text, and well liked by his peers, will nearly always move naturally on the stage and be open to further physical ideas and challenges.

Actors

If you have an actor with problems of physique or movement, look at how he behaves off stage in normal public and private life. If there is physical ease and grace there but not on stage then the source of the difficulty is likely to be an emotional or mental one caused by the acting process itself and will not be solved by addressing its outward symptoms. By giving such a physically locked actor notes about his woodenness or lack of movement you will merely add to his self-consciousness and thus compound the problem. Work with him instead on changing his inner life to match the inner life of the character. If he has an active imagination and you have the ability to put him in touch with it, his physical awkwardness will soon be replaced by the pleasure of finding the true physical life of the character he is playing.

But there will always be actors who just can't loosen up, who are just as wooden in their daily lives as they are on stage. Many such actors have short careers, choosing to leave the profession rather than continue to torture themselves with nightly stabs of self-consciousness. Others move into film and television, where a lack of physical ease is far less noticeable, or radio, where it's invisible. But others soldier on, building their woodenness into their acting personalities and achieving considerable success on stage in parts where physical stiffness doesn't matter or could be seen as a positive advantage.

Physical relaxation apart, if the theatre is to succeed in holding a mirror up to nature there should be as wide a variety of bodies on stage as there is in daily life. Don't diminish the human pageant by becoming too selective or too conventional in your casting choices. Let there be fat Hamlets, gangling Juliets and tiny Agamemnons. Let audiences see themselves as they are, not as they pretend to be.

THE ACTOR'S FACE

The lineaments of an actor's face are the most important indicators of his expressiveness, but they also have a strong influence on his personality and confidence. They may indeed be part of the reason why actors become actors in the first place, their feelings about their own faces and other people's attitudes to them being deeply ingrained from their earliest years. 'She was always a beautiful child.' 'He was making funny faces when he was two and he hasn't stopped since.' 'That profile was destined for the stage.' Of course such sentiments are mostly a lot of nonsense and come to nothing. There are plenty of beautiful bankers, hilarious dentists and nobly profiled truck-drivers in the world. But such remarks do get into the imaginations of actors at an early age and often help to form their opinions of themselves.

Whatever face an actor possesses, there are useful and un-useful features when it comes to using it as an instrument of expressiveness on stage. However, given that some theatres are so small and intimate that the audience has the same relationship with the actor's face as a film camera in close-up, and some theatres are so large that those sitting in the furthest-away seats are provided with binoculars, this is not an exact science.

Eyes are crucial. They are the windows to the mind, if not always to the soul, and provide the strongest evidence of an actor's thoughts and feelings. Large, vivid and expressive eyes are thus great assets in a stage actor. Small eyes, pale and watery eyes, sunken eyes or eyes overshadowed by craggy brows are all drawbacks.

But even a lack of expressiveness in the eye department is not a fatal flaw in an actor. It can still be made up for by mobility of features or resonance of voice, and the bigger the theatre the less the lack will be felt as the power of the voice becomes a much more salient feature of the actor's skill.

Interestingly, the power of the eyes in an optical sense has no relevance at all to the authority of the actor. Some actors are extremely myopic, almost blind without their glasses, but rather than wear contact lenses on stage, which can easily dry out under the hot stage lights, they choose to act without glasses or lenses, relying on the blurred outlines and the voices of their fellow actors but never getting more than rudimentary eye contact with them unless at very close range. The resulting misty-eyed look can come across as romantic or spiritually enlightened, adding a charm and vulnerability to the actor's general aura. Such performers often wear their glasses for the journey from dressing room to stage, but must then be reminded by stage management to take them off before making their entrance onto the blasted heath or the Roman Forum.

Actors

In the theatre the eyes have it, the rest of the face being far less important and indeed less wise to generalise about. But each facial feature also has its corresponding conventional association. Audiences and actors alike nurse their subjective attitudes about the mean mouth, the resolute chin, the noble brow or the aristocratic nose. But such conventions are rendered ridiculous in the face of the sensuous actor with thin lips, the resolute hero with the weak chin or the perfect nobleman with the low hairline and the snub nose. No feature matters much if the performance is strong and the face is being put to its proper use as a mirror for the inner life and feelings of the actor and the character he is playing.

Just as some actors adopt disguises to escape from the physical reality of their bodies, so others do with their faces. Beware the actress who always appears in rehearsal with a thick mask of make-up or the actor who can only play heavily bearded parts because the hairy face has become part of his acting personality. They are hiding. And they may be playing a part in public they will be unhappy to relinquish in rehearsal. This lack of confidence or personal dissatisfaction finds its most pernicious form in paranoia about a particular feature or about the face in general. In some actors the obsession can become so devouring that it results in a determination to fix the perceived problem, leading to the perils of cosmetic surgery and permanent disfigurement. Though far more of a problem with screen actors, theatre actors have just as much to fear from giving in to this gross perversion of the meaning of **beauty** and age.

Whatever the delineations of the actor's face, it must also be mobile and expressive. Actors on stage have to communicate thought and feeling over great distances to large numbers of people. They are competing for the audience's attention against a lot of visual interference – from the movement of the other actors to the busy-ness of the set to the décor of the theatre itself. An actor with a small head, a little mouth and deep-set eyes will be at a disadvantage in such an environment. A less talented actor with large, elastic features, a big gash of a mouth and striking, vibrant eyes will seem more talented in comparison, all other things being equal. It isn't fair, but it's so nonetheless. The unfairness inherent in this simple physical fact is illustrated most vividly when an actor resorts to

mugging, a deviant form of acting into which the talented and untalented can both lapse.

If mobility of facial features is important on the stage, the opposite is often true on the screen. This is well illustrated when a practised stage actor tries out his skills on television for the first time and struggles for control of his face, his expressions seeming contorted and unnatural. The communication of inner feelings to a camera lens is a very particular sort of skill, requiring a stillness and concentration that would seem lifeless on stage. The two sorts of acting are very closely related but require the exercise of two completely different sets of facial acting muscles. It takes actors many years before they become equally proficient in both techniques, and some actors find themselves opting for excellence or celebrity in one rather than a bare proficiency in both.

THE ACTOR'S MIND

The actor's mind is a storehouse, stocked with experience and memory, observation and imagination, emotion and thought. Some of these storehouses are well ordered, the stock up to date and easily accessible. Others are labyrinthine treasure houses so complex that even the owner is ignorant of the contents. Some are suspiciously clean, suggesting an underlying chaos just behind the goods on display. Others are like Romeo's apothecary's shop, full of weird but worthless pieces of junk 'thinly scattered to make up a show'. For every actor a different storehouse.

One of your jobs as director is to persuade the actor to let you have access to the storehouse, and to encourage him to range around it himself as freely as he can. Together you will discover things he may have undervalued or overlooked when searching on his own. Some actors will never let you in but will listen to what you want and then search for it on their own, quietly bringing back the item a few days later. Others will overwhelm you with choice, proudly but indiscriminately revealing every corner of the warehouse for inspection. From this wealth of choice you must help them select the useful from the pointless, the tasteful from the vulgar, the fine from the shoddy.

Your purpose is to help fit the contents of the actor's mind into the mind of the character he is playing – and to help excise or rather neutralise those parts of the actor's mind that are un-useful to his portrayal of the role. To do this well you must become adept at reading the minds of the actors in your charge as well as the minds of the characters they are playing – and you must be able to know at a glance the one from the other. You can't talk to an actor about his role if you have misread the actor when out of character or the role when he is in it.

It is a privilege to be allowed access to actors' minds. Don't abuse it. Don't require all actors' minds to be the same. Celebrate their diversity by discovering the true nature of each one and then using it for what it is. Don't fear discovering something unpleasant in an actor's mind or express disappointment when what you discover is not what you were looking for. Adapt the character to suit the mind as well as the mind to suit the character.

Don't require your actors' minds to be like your own. Don't require a female actor to think like a male or vice versa – unless you and the actor have made a conscious decision to do so. Don't attribute a mean motive to an actor's mind if a generous one is equally available to you. Don't be frightened of fear, cowed by strength or rebuked by disagreement.

Measure each mind not against your own, but what you know to be the most interesting in people generally, and don't value any part of a mind at an inflated price. The intellectual capacity of an actor, his learning and literacy and his speed of thought are only a part of the picture. Don't undervalue humour and humility, generosity and sociability, passion and doggedness.

An actor's mind comprises his humanity. If the theatre is to reflect an audience's true nature back to itself, only a whole actor can create a whole human image.

THE ACTOR'S SKILL

An actor may have the finest of basic natural instruments, a good active body, an expressive face, a resonant voice and a broad mind and still make a disappointing impression on stage. This might be caused by a lack of innate talent but could just as well be a result of poor technique, preparation, training or practice. As a director you must be able to tell the difference. You will meet actors at every stage of professional development and be asked for your opinion about their prospects and ambitions. If you are to advise them wisely you must be able to make accurate judgements about their strengths and weaknesses. Directors are often cast in the role of teacher or trainer, a role more or less impossible to shirk once it is visited upon you by actors hungry for instruction.

Every part of the actor's instrument is capable of training and will grow rusty with lack of practice. The body can be strengthened and made more supple by physical training, dance lessons can imbue gracefulness and balance, vocal power and dexterity can be increased by singing, breathing and articulation exercises, and the mind can be kept active by reading, argument and games of mental agility.

These elements of training and practice are the basic diet of a good drama school, but not all actors will have had an intensive drama school training, and those that have may have let their skills slip over the years into a lazy complacency. Some actors will have gone straight into the profession from university. Some will have started as child actors and gone into the adult profession without any sort of secondary education. Some will have had no formal training but picked up their skills where they could find them from the acting jobs they have done and the colleagues they have observed. In a company of actors you will be hard-pressed to find two actors with exactly the same story to tell about their initial training and the currency of their present skills.

Learn how to equalise the skills of the acting companies with whom you work, capitalising on the best techniques and disguising the worst. If your play requires physical skills that your actors do not possess, build a training programme into your rehearsal period.

THE ACTOR'S TALENT

Whatever the physical attributes of an actor and regardless of any skills he may or may not possess, there is also a thing called talent, not mysterious and indefinable but a measurable and valuable commodity far more present in some actors than in others.

Actors

The origins of talent are perhaps a matter of question, some asserting that an actor is born with his talent and that those not blessed at birth will never make up the deficit however hard they try, others that it is formed by conditioning in childhood, a response to encouragement or neglect or sibling rivalry. If there is an acting gene, inheritable from one's parents, it would be interesting to see what it looks like, this noisy little group of histrionic cells struggling for expression in a single strand of DNA.

Whatever the origins of talent, the thing itself is easy enough to spot in the possessor, though it is a matter of great unfairness that those possessed of the greatest talent are rarely possessed of the physical attributes that audiences look for in their heroes and heroines. There are actors of great genius who are just too short to be anyone's natural choice for Romeo and there are actresses just too plain to get away with being Juliet. It isn't fair. And a good, and brave, director will buck the trend and cast the talented actor anyway. But casting is not always good and rarely brave, so the short and the plain and the fat and the odd will always get short shrift, however heroic they are in their hearts or abundantly gifted in their talents.

Unlike skill, which can be acquired, practised and developed, talent is composed of a rich amalgam of related natural gifts and instincts, more or less interwoven with the actor's values, attitudes, personality and self-image.

The three most important constituents of acting talent are **imagination**, **impersonation** and **observation**. They are the gold, frankincense and myrrh of acting. Without them, actors are giftless and acting itself thriftless.

THE ACTOR'S VOICE

A good stage voice must have three virtues: resonance, musicality and distinctness.

Resonance

The resonance of a voice is largely defined by the size of the voice box and the elasticity of the vocal chords, and, to a lesser extent, by the resonating chambers in the head and chest and the capacity of the lungs. Resonance can be increased by training and practice but is greatly dependent on the size of the physical instrument.

Some actors are born with big voices and have to make very little effort to be heard, whatever the size of the theatre in which they are acting. Others, with smaller voices, must work much harder at projecting their sound into the bigger spaces and will always be at a disadvantage in the very biggest, or in any space with bad **acoustics**. Small voices that are overworked to fill large spaces tend to wear out quickly, resulting in temporary loss of the voice or, chronically, in permanent damage to the chords. They also tend to disappear altogether when the actor is struggling with a cold or the flu. Larger and more resonant voices are nearly always more cold- and flu-proof, with the actor still able to struggle on, drugged but audible.

Beware of casting un-resonant voices in big parts in big spaces.

Musicality

The musicality of a voice is defined by the range over which it has an active expressiveness and the elasticity with which it can change from one part of its range to another.

Most people talk like their parents, their siblings, their teachers and their school friends. Actors are no exception. The voices they heard in their childhood are the ones they mimic most easily and with the least self-consciousness. The natural musicality in an actor's voice will be largely a matter of inheritance, its range and tonal quality defined by the voices in the parental home, the local dialect and the prevailing social and educational culture. An actor who went to boarding school will sound more like his school friends and his teachers than an actor who went to a day school and lived at home.

Musicality can certainly be enhanced by training, but only if the actor has an innate ability to listen, absorb and impersonate. The more he develops these skills, the greater will be his vocal range in reproducing what he has absorbed. But a good drama school will be wary of training out an actor's natural dialect and replacing it with a borrowed musicality. No one else's dialect is ever quite so personally expressive as your own, however cleverly you mimic it.

An actor's natural musicality can be heard in his normal everyday voice and shouldn't change that much when he goes on stage. If it does, it may be at the expense of naturalness, an acquired musicality of speech often expressing itself as 'singing' or 'intoning', where the voice adopts arbitrary patterns of tone and pitch that are at odds with the true sense of the language. This is the 'voice beautiful' syndrome, where the sound of the voice becomes a kind of vanity, and vocal dexterity becomes a substitute for characterisation.

A voice needs an unforced musicality if an audience is to listen to it for any length of time. The bigger the part the more melodious and mellifluous the voice needs to be.

Beware of casting an unmusical voice in a leading role.

Distinctness

Distinctness depends on clarity of **diction** combined with the intention of the actor to be heard and understood.

The organs of distinctness are the lips, the tongue, the palate, the teeth, the brain and the ears. These work together to produce and pronounce the words, punching out the consonants, clipping off the word endings and winging the sound into the auditorium, the actor's ears completing the job by assessing the efficacy of the result.

Any weakness in any of these organs can be fatal to an actor's ability to communicate his meaning.

Unlike resonance and musicality, distinctness is almost entirely learnt. No child is born with perfectly inflected vowels or copperplated consonants. Most toddlers lisp and elide and fluff their words until they learn that distinctness helps them get what they want. This is not a conscious process until children grow to be aware of the social and regional implications of their dialect. They then have a choice to make. Change the dialect to make it more distinct to more people or remain happy to be understood by only the few. With actors there is no choice. They must be understood by all in order to be appreciated by all. But by the time they know they want to be actors they may have settled into peculiarities of dialect or diction that make it difficult for this to happen. This is where you come in. If there are deficiencies in the organs of speech, you mustn't be afraid to help the actor address them. Words can easily be practised, consonants enunciated and peculiarities of dialect gently modified, but they will need your ears to help them identify the problem in the first place, their own having already let them down.

Listening is the key to nearly all problems of distinctness. You can spend hours after a performance making lists of words you couldn't hear or understand and then pass them out to a cast assembled for a note session the following day. Or you can save yourself and them a lot of trouble by treating them to a few listening exercises. For instance, dot them around the theatre and ask them to project their words quietly into the space, listening to one another and themselves and repeating any word that isn't distinct to all of them. By tuning their ears in this way, the next performance will prove much more distinct and your list of problem words a great deal shorter.

Without distinctness, words lose their authority and meaning and the indistinct actor, however resonant and musical his voice may be, will struggle to claim the audience's attention. With it, any lack of musicality or resonance in the actor's voice will seem far less of a problem.

Adaptation

Adaptation has a long and honourable tradition in the theatre. From Thespis and Aeschylus onwards playwrights have adapted existing popular stories and turned them into plays. Myth, legend, poetry, romance, novels, histories, diaries, letters, biographies, films, casebooks, court transcripts and already existing plays have all been grist to the playwright's mill.

Of course, adaptation in the theatre is a relative term, and in several different senses. The original material, whatever its source, may be slavishly followed or broadly interpreted or mildly influential or radically changed. The finished adaptation may end up being faithful to the intentions and the tone of the source, or create an entirely new aesthetic true to itself but at variance with the original author's intention. The original material might be a great work of art in its own right and the adaptation an attempt to capture its greatness in a theatrical form. Or the adaptation might become a great theatrical work in itself, entirely eclipsing its original inspiration. In this case, of course, the finished work will not thereafter be known as an adaptation and the original work will become a mere source.

As a director, your relationship with these different sorts of adaptation may express itself in a variety of ways, involving you in duties, responsibilities and opportunities not normally required of you or open to you when you direct an entirely original play.

DIRECTORS AND ADAPTATIONS

1 Classic adaptations

You may be directing a classic play that was an adaptation from an original source. In this case you would be well advised to research the material from which the adaptation was made. By comparing the source material with the finished work, you will get an insight into the structure of the play and learn something about the way the story or the characters have been imagined that could be very helpful to you and to your actors in rehearsal.

2 Modern adaptations

You may be asked to direct an adaptation by a living playwright of a novel or some other literary work. In this case you will obviously read the source material and form an opinion as to the success of the adaptation. If everything is not as you would wish it, you will then have to decide how much authority you have in asking for the adaptation to be adapted further.

3 Commissioning adaptations

You may find yourself wanting to commission an adaptation and have a strong opinion about the source, what you want the final play to say and how the adaptation should be structured. In this case you will have to decide who would be the best playwright to adapt it, how much you want to influence the artistic parameters of the adaptation, even how involved you want to be in the writing process or whether to propose yourself as a co-author of the finished work.

4 Composing adaptations

You may decide to adapt an existing work yourself. In this case you must ask yourself some rigorous questions. Do you really have the playwriting skills required? Would you not be better off collaborating with a proper playwright? Once you have adapted the work, will you still be the right person to direct it? Your passionate interest in the source material will not necessarily make itself apparent in your work on the adaptation. Admiration is not a qualification.

5 Authors and their estates

You may want to adapt, or commission an adaptation of, an existing literary work by a living writer, or by a writer whose work is not yet in the public domain. There will always be complications here, and you will have to get your **performing rights** sorted out. The original author may have a very strong opinion about an adaptation of his work. He may want to adapt it himself but in your view not be the best person for the job. Or he may want to have the work adapted by someone else and not think you the right person to direct it. If he is dead, his remaining family, executors or trustees may have an even stronger and often less reasonable view about an adaptation than the author had he still been alive.

6 Adapting from workshops

You may want to use a **workshop** as part of the writing process (see below). This might involve improvisation with actors and collaboration with the original author and/or with a playwright. And it might require the skills of a choreographer and dancers or a composer and musicians.

7 Adapting from scratch

You may be working on a **devised play** or a **verbatim play** and find yourself adapting the experiences and improvisations of your actors or the memories of your real-life characters. Again, you

Adaptation

must be sure that you have the authorial skills to form what you see and hear in rehearsal, or bear witness to in research, into a performable play. If you have any doubts on this score, get help. Invite a writer to join you.

QUESTIONS FOR WOULD-BE ADAPTORS

1 *Motive*

What is your motive for making the adaptation? Do you seek to give a non-theatrical work that you admire a theatrical life? Does the author of the original work have something to say that you think is important for a modern audience to hear? Is it your intention to be faithful to the original material or are you using it as a source for some other reason? Do you want your audience to receive what you perceive to be the original author's intention or do you have some other, equally credible and creditable, intention to put in its place?

2 *History*

Why did the writer of the original work not write it as a play in the first place? Is it because it never occurred to him? Or is it because he disliked the theatre, or didn't know about the theatre, or because the theatre of his time was moribund, unequal to the task of saying what he wanted to say as a writer? If the latter, why would the theatre of today be kinder to his work than the theatre of his time?

3 *Theatricality*

Are you quite sure that the theatre is the right place for the expression of this story? Is the plot structure sufficiently theatrical? Can the events of the story be broken up into coherent theatrical scenes?

4 *Actability*

Are the characters actable? Is there enough dialogue in the story or enough evidence of dialogue for it to be extrapolated from the interplay between the characters? Has the author given the characters thoughts they cannot express to the other characters? If these thoughts are important, how will they be communicated to an audience? Do you need a **Narrator** or a narrative device? How will such a device work? How will it be integrated into the rest of the play?

5 Conflict

If the essence of drama is conflict, is there sufficient conflict in the story? How does the conflict express itself between the protagonists? Can the conflict between the characters come to a dénouement without the intervention of the author?

6 Philosophy

How philosophical is the work you intend to adapt? Does the philosophical content make the work discursive? Will this matter in a theatrical version? Is the philosophical content of the work important to its overall meaning? Must you find a way of expressing it to make the work complete?

7 Legacy

Would the author of the original work admire what you are doing? When it is finished will he thank you for it? Dead or alive, will he be pleased? Do you care?

ADAPTATION TECHNIQUES AND DEVICES

1 Themes and ideas

What is the author's theme? If he is saying something you think is important, your first duty is to make that something visible and audible on the stage. How do you want the audience to feel as they leave the theatre when the play is over? What do you want them to be thinking about? Throughout the adaptation process, don't get hung up on detail. Keep the big ideas and the major themes in your sights. Have a copy of the original text constantly by your side. Let it be your bible. Analyse it. Make notes all over it. Underline the passages you think are crucial to its meaning. Pay special attention to the passages that inspired you the most and first triggered your thought that the work should be a play.

2 Structure

Novels are usually divided into chapters, epic poems into books and stanzas, biographies into periods of a life, histories chronologically ordered into their major events. How can these structures be converted to a theatrical form? In other words, what's the story? In the theatre this nearly always means: whose story is it? With which of the characters are you expecting the audience to identify? And why would the audience make the identification? How can you present the story of this character, or these characters, in a coherent theatrical manner? How many acts are there? Does the story fall naturally into one or two or more major movements? Should the audience receive the whole work in one uninterrupted act or should there be a break halfway through? If the latter, how will the first half end? What will make the audience want to return for the second half? Or is there more than one break? How long do you intend the whole performance to last?

3 Length

How long is your source material? Assuming it is in book form, count the pages. Then time yourself reading a typical page, not too fast, at the same speed it would take for an actor to project the reading during a performance. Now multiply that time by the number of pages in the book. That's how long your show would take if you left nothing out. Now ask yourself how long the finished play should be. The best way to answer this is to consider the source material and the attention span of its likely audience and ask how long a play version *deserves* to be. How much time does the story need? How long will an audience sit still for it? How personal is it? How epic? How full of ideas? How serious? How comic? How involving in any way? Once you've decided on a rough length, subtract that time from the time it would take to read the entire source. What's left over is what you have to cut.

4 Telling the story

As a general rule, try to tell the story as vividly as you can with as few scenes as possible. Consider for a moment Shakespeare's *A Midsummer Night's Dream*. It has three highly complex plots weaving in and out of one another. It has two major locations, one 'real' and the other fantastical. It goes from palace to wood, from day to night, from reality to dream and back, and it ends with a celebration that includes a play within a play. And it does all this in only nine scenes. Or look at Chekhov's *Three Sisters*. The central characters start young and hopeful and become older and more jaded by time and experience as the play continues. There is a birthday, a marriage, a baby, a fire, a retirement, infidelities, a duel and a death. The army, garrisoned in the town, moves away, leaving the central characters to mourn their departure and hope for a better future for themselves. Nothing has happened and everything has happened. And all in four scenes, an astonishing dramatic conflation that would have taken a lesser playwright ten or twelve scenes to accomplish. How many scenes does your source story need? Remember, every time you finish one scene and start on another, the audience must reconfigure its attention. It should only have to do that when absolutely necessary for the action and the development of the characters.

5 Exposition

What is the opening scene of your play? How much of the exposition of the story can it contain? Don't leave too much for later scenes. Try to get all the conflicts in your story set up as early as possible. More than anything else, conflict is what will hook the audience's attention. As you set up all the threads of your main plot, look at the subplots, if any. Do you need them all? Is there anything you could sensibly cut to streamline the story? With novels especially there are often episodes that support the main story but are not integral to it. Can you do without them? Are there any events in the main plot that can be conflated with other events to make longer and more dramatic scenes? Can events from any subplots be drawn into main plot scenes?

Adaptation

6 *Time scale*

What is the overall time scale of your source story? What month or season does it start in, how much time goes by during the story and what month or season does it finish in? Is this the right time scale for your play? Should you change the seasonal plot for thematic or character reasons? Is your play a winter play ending in spring or a summer play ending in autumn? Is it seasonal at all? Or is it cyclical? Are there repetitious patterns of time in the story? How does time relate to the development of the characters? How old are they all when the play begins and ends? How much time goes by inside each act? Most plays have a broader time scale in the first act than in the second or subsequent acts, with time contracting further and further towards the dénouement. Is this suitable for your story? How much time passes between each of your scenes and during each scene? Do you want to lengthen the feeling of time passing or foreshorten it? How will you do this? Through narration, or as part of the visual design, or by having the characters mention the seasons or the day or the hour? Is there a 'ticking clock' in your story? Do the characters have to achieve anything within a particular time? How would your scene structure take account of this? Sometimes the visiting of multiple locations within the same short time span can intensify the feeling that time is moving very quickly. Should you be considering unconventional time schemes? Would a flashback be suitable at any point? Would the story benefit from being book-ended by a present-tense scene but with the body of the story being in the past? Could the story jump around in time, or go backwards in time?

7 *Location*

How many locations are there in your source story? How useful is it for all these locations to be honoured in your play? Can you simplify them or conflate them? Is there one overarching metaphorical location in which all the events can happen? Are you in a wood or an orchard, in a house or a garden, on a ship, or on another planet? Novelists have no limits on their choices of location. Playwrights have as many limitations as the style of their plays dictates. The more naturalistic the style the more the locations must be realised for the audience. How naturalistic will your design style be? How many locations will your **budget** allow you to depict?

8 *Characters*

Novels and biographies have no limit to the number of characters they use. They are as populated as the novelist or the biographer needs them to be, which is always more populated than the theatre can afford, in terms of space, salary and narrative coherence. The reader of a novel or a history can keep dozens of characters ticking over in his mind. If he gets lost he can flip back through the pages and remind himself who was who. In the theatre if a member of the audience gets lost he stays lost. Experienced playwrights limit the number of their characters to the essential figures needed to tell the story. A character must earn his keep.

Make a list of all the characters in the source material. Underline the crucial leading characters, those that can't be played as doubles. Cross out all the characters that are only in the subplots you have cut or that feature in unimportant incidents. With the characters that are left, make a table, with chapters or scenes on one axis and characters on the other. Once you've finished the table, see how the characters are spread across the story. Now ask yourself: could any of these characters be amalgamated? Do any of them serve similar purposes to one another in the story? Could a series of unimportant characters be amalgamated to create a larger one? Could any of the male characters just as well be female and vice versa? Are all the characters worth playing? Will the actors thank you for them? Could any of the smaller characters be subsumed into middle-sized characters to make them more interesting for actors to play? Once you have finished all your amalgamations, look at the remaining characters and decide how many of them could be **doubles**. Now look at the total number of characters you think your story needs. Can your theatre company afford them?

9 *The author's voice*

In most plays the characters convey the story, unaided by a narrative device. There are obvious exceptions: Greek plays have their

Adaptation

Choruses, as do some Elizabethan plays. Brecht has his choral devices, his ballad songs, banner headlines and storytellers, as do many modern plays written in imitation. But most playwrights eschew these devices, preferring to keep their narrative subsumed in their characters. They might give you clues to their storytelling intentions in the **stage directions**, but they mostly rely on what the characters say, how they describe themselves to one another, what they notice of their surroundings, how they react to the time of day, the weather and the seasons and, most importantly, how they interpret one another's behaviour and then react to their interpretations. In many plays a stranger, or a character returning from a long absence, arrives in the first scene or two so that the back-story can be explained to him by another character more in the know. As the play continues, similarly ignorant characters can be introduced whenever the storytelling needs to skip forward in time or gather pace. However fast the story proceeds, the audience must not be left behind. Novels, biographies and histories do not need such devices. Their storytellers are present in every line, either as third-person narrators, the god's-eye-view, or as first-person, where a protagonist character, or an auto-biographer, tells the story in his or her own words. There are exceptions to these two categories – the epistolary novel, where two or more protagonists tell the story by an exchange of letters, the multi-first-person novel, where a series of protagonists take it in turn to tell the story, or the documentary history, where the historian relies on witness statements to make up the narrative. But the commonest narratives are first- and third-person ones and they present the adaptor with two rather different challenges. With third-person narrative the first thing you have to decide is whether or not the storyteller's point of view, the author's voice if you like, is inherently important to the meaning of the work. Can it be successfully subsumed into the voices of the characters or is there something so idiosyncratic about it, so powerful, so unlike anything that any of the characters would be capable of saying or thinking, that it must be included in the play on its own account? With first-person narrative the problem is a simple one: how does the character play himself and narrate the story at the same time? If the character is telling the story, he knows how it finishes, otherwise how could he be telling it? This puts him at an advantage over all the other characters, who have no idea what their fates are to be, or a disadvantage, in that he can never be completely endangered by the events of the story. Whatever happens to him in the story, he survives to tell it. This fundamental inequality is foreign to the normal world of the theatre, where the audience have an equal view of all the characters and can judge their behaviour equally. In a first-person narrative, the other characters think and feel only as they are perceived to do by the narrator. In a play version the audience must therefore rely on the narrator for all that they know of the other characters. No scene can happen unless the narrator-protagonist is present in it or watching it from afar. This greatly limits the extent to which the other characters can have an inner life. None of them can soliloquise or talk about their secret purposes or desires to anyone other than the narrator. But if you decide to abandon the first-person narrative in your adaptation, how does this decision disable the protagonist-narrator's control over the story and therefore over the audience's attention? Who is Jane Eyre unless she is telling her own story? Or David Copperfield? Or Ishmael?

10 Narration

If you decide the authorial voice of your source material cannot be subsumed within the voices of the characters, you may need a narrator or some sort of storytelling device. Choose carefully from the list under **Narrators and Narration**, but once you have done so, take equal care that you do not overuse your choice. A storyteller can give you extraordinary narrative freedom, but freedom can lead to looseness of structure and prolixity. Be rigorous in cutting down your narrative to what is essential. Don't let the narrator outstay his welcome or the narration outweigh the rest of the text.

11 Making connections

Look at items 1–10 above and ask yourself how they relate to one another. For example, how do the big themes of the story manifest themselves in the lives of the characters or in the locations of the scenes? Does the time scale consistently relate to the lives of all the characters? Does the storyline leave any of the characters hanging at the end of the play? Does everyone get a proper resolution? Does your choice of a narrative device solve your location and time scale problems? If you include a narrator, what is his relationship with the characters and with the set? And so on. By cross-checking all these devices you may discover a missed opportunity or two.

ADAPTATION FOR MUSICAL THEATRE

Whether they are original creations or adaptations from an existing source, musicals are written by partnerships of **book** writer, **lyricist** and **composer**.

Even if you find yourself doubling as book writer or, in very exceptional circumstances, as lyricist or composer, your main role as the director of an adaptation will be to coordinate the work of these three disciplines and keep them all working in the same direction and faithful to, or more interestingly inventive than, their source.

If you are asked to direct an already finished, or partly finished, adaptation, you should look at the list of questions under **New Musicals** and make a judgement on the quality of the work and the likelihood of its being successful before you agree to get involved with it.

If you are helping to start an adaptation from scratch, your first and most important job, if you have any say in the matter, will be to make sure that the composer/lyricist/book writer team is the right one for the source material. Assure yourself that the composer can write with originality in an appropriate musical style, that the lyricist fully understands the complexity and skill required for the job and can suit his lyrics to the original author's cast of mind, and that the book writer is a proper dramatist with a play or two under his belt.

The initial ground you will all have to cover will be more or less the same as for straight theatre. Look at everything else in this entry and see how it relates to the source you are considering. Only then should you also consider the following important points peculiar to musical theatre:

1 Story structure

Don't write a note of music or a word of lyric until the basic story has been mapped out and you are all sure that the plot will bear the weight of a musical adaptation. You could do a lot worse than have your book writer sketch out the whole story as if it were a play before composer and lyricist pick up their pens.

2 Plot complexity

Avoid stories with highly convoluted plots. The more complicated the plot the harder it will be to paint it in the broad emotional brushstrokes that most musical theatre pieces require. Songs are bad vehicles for explaining things.

3 Intellectual complexity

Avoid overly philosophical or intellectual material. Complex ideas are very hard to convey in song. They nearly always end up sounding pretentious, however important they are to the story.

4 Characters

Concentrate on telling the story through the lives of the characters. Characters that sing must have something to sing about. Why are your characters singing? If they are to sing soliloquies or solo ballads, they must have sufficiently conflicted inner lives that their thoughts can only be communicated to the audience in private address.

5 Choruses

If your work employs a chorus, make sure it has a proper dramatic function. Don't have a chorus just because your composer wants to make a big choral sound at some point during the piece. Look at the narrative devices in the list above and consider how your chorus might relate to the way your story is told. If the chorus has no narrative function, why do you need it? Who are the people that your chorus comprises, and what is their relationship to the protagonist characters? If you can't answer these questions adequately, then you don't really need a chorus.

Adaptation

6 Singing and speaking

Unless your musical structure is exceptionally tight and/or the musical itself is exceptionally short, beware the perils of the sung-through musical. If the characters have a lot to say to one another, or if the author has a lot to say to the audience, the recitative sections of the score will seem endless and the composer will be hard-pressed to keep the music melodically engaging. Don't forget, it takes much longer to sing than to speak, and sung words are harder for an audience to understand than spoken words. Sung-through musicals are not worthier than book musicals or more 'artistic'. Much better to have spoken scenes than poorly realised sung dialogue.

7 How to speak

If you decide to include spoken scenes in your piece, encourage your book writer to keep the dialogue lines as short as possible. As a general rule, if the characters have long speeches you will find it harder for the scenes to go seamlessly from spoken word to song and back. Short dialogue lines are crafted in a similar way to lyrical lines and therefore make a better match with them.

8 Musical structure

Encourage your composer to express the story structure in musical terms. Look for the big musical scenes in your source material, where a single musical idea can be sustained over a long period. Look for the big songs. Where are the greatest moments of conflict for the protagonist characters? Where are they wondering what to do next? Where are they in moral or emotional quandaries? Find musical leitmotifs of theme and character that help bind the whole piece together. Don't drown the story with an over-abundance of musical ideas. Find ways in which the predominant musical ideas can be reused in different forms as the story grows. On the other hand, don't overuse a melody or a musical device in the mistaken belief that it will make the score more memorable. More likely it will just drive the audience nuts.

9 Lyrical content

Once the main musical scenes and songs have been identified, encourage your lyricist to make his content interesting and dramatically necessary. A good method is to have the book writer map out the content of each scene and song before the lyricist has a go at it. In solo ballads, make sure there is a dramatic progression through the song. If the character is in the same frame of mind at the end of the song as he was at the beginning, the song will not be earning its keep.

10 Musical and lyrical variety

Your composer and lyricist should collaborate to ensure that no two scenes or songs have an identical structure. They have plenty of techniques at their disposal: length and rhythm of line, rhyming scheme, time signature, key relationships, melody, harmony and tempo. If two songs end up feeling similar, one of them will need to be given a makeover. A good test of the musical and lyrical variety of your work is to get your Musical Director to play you a single bar randomly selected from the score. If you can't tell exactly where it comes from, it isn't particular enough.

11 Rhyme and reason

Rhyme is the mother of cliché in the musical theatre. In a serious piece, bad or clichéd rhyme will trivialise the lyrics, but good and ingenious rhyme can also make them seem over-clever, as if the lyricist is quietly applauding himself at the expense of the characters. Clever rhyme is much better suited to comic material than serious. Rhymed lyrics take a long time to get right and can hold everything else up in the process. Lyrics don't have to rhyme at all, and when they do they don't have to rhyme with absolute regularity. Rather than fall into hackneyed patterns of rhyme, experiment with schemes that give you greater freedom and the lyrical language more of a chance to breathe.

12 Letting go

Never fall in love with a tune, a lyric or a scene. Adapting a story for the musical theatre is an endlessly collaborative venture. If a

Adaptation

work is held hostage by over-preciousness from any one of its creators, it will fall into jeopardy. All partners to the enterprise must be ready to 'murder their darlings' for the common good.

ADAPTATION WORKSHOPS

Adaptations are often commissioned for particular ensembles or theatre companies. In these cases it may be appropriate to begin the whole adaptation process with a **workshop**, making the writer a collaborative partner in the ensemble.

Schedule the workshop to take place at least three months before the rehearsals proper are due to start, longer if the source work is complicated or in a very raw state.

You will need a good-sized rehearsal room and as large a group of actors as the work requires. If at all possible you should try to use actors who will see the work through to the performance stage, though this may prove difficult to schedule.

You may wish to include other important collaborators. Having a designer on board from the start is always a good idea, and a composer too if music is to be a major ingredient.

You could take a week over the work, or two or three, depending on what you want to achieve – though in some countries you may have to take account of union rules governing workshop hours and rates of pay.

What you shouldn't try to do is to write the piece during the workshop period. Writing by committee never works. Because actors are good at speaking dialogue, they will sometimes deceive themselves, and you too, into thinking they are good at writing it. But this is rarely the case. Be ready to intervene if you see your writer being fed lines by your actors and doing his best to jot them down in order not to offend. He will need your protection. Actors should be encouraged to improvise with all the freedom and brilliance they can muster, but not to think of the dialogue they invent as finished script. Let the writer take notes as he thinks fit, but let no one dictate to him what those notes should be. The idea of a workshop of this sort is to give the writer a clear set of guidelines about the structure of the finished work, together with its themes, ideas and characters. After the workshop is over, he will go away and write the play.

The structuring of the workshop is up to you and your collaborators. It's impossible to be prescriptive given the wide variety of source material you may be working on, but here are some of the things you may need to achieve and a few ideas on how to achieve them:

1 Reading and understanding the source

All members of the workshop should become conversant with the source material, but it would be unreasonable to expect them to study it too deeply in advance. You may be adapting a long and complicated novel and some of your actors may not be great readers. At some point during the first day, allocate chapters or sections of the source for your actors to read at home. You and your other collaborators should also be part of the allocation. Depending on how many actors you have, you may need to allocate two or three chapters per person, but don't give the same person two adjacent chapters. On subsequent days, when they are ready, and in no particular order, they can make reports of the chapters they have studied, précising the material to, say, a minute per chapter. Once everyone has reported, you will have in your possession a précised version of the source. You will also have a resident expert for every chapter, a valuable resource for the whole of the workshop period. You can now get the whole company to sit down and tell the story a chapter at a time. If you have a thirty-chapter novel and everyone has kept to the brief of a minute a chapter, the story will take half an hour to narrate. This can be a fascinating exercise. You get the bare bones of the story but you get with it the creative animations of your storytelling actors. Events and characters are brought into vivid relief, with different actors delineating the characters differently depending on where you are in the story. Once the exercise has been fully discussed, you can go further with it. Ask the actors to précis their material much more succinctly, say to ten seconds per chapter, and a few days later repeat the storytelling exercise. This time a thirty-chapter novel will take only five minutes to narrate. You can learn a lot from this about the essential structure of your source. Pay special attention to chapters that are very hard to précis. These will be the places where you and your audience will be most in danger of losing the plot.

2 Research

It is often important to understand the social, political or religious background of the source material and something about the life of its author. If this is the case, you can use the same **research** exercises that you might use for rehearsing a play, allocating research homework for different members of the company. It may also be useful to turn part of the rehearsal room into a research library with maps, charts and illustrations on the wall for easy reference.

3 Creating a narrative

Once you have understood the size and scope of the story you are telling, it should become clear how much of it can be told through the characters alone and how much you will need to use a narrative device. If you feel you don't need a narrator at all, you can omit this stage of the work, but if narration does figure in your thinking you should spend at least a day experimenting with different narrative forms. Take a look at the different narrative options in the list under **Narrators and Narration,** and decide which might be appropriate for your story. Take an important passage from the source, an episode that is crucial to the story but looks like it might be hard to narrate, and work on it with your actors. Once you've hacked a rough performance out of it, try a different device on the same material. And a third and a fourth. If you have a large workshop company, divide it into two or three groups and give the groups the same passage from the source to be narrated in two or three different ways. Give them an hour to prepare and then get them to perform their different versions. If nothing feels right, try other options, but if you can't decide on a narrative form on the first day, don't worry. You will still have plenty of time to experiment as you start to explore scenes in greater detail.

4 Building a story

Isolate three or four of the main events from the source; episodes that you know must be included in the adaptation because of their importance to the narrative, their dramatic vividness or their moral or intellectual authority. Choose scenes that are well spaced across the story so that when you've finished working on them they can serve as stepping-stones from one part of the source to another. You should probably avoid working on anything from the very end of the story: endings tend to sort themselves out when you get everything before them right. But if you are planning on having an interval, it may be instructive to work on the scene you think might immediately precede it. This scene will carry the weight of its own story, maybe even have a strong plot twist or a summary of uncompleted themes, but it must also send the audience away wanting to know more, feel more, experience more. Imagine what you want the audience to be thinking about during the interval. This will tell you what the tone of a pre-interval scene should be and, by inference, the tone of the whole work. Once you've chosen the scenes you want to explore, work through them thoroughly in turn. If you are working a two-session day, don't let work on any one scene run over more than one session. Try to accomplish two big things every day. If you get badly stuck on anything, move on to another scene. A solution may well present itself at a later date when you're working on something else. How you work on each scene is entirely up to you. You and your writer may have prepared scenes in advance that you want the actors to explore. You may want to use **improvisation** techniques of one sort or another so that the writer can watch scenes being played in different situations or styles. You may want to have two or more groups of actors working on the same scene so that you can compare and contrast different acting or narrative solutions. There are no set rules for workshops, only what you or your writer think will prove most useful or informative to the creative process. Be ready for your writer to guillotine your work on a scene. At any moment he might get such a clear idea of where he wants to take the material that he will fear losing his thread from an overload of ideas, or from the pursuit of what he thinks is a fruitless line of enquiry. Conversely, before you abandon your work on any scene, make sure your writer is also happy to do so. He may want to try something that hasn't occurred to you or your actors.

5 Exploring the characters

Characters in novels may be as fully realised as their authors need them to be, but they are usually much more clearly delineated by description than by dialogue. Characters in histories, biographies and letters often have very little dialogue at all. One of the most important tasks for an adaptor is to flesh out the protagonist characters in a story by turning description into conversation. Get your actors to read through whatever dialogue evidence there is, however thin, for the characters you want them to explore. Then allocate the roles and put the characters into rehearse-able scenes or improvisations. In choosing scenes or situations, concentrate on those where two or more characters are in a conflict of some sort. The best way to prove the depth and quality of a characterisation is to clash it against another character. Scenes dominated by a single character will tend to become monologues and monologues tend to make actors self-conscious rather than reactive. Writers often enjoy having an actor, or actors, in mind while they are writing a character. A sparky improvisation from an actor can provide a writer with the rhythm of a character, or a speech pattern or a set of attitudes, maybe even some lines of dialogue. But don't let a particular actor hog one of the characters. Try out different actors on different characters, regardless of age or gender. Your writer should be perfectly capable of making up a whole character from different actors' characteristics. This will also stop the actors feeling proprietorial about the characters – but explain to them in advance what you're doing so they don't feel they're being auditioned. Where final casting has yet to be decided or the roles to be cast are not yet properly defined, actors can get nervous or competitive about their future prospects, and this can harm the creative atmosphere of the workshop. You will also get a much better idea of the possible casting range for each character, in terms of age, gender and personality. If a character is proving particularly elusive, get an actor to assume the role and then put the actor/character in the **hot seat** and let the other actors and the writer fire questions at him.

6 *Experimenting with style*

You may already have decided on a performance style. Your source material may so obviously demand a particular sort of acting or production technique that you feel you have little choice in the matter. If not, you should use part of your workshop time to search for an appropriate style. Use different groups of actors to rehearse the same scene in three or four different ways: in a completely naturalistic style with real props and furniture as required, in dumb-show with the story simultaneously narrated, naturalistically acted but with mimed props, as farce. Keep searching until you find a tone to suit the source.

AFTER THE WORKSHOP

Once the workshop is over you will need to stay in pretty constant touch with your writer. As he works his way through the material, he may want to refresh his memory about some aspect of the workshop or try out a new idea or two on you. Frequent meetings are often needed to keep the work on the right track. But if he prefers to work alone, let him alone. For each writer his own method.

As soon as a first draft is completed you can reconvene the workshop for a read-through, preferably with the same actors you used in the workshop. The greater the continuity of personnel, the more informed the subsequent discussions about the work and what it will be like when it finally meets its audience.

The quality of the debate is very important at this stage. The writer will need plenty of support and encouragement before he goes off to produce the final script. A process that begins collaboratively will need to continue in the same vein. And you must be careful at this point not to respond negatively if the writer has developed the script in ways you didn't expect. You and the actors must be prepared for him to have had inspirations of his own that weren't anticipated during the workshop period. That's what writers do when you leave them on their own. So give their new ideas a proper hearing before you react to them.

By this time you should be only a matter of weeks at the most from the start of your rehearsal period, just enough time for the writer to make final adjustments to the script, and for you and your other collaborators to finalise the casting, the set and the score.

Don't panic if the work isn't entirely finished by the time you get into rehearsal. There isn't a line where one sort of work finishes and another begins. You need to be as well prepared as possible, of course, but your writer will still be with you in rehearsal, still writing and shaping and trimming as you and the actors work on the scenes. With adaptation plays, it is quite common for rewrites to be happening right up to the last minute, and beyond, into the first previews. The more the actors have been part of the process from the very start, the more they will relish the challenge of last-minute changes and understand the necessity for them.

Ad Libs and Ad Libbing

When an actor ad libs, he invents or extemporises a line not written in his text. Not to be confused with 'paraphrasing', where an actor is being lazy with the text or extemporising his way out of a lapse of memory, an ad lib is a deliberate addition, often by an actor in a comic role intent on building a laugh or stretching out a routine beyond the author's written intention.

Ad lib is short for *ad libitum*, a Latin phrase meaning 'at will' or 'at pleasure'. The word libido is derived from the same root, and in some actors it is hard to tell which is the stronger of the two urges.

An ad lib can be very useful when an actor **dries** and needs to be signposted back to the text by a kindly intervention from a colleague. Or when something horribly untoward has happened on stage and a witty actor alleviates the audience's discomfort with a pithy and apposite phrase before returning to the text as written.

Ad libbing can be highly contagious, and a serial ad libber must have his efforts nipped in the bud if you want to avoid a pandemic of ad-libbery breaking out all over one of your productions.

Ad libbing is sometimes a required technique, especially in the construction of **crowd scenes,** but directors and actors must beware the vegetable perils of 'rhubarb'.

Administrators

Always treat the administrative staff of a theatre, however junior, as your equal collaborators. Don't let their closed doors or busy demeanours put you off. Learn their names and make them your friends.

Most people take up jobs in the theatre because they love theatre. You will get the best support from them if you interest them in what you are doing and assume that they are interested in supporting you, which nearly all of them will be. If they sometimes seem a little reserved in their support, it is because they have worries other than yours and a set of complex loyalties involving every department in the theatre.

Most administrators have a wealth of theatrical experience you'd be foolish to ignore. When you find yourself in a bind, ask for their help and advice. One friend in the administrative offices of a theatre will sometimes be worth more to you than a dozen in the rehearsal room.

Agents

Agents are the middlemen in the theatre business. They represent the interests of creators and performers in their dealings with producers and other employers.

Directors, like most theatre artists, are usually self-employed. They move from job to job and contract to contract on an irregular basis with very little financial or legal security. In these circumstances managing one's own career can be a daunting prospect and an agent an invaluable protector.

Good agents are very useful beasts. They know the theatre business, who's running what, who's in and who's out, what's about to happen and what's just been cancelled, who has influence and who doesn't. They bring work opportunities to your attention. They know theatre law or they have lawyers that know it. They negotiate on your behalf when you sign your name to a contract or negotiate for **performing rights**, and they protect you from exploitation by unscrupulous producers. They ask your potential employers for sums of money that you would blush to mention and in return take a mere 10 per cent of your earnings. They give you a better sense of your real artistic and financial worth than you could arrive at by yourself. They place you to advantage in the profession by exaggerating your virtues and moderating your inflated expectations.

But you won't have to work for very long in the theatre before you hear your first negative view of agents. There are those who inveigh against them with a passion. Their patter runs thus. Agents are parasites. They have created a need for themselves where no need really exists. They never get you work. They do nothing in negotiating with employers that you couldn't do just as well for yourself. They take 10 per cent of everything you earn, even when you get a job without their help. They are never available to support you when you're down and they exploit you for all you're worth when you're up. At best they are a necessary evil, at worst a positive menace.

Of course there are bad agents as well as good agents, but those who damn them outright usually have grievous ulterior motives for doing so, the sins of the agent made an excuse for the shortcomings of the client.

GETTING AN AGENT

Most experienced and successful directors have agents. Most young and aspiring directors don't have agents and wish they had. Agents are more interested in representing successful directors than unsuccessful ones. Some far-sighted agents are keen to represent talented young directors who haven't yet proved they can be successful. Short-sighted agents tend to outnumber far-sighted ones, just as busy agents outnumber unbusy ones.

This equation makes things difficult for the young and aspiring director, but if you count yourself in that number, you shouldn't lose much sleep over it. And you shouldn't confuse cause with effect.

By and large agents don't get you work. Successful directors don't derive a living from their agents. The case is quite the opposite. Agents derive a living from their successful clients. Good directors create their own work by networking on their own account. No employer of directors is ever going to take an agent's opinion of his client on trust.

Agents will be interested in representing you the minute you have a potentially lucrative contract that needs negotiating or when you are working so regularly that the prospect of representing you looks like being a good bet. Until that time there is little an agent can do to help you develop your career that you couldn't do just as well, if not better, yourself.

If you do have a piece of work you think is good enough to attract an agent, don't just wing off a raft of generalised letters to every agent in the book. They get dozens of those every week. Know who you're writing to and why. There are hundreds of agents and none of them have quite the same client list. Most actors' agents don't represent directors at all. Some writers' agents also represent directors. Some directors' agents only represent TV and film directors. Know your agent.

Start by networking. Ask all the directors you know and admire who their agents are, and if it doesn't seem too cheeky, ask said admired directors to recommend you, but only if they know your work and can genuinely vouch for it. If you don't know any directors that well, look up the ones you admire on the various professional registers that exist, British Actor's Equity for example, or the Director's Guild of Great Britain, and find out who their agents are. The agent of a director you admire might be the right one for you or be able to recommend someone suitable for you. If you do your detective work well enough you will be able to create a list of the twenty or so agents that might give you the time of day.

If you are offered a significant contract that you feel unable to negotiate on your own, don't hesitate to ask an agent for help.

Agents

Many agents will agree to represent you provisionally on the basis of one good contract and then see how your career develops without making a hard and fast commitment to you.

POINTS TO CONSIDER WHEN EMPLOYING YOUR
FIRST AGENT

1 There are good agents and not-so-good agents.
2 Not every good agent is necessarily the right agent for you.
3 Some good agents have so many successful and demanding clients that they won't have time for you. They may not like to admit this, especially if they admire you.
4 A small agency will not necessarily be better for you than a big one. An agent with only a few clients can still be monopolised by the most successful and demanding clients they have.
5 A big agency is not necessarily a faceless institution. There may be a young agent working in it who is perfect for you and is trying to prove himself as an agent just as you are trying to prove yourself as a director.
6 An agency that mostly represents actors may be less useful to you than one that also represents playwrights and other directors.
7 Choose an agent who is genuinely interested in theatre. A lot of agents are much more excited by film and TV than they are by theatre. If attending your productions is a penance for them they will come to resent you for obliging them to attend.
8 Choose an agent who admires and understands your work. Your agent must be able to speak energetically and cogently about you to prospective employers.
9 Choose an agent you personally like and who personally likes you. If an agent shares your sense of humour and intelligence and general view of the world, he or she will think positively about you and want to see you prosper.
10 Don't think you have to be close friends with your agent. Your relationship should be founded on mutual financial interest and what is best for your career. Most agents resent having to double as therapists.

11 Agents work for you, not you for them. They may be powerful figures in their own right, but in the end they rely on your work to survive. If you start feeling like an employee, the relationship has inverted itself.

12 If your first agent doesn't work well for you then talk to him or her about it. If that doesn't help, look for another.

ACTORS' AGENTS

If you work for larger theatre companies that employ their own Casting Directors you will have little to do with actors' agents, but at the start of your career you may have to deal quite regularly with them. Here are some rules of engagement:

1 Agents can be a total pain, but try not to lose your patience with them. One of their jobs is to protect their clients from doing crappy work that doesn't pay anything. The work has to be very good to compensate for the lack of money. You need to persuade them that their clients' careers will benefit from working with you; that your career is worth the gamble.

2 Before you start negotiating with an agent, make sure, if you can, that the client really wants to work with you. This will strengthen your position. Obviously it will help if you know the actor and you've discussed the job between you. Agents don't like being sidelined like this, but there's no law against it and it saves a lot of time.

3 An actor might say one thing to you and a different thing to his agent. It happens all the time. Actors don't like being rude to directors, however inexperienced they are. They use their agents to protect themselves from people like you. Learn to read between the lines.

4 If an agent is stalling you, it's probably because he doesn't want his client to do the job you're offering but hasn't yet talked to the client about it. In this case, find a way to talk to the actor direct or give the agent a deadline, and if you don't hear back, move on to someone else.

5 If the actor you want is unavailable or unwilling to take the part you're offering, the agent may try to sell you someone else. Don't dismiss the suggestion out of hand. If the agent has read the play and knows what the part requires, the proposal might be a good one. Agents are subjective about their clients, of course, but they're often very good at casting.

Alexandrines

See **Metre**.

Alienation

'Alienation' or the 'Alienation Effect' is the usual translation of the German composite word *Verfremdungseffekt*, the theory originated by the German dramatist Bertolt Brecht, that describes the deliberate distancing or 'alienation' of the audience from a thoughtlessly emotional response to the human drama being acted out on the stage. In many ways the alienation effect was a reaction to the Wagnerian concept of **Gesamtkunstwerk** or total aesthetic experience, an idea completely alien to Brecht's social and political view.

Various alienation devices were used by Brecht and many of them put to such effective use in his work as a writer and director, especially in the productions of his own company, the Berliner Ensemble, that they have since become commonplaces of the modern stage. They include:

1 The deliberate revealing of the techniques behind scenic and lighting effects and the rejection of unnecessary masking of lighting instruments and other theatre machinery.
2 The abandonment of any unnecessary decorative adornment on stage or in the auditorium and the breaking down of any barriers between the two spaces, most noticeably the traditional stage curtain.

3 The obvious punctuation of the scenes of a play into clearly comprehensible units unaffected by the need for conventional dramatic climaxes.

4 The description before each scene starts of its dramatic content, the words being written on boards or banners, projected onto a screen or spoken or sung by a chorus.

5 Incidental music and sound effects performed in full view of the audience.

6 The presentation of the actors to the audience as ordinary people prior to their getting into their characters or the manifest adoption of character or costume as part of the dramatic incident of the play.

Few of these ideas were really Brechtian inventions, most of them originating in long-established world theatre practice of one sort or another, from Greek theatre via Shakespeare to the music hall. But Brecht was a great theatrical magpie, flying in the face of a moribund Romantic theatre tradition in Germany and collecting the most robust set of dramatic devices from wherever he could find them. The resulting fusion of East and West, ancient and modern, 'legitimate' drama and music theatre, and his peculiar mix of political dogma and personal witness gave the European theatre of the post-World War II period a new start and served to rejuvenate the plays of the past with a new energy and purpose.

As with most successful artistic innovations, the revolution of one age becomes the accepted norm of the next, and Brecht's influence is now so well acknowledged by the modern theatre that some of the terms he found necessary have become somewhat redundant, 'alienation' being the most obvious example. Once the most exciting and revolutionary of Brecht's theories, it now seems the most confusing, all the more so because of the contradictory nature of his own writings on the subject.

If the audience is to have its perceptions of the play 'alienated' so that its reactions are made more intellectually acute, what happens when its intellects are so successfully stimulated that passionate political or emotional feelings ensue? If Brecht's greatest plays – *Mother Courage, The Caucasian Chalk Circle, The Life of Galileo* or

Alienation

The Good Person of Szechwan – are brilliantly performed with all their 'alienation' techniques in place, and audiences respond by being deeply moved by them, should they feel guilty for not thinking enough or for feeling too much? Some devoted scholars of Brecht see no contradiction between his theories and his plays, but most theatre professionals are rather more worried by them.

The answer for the director is simple. If you like Brecht's plays, then direct them. Read his theoretical works with interest but take his more dogmatic opinions with a pinch of salt and learn to enjoy his contradictions. Above all, don't let any confusion you might have about the theories put you off the real value of the work. Brecht's plays are his true legacy. If he had been solely an academic theatre writer he would already be a footnote in the history of European Marxist culture.

And if you never manage to reconcile your problems with the Alienation Effect, don't lose sleep over it – just take a couple of aspirins and read *Henry V*.

Amplification

The electronic amplification of the voice is a staple technique in **musical theatre**, and a necessary one. No singer can perform a large role eight times a week, week in week out, without a little help, especially if the voice has to compete with electronic keyboards and a noisy rhythm section. Thus nearly all musicals need Sound Designers, mixing desks, **radio-mikes** and all the rest of the electronic clobber that goes with them. Thus, too, the paradox – amplification for musicals is very expensive but also constitutes an economic necessity. Without it you would need twice or three times the number of performers playing in rotation or you would have to do far fewer performances per week. Either way you would never make ends meet in the commercial theatre.

But if amplification is a simple solution to a commercial problem, it causes a whole series of other problems in its wake. Radio-mikes must be attached to the performers' clothes or taped to their heads or threaded into their wigs. Costumes must be made to accommodate mike packs. Spare batteries and mikes must be on constant stream in the wings, with sound department runners on hand to refit them or change them. Amplified voices must be played through speakers that have to be built into the set or mounted on the walls of the theatre in a manner sympathetic to the rest of the design. The sound they produce must then be balanced with the sound of the orchestra and with the other voices on stage. Different parts of the auditorium with different **acoustics** must also be balanced against each other. Thus an entire science is unleashed, and all because of a simple financial imperative.

Because of the extreme annoyance and expense of this process, you should try to avoid using amplification in non-musical theatre. Apart from anything else, it has a dehumanising effect on actors' voices. Even when used with great finesse, amplification tends to create a split vocal focus for the audience, with the actor's real voice competing with an amplified version of itself coming from another source in another direction.

Don't ever get suckered into using amplification under false pretences. If a theatre acoustic is poor strive to make it better (for possible solutions, see **Acoustics**). If the actors are inaudible get them to speak up. If theatre machinery is noisy silence it. Try everything else before you succumb to the drug of amplification. And it is addictive. Audiences can get so used to it that they expect every voice coming from the stage to be resoundingly and uniformly clear, with all the interesting idiosyncrasies of speech and tone ironed out to a uniform loudness. Worse still, actors can grow vocally lazy. The more they rely on their microphones, the less they bother to project their voices. If mikes are allowed to become standard in the theatre, actors' voices will eventually diminish to become a vestigial part of them, like the legs on a slowworm.

If all else fails then the audience's right to hear your play must prevail over other scruples and you will have to consider amplification. Here are some circumstances in which it may be necessary:

1 Venue failure

A theatre is too big or too poor acoustically for the audience to hear the actors properly. Modern theatres are often made from acoustically unfriendly materials, theatrical technology makes an increasingly loud undertow of noise with which actors often feel powerless to compete, air-conditioning plants blow and bellow from the walls of stages and auditoria, and audiences themselves can contribute to the general cacophony. In these cases Theatre Managers often install a 'sound enhancement' system consisting of microphones hidden all round the stage and speakers hidden all over the theatre. The best systems are undetectable to the audience. The worst have the actors' voices sounding from everywhere but the direction of the stage.

2 Actor failure

A particular actor has a vocal problem, rendering him inaudible. If this is caused by illness – a heavy cold or a bad throat – then you would normally just put the understudy on until the principal actor gets better. But there may be times when this isn't an option – a first night or a gala performance for instance – and you have to patch your leading actor up the best you can. A discreet radio-mike could well provide the answer. If an actor's inaudibility is caused by a lack of technique and for whatever reason he is indispensable to your production, the answer may be the same, but it won't be a temporary measure. You and your Sound Designer will have to decide how best to blend his voice with the other more competent voices on stage. This might mean a radio-mike for only the poor voice or it might mean general amplification for all the voices. You will have to decide. This is a problem quite common in the commercial theatre, where a bankable star of film or TV is heading a cast of seasoned theatre actors without the voice or the vocal technique to do the job properly.

3 Sound effects

A musical **accompaniment** or **sound effect** is so loud that the performers' voices cannot be heard above it. Radio or locally placed microphones are the only answer here. General amplification will also pick up the music and merely amplify the whole problem. Alternatively turn down the sound effect.

4 *Voice effects*

An actor's voice needs to be treated in order to provide a special effect – an echo, for example, or some other effect that can only be achieved by first amplifying the voice and then treating it. This isn't really an amplification issue, but you should be careful that the effect you achieve doesn't require further amplification of everyone else. Don't let your special effects make everything around them seem un-special.

Increasingly, it seems that amplification or sound enhancement is destined to become a norm in the theatre. This would be a terrible pity. If theatre is to survive as a living art it will only do so by celebrating what is unique to it, and a natural human relationship between actor and audience is at the heart of that uniqueness. The closer that theatre gets to the technological anonymity of the rock concert or the film the more likely it is to be subsumed by them.

Angels

Angels are the investors in commercial theatre, so called because they traditionally descend from financial heaven, bearing good tidings of comfort and joy in the shape of a large cheque. The term should really be confined to those who help with no thought of a benefit in return, as the rules of angelic behaviour would seem to dictate, but the commercial theatre can't function without investors, and if they like to be called angels, it's a small price to pay for their enthusiasm whatever their motive. They nearly always lose their money anyway and become angels by default.

The true angels are those who put money into the non-commercial theatre because they believe in its artistic, social or educative importance, and know that their reward will not be a financial one. Instead they will sit at the right hand of the Artistic Director and dwell in the glorious presence of writers, actors and directors for ever and ever. Amen.

Animals

Actors hate working on stage with animals almost as much as they hate working with **child actors,** and for very similar reasons.

Where there is quite often a real necessity for the use of real children on stage, this is rarely the case with live animals. Few plays are written in such a way that only a living creature will satisfy the demands of the drama. There are exceptions. Launce and his dog Crab in *Two Gentleman of Verona* have a partnership that is entirely dependent on live interplay. If the actor playing Launce enters trailing a wooden dog on wheels, you know he's going to struggle to make you laugh. But Shakespeare has made it easy for the actor, allowing plenty of scope for a real dog's reactions, or lack of them, to raise the necessary laughs. In a production of *Two Gentlemen of Verona* at the RSC in the 1970s a very beautiful Old English sheepdog cast as Crab had to be fired because the audience didn't find him, or the actor playing his master, at all funny. The problem was that his face was so shaggy that the audience couldn't see his eyes. He might just as well have been a puppet. He was replaced at the next performance by a bright little mutt belonging to a member of the props department, and the audience fell about within a few seconds of his first entry, largely because they could see his eyes. Whenever the dog changed the focus of his attention throughout Launce's speech he gave the actor another opportunity to play the audience's delight in the partnership. The part of Crab is one of those rare examples where a well-cast animal can enhance rather than detract from the effect of an actor's appearance.

In most cases, live animals have a negative effect on any scene in which they appear, and you should think long and hard before you employ them. Firstly, you mustn't imagine that you'll be adding to the verisimilitude of a scene if you stage it with live animals. This is partly because animals on stage tend to look and behave less like themselves than they do in their real habitat and partly because audiences are unused to extending their conspiracy of **belief** to include animals.

What you think a horse will give you on stage is size and strength, beauty and nobility and an impressive first entrance for your leading actor or singer, but what you'll get is something rather different. A horse has no room on stage to move freely, an unreceptive surface for its hooves, a sense of unease at the brightness of the lights and the unfamiliar atmosphere and a complete lack of etiquette in matters of personal toiletry. Horse-lovers in the audience will be highly attuned to any physical or emotional distress the animal might be suffering and become more concerned with that than with anything else they might be watching. Everyone else in the audience will be consumed with a wide variety of reactions and questions, none of them pertinent to the drama they are supposed to be watching. 'Where do they keep a horse backstage?' 'I wonder what his name is.' 'Whoops, he nearly knocked that actress over.' 'What's that guy doing with the shovel?' In the end your leading actor will beg you to cut the horse in exchange for an upstage centre entrance and the audience's undivided attention.

What you might imagine you're going to get from a bird of prey on stage is the majesty of flight or the watchful danger of the hunt and the kill. What you actually get is a big bundle of feathers sitting hunched on its handler's arm, very occasionally turning its head. Doves and pigeons, even when cleverly trained, fly off at the wrong time or to the wrong place to flutter about later in the evening at wildly inappropriate moments. Snakes and lizards stay so still they might just as well be stuffed. Any small animal makes the audience wonder if it's real or a cleverly handled glove-puppet, and any big animal makes the audience nervous about its behaviour.

Most animals, whatever their size, will be nervous and out-of-sorts in front of an audience and few will ever be worth the considerable expense of the trainers, handlers, licences, accommodation and transport they require. A hawk or a cat or a chicken that appears on stage for no more than five minutes will take up more like five hours of rehearsal and technical time and dominate discussions about the schedule out of all proportion to its importance.

If your play demands an onstage animal, think first of your alternatives before you saddle yourself with a living beast. Could the props department make an imaginative version of the animal in puppet form to be manipulated by actors or puppeteers, one that will delight the audience, tell the story and cost nothing beyond a bit of papier-mâché and some clever craftsmanship? Could the animal be played by an actor, or by two actors? Audiences are good at suspending their disbelief, so why not make one little extra demand of them? Is an animal visually necessary at all? Could the presence of an animal not be suggested just as well by a sound effect, or imagined by the actors and the audience in the darkness of the wings or the auditorium?

Antithesis

Antithesis is a rhetorical figure of speech that sets one word against another, very important in understanding the works of Shakespeare and his contemporaries. For a full description, see the entry on **Verse and Verse Speaking**.

Applause

Applause is a **theatrical convention** used by the audience to express its approval. The convention has it that by noisily clapping your hands together you register approval of what you have seen and heard on stage and by not doing so you register disapproval or apathy. In civilised theatre communities the minimum response to any performance, however dull, involves polite if not prolonged applause, and the maximum response involves the use of other conventions – the stamping, shouting or clapping in rhythm conventions – and the final triumphant accolade, the standing ovation.

But the applause convention is a complicated one and has many different variations, some of which you have control over but most of which you don't.

If applause was reserved for the **curtain call** only, it would be a simple matter, but it also comes in 'rounds' at other points during the evening.

ENTRANCE ROUNDS

An entrance round is the applause that a celebrated actor gets, or demands, on his entrance. Once a required homage from the audience for any starring actor, this is a ritual that has fallen into well-deserved disrepute.

Most serious actors are embarrassed to receive a round of applause just for entering, as if, like conductors in the opera house or concert hall, they should be praised for their graciousness in turning up at all. But there are actors whose opinion of themselves puts them beyond embarrassment. They learn the trick of triggering applause on their first entrance, even waiting for it when it isn't forthcoming, thus compounding the embarrassment.

Even if an actor is a major star and the audience has turned up solely to see him, he can still silence an entrance round by entering in a normal fashion, playing the reality of the onstage situation for all its worth and getting on with the text or encouraging his fellow actors to get on with it. An audience will abandon an entrance round if it feels it might be missing the dialogue and losing track of the story.

EXIT ROUNDS

An exit round is the applause an audience gives an actor in appreciation of a well-played scene or because the exit immediately follows a climactic speech or an effective piece of **business**, usually comic. Some actors learn the trick of triggering such rounds of applause and are unhappy if their most dramatic exits are made in silence, especially in comedy, where a character's big final laugh can easily be developed into an exit round by a skilful manipulator. There are plays where such behaviour is inappropriate and plays where it should be positively encouraged. You must decide. But be ready for the occasions when your opinion will be irrelevant, the audience deciding for itself and the actor claiming to be a powerless pawn in its hands.

Applause

LAUGH ROUNDS

A laugh round is applause immediately following a big laugh. When a hilariously funny piece of comic business or verbal interplay makes an audience develop its laughter into applause, the actor or actors are said to have earned a 'round'. The same event in the US is referred to as 'a show-stopper' or 'stopping the show'.

In some comic actors' books this is the highest accolade imaginable, and they zealously cultivate and treasure their laugh rounds, able to account for them or the lack of them for weeks afterwards. Overzealousness in this regard, however, can lead some actors into grotesque comic contortions, and you will sometimes need to persuade them that failure to get a laugh round is not a criminal offence, and that an audience's laughter is a gift to be relished rather than a tax to be excised.

STANDING OVATIONS

British audiences reserve their standing ovations for performances they regard as utterly exceptional and have trouble in awarding the distinction to performances that are merely excellent. In America the standing ovation has become so devalued that some Broadway wit or other was heard to say of a recent flop, 'It was so bad it didn't *even* get a standing ovation.' Be that as it may, there are certainly gradations of standing ovation depending on circumstance and expectation. The only genuine article entails an entire audience spontaneously leaping to its feet as the last words or notes die away and then applauding long and hard in real gratitude for what they have seen and wonderment that it could have been achieved. But most standing ovations don't come up to this standard.

There is the grudging standing ovation, where the audience stands because they think it's expected of them when actually they are getting up to put on their coats. These tend to last no more than thirty or forty seconds and die out by the time the cast has taken its second call. Then there's the partial standing ovation, with little patches of the audience desperate to demonstrate their devotion to the show but unable to convince the majority around them that they are right to do so. Or the selective standing ovation, which waits for a particular much-loved star to make his solo bow before jumping into action. Or the manipulated standing ovation, usually reserved for first nights, with the front two rows of the stalls pre-packed with friends of the producer instantly rising to their feet at the start of the calls so that everybody behind them has to stand to see the cast at all. Or the required standing ovation, where a star takes a solo call with arms outstretched and face beseeching, stubbornly refusing to bow or move away from centre stage until the audience has risen to its feet in homage.

Standing ovations are nice payment if you can get them, but you should let them happen and never work for them. Applause belongs to the audience, not to you. If you and your actors are to receive any, you must earn it, and not extort it dishonestly.

Apron Stage

An apron stage is one that extends out beyond the **proscenium** arch into the **auditorium,** like an apron spread out over a pair of seated knees. The term is generally used to describe a stage that is more extended than a **forestage** but not as much as a **thrust** or platform stage, though it is often used synonymously for both, having no accurate definition of its own. The front part of the Elizabethan stage is often referred to as the apron in modern reconstructions, though it was never called so in Elizabethan times.

Arena Stage

One of the most important developments in modern **auditorium** design was pioneered in the 1950s by the director Tyrone Guthrie. Influenced by the single sweep seating of the classical Greek amphitheatres and by the **thrust stages** of the Elizabethans, he created theatres at Stratford, Ontario and Minneapolis, Minnesota that redefined an audience's expectation of how it should watch and listen to a play. The audience sits in a semicircular bank of seats surrounding the stage and thus has its attention drawn more to the actors than to any scenic elements built in the upstage spaces. The actors enter and exit from upstage or from **vomitoria** shared by the audience when entering and leaving the theatre.

The arena idea became very fashionable with theatre architects in the 1960s and 70s and other theatres followed suit, notably in Chichester, in London at the National Theatre's Olivier auditorium and at the Lincoln Center in New York. Guthrie's original designs have perhaps proved less durable in practice than in theory and most of the above-mentioned theatres have adapted their spaces to make them more actor- and audience-friendly, but the basic idea has continued to exert a strong influence on theatre architecture all over the world.

The arena configuration presents directors and actors with both **acoustic** and **staging** problems very similar to those found in **thrust** and **in-the-round** theatres, the solutions for which are discussed under those entries and under **staging**.

Artistic Directors

Most theatre companies are run by a partnership of Artistic, Administrative and Financial Directors, responsible to a governing board of directors or trustees. The role of chief executive of the company sometimes resides in the post of Administrative Director, but more usually, at least in Britain and America, in that of the Artistic Director. Some boards prefer to give their administrators the executive leadership in order to guard themselves against capricious or ruinously expensive artistic decisions. Others prefer to give executive authority to the Artistic Director in order to ensure the artistic policy of the company takes precedence over any other consideration. In such cases the Artistic Director must take ultimate responsibility for the efficient administration and the financial solvency of the company as well as for its artistic policy.

Most Artistic Directors direct as well as programme the plays in the **repertoire** of their companies. If the company is small, they will tend to direct most or all of the plays. If the company is large they will direct only some of them, employing permanent **Associate Directors** or occasional **Visiting Directors** to direct the others.

If you direct plays, then at some point in your career you will either become an Artistic Director or have to come to terms with a variety of Artistic Directors in the theatres that employ you, or perhaps both. Or you will find yourself coveting an Artistic Directorship, or applying for one, or interviewing for one or being petitioned by others to put yourself forward for one.

It is a commonplace that the best Artistic Directors are not necessarily the best directors of plays, and that brilliant directors of plays do not necessarily make good Artistic Directors, though there have been, and there will always be, notable exceptions.

It is therefore instructive to consider the differences between these two functions, the talents required to discharge both jobs and the conflicts that may arise between them.

THE ADVANTAGES OF BEING AN ARTISTIC DIRECTOR

1 You are permanently employed by a company and receive a regular wage. You are thus freed from the artistic and financial insecurity of the freelancer.
2 You define the artistic policy of your company. This affords you a responsibility and an excitement denied to the freelancer or the Associate Director. Your choices of repertoire can define whole seasons of work around social, political or any other artistic themes.
3 You have commissioning power. You can decide which playwrights are worthy of commission and which commissions worthy of performance. If you are directing a new-writing company, your choices can establish a stable of writing talent that will outlive your regime.
4 You have employing power. Your choice of associate artists will define the artistic profile of your company; your Associate

75

Artistic Directors

Directors, designers, music staff and actors will speak for you, whether or not you are directing the plays they are working on. Your choice of staff in other departments will define the way your company is perceived by its artists and its audiences.

5 You can, if you wish, create a performance style unique to the actors of your company. Employing the same group of actors over a long period may result in a unifying style that helps to define the efficacy of your policy. Freelance directors have to start afresh with every new company they direct.

6 If your company is building-based, you have the security of working in a single theatre space or spaces. Your choice of repertoire can therefore be inspired by the spaces at your disposal. You never need choose a repertoire that would be unsuitable for the spaces at your disposal.

7 Your rehearsal rooms and office spaces will very likely be a permanent feature of your company and the support staff attached to them constantly available to you. These luxuries alleviate the commonest bugbear of the freelance director – artistic loneliness and the constant search for a home.

THE DISADVANTAGES

1 You are tied to a single company and to the theatre spaces associated with it. Your choice of repertoire, including all the plays you may want to direct yourself, will be circumscribed by the size of your acting company, the tastes of your habitual audience and the configuration of your theatre or theatres. A freelance director can choose his work from a long and varied à la carte menu of theatrical fare, from plays, musicals, opera, even films or television. Unless you are heading up one of the giant subsidised companies, you will always be ordering from the *table d'hôte*.

2 If you decide, for whatever reason, to create work for yourself outside the confines of your company, you will find it very difficult to square your absence with your permanent employees. When the captain leaves the ship in mid-voyage, the crew tend to feel betrayed.

3 However good you are at delegating your authority, you will have to get involved with things that hold no interest at all for you. If you are leading your company well, everyone will be interested in your opinion on every conceivable issue. You will thus have to endure hours of mind-numbing meetings about peripheral issues when what you most want to be doing is reading or rehearsing plays.

4 The smaller the company, the harder it will be to exclude yourself from the mundane practicalities of running a building. On an opening night, the artistic health of your play may suddenly seem less important to you than a clogged front-of-house toilet.

5 Your artistic life will be dominated by financial concerns. However well funded your company is by government subsidy or private sponsorship, the battle for cash will never entirely be won. More likely you will be immersed in a constant struggle for solvency. You will therefore be forced to spend a great deal of time talking money out of people's pockets into your theatre's coffers. These may very well be people you would never otherwise have chosen to know.

6 Your directorial career will become inseparably entwined in the public mind with the stewardship of your company. Even if your own productions do well, if your company is failing, your work will seem to fail with it. If your own productions do badly, your career as a company leader will still seem glossy if your theatre continues to do well. You yourself may find it increasingly difficult to separate your personal fortunes from those of your company. This may have negative implications for your career if you move back to the freelance world. The longer your tenancy of a company or companies, the more likely it is you will become addicted to Artistic Directorship, only able to direct plays from within the shelter of an organisation with all its support mechanisms in place around you.

7 If you have ambitions to be a writer, librettist or adaptor as well as a director, you will be hard-pressed for the time to realise them. Writing of any kind requires a measure of untroubled space and time, both commodities in short supply for an

Artistic Director. Playwrights who run theatres tend to stop writing, or if they continue to write, they stop writing well.

The constraints and anxieties of running a theatre company can adversely affect your ability to direct your own productions. If your work as a director suffers in this way, you must ask yourself what good you are doing, as director or Artistic Director. Would you not be happier as an administrator on the one hand, or a freelance director on the other? Or will you slowly get better at doing both jobs simultaneously? How can you be sure? Look at the following list and see how close you are to creating a happy and secure company for yourself and for those in your care.

12 WAYS TO BE A HAPPY ARTISTIC DIRECTOR

1 Get fully involved

Your enthusiasm should extend to every department of your theatre. Learn everyone's name. Treat everyone equally. Take time to listen.

2 Learn to delegate

Don't try to do everything yourself. If you micromanage the work of your colleagues, you will disable their enthusiasm and expertise and risk undermining their relationships with their colleagues. You will also lose sight of the big picture and end up doing your own work badly.

3 Promote discussion

A regular forum for artistic planning and scheduling will help you to draw all your threads together and will allow your colleagues to let off steam in a creative way. Listen carefully to what you hear. Don't feel you have to act immediately on what is proposed by others, but make it clear you have heard and digested all that has been said.

4 Befriend Admin and Finance

Form a particular bond with your Administrative and Financial Directors. They must be your co-conspirators and brothers-in-arms. If any one of you pulls in a different direction from the other two, the whole company will suffer. Learn to like one another. See also **Budgets**.

5 Conspire with the board

Don't let your board of directors or trustees be your enemies. You might not find all of them equally sympathetic, but try to make some of them part of your conspiracy to succeed, especially your chairman. Most of them will be serving because they love the theatre. Forgive them their moments of ignorance and enjoy their enthusiasms. Let them into the game.

6 Learn to love raising money

Do not disdain the company of those that are keen to give you their hard-earned cash. Create a world for yourself in which patronage is a duty and begging is noble. Believe in the necessity of art and the primacy of great theatre in a healthy society. All the best things in life must be paid for, and the best of theatre will always cost more than most people think it is worth. Enjoy proving them wrong.

7 Be generous

If you employ Associate or Resident Directors, take pleasure in their successes and sympathise with their failures. This may be hard to do if your colleagues are experiencing a run of popularity and your own work is in the critical doldrums. But don't forget, you employed them. Their triumphs are making your company look good. Consider how clever you have been to promote a director of such talent.

8 Don't be paranoid

Whatever the circumstances, don't become suspicious or peevish or fearful. If you feel threatened by one of your colleagues, find out why you feel that way and address the problem, whether it lies with him or with you or somewhere in between. Don't go to bed on two successive nights brooding on the same problem.

9 Don't sacrifice yourself

Don't become the fallback director for plays that no one else wants to direct. If you feel obliged to programme a play you wouldn't want to direct yourself, and you can't find a talented director to do it for you, don't drop yourself in it. Drop the play.

10 Commission new work

Make relationships with living writers and promote them and their plays from first idea to final performance. Your regime will be remembered for the work it has produced, and published works will be your most concrete testaments. There is nothing more gratifying than being midwife at the birth of a healthy new play.

11 Make room for others

Listen to your associates' enthusiasms and let their choices of material be reflected in the repertoire. You can't direct every play yourself and you shouldn't force your associates into directing your hand-me-downs. No one likes to be the second-choice director, especially if the first-choice director is looking over his shoulder as the work proceeds.

12 Make time for yourself

Give yourself time to read and learn, experience and imagine. Go to other people's theatres. See as much as you can of plays, operas, musicals and films from all over the world. Don't get so locked in to the day-to-day running of your company that you lose sight of your larger artistic goals. Have a life outside the theatre. Spend time away. Take holidays.

Asides

An aside is a mini **soliloquy**. In a scene in which two or more characters are conversing, one of them conceives the need to communicate an unspoken thought directly to the audience. He turns away from his interlocutors and speaks his thought, usually briefly – sometimes very briefly – but occasionally at greater length. The other players complete their side of this **theatrical convention** by seeming not to notice that the aside is being made. As the speaker turns back to his interlocutors the scene continues as if the aside hadn't happened, though the other characters may play an awareness that the speaker has had a thought he doesn't want to share with them.

The aside convention, even when used in a serious play, is a fundamentally comic one, as it nearly always features a puncturing of the dramatic tension established between the characters which in turn tends to trigger an audience's laughter.

ASM

ASM stands for Assistant Stage Manager, the most junior rank of the **stage management** team.

Assistant Directors

A staging post in the career of nearly every director is the role of Assistant Director, an assistantship being the nearest thing in the profession to an apprenticeship or studentship but without any precise definition or rules of engagement. Indeed, no two professional directors, producers or theatre companies, the most likely employers of Assistant Directors, are likely to agree on the exact nature of the role, and various expectations may arise if you are employed as one.

The problem of definition derives from the fact that no two directors are alike in their preferences and methods. Some directors like to have another challenging intellect in the rehearsal room with them and others feel threatened by it. Some directors insist on doing absolutely everything themselves, from making the daily rehearsal call to getting their own coffee and some are only too willing to delegate. Some directors love to be fed ideas while others only have use for their own. No two directors are alike, so no two assistants can ever be alike.

Assistant Directors

Nonetheless, it may be valuable to give an outline of the variety of duties and responsibilities that attach to the post and the way in which both director and assistant may find themselves responding to them and to each other.

The reason for the employment of most Assistant Directors is to rehearse and maintain the **understudies**. Any production that cannot afford to cancel a performance because of accident or ill health must equip itself with understudies, and they must be adequately prepared to go on at a moment's notice. In the commercial theatre, the understudies are often rehearsed by a senior member of the stage management team, even though he may have missed the rehearsal discussions essential to a full understanding of the play; in the subsidised sector, however, this job is nearly always done by the Assistant Director, whose relationship with the director and closeness to the principal actors makes him an ideal support for nervous or inexperienced performers. Rehearsing the understudies gives the Assistant Director a good opportunity for practising his craft, with a lick of real responsibility but without the weight of a whole production on his back.

HOW TO CHOOSE AN ASSISTANT DIRECTOR

The most important qualities in an assistant are intelligence, patience and good humour.

Intelligence, because an assistant must be at least as bright and quick as the actors with whom he works or problems may develop in understudy rehearsals. Assistants who feel intellectually threatened by the actors will often react by standing on their authority and end up making themselves ridiculous.

Patience, because an assistant spends most of his time in rehearsal watching the director work rather than working himself. He may be bursting with ideas and observations but is obliged to remain silent. The best assistants are able to think their thoughts and bide their time.

Good humour, because an assistant is often required to cope with a great tangle of scheduling rehearsals, listening to troubles, assuaging bruised egos and pleasing the director all at the same time. Laughter is a necessary safety valve.

When interviewing a prospective assistant, read his CV very carefully. Look for evidence that he has a genuine interest in the sort of play you will be working on together. Quiz him in detail about his directing experience to assure yourself that he has a real love and sympathy for actors. Ask him about other directors he has assisted and compare his impressions with your own knowledge of their work. If he has had bad experiences, find out why. Beware of disloyalty. If he bad-mouths one of his previous employers, he'll probably end up doing the same to you. And beware of flattery, which is disloyalty in disguise. Examine his career and ambition. If he has been an Assistant Director for a long time, has he become a career assistant without any real prospect of a directorial career of his own? Do you want that in an assistant? Maybe you do. Or would you prefer to share the rehearsal room with a bright young spark who'll be running his own company in a year or two? Are you strong enough to have an assistant who wants your job? Is he intelligent, patient and good-humoured? Do you like him?

As in the rest of this book I have used 'he' above for both 'he' and 'she', but sometimes gender is an issue in the appointment of an assistant. If you are working on a play that has a preponderance of male roles and you have a male stage management team, the few females in your company may feel outnumbered. A sympathetic and intelligent female assistant can help redress the balance. Vice versa in a predominantly female company.

HOW TO USE AN ASSISTANT DIRECTOR

Involve your assistant as early as you can in the preparation of the production. Share your ideas with him and take him through the design process and the casting process. The more he understands about the genesis of your production the more supportive he will become.

Don't be frightened of your assistant, even though he might be destined for a glossy career in the theatre, a career that may eclipse your own. Even if he's very talented he might not know how talented he is. Most assistants are finding their feet as directors and don't know exactly where they are going. Assisting you will be part of their training, and they will nearly always value your approval and support. Don't be embarrassed to teach your assistant something you think he needs to know.

In exchange for your support you can use your assistant as a sounding board for your ideas. Treat him as an intellectual equal, and if he has an idea that fits in well with your production, steal it. Shamelessly.

Never treat an Assistant Director as a slavey. A junior member of the stage management can bring you your coffee or nip out to the deli for your sandwich. If you use your assistant as a gofer, your cast will find it hard to see him as having any authority when he takes over as the Understudy Director or comes to them with notes during the run.

Instead, take care to build up your assistant's authority and confidence. Involve him as much as you involve the actors in discussions about the play. When you need a second opinion about something, ask him first. Listen when he makes an unsolicited suggestion, and adopt it if it's a good one. If it's a bad one, don't mock it but consider it and reject it kindly.

Encourage him to have a strong professional and social relationship with the actors and stage management. Use him as much as you can. Involve him in planning and scheduling. If it's a big-cast play, let him rough out the rehearsal call and the costume and wig fittings. Encourage him to start the understudy rehearsals as soon as possible, especially with the principal understudy players. If he turns out to be energetic and well respected by the actors and you're working on a large and complicated show, let him take second rehearsals in another room while you forge ahead with the difficult stuff.

Have time for your assistant. Talk to him during the breaks. Have the occasional dinner together. He is sitting watching rehearsals day in day out and quietly keeping his counsel. His objectivity could be of great value to you. Not being entirely inside the work as you are he may have some very interesting things to say about it.

Take your assistant seriously. You were him once.

HOW TO BE AN ASSISTANT DIRECTOR

However talented and ambitious you are, the job is assisting, not directing. Be supportive of your director even if you don't agree with his methods or have no sympathy for his aesthetic principles. Learn what you can in the time you have been given. To do this well you must immerse yourself in your director's process and save your judgements about it to a later date.

Don't make the mistake of trying to be like your director, of aping his behaviour or copying his mannerisms. If your director's any good, you will come across as a pale imitation and if he isn't any good, you'll seem all the more feeble yourself.

Don't pander to your director. Don't be the first one to laugh at his jokes or agree with his ideas. Your reactions are only useful if they remain independent of your director. You will help him most by listening best and observing the reaction of the actors to his ideas. Then watch how his ideas transmit themselves through the actors to the characters in the play.

Without betraying your independence of thought, try to put yourself in your director's artistic shoes. What does he want from the play and the actors performing it? Is he getting what he wants? If things aren't going well, is there a better way of achieving his artistic ends than the one he is employing? How can you put that to him in tactful and supportive terms?

Try to establish a balanced relationship with your director – don't assume equality but don't settle for subservience. If you are to rehearse the understudies or maintain the production throughout a long run you will need a strong relationship with the actors. They are keen observers of people. They will remember very clearly what they observe of your behaviour in rehearsal – your authority or lack of it, your tact, your kindness and your loyalty.

Offering suggestions and ideas to your director may prove tricky. Some directors are very touchy. They don't like to be challenged in rehearsal and will react badly if they think they are being shown up in front of the actors. So gauge your interventions carefully. If your director is particularly sensitive, don't say anything until you are alone with him. An idea he would repudiate in front of the actors he may very well accept in private.

85

If your director is open-minded and welcomes your thoughts in rehearsal, be grateful by not pushing your luck. It's still his production, however clever your ideas might prove to be.

If the production is an unhappy one, you may find yourself having to listen to actors' private grievances about how they are being treated or what a bastard the director is or what a crap production it's going to be. This will most likely happen in the pub or the **Green Room** after rehearsals are over for the evening. The comments might be justified or they might take you completely by surprise. The production might be a perfectly happy one and the disaffection entirely of one or two actors' making. In any event you must try to keep the faith. You will only make things worse by joining in with the prevailing bitchiness or negativity. Put the balanced view, the fair view, the useful view, the view that will help the production to be better. Then decide what to say to the director. Don't be a spy or an informer, but don't leave him hanging if you think you can do some good by reporting a prevailing unease. Be tactful. It's part of the art of being a director. Don't say anything to your director that you wouldn't be happy to have said to you one day.

Finally, if your director asks you to get him coffee, go to the canteen or the Green Room and make him a cup with three heaped teaspoons of instant coffee lightly stirred into half a cup of lukewarm water. Then add a small dash of milk to make the colour look vile and spill some coffee over the edge so that the cup looks twice used. And take a good ten minutes over it. With a little luck his response will be 'About time! *(sip)* Bloody hell! This tastes awful. I'm not asking you for coffee again.' Mission accomplished.

Assistant to the Director

Not to be confused with the role of **Assistant Director**, an Assistant to the Director is really a personal assistant with access to the rehearsal room but with no artistic authority and no professional relationship with the actors or any of the other creative staff. The job description varies depending on the needs of the director but will usually include secretarial duties as well as the management and scheduling of the director's life outside the demands of the production in hand. A busy professional director will have three or four productions looming up ahead, each one with a demanding producer, designer and Casting Director attached. The busier you become as a director, the more you will need somebody to screen the incoming scramble of demands on your time, provided you can afford the salary. From the assistants' point of view, the job is a chance to put a toe in the theatre water, mix with theatre people and decide if this is the right profession for them. Some assistants find the job so conducive that they stay with their director for decades, but most move on to other jobs after a year or two, becoming managers, agents, actors, playwrights or even directors.

Associate Directors

An Associate Director is usually a director associated with a permanent theatre company but not in charge of it.

This may mean that the company permanently employs the associate and he directs two or three shows a year as well as taking some responsibility for the overall artistic plan under the supervision of the **Artistic Director**. Or it may mean that the associate is loosely tied to the theatre company because of past achievement or present influence. His name appears on the notepaper and in the programmes, he advises the Artistic Director from time to time, and is always welcomed back to direct a show if the time and the show are both right.

The term can also be used to credit a director on a particular production for being something more than an **Assistant Director** but not as much as a **Co-Director**. This sometimes becomes appropriate if an Assistant Director employed for a number of productions becomes more to his principal director than an assistant or is unhappy to remain as an assistant. Young directors can use the credit as a step up the directing ladder, but they should beware of asking for it, and principal directors should beware of granting it

87

unless it is truly merited. Your actors will not understand a division of authority if it hasn't been clearly worked out by you and your associate in advance. A cosmetic award of associate-ship will be resented by the cast and create frustration in the associate.

RESIDENT DIRECTORS

A Resident Director is usually a junior directing post in a large theatre company where the director has not yet been awarded the distinction of an associate-ship. He will be fully employed by the company and may be able to propose plays for direction, but will also have to direct the plays that the Artistic Director wants to see in the repertoire but is unable or unwilling to direct himself.

WITH

A halfway-house credit between Associate Director and Co-Director can be expressed in the word 'with'. A 'with credit', as in 'Directed by John Caird with Ernie Sniggins' implies that the direction has been shared but not shared equally. This might mean that I conceived and designed the production but was not completely available to rehearse it, so Sniggins had to do a lot of the work for me. Or that the production was originally mine but Sniggins directed a revival of it that I was unavailable or unwilling to direct. In truth 'with' is a bit of a fudge and should only be used where no other clearer credit can be established.

WORKING AS AN ASSOCIATE DIRECTOR

At some point in your career you may be permanently employed in directing plays for a theatre company of which you are not the Artistic Director. Your work will be part of the expression of a company's artistic policy, but the definition of that policy will be your Artistic Director's, not yours. This association will require a particular set of skills from you, never entirely easy to understand and harder still to put into practice. Whatever the precise nature of your employment or the length of your contract, consider the following interrelated points.

1 Whatever your motive for being an associate, learn to enjoy the job you have rather than yearn for the job you have not.

2 Support your Artistic Director through thick and thin. He has given you work. He has believed in you. Return the compliment.

3 Whether or not you like your Artistic Director or approve of his policies, do not believe you could do his job better than him in the same circumstances. Such beliefs are vain and are rarely, if ever, put to the test.

4 All theatre companies have their malcontents and mischief-makers. Do not give them credence by encouraging them or conspiring with them. Anyone who would stab the Artistic Director in the back will be just as happy to stab you in the back if the occasion arises.

5 However unhappy the regime in which you are working, do not allow others to form an imaginary alternative Artistic Directorate around you. Such attention may be flattering, but it is also meaningless and disloyal. Rather apply all your artistic energies to the real job in hand and require others in your circle to do likewise.

6 Understand the limits of your authority. In the rehearsal room you must lead your company of actors with all the authority at your disposal. As you leave the rehearsal room, the nature of your authority must change from leader to supporter. Learn to change gears gracefully.

7 Study your Artistic Director's work and appreciate the difference between his work and yours. His job requires him to have an opinion about the value of your work. You must form a balanced view as to the value of his opinion.

8 Recognise that the job of Artistic Director can be a lonely and isolated one. Do what you can to reciprocate his interest in your work by taking a constructive interest in his.

9 Use the relative comfort of your position to supply the company with your best ideas. If they are rejected, don't let them fester by

neglect: save them up for another occasion, or propose them on a regular basis so they gain currency by repetition and familiarity.

10 Read voraciously – new plays and old, native and foreign, serious and funny, poetry and prose. Let your learning and research become a well of fresh ideas from which your colleagues can draw.

11 Don't be upset if your Artistic Director steals your ideas and makes them his own. Think of it as homage. If you become an Artistic Director you will do the same, and you won't even know you're doing it.

12 However selfless your support for your Artistic Director's regime, do not imagine it will ever convert into a right of succession. As a general rule, the longer you work as an associate, the weaker your candidacy will be when the next Artistic Director is being appointed. If your ambition is to be an Artistic Director, don't spend too long being an associate in any one company. If your ambition is to lead the company in which you are an associate, know that you will probably have to leave it and work elsewhere in order to become a credible outside candidate at a later date.

Audience

Never take your audience for granted. Never think of the audience as the enemy. Never patronise them, or feel superior to them, or be threatened by them.

They are your collaborators. Their attention and good will are as essential to your craft as that of the actor and the author. Indeed their relationship with both actors and authors must be thought of as being more important than your own and therefore essentially outside the control of the **director's authority**.

One of your most important functions as a director is that you represent the audience's interest in a play. You are, if you like, the audience's agent. From the moment you first read a play through to the first performance you must try to understand and interpret it from the audience's point of view. As a one-man or one-woman audience you are constantly imagining how your thoughts about the play will be received by the many. Thus when your first audience walks into the theatre, they replace you. If they then behave unexpectedly by reacting to your play in a way you cannot approve or understand, you mustn't blame them. The fault is not theirs but yours. You have simply imagined them incorrectly.

The more experienced you are as a director the easier it should be to accord your audience's imagination with your own. The greater your powers as a director the more you will be able to pull the audience away from their conventional assumptions towards your interpretation of the author's imaginative world. The more confident you are as a director the more freedom you will allow the audience to surprise you by their reactions.

There is a fine balance in the director's craft between inspiring the audience and controlling it. An inspired audience is one that evinces a strong collective response to a play but sustains a wide variety of individual experience within it. A controlled audience is one in which the collective response seems demanded by directorial diktat and individuals made to feel wrong or foolish if they fail to get the point.

Directors that try to control their audiences are always the ones that fall into the heresy of describing them in terms of 'good' and 'bad'.

If audiences never behave quite as some directors would like them to, they cannot, must not, be blamed for it. There is no such thing as a bad audience. An audience is as good as it is made to be by the excellence of the play and the skill and artistry of the actors.

Of course, there are audiences that cough, especially in winter, and those that stay silent when the actors would prefer them to be laughing. There are predominantly old audiences that don't hear very well and young audiences that fidget and foreign audiences that don't understand the language. But they are what they are. They've bought tickets and are there to be entertained. And they are convertible. A mature cast working on peak form will rise to whatever challenge it is given. There is no more satisfying accomplishment for an ensemble than to convert inattention to absorption or silence to hilarity. Your job is to ensure that your ensemble is equipped with the flexibility, good humour and patience required for the nightly task of conversion.

Because there is always a gap between how you expect an audience to behave and how it behaves in practice, your first public performance will always bring surprises with it. This is why **preview** performances can be so important. They allow the actors to accommodate their performances to the audience's participation. It is as if a new character has quietly entered every scene and is demanding to be part of the action. In comedy, of course, the demand isn't quiet at all, it's vociferous, and the **laughter** that attests to the new character's interest creates new rhythms within the play.

Auditioning

Auditioning is a craft. Your ability to master it will greatly affect the quality of the actors you cast and their fundamental suitability for the roles you have to offer them.

Actors come to audition for you because you ask them to be there. The audition will cost them – in money and in time. They may have travelled dozens, even hundreds of miles to be there. To suit your convenience and your schedule they may have inconvenienced themselves considerably. There could be upsetting events going on in their private lives of which you know nothing. The least you can do is treat them with professional kindred fellowship, whatever you think of their acting ability, their suitability to be cast or their behaviour in the audition. Grace, humility, politeness and generosity should be your watchwords.

There are two principal reasons for auditioning an actor:

1 To become acquainted with an unknown talent, or a talent about which you are uncertain.
2 To ensure that a known candidate is the correct choice for a particular part.

The best way to become acquainted with the gifts of particular actors is to see them in action, but always remember that an audition is only an artificial recreation of an actual performance, with you standing in for an absent audience.

Ironically, the most unsympathetic and often therefore the least effective place to hold an audition is a theatre with the actor performing on the stage and you sitting in the auditorium. The coldness, darkness and emptiness of the space, the strangeness of the acoustics without an audience present, the physical and emotional distance between auditioner and hearer – all are conducive to an unnatural and estranging atmosphere.

Auditioning is best done in a large, light rehearsal room with a dry acoustic. You can see the actor's face and form very clearly, you can vary the distance between the actor and yourself according to the quality of the work or the speech within the work, and you can have a social interaction with the actor essential for forming a judgement about his character and artistry. If a doubt remains at the end of an audition about the vocal or physical prowess of an actor, that is the time to move into the theatre and watch or listen from a greater distance.

If the only available space for auditions is the theatre itself, then start the audition with director and actor on the stage together. You can then move into the auditorium once the actor has acclimatised. Make sure the house-lights are on so that the actor is not obliged to squint into the darkness at an unknown number of terrifying judges. Directors and Casting Directors who sit in darkened theatres shouting out instructions to an actor on the stage are not only rude and unkind, they are also betraying their professional incompetence.

Whether in a rehearsal room or on a stage, when the actor starts acting make sure he addresses you directly. You are standing in for the audience, and a good actor has a relationship with the audience. It is only the fearful or embarrassed director who insists that the actor be disallowed from making eye contact. You cannot possibly make a sound judgement about an actor's talent if you are requiring him to act into the void without an interlocutor of any sort. By engaging with an actor while he is performing you will gather more about the inside of his mind and the true nature of his talent than you will ever do from watching him grape-shotting his performance into the void. If an actor starts an audition by avoiding eye contact with you, then stop him and start again. He may be surprised at this direction, having been told by embarrassed and fearful directors to avoid eye contact, but he will almost invariably be grateful for the opportunity to connect with you, and you will always be happily surprised by the instant improvement in the quality of his acting.

Actors are at their most vulnerable and often their most unnatural in the artificial atmosphere of auditions. They are being asked to respond to material with which they are often totally unfamiliar. They are performing to a complete stranger, or worse still a large group of complete strangers, who will then assess their competence to do their job and earn their living. No wonder they are nervous. Your job is to help them behave as naturally as they would be when happily performing to a live and admiring public audience. To do this competently, you must be able to identify the various ways in which an actor's nervousness may manifest itself.

It is often the most imaginative actors who are the most nervous. They may have spent a week, or sometimes longer, preparing for the audition and imagining what it is going to be like. By the time they walk into the room they have imagined themselves into the most negative frame of mind, with the part they are up for an impossible challenge and you, the director, an implacable adversary.

Nervousness can express itself in various forms:

1 *Silence*

Characterised by inaudible responses and the swallowing of words.

2 *Vain swaggering*

Most commonly exemplified by a preening walk, affected speech, sexual flaunting, overactive hand gestures and general loudness of demeanour.

3 Aggression

As if to say 'You think you're a hot-shot director, but you don't impress me, you arsehole. So don't give me the part, see if I care.'

4 Naked, gibbering terror

Undisguisable shakes, dry-mouth, deep breathing and swivel-eyed dismay.

Your job as a director is to get beneath these outward signs of nervousness and expose the talent and the character underneath – this is for your own sake, unless you want a cast for your play entirely comprised of facile smoothies. Social grace and a talent for anecdotes and jokes do not add much to a real acting talent. These qualities may coexist in the same actor but you must not confuse the one with the other.

Don't overreact to outward nervousness. Don't read silence as sullenness, or meet aggression with aggression of your own. Be courteous, friendly and welcoming and so give the actor the opportunity to lose his nervousness.

It's a good idea to spend a minute or two talking before any acting is required, unless it seems to make the actor even more nervous. The interaction of chat about the actor's career or the play or the part the actor is up for usually creates a more relaxed atmosphere and allows the actor to become acclimatised to the room and the people in it. If an actor requests to jump right in and start acting immediately, don't fight him. It may be his preferred way of losing his nervousness, or he may have found in the past that a talk beforehand tends to increase his tension rather than alleviate it.

There are practical ways you can help the chronically nervous auditioner:

1 Every audition room should have an ample supply of drinking water and paper cups. One of the commonest manifestations of nervousness is dry-mouth – easily detectable by a slight clicking sound when the sufferer speaks. Offer the sufferer a cup of water and time to drink it.

2 A box of tissues is also an advisable prop. Many actors, gifted
or not, will produce various combinations of tears, sweat, spit
and snot, sometimes in copious flow when performing emotionally charged material. Watching them mopping themselves
up with only the aid of their clothing is never a pretty sight. If
a very gifted performer does a particularly moving audition,
you may have recourse to the tissues yourself.

Never interrupt an actor in mid-flow, unless the speech or the song
is so unreasonably long that you are obliged to intervene. If you
have to do so, choose your moment sensitively. Even if an actor is
performing abysmally, don't interrupt him except to give him a
note or allow him to start again. You must never simply stop an
actor and require him to leave without another word. Auditioning
actors are your guests and should leave the room feeling as good as
a guest should feel when leaving your home. Even a deeply unconfident actor can be made to feel better with a few kind words of
encouragement.

Once an actor has completed a speech or a reading or a song,
you must decide how best to proceed. If he has piqued your interest it is often a good idea to have him repeat at least some of the
speech he has just performed but in an altered manner. Give him a
few notes about his speech and get him to do it again. Some actors
are much better at this than others. Some have made an art of auditioning and have honed their speeches or songs to such a high polish that it's hard to tell how talented they would be in other
circumstances. Don't forget that your judgement is about the actor,
not the speech or the song. If he is incapable of sensible adjustment,
however arbitrarily requested, he may prove just as intractable in
rehearsal. Some actors are afflicted with instant memory loss if
required to act their pieces in even a slightly different way. This is a
sign of creative brittleness that you will have to investigate further
before you commit yourself.

If you are particularly pleased with an actor's performance in
audition, ask him to perform something else with a quite different
quality. Find out how deep his talent is. If he is a gifted comedian,
guide him towards something more serious, if very serious try him

on something comic. By giving actors a choice of what to perform you will find out what tickles their imaginations and therefore how versatile and creative they are going to be in rehearsal.

Even if you know very early on in the audition that an actor is unlikely to be suitable for the role you are trying to cast, don't let him sense your lack of interest. Use the time to find out more about him for future reference. There will be other plays and other productions, other opportunities for other parts. You will often meet greatly gifted actors who aren't right for any of the roles on offer but whom you would love to work with in the future. Store them up and save them for a rainy day.

Try to make the audition process a pleasure both for yourself and for the actors. Remember that the audition you are engaged in might be their only opportunity to deploy their skills for a whole week, or a month or more. Auditioning can be a long and arduous process. Done well it is very tiring. Don't make the experience more enervating by wishing yourself at the end of it. Use every opportunity that arises to greet new talent, salute new excellence and make new creative friendships. There should always be a degree of flirtation in the auditioning process.

Without actors you wouldn't have a career. Your power over them in auditions is illusory. Don't make the mistake of abusing it. By doing so you abuse yourself. You also open yourself to the possibility of ridicule. Don't forget that the actor you are mistreating is likely to be skilled at mimicry and much better qualified to mock you than you him.

AUDITIONING FILM AND TV ACTORS

Don't imagine that film or videotape evidence of an actor's talent is proof of theatrical competence. The physical life required of an actor for film and television is largely limited to the face.

Actors who have only worked in film and television may not be capable of fluid physical movement on a stage. Exposure to a large stage space can make such actors seem awkward and wooden, where on film and television they seemed completely at home.

Auditioning

Stage performance also requires vocal projection, even in quite small theatres. An actor unaccustomed to the stage and without a good vocal technique will find himself having to push his voice beyond the point where his acting will seem natural.

A brief audition will tell you all you need to know about an actor's physical and vocal strength. You will be doing yourself and the actor no favours if you ignore evidence of serious weakness in audition.

AUDITIONING FOR THE MUSICAL THEATRE

The room you audition in should be a good size and have a dry acoustic. You won't be able to judge the quality or the size of a voice in a small, echo-y room. Your room must be equipped with a piano – or at least an electronic keyboard. The piano must be in tune. Don't assume that the people from whom you've rented your hall will have tuned their own piano. They may be tone deaf, or skinflint, or both. Check that the piano is in tune before you rent the hall, and if it isn't, have it tuned. Nothing will reflect on you worse in the eyes and ears of singers than a poorly tuned piano, and your day of auditioning will be excruciating for all concerned.

Employ a really good **accompanist**. Without one you'll be sunk.

If you are auditioning for a sung-through musical in which there are no spoken words, you obviously won't need your auditioners to prepare a spoken piece. You can judge their acting as well as their singing on how they present their songs. But many musicals do contain some dialogue – and some musicals have lots of it. If this is the case you must not rely entirely on sung material in auditions. You must require your auditioners to prepare a monologue as well as songs. You may meet considerable resistance to this from both performers and agents, but don't let them browbeat you. You don't want to find yourself in rehearsal listening to a singer speaking his part in a monotone or with wildly inflected vowels or empty rhetoric and realise too late that the beautiful voice you cast at the audition was masking a complete absence of acting talent. And don't let your singers get away with reading bits of your libretto to you. Make them do a piece. Their choice of material alone will tell you a lot about them as people and as actors.

Experienced musical theatre actors will present you with a variety of songs to choose from. Let them start by singing a song with which they are comfortable, something that shows off their voices to the best advantage. Don't be too picky unless they really don't know what they want to sing for you. Again, their first choice will tell you a lot about them as performers. Once you have heard their first song, ask to hear something else that will show you the breadth of their talent. If they started with a soulful ballad, ask them for something more comedic, or quick-tempo. If a female singer has blown you away with a huge belt number, find out if she has a soprano voice as well. If someone has been hilariously funny in their first song, make them try something serious in their second.

If an auditioner seems perfect for one of the roles on offer, have him sing through that character's main song or songs. If he's a good sight-reader or if the material is well known, he may be happy to work through it 'round the piano' with the Musical Director. More likely, he will want to take it away and have a look at it for a while or go away and come back on another day. Wherever possible, give the auditioner as much time as he requires.

Some experienced and status-conscious singers may not be happy about auditioning with their own pieces, preferring to sing the material for which they are being considered. If this is the case, send them the songs well in advance so they can make proper preparation.

Never stop someone in mid-flow. It's rude and unnecessary. However badly they are singing, you invited them to do so. If someone has a memory lapse halfway through a song, let him recover and start again. Auditioners are often nervous and auditions are not tests of memory. Give everyone the benefit of the doubt and want them to be as good as they can possibly be.

Don't switch off if auditioners don't seem right for the roles available. Hear them out. If they're good, they might be perfect for something else you do further down the line. If they're really good, they might even persuade you to change your thinking about a role just so you can have them play it.

In fact, don't ever switch off. Auditioners can tell if you do, and it's not fair to ask them to sing a whole song to a row of glazed-over eyes.

If auditioners have a routine they fall into – stretching or breathing or jumping about – don't disrupt it. It doesn't make you look clever to comment adversely on their appearance or behaviour. And if they have a song they specially want to sing, don't let your own taste or prejudice stop them from singing it. They may have spent hours practising it just for you and not being allowed to sing it will throw them horribly. You don't need to be controlling or severe in auditions – it doesn't make you look strong and it stops you making good judgements. Take the people and their favourite material as it comes and let yourself be affected by them and it before you pass judgement on either. Be gentle and be kind. That way you'll get the best out of everyone.

Auditorium

The auditorium is where the audience sits to listen to the play. Note well, it is called auditorium and not spectatorium. It is a space in which the author's words are communicated by the actors' voices to the audience's ears. In auditoria all over the world audiences forgive bad **sightlines**. They will pay less for **obstructed view seats**, happily craning their necks from behind pillars and peering down from vertiginous heights. What they will never forgive is not being able to hear the words.

Auditoria come in all shapes and sizes, from massive barns of three or four thousand seats to tiny rooms where the cast may threaten to outnumber the audience. One of your primary duties as a director is to choose the right auditorium for your play or the right play for your auditorium. If you get either of these equations wrong you make life difficult for yourself.

Consider the configuration of your auditorium. Is it conducive to the atmosphere of your play? Can the story of your play be shared in it feelingly? Will all the details of your actors' performances be appreciated by every member of the audience? Are all the seats in the auditorium within easy earshot of the stage? How are the sight-lines and **acoustics**? Do you feel like you're in a **playhouse**, or are the dimensions just too big for comfort?

Look at the space between stage and seats. Imagine it as a huge bubble of air contained by the architectural features of the auditorium. How wide is this bubble, how deep and how high? This isn't an exact science, but if the cubic capacity of the bubble is too great, the sound of the actors' voices will get lost on its way from stage to seats. The actors' words need to resound within this space like music resounds inside the case of a stringed instrument.

OLD PLAYHOUSES

If you're considering working in an old playhouse, think about its history and why it was built the way it was. The builders of theatres from the eighteenth century to the beginning of the twentieth created multi-tiered auditoria in order to pack as many people as possible into the small areas of ground upon which the theatres are built. At the same time they stratified the tiers to provide a variety of different seat prices for a variety of different purses. Theatre auditoria became microcosms for the British class system. The upper and upper-middle classes sat in the boxes,and the **royal circle** the middle classes in the stalls, **grand circle** or **circle**, and the educated lower middle classes in the upper circle or **balcony**. The dress circle was originally reserved for those wearing evening dress, and so on. None of this was writ in stone and of course people broke the rules all the time, aping the class to which they aspired or slumming it in a class they thought beneath them but better suited to their purse. The stratification was indeed far more important in terms of money taken at the box office than a true reflection of any real social system. But if you work in theatres like these today, how do you make sure that everyone sitting in them gets their fair share of the play? Your producer will still price the seats according to their market value, but audiences sitting in the cheap seats should be just as important to you as those in the expensive ones.

Auditorium

In the twentieth century auditoria began to be configured on more democratic lines. The number of tiers was reduced from four or five to three and then to two. The classic **Broadway** auditorium, reflected in the design of theatres all across America, is a two-tier configuration built very wide to maximise the number of seats and with a shallow stage to fit the theatre's rectangular footprint. These theatres have problems all their own. Every seat may be reasonably close to the stage, but the side seats seem out on a limb unless the action on stage is spread very flat to accommodate them.

Modern playhouses are rarely built with more than two tiers and, since the 1960s, may be influenced by any number of different architectural or theatrical fashions. Thus you may find yourself working on a **thrust stage** or an **arena stage** or in a **replica theatre**.

Auteur Director

Auteur director is a loose term applied, rather subjectively, to directors whose work seems so distinctively original that it transcends direction and becomes authorship. The term derives from film, where the dominance of the visual image over the spoken word gives the director a pre-eminent role in the creative process.

The fact that *auteur* is merely the French word for 'author' makes its use seem a little pretentious to many an Anglo-Saxon ear, *author* director not having quite the same ring and making one suspect it would never be used if it were the only term available.

The authorship referred to can assume several different forms. Some *auteurs* are so called because of the extraordinary liberties they take with existing texts. By making radical cuts, rewriting the characters, reorganising the structure or setting the play in a rigidly **conceptual** framework, they seem to put themselves on an equal creative footing with the original author. Others make up their own plays from scratch, using **improvisation** or **devised play** techniques, but eschewing the services of a writer, so becoming authors by default. Others start with a predominantly **physical theatre** approach, their work more akin to **choreography** than conventional direction but the resulting performance more akin to play than to dance.

Unfortunately the term gets bandied about where it is neither appropriate nor merited. An author that happens to direct his own plays is not thereby an *auteur* director. A director radically interpreting a more or less uncut classical text does not qualify thereby for co-authorship. It's always a little disturbing when one hears a famous play referred to as if it had become the property of a particular director. 'Have you seen Sniggins's Lear?' – not Shakespeare's any more but Sniggins's. For some directors this assumption of authorship might be the acme of their ambition, but many would blush even to consider it.

The term should really only be used in circumstances where a theatre piece originates in the unique vision of a director and where all other claims of authorship are insignificant in comparison.

Awards

The award culture is a deadly influence on theatre. It diminishes all of us, judges and judged alike. It creates division, envy and disharmony amongst those who rely for their living on collaboration, friendship and accord. It compares the incomparable. It reduces art to the level of sport.

If you are nominated for an award, you are usually four to one likely to end up a loser, but if you win, you do so at the emotional expense of your peers.

If you take your losses or wins seriously you disable your creative life by disappointment on the one hand or pride on the other.

If there are commercial benefits to awards – in that the ceremonies attract the attention of a media that loves to obsess over league tables – what is gained by the winners is generally offset by

Awards

what is lost by the rest of the theatre community, especially by those who have been ignored altogether.

The culture is now so pervasive you will be hard-pressed to have nothing to do with it, but your best position is one of ironical distance. Take none of it seriously and judge yourself only by your own lights and those of your trusted peers.

B

Balcony

The balcony is the uppermost tier in a multi-tiered **proscenium** arch auditorium, built originally for those who could only afford the very cheapest seats with the very poorest view (see **Auditorium**). In these more egalitarian times balconies are often hard to fill, and many Theatre Managers close them off unless they are hosting an absolutely copper-bottomed hit.

When balconies are in use they often contain drama school students both home-grown and foreign and the most devoted but poorest of overseas tourists anxious to get even the most vertiginous glimpse of the stage. Like many a professional director or actor, you may have seen your own first show from the balcony.

Vertigo can actually be a real problem for some balcony dwellers, giving rise to the American slang term 'nosebleed seats'. Furthermore the sightlines are usually somewhere between poor and atrocious, the acoustics strange if not bad, the atmosphere stuffy and the temperature hotter than anywhere else in the theatre, heat rising the way it does. Despite these drawbacks the balcony will often contain the majority of first-time theatregoers.

If you work in a theatre with a balcony, pay it a visit during a schools matinée. There will be a certain amount of disruptive behaviour going on from the uninterested minority, kids texting one another across the rows or playing games on their cellphones and the odd teacher doing his utmost to keep the rowdier elements in check, but as long as the show is halfway decent, the majority will be respectful and quiet. In the midst of them there will be one child, or two, who will be sitting in utter amazement at the spectacle below, impervious to the distractions of their friends or the watchful tension of their stressed-out teachers. Look at their eyes and the stillness of their heads. Look inside their heads, at the riot of imagery. Look back at the stage and see what they see, hear what they hear. They are you. They are the directors of the future, and the authors and the actors. They are the designers of sets and costumes and lighting and sound. They are the Box Office Managers, and the Stage Managers and the Theatre Managers. They are the producers and administrators and agents. Or they may just be the life-long passionate theatregoers who pay your wages and everyone else's.

Beats

In modern play texts and in actors' parlance a 'beat' is a small pause for thought or a moment of silence between characters that is too short to be called a **pause** akin to a 'rest' in music. Some actor training systems also use 'beat' to describe a section of speech or the forces of **motivation** underlying it.

There is an apocryphal story concerning the origin of the term. A Russian director, teaching the **Stanislavsky** method in New York, mispronounced or was misheard when he described how an actor's text can be split up into motivational sections, or 'bits' as he called them. Say the word 'bits' with a heavy Russian accent and you'll hear what his students heard. The mistake took root before anyone had understood it was a mistake and the term is now common currency.

Beauty

Nowhere in the **casting** process is the limited nature of your own vision likely to get you into more trouble than when you are making judgements about physical beauty or sexual attractiveness.

This is a constantly provoking issue because so many playwrights have been obsessed with beauty themselves, or with the conflict between external beauty and internal worth, and so many of their plays have a romantic relationship at their centre, the protagonist lovers describing how gorgeous their partners are. It is also the subject on which there are more quiet mutterings from the audience than on any other.

Let's imagine you are casting a 'beautiful' part. Consider the following list.

10 USEFUL QUESTIONS TO ASK YOURSELF ABOUT BEAUTY

1 Does the playwright describe the character as being beautiful in the text or stage directions or both?
2 Do other characters in the play describe the character as being beautiful, and if only one other character does so, is the character only beautiful in his or her eyes?
3 Does the character have to be beautiful in order for the plot to be credible?
4 Does the character believe him- or herself to be beautiful and if so is he or she deluded?
5 Do 'romantic' characters need to be more beautiful than others?
6 Is there a necessary relationship between the heroic and the beautiful or is that an illusion?
7 Do you find it easier to imagine an unbeautiful hero or an unbeautiful heroine?
8 How does beauty relate to sexuality?
9 Are your prejudices or preferences showing?
10 How do your own judgements about beauty accord with the judgements of others?

These questions may be useful in informing your choice of an actor to play a 'beautiful' part, but they beg a more fundamental and perhaps more illuminating one. How does beauty in the theatre relate to beauty in life or as it is perceived in magazines, television and films? This question is especially important when you consider that the theatre has a strong relationship with the television and film industries and a less strong but nonetheless significant relationship with the worlds of fashion and dance, and that successful performers from all those disciplines may see themselves as candidates for roles in the theatre.

Film and fashion have a stronger relationship with each other than either of them does with theatre, and defining beauty in either of those industries would be an impossible task, reliant as they are on such voguish and subjective values, but it is noticeable nonetheless that men and women who appear beautiful in photographs or on film do not necessarily appear so when acting on a stage. Contrariwise, actors and actresses who appear quite ordinary in real life and cannot persuade a camera of any sort to find them attractive can look extremely beautiful on stage. Why is this?

The main reason is that beauty in film and in photographs is almost entirely defined by the lineaments of facial feature. This is why members of the public are often surprised to find how short or slight film stars or models are when they meet them in real life. They have imagined a body and a stature to go with the face they have grown to admire. Because they admire the face, they endow the star with a similarly admirable physique.

In the theatre, the disappointment, when there is one, tends to be the other way around. Actors who appear beautiful on stage suddenly seem much less so at the stage door where, face to face, it is their faces alone that monopolise our attention.

What is it, then, that we perceive as beautiful when we watch the whole person on a stage? It is, I think, a combination of complementary attributes including strength of feature, physical gracefulness, personal confidence, emotional warmth and vocal dexterity and authority. The bigger the theatre the stronger and clearer the facial features need to be. Big eyes and a large mouth are able to communicate themselves as beautiful in a way exquisitely perfect little eyes and a perfectly formed but small mouth will never manage. A person with a beautiful physique but an awkward physical manner will not appear beautiful on stage. A lack of emotional or spiritual warmth in the inner actor will always affect the extent to which they are accorded to be physically beautiful. An actor whose voice is thin and reedy to the ear will have difficulty appearing beautiful to the eye.

More important than any of these is the power of suggestion. If the character an actor plays is described as beautiful and loved for his or her beauty by other characters, the audience will happily believe it too, whatever the evidence of its own eyes or judgement. This alchemy is impossible to achieve in film and television. That the theatre can generate its own idea of beauty based on a complex apprehension of human worth is one of the reasons it will always survive.

Belief and Believability

Alice laughed. 'There's no use trying,' she said, 'one can't believe impossible things.'
'I daresay you haven't had much practice,' said the Queen. 'When I was your age, I always did it for half-an-hour a day. Why, sometimes I've believed as many as six impossible things before breakfast.'

Belief is at the heart of theatrical experience and believability the test of its effectiveness.

Coleridge's 'willing suspension of disbelief' has the reader of poetry making an agreement with himself, and with the poet, that the disbelief he would normally feel while considering the events of a poem are to be temporarily suspended for the sake of a vivid vicarious experience.

The case is not the same in theatre. There the audience is continuously reminded of the fictive nature of the events it witnesses by the essential duality of performance. Actors play characters. The audience is not required to believe that the actors are the characters. In this it has no disbelief to suspend. Rather it enters into a conspiracy of belief with author and actors alike that the events being enacted on stage are a true depiction of **reality**.

Audiences know very well that the actress playing Cordelia, lying dead in Lear's arms, is not really dead nor really his daughter, but they know it will help them to understand the story and to empathise with the characters if they conspire to believe it. They are told at the end of *The Seagull* that Konstantin Gavrilovich has shot himself and they conspire to believe it has happened, though they know they will see the actor alive and well at the curtain call and that the shot was a blank fired by a member of the stage management. They know that a group of actors miming a scene in a bar are not really drinking, but they 'see' the glasses, 'hear' the clink of the toasts and conspire to believe in the ensuing drunkenness.

This conspiracy of belief is inherent in all forms of **theatrical convention,** of which there are many. As such it is a constantly shifting commodity with every member of the audience believing a little more or a little less as the events on stage evolve. Belief in the theatre is never an absolute requirement but rather a balancing act between belief and disbelief, with the author, director and actors constantly pushing out the boundaries of sustainable belief and the audience constantly rearranging its reactions in response.

Sometimes this balance becomes extraordinarily complicated. Consider what Shakespeare asks us to believe in Act IV Scene 5 of *King Lear*. Earlier in the play we have believed in Edgar's belief that his best means of escape from his brother's treachery is to disguise himself as a naked madman, Poor Tom. We have 'seen' his father's eyes being put out and the actor playing Gloucester has made us believe in his subsequent blindness. We have witnessed the reunion of father and son and believed in Gloucester's inability to recognise Edgar's voice. And we have believed that Gloucester is so driven by remorse for the wrong he has done to Edgar that he wants to throw himself from the cliffs of Dover.

We now watch while Edgar, still disguised as Tom, pretends to lead his father to Dover. We believe in Gloucester's belief that he stands at the 'extreme verge' of the cliff. Edgar's description of the drop in front of him is so vivid that we 'see' it as clearly as his blind father does. We believe in Edgar's belief that he is trifling with his father's despair in order to cure it. Then, impossibly, Gloucester jumps and we must believe that he believes he falls.

This is an extreme example of how the bounds of believability can be stretched, with pitfalls at every step of the journey, but a pair of fine actors will convince an audience of their characters' beliefs. Your job as director is to create a world in which all of these events seem natural and necessary, the only possible reality available for the audience to believe in. A successful production of *King Lear* will have members of the audience describing how much they enjoyed the 'Dover cliff scene', confusing the imagined with the imaginary.

In every play there are things that are hard to believe in and in some plays there are things apparently impossible to believe, wild coincidences of plot or maddening inconsistencies of character. In every cast there are actors whose lack of technique or taste will stretch your belief in their characters beyond breaking point.

In the great conspiracy of belief the director is cast as chief conspirator. Throughout rehearsals you must constantly use your critical judgement to decide what is believable and what isn't. And belief being such a shifting and subjective commodity, you must be ready to exert your judgement over the judgement of others. Like the White Queen in *Through the Looking Glass*, you must insist on your right to believe in impossible things, but like Alice you must maintain a healthy scepticism when faced with the downright improbable.

Billing

'Bills' are posters or other sorts of theatrical advertisement and 'billing' the prominence with which a particular artist is featured on the bill. Thus 'top billing' is accorded to the star or equal co-stars of a show and 'over-the-title billing' is when the names of artists appear on posters, or in neon lights outside the theatre, above the title of the play.

Unlike **credits**, which are always important, billing only really matters in commercial theatre, where producers use the names of stars to sell tickets and where stars vie for pre-eminence amongst themselves.

Producers use billing as a bargaining tool in contractual negotiations. Indeed it is often the very last thing to be decided, after the money and the travel arrangements and the dressing room allocation have all been agreed. You will see evidence of these deals in the fine gradations of commercial billing, with actors appearing below the title in slightly bigger or slightly bolder lettering than their fellows, or in a box, or preceded by a 'with' or an 'introducing'.

This might all sound ridiculous, but if you ever cast a show in the West End or on Broadway you could easily find negotiations over actors' services breaking down over the billing. Egged on by their agents, actors can conceive such an inflated view of their status they would rather lose a job than agree to be billed below what they think is their true worth. On Broadway the situation is made more complicated by there being an uneasy relationship between an actor's billing and his eligibility for certain categories of award.

Over-the-title billing, where the star or co-stars have their names in lights above the title of the show, can lose a show more than it gains. The more celebrated the star, the greater his box-office pulling power. If he leaves the show, and his name is replaced over the title with that of a comparative nonentity, the box office will go dead in response. So producers are forced to scratch about for celebrated names regardless of their suitability for the roles on offer. In recent years some astute producers, especially of the large long-running musicals, have reacted to the tyranny of billing by refusing to have anyone billed over the title. The show is the star, and when leading performers leave it, the title of the show remains in pre-eminent position.

Black Box Theatres

Black Box theatres are small, simple, unadorned spaces in which the play and the audience's perception of the play are deemed to be the only important elements. Their name derives from the squareness of their shape – because in the breezeblock architectural style in which they are usually built, right angles are cheaper than curves – and the blackness of their interior design – black to absorb light and provide a completely neutral backdrop so the most minimal and inexpensive designs can have a maximum effect.

They started to be built in the 1960s as a reaction against traditional ornamental theatre design where the prettiness of the auditorium is thought to enhance the audience's pleasure in an evening's entertainment. They were often built within or alongside existing theatres as alternative venues for the production of more challenging and less popular work.

Black Box theatres are usually highly adaptable spaces with the capacity to change their stage and **auditorium** shapes to suit a wide range of production styles including **in-the-round, traverse** or even traditional **proscenium** form. They generally have a technical gallery or lighting grid of some sort mounted over the entire theatre space but no capacity for flying and rarely the possibility of a trapped stage. They are often equipped with a system of modifiable auditorium seats whose configuration can be changed quickly by a small crew.

BLACK BOX SETS

A Black Box **set design** is comprised of three more or less equal sides of a squared-off box, the fourth side open to the audience. Set Designers use Black Box sets to close down larger stages into focusable playing spaces and as neutral design environments within which they can place other elements of design as required.

Blackout

A theatre is blacked out when no light is spilling onto the stage or into the auditorium from whatever source.

A complete blackout is almost impossible to achieve. In older theatres, daylight often spills in from badly masked auditorium doors or windows or from the 'lantern' above the grid. **Working lights** in the wings, flies and grid glow at the edges of the stage, **exit lights** cast a low green or orange twilight over the auditorium, video relay monitors and computer screens flicker all over the theatre, most noticeably from lighting and sound booths and on the facades of dress circles and balconies, musicians' reading lights glow in the orchestra pit and ushers flash their little lights up and down the aisles. Theatres are awash with unwanted light.

Despite the uphill struggle, **Set Designers** and **Lighting Designers** do try to achieve as near blackout conditions as they can. Their work generally shows at its best when the only perceivable light in the theatre is designed light, and they get frustrated when subtle scenic or lighting effects are spoilt by light spill. Most scenes in most plays are lit brightly enough for light spill not to matter too much. But in darker scenes extraneous light can become very distracting. You and your Stage Manager must be ready to police as complete a blackout as possible.

Working lights and musicians' lights can be turned down or the light bulbs covered with blue gel. Exit lights can be adjusted to their lowest legal level, even switched off for short periods of time. Video monitors and computer screens can be set on their lowest brightness and their edges masked from view. Daylight can be painted or curtained out. Ushers can be trained in the subtle use of the flashlight.

THE BLACKOUT CONVENTION

The blackout is a common **theatrical convention** used to demarcate the beginnings and ends of acts or scenes, and to conceal the movements of actors and stagehands during **scene changes**.

With the fading or snapping out of the lights, a portion of theatrical time is deemed to have ended or been suspended. With the fading up of the lights time is deemed to have begun or started anew. A slow dipping of the lights followed by a restoration can mean that a short time has passed while the characters remain in the same location. There are many different versions of this convention and others no doubt still to be imagined.

In its simplest form the blackout has replaced the curtains, or tabs, separating actors and audience. The final line of a scene, act or play is traditionally called the curtain line, but should really now be called the blackout line.

Blank Verse

See **Metre**.

Blocking

A square word describing an outmoded process. Blocking, verb and noun, refers to the technique a director employs to instruct a cast of actors where they are to stand, sit and move throughout a production and to the subsequent recorded pattern of positions they are obliged to adopt.

Blocking originated at a time when rehearsal periods were hopelessly short, actors did what they were told, and the stage was divided up into a grid of imaginary, or sometimes actual, 'blocks' as a guide to the actors and a record for stage management. Actors were given their 'blocking' and had to stick to it, invariably before discussion had taken place about the meaning of a scene or the appropriateness of any movement within it, if any such discussion took place at all.

The word is still used to describe the **staging** of a play, and the concept still persists in rehearsal rooms where controlling directors are frightened to engage with the complexities of real acting talent and the creation of fully rounded and unpredictable characters, or where the physical life of a production ends up being defined by the plot of the computerised 'moving lights' and an actor not in his block becomes an actor unlit.

The old-fashioned block system has been revived in recent years for the re-rehearsal of long-running mega-musicals, the singers having their moves monitored on a nightly basis by a police force of Staff Directors or Stage Managers. Any infringements of the numbered grid positions are noted and the guilty singers' names entered on a black list at the end of the performance. But this is not theatre at all. This is anti-theatre. This is the death of theatre.

Blocking should be banned – both the use of the word and the technique it describes. If you need a word to describe the physical rehearsal process, say 'staging'. Leave 'blocking' to the blockheads.

The Book

The 'book' is the text of the play. Actors are said to be 'off the book' if they have learnt their lines and 'still on the book' if they haven't.

It is also a common alternative term for the **prompt copy**, or prompt book, used by the Stage Manager or **DSM** for **calling the show.**

In **musical theatre** the 'book' was originally the libretto or spoken text as opposed to the songs, but in the modern musical it comprises the whole text of the show whether the material is spoken or sung. The book writer is sometimes also the **lyricist** and much less frequently the **composer**. The director, too, is very often responsible for some book-writing duties, the demarcation between staging and writing tending to become fuzzy in the practical hurly-burly of musical theatre rehearsal.

BOOK MUSICALS

A book musical is one with a spoken libretto – as opposed to a sung-through musical that has no spoken words at all.

Breaking Down

This is not a reference to onstage sobbing or any other hysterical behaviour. It is the process by which newly made or bought **costumes** can be made to look old, used or worn.

When actors first appear on stage in their costumes at the start of the **technical rehearsal** process, they often look awkward and unnatural. This is partly because they have yet to become comfortable in their new garb, but also because their costumes look uniformly clean and unused, as no set of real clothes ever looks (for very long anyway) in real life. If you're an inexperienced director, especially one devoted to **naturalism**, your heart will sink at this sight, but don't panic. There is much that can be done. The actors will get used to their costumes and invent more comfortable ways to wear them, and a good **Costume Designer** will already have scheduled a breaking-down process to take place as the technical rehearsals proceed. Costumes will disappear during the tech to reappear hours or days later, completely transformed.

Sometimes your view, or the actor's view, will differ from the designer's as to the appropriate level of breaking down, and you will have to negotiate. Inexperienced designers are often a little afraid to treat a set of carefully crafted costumes with sufficient disrespect.

Breaking down is important in plays that require any degree of naturalism, especially when they are populated by characters that are poor, travel-soiled, work-worn, weather-stained or wet, or whose clothes are in any way different from how they were when they were first bought or made. Only that class of characters for whom new clothes and freshly laundered linen are the common necessities of a fashionable life should escape the process.

Sometimes a designer will enlist an actor's help by agreeing to let him break down, or at least wear in, his own costume during the rehearsal process. This can be an effective method and has the advantage of accustoming the actor to his costume in the most natural of ways. Boots and shoes respond particularly well to this treatment.

Where you will have no choice in the matter of breaking down is when your costumes are hired. No hire company will appreciate having their property returned in a more broken-down state than when it left the warehouse. So if verisimilitude is your passion, check out the clothes before you hire them to make sure they seem suitably worn and soiled, otherwise make them and break them yourselves and save yourself the hire costs into the bargain.

Broadway

Broadway is the main theatre district of New York, so called after the thoroughfare that bisects it. It is the goal of ambitious theatre practitioners all across the US and an almost inevitable destination for the most successful of **West End** theatre and musical theatre productions. Unlike the West End it is not a place where serious drama puts down very strong roots, or certainly not very often, but it is undoubtedly the world capital of **musical theatre**. In any one season on Broadway you can see an astonishing variety of new musicals and revivals, from serious modern musical dramas to the most idiotic extravaganzas.

A Broadway theatre is defined – for purposes of union negotiation, contractual regulation and award eligibility – as a house of five hundred seats or more used primarily for theatre and situated in the district bounded by 6th Avenue to 8th Avenue, and 41st to 54th Streets. The Vivian Beaumont Theater at the Lincoln Centre is outside this district but qualifies as a Broadway house. Madison Square Garden, Radio City Music Hall and City Center all have larger auditoria than Broadway theatres but theatrical shows presented in those houses aren't considered to be Broadway.

There are some forty Broadway theatres. All but eight of them are owned by one of three major theatre-owning organisations, Shubert, Nederlander and Jujamcyn.

OFF BROADWAY

Off Broadway theatres have between one hundred and 499 seats and must be located in the borough of Manhattan.

OFF OFF BROADWAY

Off Off Broadway theatres are theatres in Manhattan with ninety-nine seats or fewer.

Both Off and Off Off Broadway houses are breeding grounds for new writing, directing, producing and acting talent in theatre and musical theatre. They provide a considerable variety of fare and comprise most of the artistic excitement in New York theatre.

If you make a theatre pilgrimage to New York you would do well to spend more of your time off Broadway than on.

Budgets

The budget of a production is the projection of its total financial outlay. It should include a costing of all the elements your production requires above and beyond what your theatre company has already provided for under other budgets.

Thus if you do a play in the commercial arena, where producers rarely have access to their own theatres, you will need a much bigger production budget than in an established subsidised theatre company, where many of your labour and workshop costs will already be covered.

All competent theatre companies have their **administrators**, financial controllers and **Production Managers** whose responsibility it is to balance the books, but they only do the jobs they do in order for your work to thrive, so your relationship with them and the budgets they control should be a creative one. Don't treat them as the enemy. They can find you money for what you need as well as forbid you to have it. The more they are made to feel part of the creative process, the more creative they will want to be with their budgets. But you too must always be ready to react creatively when faced with a shortage of funds.

All theatre companies, whether competently administered or not, are poor. There is never enough money. The small companies think the big ones are living in the lap of luxury, but the big companies never see it that way. Large or small, every company competes for grants, drums up sponsorship, tightens its belt, cuts its budgets and still ends up spending more than it should. Rest assured, you will never work for a company that does not put you and your collaborators under financial constraint, and the odds are that for most of your professional life you will be obliged to work in extremely straitened circumstances. To paraphrase Mr Micawber, 'Production budget £1,000, production expenditure £990, result happiness. Production budget £1,000, production expenditure £1,010, result misery.'

If you are the **Artistic Director** of a company, your annual overall budget will affect everything you plan and do, from the number of plays you programme to the size of your casts, the scale of your productions and the levels of pay for everyone involved.

You and your planners will argue and jostle and conspire, moving your limited resources from budget to budget, robbing Peter to pay Paul and Paul to pay Phyllis, reacting to the righteous and not-so-righteous demands of your heads of department, union representatives and employees, and constantly looking over your shoulder at the decaying fabric of the buildings in which you work. As a director of plays you will also have to negotiate your way round a fairly constant conflict of interests. You will want your own productions to be well financed but you will also be responsible for providing your **Associate Directors** and **Visiting Directors** with equal treatment. There is nothing more unbecoming to an Artistic Director than a reputation for featherbedding his own work at the expense of others.

If you are employed by a theatre company to direct a one-off play you will have considerably less control over your budget and no bargaining power to move money from some other budget onto your own. You will have agreed in advance the number of actors and any other performers you need, the musicians, singers, dancers, whomever. Their wages and those of the stage management team and your other creative collaborators will already have been budgeted for, and any late additions you might want to make to their number would have to be paid for out of your production budget. Where you should have some influence is on how the money is divided up for the 'physical' production – the cost of the set, costumes, wigs, make-up, lighting and sound.

Initial allocations of money for these different elements are always more or less educated guesses by your Production Manager based on previous experience of similar shows. The work you do with your designers can easily change that balance. You may decide to dispense with wigs altogether, or a sound plot. You may know in advance that your set is going to be simpler than usual but your lighting rig very complicated. And so on. As your design plans progress, you will need to keep your Production Manager in the picture so that budgets can be adjusted accordingly.

Always insist on knowing the precise size and make-up of your budget. Some Production Managers like to keep directors and designers in the dark about how much money is really available. This tactic may conceal a fundamental lack of funds, but is more often an ill-considered method of keeping all the allocations as miserly as possible. Either way, it drives designers crazy and is always counter-productive. Good, experienced designers know how to work within their budgets. If they don't know the size of the budget they can't possibly create financially responsible designs.

THE BUDGET CRISIS

Most productions have a budget crisis at some point so you should have a plan for when it happens rather than if.

The usual crisis point is a week or so after **the model** of the set and/or the **costume** design drawings have been handed in and the Production Manager has received the first costings from the scenic and wardrobe departments.

The meetings are always the same. You, your designer and the Production Manager and any other interested parties, depending on the scale of the crisis, sit in gloom around the model of the unaffordable set with the drawings of the unaffordable costumes scattered accusingly around you.

Silence. We just can't afford it. Well, it's what it is. There must be savings you can make. Do you want a first-class production or not? It's great, but we just don't have the money. The set just won't work without a rake . . . and so on. And then the haggling starts. A bit of scenery here, a large prop there. Every element is analysed and talked up or down, in or out, according to its relative cost and aesthetic integrity.

It's actually a very instructive process, or can be if you go about it in the right spirit. No one enjoys mounting an unaffordable production. No one wants the theatre company to go bust. Only a fool would envy the reputation of a spendthrift. In the subsidised theatre, you can't blithely squander public money. It's only right that the value of everything should be questioned. Not just the price, but the value.

Budgets

Every element of your production has a worth to you and your designers, and you must assess it. What can you do without? What is merely a luxury? What would be an acceptable compromise in design or material terms? What would be unacceptable? How much can you pare away before you have removed not just the skin but the whole fruit?

The meetings usually end the same way, too. With compromises and economies being made but the basic idea of the design remaining, the cut elements soon forgotten and the whole process serving to refine, and ultimately improve, the design. Some cynical designers know the process so well they try to control it by putting elements into the design they know will be cut, sacrificial lambs that are sure to fall under the budgetary axe. And canny Production Managers see the ploy coming and counter it by threatening more substantial cuts and forcing the designer into a voluntary sacrifice of his own lamb.

There are times when the gap between cost and budget is just too big to be coped with. Where the cuts required are so extreme that the integrity of the set would be hopelessly compromised. Where the baby is clearly in danger of being thrown out with the bathwater. If this happens, don't mess about. Go back to the drawing board and start again with a completely new design. Go for something fundamentally simpler, a **rough theatre** or **poor theatre** solution more suited to the company's purse. However late the date, it will be a great relief. There is much to be gained in the creative process by making a virtue out of necessity. Designs that come in under budget give you more artistic freedom in the rehearsal room. You and your designer can use that freedom to give your imaginations free rein. If you go through a whole rehearsal period feeling constrained by your budget your work will suffer. Budgets are good servants and bad masters.

Bullies and Bullying

Fear is an enemy to creativity, and those who use fear as a professional tactic will never rise to the very top of the theatre profession, or if they do will never feel completely safe there.

Of course, there are bullies in every walk of life, but it is part of your job as a director to know the theatrical ones when you see them and to neutralise their effect on the people around them. They come in different shapes and sizes, but the commonest forms are these:

1 The Director Bully

Victimises a particular junior actor or member of stage management in order to create an atmosphere of fear in the company and so distract from his own incompetence or fear of failure.

2 The Actor Bully

Usually a frightened performer taking out his fear on a more junior member of the company or stage management, or on an unconfident director.

3 The Stage Management Bully

Often a disappointed actor or director who resents a junior actor's success or cockiness or who terrorises a member of his own team in order to make himself feel more important.

4 The Designer Bully

Has usually been bullied by the Director Bully and passes on the abuse to those under his command. He is most often encountered causing offence to actors or wardrobe staff in costume fittings.

The best theatre is made in an atmosphere of mutual tolerance and creative excitement, with the right to fail enshrined in the rehearsal process. A single bully quietly at work in the rehearsal room can destroy this atmosphere very easily. You must therefore confront such behaviour as soon as it occurs, light-heartedly at first but if that doesn't work then as firmly as is necessary.

Perhaps the most egregious form of bullying comes in the form of sexual harassment, the director or senior actor victimising some member or members of the cast he finds attractive, professionally humiliating them and reducing them to tears in order to soften them up for a sexual 'rescue' at a later date. Watch out for this behaviour in bitter old stagers who have long ago abandoned any real interest in the quality of their own work.

One of the most difficult aspects of any sort of bullying is that the bully often doesn't know who he is. In other words it's easy to spot bullying in others but hard to admit to in yourself. The bully confronted with his behaviour will often be unaware that he has been causing unhappiness, especially when the cause of his behaviour is his own unhappiness. There is plenty of scope for unhappiness in the theatre and some creative artists have a peculiar talent for it.

Your awareness of bullying must start with yourself. Chart your own behaviour as rigorously as you do the behaviour of others. As the director you are under more pressure than anyone else in the rehearsal room, more constantly harried by questions, decisions, deadlines and incompetence, so you may also be the most likely to take out your frustration, or your inability to cope, on the people in your charge. But your own behaviour must be exemplary if you wish others to behave in like manner. Be patient and forbearing at all times. If you become a bully in your own rehearsals, your bad behaviour will be sure to spread to others.

The clearest symptoms of bullying are stress, uncharacteristic quietness and/or tearful, whispered conversations. Never ignore the symptoms. Make your care for the victim a clear demonstration of support.

If you feel you're being bullied yourself, talk to the perpetrator and let him know how you feel. He may tell you things that are hurtful to your *amour propre*, but better that than suffering in silence. More likely he won't even know he's been hurting you, and an airing of the grievance will make it evaporate.

If you are the bully, reform yourself. If you cannot, and your directorial technique relies on hurting your collaborators, you should seriously question your suitability for the job.

Business

'Business' is theatrical slang for physical action, usually comic and often unconnected to any particular stimulus from the text. Comic business, 'biz' for short, is best used at climactic moments of comedy to capitalise on laughter already in full flow. It is less likely to succeed when deployed from silence. Any comic business unconnected to situation or character is likely to fall into the **gag** category and should be banished from the rehearsal room.

The 'business' is also common theatrical slang for the theatre profession generally, the more inclusive 'show business' referring to all branches of the entertainment industry. Most theatre professionals prefer not to think of themselves as working in show business.

C

Calling the Show

The show is 'called' by a member of the **stage management** team, in Britain usually the Deputy Stage Manager who is responsible in rehearsal for the upkeep of the **book**, or bible of show cues. In the US the Stage Manager will call the show until one of his **ASMs** is ready to take over.

The calls in this case (not to be confused with rehearsal or performance **calls**) are the warnings to actors, stage management, stage crew, lighting and sound departments to stand by for the execution of their various **cues**, and are followed by the cues themselves. Calling a show requires a great degree of sensitivity and rhythm, and a sympathetic caller is one of the director's most essential allies during the run of a play.

Calls

A call in the theatre refers to the starting time of any session of work an actor or member of the crew is required to attend, or to the work itself. Thus the **rehearsal call** is the schedule of the day's rehearsal, specifying the time each actor is 'called'.

The performance calls include the 'half', the 'quarter', the 'five' and 'beginners', and any subsequent summons of actors to the stage. The performance ends with the **'curtain call'**, to which every actor in the theatre is summoned, regardless of status or merit.

THE HALF

The 'half' or 'half-hour' is the time, in British theatres thirty-five minutes and in American theatres thirty minutes, before the commencement of the performance. It is the time by which all the members of the cast and crew must be in the theatre so that the Stage Manager can be sure of a complete attendance for the performance. It is a serious offence to be 'late for the half'. If an actor has not signed in at the stage door by that time, the Stage Manager assumes he will not be performing his role or roles that night and instantly informs his **understudy** so that the costume and wig department and the understudy himself can make adequate preparation. A strict Stage Manager will not allow an actor who is late for the half to perform, particularly if the actor in question is habitually late, though often the status of the actor, or the un-preparedness of the understudy, or the unwillingness of one of the other principal actors to play his part with an understudy, will make for a speedy forgiveness of the culprit.

The half is called by a member of stage management, usually over the dressing-room speaker system, but sometimes by foot and mouth from dressing room door to door.

THE QUARTER

The quarter-hour call is given fifteen minutes before curtain-up in America and twenty minutes in Britain.

THE FIVE

Given five minutes before curtain-up in America, ten minutes in Britain.

BEGINNERS

Beginners are the performers who appear within the first few minutes of a play, and the 'beginners' call (in the US, the 'places' call) is their summons to stand by in the wings.

In Britain the 'beginners' call is five minutes before the actual start of the performance, allowing the actors a little grace to get from dressing room to stage in an un-panicky frame of mind. This is why all the other calls are advanced by five minutes.

The 'beginners' or 'places' call may be delayed if the stage manager is warned by the **Front of House** Manager that the curtain must be held for latecomers.

Casting

If you cast your play well you will be halfway to creating a good evening in the theatre and all the way to an enjoyable rehearsal period.

If you get the casting significantly wrong there will be little you can do to repair the damage, though your rehearsal period will be dominated by your attempts to do so.

The best preparation for casting any play is to have an intimate knowledge of the characters in it and the acting talent available to play them. If you find yourself in doubt as to the suitability of a particular piece of casting, then refer back to the text of the play to research the character more deeply, or look more closely at what evidence you have of the talents of the performer.

The casting process is informed by craft and instinct. If you are a beginner you must learn the craft first and rely on your instinct as little as you can, because until you have practised the craft your instinct will be worth little. So here follows a set of guidelines to help you match actor to character. Eventually the guidelines can disappear as your experience teaches you methods of your own. But let these serve for now.

5 GOOD REASONS FOR CASTING AN ACTOR

1 The actor is 'right' for the part

The more experienced you become, the more this feeling of 'rightness' will come naturally to you. Rightness is a combination in the actor of the following personal characteristics:

A) AGE

Many characters are not given a specific age by the playwright and, even after sensible deduction from the script, age can remain unimportant to a character's function in the story.

Sometimes the evidence in the text is conflicting. Hamlet, for instance, is described as being young and also as being thirty – but the part can be played by an actor as young as twenty or as old as fifty, depending on the brilliance and maturity of the performer on the one hand and the understanding – sometimes even the forgiveness – of the audience on the other.

The age given by the playwright may be specific but could also be something of a trap. Shakespeare gives Juliet's age as thirteen and by deduction from the text her mother's age as twenty-six. It is unlikely, however, that one of the trickiest female roles Shakespeare ever wrote could be played successfully by a thirteen-year-old actress. The experience and maturity necessary to play such a part are more likely to be found in an actress in her early to mid-twenties. But if such is the case then an actress in her late twenties playing Lady Capulet would seem more like Juliet's sister than her mother.

The relative ages of other characters in the play can become an important qualification. If King Lear is to be played by a seventy-year-old actor, then Goneril and Regan can be middle-aged, but not if Lear is only forty-five or fifty. If the actress playing Rosalind is thirty-five, then the actor playing Orlando must not be twenty, unless you want the central relationship of *As You Like It* to have a maternal subtext.

Some actors, of course, are better at playing age than others – either younger or older than themselves. This skill can become a factor in casting, especially when the pool of actors is a limited one. Beware, however, of always requiring a younger actor to play old or vice versa. It can result in the actor acquiring some tiresome habits.

B) PHYSICAL APPEARANCE

This is erroneously treated as the most important qualification but is actually often the least. It is certainly where the most subjective casting judgements are made and therefore also the greatest mistakes.

Never start off with a rigid idea of a certain physical look for the roles you are casting. My heart sinks when I hear a director say, 'I was looking for someone slender and fair,' or 'Yes, he would be good but he's a bit shorter than I was imagining.' The proper response to this is: 'Then imagine it differently.'

Casting

Physical characteristics should figure very low on your list of qualifications if the actor is qualified in every other way. If you persist in hanging on to a limiting image of a role in spite of being unable to find a competent actor to fulfil it, you will fall into the worst of all heresies and cast an actor who 'looks right' but who is wrong in every other way. Do this with every part in the play and you will end up with a thoroughly substandard cast.

If you have a strong physical preconception of a role, ask yourself how you acquired it. Try to be honest in your response. It will help you cast well and it will teach you something about your own imagination that may prove useful in other respects. There are three likely sources of preconception:

i) The author's physical description of the character
From a careful reading of the play you have noted what the characters say about themselves or one other, and how the writer describes them in the stage directions. Accurate research is important, but you should never take these physical pictures too literally or cast solely on this basis, without reference to the character's, or the actor's, other attributes. Playwrights have their own preconceptions, and they are not always useful to the performance of their plays. Sometimes they write parts with particular actors in mind. Of course there are physical requirements for the proper performance of some roles – requirements of size, strength, girth or **beauty** – but within reason this is where an actor's skill can easily compensate, helped by sympathetic casting around him and a little assistance from wardrobe and wigs.

ii) Theatrical tradition
You have seen the part played by a particular actor and his physical 'rightness' has stuck in your mind. This happens most frequently when an actor is required to '**take over**' a role that has been successfully played by another. If you fall into this trap you are also more likely to consign your chosen actor to a fruitless task of imitation – of someone he might not even have seen playing the role.

iii) Your subconscious imagination
You don't know why you 'see' the part in a certain physical way,

you just do. This really isn't good enough. A strong-willed **Casting Director** will force you to explain yourself, and you should do your best to comply. Your certainty may be the result of a prejudice that no one else in your audience will share. If you find yourself defending a hunch against a chorus of disapproval, give it up as a bad job. In any case, a good actor will become more and more like the character in **rehearsal**, and by the same process the character will come to resemble the actor.

2 The actor wants to play the part

Good actors are at their most creative when they are developing artistically. Nothing is more stultifying for an actor than being required to play the same sort of part over and over again. All artists rely on variety for a healthy attitude to their art, and actors are no exception. That is why an actor's hunger to be in a particular company, or in a particular play, or to perform a particular role, is an important factor in the casting process.

As a director you don't want to find yourself in a rehearsal room with a group of actors who feel they are repeating themselves, that the parts they are playing are well within their grasp because they have played similar parts in other plays. For this reason you should never cast an actor in a role because you have seen him being brilliant in a similar role. The copy will always be less brilliant than the original.

Make sure during the auditioning and interviewing process that the person you are considering for a role really has a passion to play it. This will be easier to assess with leading roles than supporting ones, but there is no part than doesn't somewhere have an actor desperate to play it, or desperate to be part of the company putting on the play. Sometimes this assessment is hard to make, the actor's need to be employed masking his other more specific ambitions. But if you are perceptive and diligent you should be able to make this judgement about every member of the company as you assemble them. Never peg an actor at a certain level of talent, or type of part. And don't let them do it to themselves. Inspire your actors to want what is just beyond them, and then support them in their attempt to achieve it.

Casting

The perfect ensemble of actors for any play is one in which every actor is playing a part that requires him to stretch his talent to the utmost and learn something new about his craft on every day of rehearsal. The desire an actor has to inhabit his role then becomes a crucial part of the creative process, infecting the atmosphere in the rehearsal room and thereby the energy of all the other actors.

3 The actor is capable of playing the part

A) VOCALLY

The bigger the part the more important the quality of the actor's voice. An actor with a fine, strong, resonant voice will cope with a large part without undue vocal effort. Others less gifted may struggle (see **Actors**).

Many parts are written in specific **dialects**. Some actors are better at these than others. Some dialects are so tricky that only native speakers can completely master them. Dialect plays need actors with good ears. Actors with duff ears should stick to their own dialects or risk outraging more sensitive ones. Local audiences can be very proprietorial about their dialects.

B) PHYSICALLY

Some parts are more physically demanding than others, and some are scarcely demanding at all, but they all require some degree of physical prowess.

If a part requires exceptional physical skill, have the actor prove it in **audition**. Don't take his word for it. If he claims to be an acrobat or a dancer, let him show you. If he has the skills, he will relish the opportunity to show them off. If he doesn't, you will save his blushes and your own by not casting him in a part he can't manage.

Physical dexterity is most obviously needed in comedic work. Talented comedians are nearly always physically gifted. A company of comic actors will rely on one another for the development of a physical language in rehearsal. One inept actor thrown amongst them can upset the rhythm of this language to the detriment of the whole piece and the inevitable trampling on essential laughs. A lack of competence in one actor will infuriate the others as well as you, but only you will be held responsible.

c) INTELLECTUALLY

All parts require some level of intellectual apprehension, but very few are beyond the grasp of an actor of normal intelligence. Don't be too impressed by an actor's ability to talk cleverly about the role for which he is being considered. It doesn't mean that he will play it well. Many fine actors are quite inarticulate in private. Others have little or no formal education or ability to analyse their craft or talk interestingly about the characters they are playing. Do not be deceived. They may be just as good at *playing* intellectual roles as their genuinely intellectual peers.

There are parts that are best attempted by an actor with a good analytical mind, particularly if the play is written in complex **heightened language**. They are the great, play-defining roles, like Hamlet or Faustus, where the character's journey is also the intellectual journey of the play. The best actors for these parts are the ones who understand the full complexity of the author's mind. If the actor who plays Hamlet gets intellectually lost then the audience will follow him into the same wilderness.

d) EMOTIONALLY

If comedy requires physical skill then tragedy requires emotional skill. The best actors of serious drama are those who have an easy access to their deeper feelings, and the very best will seem to have fewer layers of protective skin than the rest of us, wearing their emotions on the outside and able to exhibit them freely without embarrassment.

This access to the emotions can be acquired by practice, but some actors have it much more naturally than others. If you are directing a play that requires the characters to expose their innermost feelings and move the audience in doing so, then you need a cast that can explore these emotions with the least possible show of effort. Just as it is uncomfortable to see an actor with no comic talent trying to be funny, so it is embarrassing to see an actor whose emotions are deeply buried strenuously mining for them on a public stage. The strain usually starts in the voice but soon transmits itself to other parts of the actor's frame, resulting in a performance that rasps the vocal cords, bulges the veins in the neck, and twists the body into dehumanising contortions.

Casting

I don't mean to imply an artificial division between comic and tragic acting. Very few plays require a pure version of either, and the best plays usually require a mixture of both. The most emotional of plays are often filled with laughter and the greatest comedies are infected with sadness. Good actors should be able to play comedy and tragedy with equal skill, and the very best will play both without any discernible change in their technique.

4 *The actor is a good mix with other actors already cast*

A) PERSONALLY

This is very difficult to assess and will have to depend on your instinct more than anything else. Conflicts of personality will always be a feature even in the best-regulated ensembles, and part of your job will be to neutralise any tensions that arise.

The best antidote to unreasonable behaviour in rehearsal and on into the run of a play is to cast at least one 'leading' actor as a member of the company. By 'leading' actor I do not mean an actor playing a large leading role, but rather an actor capable of leading a company, able to inspire and exhort with his or her personality and talent. A leading actor of this sort is always confident, calm and kind, with an unaffected interest in the lives and skills of the other actors. This person is unlikely to be the social organiser of the group and is unlikely to have directorial ambitions. He or she will not necessarily be older than the other actors – but will certainly be wiser, able to see all sides of an argument when a fight breaks out, able to represent you when you are absent, and to stick up for the rights of the less powerful members of the company when they are victimised or troubled. Such a person is a director's essential ally. If you are lucky you will have two or three of them in a cast, although one is enough. If there are none at all, then beware the company's peace of mind in your absence. This role can only be fulfilled by an actor. A Stage Manager, however calm and influential, will never be able to assuage a troubled stage while a performance is in progress, or control the bad behaviour that is characteristic of a company that has lost its way.

B) AGE-WISE

I have already referred to this issue in the section above on Age, but it bears reinforcing here that the actual age of individual cast members is always a relative matter.

A school production of *King Lear* may be superb, but only because all the characters are played by children with the skills and experience and outlook of children. If you cast an adult actor as Lear and surround him with children in all the other roles, no one in the cast or the audience will be comfortable. This is an extreme example of a general truth: the age of a character or even of a performer on stage is always relative to the ages of the other characters or performers.

Awareness of the relativity of age in casting is thus one of the most important ways in which you can support the casting you have already done, especially when you have cast an actor in a leading role which he is actually too young or too old to play.

c) PHYSICALLY
Physical shape and strength and size are relative in exactly the same way as age. If you cast a stocky but otherwise unimpressively built actor as Falstaff in the *Henry IV* plays, and help him out with a bit of body-padding, it would be terribly unfair on him to cast a fat actor in any other role in the play. By surrounding him with a supporting group of short and slight-framed actors and by casting a boyish young man as Prince Hal, you can give the audience the impression of a huge man as Falstaff. By the same token, you should avoid surrounding Cassius with lean-and-hungry-looking co-conspirators, or pairing Cyrano de Bergerac with a large-nosed Rageneau.

d) PROFESSIONALLY
Training in drama schools changes over time but it changes slowly, the pace dictated by the working lifetimes of the various teachers employed in them. Hence any generation of actors will tend to share the same fundamental working methods. Problems can arise, though, when older and younger actors are cast in the same play and find it hard to develop a common language for rehearsal. The best older actors are only too happy to have their batteries recharged by exposure to new currents in theatre thinking, and the most sensitive younger actors are ready to accommodate a little rigidity in the

methods of their seniors, but when sclerotic old rigidity meets passionate young dogma then sparks can fly, and you will need to intervene to save the *amour propre* of both parties. Better to head off such battles by casting open-minded actors whatever their ages.

Some drama schools teach methods which are a law unto themselves, and the graduates of such schools are often quite uncomfortable for the first few years of their professional lives as they try to reconcile the rigidity of their training with the obvious excellence of the actors in their company who have been trained under more relaxed systems.

5 You like the actor

This might seem a shallow motive in relation to the other more practical and technical ones, but it can turn out to be the most important.

Theatre is a social art. Without harmony and balance and mutual respect it is well-nigh impossible to create good theatre. A good company of actors is a community of like-minded souls united in the pursuit of an artistic goal. Ego, ambition, small-mindedness and lack of understanding are all barriers to the creation of such a community. As the leader of the company, empowered as such by the casting process, as the proposer of the work and its aims, your vision and clarity of purpose are essential to the happiness of all.

If you have an instinctive dislike for a particular actor, for his personality or his talent, then value your instinct. Ask yourself why this actor is unappealing to you, or threatening or dismissive. It is good to be challenged in rehearsal but not when the challenger has no natural sympathy for you or your ideas. You will never like all the actors presented to you. Other directors will never like all the actors with whom you have worked and whom you like. Don't be ashamed of the choices you make and don't be frightened to base your choices on personal feeling. Such feeling can become your clearest guide when confidence in your other judgements eludes you.

All other judgements being equal, you want to end up in rehearsal with a group of actors whom you find personally engaging and who are personally engaged by you. If you like them, and they like you, then in your absence they are far more likely to like one another.

13 BAD REASONS FOR CASTING AN ACTOR

1 Pressure from the actor

An actor may think he is right for the part and attempt to persuade you against your better judgement. Most actors have an awareness of their strengths and their limitations and understand that they are not right for every part they fancy playing. Some actors are not so blessed with self-knowledge and will never admit to a weakness. Their maxim is: 'I'm a good actor. A good actor can play anything.' Very occasionally they will be right. Usually not.

2 Financial pressure

A producer or theatre company needs a star in order to raise the money for a production but the available star doesn't fit the part. You are persuaded against your better judgement.

3 Pressure from the actor's agent

A powerful agent is desperate to find work for a particular client, either because the actor is desperate himself or because the agent has lost the confidence of the actor for some other reason. The agent 'sells' you the actor and you cast him without proper research.

4 The Laurence Olivier Syndrome

A leading performer is modelling his career on some beloved icon and wants to play every part the icon played in his career. You feel obliged to cast him even though you have little or no faith in his rightness for the role.

5 Vanity casting

A major film or television performer wants to play a romantic leading role in the theatre in order to give his career an imagined legitimacy, or a star from the music business is moving past his sell-by date and sees the theatre as a possible alternative career. If you don't cast the actor then the project won't happen and you are persuaded against your better judgement.

Casting

6 Nepotism

Your own husband/wife/partner seems right for a part or you persuade yourself so, or they persuade you so. Be very careful. This is usually a bad idea. Even if the casting is genuinely good, there are likely to be problems with the rest of the cast over a perceived favouritism in the process, and your partner will have to work unfairly hard at persuading the rest of the cast it isn't so. It is also extremely difficult to keep the terms of a personal relationship out of the rehearsal room and embarrassing for the rest of the cast if you can't. If you have to cast a partner then live apart for the duration of the rehearsal period, or have an absolute rule that the play is never discussed between you outside the rehearsal room.

7 Nepotism by proxy

An actor you are keen to cast will only play the role if his or her husband/wife/partner is in the play in a decent-sized part. Even if the partner-actor is good and right for the part, beware! This sort of nepotism is rarely benign and can turn out to be a real blind. It is often the case that such actors don't really want their partners in the play – they just want you to have tried, or appeared to try, to make room for them. Perhaps they feel guilty about having a more successful career. Who knows what domestic blandishments have led to the request? In any case the partner might end up feeling mortified by getting the part for the wrong reason and by everyone else in the cast knowing or suspecting how the casting occurred. This latter is lethal if the partner turns out to be a dead weight.

8 Nostalgia

A well-known actor's career is in the doldrums and he wants to recreate a past triumph. This is rarely a good idea. Triumphs are usually unrepeatable because the circumstances in which they occurred will have changed – including the age, competence and confidence of the actor in question.

9 Compromise

A good actor with whom you love to work is perfect for a part that has already been cast with another actor. Beware! Be very careful before casting that actor in a different, inferior role. You don't want him looking enviously across the rehearsal room at the other actor and you don't want the other actor looking fearfully back at him.

10 Sentiment

You feel bad about the halting career of an actor with whom you used to work and miscast him out of personal concern. Theatre can be a familial enterprise, but be careful that your fondness does not blunt your judgement.

11 Lust

You fancy the actor in question and hope that the rehearsals will provide an opportunity for a sexual adventure. A bad idea for a number of reasons. Your perception that the actor is right for the part has already been clouded by personal passion. The liaison will probably never happen. If it does happen it will be a hopeless distraction. If it doesn't happen it will be a hopeless distraction. At worst it could result in a very bad atmosphere in rehearsal.

12 Narcissism

You cast yourself because you are the best, or the only, actor for the role. Double beware! It is extremely hazardous to direct a play in which you are also appearing. The crafts of acting and directing are both hard enough on their own. Combined, they can produce a serious conflict of interest in you and in the rest of the cast. Very few people have the skill and the patience to do this well. Better to choose between your acting and directing roles and appoint a colleague to discharge the other.

13 Narcissism by proxy

You have a real or subconscious urge to play the part yourself but for some reason can't, so you choose the actor you think most resembles you. This happens much more often than you would imagine or than many directors would be willing to admit. If you are not acting in a production it is quite unfair to lumber some other actor with trying to be you. If you want to play the part that badly then play it and let someone else direct the play.

THE CASTING PROCESS

However cleverly you choose your actors, plays are not cast in a day. Most of them take weeks of negotiation, a cast like a wall being slowly built up, actor by actor, brick by brick. You gain an actor, you lose an actor. An actor proves too expensive, or cannot agree to his billing, or will not tour, or suddenly gets a better offer. Directors create systems to help them cope with this frustrating business. This is the one I use.

1. Keep an Actors' Book listing all the actors with whom you have worked or would like to work. Update it after every visit to the theatre or cinema or viewing of television drama. Be selective. Include only the actors that you genuinely admire. Have a system for recording the names but not too rigorous a classification – most actors are capable of more than one style and in any event change with their employment and age. An alphabetical delineation that separates actors and actresses will serve you well because it can be cross-referenced with other lists and directories.

2. Make a list of all the characters in your play, including any parts to be **doubled**, and then list against them the possible candidates for playing each role or roles. If you work with a permanent ensemble your choices will be constrained by the actors in your company. Indeed, their talents may even have influenced your choice of play. If, however, you are casting from scratch, then you must have a number of different options for each part.

3. Know your own strengths and weaknesses. Who you are as a director will define how you cast certain parts. Some directors are very poor at casting young women. Others are over-impressed by physical beauty in young men. Still others are threatened by strong older women or by actors more intellectually gifted than they are themselves. The best directors learn from their experience and get to know where they cast least well. Be like them and ask others for advice where you need it most.

4. Many large theatre companies and most commercial producers use **Casting Directors**. Working with a Casting Director requires a degree of understanding and forbearance. They have their strengths and weaknesses just as you do.

5. In compiling your lists of candidates, with or without the help of a Casting Director, use your Actors' Book before you start trawling through a **casting directory**. Use a casting directory as a way of checking the age, appearance and atmosphere of your candidates, but not as a primary source of inspiration.

6. Once you have written a list of actors for each part, put the names in order of preference, but don't get too attached to a particular choice too soon. Once you have chosen an actor he still has to choose you back. Good actors are not always available, and they are choosy about what they do. Every actor is unique, but every part can be played in hundreds of different unique ways.

7. Check the availability of all the names at the top of your character lists. You do this by reference to *Spotlight*, or some other similar **casting directory** in book or online form, and then calling the relevant agent. If an actor has no agent then *Spotlight* should be able to provide you with a contact number.

8. Once you have a shortlist of available actors for each part, decide who to make your first offers to. Never, ever make an offer for the same part to more than one actor at a time. Once you have made an offer to an actor or his agent, you must stick by your choice until the part has been accepted or turned down.

9. Don't be offended when actors turn you down. You can't know what they're thinking or what else is on offer in their professional and personal life. Sometimes an actor or his agent will tell you why the offer has been rejected, but the explanation may only be a polite excuse. In any case it doesn't matter, you've been turned down – so go on to the next choice – there's always a better idea.

10. You don't have to have all your parts out on offer at the same time. Start with your leading roles and get them in place first. Be especially careful how you cast 'pairs' of parts – lovers, or marriages or protagonists of one sort or another. Make sure that the actor already cast is well complemented by a 'partner'.

Casting

11. Never cast an actor on insufficient evidence or hearsay recommendation. If you don't know the actor, then set up a meeting, a reading or an **audition**. There are very few actors so grand they will refuse to meet you prior to an offer being made.

12. In certain cases it is quite proper to discuss your ideas with the leading actor or actors already cast. Many leading actors are quite able to sustain an unprejudiced view of what is required in the cast to be assembled around them, and their experience could be useful to you. In rare cases in the commercial theatre, leading actors may have a contractual veto in the choice of their co-stars. Make sure you know about any such arrangements before you start the casting process. Producers can be coy about admitting to such things.

13. As your offers start to be accepted, look carefully at the remaining parts in the light of the actors already cast. You are building a wall but not out of identically shaped bricks. Like the drystone wall builders of the north, you are building with the boulders and rocks and stones and pebbles that are lying in the fields around you. None of them has the same dimensions, but collectively they must form a solid structure, bound together by their own shape and weight, mortar-less.

14. As you cast the final, more junior members of a large acting company, you may have to take account of their **understudying** potential, but you should also be aware that you are finishing your wall. Very small parts are usually written quite unspecifically and can be played in many different ways. Look at the people you have already cast and ask yourself what is missing from the ensemble in the way of humour or intelligence, youth or age, sexuality, gravitas or energy. Use the remaining places to plug the gaps.

CASTING A MUSICAL

In many respects casting a musical entails the same process as casting a play, and you can use the same systems for both. But your Casting Director, if you use one (and you would be well advised to use one), should be a specialist. Matching a singing voice to a role is a tricky and quite technical business requiring a lot of experience.

However well cast a performer is in terms of age, appearance, personality and acting skill, he will not be forgiven by the audience if he can't hit the top notes in his songs, or if his singing voice is bland, coarse or out of tune. The bigger the role, the more mellifluous the voice must be to satisfy the emotional demands of the role as it develops through the show. And don't imagine that a 'book musical' requires less accomplished singing voices than one that is 'sung through'. Audiences are more likely to forgive great singers for indifferent acting than great actors for indifferent singing.

Auditioning is a crucial part of the casting process in the musical theatre. Even very experienced performers will not object to singing through the songs in audition conditions. They are as keen as you and your **Musical Director** should be to prove that their voices are able to handle the songs as written. They may wish to negotiate a change of key to accommodate the **tessitura** of their voices so that the climactic notes of a song match their own best high notes.

If your musical has choruses or an ensemble, once you have cast the main roles you will have to consult your Musical Director about the vocal make-up of the rest of the cast. You will want to get the right actors for the small roles available, but your Musical Director will need to get a balance of voices for the chorus. You may need to compromise on some of your choices for the sake of having the right mix of sopranos, tenors or basses. And so may he.

MULTIRACIAL CASTING

This is an issue over which there have been more bitter arguments in recent years than any other, but it would be wrong to avoid the subject because of that. If you direct plays today you will have to deal with it and you should therefore have all the arguments at your fingertips. It is a complex matter and even discussing it can lead to misunderstanding and anger, so I hope none of the terms I use here prove contentious or offensive to anyone.

The meaning, relevance and desirability of multiracial casting will differ depending on the nature of the society you are living in. The more racially integrated your society the easier you will find the discussion and implementation of multiracial casting. Audiences in a society with repressed or ghettoised minorities or where the minorities represent only a tiny proportion of the population will tend to be the least willing to accept it. The matter is further complicated by the fact that theatre people are on the whole less racially prejudiced than average members of the population and therefore average members of their audience. As a director you may find yourself being influenced by the more conservative members of your theatrical and critical community against the idea of multiracial casting.

Here are the two main arguments that are most commonly deployed, Shakespeare's plays providing some excellent and controversial examples of them.

1 The historical accuracy argument

'The plays of Shakespeare were written at a time when there were very few African or Asian people living in England. If Shakespeare had wanted his characters to be African or Asian, he would have said so, and indeed did say so in the tiny number of instances where it was required. It is a perversion of his works to cast his characters contrary to his original intention.'

This argument can be answered in a number of ways.

a) While it is true that Shakespeare was writing at a time of very little racial integration, he was writing about a society that was fascinated by itself as a society. In order properly to reflect this original relationship with his readers and audiences, we must put on his plays today in a way that similarly reflects the society of today. If a community today is racially and culturally complex then it needs its theatre to reflect that complexity, or the community will stop going to the theatre.

b) Historical accuracy was unimportant to Shakespeare, even in his history plays, and we do him a disservice if we force his plays into an over-literal historical mould. Should we also ban the use of electric light in Shakespearean productions, or insist that 'water' is pronounced to rhyme with 'matter'?

c) There may have been an absence of African and Asian citizens in Shakespeare's England but the same could be said of Jews. Should we therefore propose that Jewish actors are inappropriately cast in Shakespeare's plays, other than as Shylock, Tubal or Jessica? Most people would agree this would be grotesque, but are we then really talking about race or rather about the outward physical evidence of race, and should that really ever be a reason not to cast someone in a part?

d) Where does it say in the text that Caliban is *not* African? Or indeed Ariel? Or many other of his characters – Oberon, for instance, or Titania or Puck? One could go further and include all the characters whose racial lineage is not mentioned or even implied in the text – most of Shakespeare's servants come into this class of parts, and his clowns too – his porters and gravediggers and soldiers and priests. But beware of this argument, for it is dangerously circular and leads back to the fundamental conservative complaint of racial inappropriateness. Indeed, African and Asian actors in Europe and America are more frustrated by this argument than any other, for they see it as the fairy-isation or clowning of their talent. They are permitted to play any part as long as it isn't a king or a queen, a hero or heroine, or any close relation of another character.

2 *The family characteristics argument*

Those who don't object in principle to the idea of multiracial casting may still have difficulty accepting casting that seems to confound the laws of genetics.

Here there is far more difficulty for the liberal conscience in that audiences can have an attachment to rigorously naturalistic production values and therefore object when what they see on the stage seems not to fit with an application of those values.

Consider the following awkward practical questions:

a) You believe that the best actress available to you to play the part of Juliet is a black actress. Do you look for an older black actor and actress to play her parents, Capulet and Lady Capulet? If you do so, do you also decide that all the Capulets should be black and all the Montagues white? If you follow that course, can you say that it was your original intention to make *Romeo and Juliet* a play about racial conflict? Not a bad idea in itself perhaps, but is that what you wanted to do when you cast a black Juliet? If you don't cast black parents for your black Juliet, are you happy that some members of the audience will be unhappy with the apparent racial inconsistency? If you see this as a problem, is there a solution to it?

b) You are directing *Othello* and the best actor in your company to play the part is white. Is it any longer acceptable for a white actor to play Othello and if so, does he wear black make-up? The part was played by white actors almost exclusively for four hundred years and has therefore become one of the parts that great white Shakespearean actors aspire to play. Should they still be allowed to do so? If a white actor plays the part, then can you still have black actors in the supporting cast? Won't they make the white actor play-ing Othello seem ridiculous? Can you really ban black actors from your production of *Othello*? Shouldn't you choose another play?

c) You have a black actor playing Othello. You deem it important that Othello's blackness should be a unique characteristic in the play. Do you therefore have no other black actors in your produc-tion of *Othello*?

d) If it isn't a good idea for a white actor to play Othello, is it a good idea for a non-Jewish actor to play Shylock? Is there a difference?

e) You are directing *The Merchant of Venice* and the actress you have chosen to play the part of Portia is black. How do you play the scene with the Prince of Morocco where Portia states her unwillingness to be married to someone 'of his complexion'? Do you cut the lines? Or cut the scene? Or change Morocco's colour? Or make Portia racially self-hating? If the society you are exploring in the play is fundamentally anti-Semitic, how does a black Portia fit into that picture? In what way does it change the nature of her relationship to Shylock in the court scene?

f) You cast a black actor as King Lear. Do you cast all three of his daughters black? Or do you cast them all mixed-race? Or do you cast Cordelia black and Goneril and Regan white or Cordelia white and the others black? How would the relative races of the actors playing these four characters affect the meaning of the play? How would these meanings be changed if the play was being produced in London, or New York, or Atlanta, or Cape Town, or Lagos?

'COLOUR-BLIND' CASTING

While there will always be a case for racially specific casts, especially when a play's theme is race or centres around a particular cultural or racial community, there is also a case for treating all other plays as opportunities for colour-blind casting. This means that you cast every part with the best possible actor available regardless of his race, culture or colour. Of course this is much easier said than done. An actor's race or colour is part of what makes up his character and therefore his talent. How do you take account of every other aspect of an actor's physical form – his age and beauty and size and weight – but not his racial characteristics? It's harder to accomplish than you would imagine. To be truly colour-blind in your casting process and to honour the play, the author, the actors and the audience without offending or patronising someone in the process is probably impossible, but there are many who believe it is the only honourable aspiration when casting plays for a multicultural, multiethnic audience.

Casting Directories

Most countries with strong theatre and/or film traditions and a large pool of acting talent have casting directories. These are catalogues of actors' faces, arranged in alphabetical order of their names and sometimes broadly 'typed' by age and gender. The companies that publish them take an annual fee from the actors who appear in them and they are sold to Casting Directors, agents, theatre and film companies, advertising agencies, and any other individual or organisation that has an interest in casting actors.

In Britain the most important casting directory is *Spotlight*. The company that produces it also publishes *Contacts*, a directory, brought out annually, of the contact names and addresses of every theatre, film and television organisation, agency and training school in the country. *Contacts* is an essential reference book for anyone working in the theatre in Britain.

In the US an equivalent to *Spotlight* is *Players' Guide*, which is available on disk, but imdb.com or imdbpro.com are also now very widely used.

Casting directories like *Spotlight*, whether in published or online form, are indispensable aids, but a poor way to start the casting process. There are some twenty thousand entries in *Spotlight*, and trawling through all of them will invite suicidal feelings. In any case, after only a few hundred entries you will start to grow 'face-blind', unable to remember what you are looking for or why. *Spotlight* is best used as a method of checking the faces of actors that have already been proposed, or as an *aide-mémoire* for actors you are a little hazy about.

Casting Directors

Casting Directors can be influential in helping you to choose your actors, but you mustn't let them do your job for you. Don't let them persuade you to take someone against your better judgement. They sometimes have relationships they value with actors, agents or even other directors, and may be guilty of making unobjective judgements about the actors they propose to you. The best Casting Directors know this and will stop pushing someone they can tell you aren't keen on.

You know the play best. You know what you want to do with it. Take time to explain in great detail what it is you are looking for in every part. A good Casting Director will abandon his preconceptions in favour of your vision, provided it is clear and well-reasoned.

A Casting Director will save you an enormous amount of time and trouble in the administration of the **auditioning** process, the following-up of offers and the negotiation of contracts and salaries. He can also be a sympathetic advocate in persuading actors and their agents to accept roles about which they may be doubtful.

Casting Directors also find themselves cast as arbiters between overambitious producers or directors and the realities of the market place. Producers love stars, but most stars don't want to play the parts producers want them to play. A knowledgeable Casting Director will know who is likely to say yes to which role at what price and so save a great deal of time and anxiety in the process.

Child Actors

There is a maxim amongst theatre actors that one should never appear on stage with children or animals, both being regarded as equally damaging to their professional status, *amour propre* and peace of mind. Though this might seem an unnecessarily proscriptive belief, there is much truth in it.

A great deal of the charm that children and animals possess in real life relies on their lack of self-consciousness. On stage a lack of self-consciousness usually equates to a lack of awareness and a lack of skill. Everything that seems real on stage is actually cleverly contrived, and the presence of true innocence, naïveté or unawareness will always become riveting by contrast. Thus what actors are really worried about is that an animal or a child will monopolise the audience's attention in exactly inverse proportion to its skill, sophistication or desert. In other words, if an actor shares a stage with a child or an animal, he may as well not be acting for all the difference it will make to the audience. Few actors will ever willingly accept such a constraint on their craft. But they sometimes have to.

Many plays are written with parts for children, and if you work on such plays in a naturalistic style you will have to cope with the challenge, not to say the problem, of children on stage. Before you do so, make yourself certain that the child or children will be worth the trouble. Could you not cut them? Or have them played by adults? Or replace them with puppets?

The three main difficulties in working with children are those of integration, disruption and expense.

Children need to be chosen very carefully from a large range of candidates if you want to find really talented ones. They need a lot of rehearsal time with constant repetition if they are to be properly integrated into a professional adult ensemble.

Most children go to school during the day, so the scenes in which they appear have to be scheduled after school hours or at weekends, thus disrupting the rest of the schedule.

Most countries have child labour laws that restrict the amount of rehearsal time and the number of performances that any one child can work. Licences for children to appear on stage have to be applied for well in advance from local authorities. Head teachers of schools may also have to be consulted.

When children get ill they can't just 'soldier on' as actors are required to do; they disappear for days at a time. So you usually need two or three teams of children for each role, adding to the expense and disruption.

However many children you end up with, some of them may turn out to be unreliable in performance, the younger they are the more likely their concentration will waver and destroy the reality of the action around them. With different children playing different performances the adult actors have to get used to a variable quality of concentration in the scenes in which they appear.

Finally, children must be paid. In some parts of the world they are paid the same as adult actors, but even when badly paid, they can constitute a considerable production expense. They always need to be chaperoned, and chaperones must be paid. On tour, they must also be taught and the tutors paid and the children, the tutors and the chaperones all transported to and from the venues and their day-to-day expenses defrayed.

If you haven't been deterred by any or all of the above then good luck to you. There is another side of the coin. Well-trained and well-behaved children can be a delight in rehearsal. They can humanise a rehearsal room and fill it with a charming normalcy and sweetness. It's hard for anyone to be pretentious in the presence of children, or harder than usual anyway. And you may have the good fortune to employ an actor as a child who later turns into a considerable adult performer. You will know you have worked in the theatre for a long time when a child actor with whom you once worked offers you a job in a theatre company for which he is now the Artistic Director.

If you do include children in one of your casts, try to give them as normal a life as you can. On evening performances, don't let them hang around for the curtain call. Send them home after their final appearances. They will be more use to you if they get to bed as early as possible and have a normal school day in the morning.

With double or triple casts, tell the children well in advance which one of them you want to do the opening night so they, and their parents, don't spend anxious weeks worrying about which of them is best.

Work children hard, but treat them with the same respect and kindness you use for adult actors.

Keep pushy parents at arm's length and never let any parent into the rehearsal room. No child behaves normally if it knows a parent is watching. The acting experience you want is the child's, not the parent's, though often enough the child is living the experience for the sake of the parent. If you find this is the case, liberate the child from dependency on the parent's approval with carefully aimed encouragement. A little praise goes a long way with a child and can earn you the right to extend his capabilities beyond most parents' expectations.

Choreography and Choreographers

Choreography is the art of making dances or, more generally, the composition of any formally organised movement on stage, usually but not always backed by a rhythmic or musical accompaniment.

The term can also be used more loosely to describe any movement the characters of a drama make on stage that is especially complex, graceful or stylised.

The more formalised the episodes of movement in a production, the more you will require the collaboration of a choreographer, or at least a **Movement Director**.

Many plays and most musicals include sequences of **dance**. If you are doing a period piece, the dances should probably bear the same stylistic relationship to your production as the set and costume designs and the music. This requires an expert touch. Unless you have been properly trained, don't imagine you can take on such a job yourself. Your actors will lose patience with you very quickly.

In choosing a choreographer, be careful to go for someone who will work in a sympathetic style to your production. Some choreographers are capable of working in a variety of styles, but many of the best ones have a distinct style of their own and will be unhappy about compromising it. Make a careful study of a choreographer's work before you engage him.

There are choreographers that specialise in working on theatre pieces and can easily adapt their techniques to accommodate for the inevitable lack of competence they meet in an acting company. Those who work mostly in the dance world find it harder to make allowances. You should avoid employing a starry choreographer if all you have to offer him is a company of cock-footed actors.

If experienced choreographers are unavailable for your production, unwilling to work with you or too expensive for your purse, look for new young choreographic talent in fringe dance venues. There are always exciting young choreographers only too happy to work on a theatre piece, but you won't know who they are if you don't seek them out. Look for guidance from any dancers you know. The dance world is small and its village pumps teem with professional gossip.

In rehearsal, don't micromanage your choreographer's time. Leave him plenty of time to find his own relationships with the actors. The more he gets to know them, the more he will be able to play to their strengths and disguise their weaknesses. On the other hand, don't leave him entirely to his own devices. If he follows a wrong path for too long, he will resent having to backtrack just because you haven't been paying attention.

Throughout rehearsals, talk to your choreographer about the story of the play and what you want it to mean. The more he understands your vision, the more integrated his work will be with yours.

Chorus

Choros is the Greek word for dance, the Chorus of the Greek theatre originating in the 'dithyrambs' or choral hymns of the bacchanalian song and dance festivals. No one knows the precise moment when dancers first started to speak, or when solo members of the choral ensemble first started to assume the roles of individual characters, but even after Greek plays were fully developed into character-driven dramas, the Chorus continued to have an important part to play and its use has continued in the Western drama all the way up to the present day.

In the theatre, the Chorus more or less died out with the development of naturalistic drama, though it has made brief reappearances in the modern age in poetic and political drama by writers as diverse as Brecht, Eliot and García Lorca.

Where it has survived very healthily is in the world of **opera** and **musical theatre**, the sung word being more conducive to choral utterance than the spoken, or at least more acceptable to audiences' ears. We seem to be able to take quite seriously thirty or forty woodsmen or villagers all singing the same thing, where if they were speaking we would find what they say risible. But such is the nature of many a **theatrical convention**.

Composers of grand opera and large-scale musical theatre have always had a vested interest in perpetuating the use of the Chorus. Without it they wouldn't be able to make the sweeping emotional choral statements that alone can compete with the noise of an orchestra going at full tilt. But in writing their works they have often paid more attention to how the Chorus sounds than to the meaning of the words it is singing. This can be a problem for directors of opera or musicals, especially when they are trying to work in a naturalistic style. The lyrics of a Chorus are prone to self-contradiction and repetition. Trying to fit them into the conventional rules of character and motivation can be a thankless task.

For further discussion of this subject, together with advice on how to work with a professional opera chorus, see under **Opera**.

Chorus

Various forms of choral device, ancient and modern, can be found under **Narrators and Narration**.

The Circle

In Britain, the circle is one of the upper tiers in a multi-tiered **proscenium** theatre, so called because the seats are arranged in curved formation overhanging the stalls or any other lower tier. Some theatres have more than one circle, and theatre builders or managers often add the words 'royal' or 'grand' to 'circle' in order to differentiate them and to persuade theatregoers that their seats are in a privileged position.

Circles vary enormously in quality of **sightline** and **acoustic**. Some provide an excellent view of the stage, especially from their front-row seats, but some have a sightline that is considerably above the actors' eye-line, and their seats have to be priced down accordingly. There are often acoustical problems associated with the seats at the back of the circle, especially when there is an **overhang** from a higher tier of seats above it.

Co-Directing and Co-Directors

Co-directing is not easy. Two directors working together on the same production must both be very sure of their techniques, flexible in their methods and peculiarly lacking in ego in the way they work with their actors and other collaborators. Few competent directors possess such a temperament.

If you do consider a co-directing partnership, you and your partner should have a good reason for doing so – not just a mutual admiration, a desire to work together and learn from each other, or an inability to decide who should be captain and who lieutenant.

The best reason for co-directing is when the scale or complexity of the work demands it. This might be true of plays with huge casts, plays of great length, plays mounted in a complex environment, plays being written as they are rehearsed, community plays involving large numbers of amateurs and professionals or plays that require directorial authority in a number of different disciplines. Any production, in fact, that would be hard for a single director to contemplate managing on his own.

Plays that respond least well to co-directing are those that require a close intellectual relationship between director and leading actor. The actor that plays Hamlet, Hedda Gabler or Oedipus is often an implicit co-director. These great parts are best cracked open by a concerted effort of director and actor working in privy counsel. A third party with equal authority can only serve to confuse the picture.

The danger inherent in co-directing is a confusion caused by dilution of directorial authority. Two voices with an equal say are only authoritative if they are saying the same thing. Designers, authors, composers, Stage Managers and actors, all used to a single voice, can be disconcerted or even embarrassed if the instructions coming from two different authorities seem to be in conflict. Mischief-makers can even take advantage of such confusion and try to drive wedges of discord between co-directors and their collaborators.

The best antidote to divided authority is openness. Co-directors should tell their collaborators that if ever they feel they are in receipt of conflicting instructions they must not be afraid to say so quite openly and without fear of causing further conflict. Whatever the problem, it should be openly discussed in the presence of both directors and the conflict amicably resolved. And there should be conflicts.

Conflict in rehearsal can be very creative as long it is properly controlled. Therein lies the great potential of co-direction. In rehearsal, or design meeting or any part of the creative process, if one director has a good idea, then it will be worth challenging by the other. If the challenge is more persuasive than the idea, the idea will fall, if less good, the idea will prevail. Thus co-directors can rescue each other from the implementation of poorly thought-out ideas and turn half-baked ideas into fully cooked ones. They can achieve this most successfully in the full flow of rehearsal if they allow themselves complete candour in the presence of all their other collaborators. By according to others the same rights of challenge and debate as they accord themselves, conflicts can be resolved collectively as soon as they are identified.

At the end of each rehearsal day, co-directors should discuss between them what has been achieved, what the targets are for the next day and how duties should be divided between them.

If they are working in two different spaces with different groups of actors, they should discuss in great detail what they plan to accomplish, so each can contribute advice to both endeavours. They should also plan to coordinate their rehearsals in the last hour of the day so that what has been achieved can be shared by both groups and subsequently discussed by both directors.

If they are working in the same space, they should decide in advance who is to lead the rehearsal of each scene, improvisation or sequence of work and who is to be held in reserve for supplementary support and challenge.

Co-directing takes great sensitivity and generosity, but it can be rewarding if the work really requires it. In those circumstances you can recharge your directorial batteries by plugging into a talent you admire, you can learn at the feet of a more experienced director or be challenged by the ideas of a younger, you can even form an enduring partnership with someone to whose ideas and style of work you are deeply sympathetic.

Collaborators

There is an art to choosing your collaborators that only time and experience will perfect in you. Your ability to choose well in your **designers, composer, Musical Director, choreographer, stage management** and **actors** will, more than anything else you do, define the characteristics of your work – if you like, your style as a director.

Start by defining the order of choosing, as it is sometimes advisable to involve one or other of your collaborators in further choices. A **Set Designer** may have a strong view as to who should design the **costumes** and who should **light** the show. Consultation is crucial in this matter. You really don't want to be working with a Set

Designer who despises the Costume or Lighting Designers because of artistic incompatibility or a bad past working experience.

If you have a strong and long-lasting relationship with your leading actor or actors you may wish to involve them in choosing the other members of the creative team, or at least ask their advice if you are not sure you are making the right choice. Some actors are wary of getting involved in these decisions, but others are happy to share their views, and it would be foolish of you to ignore them. After all, it's the actors who have to walk around on the set, wear the costumes, sing the songs and find the light.

Whatever you do, choose carefully and take your time. Get to know your putative collaborators. Talk to them, but don't be too led by what they say of themselves. Rather judge them by the quality of their work. If you haven't seen this in action, in performance, then look at their portfolios or any DVD footage they might have and take a good look at their biographies. You can tell a lot about creative artists by the company they have kept. Do you admire the work and the judgement of their past collaborators? If you have any persistent doubts about your choice, contact a colleague director or actor who has worked with them in the past and ask about their strengths and weaknesses, their ability to collaborate, their adaptability and their friendliness. Before too long you will build up a picture of the candidate and get a feeling for the rightness or wrongness of the appointment.

Just as you should keep a careful record of all the actors you admire for easy reference when **casting** a play, keep a similar log of all your other potential collaborators. The more experienced you become in the theatre, the more your opinion will be solicited on the appointment of artistic partners, and you should never be stuck for an answer.

Comedy

The most fundamental rule of comedy for those engaged in writing, directing or performing it is that it must be taken seriously. If it isn't taken seriously it won't be funny and if it isn't funny it isn't comedy.

Comedy

In a stage direction for the first scene of *Peter Pan*, Barrie describes how he wants the actors in his play to behave. He starts by giving advice to the actor who will play the dog-nurse, Nana, but develops his remarks into a recipe for comic acting generally:

The Nana must go about all her duties in a most ordinary manner so that you know in your bones that she performs them just so every evening at six; naturalness must be her passion; indeed it should be the aim of everyone in the play, for which she is now setting the pace. All the characters, whether grown-ups or babes, must wear a child's outlook on life as their only adornment. If they cannot help being funny, they are begged to go away. A good motto for all would be 'the little less and how much it is'.

An actor trying to be funny will always have a disastrous effect on a comedy – the greater the effort, the more dismal the result.

If you are directing a comedy, try to cast actors that are funny in themselves, funny as people. If an actor has no sense of the absurd, if he can't tell a joke or embellish an anecdote, laugh at his own foibles, mock authority or play the fool, then he will almost certainly make heavy weather of a comic character.

Comedy requires a degree of physical skill from actors. Beware casting a clumsy or lumpen actor in a comedy. He will drop his own laughs and tread on everyone else's.

Comedies are fast and they get faster as they reach their climaxes. Actors that are naturally slow of speech or thought will not be able to keep up and will drop the ball when it is passed to them.

When rehearsing a comedy, concentrate on the situations before you consider any comic **business** that might accompany them. Trust the play. If the situations are funny in themselves, the play will be funny.

The more improbable the events of a comedy become, the more seriously the actors must take them. Wild coincidences, obvious disguises and impossible collisions of interest need intense **belief** from the actors if the audience is to swallow them. **Farce** is the most serious and technical of all the comic forms.

However inventive the actors are in rehearsal, and rehearsal rooms should be alive with **laughter**, never let **corpsing** become habitual or an acceptable way of raising further laughs. Keep the room disciplined.

Above all, be true to the **reality** of the characters' personalities, difficulties and obsessions. The liberating phenomenon of laughter occurs when an audience recognises its own behaviour in the events on stage. Those events must therefore be strongly attached to reality or the illusion of reality. The more real the events seem to be, the more naturally the laughter will flow and the more liberated the audience will feel by the time the play ends.

Commedia dell'Arte

Commedia dell'Arte was a popular style of improvised masked comedy that flourished in Italy from the sixteenth to the eighteenth centuries. Its plots and characters became thoroughly absorbed into French theatre and Italian opera and persist today in many other Western theatre forms. The plays of Molière are perhaps the most sophisticated expression of the Commedia form, and they have an obvious correlative in the moral comedies of Ben Jonson.

The plots of the plays were based around stock comic situations, usually involving thwarted young love, jealously guarded and/or adulterous marriages, and the ultimate triumph of youthful spirits over aged greed and stupidity.

The stock characters include Arlecchino (Harlequin) and Columbina the male and female clowns, Pantalone the jealous old miser, Pedrino (Pierrot) the loyal, innocent servant, Scaramuccia the bragging buffoon, and Pulcinella the deformed and pitiful loner, who grew into the mad and violent figure of Punch in the English Punch and Judy shows.

In almost any comedy written from the late sixteenth century onwards you will find some relative, however distant, of these stock characters, but then they are so archetypically human you can also see them in the world around you wherever anyone's behaviour holds them up to well-earned mockery.

Commedia dell'Arte

The skills for which the Commedia performers were renowned are enjoying a remarkable resurgence today in training schools all across Europe. Young actors fascinated by **physical theatre** are supplementing their drama school or college educations with lessons in clowning, acrobatics, **improvisation** and **mask** work.

Company

The idea of company is essential to the best sort of theatre.

Theatre is the most collaborative of arts. We who work in it can only do so by the grace of our companions. The longer our careers, the more we learn to depend on the companions that suit us best. It is the most natural desire in the world for us to seek to bind our companions together into permanent ventures, companies where our preferred companions will be constantly available to us.

Company allows us to create artistic policy, to support the work of particular playwrights and develop styles of acting and production appropriate to them. Company inspires us to choose the best talent available to us in all the theatre disciplines, and then stick to our choices, creating permanent ensembles of distinctive worth (see below). Company has the patience to develop careers, in acting, directing, authorship and design. Company allows us to fail honourably and reinvent ourselves in the wake of failure. Company can be alchemical, turning failure to success.

Company, in short, is what differentiates theatre as an art from theatre as a business.

But even in the commercial theatre, where few of these aspirations ever apply, the idea of company still creeps into every venture. Every production has a 'company' of actors administered by a 'company manager'. If you call an entire cast to **rehearsal**, it is a 'company call'. On the **first night**, invitations go out to the 'company party'. Years after a production has folded and the actors are all blown to the wind, you will hear one of them say, 'What a good company that was,' or 'That was a strange company, wasn't it?', and the social organisation of the cast will be remembered and anatomised. Good or bad, happy or unhappy, it is the idea of company that endures.

At whatever stage you are in your career, this idea will persist whether you will or no, and if you organise your thoughts to suit the idea, it will predominate. Treasure it. Develop it in yourself and in others. Form companies. Aspire to be an integral part of a permanent ensemble. That's where the best work is. That's where conditions for the best work will give you the greatest security, the easiest authority and the deepest satisfaction. Company is the thing.

ENSEMBLES

An ensemble is a theatre company whose actors, directors and other creative artists stay together over many years, embodying the ethic outlined above. However, pure ensembles in which the same group of actors play all the parts, whatever the demands of the repertoire, are actually very rare.

Most ensemble companies employ a core of permanent members, a supplementary group of probationary members and occasional additional actors where the demands of the **repertory** require greater numbers or when the permanent and probationary members are unavailable to discharge all the parts in the **repertoire**.

The strength of the ensemble idea resides in the spirit of company that inspires all the best long-term theatre projects. Members of an ensemble grow to have a keen awareness of one another's talents, an ease and enjoyment in playing together, a commitment to a shared ethic of performance and company organisation and an almost familial relationship with their audience.

If ensembles have weaknesses, they lie in the way familiarity can breed contempt, the tendency for the weakest members of an ensemble to cling on to their positions regardless of talent, the difficulty of introducing young performers into an ensemble that slowly grows too old to play younger roles, and, if a single director is in sole charge of everything, the possibility of long-term artistic atrophy.

The best-regulated ensembles, like the Moscow Art Theatre or the Royal Dramatic Theatre in Stockholm, are at least partly run by the actors. Actors help to choose the repertoire, regulate many of the working practices and are involved right up to board level with the selection of the **Artistic Director**. It is actor involvement, more than any other factor, which helps to keep the best ensemble companies perennially fresh and artistically ambitious.

Ensembles, whether well regulated or not, need a lot of subsidy. The permanent employment of actors on set salaries whether they are appearing in productions or not can be extremely expensive, especially if they have the right to refuse roles they are offered without suffering any financial consequences. This is why most permanent ensembles enforce a system of financial penalties if actors consistently turn down roles they think aren't worthy of their talents or status. A first refusal gets a warning, a second a reduction to half-salary and so on until only a nominal retaining fee is left. In this way each actor finds his natural level in the artistic market in which he is to some extent a commodity.

The term 'ensemble' is also commonly used to describe any group of actors that appear in more than one play during a single repertory season. The Royal Shakespeare Company, for example, employs actors on annual contracts to appear in many different productions and may renew some of those contracts from one year to the next. There are no lifetime contracts, no casting rights and no participation in artistic governance, but the actors employed at any one time may still consider themselves to be part of an ensemble.

ENSEMBLE PLAYS

An ensemble play is one that offers a large number of more or less equal-sized and interesting roles. The term is widely used by directors looking for suitable plays for permanent ensembles to perform. If you have a group of, say, twenty permanently employed actors, all of them hungry for juicy, play-defining roles, you don't do *Hamlet* or *Henry V*. If a play has a huge central role it will be unlikely to qualify as an ensemble play. In Shakespeare, most of the comedies qualify, as do the late romances, but *King Lear* is also an ensemble play and so is *Troilus and Cressida*.

Russian drama is full of them. The plays of Ostrovsky, Gorky and Chekhov are, almost without exception, great ensemble plays. The Restoration period of English drama is also a rich source.

ENSEMBLE PRODUCTIONS

This term describes a production style where an ensemble of actors is given a storytelling role. Typically, the whole ensemble of actors is presented at the start of the performance, however large their roles, and remains more or less permanently on stage as witnesses to the events of the drama. They may have a choral function, help to change the stage environment from one scene to the next and play a large variety of subsidiary roles with a minimum of disguise from one role to the next.

Company Managers

The Company Manager is responsible for the administration of an acting **company** and the health, security, pay and well-being of each of its members. He liaises with other departments for the proper use of the actors' time and organises the rehearsal and technical calls to minimise collisions of interest. He reports to the director on artistic issues and the producer on financial and business ones, and to both director and producer he communicates personal problems within the company that threaten to jeopardise a performance.

A good Company Manager will be your eyes and ears once a play is up and running, especially on tour, where he supervises travel and housing arrangements and keeps the company on an even emotional keel.

If you want to know what's going on in the lives of the actors, who's happy and who isn't, who's kind and who's bitching, who's behaving and who's being naughty, Company Managers will nearly always be the most reliable authority. If they don't know what's going on then they aren't doing their job properly.

COMPANY STAGE MANAGERS

In small or less affluent theatres, a Company Stage Manager combines the functions of the Company Manager and the Stage Manager in a single job.

Company Managers

In American theatre, the Production Stage Manager is the equivalent of the British Company Stage Manager, responsible for the cast and the stage management team and answerable directly to the Producer or Administrator.

Complimentary Tickets

Complimentary tickets, or 'comps' as the profession calls them, are the free tickets that a producer or a theatre owner may hand out from time to time to a variety of people for a variety of usually cogent commercial reasons. But just as there is no such thing as a free lunch, the real cost of a complimentary ticket is hidden and may have to be repaid in some other kind.

Successful theatre companies have clear policies on complimentary ticketing in order to avoid corruption or insolvency, or both. In state-subsidised theatres, where public money is involved, great care must be taken. Every complimentary ticket issued represents an implicit burden on the tax-paying public. In the commercial theatre, the cost of a complimentary ticket is immediately reflected in the weekly profit or loss to the investors and therefore a reflection of the commercial competence of the producer. So managements are understandably mean with their comps, though there are certainly plenty of constructive ways in which they can be used.

A couple of **first-night** comps are generally issued to the actors and other members of staff and crew for their family and friends – out of contractual obligation, tradition or kindness, together with a calculation that the presence of family and friends at a first night will give the whole event a festival atmosphere that will add to its chances of critical acclaim. Comps are also given to celebrities on the first night, or indeed at other times, to add status to the show, pick up any attendant publicity and encourage other, un-famous, members of the audience to pay to sit in the same seats at other performances.

Comps can also be given to fellow professionals that are prospective employees or clients of the producer in order to woo them into a partnership or a sense of shared interest. They may be used in lieu of cash as a reward for services rendered when ready cash is unavailable, inappropriate or unbudgeted for. They are usually supplied without too much resistance to members of the **creative team** when they are revisiting a show to check on its progress.

PAPERING

From time to time comps are given to members of the general public when the auditorium would otherwise look so thinly populated that the actors would become discouraged and the play would be made to look like a flop. This is known as 'papering the House'. Papering is done in consultation with the **producer** and the **Theatre Manager** when you decide it is better to have an audience watching your show for free than to have no audience at all.

For reasons of box office accountancy and convenience these audiences are not given proper tickets. Instead they are given informal slips of paper upon which their seat numbers are scrawled – hence 'papering'.

Papering is usually a sign that a show is in trouble or going through a bad patch at the box office, but it can be a positive strategy for survival, especially if you believe your show has a real chance of commercial success but is suffering from a dearth of publicity or a seasonal blip. A non-paying audience will still talk about the show and will talk it up if they have enjoyed it. But of course they will also talk about how they got free tickets, and then everyone will want one. You may sometimes find yourself caught in an argument between a producer who is fundamentally against papering and a cast who have a deep-seated aversion to playing to small houses and get very beady when a producer refuses to issue any paper, especially to all their friends and relations.

The most common and uncontentious time for papering a House is during previews, when a very good show might still be in need of some positive word-of-mouth approval and when the actors are most in need of good, big audiences in whose company they can best develop their performances.

Most producers or Theatre Managers do have a 'paper list',

which they haul out when audiences are thin. It usually includes a number of local nurses' homes, students' hostels and sundry charitable institutions. It somehow seems easier to give away a lot of free tickets if the recipients are people who couldn't afford to pay for them anyway.

UNCOMPLIMENTARY BEHAVIOUR

It remains a source of constant annoyance to actors and other theatre professionals that people presume on acquaintanceship for complimentary tickets. They wouldn't ask for free pork chops because they know the butcher or free stamps because their nephew's best friend knows the postman, but they have no qualms at all about asking their theatre friends for free tickets.

Inexperienced actors, directors and designers are often too embarrassed when asked for comps to turn down the request, so they delve into their own pockets and stump up for the tickets themselves, not letting on to their ignorant friends that they have done so. They soon learn that a polite strategy of resistance is a far better policy. The commonest solution is to say, 'I can get you tickets, but they can't be free, I'm afraid.' Or, 'I can't even get comps for myself, I'm afraid, so there's little chance I could get them for you.' Astonishingly, some people still get a little huffy if turned down in this way, especially in the subsidised theatre. Let them be. It's hard enough to earn a living in the theatre without having to add a personal subsidy to the public one.

Composers

If your play requires a significant musical ingredient, there is no greater privilege you can accord yourself than that of working on a new score with a living composer. Your choice of composer will obviously be influenced by your choice of play, its period, its themes and its style of language. It will also be affected by your own artistic preferences – for historical authenticity, cultural specificity or modernity.

Composers come in many different guises. There are composers who specialise in theatre – whose familiarity with theatrical forms has made them experts in the composition of integral, incidental and atmospheric **music**. There are composers who are clever pasticheurs, able to capture the musical style of a particular composer, school or period. There are composers of **musical theatre** or **opera**, only too happy to apply themselves to the differing demands of a play. Many singer-songwriters have been theatre folk in their time or fancy themselves as such and are flattered to be asked for a contribution to a form they admire.

Composing is a lonely business, and composers are often starved of artistic companionship. If you think your play would benefit from a new score, get to know the work of modern composers. Listen to new music programmes on the radio, go to concerts or buy CDs of the latest stuff being written. You will soon get to know what you like and what excites you and challenges you. It's a short step from there to contacting a composer or his agent and then meeting to discuss terms. Composers spend most of their time on their own, squeezing notes onto a silent page, their only artistic contact being with the players for whom the music is being composed. Many of them love the theatre – and get a great charge from the rehearsal room, its atmosphere, its energy and its population.

For the price of a modest fee you can help to create a new theatrical score, introduce or reintroduce a composer to the excitement of the rehearsal room and give yourself the challenge of a new artistic influence and the possibility of a developing alliance.

Don't be shy. And don't be un-ambitious. However celebrated your choice of composer or however much in awe of them you are, the worst thing that can happen is that they say no. You can only ask.

Concept and Conceptual Design

Concept is a troubling term. It conjures up different ideas in different people. It is habitually used by some and entirely eschewed, even despised, by others. In its simplest form it is used synonymously for 'idea', but it has more complex applications in notions of conceptual design and direction, and in some theatre communities these are so current that one must take some account of them.

In broad terms, the idea of conceptual direction or design is an intellectual construct much loved by those for whom theatre is primarily an intellectual pursuit.

In more traditional ways of thinking, the director and designer conceive of an idea or a number of ideas, drawn from the world that the author conjures up in the text of a play, ideas that find concrete form in an appropriate environment of set and costumes for the characters of the drama to inhabit.

Concept implies something rather different. Here, the director and designer conjure up a world of their own contriving, an environment that may be inspired by the author's text but not necessarily described within it. A line in the text, or a theme or even a feeling or atmosphere, can spark off a chain of visual images in director and designer that develops into a parallel reality that tells its own story about the events of the drama, a story not imagined, perhaps even unimaginable, to the original author. Therein lies both the strength and the weakness of conceptual productions. If the parallel world is well imagined it can provide a thrilling gloss on an original story. If poorly imagined, the results can seem arbitrary in the extreme, an insolent slap in the face of the author, the conceivers smugly asserting their superiority to the text while audiences look on in angry bemusement.

This 'conceptualising' of a play often expresses itself in purely imagistic form. The text of the play stays the same but the images shift as the designer's mind wanders through it. For this reason, designers of 'conceptual' productions often feel so constrained by the presence of a director they prefer to combine both roles in themselves. Directors talk to them of 'motivation', 'sense' and 'reality', terms that seem inappropriate to their process. They prefer their own reality, consider 'sense' to be a nonsensical construct and 'motivation' an irrelevance. The characters must move through their productions as the concept demands, so the performers must follow wherever they go.

The plays that respond best to the conceptual treatment are those that rely least on naturalism and that are less character-driven than ideas-driven. Where the plot already constrains the characters away from a conventional depiction of reality, a conceptual design can do little further harm to the relationship between the characters and may even help in focusing the audience's mind on the ideas of a play rather than its human predicament. Into this category one might place the plays of Ibsen, Racine, Camus, Sartre and Eliot, even perhaps Shaw and certainly the late Shakespearean romances.

However well or badly, suitably or unsuitably conceptual design is achieved, most traditionally trained performers do not much like working with purveyors of concept. They play along as their professional conduct requires them to do, but they often feel used, even abused, in the process. The questions they ask in rehearsal are ignored, answered only obliquely, sometimes even mocked. Their own methods are useless to them without the possibility of physical or mental application. So they go through the motions, stand where they are told to stand, and fit into the conceptual image as best they can. The anger comes later, as they remember the feelings of indignity that attended their powerlessness.

Of course, some actors love being in conceptual productions, the trick of their minds being well satisfied by the combination of theory and image that informs them, and the most consistent of conceptual directors and designers take care to surround themselves with actors such as these. The best examples of this sort of work are often found in ensembles permanently dedicated to them led by **auteur directors** or director/designers working through a theatrical language all their own.

Whether you will or no, you will have to respond, sooner or later, to the idea of concept in your work. Of a new production, in theatre or **opera**, you will often be asked 'What is your concept?' If you have one, then go ahead and describe it as best you can. But if, like many directors, you feel the whole idea of concept to be foreign to you, don't be abashed. Say, 'I don't have a concept. I'm just trying to do the play the best I can.'

Conductor

The conductor, in **opera,** is responsible for the musical interpretation of the work and the excellence of its execution in performance. In **musical theatre,** the more commonly used term is **Musical Director.**

Conducting from an orchestra pit takes a very special talent. Not all good conductors are good pit conductors. The conductor of a symphony is a solo performer in his own right, visibly demonstrating to players and audience alike what he feels about the work he conducts. The conductor of a concerto should cede the solo spot to the instrumentalist and be happy in the role of sensitive accompanist but, happy or not, sensitive or not, he is still visibly in control of all the other players and the concerto as a whole. The conductor of an opera must control the **orchestra** and accompany the singers, like a sort of multiple concerto but he should be invisible to the audience. The more attention he gets from the audience, the less likely they are to be enjoying the opera.

Whether it be in opera or musical theatre, try to ensure the conductor spends as much time with you in rehearsal as possible. Don't get involved in productions where the conductor flies in two days before the performance. He won't know what the singers are doing and he will have little patience with anything that doesn't accord with his own well-trodden path through the work.

A good pit conductor watches the stage like a hawk. He knows the score so well and has such innate control over his orchestra that he will rarely need to look down. His hands will make a single ensemble out of singers and players while his eyes and heart move with the story unfolding in front of him. He will feel the tempo that suits each singer, giving them leeway when they want to let loose and pushing them on when they get too indulgent.

It is quite proper for a director in opera or musical theatre to talk to a conductor about tempo. If you feel things are dragging or rushing on too fast, have a quiet word. Don't demand. Discuss. You may have to compromise but a good conductor will want to help you solve the problem.

Corpsing

'Corpsing' is theatrical slang for an actor's uncontrollable burst of inappropriate and unmotivated onstage laughter, known in the American theatre as 'breaking up' or 'losing it'.

A 'corpse' is usually triggered by some unexpected or absurd incident that so catches an actor off guard that he briefly drops out of character into a private reaction. The term was coined in the late Victorian theatre and originally referred to any mistake by an actor on stage, including **drying**, that would seriously put a fellow actor off his stride. Thus an actor 'corpsing' another actor's **business** would be guilty of killing off his theatrical moment. But in the modern theatre, to 'corpse' someone always implies laughter in reaction to the 'corpse', though the origins of the term are still apposite.

The effect of a truly bad corpse can be to render all life on the stage utterly moribund, and if the corpse spreads from one actor to another the believability of a play can be seriously compromised for some time after the crime has been committed.

The severity, and therefore forgivability, of a corpse can only be defined by the relative inappropriateness of the situation in which it happens. For an actor playing a riotously funny scene in a seemingly uncontrollable farce, a corpse can happen all too easily and can be forgotten just as quickly by actors and audience alike. For the actress playing Cordelia to corpse while lying dead in the arms of King Lear would be a gross piece of professional misconduct.

Having said that, some very good actors are terrible corpsers, always teetering on the edge of hilarity and liable to be set off by any slight divergence from their normal stage routine, especially in a **long run** where performances can become habitual and unexpected divergences seem all the more hilarious.

Some actors are capable of maintaining their poker faces even under extreme provocation and pride themselves that their corpses are never detectable to an audience. There are all sorts of strategies for keeping a corpse contained – some actors turn the laugh into a 'real' character laugh and somehow blend it into the lines they are speaking, others simply turn upstage and walk about until they've pulled themselves back under control, others hide behind their fellow actors, or suddenly take an intense interest in the backs of their own hands. Whatever it takes. And the provocation will sometimes seem extreme – the splitting of a pair of trousers on stage, or a very audible fart, or an actress walking up the back of her own floor-length dress, or a really stupid-sounding sneeze coming from the audience. Anything can do it. The best actors recover quickly and the best productions provide them with the right intensity of atmosphere for such recovery.

Occasional corpses triggered by untoward circumstances are not going to cause you much grief, but you may have to intervene if one of your productions is plagued by corpsing. It happens from time to time even in the best-regulated shows and is usually caused by boredom amongst the actors or an inability to remember the true importance of the moment that is causing the merriment. The solution is to go to a performance, take copious notes, and alleviate the actors' boredom by freshening up their characters and motivations. A persistent corpse on a particular moment may need a touch of actual rehearsal.

You will occasionally meet a rogue actor whose boredom, childishness or bloody-mindedness causes him to exploit any fragility in his fellow actors' concentration. There is little you can do about this other than have a 'serious talk' with the offender. But such silliness is actually not that common, and the more professional members of an acting company will generally sort out the problem for you. Indeed, some actors get so infuriated by deliberate corpsing or provocations to corpse that they become quite violent in stamping it out at source. Few serial corpsers have not felt the lash of their colleagues' tongues at one time or another.

Actors in farces or very broad comedies will sometimes use deliberate and controlled corpsing as a device to induce or prolong audience laughter, usually in a climactically comic scene. Deliberate corpses usually originate in unplanned corpses that are so obvious and uncontrollable they have to be shared with the audience. The audience responds with conspiratorial delight and the next night the actors can't bear not to repeat the experience. But this is a dangerous practice. For every dropping-out of character there is a loss of belief in the comic situation and therefore an ultimate cost in loss of laughter later on in the scene or the play. If a deliberate corpse is rehearsed into the business of a comedy or farce it must be followed immediately by a redoubling of serious comedic intent from the corpsing characters. But even if it can be controlled in this way, a deliberate corpse will always feel like something of a cheat. The audience are being led to believe that the actors have lost control when the opposite is the case and in fact they are coolly manipulating the audience's laughter. Thus what should be a joyful sharing of laughter through recognition can easily become a cynical milking of laughter through professional control, and no comedy will remain funny for long in such a heartless atmosphere.

Shakespeare made his feelings about corpsing very clear in Hamlet's advice to the Players: 'let those that play your clowns speak no more than is set down for them, for there be of them that will themselves laugh to set on some quantity of barren spectators to laugh too, though in the mean time some necessary questions of the play be then to be considered. That's villainous, and shows a most pitiful ambition in the fool that uses it.' Quite so.

Costume Design and Designers

Most theatre designers are trained in both **set design** and costume design, and many continue throughout their careers to ply both trades with equal expertise and enthusiasm. But the craft of designing **costumes** is so demanding and time-consuming that many designers choose to specialise in it or abandon it altogether to concentrate exclusively on set design.

A Costume Designer has many hurdles to jump from the blank drawing tablet to the populated stage. The costumes must be researched and imagined before they can be drawn. The drawings must be characterful, evocative, accurately coloured and textured and be appealing to director and actors, who will want to discuss them, negotiate over them and suggest alterations to them. The agreed designs must then be presented to the **Wardrobe** Supervisor and advice given on choice of materials and method of cutting and making up. Trips must be made to shops, warehouses, markets or costume stores, to buy material, rent existing costumes or, in modern productions, buy or borrow off-the-peg clothes.

Then come the costume fittings (see below), the most time-consuming, arduous and potentially frustrating part of the job. This is what separates the costume-designing sheep from the set-designing goats.

Even after the actors are happy with their costumes and the clothed characters have inhabited the stage, the Costume Designer will sit in the theatre making judgements about the finished work and flitting from auditorium to stage to dressing rooms to wings adjusting straps and belts and buckles, tightening and loosening corsets, **breaking down** material to suggest wear and tear, and exhorting actors to wear their costumes appropriately – with style, flair and a sense of custom.

Your relationship with your Costume Designer is one of the most important in the production process. He is an essential link between the characters in the play and the actors who are to play them, so your view of the characters and his must be integrated. Talk with him in great detail about how you see the characters and share with him your views about the actors, their preferences, foibles and temperaments, their size, shape, age, sexuality and self-confidence and what sort of help they will need in the portrayal of their characters.

You will sometimes have to join forces to devise strategies for getting actors to wear things they don't want to wear, or stop them wearing things they shouldn't be wearing, for their own good and the good of the production. The best Costume Designers can work a strange magic on the characters, making fat actors look thin, camp actors look butch, plain actors look beautiful, dull actors look interesting or ham-footed actors look graceful.

You will know when you've found a good Costume Designer. You'll be sitting in the darkened auditorium during the **technical rehearsals** and some character or other will walk onto the stage and the appearance will so delight you that you will glance over at your designer in approval and a smile of conspiracy will pass between you, a smile full of the joys of transformation and imagining.

COSTUME DESIGNERS AND ACTORS

The relationship between Costume Designer and actor is critical. The best Costume Designers love actors and suffer their fears and vanities kindly. They love sharing the actors' process of building up a character in **rehearsal** and enjoy adding structure and detail to it. A Costume Designer divorced from the rehearsal process will tend to have an unhappy time with the actors in costume fittings, and will often ask for your support in forcing the actors to wear costumes with which they are unhappy.

The best costumes are designed with a strong sense of style and form and colour, but with an equally strong sense of the needs of the actor. You should encourage your Costume Designer to spend as much time in rehearsal as possible, talking with the actors, reacting to the physical life of a scene and being ready to adapt the costumes to suit the requirements of the action. A good flow of ideas between actor and Costume Designer can be very helpful to the actor, giving him new thoughts about how his character might move or suggesting opportunities for dramatic use of the costume as designed. Some Costume Designers are secret actors and love nothing more than to parade about demonstrating the efficacy of their designs. When this is the case, encourage them to do so. A single gesture is sometimes worth a hundred words.

REHEARSAL COSTUMES

In any rehearsal period, if you or your actors think a costume or any element of a costume they are to wear will significantly affect the way they move, feel or behave, you should have a version of it available in rehearsal. This is particularly relevant in period drama when actors have to wear costumes that are unlike anything they wear in their everyday lives, but there are many other occasions when rehearsal clothes can really help an actor to find a character.

Get your Costume Designer into rehearsal so he can assess the way his costumes are likely to be worn and what elements can be brought into rehearsal to acclimatise the actors to the finished costumes they will wear in performance.

Costume Design and Designers

An experienced designer will have a good eye for movement, line and style, and may be an excellent source of fresh directorial momentum. As in so many aspects of the theatre, collaboration, discussion and the free exchange of ideas are the best ways to obtain a happy result in costuming a show.

Talk through the costume plot with Costume Designer and **Stage Manager** and decide on the clothes you will definitely need in rehearsal. It may take some time to round up everything, so make you sure you ask for it well in advance.

If your play is pre-twentieth century, your actresses will almost certainly need long rehearsal skirts and some version of the crinolines that go underneath them. If they are going to be playing in real corsets and are unused to wearing them, they may need a week or two to acclimatise. When you get on stage, Costume Designers are always trying to tighten up the women's corsets so that the costumes look accurate for the period and the right shape for the designs, while actresses are always trying to loosen them so they can breathe. If you have rehearsal corsets, the actresses can get used to breathing in a different way and the Costume Designers can get used to the corsets being drawn looser than they would like.

Hats are important. If a designer has designed a hat as part of the costume because the character would be wrong without it, it is crucial for the actor to get used to wearing it, or carrying it when it's not on his head. It's very throwing for an actor to have to change his physical performance at the last minute just because of a hat, or a cloak or a pair of gloves.

Anything that is carried is important, though you may have to negotiate here between two different departments as to what are rehearsal costumes and what are **rehearsal props**. Hats are costumes, but canes are props. More confusingly, umbrellas are props but parasols tend to be costumes. And no one ever owns up to being responsible for swords, unless the theatre has an armoury, but swords and sword-belts, guns and holsters, daggers, cudgels and sword-sticks, all affect the way a costume falls and a character moves.

Shoes are especially important. The weight and style and shape of a shoe or boot can radically affect the way an actor moves and feels as his character. Indeed, an experienced Costume Designer will know that he has to get the actual boots and shoes into rehearsal as soon as possible, or else the actor will fall in love with the pair he has grown accustomed to in rehearsal and will find it hard to relinquish them.

Some actors are great dressers-up and make the adoption of rehearsal clothes part of their acting process, becoming more and more kitted out as the weeks go by. These tend to be the actors who seem most comfortable in their costumes when they finally get on stage. Others less inclined to dressing up may need to be encouraged to do so if you can see that some element of their costume might cause them a problem further down the line if not practised with in advance.

COSTUME FITTINGS

The costume fitting is an important creative event for actors, Costume Designers and wardrobe staff, and a potentially distracting one for directors.

Within the first few days of rehearsal, often on the very first day, the actors must be measured by the wardrobe staff. By taking accurate measurements of every inch of every actor, the cutters and stitchers will be able to make up the roughly tacked-together costumes for the first fittings, or use the measurements as a guide for the purchase or rental of already made-up costumes. The subsequent first fittings usually happen after a couple of weeks of rehearsal and the final fittings in the few days before the cast first goes on stage. Every fitting takes time, and that means time away from rehearsal, sometimes at critical and inconvenient moments. Directors must learn to live with these incursions, and work with the Stage Manager to create a fitting schedule that causes the least possible disturbance to rehearsals but accords it a proper place in the creative process.

For the designer, the first fitting is a moment of truth. Will the costume look the same on the actor as it looked in the drawing? Will it suit the actor's shape, colouring and personality? Will the actor like the costume and feel comfortable in it?

Costume Design and Designers

For the actor the first moment of putting on the costume is exciting and nerve-racking. By the time the first fitting comes along, the actor will understand the character pretty well, know how he thinks and moves and presents himself to the other characters in the play and to the audience. He will have seen the costume drawing on paper, but the costume itself will be a different matter. Will it help him to develop a believable character? Does anything in the shape of the costume, or its colour or material or weight, help to define the physical life or the self-image of the character? Does the costume 'feel right'?

On costume-fitting days you will know how things are going by the actors' demeanours as they return from their fittings and by the designer's attitude at the end of the day. A good day in the fitting room can have a hugely positive effect on rehearsals, with the actors gleeful at the prospect of the gear they are being licensed to wear. A bad day has to be recovered from, with readjustments of attitude, character or design from actor or designer or both.

On some occasions you may be asked to attend a fitting, or even insist yourself on being present at one. Indeed, if there is a serious clash of temperaments over a costume or some aspect of a costume, the actor and the designer will look to you for a resolution. These disagreements can sometimes be quite heated, with the actor feeling that a costume is being foisted on him by an unsympathetic designer or a dogmatic design concept, and the designer feeling that the whole look of a show is in danger of being compromised by the demands of an egotistical and unreasonable performer. Both designer and actor will appeal to your artistic loyalty, the one referring to the private and crucial talks you had in establishing the designs in the first place, and the other to the private and crucial rehearsal process that has established a character that would never wear such a costume, or such a belt, or such a pair of socks. Your best bet on these occasions is to assert the importance of your loyalty to both parties by helping them see the value of each other's point of view. If you deal even-handedly with both, both are likely to bend a bit. But there may be times when an actor is so wound up about a costume that it seems nothing will do to please him.

In the last few days of rehearsal especially, some actors can behave unpredictably as their first-night nerves start to get the better of them. On these occasions the costume, wig, shoes or props are made the excuse for neurotic or fearful behaviour, and you must beware. You don't want a perfectly good costume to be cut or unnecessarily altered just to assuage a swithering ego. And if you support an unreasonable demand for change you will end up alienating one of your most important collaborators and earn yourself a reputation for appeasement.

Start by diagnosing the problem. Why is the actor worried? It could be a neurosis over body shape – the costume makes him look fat, or old, or ugly. It might be envy – that someone else's costume looks grander or prettier or sexier. It might be superstition about a particular colour or type of material. It could be anything. But however silly or unreasonable the reaction, the actor has to go on stage feeling comfortable, so you must talk it out and find a solution. A bit of talk usually does the trick with nervous actors, the dialogue with the designer flushing out the specific problem behind the general unhappiness. Sensitive wardrobe masters or mistresses are also very wise counsellors in these situations, helping to smooth the ruffled feathers on both sides and coming up with simple and imaginative solutions.

If a costume really does seem a hopeless case, you and your designer may have to go back to the drawing board. As you do so, take care to involve the actor every step of the way so that the same misunderstandings are not repeated a second time. That way you will either end up with a redesign or else come full circle, with the actor agreeing to wear the costume as originally designed. Costume Designers are fond of such stories – delighting in how they outwitted some monstrous diva or other with a couple of snips of the scissors and a little dollop of flattery – but most of them are also generous and diplomatic and regard the stroking of egos as an integral part of their job.

Costumes and Clothes

Clothes are worn by real people. Costumes are the clothes worn by actors when pretending to be people, real or not. It is therefore axiomatic in the theatre that if you want the actors and their actions to seem real, the costumes they wear should look and feel and play as much like real clothes as you can possibly make them. As a general rule, if costumes look like costumes rather than the clothes that the characters happen to be wearing, then something has gone wrong in designing them, or in making, fitting or wearing them.

On occasion the distinction between clothes and costumes can appear meaningless. There are plenty of stage characters written to be so self-conscious or theatrical in their appearance that they might as well be wearing costumes rather than clothes. On the other hand, actors are often obliged to dress up in their daily lives in gear that they would never contemplate wearing as ordinary clothing.

This distinction can become extremely subtle when actors appear in public rehearsals or readings. On these occasions you will be asked, as the director, what you think the actors should wear – casual clothes, or smart clothes or dark clothes or bright clothes – and your answer, whatever it is, will instantly redefine the actors' clothes as costumes. Most actors have an extraordinary capacity for disguising or characterising themselves. It's an integral part of their craft. They even come to auditions wearing costume of a sort. They often calculate quite carefully the impression they want to make while reading for a part and dress themselves accordingly, hoping that the effect will be so subtle that the director and Casting Director will have no idea they have made the effort, as indeed some of them never do.

Many apparently important things are ultimately inessential to the basic art of theatre, but costume is not one of them. You can do without sets if you have to, or lights or music or a written text or even a theatre, but costumes are almost as essential to theatre as the actors who wear them. Just as the characters of a play help the playwright to tell the story, so the costumes tell a story about the characters.

Costumes can be both expressive and informative. They can denote social status, affluence, age, aesthetic taste, self-awareness and fashion. They can signify tradition, religion, profession or pastime. They can act as indicators of psychology, politics, personality or personal hygiene. Costumes can be worn tidily or untidily, tightly or loosely, fitting or ill-fitting, flamboyantly or humbly. They can be artificially broken down to indicate wear, hard usage and poverty. They can be dipped and dyed and damped and distressed to any possibly imaginable hue or texture. They can be cut and shaped to change an actor's appearance, to make him look fatter or thinner, taller or shorter, older or younger, misshapen or crippled or ill. The choices are countless and the combinations of choice almost infinite.

Courtyard Theatres

Real courtyard theatres hardly exist today. The term refers back to medieval times when travelling theatre companies would play on temporary stages erected in the courtyards of inns. The audience would stand on the ground level flagstones or cobbles of the courtyard or sit at the windows of the rooms overlooking the stage. Thus would an ordinary architectural structure be adapted for theatrical use and the 'strolling vagabond' players be kept where they belonged, in a place of little or no moral repute.

Some theatres today are built in imitation of this design with a stage at one end of the structure, a ground floor 'pit' of theatre seats looking up at the stage and, surrounding the pit on three sides, two or three layers of squared-off galleries with one row of good seats on each level and an optional further row of generally much poorer seats immediately behind them.

The virtue of the Courtyard shape lies chiefly in being able to accommodate a relatively large number of people on a very small patch of land with most of the seats excitingly close to the stage and with very little wasted space. As with **in-the-round** and **thrust theatres**, Courtyard theatres tend to be more economical to run than conventional **proscenium** spaces. This is because comparatively little of the stage is completely visible to all members of the audience, so a lot of costly scenic imagery is neither necessary nor desirable.

Covers and Covering

See **Understudies**.

The Creative Team

A catch-all phrase describing the collective talents of director, designers of set, costumes, lighting and sound, composer, choreographer and any other primary creative talents at work on a production but not including the author or the actors. The phrase is generally used to differentiate the senior artistic personnel of a show from the producorial and stage managerial teams, led by the producer in the commercial world or the Artistic Director and administrator in the subsidised sector.

As director you will generally be regarded as leader of the creative team, even when directing an opera where the conductor may have more ultimate artistic authority but little or no relationship with the other members of the team.

In **musical theatre** the creative team includes the **orchestrator** and **Musical Director** but not the **composer, lyricist** or book writer.

Credits

Credits are the published acknowledgements in **programmes**, playbills, leaflets or play texts of who has done what in a production, as opposed to the **billing**, which is the selective advertisement of some of those acknowledgements.

Crew

The crew in any theatre is the backstage staff. The term can apply to any of the technical departments that work primarily on and around the stage; thus stage crew, flying crew, lighting crew, sound crew and so on. Wardrobe, Wigs, Music and front of house all have staff, not crew.

Critics

Critics do not have a direct relationship with you or with how you work. Their primary professional relationship is with their readers, who may or may not be members of your audience. *Your* relationship is with your audience, who may or may not be readers of any particular newspaper or its critic. Indeed, members of your audience may not read the critics at all. So be very careful how you think about critics and how you imagine they might be thinking about you.

By and large, they are an intelligent and professional tribe. They have their likes and dislikes just as you do, their prejudices, preferences and peccadilloes. But if you conceive some reason to think of any one of them as being beyond the pale, consider your own likes and dislikes. How have you described the work of your peers in the last few years? What sweeping denunciations of their work have you been guilty of? How unfair have you been? How prejudiced? How mean-spirited? If you had been a critic, and your opinions published, would you have written the same things you have thought and spoken? If not, why not? And if so, how many people would you have upset in the process?

There are good critics and bad critics, just as there are good directors and bad directors. Good critics will sometimes be mistaken and bad critics will sometimes get it right, whatever 'right' may be. Either way, theirs is a deeply subjective craft – just as yours is.

Most critics take as much pride in their work as you do in yours. Do not make the mistake of judging their efforts by the same standards you use for your own. Indeed, you should avoid having an opinion about their efforts at all, especially where your own work is concerned. Just because they judge your work doesn't mean you should feel obliged to judge their work in return.

It's easier to ignore the critics when you are well established as a director and sure of your talents. But however experienced and confident you are, critics will still have power to wound you if you make the mistake of taking any one of their judgements seriously or personally.

There is no sadder sound in all of theatre than that of a director, actor or playwright trotting out a brutal phrase that some critic has used to describe his work in the past. The critic has probably clean forgotten what he said, but the artist harbours the injury as a personal disfigurement to be carried for life.

If you read the critics at all, and there is a very good argument for letting them alone, read them as a collective statement. Do not believe the good and ignore the bad or vice versa. If you bolster yourself with a good notice from a particular critic you will be all the more disappointed when the same critic reviews you negatively in the future.

In any case, the vanity that derives from believing in a good review and the depression that derives from believing in a bad have exactly the same effect on your work in terms of distraction. You should be striving to invent your next piece of work, not dwelling in pride or shame on the last one or on some stranger's opinion of it. As Picasso is said to have said, artists should have the same relationship to critics as birds do to ornithologists.

Critics, collectively, can have a powerful effect on the atmosphere of a **press night**, and you should certainly consider strategies for helping your actors to cope with these occasions, but in doing so, try to think of the critics as a colony rather than as a number of individual characters.

After your show has opened, read, if you must read, in order to get a general feeling for how well your work is going to fare at the box office and for what a generality of readers will take from what they read of your show. After you have read them all, if you can quote from any one of them a week later then, good or bad, you have taken them too much to heart.

Above all, never change your opinion of any of your fellow artists because of what any or all of the critics might say. Believe in your own choices and hold the faith.

Crossover

A crossover is a show-time performance route for actors, stage management and crew between the **wings** of a **proscenium** arch theatre or between any otherwise inaccessible entrance and exit points in other types of theatre.

In proscenium productions the crossover is usually between the upstage limits of the set and the back wall of the stage, but if the set takes up all the available stage space, the crossover must migrate to a backstage corridor or to the **understage**. If this is necessary, the actors will take longer to get from one side of the stage to the other, which may have implications for speedy exits and entrances and **quick changes**.

When a **cyclorama** is backlit, special care needs to be taken that actors and crew don't wander accidentally between the lights and the cyc, casting huge shadows as they pass.

Crossover Artists

Crossover artists are singers or musicians who work in more than one musical genre, the term usually implying, fairly or unfairly, that the artist is slumming it in a genre unworthy of his talent. Widely used to describe **opera** singers who perform and record in musical theatre or popular music of any description.

Crowd Scenes

Directing crowd scenes is difficult and time-consuming but a great pleasure if you set your mind to it.

Most crowd scenes occur in plays that treat of the relationship between personal ambition or conscience and public approbation. **Opera** is full of them. The composers of opera have always sought out stories that address great historical or social themes so they can deploy the choral forces that give their music grandeur.

Choruses are singing crowds.

An onstage crowd is almost always required to represent a greater number of people than it actually comprises. Herein lies the first principle of directing it. A static group of onstage figures, however large, will seem to grow smaller as time passes. As the audience's eye grows accustomed to the form of a crowd, it picks out individuals one by one until it has subconsciously learnt them all. As the people in the audience will always, one hopes, outnumber the people in the crowd, one static group easily feels its numerical superiority to the other. But if the crowd on stage is constantly moving, no such scrutiny is possible. The possibility of movement is not accorded to the static audience, and the more you can capitalise on this difference between one group and the other, the more numerous your crowd will seem to be.

In choreographing the movement of a crowd, give it as much character detail as you can. Give every member of your crowd a proper character to play and believe in. Don't have people moving for the sake of movement, let them be motivated by thought and feeling just as the principal actors are. They can move to get closer to the centre of the action, or further away, to talk to one another, to form alliances, to express opinions on what they are hearing or witnessing, to militate for action or call for calm.

With a big crowd, form smaller groups inside it that will help to inform the interest of the whole. Make families, huddles of friends or cousins, pairs of lovers, married couples, groups tied together by opinion or politics or social class.

Make sure no individual member of a crowd distracts from the central focus of the scene by badly timed movement or overacting. However characterised a crowd becomes, its usefulness to the story is as a group, not as individual members of that group. The greatest interest will nearly always lie with the principal characters and how they are affecting the crowd or being affected by the crowd.

Keep at least some members of your crowd downstage of the characters that are addressing them, so that the actor with the speech has someone to talk to other than the audience. Having said that, the audience is often, by inference, an extension of the onstage crowd, unless you deliberately have your principal actor playing away from the audience in order to exclude it. More likely you will want to capitalise on this relationship between crowd and audience. By putting members of the crowd in the aisles of the auditorium, or on the edges of the balconies, you make the auditorium a public forum and everyone sitting in it a temporary member of a much larger imaginary crowd. You can do this, of course, with no onstage crowd at all. Many are the small-scale productions where two backlit barrackers have stood in the audience as token of a thousand.

RHUBARB

The term 'rhubarb' is used to denote the meaningless noise produced by actors in a crowd scene to simulate the sound of a real crowd. I've never heard an actor actually use the word 'rhubarb' in a scene other than in jest, the noises they produce being more akin to the sound of 'Hraaroargharorgh . . . rabaharargargh', which I suppose do roughly approximate to 'rhubarb'.

Rhubarb sprouts up most commonly in scenes where a small group of minor characters is assembled, usually upstage, and is obliged to react in an angry or concerned manner to a principal actor's pronouncement. For instance, dense patches of rhubarb frequently spring up in Shakespeare's *Julius Caesar* or *Coriolanus*.

The antidote to rhubarb is for each actor to have something sensible and appropriate to say, though there are dangers here too. It is never pleasant to hear the voice of one member of the crowd in the forum rising above the others with 'That's right, Marcus Antonius, my old mate, you tell 'em.' But better that than rhubarb.

Cues and Cueing

In the theatre, a cue is a trigger for action. The last phrase of every actors' speech is nearly always a cue for the next actor to speak. Actors' entrances must be timed from offstage to on, their cues coming a phrase or two before they appear, depending on the distance they have to travel and the speed of the action. During a performance, cues recorded in the **prompt copy** are given by the **Stage Manager** or his deputy to every part of the theatre as triggers for all sorts of action.

The accurate picking-up of cues is crucial to the fluidity of a performance, but one of your jobs as a director is to disguise their very existence. If an audience becomes aware of a cue for action, the action itself loses its spontaneity and power. Cues are never more obvious than when they are being dropped. An actor that leaves an unnecessary **pause** before he speaks drops his cue. When he finally speaks, he seems to be reacting to the silence of the dropped cue rather than to the previous actor's stimulus. When cues are dropped or mistimed by the technical departments the rhythm of the scene is disrupted and with it the actors' sense of accustomed reality.

CUE LIGHTS

Cue lights are small electrical units comprised of one red and one green light. The red is the 'warn'. When the red light comes on, the actor or crew member 'stands by' to perform his cue. The green is the 'go' or cue, indicating that the cued action must immediately be performed. In the US, a single red light is used, on for 'stand by' and off for 'go'.

Cue lights are used when the performer of the cue cannot hear or see a live cue for action and must be given a cue by proxy or when he is deemed incapable of making a cueing judgement on his own.

Because of the split-second time lag between the Stage Manager's finger flicking on the cue light and the performer seeing it and responding, cues must be anticipated in order to land the action of the performer in exactly the right place.

The deployment of cue lights should be worked out prior to the **technical rehearsal** by the Stage Manager and the lighting department. Lighting and sound desks need them, as do **conductors** in their pits and crewmen all around the stage and flies, though in some theatres some of these departments prefer a system of taking their own cues. The smaller the theatre the fewer cue lights you will need. In very small theatres you may be able to dispense with them altogether.

In **proscenium** theatres, upstage entrances, where the actors cannot see the action without being seen themselves, will need a light as will any entrance position that puts the actor out of earshot of the stage. Some actors demand them whether they can see and hear or not, unwilling to trust their own judgements or frightened that a lapse of concentration could make them miss an entrance. Some don't like them at all, preferring to rely on their own eyes and ears and enjoying the sensation, before they enter, of integration with the scene they are about to join.

You and your Stage Manager should be sensitive to these demands either way, but as a general rule you should avoid an overdependence on cue lights. Let your actors and crew take their own cues if they possibly can. Always better to rely on human agency rather than mechanical device. If every cue is given by the Stage Manager and the Stage Manager has a bad day the performance will be horrible. When people take their own cues, they get more involved with the action and make more imaginative contributions to it.

Curtain Calls

Curtain calls are a complicated business and the art of making them is an important study for the director. If you get the curtain call wrong you can create individual and company unhappiness amongst the actors, confusion in the audience, and end your play on a wrong note every time it is performed. If you get the call right you will create the appropriate punctuation to the end of your play, a balanced accreditation for the acting ensemble and the perfect atmosphere for the audience's departure from the theatre. There is much at stake.

First things first: what is a curtain call for? The idea is contained within the term itself. In the days when all theatres had a curtain dividing the audience from the actors, the actors were 'called' to the stage by the audience so that the curtain could be raised and the actors praised.

A curtain call does three things – it acknowledges that the play is done and that the characters were just actors who can now reveal themselves for who they really are; it gives the audience the opportunity to express their gratitude for the excellence of what they have just witnessed; finally, it allows the actors a moment to bask in the approbation of their public. In other words, the curtain call restores the balance of reality between the actors and the audience, restoring both parties to their everyday lives through a mutual act of appreciation.

By being free to express their feelings about the play, the audience are also taking control of the theatre for the first time in the evening. Throughout the performance of any play the actors should be more or less entirely in control of their audience. Even when the audience is laughing uproariously or applauding a piece of **business** or the end of a scene, the actors retain the capacity to stop them in their tracks. **Laughter** or **applause** can be cut short by the forceful interpolation of a line or a new piece of business or, quite artificially, by a lighting or sound cue. The curtain call is different. Here, effectively, the audience is in charge, and a wise director and cast will not dispute their right to supremacy, but encourage them in it.

There is rarely, if ever, a good reason not to have a curtain call, though such a course is suggested surprisingly often by actors and directors alike, usually when they are engaged on a production that seems to them to be so serious in its purport that a curtain call would be a frivolous or self-gratifying way to end an otherwise pure theatrical event. It's an easy mistake to make, but it's a mistake all the same. Even if your play takes place in a concentration camp or a cancer ward, it's still only a play, and your attempt to make your portrayal of the events as serious a matter as the events themselves would be construed as an act of self-aggrandisement. Indeed, you could argue that the more serious the matter in a play, the more seriously the audience will need to be returned to reality when the events of the play are over, and that the curtain call is the perfect medium to soften their landing. Quite apart from any other considerations, if an audience is clapping at the end of a play, the tension has been broken anyway. It is vain for a cast to try to stem this tide, and will only come across as rudeness. Besides, an audience required to leave the theatre in a reverent silence is very likely to rebel against such enforcement and will leave making faces of mock solemnity at one another. Even in church the congregation gets to sing the final hymn.

In creating a curtain call you must first consider the attitudes of the various stakeholders.

1 *The audience*

They will decide how much they have enjoyed the play and therefore how long they are happy to applaud it for. They will have their favourites amongst the actors, based on that evening's performance and any prior experience. They will also be aware of the time and may have buses or trains to catch, cars to redeem from car parks or babysitters to release from bondage.

2 *The actors*

They will have been on and off stage all evening. The more experienced amongst them will have a strong sense of how the call should be structured. Some of them will also have an expectation that they will be specially featured in the call, based on the size and centrality of the parts they are playing and their view of their own celebrity. In the commercial theatre, certain actors may even have their position in the curtain call enshrined in their contracts.

3 *The producer*

Very rarely in the subsidised theatre, but quite commonly in the commercial theatre, the producer may want to voice an opinion about the curtain call, especially if he feels that a very expensive star is not being allowed to shine to the best commercial advantage.

4 *You*

The curtain call is part of your show and therefore within your artistic remit. After weighing all other interests, you must decide how the call is to be constructed. The first choice you have to make is whether to have a 'company call' or a 'hierarchical call'. If you decide on the former, your course will be relatively easy, as long as it's the right choice. If the latter, then you must tread carefully, for there are many pitfalls.

COMPANY CALLS

The company call is suitable for ensemble plays (see **Company**) where no one part dominates the action, or for ensemble companies where the actors have agreed that the integrity of the ensemble is more important than the relationship any one of its members might have with the general public. This is particularly true when ensemble companies play in small theatres. In such circumstances a hierarchical call can seem overblown and invidious, though even in the most democratic of ensembles, certain roles do single themselves out for special treatment. An audience might feel shortchanged at the curtain call if the actors playing Hamlet or Rosalind or Hedda Gabler don't get some sort of a solo call, however brief.

The company call is best achieved by having the actors range themselves around the stage in no particular order, avoiding the temptation to form a line of any sort. The formation of a line instantly suggests a more conventional arrangement with the most important actors in the middle and the least important somewhere upstage behind the line. Once all the actors have assembled on stage, they take their lead from one of the actors standing nearest to the audience and take two or three bows and then get off the stage. If the applause is sufficient to warrant a return, you can ring the changes with the actors standing in different positions from the first call, the actors who were obscured upstage taking their turn at the front. If a third call is required, that is your opportunity to have the leading actor or actors appear briefly for a solo call before paging on the rest of the company for a repeat of the first two calls.

There are many different possible variations on the company call and you and your actors will have your favourite routines, but the principle remains the same: that a company performs as a company and must therefore be appreciated as a company, all stars shining with equal distinctness whatever their magnitude.

HIERARCHICAL CALLS

A hierarchical call serves a number of purposes. It gives the audience the chance to be reminded of the excellence of particular actors, often long after they have enjoyed their featured moments on the stage; it gives the actors the chance to be individually appreciated for their efforts; if properly constructed, it allows the director to 'build' the applause through the call, making the best of the available reaction. But there are hazards, and you need a system to help you avoid them.

Start by making a list of the characters in the play rather than the actors playing them, starting with the least and working through to the most important. Now separate them into groups. Bracket together any characters of more or less equal importance and/or any characters that have a family, thematic, romantic or antagonistic connection. Don't think of giving relatively minor characters a solo call just because they are thematically isolated. Find a group for them even it isn't a very good fit.

Groups of characters will form the basis of your call. Juggle them around until you are happy that they represent a satisfying order. If any group is too large, think how you can subdivide it into two or three smaller groups. If you decide on one or more solo bows, make sure they are at the end of the call, and avoid having too many of them, as they tend to devalue one another as they accumulate.

Now write out the call in order, like this one for *Twelfth Night*:

1st Line: Valentine, Curio, Officers, Maids (Use two lines if necessary)

2nd Line: Sea Captain, Antonio, Priest
3rd Line: Belch, Maria, Aguecheek, Fabian
4th Line: Orsino, Olivia, Sebastian
5th Line: Malvolio, Feste
Solo Call: Viola

Here, the second line makes Antonio a little more important by putting him in the middle of a line between two lesser characters. You could put Fabian in the same line, but by doing so you would diminish the importance of Antonio. But Fabian does slightly weaken the third line, which has three very big, funny parts in it and one small and not very funny one – Fabian. In the fourth line, Olivia is placed between the man who loves her and the man she marries, freeing up Viola to take the final solo call on her own. The actor playing Malvolio may be a bit of a star, but the character sits well with Feste in the penultimate line. You could argue that lines 3 and 4 should be the other way around, because the strongly comedic actors will build the applause better if they are placed later in the call, but then Olivia, Sebastian and Viola would end up two lines away from one another.

Here's another try . . .

1st Line: Valentine, Curio, Officers, Maids (Use two lines if necessary)
2nd Line: Sea Captain, Fabian, Priest
3rd Line: Antonio, Sebastian
4th Line: Belch, Maria, Aguecheek
5th Line: Olivia, Viola, Orsino
6th Line: Malvolio, Feste
Solo Call: Viola

This probably builds the call better, with the parts getting bigger and funnier as it progresses. Fabian is given marginally more importance than the two actors either side of him, Antonio and Sebastian are linked – as they are for most of the play – and the fourth line has the three main conspirators together. You can't put Olivia and Orsino together as a couple because the whole point is they aren't a couple, so Viola goes between the man she loves and the woman who loves her. Then, after Malvolio and Feste have taken their call, they would have to page Viola forward for a solo call. A little awkward perhaps.

So what about this . . .?

1st Line: Valentine, Curio, Officers, Maids (Use two lines if necessary)
2nd Line: Sea Captain, Fabian, Priest
3rd Line: Antonio, Sebastian
4th Line: Belch, Maria, Aguecheek
5th Line: Olivia, Sebastian, Viola, Orsino
6th Line: Malvolio, Feste
Solo Call: Viola

In this version Sebastian would take his bow with Antonio and then rejoin at the fifth line for a second call with his sister, his wife and her husband-to-be. This has the advantage of keeping the couples together in one line without isolating Antonio in his, and by putting them all in the final line, Viola can take her solo call more easily by stepping forward from the line after Malvolio and Feste have taken their bows.

If you have an out-and-out star playing Malvolio, as is sometimes the case, you may feel you have to give him a solo call, thus . . .

1st Line: Valentine, Curio, Officers, Maids (Use two lines if necessary)
2nd Line: Sea Captain, Priest
3rd Line: Antonio, Fabian
4th Line: Feste, Belch, Maria, Aguecheek
5th Line: Sebastian, Olivia, Orsino
6th Line: Malvolio
Solo Call: Viola

. . . but this would be a shame. It honours the actor playing Malvolio but emphasises the 'solo turn' nature of the role. It also pushes Feste into the same line as Belch, Maria and Aguecheek where he doesn't really belong, and makes Viola herself seem more of a solo turn than she is in the play. No, Malvolio really does belong with Feste. Let's go back to one of the previous versions.

And so a hierarchical call is shuffled about until it becomes satis-factory to all parties. None of the above versions is the 'right' one. Any one of them could work, or some other variation of your own. Or you might decide, after an hour or two of fruitless shuffling, that a company call would be more appropriate for what is after all, a great company play.

Hierarchical calls are never easy. One or other of the actors may feel that he, or his part, is being undervalued. Two actors who thor-oughly despise each other may find themselves sharing a line. A modest actor may feel over-promoted or a grand actor under-revered. You are the director. You know your company and you know your play. Only you can decide how best to honour them both without injury to either. Good luck.

BUILDING A CALL

A perfectly built hierarchical call will have the audience applauding more enthusiastically as each line appears, with a crescendo at the final solo call or the company call that follows it. A badly built call will induce isolated pockets of enthusiasm that die down as less popular lines of actors appear. This can be embarrassing for the actors in the unpopular lines, and wasteful of the enthusiasm gen-erated by those in the popular ones. You must therefore try to put the actors who are likely to get the strongest audience reaction as near to the end of the call as practicable, without over-promoting a part. You'll be guessing of course, as in most theatres the call has to be made and rehearsed before the actors ever see an audience, unless you have the luxury of previews, in which case you can delay putting in your hierarchical call until after the second or third pre-view, by which time you'll have a better idea what the audience's response is likely to be. After you've opened your show you may find that the call you have built is outstaying its welcome. The actors will be the first to tell you if they feel they are 'milking' the applause, and will oblige you to cut down the overall length of the call or the number of bows within it.

MILKING A CALL

A call is 'milked' when the number of bows or the length of any one bow exceeds the enthusiasm an audience is willing to express for it. This most commonly occurs when an actor stands for too long in front of the audience before bowing, or stays after bowing for a second or third bow while the rest of the company are left stranded upstage waiting for the call to continue. Milking also happens if a Stage Manager misjudges an audience's response and sends a company back on stage for a call that has not been earned. The audience then feels it has to resume clapping even though it was reaching for its coats and edging towards the aisles. Nothing makes a cast more dispirited than bowing to tepid applause.

No two judgements are ever quite the same on the subject of milking, which is why no one actor should be allowed to decide that a cast should return for a second or third call.

RETURN CALLS

The decision to return for a second or third call can become a real bone of contention between actors and stage management. In some extravagantly popular shows the calls can go on for a quarter of an hour or more and strategies have to be devised to persuade the audience to go home. In some thoroughgoing turkeys the applause will be petering out before the cast has left the stage from its one and only call. More usually a decision has to be made after the first call whether to return for a second and after the second whether to go for a third.

The best system yet devised has the Stage Manager deciding the issue. He stands in the wings, usually by the prompt desk, listening carefully to the level of applause in the auditorium, but also sensitive to the feelings of the actors who have just left the stage. One half of the cast will be clustered around him, waiting for the nod to go back on. The other half will be on the other side of the stage out of contact with the Stage Manager. This is why cue lights (see **Cues**) are usually required in policing a call, especially when a large cast is involved. As the actors leave the stage from the end of the first call, the cue lights in the wings are on red. If they go to green, the actors return to the stage. If the red lights go out, they go to their dressing rooms.

COMEDY CALLS

At the end of a comedy you may want to consider a continuation of comic business into the call. This is tricky and can be a mistake unless the audience is really primed for it. If the last scene of the play has played without much laughter, a comic routine in the call can feel like an imposition and the actors required to work it will be embarrassed. The best comedy calls are based on already established character traits, and play lightly, swiftly and ironically between the actors. Don't let the comic business take over the call. Anything too entertaining will seem like an added comic scene and the applause will peter out as the audience gets more and more involved with it.

MUSICAL CALLS

In **musical theatre**, though rarely in **opera**, there can be a musical ingredient to curtain calls. Orchestral arrangements of the most popular tunes from the show keep the festival atmosphere of the show going and often feature a sung reprise of the most memorable chorus. In dance musicals, calls can be developed into such fully choreographed routines they form an integral part of the show. These celebratory dances have their antecedents in the post-show 'jig' performed by players of the Elizabethan theatre. Indeed, many Elizabethan and Jacobean comedies call for a dance in the final scene as a joint celebration of the events of the play and the good efforts of the performers.

ARTIFICIAL CALLS

In long-running shows, or in theatre companies that develop their own peculiar traditions, curtain calls can become matters of great artifice. Flowers rain onto the stage, apparently from the hands of ardent fans, but actually from a platoon of crouching ushers. Bouquets are presented to stars at the final line-up, only to be taken from them in the wings, put in water overnight and used again the next day. Calls are carefully rehearsed to seem unrehearsed, a ragged line of actors staring open-mouthed into the auditorium as if astonished that the play has been enjoyed despite the fact they have played it two hundred times. As they leave the stage in disarray, one leading actor returns too quickly as if by accident and then seems deeply embarrassed to be singled out for special praise, beckoning the other actors on to save his blushes.

This sort of nonsense can be quite effective in building a call, but should never be necessary. If the audience has enjoyed a play, the cynical exploitation of their approval will be distasteful, at least to some. If the play has not been enjoyed, the nonsense will be as excruciating for the actors as it is for the audience.

OPERA CALLS

Opera calls are a law unto themselves. Most of them have a simple formula. The first call is for the chorus, led by the Chorus Master, then come the smaller parts in groups, then the soloists. Solo parts in opera are thought of in a more distinct way than in the theatre, and each major soloist expects to be accorded a solo call. Building a call is difficult in these circumstances. Each soloist likes to wait for four or five seconds before he comes on so that the applause from the previous singer has had time to die down. Then, when he enters, he seems to get more of a response, especially when entering in the wake of a more popular performer. Audiences in opera have become inured to this technique and only clap when they see someone they like, making continuous applause impossible to sustain. If you direct opera, you should try to fight this self-serving and competitive habit, but with strong-willed singers you may have to abandon the attempt. At least if they know you don't approve, they may limit their delaying tactics to a minimum.

Final opera calls always involve the **conductor**, who makes his way up from the pit. He then acknowledges the **orchestra**, who bow from the pit though, embarrassingly, members of the orchestra may well be on their way home before the acknowledgement happens, making it seem like the conductor is thanking the chairs and the music stands. On opening nights you too may be called to the stage along with your creative team. If you are, you would be well advised to have ascertained the traditions and temper of the audience in advance. Some well-established houses are blessed with supporters as conservative as they are fervent. They will forgive minor musical faults but grow cantankerous if they feel a director or designer has foisted an inappropriate **concept** on them. Thus they may rapturously applaud the conductor and a few moments later roundly boo the creative team. If this happens to you, be prepared with a friendly smile as token of grateful acceptance that your work has succeeded in being adventurous and thought-provoking. In these circumstances a second round of boos may well indicate that the booers are themselves being booed for their ingratitude.

CURTAIN CALL ETIQUETTE

In view of all of the above, here are some simple rules of etiquette for actors taking curtain calls.

1 *Be energetic*

Dawdling always looks complacent and tiredness looks like ingratitude. Calls should be taken at a brisk pace.

2 *Be cheerful*

Don't continue to play the atmosphere of the play after the play has finished. However serious or tragic the events of the play have been, it is pretentious for actors to hang on to them when they are no longer in character. The actor that seems to be suffering a personal bereavement over the death of his character or wrestling with nervous exhaustion over the depredations his soul has suffered for the sake of his art is just a big fibber.

3 *Don't sulk*

Don't begrudge the audience its response. You may feel they haven't laughed enough or been silent enough or coughed too much, but they don't know you feel that way. Most audiences think they've been good audiences and it's churlish to make them feel otherwise.

4 *Don't wait*

Waiting for the applause from the previous actor to die down before you take your call is an old trick and a cheap one, and your fellow actors won't thank you for deploying it. See also Opera Calls above.

5 *Don't be a robot*

Mechanical bowing looks rude. When you arrive at the front of the stage, look around the audience before you bow. By appreciating the applause before you acknowledge it, you make the acknowledgement the more gracious.

6 *No false modesty*

Gestures of self-abnegation seem, and usually are, fake. It is not for you to tell the audience they are wrong to have enjoyed your performance.

7 *No triumphalism*

You haven't trekked to the South Pole or won an Olympic medal. Being an actor is no more heroic than any other profession and much less than some.

8 *No early escape*

If the audience goes on clapping, you go on bowing. It's up to them, not you, to decide that the curtain call has gone on long enough.

Cuts and Cutting

A great many plays are longer in written form than they can afford to be, or deserve to be, in performance. Some good, even great, plays are better performed with judicious cuts than without them. A moderately good play can often be made into a better one by careful pruning. Only thoroughly bad plays are proof against the benefits of cutting, unless by making them short we endow them with their only merit.

There is good evidence that Shakespeare's plays were cut for performance or indeed expanded for publication. Either way, the description, in the prologue of *Romeo and Juliet*, of 'the two hours traffick of our stage', tells its own story. Two hours, with or without an interval, is too short a time in which to perform all but the very shortest of Shakespeare's plays. *Romeo and Juliet*, which takes three and a half hours to perform uncut, is by no means the longest.

Of course, time is relative in the theatre as it is everywhere else. Plays that are very long may also be entirely engaging and bad plays can seem eternal even when very short. If you wish to cut a play you should have good structural reasons for doing so, not just a desire to cram it into a preordained time slot. The current fashion for ninety-minute plays performed without an interval is causing many plays to be cut beyond recognition. It is a fashion that should be resisted, unless we want to reduce the ambition of theatre to the same scale as that of cinema.

When to cut and when not to cut? As far as overall length is concerned, there are no absolute rules. It would nevertheless be true to say that most modern audiences do not like sitting for more than an hour and a half without an **interval**, and that any play lasting more than three hours with an interval would be regarded by most audiences as long. At the end of an evening in the theatre, people have buses and tubes to catch or dinners to eat. They will sit on into a fourth hour, or even a fifth, if they are prepared and if what is happening on stage is compelling. If not, they will become restless after two and half hours and increasingly mutinous after three.

When you cut a play, cut boldly if you can. Look at the structure. Are there whole scenes you can cut, or characters, or groups of characters? Can you amalgamate any scenes? Can a three-act play written to be performed with two intervals be reduced to two acts and one interval? In a classical five-act play, does the placing of a single interval suggest cuts in the material before and after it? Does the play have the sort of onward momentum that would suggest a performance without an interval? If so, how much would you have to cut to keep the play within a single act format without losing any of its central argument? Within scenes, can you cut entire speeches? Bold cuts are often the easiest to achieve.

If your cutting must be in more detail, cut for sense, but be careful not to disrupt the rhythm of the author's language. Make sure the remaining dialogue retains a robust meaning and that the speeches from one character to the next are still clearly motivated. This is harder to do with poetic language than prose, but writers of prose have their rhythms too and cutting is never as easy as it seems.

Your bold, structural cuts should be made before you go into rehearsal. Indeed, if they involve the cutting of characters or large parts of characters they must be done before you cast the play. No one likes to be told in the first week of rehearsal that three-quarters of his part has had a blue pencil drawn through it. Big cuts may also affect your set, costume and lighting designs. Cut bold and cut early, if you possibly can.

If you decide to make smaller cuts, these are best done in the first few days of **rehearsing a play**. The actors will have looked at their parts very carefully before rehearsals begin and may not take kindly to your microsurgery, however good at it you profess to be. So take care to explain the need for textual cuts and explore them in the company of the actors while you are making a first examination of the text.

Try to have all your cuts agreed by the end of the first week of rehearsal. Actors hate last-minute cuts. They learn the rhythms of their speeches as well as the thoughts behind the words, and they are easily thrown if these rhythms are tinkered with just before they open. If you know your play is too long, don't go through rehearsals thinking you can cut the boring bits once you've found out where they are, or that the sheer speed of the finished performance will come to your rescue. You can't and it won't. Apart from anything else, the minute enquiry into bits of text that end up getting cut is such a waste of everybody's time.

Of course you can't always know, and mistakes will always be made. Sometimes the structure of a play or a musical only properly reveals itself to you in performance. If your run is short, there won't be much you can do about this, but the longer the run, the more anxious you and your producers will be wield the knife, if wielded it must be, and your **preview** performance period will give you the opportunity to do so. But be very careful how you proceed. Don't cut in a panic. Cut with a view to curing the structural problem, but do as little damage as you can to the meaning of your play and the morale of your company. Consider what each cut means, large or small. How will it affect the timing of the events immediately after it in terms of character motivation and clarity of **storytelling**? Will there be knock-on effects in terms of lighting, sound, **quick changes** or **cueing** of any sort? How upset will the person be who is losing the scene or the speech or the song? How upset will everyone else be on his behalf? How frightened will everybody be that their speech or scene or song will be next? Put yourself in their shoes. What are the cuts really worth? Will they serve to help the play or are they just sacrificial lambs offered up to appease the angry producorial gods?

Cut bold, cut early, cut kindly.

Cyclorama

A cyclorama, abbreviated to cyc (pronounced 'sike'), is a curved cloth erected at the back of a stage to contain the downstage space, mask the upstage areas and create a lighting screen for the **projection** of atmospheres, abstract effects, colours, the illusion of distance, or the projection of scenic panoramas.

If you think your play needs a sky, a cyc is the best way to achieve one. Even in plays set entirely indoors, cyc skies can add an interesting perspective or context.

Cycs often have **scrims** set in front of them. By backlighting the cyc and front-lighting the scrim you can create a greater sense of depth.

D

Dance and Dancers

Many plays have dances in them. Dance and theatre derive from common origins and, when the context permits, it is as natural to see the characters of a drama express themselves through dance as it is to see dancers in a ballet express themselves dramatically.

In the modern age, dance is far less common in tragedy and serious drama than it is in comedy. Dances in serious plays usually spring from the requirements of the plot and are simply a portrayal of social events, like the ball at the beginning of *Romeo and Juliet*. But comedy and dance have a closer relationship. As comedies reach their happy endings, the ebullient spirits of the central characters can easily brim over into a physical celebration of their reconciliations and future joys.

Serious or comic, the dances in plays that have them do not usually require a taxing degree of professionalism from the actors. Actors learn to dance at drama school, and few actors are so heavy-footed that you would rather leave them out of a dance than see them having a go. In any case, if an actor is truly awful at dancing, you can easily deflect the fault onto his character and so build it into the fabric of a scene. If there are bad dancers in life, there should be bad dancers in plays. These are considerations that you and your **choreographer** or **Movement Director** must resolve in rehearsal. All choreographers know that the best dancers go in the front row and the worst get hidden at the back.

In **musical theatre** and **opera**, dance is a thoroughly integrated discipline. Because those forms are driven by their musical content, the events on stage are anyway to some extent stylised. The performers sing rather than talk and are accompanied by a semi-visible orchestra. Lyrics repeat themselves and songs and arias have purely musical interludes. It is a short step from there to further leaps of stylisation, further escapes from naturalism. Again, it is easier to make these leaps in comedy than in tragedy, but wherever music is played as an accompaniment, its rhythms will be insinuated into the bodies of the actors or singers performing to it. Once a rhythm starts to pulse through a body it is hard to stop it from getting through to the feet.

If you direct a dance musical, an opera with a ballet in it or a play with a lot of dances, be careful how you cast it. The Terpsichorean Muse is easily offended. Terpsichore derives her name from two Greek words, *terpsis* meaning delight and *choros* meaning dance. An audience will find it hard to sustain a delight in dance if the dancers they are watching are not themselves delightful.

In opera, the dancers are a class apart. They never sing and the singers rarely, if ever, dance. Indeed many grand operas have ballets in them that are barely integrated with their plots. Composers were required to add them because audiences expected to see the opera corps de ballet strutting its stuff. These interludes give the modern opera director a real headache. Cutting them may be an option, but not when the music in them is a much-loved feature or when the **conductor** insists that the opera must be performed uncut. Directors are often required to fill these acres of undistinguished music with some sort of narrative and generally fail in the attempt, especially when they have no trained dancers at their disposal. It is a mistake to try to attach dramatic meaning to music that has no clear thematic relationship to the work proper. Unattached meaning always comes across as pretension. Much better to use the music as written, as a respite from the narrative, a sort of cleansing of the palate before the next course is served – dancers as sorbet. But then you won't always have dancers at your disposal, so perhaps the sensible rule here should be, if you don't have dancers, don't do the ballets.

In musical theatre the case is very different. Dance musicals require a high level of singing and dancing skills from their performers. Casting one of these shows always involves a degree of compromise. Your leading performers will have to be good singers and may be forgiven for not being great dancers, but your chorus must be able to do both – though some of them will be much better at one discipline than the other. You, your choreographer and your Musical Director should choose some excellent singers who can dance a bit, some excellent dancers who are at least not tone deaf and a rump ensemble who can do both things reasonably well.

In plays and musicals, beware of giving dancers spoken lines unless you're sure they can handle them. Dancers and actors are very different beasts. Actors are trained in movement, voice, character and motivation. A weakness in one skill will be compensated by strength in another. A dancer is trained in movement alone. All his expressiveness is concentrated in his body, the fleetness of his feet and the fluidity of his movement. He may be a good actor, but his acting skill will manifest itself in his body. He may find it hard to express himself from stillness, to motivate a thought without an accompanying movement. If you require dancers to act naturally, the result is often strangely wooden, their bodies frozen by self-consciousness into very un-dancer-like postures. But the greatest shock comes when dancers speak. They can fill a large theatre with the power of their movements, but their un-projected voices seem thin and characterless in comparison. Only give a dancer a spoken line if you're absolutely sure he can honour it, sure that he will be able to sustain the rhythm, energy, character and pace of the trained actors around him.

The integration of actors and dancers is becoming more and more important with the emergence of new forms of theatre that integrate dancing, acting, physical storytelling and clowning. Whether one calls this **physical theatre** or **dance theatre** or just plain theatre, it requires the skills of a new sort of performer, physically imaginative but motivated from within by the same processes that inform the best sort of acting.

Dance Arrangers and Arrangements

Now an outmoded position, the Dance Arranger was the musician acting as a sort of assistant to the **composer**, responsible for writing the dances or ballets in **musical theatre** when the composer lacked the skill, the time or the inclination to write them himself.

The composer, usually in consultation with the **choreographer**, would give the Dance Arranger a brief regarding the style and duration of the dance and the melodic material from which it would be drawn, and the Dance Arranger would do the actual composition of the music. The job lost its currency when musical theatre, in deference to the public taste, abandoned the convention of peppering the action of musicals with dances, however slim the context in the plot.

The Dance Arranger was often also responsible for orchestrating the score from piano sketches provided by the composer, a function now performed by the **orchestrator**. Occasionally a new piece of musical theatre, written in a retro style, may still require the orchestrator to double as a Dance Arranger.

Dance Theatre

Dance theatre is dance that aspires to tell dramatic stories. This aspiration can take many different forms, but dance theatre companies are all alike in wishing to break away from the codified storytelling of classical ballet on the one hand and the wordless abstraction of contemporary dance on the other.

Dance theatre may express itself in **abstract** or **conceptual** form, but more often it strives to make a coherent political or social narrative out of the relationship between the dancers and the design environment in which they appear. There is often a reliance on video and film imagery and other quotations from contemporary culture, and a breaking-down of the barriers between dancing and acting.

The term is by no means definitive. Some contemporary dance and even ballet companies create similar work. It will be interesting to see if dance theatre develops into a distinct form or if the ballet companies slowly subsume the more abstract forms of modern dance while the work of contemporary dance and dance theatre companies re-form to create a single new contemporary tradition.

Dark Theatres

A theatre is said to be 'dark' when no show is playing. 'Going dark' is the constant fear of all theatre owners and managers, who must continue to pay for the upkeep of their buildings and the wages of the permanent stage and front-of-house staff whether or not the theatre has an income at the box office.

Dénouement

The dénouement of a play is the unravelling of the plot or story, from the French word *dénouer*, to untie. More particularly, it refers to the final issue, or outcome of the plot, including the climactic point of irreversible change in the lives of the characters. In some plays this is an obvious and singular event to which the whole drama has been inexorably leading – the suicides of Konstantin in *The Seagull* or Hedda in *Hedda Gabler*, for example – but in many plays the dénouement is harder to detect or only present in an unusual form.

It is always worth locating the dénouement of a play because of the decided effect it has on the way the audience responds to its final events. Once the dénouement has been reached the dramatic tension on stage is lowered and the audience feels its stake in the proceedings begin to diminish. But the actors still have to get to the end of the play. As a director you can help them bridge the gap between the dénouement and the end by adjusting the pace of the action, the **motivation** of the characters and the intensity of the stage picture. But you must first understand where the dénouement belongs.

TRAGIC DÉNOUEMENTS

In tragedy the dénouement is nearly always associated with a death, usually the death of the central character as in *Macbeth*, or the more modern examples above, but not always so. In *Othello* the dénouement is undoubtedly the death of Desdemona rather than that of her husband. Once Othello has smothered Desdemona, the tragedy has reached its inevitable conclusion. What happens to Othello thereafter is almost as unimportant to the audience as it is to Othello himself. He kills himself, as we know he will, as he must. How could he go on living? Even the precise fate of Iago is left undecided. What does it matter in the face of Desdemona's appalling demise? Similarly in *King Lear* it is the death of Cordelia rather than of her father that provides the point of the dénouement.

In *Hamlet* the dénouement is far harder to ascertain and is probably best described as a series of alternative dénouements, unless you think of Hamlet's prophetic comparison of his own death to 'the fall of a sparrow' as the only important spiritual dénouement. In terms of the dramatic action, the deaths of Laertes, Gertrude and Claudius are all necessary events, but Shakespeare avoids turning the play into a common revenge tragedy by having all three of them die while Hamlet himself is already dying. Thus the dénouement is drawn out across the final scene and arrives at its period just before Hamlet's death, when he persuades Horatio to go on living so that his, Hamlet's, story can be told. Shakespeare's technical mastery here gives the director a major headache in sustaining the dramatic tension after the death of his hero, the poor actor playing Fortinbras having to play the last scene to an audience that has no stake whatever in his kingship, no belief in his right to claim it and no patience left for any further dramatic gestures from anyone.

In *Romeo and Juliet* the dénouement is similarly elusive. Romeo goes to Juliet's tomb thinking her dead. He kills Paris and then himself, his own death being the most agonising to contemplate because we know what he does not know, that Juliet is still alive. But is his death the dénouement of the whole drama, or the first of several? Can we care more about the fate of Juliet than she does herself after her husband has died? Juliet kills herself in the second dénouement of the series. Friar Laurence discovers the dead lovers and tries to flee but is captured and returned to the tomb, where the lovers' parents have gathered to find their children dead. He then tells them what has happened. Like Horatio in Hamlet, he is the only one to know the whole story. As he tells it, a third dénouement occurs, or the final element of a single protracted dénouement, the Capulets and Montagues hearing how their enmity and moral blindness has caused the deaths of their own children. The director's task here is a difficult one and impossible without a very fine actor in the role of Friar Laurence. The audience knows that the lovers are to die – they are told so in the prologue and the lovers themselves are haunted by images of death throughout the play – but the other characters are not so well informed. It is only through Friar Laurence's narrative that they learn what they need to know and the audience can fully engage its feelings as witnesses. The final decision by Capulet and Montague to build a joint memorial to their children is the period at the end of the dénouement rather than a significant element of it. If a director short-changes any element in this complex series, the events of the whole drama are rendered pointless. But the scene is a long one and the audience needs to be nursed through it with care. Place the emphasis too indulgently on the deaths of the lovers and the audience will get twitchy by the time Friar Laurence is halfway through his long speech. Cut Laurence's speech and the audience will know everything but the Capulets and Montagues nothing. How can the audience feel that the deaths have meant something if nothing has been learnt by the society that caused those deaths to happen? This is one of the trickiest dénouements a director will ever have to handle.

COMIC DÉNOUEMENTS

In comedy the dénouement rarely involves a death, though there are exceptions to the rule – *Love's Labour's Lost*, for example. Comic dénouements usually involve the fathoming of a mystery, often featuring the revelation of a concealed identity. In most comedies this is a mystery to the characters but not to the audience, as in *Twelfth Night*, where only Viola and the Sea Captain know that she is masquerading as a man but where even she doesn't know that her brother Sebastian is alive and that she has been mistaken for him. Thus the dénouement occurs when Viola, Sebastian and all the other characters simultaneously have this central secret of the play revealed to them. In a moment of peculiar magic the dénouement finds its focus on the first mention in the play of the name 'Viola', as Sebastian recognises his lost sister and reclaims her identity for her and for her audience who, if they haven't seen the play before, have watched her throughout the action as an anonymous shipwrecked girl who calls herself 'Caesario'. All that remains in *Twelfth Night* is for the subplot to reach its own dénouement with the revelation to Malvolio of how he has been humiliated at the hands of his enemies.

In moral comedies, like those of Molière and Jonson, the dénouement is nearly always a revelation of the truth to the character who has the most to learn from it and has suffered the most from the being kept in the dark, as is the case with Malvolio.

In a well-constructed farce the dénouement, usually a revelation of identity, happens at the moment of greatest confusion in the final scene and therefore also the moment of greatest hilarity in the audience. If the dénouement itself can provide the biggest or most prolonged laughter, the farce has been well constructed indeed.

The more subplots there are in a play the more work the author has to do to drag all the events towards the same dénouement. In *As You Like It*, Shakespeare has so many irons in the fire he needs to introduce a **deus ex machina** in the character of Hymen, the god of marriage, to pull everything together, and by doing so he rather obscures the moment of delight when Orlando realises the true identity of Ganymede. Here the director and the actors must supply what is missing in the text and give the lovers a satisfactory dénouement of mutual understanding.

Consider now *A Midsummer Night's Dream*, where the mortals, fairies and mechanicals are in the same play but move along on parallel plot-lines. The dénouement here is one of Shakespeare's cleverest constructions and at first the hardest to locate. You can't place it at Bottom's return to his companions because all the mechanicals, including Bottom, remain in the dark about what has happened to him. Similarly the lovers may wake up after their hideous night in the dark, but they are not much the wiser for it, Demetrius's eyes being still deluded by Puck's magic juice and remaining so through the end of the play. Theseus and Hippolyta discuss what has happened to the lovers, and if the actors playing them have doubled the parts of Oberon and Titania as Shakespeare may have intended, the audience will certainly feel that an understanding is beginning to dawn on them – but it's nothing you could call a dénouement. In the end it is only the fairy world that is accorded a full understanding of the events of the play, but the rituals they enact as a final blessing on the mortal world happen long after the drama has been satisfactorily resolved. So where do we look for a dénouement? The answer is surprising, but in a good production of the *Dream*, obvious. The dénouement occurs at the moment when all the plots collide, when the fairies have been mortalised in the characters of the court and choose an entertainment to while away the hours between wedding and bedtime. Enter the Mechanicals and their preposterous tragedy-within-a-comedy, 'Pyramus and Thisbe', the longest and most hilarious dénouement in all of drama, drawing together as it does the themes of love, loss and sexual ownership that dominate the play proper.

In most comedies the audience already knows what the characters don't know, so they witness the dénouement but are not surprised by it. Their pleasure comes from observing the astonishment, delight or humiliation of the mystified characters as they understand the truth for the first time. But sometimes the audience, too, has been mystified and the dénouement comes as a revelation to them as it is does to the characters, casting the audience as another character in the drama. This is true of *The Winter's Tale*, where the audience is as taken in by Paulina's secret preservation of Hermione as Leontes is, and therefore seems to have as much to gain as he does in learning the astonishing truth and the lesson it contains. This is a very brave piece of plotting on Shakespeare's part and it challenges a director to be brave in response. But if you misjudge the mood by a hair, the audience will break into inappropriate laughter or roll its eyes at the improbability of it all.

Similarly in Jonson's *Epicoene*, the dénouement's revelation that the silent woman is really a boy in disguise was a revolutionary piece of plotting at a time when the women's parts were, in any case, all played by boys. It is now impossible for a director and actors to pull this scene off with the same brilliant *esprit* as it must have had in its original conception, unless the actor playing the boy playing the girl is so convincing as a girl that he might as well be one.

In *The Merchant of Venice*, Shakespeare provides two dénouements – the first a surprise to the audience, the second only to some of the characters. The first, and by far the more powerful of the two, is when Portia turns the tables on Shylock by insisting that his pound of flesh must contain not a drop of blood. This provides the play with such a turnaround that the second and more conventional dénouement involving the revelation of Portia's and Nerissa's concealed identities cannot possibly compete. The director's task here is unenviable, the first dénouement preceding the second by two scenes and three hundred lines of dialogue, and he must work hard to sustain the tension if the audience is not to wilt by the end of the play.

There are plays that are more or less dénouement-free. Search through the last act of *Henry V*, for instance, and you'll be hard-pressed to find one. And of course many plays written in more modern times deliberately break the conventional rules of dramatic structure. In a play that offers up a 'slice of life' or in a documentary drama written to investigate a social or political issue, a dénouement of any sort might seem inappropriate or counter-productive. But even in these cases, an audience still has to be engaged throughout the play, and in seeking to keep them so you might find evidence of dénouement in the least promising places. But you'll have to look for it.

The search for the dénouement in any text is always a worthwhile exercise. By locating the final turning point of the drama you create a target for yourself and for the actors. From the first word or action of the play the dénouement is what you're all aiming for. As you analyse the text, you must chart the stepping-stones of character and plot that will take you there. The more these moments are observed and emphasised where they feature in the story the more potent the dénouement will be when it finally occurs.

The correct identification of the dénouement in any play is one of the most salient aspects of the art of **storytelling**, which in turn is your most important responsibility as a director.

Deputy Stage Manager (DSM)

DSM stands for Deputy Stage Manager, the lieutenant or second in command of a **stage management** team in British theatre.

Design and Designers

There are four main categories of design in the modern theatre: **set, costume, lighting** and **sound**. Wig and make-up design are important disciplines but more or less subsidiary to costume design.

In any production you may have as many as six or as few as two separate designers working with you to create a visual and aural environment for your actors to play in and appropriate appearances for their characters. When planning a production, your most important task, next to **casting**, is choosing your team of designers.

THE DESIGN TEAM

The design team is the collective term used for all the designers working on a production. In choosing each member of your team look for a combination of artistic talent and collaborative skill. However artistically gifted any one member of your team may be, for his talent to mean anything he must be able to collaborate with his co-designers and with you. A design maverick pulling against everyone else will create tension and disharmony and make it impossible for everyone else to do their best work.

Put your team together carefully. As with all your other **collaborators**, don't throw out a lot of offers at the same time. Start by contracting your Set Designer, as he may want to design the costumes as well. If he doesn't, involve him in the choice of Costume Designer. This is a crucial relationship. The Set and Costume Designers must work harmoniously throughout the production process. Many Set Designers have Costume Designers with whom they have worked happily in the past. Take advantage of these relationships.

216

The job of designing costumes suits the miniaturist more than it does the structuralist, the eye that takes delight in the minutiae of human behaviour and how people consciously or unconsciously present themselves to the world. The structuralist is more interested in the big picture, how the themes of a play can manifest themselves in the stage environment. But there are many designers who can only work within a unified artistic vision. For them, the line, colour and texture of a set must be uniquely reflected in their own costume designs, and they are always loath to relinquish part of their vision to another artist.

As director, you will sometimes have to choose whether you use one designer for both disciplines or two. As a general rule, the bigger the cast, or the more **doubling** there is, the more likely it is you will need two designers. But there will also be occasions when your chosen Set Designer will be unwilling or too busy to take on the costumes as well. That's why you should always appoint your Set Designer first. If he wants to do the costumes as well, that's fine, but if he doesn't, he can then advise on the choice of Costume Designer. If you appoint a specialist Costume Designer first, you may find it harder to attract a Set Designer to match, or the Set Designer you want might be unhappy about not designing the costumes or have had a bad experience with your chosen Costume Designer in the past.

In practice, of course, you may not have a choice in the matter. You may be running or working for a theatre company where even one designer is a financial luxury and two impossible to contemplate. Even in quite affluent circumstances, producers will sometimes be unhappy about appointing two separate designers. From a budgeting point of view, it's certainly easier for the producer to control the spending on a production if he is negotiating over costs with a single designer. Two designers can be competitive over how the available funds are allocated and a producer can get caught in the crossfire, whereas a single designer can be more easily persuaded to cut something from one of his budgets in order to afford something he yearns for in the other. You may sometimes find yourself in the hot seat at **production meetings** where budgets are haggled over and adjudications being made between the financial demands of your various designers. On such occasions, the fewer designers the better.

Your Costume Designer will usually want to design the wigs and make-up, or at least make a significant contribution to their design. If the show is so large that separate designers are needed, your Costume Designer should help you choose these collaborators unless they are permanently employed by the theatre for which you are all working.

Set Designers and Lighting Designers must also develop a close relationship. Battles will ensue if the mutual self-interest at the heart of this relationship is not kept healthy by them and by you. Let your Set Designer help you choose your Lighting Designer.

For a play, the appointment of your Sound Designer will be your call, but he and the Lighting Designer must collaborate on technical and artistic matters – the placing of equipment in the limited space available for it, and the illustration of sound cues with lighting cues and vice versa. For a musical, your composer, orchestrator and Musical Director will want to have a say in the appointment of the Sound Designer.

Even departments as seemingly disparate as lighting and wigs have a reason to collaborate. Do you light the actors' eyes under the fringe of a wig, or move the fringe so the light can get to the eyes?

You must act as chairman of your design team. However happy and balanced the individual members of the team may be, there will always be discussions, debates and arguments about how the different elements of the production fit together. Call your team together on a regular basis, lest any conflicts of interest get out of hand.

The best forum for general discussion is the **production meeting** where your team meets the heads of the technical departments to monitor the progress of work done. But there may be a need for smaller meetings between particular members of your team from which the best exercise of your chairmanship may be your absence.

Deus ex Machina

Literally translated from the Latin, 'a god from a machine', meaning a god brought onto the stage by a mechanical device – the machina (Greek μηχανή)or crane of the ancient Greek theatre. In modern times this is usually a flying piece substantial enough to carry at least one actor, lowered from the fly tower to the stage or the space over the stage.

The first known deus ex machina in dramatic literature occurs in Euripides' *Alcestis*, with Heracles flying in to wrestle Alcestis back from Hades. In Shakespeare, Hymen the god of marriage ties up all the threads in *As You Like It* and Jupiter, more improbably, resolves the conflicts in *Cymbeline*.

Aristotle in the *Poetics* was the first to argue against the device, insisting that stories should be resolved by the characters within them and not by outside agency.

The term is also used more generally to describe any contrived solution to the otherwise insoluble difficulties in the plot of a play.

Devised plays

Devised plays, usually referred to as 'actor created theatre' in North America, come in many guises today, but the idea is a comparatively new one, deriving from experiments in dramatic form by various directors and companies from the 1950s onwards.

Perhaps the most influential pioneer of the form was Joan Littlewood, working with her Theatre Workshop at Stratford in East London, but her work was so successful and the ideas behind it so powerful and popular that many other directors and companies pitched in to develop the genre further. In particular Peter Cheeseman at the Victoria Theatre, Stoke-on-Trent, created a large number of devised plays in a drive to make the repertoire of his company more relevant to the community in which it was working.

The most notable artist to emerge from the genre is undoubtedly Mike Leigh who, in a lifetime of devising plays, has taken the raw idea and turned it into a vibrant dramatic form. Other European directors have also experimented with the genre, notably Arianne Mnouchkine in France with her *création collective* and Suzanne Osten in Sweden with her remarkable devised plays for children.

The usual format for creating a devised play is for a director and/or writer to decide on a basic theme or story for a play, assemble a group of actors to explore it, and use **improvisation** and **research** techniques to arrive at a performable text. But some director/writers, like Mike Leigh, prefer to start with the characters and let the story emerge from their interaction.

Whatever methods you use, the devising of plays is a complex process involving considerable collaborative skill from all involved. It works best when controlled by strong authorial leadership. If you want to direct a devised play, you should either employ a writer to work with you or be prepared to fulfil that role yourself. If you don't have a strong authorial influence guiding the process, a weak one, more inspired by ego than talent, will very likely emerge from within the group.

The great strength of devised theatre lies in its power of witness. When a play is created out of the personal experience, imagination and research of a group of actors and those actors go on to perform the roles they have created, their ownership of the material and their passion for the subject matter can make it seem as if they are testifying to their own thoughts and feelings rather than playing parts assigned to them. But this immediacy of atmosphere often disguises a weakness of dramatic form, and it is rare for devised plays to become staples of the standard theatre repertoire. If they are revived the new cast often struggles to inhabit the roles as vividly as their creators did.

Devising is a form of **adaptation**, with the dramatic material being adapted from imagination and experience rather than from an established source.

Dialect

The word dialect, in the theatre as in daily life, has two different though closely related meanings. It is the manner of speaking peculiar to a particular person or class of people, their natural conversational idiom. It can also mean the distinct local form of a language, differentiated from the 'standard' 'received' or 'literary' form by peculiar usages of vocabulary, pronunciation or grammar – as in a Yorkshire or West Indian dialect. These two meanings have become more or less conflated in modern theatrical parlance – the task for the actor being the same whether he is learning to speak an idiomatic usage or a linguistic form – and the word **accent** is a commonly used alternative to both.

RECEIVED PRONUNCIATION

The standard and once broadly accepted theatrical default dialect in the English theatre, known variously as BBC English, Standard English or RP (Received Pronunciation), is fast becoming a thing of the past. English drama schools used to drum RP into all their students, surgically removing their natural dialects in the process. This seemed an appropriate technique in the days when most plays were written about upper- and middle-class life, but since the social and theatrical revolutions of the fifties and sixties, it has seemed increasingly daft. Announcers on the BBC are now employed from every possible regional and class background and standards of dialect are impossible for anyone to assess with any objectivity. From whom, then, should any of us be receiving our pronunciation?

Actors are still trained in RP, but they are no longer required to obliterate their own regional or class dialects in the process. It is still widely used, especially in productions of classical plays or any others written in **heightened language,** but in most respects the cultural and regional barriers have broken down to such an extent in modern Britain that a consensus theatrical dialect is neither achievable nor desirable. Actors from a wide variety of backgrounds, ethnicities and dialects happily coexist on stages all around the country in plays that only fifty years ago would have been considered the cultural property of a single class, a class receiving its pronunciation as it imagined it had always been received and would always be received.

Dialect

In the absence of clear aesthetic or cultural guidelines, issues of
dialect provide the director with a number of interesting problems
and choices. Some plays are written wholly or partly in dialect.
Some plays may benefit from being performed wholly or partly in
dialect, whether written in dialect or not. Some actors are much
better at dialects than others. Some actors are possessed of strong
regional dialects that they are incapable of losing or unhappy about
losing. In order to address these issues, you should ask yourself a
series of questions about the play you are directing and the actors
you plan to cast in it, or have already cast in it:

1 Has your author set the play in a dialect-specific region or culture?
2 Is the dialect associated with the geographical or cultural background of your play crucial to its social or aesthetic integrity?
3 Do you intend to set your production in a dialect-specific
  region or culture not originally intended by the author of the
  play? If so, will this require any of the dialogue in the play to
  be rewritten in any way?
4 Do the characters in your play all share the same dialect? If not,
  how important is it that the actors differentiate between one
  dialect and another?
5 Has the text of any or all of the characters been written phonetically as a guide to the pronunciation of dialect? How accurate
  and consistent is this text and how important is it for the actors
  to observe it?
6 How important is dialect in relation to casting your play? If
  important, should some or all of your actors be native speakers of the dialect or dialects spoken by the characters?
7 If your actors are not native speakers of any required dialects,
  how good at dialects are they? If not good, how deleterious
  will their lack of skill be for your production?
8 Have you employed or are you thinking of employing an actor
  who speaks in an unalterable dialect not demanded or suggest-

ed by the text? How will his dialect affect the character he plays and that character's relationship with the other characters?

Once you have considered these questions, it is up to you how to proceed. Questions of dialect rarely have right or wrong answers, only ones that are appropriate or inappropriate to a particular production.

Most directors would opt to perform the plays of Tennessee Williams or Sean O'Casey in the dialects originally intended by their authors, but you may take a different view. You might wish to set the plays in a different region or culture or you might find yourself working with a cast of performers so poor at dialects it would be better to let them use their own than murder the originals.

You may be working with a permanent ensemble and be choosing your plays to suit the natural dialects of your performers.

Or as with colour-blind **casting**, you may wish to cast your plays dialect-deaf, with your actors using their natural dialects whatever parts they are playing.

DIALOGUE WRITTEN IN DIALECT

When playwrights write characters in phonetically spelt-out dialect, there is quite often a tension between the look of the word on the page and the way it sounds in the mouth of the actor. This is sometimes caused by inaccuracy or inconsistency with the phonetic dialect being used, in other words sloppy writing. In some cases the playwright even seems to be patronising the character in his choice of dialect. Sometimes the pronunciation of the vowel sounds in the dialect has dated since the play was written and the words are no longer spoken or heard in the way they were originally written down. Sometimes the phonetic choices seem so extreme or so foreign to the modern ear that an audience would be hard-pressed to understand them. And sometimes the actor's own native dialect clashes phonetically with the dialect on the page.

As a general rule, you don't need to be slavish in the reproduction of phonetic dialogue. Once you've understood what the playwright was after, you can let the actor adapt the text to suit his own dialect or choice of dialect, or find a modern equivalent to the dialect suggested in the text and change the phonetics accordingly.

TRANSLATED PLAYS AND DIALECT

It is easier in some ways and harder in others to decide on matters of dialect when you are directing a play in **translation**. It would obviously be ridiculous to perform a Chekhov play in English with the actors using Russian 'accents'. But what dialect should they use? What account must you take of class, or geography or nationality, in seeking for correlative dialects to the ones in the original Russian? How does a Norwegian character in a Strindberg play sound when performed in English rather than Swedish? How accurately or imaginatively has your translator treated dialect in his work? Has he put a regional or cultural spin on the characters in ways that you should be aware of when you cast the play? Are any of the characters in the original play written in a dialect that has been ironed out by the translator into a more standardised English?

If ever you direct a play in a foreign language you will have to deal with this problem from a completely different point of view or with a different pair of ears. For instance, the Ireland of Sean O'Casey or the Deep South of Tennessee Williams are phonetically unexplorable in Swedish or Russian productions of their plays. What dialects do you use in those languages as correlatives to Irish and Deep South? To what extent is dialect important as a feature of social and regional identity?

A DIALECTICAL CONUNDRUM

You are doing a World War II play with English, French and German characters. In scenes between the English and the French characters, the French speak English with French accents, but how should they sound when speaking to one another in scenes between themselves, when the English they are speaking represents French? Do they continue to sound French? If not, what English dialect should they adopt? Similarly, if it would be ridiculous for the

German characters to speak to one another in English with German accents, what accents should they use? BBC English? And what about when the French are speaking to the Germans in French? Or in German? Do they speak English with French accents slightly tinged with German? And would the German accents be French German accents or English German accents? What do you do?

Dialect Coach

Whenever you direct a piece of theatre that involves your actors in the use of foreign or otherwise difficult dialects, a Dialect Coach will be of great assistance.

Choose your Dialect Coach carefully. Some very good coaches are good at many dialects, but most are much better at some dialects than others. Scan their biographies for what they have done, and if the dialect you are seeking is not there, find out why. You don't want the Dialect Coach learning the dialect at the same time as the actors.

The best Dialect Coaches not only teach the rhythms and vowel sounds of the language but also analyse the linguistic structures underlying the dialect and even the social and behavioural attitudes that most affect it.

If you or your actors can't afford a Dialect Coach, then tapes or CDs are a cheap alternative. A Dialect Coach will in any case give your actors recorded material as a coaching aid. You can also research suitable films and television or radio plays from which your actors can crib the dialect they need. But beware – you will be getting a dialect at second hand. An actor in a film or on tape may already be copying someone else's imitation of the required dialect.

Some dedicated actors take their lines to a genuine speaker of the dialect they are trying to imitate – and record the speaker reading their part. This is perhaps the most accurate way of learning a dialect, though the actor has to be careful not to copy the speaker so slavishly that the recording defines the way he plays the character.

Dialect Coach

Without doubt the most efficient way of introducing an accurate dialect into a rehearsal room is to cast one or more characters in the play with actors for whom the dialect is native, or who have a very close geographical or familial relationship with it. Most actors are natural parrots, and the tunes of a dialect are easily caught by attentive pairs of ears.

Diction

Diction in the theatre refers to the actor's enunciation of his words. An actor with good diction speaks clearly, enunciating every necessary consonant. Poor diction is characterised by dropped consonants, elided vowels and fluffed lines. But good diction alone does not guarantee audibility. An actor with the most perfectly clipped consonants may still lack the vocal **projection** necessary to fill a large theatre space. Conversely, an actor with a hugely resonant voice may be perfectly audible but still be incomprehensible through a lack of sufficient diction.

Diction is taught in all good drama schools, but actors get rusty however well they're trained, especially when they've spent long periods working in television and film where the enunciation of words is far easier to accomplish and mistakes can easily be rectified by multiple takes or post-syncing.

Most actors have no objection to having their training topped up with vocal exercise and will welcome the opportunity to engage in vocal warm-ups when required by a director or a **Voice and Text Coach**. Some plays positively demand this work – plays where the text is complex or archaic or where the action requires a fast and furious verbal delivery with every tongue and set of teeth present and correct and all consonants reporting for duty.

There are hundreds of different diction exercises, and many actors will have their favourites. Here is one from the late and much-loved Kathleen Stafford, for many years the voice and text teacher at the Bristol Old Vic Theatre School. The words are to be spoken in strict rhythm and as fast as possible without **fluffing** a single consonant or eliding a single vowel. Breaths may be taken at the end of each paragraph. If you make a mistake, repeat the word you have stumbled on ten times, then start from the top again.

Revolution Qualification Irritation Variation
Magisterial Curiosities Continuity Accessible
Incongruity Simplicity Recognition Speculation
Association Independent Particularly Horrible
Traditional Prosperity Constituencies Possible
Susceptibilities Official Nominally Materially

Abstemiousness Authoritative Anathematise Confederacy
Contemporary Corroborative Exclamatory Effeminacy
Extraordinary Hereditary Incendiary Immeasurably

Heterogeneous Hydrophobia Incongruity Miscellaneous
Malleability Metaphysical Mythological Pertinacity
Penitentiary Pusillanimity Philosophical Physiological
Physiognomy Phraseology Simultaneous Systematical
Unaccountable Uniformity Universality Unsearchable

Directing in a Foreign Language

If ever you are invited to work abroad, don't be put off by the difficulty of working in a language you don't understand. If you really know your play inside out, you won't have too much of a problem. The relative lengths of the speeches, the **motivations** of the individual characters and the psychological interchange between them are all clear guides to where you are in the text. The precise meaning of individual words is far less important than you might imagine.

You need not worry, either, about being able to make qualitative judgements concerning the actors' performances. Good and bad acting are good and bad in any language and easily recognisable as such. And actors' minds are the same wherever you go – even after allowing for obvious cultural and behavioural differences. The only significant difficulty you will encounter is one of communication on the rehearsal-room floor, and here you will find that your work is as good as the quality and sympathy of your **interpreter**.

Whatever challenges you might encounter are as nothing to the extraordinary benefits you will gain from immersing yourself in an alien culture and opening out your artistic horizons. If ever you feel stuck, or jaded or cynical about your work at home, work abroad for a while. Then come back home with new eyes and new energy.

The Director as Employer

There is a constant conflict in the life of the director between his creative role on the one hand and his power as an employer on the other.

Very occasionally a director will be employed by a producer after the actors have been cast and the creative team chosen, though this happens in **opera** much more frequently than it ever does in the theatre. In all other circumstances, directors have significant powers of employment over their creative collaborators whether they are working as employees themselves or as **Artistic Directors**.

In small theatre companies, where the director often *is* the producer and therefore also the employer, a conflict of interest immediately arises. It is far harder for an actor to question a director's artistic judgement, or even to have a simple artistic discussion with the director, if the director has a firm grasp on the actor's purse-strings.

Even where a director is not in charge of a theatre operation he is still, indirectly, a paymaster. I have dedicated whole entries of this book to the art of **casting** a play and choosing one's **collaborators**, with the tacit assumption that it will be the director who has the final say in the process and therefore a power of employment over the people he chooses. The relationship between director and collaborators is thereby partly defined by financial gratitude, or by its negative obverse, financial resentment.

You must never forget this is the case, though you will often find yourself trying to break down the barriers that this contract creates. A good director creates equality of interest in the rehearsal room in spite of the dependency implicit in the casting process.

It is instructive to consider how you would feel if the dependency went in the other direction. What would happen if theatres were run not by directors but by actors or by playwrights? Would you, as the director, be less capable of doing your job if you were employed by the author or by the cast? One would hope not. But it would be very interesting to experience such an exchange of roles. You would find out how much of your authority resides in your artistry and how much in your power as an employer. Certainly the terms of your relationships in rehearsal would be significantly different, and you would have to hope that the author and the actors would be as sensitive to your feelings of gratitude or resentment as you should be to theirs.

The Director's Authority

At the heart of theatre is a triangular relationship between Author, Actor and Audience.

The Author writes plays for Actors to perform to an Audience. The Actor plays the Author's work to the Audience. The Audience hears what the Author has to say through the work of the Actor.

Put it another way – the Author needs Actors to bring his characters to life for the Audience. Actors need an Author to provide them with characters to play to the Audience. Audiences need Actors to bring an Author's characters to life for them.

Authors need Actors. Actors need Audiences. Audiences need Authors.

So who needs a director?

If you are seriously considering a life as a theatre director you must contemplate this triangle on a regular basis, because your relationship to it is essential to your effectiveness, satisfaction and pride as a director. Indeed, your first task as a director is to learn how to dedicate yourself to the supremacy of the triangle. If you get nothing else right in the theatre, you will have made a good start if you can help to make healthy connections between the three points of the triangle. If you construct the triangle well, it will bear a great deal of weight. If it can then stand up without your help it will be the proof of the integrity of your work. If you ignore the triangle or accord it no value, one or two or all of its component parts will turn against you. It will become your own Bermuda Triangle and you, like many an aspiring director, will lose yourself inside it, never to be seen again.

Directing is a craft – a creative and collaborative craft – working with other arts and crafts to create a theatrical event dominated by the triangle of Author, Actor and Audience. But we will only understand **the director's craft** if we can disentangle that which is essential to it from that which is co-relative or peripheral. To do so we must examine our role in a variety of guises, for directors nearly always do more than just rehearse the actors. The three most common examples of this complication are the **Artistic Director, the auteur director** and **the director as employer**. In their different ways these roles, sometimes practised separately and sometimes together, involve us in the same thing, the exercise of power – power over the author, the actors and the audience. But power is not authority and you must try not to be one of those directors who confuse the one with the other.

The Director's Box

Some large theatres and opera houses have a small observation room at the back of the stalls or dress circle so that the director and any other members of the creative team can watch the play or the opera without the inconvenience of having to sit with the general public. This room is usually called the Director's Box, and indeed in older theatres it is often not much bigger than a large box.

There are obvious disadvantages for the director sitting amongst the audience during a **preview** performance, disadvantages to the director and the audience. It is difficult to write **notes** in the dark. Most people need to see what they write in order to write legibly. Reading your own notes after an evening of hasty scribbling in the dark can be quite bewildering. Crucial words become indecipherable squiggles, notes get written on top of other notes, making both illegible, and the words themselves have a habit of growing bigger and bigger as the evening goes by, the final notes taking up a whole page each. But if you use a flashlight, or one of those natty little ballpoints with a light in the nib, the poor punter sitting next to you will be disturbed all through the evening by the light dancing around at the corner of his eye. Even without a light to help you, your constantly flicking your attention from stage to page can be very annoying for the person sitting next to you. In a very quiet play the noise of the writing itself can be a distraction – the more emphatic the note, the more annoyed the sideways glance from the person next to you. And the bitter irony here is that you will often be asked which newspaper you are the critic for.

In these circumstances, it's easy to see how irresistible a Director's Box can become. You sit in comfort at a proper desk, your notebook lit by a dimmable lamp to exactly the right intensity for you to see stage and page as you wish from one moment to the next. Your notes can thus be written calmly and legibly, perfectly ordered for future use. A sliding glass panel in front of you can be opened so that you can hear the actors' voices as the audience hears them and share in the real sound of the laughter and applause, or closed so that you can chat to your assistant or members of your creative team about the show while the actors' voices are piped to you through a speaker over your head. You can come and go as you please without disturbing anyone, no excuse-me-ing along a row of knees or huddled running up the aisle. Most importantly – and here the advantage can also be a disadvantage – you are sitting in a place unlike anywhere else in the theatre. No other member of the public is sharing your view. Your judgement of the performance is entirely discrete (and discreet) and therefore made more objective, your work, the actors' work and the work of your designers quietly appraisable from a cool distance. If you've had a difficult or emotionally charged technical period and been left a little ragged in the process, the box can seem a haven of comparative calm, comfort and privacy, but you shouldn't get addicted to it.

Part of your job during the preview period is to assess the play as the audience sees it and hears it, to share the atmosphere in the theatre, to feel the dilemma of the characters as the audience feels it, to laugh as the audience laughs. It is easy to make visual judgements from the Director's Box but much harder to make emotional or instinctive ones. Objectivity has its limits.

Thus, if your theatre has a box, you probably won't be able to resist taking advantage of it, but you should ration the time you spend there. Perhaps never sit there on two consecutive performances. Or use it at the start of previews when your scribbling is in full spate and get back into the auditorium when it has calmed to a trickle.

The Director's Craft

Directing is a complicated business. Ask a sample of directors what they do for a living and you will receive a startlingly diverse set of answers. Some see it as an art, some as a craft, some as a vocation and some as a business. Some will describe themselves and their vision as central to the art of theatre and others will deny they have a vision at all and say that a vision is none of the director's concern. Some directors have made themselves the centre of their own theatrical world while others insist that a necessary feature of their craft is to remain a servant to the primary creative and interpretive arts of writing and acting. Many directors are themselves confused about their various roles, unable to balance the way they work in the rehearsal room with what they expect of themselves in the office or the study.

A further sample of theatre professionals will give you quite another set of definitions. I have heard the role of the director described by various theatre people – with a variety of motives for doing so – as artist, craftsman, collaborator, enabler, fixer, psychologist, therapist, parent, controller, conductor, general, leader, guru, magician, manipulator, puppet-master, researcher, cherisher, dreamer, visualiser, visionary, self-appointed expert, necessary evil, unnecessary evil, glorified Stage Manager, putter-on of plays, breaker-down of barriers, builder-up of confidences, provider of concepts, instructor, interpreter, inspirer, irritant, irrelevance, tyrant, bully and bastard.

Perhaps there are as many definitions of directing as there are directors or directed. But why should this be so? Other jobs in the arts are not so dogged with uncertainty of definition. Most composers, painters, novelists, sculptors, dancers or conductors can tell you in a sentence or two of uncomplicated prose what they do for a living. And if they can't, then you could be forgiven for suspecting them of deliberate mystification – of fudging the description in order to disguise the fact that they're not doing it very well. There is certainly a great deal of such mystification surrounding the role of the director.

If you seek to define what you do as a director, you must start by disentangling the notions of art and craft. For the purposes of this book, theatre is the art and directing is the craft – hence the title. As a director you may very well be an artist, but only because you are practising the art of the theatre. The directorial skills you use, whether creative or interpretive, technical or psychological – these skills add up to your craft. You may *be* an artist but directing is *not* an art. If you persist in thinking it is, try doing it all on your own and see how many people will turn up to appreciate your efforts.

In order to understand how the craft of direction can be creatively applied to the art of the theatre, you must first understand what theatre is, but you must also be able to break down your craft into its component parts so that you can see where craft ends and where art or mystification begins. You must disentangle the director as craftsman from the director as employer or manager (see also **The Director's Authority**). You must define the role of the producer and how it is different from the role of the director, though you may from time to time find yourself doing both jobs at the same time. And you must examine the way in which the director works with all his other artistic collaborators.

Once you have done all this disentangling, you may find you have very little left to define. You choose a play, you cast and rehearse the actors and you put the whole thing on the stage for an audience. That's it.

Will you be remembered for doing it? Perhaps – but only for as long as your audience's memory lasts.

The Director's Motive

What is your motive for being a director or for wanting to be a director? It's a question well worth asking yourself, and re-asking at regular intervals throughout your career.

The theatre world is full of unhappy directors or directors who are only happy from time to time. The cause of their frustration is often a disconnection between the motive they think they have for being directors and the work they actually find themselves doing or the artistic and financial value of that work to themselves and others.

When directors start out on their careers they may be inspired by all sorts of different motives: a love of theatre, a desire to pursue a life in the arts, a fascination with dramatic texts, a talent for analysing language and behaviour and an urge to share that talent with others, a belief that theatre can be a force for political or social change, a conviction that the arts are necessary to the health of the nation and that theatre is a crucial part of the public debate.

Few directors set out with money as a motive, or the power a director's status might earn them. Seekers after money or power would be better advised to opt for careers in banking, politics or law. Some directors do eventually make a lot of money and some become influential in the theatre or in the wider world of the arts, but again, few of them plan it that way. How ironic, then, that most of the unhappiness that occurs in the directorial fraternity is caused by a lack of money or feelings of powerlessness.

It is very hard to make a living as a theatre director. If you work as a freelancer in the subsidised sector the fees you command will be irregular and afford you no more than a bare subsistence. As an **Artistic** or **Associate Director** your income may be steadier, but it will never be princely. If you work on the fringe you will be paid a pittance if anything at all. In the commercial theatre, your initial fees may be even lower than in the subsidised theatre, but you do have the possibility of making more in royalties if your show runs for a long time and recoups its capital costs. If.

The struggle for financial survival, for yourself and for the theatres in which you work, will have an influence on everything you

234

do. It affects where you work, the plays you choose, who you cast in them and what your production values are. And here's the rub. Many of the decisions that seem to be forced on you for financial reasons will fly in the face of the motives that inspired you to become a director in the first place. Unless you become very thick-skinned, or very cynical, this will not make you happy. Your maturity, credibility and self-regard as a director will depend in large measure on how you resolve these conflicts between your financial and your artistic motives.

Of course, motives can develop over time as new interests or enthusiasms assert themselves or as the circumstances of your life change your artistic outlook. But there is one sort of change that is lethal to the maintenance of artistic integrity. Some directors have a fragile grasp of their motives for what they do. They may have had a clear view when young but they lose their way in the hurly-burly of artistic and financial conflict. In place of the beliefs they have lost, or perhaps never possessed, they look for security in the exercise of their authority. They seek to protect the value of their careers by undermining the value of everyone else's and make authority their overriding motive. They become bullies. Rehearsal becomes a torture to them and to everyone in their charge. The mistake they have made is to let the frustrations and disappointments of their careers interfere with their artistic motive. They have confused their lives with their art.

The best way to safeguard your directorial motive is to insist at all times on the artistic integrity of the rehearsal room. If ever you feel that your rehearsal process is being compromised by motives that you deem a danger to the artistic health of your work, you must recognise the associated risk – that your own motives, the ones that make you a good director, may be diluted or discarded in the pursuit of someone else's agenda. However these conflicting motives are generated, whether from ego, pursuit of status, financial worry, fear of failure or critical disapproval, insistence on moribund tradition, censorship or pointless political correctness, you will have to re-examine your own motives and test their strength against the strength of the opposition. As you negotiate your way to a resolution you must know where to draw the line.

The Director's Motive

Compromise is all very well, but not if it devalues the worth of your basic talent. If you consistently subordinate your motives to the motives of others, for whatever reason, your work will eventually become worthless both to yourself and to your employers. If you can't please yourself you will lose your ability to please an audience. In theatre, it pays to be true to the dreams of your youth.

The Director's Temperament

No director is perfect. However talented or technically brilliant a director might be, there is always some hidden flaw. But then again no director, however limited his gifts, will be entirely without some hidden virtue.

How can one assess good and bad temperament in a director? Actors do it for us all the time – so do authors and designers, composers, choreographers and producers. We are judged and discussed, analysed and categorised, preferred and ignored, praised and damned by them. We share with one another our judgements about them but are rarely privy to their judgements about us.

How, then, can we assess ourselves? How can we know when our temperaments are serving us well and when they are letting us down and causing grief to our collaborators? How can we seek to improve ourselves?

From observation and anecdote, from assisting and co-directing, from stories of happy rehearsal periods and accounts of directorial bad behaviour that make the blood curdle, I propose the following list of temperamental vices and virtues.

The Seven Deadly Directorial Sins I have learnt to despise in myself and in others are: Self-Regard, Pomposity, Bitchinesss, Paranoia, Stupidity, Tyranny and Laziness.

The Nine Cardinal Directorial Virtues I admire in others and seek to possess myself are: Kindness, Patience, Perseverance, Generosity, Intelligence, Imagination, Flair, Perspicacity and Humour.

Strive to control the sins and cultivate the virtues and you stand a reasonable chance of possessing and maintaining a director's temperament.

Distressing

Distressing is an extreme version of **breaking down,** the process by which **costumes** or **props** are treated to indicate hard usage, filthiness or poverty.

Doubles and Doubling

An actor 'doubles' when he plays more than one role in a play. The term is the same however many roles he plays, so you never say an actor 'triples' or 'quadruples' a role. Thus an actor might say 'I'm playing a very interesting double of Clarence and Richmond,' or 'I'm playing the role of Kent, but doubling a number of other small parts.'

Doubling is a very common **casting** device, especially for large-cast plays, and is often forced on theatre companies by financial constraints on cast size. But there are also good artistic reasons for doubling roles, even when financial constraints are not an issue.

Plays with very large casts are not generally well served by having a different actor for every role. It isn't good for company morale to have actors hanging about in the dressing room all night for the sake of a single brief appearance. It's a waste of their energy and patience and skill. A decent actor can take on three, four or five different small roles in one evening and differentiate the characters sufficiently for the story to be appropriately told.

Depending on the performance style you are using, a doubling actor need not physically disguise himself too much as he moves from one part to another. Audiences are quite used to making the imaginative leaps that doubling requires of them and enjoy the skill the actors use in moving from role to role.

SMALL COMPANY DOUBLING

This is doubling at its most extreme. Let's say you work on a regular basis with a small ensemble of four or five actors but you feel constrained by having to stick to a repertoire of small cast plays. The play you really want to do is *Macbeth*. So why not do it? If you have a company comprising three men and one woman, one of the men can play Macbeth, the other two can play all the other male characters and the woman plays the Ladies Macbeth and Macduff. Or the woman plays Macbeth and the three men play the witches and all the other characters, male and female. Or the three men share the part of Macbeth and the woman plays all the other characters. And so on. However your company is comprised, you arrange the doubling to suit the talents of the actors and your interpretation of the play. Indeed the doubling itself will significantly affect your interpretation. If the actor playing Lady Macbeth also plays a witch, that has a meaning which gets into the fabric of the play. If the same actor plays all the people that Macbeth kills, that too has a meaning. If your cast is entirely female except for the actor playing Macbeth, you may be adding a social or political spin to your interpretation of the play.

Small company doubling demands special attention from a director and his actors with regard to **storytelling**. The audience is not going to be fed the delineations between the characters that it is used to, so the acting and/or aspects of the costume design and make-up must come to its aid. However you achieve it, there should be a vivid differentiation between each of the doubled characters.

PRAGMATIC DOUBLING

You may decide to double two or three parts for what you think are purely pragmatic reasons. The parts may be sufficiently separated within the play and are easily playable by a single actor. You can't afford a large company, so you reason that this is a gift horse into whose mouth you should not look. You cast the parts as a double and work with the actor to make the idea stick. But the minute you have made your decision, you will find that the double starts to have a thematic effect on your production. The work that the actor does to differentiate the parts gets into the fabric of the production. The physical, vocal and emotional patterns the actor habitually uses get into his characterisation of all of the doubled roles. If you, and he, try too hard to avoid these similarities, he will end up disguising himself and will seem to the audience to be working in a different performance style from the rest of the cast. However pragmatic you think you are being in the choice of your doubles, the fact is that all doubling, however it is achieved, will have a thematic or stylistic value within a production.

THEMATIC DOUBLING

Sometimes a double strongly presents itself from within the text of a play, particularly when the two or more characters involved do not appear in the same scenes, or are thematically linked in such a way that doubling them makes good artistic sense. Here are some examples from Shakespeare:

In *Macbeth*, King Duncan is murdered in Act II Scene 3. In the very next scene, a scene that is often cut, an Old Man appears and talks about the terrible times he has lived through but how much more terrible the events of the previous night have been to anything he has known before. If you have the same actor playing both the roles you make a strong statement about immortality, or about life going on in spite of terrible events. At the end of the play another older character appears for the first time, Old Siward. His son is the last person Macbeth kills before he himself is killed. His brave acceptance that his son died in a good cause and is therefore 'God's soldier' is made all the more moving if there is a thematic link with the king whose murder started all the mayhem in the first place. Having the same actor playing both roles points this up, and you can make the double more or less obvious by how he physically appears in the scenes. If you have only one older actor in your company, having him play all three of the older roles in this play makes economic sense and also gives the actor more to do during the performance. It is tempting to imagine that Shakespeare intended these doubles when he wrote the play.

In *Hamlet* it is quite possible for the same actor to play Hamlet's uncle Claudius and the Ghost of his father in the same performance. They don't appear in the same scenes, and much play is made of how dissimilar they are, making it a very interesting double for a good actor to play. It is a common double in productions of the play and one that makes a strong artistic statement. Good and evil can be apparent in the same man. Good and evil are simply two sides of the same human coin. Queen Gertrude in essence marries the same man twice. In grieving for the death of his father and righting the wrong of his murder, Hamlet has to fight the image of his father and therefore the image of himself. All interesting psychological stuff. But consider a different double in the same play. If you have two different actors playing Claudius and the Ghost, but have the Ghost actor also playing the Player, he appears as the Player at a moment in the story when Hamlet is at his most desolate, he and Hamlet have an instantly good rapport, as a father and son should have, and the Player can then appear in 'The Murder of Gonzago', the play within the play, as the King who is poisoned in the orchard. Thus the same actor can play the Ghost of Hamlet's father and the character that represents Hamlet's father in the scene that tips Claudius further and further into his self-destructive spiral of guilt. This is a very subtle double. As is the double in the same play of Polonius and the Gravedigger. Polonius is accidentally killed by Hamlet in Act III Scene 4, an event that is the moral turning point of the play, and can be resurrected as the Gravedigger in Act V Scene 1, in a scene that provides Hamlet with the opportunity for some of his most profound and positive philosophical thoughts.

In *Cymbeline*, the characters of Cloten and Posthumus never appear on stage at the same time. Just like the older Hamlet and his brother Claudius, they represent the good and evil sides of one man. Shakespeare could easily have opened the play with both characters on stage, indeed the plotting would have been made a lot easier if he had done so, but he chose not to and throughout the play creates plenty of time for one actor to make the change between the two characters. If this is not persuasive enough, later in the play Imogen mistakes the headless corpse of Cloten for the body of her husband Posthumus in what becomes a pivotal point in the plot. This is a thematic double that may seem so necessary to the meaning of the play that it would be perverse not to adopt it.

Similarly, in *As You Like It*, the two Dukes, Frederick and Senior, are rather unsatisfactory roles if played by two different actors, but make a fine double for a good actor.

Other doubles can seem interesting or easy at first sight but are actually troublesome in performance. Viola and Sebastian in *Twelfth Night* are so alike that even their lovers can't tell them apart, so having them played by the same actor would seem to solve the identity problem in the body of the play, but is actually a bad mistake. The final scene relies on an emotional reunion between the two characters, and if a production has to employ a late-appearing double for one of them or rely on stage trickery of one sort or another, the heart gets knocked out of the story just as it reaches its conclusion.

Conversely, in *The Winter's Tale*, the double of Hermione and Perdita is a deeply satisfactory one even though both characters appear together in the final scene. This is because Shakespeare supplies the trick that is required to make the double work. By having Hermione's statue come to life he reunites mother and daughter but he then wisely avoids any subsequent conversation between them, which he wouldn't have done if he had intended the parts to be played by two different actors. The use of a late-appearing double for Perdita makes the scene work and allows one actor to make the thematic double work in the body of the play.

Finally, a double in *King Lear* of Cordelia and the Fool is tantalisingly hinted at in the text but may prove more thematically interesting than appropriate in performance. The characters never appear together, though they could easily have done so had Shakespeare wished it. They are thematically linked in that they are the two characters that tell the truth to Lear. The Fool accompanies Lear throughout the time when Cordelia is absent and disappears at the point when Cordelia returns. When Lear holds the hanged Cordelia in his arms at the end of the play, he says: 'And my poor fool is hanged.' It is perhaps the most strongly indicated double in all of Shakespeare, but you need a very particular actor to perform both parts equally well and unless you have such an actor at your disposal you should eschew the double.

STAR DOUBLING

Getting two starring actors to appear together in the same play can be problematical unless their roles are identical in size and importance. No star likes to play second fiddle, especially if the other actor is a rival of one sort or another. Doubling of the leading roles can sometimes be a neat solution to this problem, both stars playing the leading role and the secondary role on alternate nights, or two nights on, two nights off, or whatever. Richard II and Bolingbroke, Romeo and Mercutio, Becket and Henry II, Valjean and Javert, are well-attested examples. But you should only consider this option if both actors genuinely want to explore both roles, are genuinely happy at the thought of supporting each other in the leading role and are sure to remain friends in the attempt. Star doubling based on the demands of the box office or the massaging of egos will generally come to grief.

Downstage

A commonly used directorial **stage direction**.

Dramatis Personae

Latin for 'The People of the Drama', the list of characters printed at the start of a published play. The term is rarely used in modern play texts and programmes. Common variants are 'Cast List', 'Character List' or 'Cast of Characters'.

Dramaturgy and Dramaturgs

Dramaturgie is a German term taken from the Greek word δραματουργία, meaning dramatic composition. Dramaturgy is the craft of analysing the structure of dramatic texts and the theatrical style in which they are performed. The term may be used more loosely to describe the dramatic structure of a play or the theoretical basis of a production.

Dramaturgs are called Literary Managers in some theatres. The two terms have until recently been used more or less interchangeably, theatres with Literary Managers regarding the term dramaturg as high-flown and arty, and vice versa for theatres with dramaturgs.

In recent years dramaturgy has become a serious study in many European and American universities and drama schools, and it now seems likely the dramaturgs will prevail over the Literary Managers. But whatever they call themselves, their duties are more or less the same, and while they used to be found only in larger subsidised companies, they have now become more and more common in smaller operations as well.

Dramaturgs are responsible for researching, developing and proposing a **repertoire** of plays. They report directly to the **Artistic Director** and are often key figures in the definition of artistic policy.

Theatres vary enormously in what they require of dramaturgs or Literary Managers, but their duties might include:

1 Reading **new plays** submitted to the theatre for production.
2 Communicating the theatre's response to playwrights and their agents.
3 Trawling through the dramatic literature of the past for suitable plays to include in the repertoire.
4 Commissioning new works from living writers.
5 Developing new plays and **adaptations** from first draft to first day of rehearsal.
6 Helping to develop the careers and craft of writers, caring for them, listening to their professional and personal problems and advising them on themes and subject matter.
7 Commissioning 'versions' and **translations** of foreign-language plays.
8 Editing and copying scripts for rehearsal.
9 Consulting with the Artistic Director on choice of repertoire.
10 Working with directors to **research** the historical and social

background of a play and styles of acting and scenography associated with its performance history.

11 Creating publishable material for inclusion in **programmes** and advertising literature.

12 In foreign-language performances and **opera**, writing, editing and managing the operation of the **surtitles**.

A good dramaturg can be an influential voice in a theatre company. His ability to read plays and to separate the wheat from the chaff, to spot and encourage talented writers whatever their level of experience, to broaden the artistic view of a theatre company and take some of the artistic weight off the shoulders of the director are all necessary talents in a busy and productive company.

Dramaturgy can be a career in itself. There are certainly enough old plays to be read and new plays to be written for a lifetime commitment. But the job can also be a useful stepping-stone for aspirant directors, producers and writers.

A study of dramaturgy is essential to a director, but students of dramaturgy are not thereby made good directors. What dramaturgy does not teach, or seek to teach, is the practical, imprecise and human craft of working with actors in rehearsal.

If you work with a dramaturg you must be careful not to forfeit your artistic authority in the process. To a great extent, a good director must be his own dramaturg. If you leave all the theoretical study and research to someone else you may as well let him direct your production while you're at it.

Reformed **critics** make very good dramaturgs and Literary Managers, though surprisingly few of them are adventurous enough to make the move.

Dressers

Dressers are members of the **wardrobe** department assigned to a particular actor or group of actors. They prepare costumes, keep dressing rooms tidy, help with **quick changes**, make cups of tea, run errands and usher visitors from stage door to dressing room. In the commercial theatre, leading actors usually have a dresser apiece, some of them long-standing personal servants and counsellors with an intimate knowledge of their principals' habits and preferences. The rest of the cast have to share a dresser per dressing room or stairway.

The number of dressers needed per show is defined by the size of the cast, the grandness of the leading actors, the number of costume changes per character and the complexity of the quick changes, if any.

In small and poor theatres, dressers are unheard-of luxuries. If an actor needs help with his costume, another actor helps him.

Dress Rehearsal

The dress rehearsal is the final run-through on stage, 'dress' because the actors perform in full costume, wigs and make-up, sometimes for the first time, though these elements may have already been added during the **technical rehearsals**.

Common abbreviations are 'dress run', 'the dress' (when there is only one) and DR. In **opera** you may have a 'piano dress' without orchestra, and an 'orchestra dress' with.

The dress rehearsal should be a natural follow-on to the 'tech' and is usually programmed for the final evening before the first performance. If you finish your tech early you may have time for two 'dresses', but in practice this rarely happens. More commonly, one or two dresses are planned but the director overruns the tech and everyone has to make do with one dress, sometimes as late as the afternoon of the first performance day. You should avoid this if you can. Dress runs should never be done in a panic. They are the only opportunity for the cast, creative team and crew to prove the work of the tech and run the play without stopping, however many mistakes might be made in the process.

Good actors learn important lessons from a dress run. They are properly on their own for the first time, running the play without your intervention. They start to learn the rhythm and tempo of your production, they grow into the set and costumes, they use more and more of their instinct and skill to find appropriate levels of projection for their performances and they start to feel the lighting, sound and music cues as an integral part of the stage environment.

You will watch the dress run from the auditorium and must learn to cope with the inevitable feeling of powerlessness that sits with you. For the first time since the start of rehearsals your participation must be silent and invisible. You will be frustrated at every turn, no doubt. You will watch in dismay as actors forget what you asked them to do in the tech and make mistakes they've never made before, as lighting, sound and music cues are mistimed or forgotten, as props misbehave and furniture is set off its marks, as flying pieces fail to come in or come in too quickly and bang onto the stage, as quick changes are missed, working light spills onto the stage and heavy weights are dropped in the wings with deafening clatter.

Don't panic. Everyone is learning. And you must learn too. Take copious **notes**. Notes about everything. You have a day of rehearsal tomorrow and maybe even another day after that. Every little thing that goes wrong can be put right with a note or a little bit of onstage rehearsal. As you write your notes, underline or put a box round things you know will need proper attention. I always put an R in a circle next to such notes – R for rehearsal.

Every little note is a thing that will be mended once the note is given. And when everything is mended the play will be much, much better. But you have to take the notes. You'll never remember it all without them.

Don't take too many actors' notes at a dress rehearsal. A lot of the mistakes the actors make they will know they are making and will never make again. Talk to them beforehand and ask them to take mental notes for themselves. When you meet to discuss the dress later that evening or the next day, ask them what they thought of their own work, what surprised them or annoyed them, what they enjoyed and what they were frustrated by. Your notes and theirs must form a joint manifest for the next run or for the first performance. If you bombard them with notes they will lose trust in their own judgements and risk losing courage in their performances.

As you watch the dress you must also have an eye for the big picture. Be ready to form critical judgements about the value of your own work. Don't get lost in the little mistakes. They will all be got right with time and patience. Look at the stage as a whole, follow the story and feel the balance between the characters as it evolves through the play. Are there scenes that should be cut, or scenic devices that are overwhelming the action? Are there bits of direction that seemed good in rehearsal but now look like impositions on the actors or the dramatic flow of the play? Have you got in the way? In most productions of most plays your work should be invisible by this time. But is it? Or do you feel embarrassingly present, standing on stage waving, as it were, to your mum and dad, your friends, your fellow directors or the critics?

This is quite normal. And it is just as normal to watch a horrible car crash of a dress rehearsal and feel that your work is total rubbish, that you have no business being a director and that everything is crap. Quite normal and quite understandable. With everyone on stage making mistakes every few minutes your work is bound to look less than finished, but you mustn't lose heart. Keep taking the notes. You are the rock upon which this whole edifice is built. If you crumble, it will tumble. Keep the faith and keep taking the notes. Everything is fixable. One way or another.

PUBLIC DRESS REHEARSAL

It is common practice to invite members of the public to the final dress rehearsal. In opera some companies even sell tickets for dress rehearsals, treating them like the theatre treats **preview** performances.

Public 'dresses' make actors nervous, especially if there hasn't been a dress rehearsal prior to the public one. Things go wrong in the first run of a play and actors are understandably reluctant to have their insufficiencies exposed to public view. If technical mistakes are made, they are easily thrown and can suffer real embarrassment as a result. On the other hand, if you fall behind your schedule and a public dress rehearsal looks like being a burden, don't cancel it without careful thought. You gain a lot from having an audience in. The actors find it much easier to pitch their performances into the auditorium. In a comedy, laughter is a considerable tonic and instructs the timing of the dialogue and any accompanying business. In serious drama, the atmosphere of attention that an audience supplies can tell you more about your work than you will ever learn from a dry run in front of empty seats.

Unless your production is in real meltdown you should keep your doors open as proposed. Allay the actors' fears by announcing that you will talk to the invited audience from the stage just before the start of the show. This will usually make them feel sufficiently protected to agree to reap the benefits of an audience's presence.

Your **pre-performance** speech should warn the audience that you are running the play for the first time and that things may go wrong. If technical mistakes happen the actors will stop for a few moments and resume as soon as things have been put right. By making the audience feel complicit in the adventure of a first run-through you will lower the temperature for actors and audience alike. Then, if things run completely smoothly, the actors and crew will feel they have been all the cleverer and the audience will be almost disappointed that nothing went spectacularly wrong.

GYPSY RUN

On Broadway, the final afternoon dress rehearsal before a first preview is often designated as a 'gypsy run' or 'gypsy run-thru'. These can be very exciting occasions as they afford an opportunity for the local 'gypsies', traditionally the dancers and choruses of the neighbouring Broadway shows but now any New York thespian who can manage to blag a ticket, to see a show they might otherwise miss owing to the uniformity of Broadway performance schedules.

Gypsy runs are sometimes the most appreciated performances a show gets, especially if it closes shortly after opening, as Broadway shows have a persistent habit of doing.

Drying

An actor 'dries' when he forgets his lines. The subsequent ghastly silence while he flails around in his brain for the missing text is known as a 'dry'. It is only alleviated when he remembers the line or is fed it by a fellow actor. As a last resort, the **prompter** shouts it out and the play continues.

In American theatre, drying is known as 'going up' or 'blanking', as in 'I went up horribly halfway through the scene, but I think I got away with it,' or 'I totally blanked.' 'Going up' can be further shortened to 'up' as in 'She was up'.

An actor who habitually dries, or goes up, is suffering from one or more possible ailments:

1 He hasn't learnt the text properly.
2 He knew the text but has been off for a while and has now forgotten it.
3 He has learnt the text, but not the thoughts behind the text, so a slight lapse of concentration knocks the text from his mind.
4 Another actor has put him off either wilfully or accidentally.
5 Some other unaccustomed incident onstage or in the auditorium has caused him to lose his concentration – a noise in the wings, sounds from the street outside or disturbances in the auditorium. It could be as minor an incident as the absence of an accustomed laugh.
6 He is old and his memory is going.

ANTIDOTES FOR DRYING

1 A drying actor will already be painfully aware that he is letting down his fellow actors. Help him to learn his text better by taking him through it – or suggest that a member of stage management hears him through his lines before rehearsals start. If the problem persists in performance, give him a personal top-up **line run** on a regular basis throughout the run of the play.
2 If any actor or cast of actors have been off for a while, a line run of the whole play is a very useful *aide-mémoire*. This work has the sting taken out of it if done at great speed.

Drying

3 Find the cause of the problem. This will often be a mis-learnt thought somewhere in the sentence prior to the dry. Identify the thought and help the actor think his way around it.

4 Accidents will happen, but wilful fooling around on stage is inexcusable – an insult to audience and actors alike. Cut it out.

5 An actor's concentration should be proof against such stuff, but your intervention or that of the Stage Manager may sometimes be required to sort out any persistent problem.

6 Kindness, sympathy and repetition will usually do the trick.

See also **Nubbing; Prompts and Prompters.**

DSM

See **Deputy Stage Manager.**

E

Education

What is the best education to equip you for life as a director?

Though I have given advice on this question to hundreds of aspiring young directors over the years, I don't think I have ever given quite the same advice twice. Every case was different, so the advice had to be adapted to suit. Indeed it was halfway through the composition of just such an attempt to be helpful that I first conceived the idea of writing this book. I thought if I could get all my thoughts about a director's education into one volume I would never have to write a letter like that again. I would simply refer all questioners to the book and turn my answers into hard cash at the same time.

The two commonest questions are 'Should I go to university?' and 'What subject – or subjects – should I study at university?'

These are good questions, though it has to be said a university education is by no means the only way to begin. Many directors start life as actors, or Stage Managers or choreographers, and may have been to university but may just as well have trained at a drama or dance school, or simply left school and gone straight into the profession. So perhaps a better question would be – 'What do I have to know to be a good director?', and the short answer to that is – 'You have to know everything.'

One of the great advantages to being a director is that your education never ends. Some would be horrified by such a prospect, but I have found it to be the single most unalloyed pleasure in my career. Every play brings a new set of intellectual challenges – new language to explore, a new writer's mind to fathom, a new period to research, new history, new politics, new religion, new social circumstances, as well as new art, architecture, music, dance and a new set of characters with a new set of human stories. Of course you get help – from designers of sets and costumes, lighting and sound, from dramaturgs and Associate Directors – but they can also drive you to further acts of wilful self-education. And then there's the cast. Every new actor in your life becomes another psychological and social study, some requiring much more work than others, but all needing to be understood, cherished and encouraged. If you also work in **opera** or **musical theatre** there are new scores to learn, with the musical and lyrical languages of new **composers**, librettists and **lyricists**, and another new set of collaborators – **conductors** and **Musical Directors** and singers – all hungry to teach you or to be taught by you, or both. Every new theatre, every new audience, every new town or country you work in, every new dialect or language you meet – all of these require a new intellectual response from you. If you are a busy director doing three or four productions a year or more, these challenges are thrown at you so regularly that you have no choice but to consider yourself in full-time education.

Thus any education you have acquired prior to your directorial career can only be seen as a preparation for the further education that your career will require of you. But what's the best way to get started? What are the most important things you need to know?

UNIVERSITY

If a university education is not essential, it cannot help but be useful – but then so can the study of a lot of other things. Many universities now offer a specialised degree course in drama, including practical as well as scholastic practice in the theatre arts. These courses have the advantage of steeping you in the world of drama from Euripides to the Simpsons, but with the possible disadvantage of giving you an over-specialised view of the world. Drama, after all, is not about drama. Drama is about people, and politics, and history, and sex, and society and anything else that happens to be on the dramatist's mind. A degree in politics or history or psychology or the history of art may be just as valuable to a young director, perhaps more valuable in the long run, than a degree in drama.

But here you must also consider the **director's motive**. There are many different reasons for wanting to be involved in the theatre, so

there must also, perforce, be many different trainings for the theatre. If the theatre is to be a multi-faceted form, then it's necessary
for directors and their collaborative artists to be drawn from as
wide a variety of educational backgrounds as possible. So, to help
you answer the question, 'How do I adequately educate myself as a
director?', please add the further questions, 'What sort of a director do I want to be?' and 'What sort of theatre most excites me?',
and then the double question, 'What do I know already and what
do I feel I most need to know?'

Wherever you go to university and whatever you study while
there, you will still be more or less ignorant about the professional
theatre when you first start out in it, but at least you will be intellectually prepared for some of the questions it will ask you.

One of the reasons for this is that directing is a lonely job performed in the midst of a mass of people. In order to become better
at it you have to practise it, but you can only begin to practise it in
the company of people who know more about it than you do, and
essentially without another director present. The people you are
working with – the actors, authors, designers, technicians and
Stage Managers – all work with lots of other directors. You, the
director, are the only person who never gets to work with other
directors. So you become self-defining. A person of strong character can be made even stronger by this experience, but a fragile personality will become more and more brittle. Education should
make you stronger and less brittle when the extraordinary pressures of the job threaten to overwhelm you. But there is a lot you
need to know.

LANGUAGE

Your first absolute necessity is an expert knowledge of your own
language and how it works. If you direct plays in English and have
an ambition to direct the best plays, then you will find yourself
working on Shakespeare, his contemporaries, and the extraordinary literary tradition that the Elizabethans spawned and which is
still alive today. The language in these plays is rich and complex
and the actors with whom you work will expect you to know what

it means. Some of them will be experts themselves and will need only a modicum of guidance, or may indeed be able to guide *you* when you go astray, but most actors will need help, and some will need a great deal of help. Your interest and expertise in the English language will be your most important intellectual tool throughout the process of dissecting and analysing the play for yourself and then, in rehearsal, for the actors.

Some of the greatest plays in the English language are written in **verse** or in a mixture of verse and prose. You will need to know what blank verse is and how it works – its rhythmic structure, **metre,** internal rhyme, imagery, symbolism and metaphor – and how the rhythm and tension of the language relates to its meaning.

IDEAS

Ever since the Greeks, the theatre has been a forum for new ideas. In the two-and-a-half thousand years since Euripides, Sophocles and Aristophanes, many finely constructed plays have been written by authors whose minds have been largely concerned with entertaining their audiences – with craft, wit, nonsense or mad physical comedy. But the greatest plays, whether serious or comic, are packed with ideas, argument and debate. If you rehearse these works in any detail you will find yourself discussing their meaning and their value, so your mind needs to be equipped to consider such matters.

There are some professional directors who are uncomfortable with this approach, branding such debate as irrelevant or pretentious, but their work tends to skid across the surface of the greatest plays, leaving their meaning a mystery to actors and audience alike. They fill the stage instead with a physical, imagistic and emotional life that has no relevance to the internal structure of the work. You don't want to be that sort of director. You will disappoint your colleagues, your audience and ultimately yourself. You will also spend an inordinate amount of your time and energy disguising your ignorance with acts of pointless stagecraft or exhibitions of overblown emotionalism. Save yourself and everybody else the torture of watching such work by training yourself to think in a clear, logical and disciplined manner.

You must, in fact, accustom yourself to thinking as deeply as did the playwrights upon whose work you are engaged. This means you must be able to analyse and understand the fundamental ideas upon which the plays are based, the motive of the playwright for writing them and the way in which these ideas manifest themselves in the lives of the characters. You must become fascinated by thought itself. Ideas philosophical, political, moral, ethical, historical and social must be your constant companions and your ultimate strength.

PEOPLE

Plays are about people and these people are performed by other people. You will need to understand both the fictional characters and the real performers and how both groups animate each other. The character on the page has to be brought to life by the actor, but the actor has no life on stage without the character. Your understanding of this essential chemistry will largely rely on your knowledge of people, whether 'real' or 'fictional'.

If you are interested in theatre you are probably already a people-watcher, but your study of human beings and how they behave must go deeper than mere observation. What people do and say is motivated by what they think and feel, which in turn is informed by their parental and social conditioning, their beliefs, the power of their intellects and their psychological make-up. The better the playwright the more truly this human detail will inform the characters of a play. The better the actor the more accurately and feelingly this same detail will appear in performance. The better the director the fewer will be the stones left unturned in pursuit of this veracity and depth.

Make other people your constant study – their behaviour, their psychology, their emotional, sexual, intellectual and spiritual lives. Don't waste time studying yourself or your own thought processes. Introspection is not a useful characteristic in a director.

Education

Obviously the literature of the theatre must be your first concern, and you must be as widely read as possible, from the Greeks and the Elizabethans through to the Restoration, nineteenth-century European drama and on to the twentieth century and contemporary drama. When it comes to choosing a play to direct you will need the broadest possible range of choices, so you must cultivate an appetite for plays of all periods and cultures.

You must also learn *how* to read a play, animating the characters for yourself as you go along and imagining the tensions and atmosphere of each scene. Reading a play well takes a great deal of concentration for, unlike a novel, there is a lot of filling in to be done, the author expecting you to visualise from the page what will eventually be flesh and blood on the stage. The theatricality of some plays comes jumping off the page for all to see, but others move more stealthily and need a more subtle understanding. Many fine directors are not such fine readers, rejecting some of the best plays they are offered through a lack of this imaginative reading skill.

In immersing yourself in the literature of the drama, you mustn't ignore other forms, especially poetry and the novel. Many playwrights have written poetry as well as plays, and others have written novels and stories as well. If you are studying a play and are having difficulty putting yourself into the mind of the writer, then a trawl through the rest of that writer's output can be very revealing. Chekhov, for instance, wrote only a handful of plays and his style is extremely difficult to pin down. In his scores of short stories, however, he is far less elusive. By examining them you can get a very clear view of his habitual mode of thought. You can then apply what you have learnt to an analysis of the characters in his plays. You will get similar insights into their plays from Brecht's poetry, Shaw's prefaces and political essays, Shakespeare's sonnets, Wilde's stories and poems, Strindberg's short stories and diaries and so on.

Most poets and novelists never wrote plays at all, but an understanding of their work is essential to an understanding of the theatre as a whole. Dickens, for instance, who has been dubbed the greatest English playwright never to write a play, had a major influence on the modern theatre through the extraordinary vividness and theatricality of his characters and the power of his social invective. Famous for spellbinding audiences with readings from his own novels, he was also a keen amateur actor, mounting new plays and revivals with some of the great theatrical figures of his day, influencing them and being influenced in return. Perhaps his own greatest influence was the Elizabethan/Jacobean playwright Ben Jonson, whose extraordinary characters afford actors some of the most compelling parts in the English stage repertoire. Countless other novelists and poets have had a similarly close relationship with the theatre, writing for it and about it, flirting with it and losing their hearts to it. Only a handful of writers have been able to resist the theatre entirely, remaining completely uninfluenced by it.

So you must learn to think of English literature as being all of a piece. To study only one part of it would be to miss out on the whole amazing structure and thereby to misunderstand the place of drama within it. The literature of other languages and cultures is similarly interlocked with the English literary tradition. Once you embark on an exploration of any one part of world drama, the rest of it beckons to you with a tantalising smile on its face.

FOREIGN LANGUAGES

Knowledge of other languages is by no means essential to the director's craft, but it can be extremely useful. The richness and variety of English and American drama is extraordinary, but other cultures and languages have their own important dramatic traditions and their plays are best understood by those who have some understanding of the languages in which they were written. The dramatic literatures of France, Spain, Germany, Italy, Russia and Scandinavia have had a particularly strong influence on English plays and playwrights and continue to do so. Excellence in any of those languages will give you an enormous head start when it comes to working with living writers in those languages, studying translations of the original texts or working with translators on new versions of the plays.

If you have a taste for Greek and Roman drama and wish to understand the true structure and imagery of those plays, then classical Greek and Latin are invaluable studies.

English-speakers in the modern world are both lucky and unlucky. Lucky in that most of the world seems to want to learn English and has at least a passing knowledge of the language through the pervasive influence of the British and American empires of the last three hundred years. Unlucky because the desire of others to learn our language makes it far more difficult to pick up theirs. If you ever have the good fortune to work abroad you will have to cope with this paradox on a daily basis, but you would be well advised not to take advantage of it and become the sleeping partner in what is already a most uneven deal in the business of languages. Equip yourself instead with a mind capable of appreciating the beauty and integrity of other languages than your own, even if you can never fully enjoy all the subtleties of them. Then your work with actors, playwrights, translators, interpreters and producers in their own countries will afford you all the more satisfaction. You will simultaneously enrich your understanding of the language and culture you were brought up with. To study any foreign language is to study your own more deeply.

THEOLOGY AND MYTHOLOGY

It was said of Shakespeare by Ben Jonson that 'he had small Latin and less Greek', but he was certainly intimately conversant with the mythology of those cultures. You can scarcely turn a page of one of his plays without coming face to face with some reference to the Greek or Roman heroes, gods, philosophers and statesmen. Indeed, the plots of nine of his plays are directly drawn from classical history or mythology, and many of the others are full of classical borrowings. The same sources and influences are to be found in the work of nearly all his contemporaries, and so throughout European drama right up to the middle of the twentieth century, when a study of classical history and mythology finally started to go out of fashion. As a director rehearsing these plays you will find that ignorance of these stories, characters and ideas will be an embarrassment to you. A detailed study of them will yield rich and lasting rewards.

An even greater influence on European plays written in the modern era is the Bible, and in England the Book of Common Prayer. Most dramatists of the last five hundred years were educated in schools attached in one way or another to the Established Church and would have attended church services on a regular basis whether they wanted to or not. They were therefore intimately acquainted with the language, imagery and ideology of the Bible and the Judaeo-Christian doctrines proposed by the writers of the Bible. If you wish to understand plays written in the shadow of this tradition you must have some knowledge of the texts that so influenced the theological and philosophical ideas within them. Some plays challenge the religious and theological ideas of their time and some plays take them for granted, but all are affected by them and so must you be.

ACTING

To be a good director you have to know about acting, and the best way to know about anything is to experience it. You cannot possibly empathise with your actors if you haven't felt what it's like to play a character, learn your lines and moves, be directed by a director, integrate with your fellow actors, wear costume and make-up and stand in the bright lights in front of a dark, populated void. The thrill of it, the terror of it, are things you need to know. Even if you're a terrible actor and you dissolve to a jelly when put on a stage, it's something you should do at least once. The more you do it, the more you will learn what it is that actors require of directors. You will understand empirically their cravings for information, clarity, security and admiration.

Working as an actor is one of the best ways to train as a director. Many fine directors were actors once. Some of them also went to university, some to drama school and some to neither. All of them acquired a further education in directorial skills by their attentiveness in rehearsals.

Education

However big or small the part you play as an actor, you can't play it with veracity if you don't know what the words mean. In finding out what a character is saying, the actor must study. In listening to what the other characters are saying, he must study further. By inventing an interpretation of the character appropriate to himself, he must study his words and all their potential meanings in great depth. By sharing a room with a cast of reasonably intelligent colleagues, a good director and a fine play, he cannot help but be exposed to all the linguistic tools of his trade. In this heady atmosphere of study and interpretation, many actors previously uninterested in directing have had the craft excitingly opened out to them.

STAGECRAFT

However you acquire the intellectual tools of your trade, there are still things you can only know by practical usage. These are the things that comprise nine-tenths of the contents of this book and they take years to learn. Lighting, sound, music, dance, fights, costume, wigs, make-up, scheduling, rehearsing, staging, opening, closing and all the rest of it. Where do you begin? You walk into a theatre on the first day of your tech and your designer says, 'We can't fly our mid-stage scrim on bar twelve because the LX truss just upstage of the bridge is permanent. Any further down and our trap would get pushed onto the iron line. Downstage of the iron we'd be punching into the pit and in any case there would be **sightline** problems from the mezzanine. Further upstage the scrim would get so close to the cyc there's no room for the cloud projector and we know we can't use a BP. I don't know what to do.' And you have to know what he's talking about!

Most directors pick up this stuff as they go along, but a good short cut is a sojourn, however brief, in the fascinating and instructive world of stage management. Here you will learn how to manage rehearsals, round up **props**, tape out a floor, marshal actors, keep a **prompt copy**, record and call **cues** and all the rest of the things that directors and actors take for granted. This is another good route on the way to directing, but if you take it, be careful not to spend too much time admiring the scenery before you arrive at your destination. Stage Managers and their teams look at theatre through a special lens of their own and their image of actors, directors and designers becomes a little distorted over time. This comes from having great responsibility but little or no artistic authority. Good Stage Managers cope with this well, but as the years go by they become more and more expert at solving problems and less and less capable of originating ideas. You need to be in practice to have original ideas, and such practice requires a degree of solitude, in and out of rehearsal. Stage management is the most useful job in the theatre but it is also the most social. There is no solitude in stage management.

Ensemble

See **Company**.

Environment and Environmental Design

A design 'environment' is a **set design** that creates a single coherently imagined space suitable for all the scenes of a play whatever their geographical or atmospheric demands. Directors and designers might introduce temporary scenic elements for one scene or another while making no attempt to disguise the permanent nature of the surrounding environment.

'Environmental design' is a loose term describing a set design not bound by the normal perimeter of the stage. It can spill into the **auditorium** or even into the foyer or street, the idea being to make the audience feel they are entering and then living in the same theatrical reality as are the characters onstage.

Environmental design is most effective when it removes at least some of the conventional surroundings of the normal auditorium space. It is hard to convince an audience it is living an onstage reality if you seat it in its familiar serried rows of seats. For this reason, **promenade performance** and environmental design can be highly complementary devices.

Eponymous Roles

An eponym is a person from whom a thing or a place takes its name. So William Archibald Spooner is an eponym for 'spoonerism', Adolphe Sax for the saxophone and Romulus for Rome.

An eponymous role is a role that gives its name to the title of a play. These are usually play-defining roles, the parts that actors most crave to play, but there are exceptions. Few actors would celebrate too noisily when cast in the eponymous roles of *Julius Caesar* or *Cymbeline*.

Exit Lights

In order to comply with modern standards of safety, every door leading to an auditorium exit must have a light above it, permanently aglow, clearly marking it as an exit in case of fire, or in some parts of the world, earthquake. Ideally these lights should be shining at a level that doesn't distract an audience's attention from the action on the stage, but the fire officers who are responsible for them are not generally endowed with an artistic temperament, and if the lights are far too bright it can prove something of a struggle to get them down to a level that is acceptable to all parties. You will find them most irritating when you are trying to achieve a very dim and subtle lighting state on stage and the exit lights cover everything you and your Lighting Designer are doing with a ghoulish green glow.

A true **blackout** is all but impossible to achieve in the modern theatre, a fact that can be a real frustration for directors and designers. But then again very few audiences are consumed in theatrical conflagrations these days, so there are definite compensations.

Exits and Entrances

Exits and entrances occur at a border between two realities. As actors move from off stage to on, they move from the reality of wings, dressing room, Green Room and backstage corridors into the imagined reality of the play. They come from a desultory society of companionship, gossip, professional hierarchy and petty rivalry and enter a sharply focused world of specified action and emotion. As they leave the stage they cross the border in the opposite direction.

These crossings represent a well-established **theatrical convention,** in that the audience conspires to believe in the onstage reality and agrees to ignore all evidence of the offstage one, but wherever they occur there is always a danger that the actor will blur the two realities.

If an actor is ill prepared for an entrance you will often see evidence of it in the way he takes his first few steps onto the stage or in the way his first lines are delivered. He brings the offstage gossip with him, or his personal worries or his dispute with the Stage Manager. Some actors are much better than others at switching on their performances as they enter, but a performance that can be switched on like an electric light is not necessarily a desirable thing.

All actors should be encouraged to prepare their entrances well in advance. Talk to each actor about where his character has just come from. What is the offstage event that might have inspired his entrance? Has he seen the onstage characters from afar or has he just caught sight of them? Is he hurrying to join them or on his way to somewhere else and making a last-minute detour when he sees them? What state of mind is he in and how are his preoccupations manifested in his body language?

The same sort of questions can be posed when a character makes an exit. Where are you going? How urgent is your journey? How long is your journey? Whom will you meet next? How do you feel about the onstage encounters you are leaving? Is there any unfinished business left behind you? Will you ever see those characters again? When? Where? How?

Exits and Entrances

A badly prepared exit is evidenced in a falling-off of performance energy as the actor leaves the stage or a change in body language just before he reaches the wings. His mind is already in the dressing room or the quick-change booth or on the bus home. This inappropriate mental energy is always destructive of onstage atmosphere. The remaining characters have to pull the stage reality back into focus away from the blurred border created by the exiting actor.

In most plays, characters speak as soon as they enter. This is a generalisation, of course, but a useful one to consider. The author brings a character into a scene in order to hear what he has to say. His entrance can be thought of as a preparation for speech. Similarly, a character will generally make an exit immediately after his final speech in a scene. Subsidiary characters, saying little or nothing, may enter and exit with a leading character, but their motivation and movements are usually defined by their relationship to their principal. Thus it is that an audience's attention to the text of a play is significantly controlled by the way the characters enter and exit.

Talk to your actors about the relationship between the physical life of their entrances and the motivation and direction of their subsequent first lines of text. If a character enters halfway through a scene, talk to the onstage actors about how they prepare for it, how much they should anticipate it, fear it, or be surprised by it. If the entrance is unexpected, they must know how they would have continued the scene had the new character not arrived. If expected, how should their text be affected by the expectation?

If an entrance or an exit is unattached to text, be very careful that the actor making the move doesn't pull focus away from the speaking actor or the central focus of the stage. There is nothing more interesting than the entrance of a new character on stage and therefore nothing more potentially distracting. Similarly a character leaving a scene without a textual exit can pull a great deal of focus. Trying to be invisible or hiding behind other characters will only exacerbate the problem. Encourage the entering actor to focus on the speaking actor as soon as he arrives on stage. If the audience's eyes are drawn to him, they will know from the direction of his attention where their attention belongs. The exiting actor, if his exit isn't the focus of the scene, should keep watching the speaking actor for as long as he can, then choose his moment carefully when the audience's attention has just been drawn to some other onstage focus.

FALSE EXITS

A false exit occurs when an actor seems to be leaving the stage towards the end of a speech or scene but unexpectedly turns back to the other characters or to the audience, thus creating a little bubble of extra attentiveness in which to deliver his actual exit lines before leaving the stage.

A useful device, but tiresome when overused. Some actors get addicted to false exits and have to be weaned off them bit by bit. In comedy, a first false exit can be funny and a second funnier, but a third kills the joke.

Extras

Extras are the anonymous characters that provide the human background in films; the passers-by, fellow travellers, diners, worshippers and all the rest going about their daily lives usually unaware of the human drama going on a few yards away from them. They are practically unknown in the theatre, which can't afford them and wouldn't benefit from using them if it could.

Extras are necessary in films. Without them the scenic backgrounds of public locations would look empty and unreal, but however many extras a film director uses, the camera will usually be focused on the leading performers, the extras relegated to a fuzzy human atmosphere in the background. No such artificial focusing is possible in the theatre, where the more extraneous people there are in the background of a scene, the greater the risk the audience will be distracted by them.

When large numbers of background characters are required in the theatre, as in **crowd scenes**, it is usually because the leading

Extras

characters need the onstage reaction of the crowd in order to motivate their words or actions. But even then, the actors are never
mere extras. They are necessary interlocutors without whom the
leading players would be diminished. A leading player that forgets
the importance of the actors around him, however small their
parts, should be gently reminded of the reality of the situation he is
playing.

F

Farce

Farce is a style of **comedy** in which credulous characters are sucked into a series of increasingly improbable events. A good farce obliges the audience to believe both in the characters and the events to the point where laughter is their only recourse.

The best farces are beautifully constructed machines. Characters just like us find themselves in impossibly compromising situations, usually caused by their own venality or vanity. Attempts to rescue themselves only result in further ignominy until venality and vanity drive the plot to explosive climaxes of laughter, embarrassment and ultimately some sort of happy resolution or appropriate humiliating punishment.

Farces are nearly always about human weakness cruelly exposed, and we laugh because we can easily imagine ourselves so weak, so cruel and so exposed.

Farce is like comedy on acid. It has to be fast from the very start and must finish fast and furious, but it must be accurate throughout. If you direct farce you must spend hour upon hour of painfully detailed rehearsal time honing the physical and linguistic routines and rhythms that will eventually release the audience's laughter. Nothing in farce can be left to chance.

Farce actors are technicians of comedy whether they play the endearing silly asses, the pompous old farts or the manic obsessives. No actor will succeed in farce if he tries to be funny all the time. Farce is a serious business.

Every director should direct a farce at some point in his life. All you need is a satirical sense of humour, a tolerance for human weakness and a love of harmless mockery. There is no more wonderfully releasing sound than an audience driven to tearful hilarity by a company of skilled farceurs in full preposterous flight. Once you've done it, you will know why some actors and directors get seriously addicted.

Feedback

Feedback is the distortion of amplified sound – a common ailment in **musical theatre** productions, not to be confused with foldback.

Fights and Fight Directors

Fights on stage are difficult to make real and dangerous to perform. The more real a fight seems, the more potentially dangerous it is.

Stage weapons are dangerous things. Even blunted knives, edgeless swords and wooden staves can cause nasty injuries when wielded at speed, or tripped over or flailed in unexpected directions.

Unarmed combat can be just as lethal. An elbow can knock a tooth out, a knee can painfully rearrange a groin and a slap can deafen an ear.

Fights need to be carefully choreographed over many hours of painstaking rehearsal. Never take short cuts with this process. Your play and your players will suffer if you do.

If you can possibly afford one, employ a Fight Director. They are the experts. They know how to make a fight look and sound real and dangerous but actually be completely safe. They know how to accommodate their work to the skills, or lack of them, of a company of actors. They know about swords and knives and knuckledusters and guns and how bodies respond to being hurt, maimed or killed. They know how to angle the actors' bodies so that the thrust of a sword or the smack of a fist seem completely real from all parts of the auditorium. They know how aggressive noises can heighten the sense of danger in a fight and mask any unreality in the sound of the weapons. They know what weapons belong to what periods of history and how they were worn and handled, cleaned and maintained. They're usually the gentlest people in the world, but their business is violence. They dote on it.

The best Fight Directors tell stories with their fights and help you to tel' the story of the play. Treat them as you would a **choreog-**

rapher. Show them the scene that has the fight in it. Talk to them about how long you want the fight to be and what the story is. Let them talk to the fighting actors about their characters and how they perceive the violence they are involved in.

The temperature of a fight depends on the temperament of the characters. Fighters can be angry or cool, methodical or out of control, murderous, retributive or psychopathic. Fights can develop as they progress, becoming increasingly violent or slowly burning themselves out. They can veer from side to side with one fighter seeming to win before being overcome by another. They can involve accidents and unexpected reversals of fortune. They can be seriously, stomach-churningly real or hilariously funny.

Stay with your Fight Director for his first session until you are sure he has the right idea and that the fight will fit in with the style of your production. Thereafter you should let him work alone with the actors. They will need a lot of practice and he will know how much repetition they can take before physical or mental tiredness sets in. With long fights, little and often is the best way to schedule rehearsals. You should look in every few days just to make sure they are on course, and as soon as possible you should integrate the fight into the scene so it doesn't become a stand-alone event.

Once a play is up and running your actors will still have to attend top-up fight rehearsals. When actors get complacent about fights, accidents start to happen. In a short run, your **Company Manager** should police a regular schedule of fight rehearsals. Five or ten minutes before each performance would be a normal routine.

In longer runs, your Fight Director should return every week or so to correct any emerging bad habits, make sure the **sightlines** still hold good to maintain the apparent reality of the action and ensure the continuing safety of the performers.

If you can't afford a separate Fight Director, include an actor in your cast who will be happy to supervise the fights for a small extra fee, or no extra fee. Actors learn to fight at drama school and many of them take the trouble to get a certificate in stage fighting. But with or without a certificate, you will find many an actor only too happy to organise some mayhem for you. Most Fight Directors were actors once, and some of them continue to be when they get the chance.

Film Actors and Acting

Successful film actors and their agents exert a considerable influence on the modern theatre and one to which no theatre director, however celebrated, can be immune. Most film actors in Britain are trained to act in the theatre, though many of them go straight from theatre school into films or only act in theatre at the very beginning of their careers.

However celebrated film actors become, there is often a nagging doubt in their heads that their celebrity has been at the cost of their true calling, that you can't be a truly great actor without having played the truly great parts – the Hamlets and Richard IIIs, the Cleopatras and Medeas – or trodden the famous boards of the Old Vic or the Royal Shakespeare Theatre or Broadway.

The ghost of Laurence Olivier stalks many an actor's dreams, rattling his theatrical chains and quietly intoning, 'You can have it all, you know, Hollywood, the West End, Broadway. Acting, directing, producing. You can be me!'

If film actors do return to the theatre it is often after many years of exile – and however many clouds of glory they may be trailing, their stage acting muscles are likely to have grown slack. The clouds of glory, of course, are of great interest to theatre producers. Audiences love film stars and are happy to pay top prices for the chance to see their idols in the flesh. So deals are struck. The film stars get to play the great parts and the theatre producers reap the financial rewards of their celebrity. You too would hardly be human if you didn't have some yen to rub artistic shoulders with the giants of the silver screen with all the influence, confidence and affluence they bring in their wake, though there are some amongst you who will sniff disdainfully at the very thought of such a thing. But whatever advantages you might gain from association with their celebrity, it will be their lack of technical competence that will require your professional attention.

The tools of the film actor's trade are, in order of importance, the mind, the eyes, the face, the voice and the body. The camera reads the mind of the actor through the eyes, and the face supplies most of everything else. The voice is important, of course, as a conveyor of meaning and character and emotion, but it rarely if ever needs to be projected. A sound boom hovers over the actor's head, an ever-present spy listening attentively for the smallest details of thought and feeling. The film actor's body is even more cocooned from the harsh demands of the stage. Watch any film and count the number of times the camera shows you the leading actor's feet, whether still or in motion. Excluding action movies, where the athleticism of the central characters is part of their charm, physical activity in most films is a scarcely required commodity.

When a film actor returns to the stage after a long absence, the muscles of voice and movement are the ones most likely to be out of shape. If the actor has dedicated some years of his early career to the theatre, the muscle memory of voice and movement will return without too much trouble, but the actor unfamiliar with stage technique may be in for a nasty shock as his confidence, ambition and self-esteem are undermined by an unsupported voice and self-conscious movement. If he tries to cut corners and brazen out his lack of technique by strutting and bellowing, he will be punished by the critics and add to his and your producer's woes by losing his voice after the first few performances. What he should do, and what you should encourage him to do, is go back into training before rehearsals start – take dance or movement classes and sign up with an experienced vocal coach. That way he won't be caught short on the first day of rehearsal when he finds himself amongst a company of actors with a quarter of his celebrity but ten times his vocal and physical competence.

Another major tool of the stage actor's trade but one hardly used in film is the art of memory. Film actors tend to learn their lines at the last possible minute before shooting and thereafter have no reason to remember them ever again. They get used to the idea of receiving the 'pages' they need for their next scenes to be shot and adapting to last-minute changes in the script. Their memories are thus trained into a rhythm of quick study followed by instant forgetfulness. Actors who play constantly in films or on television are often hard-pressed to remember more than a few lines from any of the parts they have ever played. Stage actors on the other hand are able to recite screeds of complicated dialogue from parts they played many years before in productions they can hardly otherwise recall. Thus film actors may need to retrain their memories just as much as they do their voices and bodies. They can help themselves by learning their lines early on in the rehearsal process, and you should help them retain their lines and their moves by giving them plenty of opportunity for **repetition** in rehearsal. Repetition is the most important aspect of memory training and will also inspire the greatest confidence in an actor with a rusty vocal or physical technique. Repetition allows the actor to practise, memorise and relax all at the same time.

There are, of course, many actors who manage to sustain a film and a theatre career simultaneously and who revel in the change of gear required for the proper exercise of both. But they recognise, as only they can know from first-hand experience, that the two disciplines draw on two very different kinds of technique, even if the artistry at the heart of the actor is the same for both.

Fire Curtain

See **Iron**.

First Nights

The first night of a play used to be the first time it was performed to a paying audience, but in modern theatre parlance it has become synonymous either with **press night**, when the play is deemed fit for critical consumption, or **opening night**, which might be the same evening but might also be a day or two later.

Some theatres still use the term in its original meaning, usually theatres that are mounting their play for only a few performances and cannot afford the luxury of preview performances or whose box office returns will be unaffected by the judgement of the critics.

In most **opera** houses and many a large subsidised theatre company in continental Europe, a first night is always a first night.

Flame

Many plays require the use of flame. Candlelight, torchlight, matches or lighters for cigarettes, the burning of letters or flags or heretics – all require flame, or some representation of flame.

Theatre Managers and local fire departments are understandably paranoid about 'naked flame' on stage. The very phrase implies something indecent. In the days before electric light, theatres would regularly burn down because of uncontrolled candle or gaslight, and today there are strict laws governing the use of flame in public places. All theatres now have **smoke** alarms, **irons** and sprinkler systems.

Every theatre you work in will have a slightly different policy about the use of naked flame. This will depend on the attitude of the local fire authority, the efficiency or modernity of the fire systems in the theatre, the material with which the theatre is built and the artistic sympathy or otherwise of the theatre administrators.

In some cases you will be given no leeway at all. In a wooden theatre with narrow exits and no iron you won't even be allowed to light a cigarette. In a properly equipped modern theatre you may get away with a candle or two and even specially made hand-held torches that go out if accidentally dropped. Small local flames that are under an actor's control can always be argued for. It is much harder to justify flame that seems to take on a life of its own. Burning paper, for instance, can flare up in unexpected ways, or flutter to the stage surface still alight.

The use of naked flame always involves extra expense. Fire departments have to be summoned to inspections, paperwork filled out by technical departments and sometimes an extra fireman employed to stand in the wings while a single candle burns on stage. Scenery or costumes in close proximity to the flame must be flame-proofed with fire-retardant chemicals. Characters carrying candles and torches and anyone else close to them must have their hair or wigs scraped back to avoid any possible contact with the flame. The whole business becomes a royal pain in the arse and you often end up wondering if it's worth the candle – so to speak.

Ask yourself what your alternatives are. Do your characters really have to smoke? Could you use electric candles? Some of them look quite realistic from a distance. Ironically, the smaller the theatre, the more you will want to use real candles – but fire officers also get more nervous in small theatres than large ones. Can you use a lighting effect to suggest fire? Can the flames that consume your letter be in an enclosed bin, or out of sight of the audience in some way – in a stove or through a trap-door grille in the floor? Could candles be placed inside lanterns and still be called candles in the text? Or are you working in a style where a non-naturalistic solution would be acceptable, even preferable? Ribbon as flame. Music as fire.

You may decide, after all, that flame is essential. You need the danger and heat of the torchlight, the warmth of a room full of candles, the lonely image of a single candle flame burning or being snuffed out. If you so decide, be ready to fight your corner. You may be told it's impossible, but don't give up right away. Find out what has been allowed in your theatre in the past. Find out who is saying no this time and why. Find out if the decision is a matter of law, or policy or expense, or a combination of all three. Ask for a meeting with the naysayer and offer to demonstrate the scene to prove its safety. Arrange for budgets to be adjusted to allow for the extra expense.

If you argue your case sensibly and politely you can often turn a decision round. Fire officers don't have such interesting lives that an hour in the theatre with some nice actors will be such a burden to them. And a couple of first-night tickets might not go amiss. Push it as far as you can and just hope you don't run into block-headed bureaucracy on the way. There won't be anything you can do about that.

Flies and Flying

From the **deus ex machina** of the Greek theatre onwards, machines have been used to deliver scenic devices and people onto the stage from the space above the actors' heads.

As **proscenium** arch theatres developed from the late seventeenth century onwards, stage machinery became more and more sophisticated, with flat scenic pieces being pushed in from the wings on grooves and painted cloths raised and lowered from towers built over the stage.

No modern proscenium arch theatre would be complete without an integrated flying system. The 'flies', as they are colloquially known, comprise a 'fly tower', the tall, square structure built over the stage into which the 'flying pieces' are raised, a 'fly floor', the raised gallery on one or both sides of the stage from which 'fly men' operate the 'flylines' or the machinery that controls them, and a 'grid', the framework structure spanning the roof of the fly tower from which the 'flying bars' or 'barrels' are suspended.

In a theatre with a full-height fly tower, the grid is built high enough above the stage so that a piece of scenery, cloth or **scrim** that takes up the entire height of the stage when visible to the audience will completely disappear from sight when flown out, or 'gridded'.

The flying bars all run parallel to the front of the stage. Depending on the size of the theatre and the closeness of the rigging, there may be anything between 20 and 120 of them. One of the furthest downstage bars will usually have the theatre's own front curtain or **tabs** rigged on it, either immediately in front or immediately behind the **iron**. In most non-commercial theatres there will also be two or three more or less permanently rigged lighting 'bridges' hanging at regular intervals up and downstage. When you put a new show into a theatre, all other flying bars should be available to you, though in theatres that operate a **repertoire** system, flying pieces from other shows may be stored in the flies to ensure quick changeovers from one show to another. In commercial theatres, the fly tower is usually completely empty, the front tabs being the only permanently available flying piece.

Flies and Flying

Some modern flying systems are equipped with electric winches, usually controlled by computer programmes. These systems can be extremely troublesome. They operate at slow and un-variable speeds, the software they use dates very quickly and is incredibly expensive to replace, and when the systems go wrong, which they often do, no one ever seems to know what the problem is. You ask for a cloth to fly out quickly and you're told, 'Sorry, that's the top speed.' You want a cloth to fly halfway in quickly and then very slowly onto the stage surface and it takes a fly man three hours to programme the computer to do what you want. Then, if you change your mind, the fly man and the computer both have nervous breakdowns.

Much better is the tried and tested counterweight system. Each flying bar is counterweighted against a cradle loaded with weights; the greater the weight you hang on the bar, the more weights you need in the balancing cradle. A good fly man can balance his flying pieces so that all they need is a gentle pull on a rope to move swiftly through the air. By putting 'deads' or strips of coloured tape on the hauling ropes he will know exactly where each piece is as it makes its ascent or descent. He can fly pieces very fast or at a snail's pace. He can vary the speed of a piece throughout its flight. He can slow down a piece over its last few inches of travel so that it lands on the stage with butterfly gentleness. He gives flying an essential human touch, a touch no computer will ever have, however well programmed. This is an invaluable ingredient in a show with a lot of flying. What's more, if something goes wrong your fly man will be able to tell you. Encouragingly, this message seems to be getting through to a new generation of theatre architects, and many new theatres are now being built with manually operated counterweight systems.

Most flying pieces are flown parallel to the front of the stage in line with the barrels from which they are suspended. If you want a piece to fly at an angle, you will need to have special lines 'spotted' from the grid and pulled in and out by a temporary counterweight line or an individual electric winch. Of course, if you fly anything at an angle you make it impossible for other bars to be flown past the angled piece and so reduce the overall number of bars available to you for other pieces to be flown.

You will also have a problem if for any reason you want a flying piece to swing up and downstage or from side to side. More than a few feet of lateral movement in any direction will cause the barrel from which the piece is suspended to clatter into the adjoining barrels. This will cause a frightful noise and is also quite dangerous, as anything hanging in the vicinity of the moving barrel could be dislodged by the collision. This problem is writ large if you ever try to fly people from lines attached to the grid.

FLYING PEOPLE

You cannot use a standard flying system for flying people. You need static pick-up points and a completely clear flight trajectory, and you get neither if you suspend a line from a standard flying bar. You must either drop lines direct from the grid or from a rigid structure hanging between the grid and the stage, just out of the audience's **sightline**.

Flying people is a hazardous and complicated business governed by a combination of traditional best practice on the one hand and strict health and safety laws on the other. Flying people is for experts, and if you ever do a play that requires people to fly you would be insane not to use one of the specialist firms that make it their business. There are special harnesses, special wire, special connecting clips, special winches, even special blacking for making the wires as invisible as possible.

Performers need weeks of training before they learn to fly elegantly, safely and comfortably. Different sorts of harness require different postures, postures that are sometimes agonising to sustain over even short periods of time. Different body shapes require harnesses to be adapted to avoid undue mid-flight pressure on vital and sensitive parts. All this takes a great deal of rehearsal time.

If you plan to fly people in your show, start training them early, train them every day, starting with short sessions and slowly building up their stamina as the weeks of rehearsal go by, and always have an expert present.

Fluffing

Fluffing is the term used to describe the misspeaking by an actor of a word, phrase or line of dialogue. Fluffing can have a variety of causes, the most common being an actor rushing through his words without a sufficient number of thoughts in accompaniment. When the tongue is running faster than the brain it is more likely to trip. But fluffing can also be caused by the mis-learning of a thought behind a line, the tongue pronouncing the actor's thought in spite of his conscious intention.

Most professional actors are reasonably fluff-free, though none are completely so. Professional musicians are expected to be able to play all their notes cleanly and in the right order as a minimum professional requirement, but even the most dazzling virtuoso sometimes fluffs his notes. An audience will forgive a professional actor for the occasional minor fluff but will quickly lose faith in him and the character he is playing if fluffing proliferates. (Trying saying those last three words out loud without fluffing.)

If an actor is persistently fluffy, it usually indicates a lack of training or practice. The best remedy lies in vocal and textual exercise – the systematic training of the lips, tongue, palate and chords so that the actor can manage the most intractable of sentences. A good **Voice and Text** Coach will help enormously, as he can identify a particular vocal problem and suggest specific exercises to cure it.

By some strange psychological trick, fluffing can also be catching, just as yawning is. You can be sitting in an auditorium and witness a fluff in one actor and be reasonably sure you'll hear another before too long. Occasionally, unless checked, fluffing can reach epidemic proportions. The antidote to this is a pre-rehearsal or performance voice workout for a whole cast. Many actors enjoy such a return to their drama-school days and it will always do the trick, creating a group feeling for vocal accuracy and a sense that a single fluff will be letting the side down. Most well-trained actors will have a store of horribly difficult **tongue twisters** or **diction** exercises and will happily compete to outdo one another in the virtuosity of their execution.

Fly-Man

Fly-men are members of the stage crew who work in the flies of a theatre. They may be flying specialists or they may be seconded from the 'deck' crew who work on the surface of the stage. In any production that deploys flown cloths or scenic pieces, a good fly-man will be an essential part of your technical team. There is a real skill to flying, and a lack of technique will result in pieces arriving at the wrong speed, or hovering too long before landing, or being over-pulled and smacking into the surface of the stage.

See also **Flies and Flying**.

FOH

See **Front of House**.

Foldback

Foldback is amplified music as heard through speakers by the performers in **musical theatre** productions, not to be confused with feedback.

Follow-Spots

Follow-spots, known colloquially in the theatre as 'limes' or 'pins' (pinspots), are high-powered, manually operated directional lights that are plotted to follow leading actors around the stage.

They are usually installed high up in the **auditorium** behind the uppermost seats so that their beams illuminate the actors' faces when they are facing downstage, but they can also be located high up on the sides of the auditorium or even on perches overhanging the wings of the stage. These are called 'onstage spots'.

Follow-spots are rigged in high positions so that their beams of light silhouette the actor against the surface of the stage rather than the surrounding scenery. The shallower the angle of inclination, the more likely the light will spill onto the scenery behind or beside the actor. A badly rigged or badly plotted follow-spot will create a halo of light on the scenery just beyond the actor, drawing the audience's eye away from the actor's face.

Follow-spots operate best in pairs. A spot rigged on auditorium left will be plotted to light the face of an actor standing on **stage left,** and the **stage right** actor will be lit from the auditorium right spot. In other words, the spots find the actors' faces diagonally across the theatre space. If the actors change positions on the stage, the follow-spot operators change actors. These changes are sometimes quite tricky and may need to be practised in **technical rehearsal**.

If you are working on a **thrust stage** or in a very large **in-the-round** space, having four spots, two front of house and two onstage, will allow you to simplify your lighting plot and be sure of lighting your actors' faces wherever they are standing on the stage. Four follow-spots are expensive in terms of labour but will cut down your tech time quite substantially.

An inexperienced follow-spot operator will focus his spot on the actor's whole body, rather than on his face. The beam of a follow-spot is distinctly brighter at its centre, so if the whole actor is being followed, the centre of the beam will fall at his waist, making his belly or his belt his most brightly illuminated feature. Not a good idea. Encourage your operators to focus the 'hot-spot' of their limes on the actors' faces where they belong.

Footlights

Footlights are theatre lighting instruments set along the front of the stage, and thus at the actors' feet, to illuminate the actors' faces from below. They used to be the closest and therefore the most effective way of lighting the actors' faces, but they have largely fallen out of fashion in the modern theatre as they tend to distort the facial features and throw unwanted shadows on the back wall of the stage or scenery. Modern lighting, with its ability to focus strong light very accurately over great distances, has largely obviated the need for footlights, but they are still quite frequently used for special effect to denote firelight, candlelight or sunset, to throw spooky-looking shadows, or to create a deliberately old-fashioned pantomime atmosphere. The lighting instruments used as 'footlights' today are usually little 'birdie' lights that are easily disguisable and small enough not to obscure the view of people sitting in the front few rows of the auditorium.

Even in theatres where there are no actual footlights, the term is still used to denote the very front of the stage, with actors being instructed 'to come right down to the footlights'.

Some older actors of a sentimental cast of mind still refer to 'Dr Footlights', an imaginary physician who cures all illness and injury, by which they mean that the best cure for any ailment is a performance in front of an admiring audience.

Foreign Languages

See **Directing in a Foreign Language; Education; Interpreters.**

Forestage

In a **proscenium** theatre the area downstage of the proscenium arch, and therefore closest to the audience, is called the **apron** or forestage.

In some stage designs, director and designer decide they want the forestage to push out over the front of the auditorium in order to put the audience more intimately in touch with the action, the furthest limits of the forestage being prescribed by the **sightlines** from the upper levels of the auditorium.

Such design decisions always have a commercial implication,

however, as the seats lost by the inclusion of a forestage are usually amongst the highest priced in the house.

The dimensions of any specially adapted forestage are therefore a matter for discussion with the producer and the Box Office Manager. Usually the loss of one row can be reasonably borne, the loss of two borne with considerable resistance and the loss of three or more stoutly refused unless there can be substantial relocation of seats elsewhere in the house or on stage, or the design of the auditorium allows for the re-pricing of seats that have been brought closer to the action and are thereby made more valuable.

In many theatres there is a provision for a considerable area of forestage when the orchestra pit is not in use, although in such spaces there is often also the capacity to lower the forestage to auditorium level, carpet it and fill it up with two or three rows of prime auditorium seats.

A forestage that pushes out so far into the **auditorium** that the audience has to be configured on three sides is called a **thrust stage**.

The Fourth Wall

The fourth wall is the notional wall separating the stage from the auditorium in naturalistic drama. The term derives from the naturalistic theatre tradition of building three walls of a room on the stage and leaving the fourth or audience wall blank or with only a few token objects to suggest the completion of an actual room. Thus the audience looks into the room through its imaginary fourth wall.

The term is now used much more inclusively to mean the imaginary barrier separating the actors from the audience whatever the stage setting or production style. Even in theatres-**in-the-round**, where all four walls are imaginary, 'the fourth wall' can describe the boundary between the private reality of the actors' space and the public space of the auditorium.

The fourth wall is the most commonly accepted **theatrical convention** of the modern drama. An audience accepts without complaint that a room they are looking at has only three walls, that a window, a fireplace, a portrait or the masonry of a fourth wall is necessarily transparent even when every other construction on the stage seems to be real. They have no choice but to accept it, just as they must accept the actors' behaviour that accompanies this convention – the behaviour that has every character directing their faces and speeches towards the fourth wall rather than away from it. It was the fundamental objection to this convention that made Strindberg write his revolutionary preface to *Miss Julie* in which he proposes a theatre where reality can be perceived in a more natural and inclusive way, and which gives so many actors and directors such pleasure when they work on **thrust stages** or **in-the-round** stages.

The fourth wall is essentially an invention of nineteenth-century naturalism – made all the more vivid in the minds of modern directors, actors and audiences by comparing what is achieved on stage with what is achievable on film, where the breaking of the filmic fourth wall – by directly addressing the camera – happens so rarely. By putting scenic replicas of real life on three walls of a stage, we cannot but ask the question why the fourth wall is not similarly adorned. In the Greek theatre, or that of the Elizabethans or in Restoration drama, the theatre itself is the world of the play. When the surroundings are vividly described in the language of the play there is no need for a literal depiction of them on stage. There is also no need to draw attention to the presence of two different realities. In a strictly naturalistic play we are shocked when an actor 'breaks the fourth wall' by addressing the audience directly. In non-naturalistic drama, the audience can slip from being uncomfortable voyeurs of the intimate secrets of human life to being full co-conspirators in the drama without any thought of a broken convention.

In any play written before the age of **naturalism** the fourth wall is automatically broken when a character enters on his own, or is left on his own by other characters exiting, and embarks on a **soliloquy**. As he addresses the audience, his only possible interlocutors, the fourth wall ceases to exist. And so it is with **asides** or any other bits of apparently improvised banter with the audience. For this reason it is difficult, even perverse, to attempt a naturalistic production of a pre-naturalism play. You carefully build a fourth wall only to have it knocked down every time a character makes an aside. The fourth wall ends up looking like an imaginary pile of bricks.

Fringe Theatres

Fringe theatres are small theatre spaces that operate in reduced financial and contractual circumstances outside the commercial theatre establishment.

In central London, any theatre that isn't **West End** can consider itself to be part of the fringe. The term is derived from the 'fringe' events of the Edinburgh festival and, like them, the fringe theatres of London often provide the most interesting fare on current offer.

Whatever the quality of its productions, the fringe is a breeding ground for new talent in writing, acting, directing and theatre management. New theatre companies and venues spring up every year and old ones expire. Like sea turtles' eggs. Dozens are laid for only a few little turtles to survive in their mad scramble for the open sea.

Fringe theatres are the perfect places for young, aspiring directors and actors to develop their craft. They inspire experiment, incubate success and protect from failure. A noble failure in a sixty-seat theatre, where an audience of twenty can make the space seem comparatively full, is far easier to disguise than in a four-hundred- or six-hundred-seater.

By the same token, an uproarious success will still only be able to sell sixty tickets a night, so it's as hard to be vainglorious on the fringe as it is to be depressed.

Front of House (FOH)

The 'house' is the theatre and the 'front' of the house (in theatrical slang, FOH) is all those parts of the theatre that are accessible to the public from the street: the foyers, the box office, the bars and all the different levels of the **auditorium**. When applied to **lighting** instruments, loudspeakers or monitors, anything rigged 'FOH' is on the audience side of the **proscenium** arch.

Front of house is further divided in terms of public access. The street doors of most theatres open well in advance of the start of the play so that the audience can collect tickets, meet friends, check in coats and buy drinks, but the auditorium is still out of bounds.

At the half-hour call, or shortly thereafter, the 'house' is opened. This means the ushers open the doors between foyer and auditorium and allow the audience to occupy its seats. The Stage Manager or his deputy warns the actors over the dressing-room speakers that 'the house is now open', and from this moment actors are not allowed to appear on the stage unless the production style specifically requires them to do so.

At the end of a performance, the audience goes out through the front of house just as it came in, and the actors leave through the **stage door**, just as they came in.

Most theatres have an access door on one side of the auditorium that leads directly to the wings. This is called the pass door. It allows actors, creative team, crew and Stage Managers to pass to and from the auditorium and backstage but is out of bounds to the general public. During **technical rehearsals** the pass door is in constant use but is more or less sealed during performances.

FRONT OF HOUSE BELLS

The **Deputy Stage Manager** is usually responsible for ringing the front of house bells. These are operated from the prompt corner and sound in the foyer areas of the theatre as a warning to the audience that the performance is about to begin, often accompanied by a live or recorded announcement to that effect, the lights in the bars being flashed on and off and, on Broadway, ushers shouting, 'Curtain going up!'

Actors like to start the performance on time and audiences often prefer to dawdle and chat on their way in to the auditorium, so the bells and the announcements are more inspirational than honest. Thus the three-minute warning tends to happen five or six minutes before curtain-up, the two-minute warning a minute after that, and the final and urgent warning a good three or four minutes before the curtain will actually rise. In spite of bells and warnings, shows very rarely go up on time, and most theatres reckon on a normal starting time being some two or three minutes later than advertised.

FOH bells can also be used by the DSM to warn the front of house bar staff that an interval is about to happen. This can be very annoying if the bells are audible from the auditorium and are rung at a sensitive moment in the play. A good DSM will find an appropriate moment to ring the interval bells, under audience laughter, for example, or during a rowdy bit of stage action. If there is no appropriate moment, you should instruct that the bells are not rung at all. There are plenty of other ways of communicating with the front of house, or the bar staff could just look at their watches.

A short blast on the FOH bells is also a good way of giving the staff their 'go' for the admittance of latecomers.

FRONT OF HOUSE STAFF

Most front of house staff work in the theatre because they love it and want to be a part of it, but their contribution is undervalued by others in the theatre and most unfairly so. A well-trained staff can enhance an audience's experience of coming to the theatre and a complacent or over-officious staff can spoil it. While the artistic fare on offer from the stage may vary greatly in quality, the ministrations of the front of house staff should never do so.

As a director, you want the patrons of your plays to be sitting down to enjoy your work in a genial atmosphere surrounded by helpful and cheerful staff. If they have been patronised, shouted at, made to feel small for not having the right change for a programme or herded like cattle down the aisles, they will very likely start their evening in a recalcitrant and unreceptive frame of mind and the actors will have an uphill struggle to cajole them out of it. If you find yourself directing a play in a theatre where the FOH staff have come to believe that the whole place is being run for their convenience then you should have a little chat with the **Theatre Manager** and try to inspire a more helpful attitude. Most problems of this sort are usually caused by thoughtlessness rather than malice.

FOH staff members are often students doing part-time work, so they may not be as disciplined as they ought to be. While the play is being performed they can get bored; boredom leads to chat, chat leads to laughter and laughter leads to hilarity and raucousness. Staff may sometimes need reminding that in a theatre everywhere except the stage should be silent, and that very few foyers are properly sealed off from the auditorium. In many theatres, an audience member sitting near a foyer door will be able to hear even a whispered conversation happening just the other side of it. A jolly convention of ushers can become deeply irritating.

G

Gags

Gags are pieces of gratuitous comic **business** invented by insecure actors as a poor alternative to true comic invention. The US term is 'shtick', taken from the Yiddish word meaning a 'bit' or 'piece' of comic business.

'Gags' and 'schtick' should be outlawed when you rehearse any play, especially a **comedy**. Gags are like farts. A gagging actor may raise a cheap laugh but he will create an odour of unfunniness around him that quickly spreads to all parts of the rehearsal room.

Games

Theatre is play. Actors are players. Good actors play as children play – uninhibited, imaginative, concentrated and with a mutual trust in the rules of the game. But the freedom to play is much stronger in some actors than in others, and the circumstances of rehearsal and performance often militate against anyone playing. Companies of actors are usually comparative strangers to one another when they start rehearsing. Differences of age, experience, gender and skill can create artificial social barriers within companies that cannot be broken down by good will alone. Theatre games, carefully applied, can be helpful in breaking down these barriers and in creating an atmosphere in which unselfconscious play is possible. They can also serve as a gentle precursor to more challenging and specific **improvisation** work.

The distinction between improvisation and theatre games is a subtle one. Some games can become improvisations if played well by skilful actors, and some improvisations are little more than applied games. For the purposes of this book, theatre games are exercises played for their own sake. They might be played within a rehearsal process, but they do not relate to the text or the subject matter of the play being rehearsed other than in a general way. Improvisations are exercises that have a specific application to work being done on a play, involving the characters of the play or its situations, themes and structure. They can even be used in the writing of **devised plays** or **verbatim plays**. Most theatre games are useful for the development of acting skills but don't require the players to be talented actors. Most improvisations require real acting skills.

You should be careful when using games as a rehearsal aid that they do not become an end in themselves as part of a neurotic rehearsal ritual or are used as an avoidance tactic when a clear onward path for your production is eluding you.

In the first few days of rehearsal games are particularly useful for setting the tone of the work or creating an atmosphere of mutual trust and play. As rehearsals continue towards the opening night you should only use games if they are clearly earning their keep. Games that are entertaining and instructive in the first few days quickly lose their charm when competing for real rehearsal time. If you want to deploy or redeploy a game at a late stage in rehearsal, be sure you have a demonstrably good case for doing so.

There are hundreds of different theatre games, indeed whole books have been written on the subject by passionate enthusiasts. In some countries the playing of theatre games has become a popular entertainment in itself, with actors from different theatre companies competing for prizes. Television shows have been created in imitation of this fashion and a special breed of sharp-witted actors has emerged, better at playing theatre games than any other sort of acting.

This entry will not pretend to compete with the experts in the field or attempt a definitive list of games. In any case, many directors will already have their own favourite theatre games and training routines. It will rather serve as a brief outline of where games might be useful in rehearsal and how different games can be applied to solve problems, create opportunities for uninhibited play or explore areas of vocal, physical and mental training.

Games

You should always let actors know in advance if you intend to play theatre games as part of your rehearsal process. Many games are physically challenging, and actors will need to wear rehearsal clothes or workout gear when they play them. If actors are worried about spoiling their clothes or are straining against tightly fitting garments, they won't be playing the games properly.

As you play your games, leave some time between each one for the actors to react to them, what was difficult about them, or surprising or enlightening. These games are only useful if they are properly understood and the skills and lessons learnt from them assimilated by the players.

INTRODUCTION GAMES

These are only really necessary for large groups where the learning of identities and personalities is a problem. They are especially useful for large groups that are working together for short periods of time, in **workshops** for example.

1 Compliments

The actors spread out all over the room. In a period of, say, two minutes they must all introduce themselves to one another by name in very brief one-on-one encounters. Each introduction must include a pair of compliments. The compliments must be particular, and genuine, no actor using the same compliment twice. The combination of putting a name to a face while giving and receiving a compliment makes the name stick in the mind very successfully. An efficient, funny and revealing game.

2 Name Catch

The company stands in a circle. A ball or a beanbag or whatever is thrown from one person to another, but just before each throw, the thrower calls out the name of the receiver. Obviously you start by only throwing to someone whose name you know, but you soon learn all the other names in the process of the game. The game should be played very quickly, without pausing for thought or dithering over whom to throw to. For large groups two or three balls can be used at the same time.

3 Name Painting

The company stands in a circle. Each person in turn speaks his name but in a way that imprints itself on everyone else's memory. Singing, shouting, whispering, large gestures, extravagant accents, and any other histrionics can be deployed, but no two deliveries should look or sound the same. When everyone has finished, the success of the game can be tested. Call out someone's name. The whole company must repeat the name in chorus, but with exactly the same vocal and physical delivery as the name's owner.

WARM-UP GAMES

These are designed to get minds and bodies active before starting on the real work of improvisation or rehearsal.

1 Cat and Mouse

This is the children's party game. The company stands around the room in pairs, with both members of the pair facing the same way, one behind the other. One pair is selected to be the first cat and mouse. The cat runs after the mouse. If he manages to tag him, the roles are instantly reversed, the mouse becoming the cat and the cat the mouse. The mouse can escape from the cat by hiding behind any one of the other pairs standing in the room. As he does so, the person standing at the front of the pair is forced out into the room and becomes the mouse. The cat must now catch this new mouse before he too darts behind a pair releasing yet another new mouse. This game should be played fast and furious until everyone is thoroughly out of breath.

2 What Are You Doing?

Played in pairs. One actor mimes an activity, cleaning his teeth for instance. The other actor asks 'What are you doing?' The mimer replies with a lie while still miming cleaning his teeth. 'Flying a kite,' he might say. The second actor instantly starts to mime flying a kite. The first actor stops cleaning his teeth and asks 'What are you doing?' 'Driving a car,' lies the second actor while still flying his kite, and the first actor starts a car-driving mime. And so on. The game should be played as quickly as possible, with the mimes as accurate and concentrated as they can be.

3 Port Starboard

A simple, brief and exhausting game. The company stands in the centre of the room. The room is a ship. One side is designated the port side, the other the starboard. The captain – and it might be you – shouts out one of four instructions: 'port', 'starboard', 'man the mast' or 'batten the hatches'. The company must instantly obey the captain's command. 'Port' means they all rush to the port side of the ship and 'starboard' the starboard side. 'Man the mast' requires everyone to get off the floor onto furniture, up ladders, onto window ledges or wherever, as long as it's up. 'Batten the hatches' means everyone flings themselves on the floor. The orders should come thick and fast, without any pauses for rest. Once everyone gets the hang of it, the game can be played competitively, the last one to complete each order dropping out. This way the fittest people with the quickest reactions get the most punishing exercise, which is how it should be.

PHYSICAL GAMES

Some actors are more physically in touch with themselves than others, their acting personalities based on a strong sense of their own physicality. These are actors who could just as well have been dancers or gymnasts, indeed they may have been. Other actors can be far less free with their bodies and some may be physically quite locked. These games are suitable for all actors, regardless of their physical prowess, but they can also be used to find a median physical life for a whole company, pulling the less physically aware up to the same level as the fit and agile.

1 Mirrors

The company divides up into pairs of roughly equal heights. Actors in each pair stand facing each other just far enough apart so that outstretched fingertips do not meet when reaching towards each other. One person is the object, the other the mirror. The object actor moves in front of the mirror actor. The mirror must exactly reflect what the object is doing and at exactly the same time. This is a co-operative game, not a competitive one. If the object moves too quickly or too suddenly, the mirror stands no chance of making an accurate reflection. To start with, the two players should maintain eye contact at all times. If the two pairs of eyes stray away from each other it is almost impossible to maintain a peripheral observation of the other actor's whole body. The more physically agile and fit the actors are, the more complex the movement can be, but neither actor should stretch the movement beyond the other's physical capabilities. After a while the actors should change roles, mirror for object and object for mirror. For the exercise to be completely fulfilled it should be difficult for an external observer to tell which actor is the mirror and which the object. As a final variation, the pair should continue the exercise without an allocation of roles, creating two perfect mirror images but with neither actor seeking to initiate the movement. This is not as difficult as it sounds. If played well even the actors will be unable to say which of them is initiating the movement.

2 Group Mirrors

To be played as an extension of Mirrors. Actors form fours, two being the mirror and two the object. Exactly the same rules apply, though obviously far more variations of movement are possible, with actors being able to support or lift one another or get tangled up together in any number of ways. The stress here should be on all four actors maintaining a constant awareness of the shape of both object and image. Again the pairs should change roles after a while and then continue into the 'auto-initiation' version as in Mirrors. Larger groups can then be tried with three or four or more on each side of the mirror. Here it is important that the groups start with very accurately mirrored positions before any movement is initiated one way or the other. As a final exercise the whole company can be divided into two groups, however large, with the object and image covering the whole of the rehearsal room floor. Strangely, the auto-initiation version is often easier the greater the number of actors involved in it. A very good company-forming game.

3 Fun House Mirrors

The rules are the same as for Mirrors, but here the mirror actor must distort the image he is given by the object actor. The object actor makes simple and natural movements, gestures and facial expressions and the mirror actor reflects them back grotesquely. A good exercise for breaking down physical inhibition, but also a study in control. Neither actor must allow the silliness of the images to break their concentration.

4 Machines

One actor goes to the centre of the rehearsal room and starts a repetitive action with an accompanying sound. Whatever position he adopts and however much of his body he uses for the move-ment, he must be able to repeat it in a strict machine-like rhythm for a considerable time. Once he has set up his rhythm, other actors can join him, one at a time fitting their positions, movements and sounds into his. The movement of the first actor must seem to acti-vate the second, but subsequent actors can join onto whatever moving part of the machine they choose as long as the movement they adopt follows the strict rhythm already laid down by the pre-vious actors. The challenge for the actors is to be as adventurous as possible with their choices of physical position, movement and sound while still being able to maintain a repetitive motion without flagging or slowing down. Once everyone has joined in and the machine is running like clockwork, the controller can order varia-tions of speed. Start by slowing the machine down. The challenge here is for the actors to slow down to a crawl, or even grind to a complete halt, without changing their speeds relative to one anoth-er. Or the controller can order the pace of the machine to be cranked up to danger level or beyond to see how many of its component parts can handle the pressure and which of its parts breaks first. A well-oiled machine is a real test of a company's ability to work as a physical unit. It can also turn into a considerable physical workout.

5 Custom-Built Machines

The rules are exactly as they are for Machines, but here you start with an agreed title for the machine and the actors must all adapt their contributions to take account of it. You can make imaginative versions of machines that might exist in real life – for cake-baking or sausage-stuffing or wood-carving or whatever. Or you can make more institutional, metaphorical or emotional machines – a hospital machine or a war machine or a happiness machine – or an unhappiness machine. Let the actors throw out suggestions and make the machines as an instant response. With Custom-Built Machines the actors' imaginations and sense of fun are being exercised as much as their bodies.

6 Personal Machines

The same rules apply as for other machines but here the title must be the name of some person or group of people known to the whole company of actors. Current politicians, pop groups or other celebrities make for good material here. With Personal Machines the sounds that accompany the actions can include snatches of words or phrases associated with the subject as long as they can be uttered within the strict rhythm of the machine. Actors can also make machines for one another. A member of the company can be chosen at random and a machine created of all his mannerisms, movements, customary phrases and attitudes. He can then watch himself being personified in machine form. This can be a very entertaining exercise, but you will need to have plenty of time for it if everyone is to have a go, especially if you're playing it with youngsters who'll be disappointed if they get left out. If you start playing this game, you must also be ready to watch a Director Machine, potentially a painful experience.

Games

7 *Slow-Motion Wrestling*

Actors get into pairs and wrestle each other in slow motion. This is an exercise in balance and physical co-operation and trust. The actors must exactly co-ordinate the speed of their slow motion and be as adventurous as they can be in the positions they adopt without ever falling, or breaking the tension between them, or losing control of the action. Every part of the body and face must sustain the slow-motion exercise, from the tips of the toes to the end of the nose. The controller should cruise the room, quietly pointing out where couples are infringing the rules, moving too fast or out of synchronicity. He can also give general instructions to all pairs at once to slow down the motion or speed it up by very careful degrees. The slower the motion the harder the exercise. After a while the actors should change partners, not always choosing partners of equal weight and size. The greater the disparity of weight and size, the more physical empathy there needs to be from both partners. Like the Mirrors exercise, Slow-Motion Wrestling can slowly be developed into threes and fours and larger groups until you have a whole company of actors wrestling with itself in perfect balance.

8 *Happy Knees*

A silly but effective game. Without referring to each other, the actors write down twenty or thirty different body parts on individual slips of paper and put them all in a hat, say two or three slips per actor. They then write down twenty or thirty different adjectives and put them into a different hat. There must be a lot more slips of paper than actors. One of the actors draws two slips of paper, one from each hat, and must silently play the resulting combination of body part and adjective. He mustn't act out the adjective in his face while moving the body part, he must animate the body part with the feeling suggested by the adjective, hence the title of the game. The other actors must guess the body part and the adjective solely from the way the actor uses the body part in question. It's harder than it sounds and requires a great deal of imagination, physical invention and energy. Imagine trying to communicate proud ears, or neurotic shoulders or a tragic pelvis. You get the idea.

MIMING GAMES

Mime is an important part of the actor's art. Miming games are a good way of sharpening up your actors' mimetic skills and at the same time stimulating their imaginations.

1 Creating an Object

The actors sit or stand in a circle. One actor starts by creating a mimed object. He must make it clear what it is by the way he handles or uses it. Once he has clearly demonstrated the object's shape, size, weight and use he carefully passes it to the person next to him. That person receives the object and starts by using it in exactly the same way as the originator has used it. He must then change it into something else, not suddenly and capriciously, but using the movement and shape and weight of what he has started with he must slowly metamorphose the object into something new. When he has successfully demonstrated the new object he carefully passes it on to the next actor and so on until the changing object has gone full circle around the company. No actor should devise in advance what he will change the object into. Rather he must wait to be surprised by what he receives and even surprise himself by what he changes it into. The rest of the company must remain constantly attentive. It is for them to judge the success or otherwise of the mimes they are witnessing. The mimer must feel their attention and sense when he has successfully communicated his mime before passing the object on.

2 Discovering an Object

Place an everyday object in the centre of the room, a chair or a blanket or a sheet of paper, anything at all. In turn the actors must approach the object, seeking to understand what its use might be, as if they were from another planet, one without chairs, or blankets or sheets of paper. This is an exercise in invention but also in the inventive use of mime. How do you wear a chair, for instance, or keep warm under a sheet of paper or get a musical note out of a blanket? The last person to approach the object can discover its real, everyday use, much to the enlightenment of everyone else.

3 Changing an Object

This game is played in pairs or small groups. Each pair is given a real object and must change it, by agreement, into a variety of other things, creating an imaginative scenario as they make their changes. But this is a mime game, so no dialogue is allowed, or even homemade sound effects. Thus a chair could start life as a chair but soon become a telephone, an elevator, a speeding car or a bomb as the actors' story unfolds around it. Whatever else the actors invent, the concentration must remain on the object, giving the object new life, and a new personality as the story develops.

LISTENING GAMES

Listening is a crucial skill for an actor. An actor who cannot listen, to the atmosphere around him and to the constantly changing inflections of the other characters on stage with him, will never be able to adapt his performance to suit his environment. Listening games are designed to give companies of actors a collective awareness of the sounds all around them and an ability to be completely absorbed in their characters without making themselves deaf to external influence.

1 Double Stories

Played in pairs. The actors sit on the floor facing each other. They have one minute to tell each other exactly what they have done so far that day, from waking up onwards. They must speak clearly, continuously and simultaneously. This is an exercise in thinking and listening at the same time. There mustn't be little gaps for thought in which the actors can hear each other speaking on their own. The controller should have his eye on the clock and signal when the minute is up. At this point the actors take it in turns to recount to each other all that they have understood from each other's stories, in as much detail as possible. If they have heard and understood everything then the retelling should take roughly a minute, but first attempts at this game are often wildly inaccurate and the retelling sketchy and brief. Change partners and try the game again, but in a more challenging way. Both actors must tell a story of their own devising, a fairy story or an adventure story or whatever. The rules are the same as before, both partners speaking and listening simultaneously, but this time the actors should use actions and characterisations for their stories. The characters should be vividly represented, both physically and vocally, and the action mimed as accurately as possible. The actors should have the freedom to range around the room, but each pair must be careful to remain close enough to each other to appreciate every detail of the stories being told. Once the minute is up, they must retell the stories but with every detail of plot, character and action in place, following the same route around the room that the original stories took. The challenge for both actors in this game is to be able to reproduce the other actor's story in every detail and to make their own stories so generously vivid that they are all the easier for a partner to retell.

2 Radar

Played in pairs, blindfolded. Each pair of actors agrees on a sound that can be continually repeated and that is easily recognisable to both players. The blindfolded players then disperse themselves all over the room, the controller making sure that every pair is properly split up. On a signal from the controller the pairs must reunite, using their agreed sounds as radar. The greater the number of players, the louder the cacophony and the harder the game. Once a pair has reunited, the players can remove their blindfolds and watch the efforts of the remaining pairs. As pairs find one another, the noise reduces and the game becomes easier. A variation of Radar is Jamming Radar, which is much more difficult. In Jamming Radar, when a pair has reunited, the players remove their blindfolds and jam the radar of the other pairs by imitating their sounds. There must be no physical contact – the interference must be purely sonic. Here the challenge for the pairs is to invent a truly inimitable sound. The challenge for the jammers is to imitate the sounds so accurately that the remaining pairs are thoroughly confused. As the game develops, the jammers start to outnumber the pairs, making reunion almost impossible. The controller may have to intervene if unnecessary pain is being inflicted.

3 Playback

A group of actors sits and listens for exactly a minute. Even in a quiet rehearsal room there are many sounds to be heard inside and outside the room – traffic, birds and animals, aeroplanes, clocks, creaks and coughs. After a minute the group must discuss what they have heard and then reproduce the sounds in a synchronised playback lasting exactly a minute.

4 Mirror Words

This is just like the physical Mirrors game but with words instead of actions. Pairs of actors stand facing each other. One of them speaks, slowly and distinctly, while the other mirrors the words as accurately as he can, in pitch, inflection and dialect. As with Mirrors, the partners then change roles, the mirror becoming the speaker and vice versa. Finally the pair speaks simultaneously with neither partner seeking to initiate the words. The resulting sentences are often surprisingly sensible, even when both partners are completely unaware of where the words might be leading them.

5 To Be or Not to Be

The company stands in a circle. One actor starts with the word 'To'. The next actor has 'be' and the next 'or' and so on until the whole line is completed with the word 'question' – at which point the next actor starts with 'To' again, the line being repeated over and over again around and around the circle. Make sure there aren't exactly ten, twenty or thirty actors in the circle or actors will get the same word every time the line comes round to them. The challenge here is for the actors to sound collectively like a single actor. As the word moves around the circle, each actor must listen to the tone of the line as it approaches him and make his contribution fit in without breaking the rhythm, the inflection or the pitch. As the game continues, emotional tones can be added to the line so that it slowly changes through different feelings and attitudes, but no one actor should be wilfully affecting the way the line develops. This is an exercise in collective listening and mutual sensitivity. The game can be varied to include different and longer texts, perhaps bits of text from the play you are working on.

THINKING GAMES

The mind needs exercise just like the body and the voice. These are games to wake everyone up, to get the brain cells humming in tune with the rest of the body. There are hundreds of games such as these.

1 Fizz Buzz

Players sit or stand in a circle. In a strict rhythm they go round the circle counting from 1 upwards, one number at a time, one person at a time. In the simplest form of this game any number with a three in it or that is divisible by three is substituted with the word 'fizz'. Thus the counting round the circle goes: 'one two fizz four five fizz seven eight fizz ten eleven fizz fizz fourteen', and so on. Once this has been mastered you add the word 'buzz' for numbers containing five and multiples of five, but you keep 'fizz' for the threes as well. Thus: 'one two fizz four buzz fizz seven eight fizz buzz eleven fizz fizz fourteen fizz-buzz sixteen seventeen', and so on. All numbers divisible by both three and five are substituted by 'fizz-buzz'. You can further complicate the game by adding the word 'ding' for sevens and multiples of seven. Thus: 'one two fizz four buzz fizz ding eight', and so on, with twenty-one becoming 'fizz-ding', thirty-five 'buzz-ding' and 105, if you get that far, 'fizz-buzz-ding'. If you need a further complication, and you'd be surprised how quickly even the maths dummies catch on to this game, you can change the direction of the counting round the circle whenever you reach a double multiple, a 'fizz-buzz' or a 'buzz-ding' or whatever. At advanced nerd level you can also add the word 'crash' for prime numbers. Thus: 'one crash fizz-crash four buzz-crash fizz ding-crash eight fizz buzz crash fizz fizz-crash' and so on all the way up to a climactic 'fizz-buzz-ding-crash' at the number 1,753, but this will definitely constitute cruel and unusual punishment for most members of the acting profession.

2 *This is a What?*

The players sit in a circle. One person starts by passing an object to the person sitting next to him, left or right doesn't matter as long as the object continues in the same direction on either side. As the starter passes the object he falsely identifies it. Thus if he passes a pencil, he can say anything but 'This is a pencil.' Let's suppose he says 'This is a crow.' The person next to him takes the pencil but then passes it back to the starter saying 'This is a what?' The starter takes the pencil back and re-presents it to the second player, repeating 'This is a crow.' On the second presentation the neighbour understands what he has been passed and takes the pencil, saying 'Thank you' as he does so. He then passes it to his next neighbour, the third player, saying 'This is a crow.' The third player passes it back, saying 'This is a what?' By now the second player must feign to forget what the object is called and must pass it back to the starter, repeating 'This is a what?' as he does so. The starter passes the object again, saying 'This is a crow.' The second player receives it without comment and passes it to the third player, repeating 'This is a crow'. The third player, receiving the object for the second time, now understands what it is called and says 'Thank you'. He then passes it to the fourth player, saying 'This is a crow,' but the fourth player returns it with 'This is a what?', and it then returns all the way back to the starter, each player feigning to forget the name of the object with a 'This is a what?' to their neighbour. Players only say 'Thank you' when receiving the object for the second time but not on subsequent occasions. When the object makes its return journey they must have forgotten its identity on every occasion. Only the starter can correctly identify the object every time it returns to him. When the object has gone all round the circle and is presented to the starter for the first time from the opposite direction with the words 'This is a crow,' he receives it with the words 'I know,' and the game ends. This is a game far more complicated to explain than it is to play, and once understood the players can pick it up and play well and quickly. So quickly, in fact, that further complication will be needed to make the game more taxing. You do this by having more than one object going round the circle at the same time, each originating at a different part of the circle and using both directions, forcing players to deal with objects coming at them from two different directions at the same time. Thus you could have a pencil and a ball going round the circle one way as a 'crow' and a 'banana' while a coin and a pen go the other way as a 'shoe' and a 'buffalo'. You can confuse things further by calling the objects by each other's names: the pencil could be called a 'ball', for instance, or the pen a 'pencil'. Or all the made-up identities could rhyme, as in a 'crow', a 'toe', a 'bow' and a 'throw', or, worse still, rhyme with 'what'. The challenge of the game is for the players to hold a number of conflicting images in their heads at the same time while obeying a strictly imposed set of repetitive rules. Just like acting.

WORD GAMES

Actors must use words skilfully and confidently and will be well acquainted with all manner of technical **voice and text** exercises and **tongue twisters**. But they must also be able to think quickly around the words they use, to make connections of meaning and rhythm within the text allotted to them, and to find unexpected and exciting interpretations of their text in the very moment of speaking it. These games are devised to bring a dose of verbal wit to sleepy minds.

1 One-Word Stories

The company sits or stands in a circle and tells a story one word at a time, one person at a time. As the story moves around the circle

Games

each player has the opportunity to take it in whatever direction he chooses but without infringing the basic rules of grammar. The game should be played quickly and smoothly and without pauses for thought, as if a single person was confidently telling the story on his own. The players must work collaboratively and not always try to best one another with surprise twists and turns of grammar and vocabulary, the ifs, ands and buts being just as important to the story as the active verbs and nouns. A mistake beginners often make is not being able to let a sentence come to a conclusion, endlessly extending it with ands, buts and sos. Short sentences should be strongly encouraged to stop the story getting bogged down in grammatical errors and misunderstandings. The secret of this game is for each player to leave his choice of a word to the last possible moment. Words prepared two or three people in advance are often inappropriate once the story actually arrives at the player.

2 One-Syllable Stories

This is much harder. The rules are the same as for One-Word Stories but each player is only allowed a single syllable before the story passes on. Thus a player can change the direction of the story with his word but also from within a multi-syllable word.

3 Punchline Stories

A nice variation of both the above games is to give the players a destination sentence or punchline for their story. It could be anything: '. . .and that was how Jenny finally found her mother,' for instance, or '. . .which is why I never, ever, go skating.' Let the players invent punchlines of their own and then work their stories towards them.

4 Cut and Paste

This is an excellent game for teaching young actors about the structure of language and the choices they have in the way they use their words. Divide the company into groups of seven, eight or more players – the more players in each group, the harder the game. Write a sentence on a sheet of paper and then cut it up into its component words, one sentence for each group, the number of words in each sentence being the same as the number of people in the group that receives it. Each group gets its sentence in fragmented form, one word for each player, and must then reassemble the sentence in its original form. Once the words have been understood and memorised by each player the fragments of paper are given back to the controller. Thus the words have to be put into the right order by arranging the members of the group rather than the fragments of paper. Once the group has organised itself into the correct sentence order, it must speak its sentence one word at a time, one person at a time, but sounding as much like a single speaker as it can. You can make the game harder by introducing more and more complicated sentences to larger and larger groups. To make it even more difficult you can also play Cut and Paste with syllables rather than complete words. You can also use short poems, the rhymes helping the players to figure out the structure of the verse. Limericks give very good value in this game, but if you want to stretch the players to their limits, use an extract from Shakespeare or one of his contemporaries where the **heightened language** is much harder to work out.

TOUCHING GAMES

Some actors are physically buttoned up, happier to act with their heads and hearts than with their bodies. Actors can also be shy, uncomfortable with touching and being touched. These games are designed to break down physical barriers between actors and get them to use their own bodies more freely and creatively.

1 *Finding Hands*

The players are all blindfolded and the controller arranges them into a circle facing inwards and holding hands. The game is played in total silence. No player should know the identity of the two people either side of him until the end of the game. The players start by thoroughly examining the hands on either side of them, using touch alone. Once they are sure they can recognise the hands again, the controller splits up the players, leading them all around the room until they are thoroughly disoriented. The challenge for the players is to remake the circle exactly as it was by reuniting with the hands on either side of them. With a large group this can take quite some time. If a mistake is made, with two players holding onto the wrong hands, it must be unmade by another player insisting, by touch alone, that he has a better claim to the hand in question. The game slowly works itself out, starting with short chains of people certain of the hands they are holding, then those chains uniting with other chains until the circle is complete. The controller might have to intervene if there is a complete stalemate, with players doggedly holding onto the wrong hands while other players are left out of the circle. In this case the game should be stopped, the errors identified and the game replayed with a different circle.

2 *Finding Faces*

Similar to Finding Hands, this game can be played in pairs with the controller splitting up the pairs all over the room and the pairs having to reunite, or it can be played in a big circle, just like Finding Hands. The players must keep their eyes shut rather than be blindfolded, otherwise the faces cannot be properly explored by touch.

3 *Finding Bodies*

Easier than the previous two games because players can use the entire body, face, hands and everything else, to find their partners or their places in the circle. The chronically shy get a bit hysterical playing this game, but it's good for them.

4 *Statues*

Played in pairs. Players take it in turns to sculpt one another into different shapes and attitudes, the sculpted player yielding to the pressure of the sculptor's hands and holding steady in whatever position he is put. The game can also be played with one sculptor and two or more sculptees, forming groups of sculpted figures linked together in a single structure. Or two or three sculptors can work together on an enormous structure of interrelated figures using the whole company. A variation of this game has the sculptor working on his sculpture without any physical contact, the sculpted player having to react to the flow of the sculptor's hands as they move close to his body, his physical shape moulded by the sculptor's intentions alone.

TRUST GAMES

Trust games are the natural follow-on to Touching Games, and are designed to help create an atmosphere of mutual trust in a company, especially when the work requires a high level of physical interdependence from the actors. By creating the necessity for physical trust, they can also help to create the basis for mental and emotional trust.

1 Falling

The company splits into pairs, actors of roughly equal height and weight. One actor is the faller, the other the catcher. The faller stands rigidly upright, feet together, eyes closed. The catcher stands behind him, feet broadly braced one in front of the other. To begin gently, the catcher holds his hands no more than a few inches behind the faller's back. On a quiet instruction to fall, the faller lets himself fall backwards onto the catcher's hands, keeping his body rigidly flexed as he does so. The catcher then gently puts the faller back into an upright position. After a few tries at this, the catcher moves a little further back so that the faller has further to fall before he is caught. The further the catcher moves back the more he must brace himself to take the full weight of the faller. A slip at this point will obviously destroy the whole point of the exercise. With sufficient support from the catcher and absolute trust from the faller, the faller can almost reach the ground before being caught. Once the faller has managed a good long fall, catcher and faller should change places to see what trust exists the other way round. Some actors take very easily to this exercise. Others find it far harder. Some people are much more physically trusting than others, but the others usually take great delight in learning to

Games

overcome their fear. Large people and old people have to be taken special care of. As a general rule, the heavier or frailer someone is the more they will be hurt by a fall and so the more fearful they will be about falling. In these cases, you should deploy two catchers for one faller.

2 Falling and Carrying

A small group of at least four catching actors stands in a tight circle, feet braced, hands flexed in front of them, the size of the group depending on the size and weight of the faller. The heavier the faller the more catchers will be needed to catch and carry him. The falling actor stands in the middle of the circle, feet together, body rigid, eyes closed. To start with, the hands of the catching actors should be very close to the faller's body. One of the catchers gives the faller a little push to get him going; it doesn't matter in which direction. As he falls onto the hands around him, the catchers push him back just past his upright position so that he falls in a continuously irregular motion against the catching hands. As the faller learns to trust the catchers, they slowly move further away from him so that his falls become progressively steeper and steeper in every direction. Once he has completely yielded to his catchers, they can pick him up and float him around the room, gently raising and lowering him as they go. For the faller this can be a really delightful experience, well worth trusting his catcher colleagues for.

3 Falling from a Height

This is the ultimate trust game. A faller stands on a raised level, table height to start with but from greater heights when the exercise becomes familiar. Six or eight catchers stand below him facing one another in two lines, their arms firmly interlocking. The faller closes his eyes and on a command from one of the catchers he falls forward and downwards into their arms. Like skydiving but with people as your parachute, or rather, your haystack. Some players will find this game quite impossible, but most will be able to do it with a little encouragement and carefully graduated steps.

4 *Guiding the Blind*

The company divides into pairs. One member of each pair is blind-folded, the other sighted. The game starts with the blind player being gently guided around the room by his sighted partner, who helps him avoid obstacles and tells him where he can sit or lean or lie. As the game develops, the guide walks with his blind partner but without touching him, using his voice alone to help him navi-gate around the room and achieve simple tasks. However many couples there are playing the game, the blind partners must be able to recognise their guides by their voices alone, even when separat-ed by some distance from one another. Once a good trusting bond has developed between all the partners, they change roles and the game is repeated but in the same pairs. As players get used to trust-ing their guides, they can get more adventurous with their move-ments. As a finale to this game, try blindfold running. The blind partner stands at one end of the room and on a command from his guide, he runs across the room towards his guide until told to stop. To start with, the blind runners will tend to grind to a halt halfway down the room, but with increasing trust in their guides they will be able to manage the whole run without stopping. This can be a very exhilarating game.

TRUTH GAMES

Be very careful how you use these. They are only suitable for actors interested in learning about one another's strengths and weakness-es and happy to explore their relationships with one another. They can also be valuable exercises for young actors learning their craft, understanding how to separate their basic personalities from their conditioning and their egos.

Truth games are at their most unpleasant in the hands of an ego-tistical director intent on exploiting his control over a company of actors at the expense of their feelings and sympathies for one another. If you are not certain of your motive for using these games and ready to handle any personal upsets that might occur in their wake, you had better leave them alone.

Games

1 *Categories*

This is an easy game to play and is excellent for large companies of
actors that are getting to know one another in workshops or drama
classes. The controller asks the group to arrange itself into a series
of categories. Start with height, for instance. The tallest actor
stands at one end of the room and the shortest at the other with
everyone else in height order between them. If there isn't a long
room for a straight line, bend it into a circle with the controller
standing at twelve o'clock, the tallest person at one and the shortest at eleven. Once the line has been organised, ask the players if
there are any surprises. Did they think someone was taller or shorter than they actually are in reality? Now go on to weight. Who is
the heaviest actor and who the lightest? Some honesty may be
called for here. And then age. Here is where you will encounter
your first surprises, not just because some people are older or
younger than they seem, but because they think of themselves as
older or younger and are surprised to find themselves nearer one or
other end of the line than they imagined they would be. You can
think up your own categories as you go along, but depending on
the make-up of the group you might include intelligence, wit, affluence, class (a very interesting one for UK players), beauty, sexual
attractiveness and so on. Of course, the ordering within some of
the categories will prove extremely subjective and subject to various forms of double-think. Some players will be ignorant as to their
beauty or sexual allure, others will be over-proud of it, and still
more will be unable to assess it with any honesty. No one likes to
be thought vain, though come to think of it vanity would make
another good category. In these cases individual players may find it
hard to put themselves into their correct place in the line and their
colleagues will have to insist where they are to go against their
wishes or natural inclination. But this is where the game gets interesting, with the group exerting its influence over individual egos
and prejudices. Repeat the game with however many categories
you want to explore. Actors may be self-involved creatures, but
they are also keen observers of the social structures around them
and how they fit into them. Every category will have its surprises.

2 Stolen Identity

One member of the company secretly assumes the identity of another. He is then put in the **hot seat** and the company fires questions at him, which he must answer truthfully to the best of his knowledge. If he doesn't know the answer to a question he can say so. The questioning continues until the company finds out who he is being. This game is revealing in a number of ways. It reveals the prejudices of the thief towards the personality of his assumed identity, it reveals the prejudices inherent in the interrogators' questions, and it reveals information about the subject that may not be common knowledge and may indeed be a secret, even to the subject.

3 Thinking the Truth

This is a game for groups of actors that really want to get to know one another and their feelings about one another on a deeper level than they have been able to achieve in the normal run of **rehearsal** or **workshop**. It is also a good game for groups that have grown close but have developed some dysfunction in the process, through personal animosity, boredom or social complacency, a psychotherapeutic exercise for companies that have forgotten how to talk amongst themselves. Perfect for second- or third-year drama students. The company splits up into pairs, randomly chosen. The members of each pair look into each other's eyes and respond to the controller's questions. They must express nothing with their faces. They must only consider the questions as they are asked. The controller can ask any questions he wishes, in whatever order he wishes, pausing for ten or fifteen seconds after each question for the pairs to consider their silent answers. He might ask 'Do you think the person you are looking at is attractive?' 'Do you think they are more or less intelligent than you?' 'Are they talented?' 'More than you?' 'Do you think the person you are looking at is lucky?' The controller can turn the questions around by asking, 'Do you think the person you are looking at finds you attractive?' 'Do they think themselves superior to you?' 'In talent?' 'In physical prowess?' 'In intelligence?' And so on. After ten or twelve questions, change the pairs around so that everyone has a different partner and repeat the process. Some of the questions will bear exact repetition, but controllers should avoid a predictable cate-chism. Anticipated questions are far more easily ducked than unex-pected ones. To this end, it is a good idea for the control to circulate through the company as the game is played. If there is an odd number of players, the odd-man-out can become the new con-troller for each round, if an even number then you can have two new controllers each round, asking questions in turn. The beauty of this game is that everything is thought but nothing said. Much is learnt but nothing recorded. Players can read, or think they read, the truth in their fellow players' thoughts, but in the process they can learn, if they are open to learn, just as much about their own feelings and prejudices towards others. A quietly explosive and self-revealing game.

4 *Life Plays*

This is a fascinating game. Divide the company up into small groups of, say, four to six players. Each group chooses one of its players to be the subject of a life play. That player recounts an important event from his or her life, an event with a strong emo-tional, even confessional, content, something that may be difficult to recall with equanimity but which the player is prepared to explore. Each group must then devise a short dramatisation of the event in whatever style they like. Dialogue, if included, should be kept to a minimum. Groups can waste a lot of time trying to script an accurate account of the subject player's memory and get bogged down in writing and memorising the lines. The plays should have a performance time limit, say of two minutes. The players whose experiences are the subject of the plays should help to direct them and may act in them but not playing the role of themselves. There should also be a time limit for the rehearsal of the finished plays. After a set period, say twenty minutes or half an hour, the con-troller should warn the groups that they have five minutes of rehearsal left. After the five minutes is up, all the groups should do a simultaneous dress rehearsal, then the plays should be performed, one at a time, for the whole company. After each play the subject player should talk briefly about the real event behind the drama and the rest of the company can then discuss the event and its dramatisation for a few minutes before going on to the next group's performance. Once all the groups have performed and discussed, split the company into new groups each with a new subject-player. For the game to have meaning, every member of the company must have his or her turn. This makes for quite a time-consuming process, so you may have to give up a whole morning or afternoon to it, or split it up over a number of days. However you do it, this game has real company-binding power. If played seriously and carefully, it can also have a strong emotional effect on the subject-players, an effect that may be therapeutic but can also be upsetting. The whole company should be ready to supply after-care if necessary.

ACTING GAMES

These games all require some acting skill and are useful preparatory exercises for real improvisation work. Indeed, when played well, they can easily develop, or be developed, into improvisations. They all require some measure of spontaneous textual invention. But here one should add a warning. These games can easily be hijacked by the witty wordsmiths. Acting games should be played with lightness of touch, swift changes of direction and minimal dialogue.

1 Parallel Lives

Played in pairs. The controller gives a different situation to each player, but neither player is told the other's situation. They then play a scene both assuming that the other is a character within the reality they have been given. Thus both players might be sitting on a bench, one waiting for a bus and the other waiting for the arrival of his first child. The players must converse but must maintain the reality of their own situation without breaking their partner's reality. The rest of the company watches and tries to guess what the situations are. You can play the game with a time limit – say a minute – or until one of the players has guessed the other's situation. But played competitively the game takes on a distinctly different quality, with each player trying to manipulate the conversation so that his partner gives away his secret situation. It is more interesting to play the game collaboratively, but in that case a lot depends on the quality of the set-up. Controllers can influence the way the game is played by the specificity of their instructions. The players might both be told they are strangers to one another, or player one might be told he is a stranger to player two and player two be told he is player one's father. Or both could be told they are father to each other. The permutations are infinite. The challenge of the game is for both players to maintain their own realities when a conflicting reality is being played in close proximity.

2 Changing the Plot

The controller puts one player into a situation. The player plays the situation while the rest of the company watches for an opportunity to join in. As each player joins, he must bring a new situation with him, but based on some evidence he has picked up from the previous situation. As the situation changes, players already in the scene must immediately adapt to the change, either modifying the character they are already playing or making a complete change to a different one. So, the first player might be waiting for a bus. He keeps glancing at his watch. The second player joins, limping, and asks the first player how he injured his wrist, changing the situation to a doctor's waiting room. A third player joins and changes the situation to a football dressing room after a hard-fought match. A fourth turns the scene into a battlefield. And so on. The progression can be as logical or illogical as the players wish, but each change must be based on some evidence of action or word in the previous situation. The challenge here is to be inventive, collaborative and flexible, able to concentrate immediately and unquestioningly on a series of constantly changing realities.

3 Borrowed Arms

Played in pairs or fours (double pairs) or larger groups of pairs. In each pair one player stands behind the other. The front player folds his arms behind his back. The back player interlocks his arms as far as he can reach under the front player's armpits. Thus they form a single person, the back player providing the arms and the front player providing everything else, including the voice. The only shared, or amalgamated organ is the brain. As the front player speaks, the back player must accommodate his gestures to suit the words and vice versa, the back player's gestures having to be incorporated into the front player's words. Played in its simplest form, the front player makes a speech on any subject whatsoever, perhaps one suggested by the rest of the company, and both players strive to fit the arms to the words and the words to the arms. There is some element of competitiveness in each pair as the front and back players try to catch each other out with word or gesture, but this is essentially a collaborative game with both players trying to make physical and verbal sense of the speech as it develops. Once everyone has had a go, swap partners and develop the game into its double pairs version, with one pair of players holding another pair in conversation. This is where the game gets interesting and the competitiveness between the partners largely disappears. Some structure may be useful in the selection of situations. The controller could propose the same situation for all the double pairs. Start with something simple – 'The Job Interview' for instance, or 'In the Confessional' – whatever simple one-on-one situation takes your fancy. This would seem at first to be an essentially comedic game, but it need not be so. Once the players have got over the inherent silliness of talking with someone else's arms, it can become a very interesting acting exercise, but it must be played with sensitivity and generosity. Front players should avoid cheap deflation lines like 'Why are you making those funny movements with your fingers?' or 'What's the matter with your arms?' and back players should be careful not to be over-busy with their movements. Great subtlety can be achieved with thoughtful dialogue and sympathetic gestures. Played at its best, an external observer should start to believe that each pair is a single character, thinking and gesturing with a complete unity of purpose. Once players get really good at it, the situations need not be proposed in advance but can grow out of the gestures, or changes as the gestures and the dialogue change.

You can also play the game with larger groups of pairs – with everyone at a cocktail party or a funeral or wherever.

4 Obsessions

Played in pairs or groups. You give all the players in the game the same situation to play, but you give each individual player a private obsession unknown to the other players, together with a symptom of his obsession. When his obsession is triggered off, he must exhibit his symptom. The object of the game is for each player to conceal his own obsession while trying to discover what the other players' obsessions are. When a player's obsession is discovered he drops out of the game. The last player to drop out is the winner. Let's say there are four players. They are sitting in a bar. Player 1 is obsessed with Player 3's hair. Whenever Player 3, or anyone else, touches it he must look up, take a deep breath and say 'Rapture'. Player 2 is obsessed with the word 'drink'. Whenever the word is mentioned he must sneeze. Player 3 is obsessed with having a baby. Whenever babies are mentioned he starts to cry. Player 4 is obsessed with money. Whenever money or anything to do with it is mentioned he must say 'garage' very quietly. The game can be played with great subtlety, the obsessions quite serious and the symptoms very hard to detect, or it can be played wildly, with mad, nonsensical obsessions and ludicrous symptoms. Either way, the players must be faithful to the situation they are given, consistent with their obsessions, imaginative with their dialogue and constantly observant of the other players' behaviour.

Gauze

From the Persian word for silk via the Spanish word *gasa*, gauze is now usually made of cotton and is used in the theatre for making transparent scenic cloths, now more commonly called **scrims**.

General Manager/Director

In the subsidised sector of theatre and in opera, the most senior **administrator** of a permanent company is often called the General Manager or General Director. He may also be the chief executive of the company, directly responsible to the board, or he may be a board appointment serving an executive **Artistic Director**.

Gesamtkunstwerk

This is Wagner's idea of the 'total work of art', more simply described by the term **music drama**, a synthesis of music, theatre, dance and allied visual arts, melding together to provide a uniquely satisfying art form where the parts are all subservient to the whole. The idea seems a little pretentious now but it had the effect, during Wagner's lifetime, of persuading the disparate creators involved in the making of **opera** to become more aware of one another's contributions.

At Bayreuth he built an orchestra pit below the level of the stage, making it invisible to the audience, and insisted for the first time on the auditorium lights being extinguished during the performance. In everything he did he tried to place the drama on an equal footing with the music, thus pulling opera away from its moribund tradition of an animated concert performed in front of painted cloths.

Get-Ins and Get-Outs

The 'get-in' (or 'load-in' in America) is the process of moving the technical elements of a production into the theatre, whether for a single run or for a series of touring performances. The 'get-out' is the same process in reverse.

In most theatres, the get-in will start right on the heels of the previous show's 'get-out' in an attempt to get to the next paying audience as quickly as possible.

Get-Ins and Get-Outs

The assessment of how long a get-in is likely to take is an important aspect of the Technical Director's job, and if miscalculated, a subsequent delay can have a serious knock-on effect in all departments and may delay the start of the **technical rehearsals**. In **musical theatre** especially, the get-in must be planned like a military operation to make sure that all the elements of a production get put into the theatre in an order that is mutually agreeable to every department.

If you are present at a **production meeting** where the get-in schedule is being discussed and you have a say in the matter, always advise that a realistic amount of time be allotted for the get-in, as you will be the one to suffer if the technical rehearsal gets squeezed by an overrun.

Gobos

A gobo is a perforated steel plate placed between the lens and the lamp of a **lighting** instrument in order to project a pattern of light onto the stage. The term may be derived from a contraction of the words 'Go Between' or stand for 'Goes Before Optics'. No one seems to know.

Gobos are extensively used in **lighting design**, most commonly to suggest the way natural light breaks up as it passes through permeable structures. Thus sun or moonlight streaming through leaf shapes or bare branch shapes creates the impression of trees in summer or winter. Various types of window shape suggest rooms or buildings of particular architectural form. Barred light is a prison cell, slatted light a shuttered window, and so on. The 'break-up' of light can also be used in a more atmospheric than figurative way and, mixed with various colours, can create purely decorative patterns on the floor and walls of a set.

Don't be deceived by gobos. They sometimes do less for you than you might think. They are particularly limited as storytelling devices. A little patch of patterned light on the floor may be obvious to you but entirely overlooked by an audience. Gobo light needs to be quite intense to have any real effect and is at its most effective when strongly focused on the actors rather than just the scenery. Audiences watch actors' faces more than anything else on the stage. If gobo light has no discernible effect on the actors' faces, you might question the point of it.

Gobo light patterning has become something of a cliché, and there are designers and Lighting Designers who have come to despise it, especially the leaf and window shapes that have become universal signifiers for romantic wood and domestic interior, warm yellow light for sun and cool steel blue for moon. No moonlight in nature was ever as strong as stage moonlight. Such designers prefer to look for pure design solutions to storytelling problems and will only use broken light in an abstract form.

God-Mike

A god-mike is a microphone used by a director or choreographer in **technical rehearsals,** so called not because directors and choreographers are gods but because the mike makes them sound so. Useful.

The Gods

Theatrical slang for the uppermost **balcony** in the auditorium, so called because of its lofty position rather than for any dignity it confers on its occupants, though seasoned theatre professionals will know that the cruellest judgements are often made from those Olympian heights.

Going Up

In Britain the show 'goes up' when the performance begins on stage, and ends when it 'comes down', the expression referring to the rise and fall of the stage curtain.

In America an actor 'goes up' when he forgets his lines, the equivalent of **drying** in Britain.

The Grand Circle

In a multi-tiered **auditorium**, Theatre Managers use words like 'grand' and 'royal' to describe the various tiers of a theatre in order to make people feel good about paying a lot of money for what may be quite poor seats. This is fundamentally an appeal to the audience's snobbery. People who would never consider buying tickets for the balcony would happily agree to sit in the grand or the royal circles, where they could imagine they were surrounded by lots of other grand and royal people.

Grand Guignol

The Grand Guignol Theatre opened in Paris in 1897. It started out as a theatre specialising in intensely naturalistic plays depicting the lives of the Parisian underworld, the sort of people whose lives were ignored by the mainstream drama. Within twenty years it had degenerated into a house of horror drama, recreating in grim detail the most violent examples of human cruelty. Its closing, for lack of public support, in 1962 was salutary. The last Artistic Director, Charles Nonon, declared 'We could never equal Buchenwald. Before the war, our audience thought what was happening on stage was impossible. Now they know these things, and worse, are real.'

The term is now used to describe any theatrical performance that indulges in over-the-top violence, gratuitous horror or excessive bloodletting.

Green Room

The Green Room is the actors' common room, usually placed conveniently near the stage for communal use during performances.

Nobody really knows how the Green Room got its name, though there are dozens of more or less equally spurious-sounding explanations. The most likely of them proposes that the Green Room housed the potted plants and shrubs used to adorn the stages and auditoria of open-air theatres during performances. The room would thus be empty while the play was in progress and so available as a resting and waiting room for the actors between their appearances on stage. Hmm . . . maybe.

H

Hair and Make-Up

When your actors assemble for a first day of rehearsal you may be a little surprised by the appearance of some of them. Even the actors you know well may look different from how they were when last you saw them. Some will seem older or younger than you remember them, some fatter, some thinner, some more or less attractive, confident, healthy or fit. None of them will look as they do in their publicity photographs and they will rarely be sporting the same hairstyles.

As you peruse the faces around you, what you see is how each actor sees himself or at least how he has chosen to appear that day to you and his fellow actors. You will see faces unadorned and faces made up, faces wearing glasses and faces without, hair abundant and scanty, thick and thin, natural, highlighted and dyed. You will see all sorts of disguise reflecting all sorts of vanity or insecurity.

The best actors are often the least troubled by personal vanity. They treat their faces and their hair as part of the tools of their trade and will change themselves as much or as little as they think right to suit the character they are playing. A great part of their talent lies in their ability to reveal themselves as they are, and to do this they must accept the features they were born with. Most good actors know their faces well and have an instinct, born of experience, artistry and perhaps a little vanity, that tells them what the appropriate make-up for a character will be. They have their little kits of favourite powders and potions, brushes and sponges, creams and cleansers. And they know, too, how to listen to advice, how to take advantage of the expertise of a make-up and wig department.

Even so, there are fine actors who are not blessed with such confidence. They have a 'thing' about some aspect of their face and unless persuaded otherwise will want to dress their hair or apply their make-up in an attempt to fix what they see as their problem. Inexperienced actors, meanwhile, often have to be persuaded to the view that when it comes to make-up, less is usually more. Young actors may have spent two or three years at drama school playing parts wildly unsuitable for them and have accustomed themselves to use make-up as a casting supplement. In the professional theatre actors are generally cast more accurately, the rightness of face for role being one of the main considerations for casting them.

On the first day of rehearsal, every face presents a challenge or, if not a challenge, at least an opportunity. The opportunity is for you and your actors, together with your **Costume Designer** and designers of hair and make-up if you have them, to make the most of what you've been dealt, to change where change is appropriate and leave well alone where it isn't.

Start your discussions about the appearance of the characters in the first day or two of rehearsals. Some actors will have been worrying about how they're to look, and the longer you leave the discussions, the more the worry can grow. Some decide in advance how they want their character to appear and may even have started to groom themselves appropriately. This is all very well if they're on the right track. If not, they should be headed off before a bad idea gets entrenched.

Talk to each actor separately but involve other interested parties. If you're working in a small company the only other person will be the Costume Designer, who will very likely be designing the set as well. In a more prosperous set-up, you will also have a hair and make-up person to consult and/or a member of the wig department.

Talk about the character and his place in the story; his age, status, sexuality and view of himself. Talk about how the facial form and the hair of the character will relate to the costume in terms of colour, period, form and fashion. Talk about how the character might change in appearance as the story unfolds. Where appropriate, talk about the advisability of a wig (see below), but consider the difficulties and expense that wigs bring in their wake.

Above all, don't forget that your raw material is not just the physical form of the actor but the whole person. Whatever you propose, you must take the actor with you. His feelings, fears, habits and self-image are part of the picture. One actor may need no encouragement to shave his head or dye his hair green. Another may need persuading to any serious alteration of his accustomed look. A third will resist anything other than the most superficial change. This last case is especially true of actors whose appearance has become a trademark to them. Long, luxurious hair that has taken years to grow, or cultured blondeness, or a characteristic beard may be permanent features you will be powerless to change.

MAKE-UP

If naturalness is the aim of theatre, an unadorned face will rarely look natural in a large theatre under intense artificial light. If an actor is to change the shape of his face or the tonal quality of his skin, or seem to be younger or older than he is, or look weathered, scarred, wounded, dirty or ill, he must make up his face to suit his character. If a Costume Designer creates clothes in a narrow range of colours, a correspondingly sympathetic range of skin tones may be necessary in the cast that wears them. If the Set and Costume Designers have created a fantastical environment for the world of the play, the characters must be given faces to match the fantasy.

As a director you will often be called upon to adjudicate a conflict of visions and opinions in your collaborators. Your designers of set, costume and lights will all have a view about the general level of make-up in the cast, and every one of your actors will require guidance of one sort or another.

In naturalistic plays, actors should be encouraged to use as little make-up as possible. Whatever the challenge involved in portraying a character, an actor shouldn't expect his make-up to do more than, say, 5 or 10 per cent of the work. When make-up is required to correct a **casting** mistake or cover for a failure of acting technique, it puts the actor into a different visual style from the cast around him. Drawing wrinkles on the forehead of a young actor will not make him look old any more than blackening the skin of a white actor will make him look African. The true architecture of a face should always be clearly perceivable through whatever make-up is applied to it.

Beware all obvious 'character' make-up – the daubed stubble, the twinkly laugh-lines, the highlighted duelling scar. Beware, too, the 'comedy' make-up that tips the wink to the audience, the bushy eyebrows, the prosthetic or blacked-out teeth, the improbably rosy cheeks. Make-up is a subtle craft and must be employed with taste, discretion and a careful eye on the larger **stage picture** – the relationship between the characters, their costumes and the set they inhabit.

In larger theatre organisations, make-up and wig departments have a certain amount of autonomy, and one has to be careful sometimes that it doesn't get out of hand. The best way to approach the leaders of these little empires is to make it clear from the outset that you expect them to work under the artistic guidance of the Costume Designer. In the end the appearance of the characters must be in the artistic remit of Costume Designer, director and actors. No actor should be expected to wear a make-up he hates for whatever reason, but least of all because the head of a make-up department 'sees it that way'.

Make-up, of course, is used in everyday life as much as it is in the theatre. In this respect you and your designers may encounter in your actors some interesting combinations of vanity, self-delusion or fashion addiction. Most actresses come to rehearsal wearing at least some make-up, and some of them wear a great deal. Actors and actresses alike have a view of themselves, a self-image that they are more or less happy to abandon as they go through the process of becoming their characters. The actors that will give you the greatest problem are those whose self-image is significantly different from how they appear to everyone else. The fake tan, the thick false eyelashes, the coloured contact lenses, the overambitious lipstick, the dyed moustache and the preposterous toupee may all be cherished adornments and talking actors out of them can be a tricky exercise in tact, diplomacy or counter-flattery. You will win some of these battles and lose others. Self-image is a manifestation of self-worth and can never be lightly brushed aside. Rough treatment will tend to result in defensive entrenchment.

However self-conscious or blasé your actors are about their appearance, when you talk to them about make-up, don't start by talking about how they appear in real life. Talk about their characters and how they appear to themselves and to the other characters in the imaginary world of the play. If the actor is shy, dowdy or prone to self-beautification, refer him obliquely to the shyness, dowdiness and vanity, or lack of those things, in the character. If the actor hides behind adornment in his daily life, you should challenge the right of the character to follow suit. The more you inspire an actor to enquire into the fundamental truth of his character, the more likely he will be to forget his own outward appearance in the excitement of transformation.

WIGS

If you're doing a period play and you want the hairstyles in it to look authentic, or if any of your actors need a significant change of appearance to play their characters, you should think about wigging them.

You may not be able to afford wigs, in which case you'll have to do your best by other means – using make-up, hair-dye and styling. If, in spite of the expense, you decide that wigs are essential, don't be tempted to buy them off the peg. Wigs must be properly fitted to the head to look right. Fitting them is a skill. So is maintaining them over the run of a play. If you use wigs, you need a qualified wig person to look after them.

The larger established theatres have their wig and make-up departments with dozens of wigs in stock that can be adapted to heads of different sizes. They will also be able to make wigs from scratch, though this is an extremely time-consuming business. If you and your designer want new wigs for a production, you'll have to get the designs to the wig department in very good time.

In smaller theatre operations and in commercial theatre, you'll have to buy in the services of a wig person. Find someone your Costume Designer likes and whose work you have seen and appreciated. Once you have made the appointment, go through the cast list and decide how many of your actors need to be wigged. Try to avoid a wig if at all possible. When in doubt, natural hair is always better as long as it looks and feels right. Decide who needs a full wig – covering the whole head – and who could make do with a 'piece' added to the existing hair, or a toupee glued to a bald spot and combed in to match existing hair.

If you can't make up your mind whether to have wigs or not or whether a particular actor would benefit from one, consider the following points.

TO WIG OR NOT TO WIG – THE ARGUMENTS FOR AND AGAINST WIGGERY

To wig . . .

1 Wigs are an indispensable part of costuming the characters of period costume plays. The fashions of the past were created with certain styles of hair in mind. Without the right hairstyles the clothes lack the balance they were designed to have.

2 Very few actors happen to have the right hairstyles to suit the costumes designed for them. You don't cast an actor just because he has the right hair for the part.

3 The physical appearance of an actor can be so different from how you expect his character to look that a wig becomes a necessary part of his characterisation.

4 In Europe and America, the fashion for short hair in women largely started at the beginning of the twentieth century. Before that, most women, certainly those in the upper echelons of society, grew their hair long. Today, most actresses have shorter hair than the period characters they play.

5 Many actors keep their hair short in the expectation that they will be given a wig when they play a period part.

6 By wigging the actors, Costume Designers have more control over the appearance of the characters. When actors use their own hair they change it week by week according to personal preference or fashion. Wig hair doesn't grow.

7 Even if an actor has the right hair for a period part, it's a boring and time-consuming business having it prepared for every performance. A wig is prepared in the absence of the actor, a wig-cap fitted on his head in a minute and a wig put on top of that in half a minute.

8 Hair that has to be tortured and teased into shape every night will turn to rats' tails after a few weeks. Actors anxious to preserve the quality of their hair usually prefer the wig to get the torturing and teasing.

9 An actor who is bald or thinning on top tends to get cast in parts too old for him. This is scarcely fair. Wig him up so he can play parts his own age.

10 In **musical theatre, radio-mikes** have to be hidden somewhere. The best places for them are poking out behind the ear, high up on the forehead or just below the cheekbone, places easily concealed by carefully dressed wigs or whiskers.

. . . or not to wig

1 The hair of a wig never quite behaves like real hair however beautifully the wig is made. It doesn't have the flow and bounce and feel of real hair.

2 Actors never treat wig hair as they would their real hair. They are reluctant to run their fingers through it for fear of disarranging it or dislodging it entirely. Actors compensating for this problem make it worse by indulging in studious acts of self-grooming.

3 Actors treat one another more gingerly when wearing wigs, especially in scenes that demand close physical contact – dances, fights and love clinches.

4 A badly designed wig can affect the entire body language of an actor. Self-consciousness about the wig spreads to general physical unease.

5 For wigs to fit properly, the lace has to extend onto the actor's forehead and temples. In some actors this may mask an expressive part of the face.

6 The lower the natural hairline of an actor, the harder it is to get a good fit for a wig. Bald or receding actors, or actors with lots of forehead, have an easier time of it.

7 Actors with abundant hair are poor wig subjects. If their hair is precious to them and cannot be cropped, they must pin it up, bundle it into a cap and have the wig fitted on top. If the actor's

head is big in the first place, the final appearance can seem monstrous.

8 The smaller the theatre the more detectable wigs are to the audience. In very small theatres the wigged characters may look theatrical and artificial compared to the un-wigged.

9 In any size of theatre it is a challenge to integrate wigged and un-wigged characters into the same style of appearance.

10 Over a long run, the dressers of wigs tend to set them into hard and artificial-looking shapes. A wig that looked natural on opening night looks like a hat a month later.

If you get into **technical rehearsals** and any of the wigs look wrong, don't hesitate to change them, or cut them. Just like costumes, wigs need work. And actors need to get used to wearing them. But there will always be occasions when you and your designers realise you have made a mistake. If this happens to you, swallow your pride and cut the wig. Don't let the poor actor suffer needlessly.

There may also be occasions when an actor insists on wearing a wig that is utterly wrong for him and makes him look preposterous. This will very likely be because of personal vanity. He'll be hiding a bald spot or hate the fact he's grey or have some image of his character that is wildly different from what comes across in his performance. Talk him out of it. Or talk his performance up and his wig down. By making him feel better about himself in every other way, he'll stop feeling bad about his hair. Get him to try different wigs, or no wig at all. Help him to see himself as you see him and to accept that that your view is a better one than his.

FACIAL HAIR

If a character requires facial hair, encourage the actor to grow his own. Stuck-on facial hair is never a good idea and should be avoided if at all possible. It rarely looks real, it irritates the skin, it tickles the mouth and the nose, it stops the actor speaking naturally and it can fall off or end up stuck to someone else's face.

Canny actors start growing their whiskers long in advance of rehearsals even when a beard may not be indicated in the text.

Then, if they decide to play without whiskers, they shave. Easy.

Actors who can't grow beards, or whose beards are too scanty to be effective, can't benefit from this system, but then they never look good with stuck-on beards anyway.

Talk to your male actors at the start of rehearsals about how whiskery their characters should be. Some might look good with two or three days' growth, so the actor should schedule his shaving days to fit in with performances. Others should trim their beards to fit the fashion of the times or the personal vanity of the character. Talk to the make-up department, too, about combining real whiskers with appropriate levels of facial shading.

For female characters disguised as males, a stuck-on moustache or beard is only advisable for broad comedy or farce. An actor playing one of the great classical breeches roles – Rosalind, Viola or Imogen, for example – should be dissuaded from masking her expressiveness with such a disguise. If the other characters are to be fooled by a fake moustache they must be crassly unobservant. You, and the actor, should rather put your faith in the conspiracy of belief that makes her male.

Hanamichi

The hanamichi is the broad platform or runway extending out from the stage into the auditorium in the Kabuki and Noh theatres of Japan, literally the 'flower path'.

The origin of the name is unknown, but may have come from the world of Sumo. As the wrestlers entered the arena to fight they used to come garlanded with flowers. What a good thought. Why did they give that up?

In Kabuki theatre, the hanamichi always runs through the left side of the auditorium to stage right. In Noh theatre it runs parallel with the auditorium left, stage right, wall.

The term is sometimes used in European theatre to describe any walkway that projects out through the auditorium from any part of the stage.

Heightened Language

Heightened language is language rich in imagery or other poetic device, 'heightened' in that it is deemed to be 'higher' in levels of poetic imagery or imaginative intensity than naturalistic language.

The term is most commonly used to describe the work of Shakespeare and his contemporaries, but it can be applied to any drama that is rich in poetic device, from the Greeks to the modern day.

If heightened language takes a **verse** form, actors must be encouraged to observe the rules of **metre** that define it. Heightened language cannot be spoken as if it was naturalistic speech, nor orated as if it was opera without the singing, but rather observed, so that the figures of speech it contains seem part of the speaker's natural expression.

Hot Seat

Hot seat is an **improvisation** technique used to prove the detail and depth of an actor's invented character. The actor is placed on a chair in the middle of the room and quizzed by the director or his fellow actors. He is obliged to stay completely in character and to answer as truthfully as the character would answer. The questions can be quick-fire – to prove the speed of thought of the actor, or deeply searching – to prove the emotional or psychological accuracy of the actor's invention.

Hot-seating a character can help the actor come up with answers to questions he hadn't previously considered and that may be of importance to the playing of his character. It can also teach other cast members how their own characters might relate more interestingly to the hot-seated character. It will also expose any shallowness of perception or fatuousness of response. A very useful rehearsal tool.

The House

The 'house' is theatre slang for an auditorium full of people, or not so full of people. Thus if you say, 'How big is the house tonight?' you are asking how many tickets have been sold. 'The house is completely dead tonight,' would refer to a silent or unresponsive audience. A 'House Full' sign outside the theatre means that all tickets have been sold for that performance, or that the manager wants you to believe they have.

I

Iambic Pentameter

See **Metre**.

Impersonation

A useful skill in an actor, though like mimicry, its close cousin, not to be confused with **acting** itself. Impersonation is the imitation of the physical, vocal and mental characteristics of another person. At its best it is an art in itself, the finest impersonators capturing their subjects and improvising their patter so accurately that the audience is made to feel it is in the presence of the subject rather than the impersonator, its laughter of recognition being the outward sign of the impersonator's success.

Many actors are fine impersonators, the talents of the two crafts having common origins in observation, memory and mimicry. But the art of acting is a far more complex business than mere impersonation, and the actor who relies too much on his ability to copy the behaviour of real people will always fall short when it comes to the invention of an original character. The best actors are capable of using their skills of impersonation when useful to them, when working on satirical comedy, for instance, or playing a character drawn from real life, but are wary of relying on their facility at other times.

Every acting company has its impersonators, and the pleasure they take in their skills will become a feature of any relaxed rehearsal process. The character of the impersonator will define who the targets are and how kind or unkind the impersonations. The only certainty is that the director will feature as one of the main subjects of satire. There is absolutely nothing you can do about this. Directors do most of the talking in rehearsal, giving the mimics and impersonators more than ample time to listen, learn and go in for the kill. Be indulgent with your impersonators. Think of their accuracy as a compliment to your uniqueness, and consider how insignificant you would have to be to be ignored by them.

Improvisation

Improvisation is the art of extemporised drama. In its commonest form it is the unpremeditated creation by actors, usually under the instruction of a director, of characters, dialogue and situations.

Improvisation has a wide set of applications, and this entry does not pretend to be exhaustive or methodological. Many fine books have been written on the subject and many more will be written in the future, but not by me. The books that most inspired me as a young director and subsequently helped me to form my own system were *An Actor Prepares* by Konstantin **Stanislavsky**, *Towards a Poor Theatre* by Jerzy Grotowski and *Improvisation for the Theatre* by Viola Spolin. But you must draw on the books and practices that suit you best and refine your own method as a reaction to them.

There is an inherent paradox to improvisation. The term implies spontaneous creativity and discovery but in most of its applications it works best when carefully prepared for and its techniques controlled and monitored. The directors who use improvisation most creatively are those that have built it into their own rehearsal systems. They know what they want to get out of each exercise and they apply what it teaches them as an integral part of their work.

Improvisation for its own sake is more or less worthless in a rehearsal room. You and your actors might get considerable value from the playing of improvisation **games** in the first few days of rehearsal, but the closer you get to opening your play the more necessary it becomes to justify these exercises as part of the rehearsal process. If actors can't see the concrete benefits in the work you ask them to do, they lose patience with it. This is why you need to make your improvisation technique your own. If the work demands it, your actors will be as excited by it as you are. If it feels tacked on or borrowed from some other director's system, your actors will get frustrated with it and with you.

Whenever you use improvisation, first know what you want to achieve by it and then prepare, monitor and apply the exercises with care. Here are some of the situations in which it might prove useful.

THE USES OF IMPROVISATION

1 As a primary creative source

There are theatre companies that present long-form improvisations as public performances. These are the high-wire improvisers. No author, no text, no safety-net. Just a collection of actors' imaginations and let the story be what it will be.

2 As an authorial strategy

Improvisations can be used in the writing of **devised plays, verbatim plays** or **adaptations**. In workshop rehearsals a writer, director and actors may use improvisation to explore basic **research** and to create scenes and characters that the writer can then refine as part of his final text.

3 As a *company-building device*

Because improvisation requires intelligence, imagination, generosity and wit, a group of improvising actors soon gets to know itself, for good or ill. This is the main value to be derived from the playing of theatre **games**, of which there is a varied but by no means exhaustive selection in this book. Improvisation games can build confidence, break down social, sexual and behavioural barriers, and supplement actors' training. Some of them can be adapted to solve problems that arise in rehearsal between actors or their characters.

4 As a rehearsal technique

In rehearsal, improvisations can help to enrich the historical, social or psychological background of a play. Actors in groups or individually can be given exercises to help flesh out the lives of their characters as they might be lived outside the scenic structure of the play.

Improvisation

Where do the characters come from? How do they live? Have they had relationships to one another before the events of the play begin? Might there be meetings between the characters contemporaneous with the play that are un-staged by the author? All such events, however imaginatively conceived, can be improvised and may answer important questions about the characters and how they relate to the story.

5 As a resource for individual actors

Some actors need help with imagining the inner lives of their characters. The fundamental building blocks of character can all be found in the actor's imagination, provided the actor has one. Improvisation starts in the mind – the broader the mind the better the improvisation. **Hot seat,** and exercises like it, can be very useful in deepening an actor's perception of his character's intellectual, psychological and spiritual make-up and therefore how he would react in the presence of other characters. The physical life of a character can also be opened up by improvisation. Actors who are physically limited in their expressiveness may more readily unlock themselves in improvisation than be unlocked by instruction.

6 As directorial inspiration

Directors get stuck. They get ideas in their heads that prove incommunicable to their actors or audience. They have staging ideas that seem unworkable or to which their actors cannot or will not subscribe. No amount of talking or persuasion or debate seems to help. Try improvising. Put the scene in a different context. Make a radical change to its physical life. Relocate it or play it at a different pace, or in a different mood or style. Something will happen. You may not come up with answers you expect, but the ones you don't expect may be more interesting. Or you may find yourself being presented with questions that hadn't occurred to you, ones that make the problem you thought you had seem completely irrelevant.

7 *As artistic or stylistic leavening*

Actors get stuck. They conceive a part in a way that cannot be shared with you or with their fellows. Two or more actors playing a scene together may be so out of sympathy with one another through inappropriate character choice or conflicting acting systems that the dough of the scene refuses to rise. Add some improvisational yeast. Change the motivation of the characters, or their ages or genders. Redefine the relationships: lovers as parent and child, parents as lovers, friends as strangers, enemies as co-dependent spirits. Have the actors play each other's parts. Speak the scene with different words. Add other characters. You may not get immediate results, but some little bubble of fermentation in the mind of one of your actors may be all you need.

PROVISO

Improvisation is a technique, not a virtue. Using it won't make you a better person or a more imaginative director. There are evangelical improvisers, directors and actors, so passionately attached to the practice they cannot understand others not being similarly inspired. Don't get door-stepped by them if it isn't your thing. If you don't like improvisation or can never find a suitable application for it, then don't do it. You won't be doing anything wrong.

Ingénue

From the feminine form of the French *ingénu*, meaning 'ingenuous', the term describes the type of a young innocent female protagonist or the actress who plays her – as in 'For an ingénue role it's quite an interesting part,' or 'She went on playing ingénues far longer than she should have done.'

The term is dated now and only used by old-fashioned theatre buffs, though it is still employed in musical comedy and operetta, particularly in America.

Intermission

The American term for **interval**.

Interpreters

If ever you find yourself **directing in a foreign language**, your interpreter will be an essential collaborator, and the quality and sympathy of his work will greatly affect yours. Choosing the right interpreter could turn out to be a crucial piece of casting. A lazy, ignorant or unsympathetic interpreter will make you seem lazy, ignorant and unsympathetic. Because you don't know the language he is speaking, it's very hard for you to know for sure how well or how badly he is transmitting what you say to others. But you will soon start to get a good idea if all is not right – by your actors reacting perplexedly, or not laughing at an obviously funny joke, or taking you seriously when you were talking ironically – and you must not hesitate to change your interpreter for another if you find yourself thus hampered.

A good interpreter will work with your mind just as a good translator works with a text. He will listen with diligent attention, stop you if you are saying more than he can remember at one hearing, ask you to explain yourself if he hasn't understood your intention, demand of himself the precise form of words to communicate your meaning, get your wit and transmit it wittily, and in every way reflect the true quality of your mind and the true tone of your voice with as much detail and complexity as he can.

Your relationship with your interpreter should be so close that after you go back to your own country, the actors should continue to hear your tone of voice when they talk to the interpreter you leave behind you. Sometimes they will so identify your interpreter with you that they will expect him to be able to talk as if he was you after you've gone!

There are techniques to be learnt in the use of interpreters. You cannot speak as fluently and continuously as you are wont to do.

338

You must pause frequently so that the interpreter has time to catch up. This means you'll find yourself with much more time than is normally available to you for planning what you're going to say next. This may throw you at first, but once you get used to it, it's a very relaxing method of discourse. Any jokes you make must be comedic time bombs – dropped as precisely as you always drop them but only exploding a few seconds later, when the interpreter has cracked them open for you. Again, this can be disconcerting at first – especially if there's someone in the room who can understand you perfectly well and chortles to himself in advance of everyone else – but you soon get used to timing things a little differently and playing your humour deadpan enough not to give the game away in advance. Similarly, you must get used to listening to everything twice over – once when your interlocutor is talking to you and once again when the interpreter translates what he has said. Don't be thrown by this – and don't look off into space while you wait for the interpreter's version. Engage your interlocutor just as you would if you could understand everything he is saying. Don't be afraid of stopping him if he goes on too long, and, when the interpreter is speaking, divide your attention between him and the interlocutor. Then, when replying, speak directly to the interlocutor as if he can understand every word you are saying – that way, if not your words then the attitude and feeling underlying them will have their fullest impact on him. When you have finished speaking, continue to watch his reaction to your words while your interpreter is communicating their meaning.

Above all, enjoy your relationship with your interpreter, spar with him, joke with him, play linguistic games with him, stretch his understanding of your language and the usefulness of his own to the absolute limit – the pleasure you take in each other's company will communicate itself to your listeners and help them to relax and listen all the better.

Intervals

The history of intervals, or intermissions as they are known in America, is a fascinating one and worthy of a comprehensive study.

Intervals

It won't get one here, but the relationship between the structure of a play and the social event comprising its performance is something every director should think carefully about when preparing it for public consumption.

Theatre is a social event. Few people go to plays alone. They go in couples and groups. They may arrive together or they may meet at the theatre. They may be seeing one another for the first time in hours, days, weeks or months. They will have all sorts of things on their minds and all manner of news to share. They may be excitedly anticipating the play, but more likely they will be catching up on completely unrelated matters. These preoccupations will recur during the interval or intervals, if you have them, and continue on into the night after the play has finished. Members of your audience may talk about the play for weeks to come, or they may stop talking about it within a few seconds of leaving the theatre. You hope the former, but you also know that no one in your audience will ever have the same exclusive and obsessive interest in your play that you and your author and actors do. When considering an interval for your play, whether to have one, or more than one, and how long it, or they, should be, you are considering not just the impact on the shape of your play but the relationship between your audience's social life and their appreciation of your work.

Intervals also have a financial aspect. Foyers are market places. Drinks, meals, sweets, programmes and souvenirs are hawked and consumed. Without an interval, commercial opportunities are significantly reduced. Some theatre owners have interval rights enshrined in their contract with producers. If an interval is omitted, a financial penalty must be paid in lieu.

The no interval issue has become particularly apposite in recent years with the rise in popularity of the ninety-minute play. New plays are written with no possible interval break and old plays are trimmed to fit the fashion. No doubt the fashion will pass, just as the five-act, four-act, three-act and two-act fashions have. Plays will get longer again and intervals be made to match them. Whatever the length of your play, and whether it be new or old, your decision about an interval won't, one hopes, be entirely defined by fashion.

Some plays choose their own intervals. Their structure is so conventional or an interval so strongly indicated it would be foolish to deviate from the author's intention. But surprisingly few plays are this clear-cut. A classical five-act play may not have an obvious break after any of its acts. A four-act play could be split in the middle, or have two or three intervals of different lengths, or none at all. A three-act play may have had two intervals when it was first performed, but seems no longer to deserve the extra overall length that two intervals would give it.

When making your choice, there are several things to consider. First of all comes timescale. Most audiences won't sit for more than an hour and a half without beginning to get restless. Bladders get full. Legs get stiff. Concentration lapses. If they've read in their programmes that the whole play lasts an hour and fifty minutes without an interval they may cross their legs, or stretch their legs, and give you the extra twenty minutes, knowing the end is in sight. That's if the play is good and they have something worth concentrating on. If the play is less than spellbinding, you may well lose them.

If you feel your play would do better with an interval, perhaps even that it might be pretentious not to have one, but there isn't a clear-cut place to put it, consider the balance of the play. The conventional wisdom here is that the first act should always be longer than the second. This is based on the notion that audiences concentrate better at the beginning of an evening than at the end. If they go back into the auditorium after a single interval with more than half of the play still to be performed, they may do so a little penitentially. Conversely, an audience that has seen between a half and two-thirds of a play before the interval feels it has earned its drink, and that a play worth its salt should be able to get from the interval to the next drink, or dinner, in an hour or less. I generalise of course. But so runs the conventional wisdom.

It is also generally true that weighting a play towards the first half is a good idea in terms of structure. The exposition of a plot is not usually interesting enough stuff in itself for an audience to feel an interval has been earned before it is over. The story needs to have developed, something irreversible needs to have happened, before there can be a pause for thought. In most plays this only happens when over half the story has been told. Exposition after the interval is always a hard sell.

Consider, too, the themes of your production. Do any of your ideas, or those of your designer, help you to decide where your interval should be? Does your take on the story give it an uninterruptible thrust up to a certain point? Would it be appropriate to highlight a cliffhanging moment that would send the audience out longing to know what happens next? Is the storyline of one of the characters more important than the others? Which character do you want the audience to be thinking about most as they sip their drinks? Is there a cyclical aspect to the production that would suggest the interval moment should have a strong visual or emotional relationship to the beginning or end of the play? How artful do you want to be?

There may be strong reasons for having more than one interval. If a play is very long, or its structure clearly tripartite, you may be driven to this conclusion. But you don't have to have two equally long intervals. You can have one proper interval of say twenty minutes and one short break of five. Or a fifteen and a ten. Or two twelves. What you need to consider here is the overall time the intervals take. Two twenty-minute intervals make for forty minutes' foyer time. Some audience members will run out of things to say to each other. Others will be start worrying about the bus home. If the play is not being enjoyed, long intervals only make things worse.

Lastly, unless there are compelling reasons for it, you shouldn't let the changing of your stage settings add time to your intervals, or worse, require you to add otherwise unwanted intervals. Sets must sometimes be changed, of course, but if the changes can't be done as part of the action or within the time of a normally scheduled interval, the tail will be wagging the dog.

In-the-Round

Theatre-in-the-round is a configuration of **auditorium** that has the audience sitting all around the stage.

Most in-the-round spaces are not round at all, but square, the audience sitting on four more or less equal sides, with diagonal entrances cutting through the seats to the four corners of the stage.

Whatever the shape of the stage, the term defines an acting space and a **staging** style where the audience completes the background to the action. Wherever any audience member sits, other members of the audience are in his direct **sightline**. As he watches an actor moving across the space, his attention is reflected back to him by the same attention in the audience on the opposite side. Herein lies the strength of the in-the-round principle. Whatever happens on stage is caught in a context of communal witness. The actors and their characters have no neutral hiding place, no designed world that is theirs and theirs alone. Whatever environment they live in seems as accessible to the audience as it is to them. In a well-imagined production this can draw the audience into the world of the characters almost as if they were participants in the drama. This is in-the-round at its best, with actors and audience seeming locked into the same story.

There are drawbacks. Audiences don't always behave themselves. People fidgeting in the front row or falling asleep or trying to creep out to the toilet seem extraordinarily present. In smaller spaces the actors are never more than a few feet from one member of the audience or another, so their powers of concentration are tested every second they are on stage. Some of them cope with this better than others.

And there are staging problems. Wherever an actor stands, unless it is at the extreme corners of the stage, he masks the action from some part of the audience. Actors have to be kept on the move, far more than in a **proscenium** setting, more even than in **courtyard, traverse, arena** or **thrust** configurations. In inexperienced directorial hands, this can make for an awkward performance style, with actors constantly circling the stage trying to keep out of each other's way.

In-the-Round

Designers need to adapt their techniques to match the space. The floor becomes very important, its texture, colour and style. Pieces can be flown in the space over the stage but rarely made to disappear from sight when not in use. Furniture cannot be over-heavy or tall. In a multi-location play, anything lugged on has to be lugged off again in full view of the audience. A chair with a tall back can obscure the sightlines for a whole wedge of the audience. The settings that answer best are minimal and/or permanent environments. An unadorned stage with an evocative floor and subtle lighting and perhaps a few sticks of furniture moved about by the actors serves well for even the most complex of stories. Or a permanent environment can be created for a more naturalistic style of staging. An entire house-and-garden's worth of architecture and furniture can be assembled for a naturalistic drama, with delineations for different rooms and everything carefully arranged so the sightlines are sympathetic all round.

If you are working in a **Black Box** theatre or some similarly adaptable space and you think an in-the-round configuration might suit your play, do a little research before you settle your mind to it. Make sure the theatre can really give you what you want and not some bastard version of it. In-the-round doesn't work if one of the sides is conspicuously smaller than the others or if a single bank of seats on one side dominates the other three sides. People sitting in the smaller banks of seats can feel embarrassingly part of the action in relation to the larger banks. Or those sitting at the back of a single large bank can feel sadly left out. The sides don't have to be exactly equal, but there should at least be the illusion of equality in all parts of the house.

Intimate Theatre

This is a very loose term, used subjectively by many different theatre practitioners in various circumstances. It generally refers to the performance of plays in small spaces where the audience sits in such close proximity to the action that the drama seems intimately involving. Wherever the atmosphere exists for real intimacy between actor and actor or between actors and audience, then intimate theatre can be said to exist.

But the word is often used in more relative terms. A commercial producer will describe a West End or a Broadway theatre as being intimate because it contains merely a thousand seats rather than fifteen hundred. A director will ask a designer to try to achieve 'an intimate feel' on a vast desert of a stage and will be well pleased when audiences or critics describe the resulting production as 'surprisingly intimate'. A bleak little function room over a pub can be described as 'intimate' in order to avoid using words like 'squalid', 'airless' or 'cramped'.

The Iron

The iron is theatrical slang for the safety curtain, the fireproof wall that hangs in the fly tower immediately upstage of the **proscenium** arch and drops to seal off the stage area from the **auditorium** in the event of fire. Thus if a fire breaks out on stage or backstage then the audience can be protected for as long as it takes to evacuate the theatre. If a fire occurs in the auditorium, the safety curtain seals off the stage and prevents the fly tower from becoming a chimney. The safety curtain is a legal requirement in every theatre with a fly tower, and fire departments are rigorous in policing its integrity and efficiency. Nobody in the professional theatre calls it the safety curtain. It is always the iron.

The iron affects the work of the director in two ways:

THE OPERATION OF THE IRON

In Britain, the law states that the iron must be raised and lowered in the presence of the audience at least once during the evening. It doesn't state how many members of the audience must watch the operation, just that it must occur. This is a precaution against dishonest Theatre Managers who are thereby prevented from performing the play with a faulty iron. With a whole audience as potential witnesses, managers cannot take the risk of losing their licence.

The Iron

From your point of view as a director, however you have designed your production, whatever the relationship between actors and audience, whatever atmosphere you have managed to achieve on stage, whatever continuity of image you have dreamt up for the audience, at some moment in the evening there will be a quiet hydraulic hiss and an impenetrable iron wall, often very shabby or kitsch in appearance, will descend from the flies and seal off the stage. The choice of when it rises again is yours, which may provide you with an artistic or a practical opportunity. With the iron in, the stage can be re-dressed out of sight of the audience, actors can leave the stage or position themselves on it, messes can be cleaned up, and tall-o-scopes, or cherry-pickers, can be deployed to refocus lamps or change light bulbs.

THE IRON LINE

This is a notional strip of stage surface running just upstage of the proscenium where the iron rests when it has fully descended. The surface of the stage along that line must be uniformly flat, so that when the iron is lowered a seal is created right across the stage. The fire inspectors will allow no irregularity of stage surface along that line, and no permanent scenic piece or even furniture must be placed there.

On any set that uses a forestage, or which thrusts out into the auditorium across the iron line, you and your designer must be aware of this stipulation and design yourselves around it. Sets that rely on an irregular stage surface must either confine their irregularities to the areas up or downstage of the iron line, or successfully incorporate an integral iron line into the design itself so that the audience's eye isn't drawn to a regular straight line in the middle of an irregular pattern. Sets that require a lot of furniture must deploy the furniture so that the iron can fall unimpeded by it. Once the show is under way, small pieces of furniture and any other easily portable items may be moved into positions along the iron line, as long as a member of the stage crew is deputed to move them in the event of the iron being lowered. Some fire departments are stricter than others on this point.

With sensitive design and direction the audience need never be conscious of the existence of the iron line.

Irony

There are certain types of play that require an ironical delivery in the realisation of their characters. The plays of Bernard Shaw, Oscar Wilde, Noël Coward and Luigi Pirandello, or at least some of them, fall into this category. The author's wit and intelligence communicates to the audience by insinuating itself between actor and character. Actor and character seem to conspire together to say, 'I speak this line, but you know I don't really mean it,' or 'I'm a real person, but so is the actor playing me, and so is my author.'

Comedies of manners, plays written to celebrate the wit of the author or the style and brilliance of the performers, can all use irony to great advantage because they can all say, 'You don't need to believe in this to understand and enjoy it,' or even 'Your sophisticated unbelief is necessary to your enjoyment.'

In most other plays, this sort of irony is the enemy. In tragedy, serious drama and comedy, even in farce, or especially in farce, an ironical distance between actor and character is lethal to the audience's **belief** in the drama.

Of course I don't mean you have to remove all sense of irony from the mental processes of the characters. There must be ironical characters in plays just as there are in real life. But while the characters must be free not to mean what they say, the actors who play them must always be in earnest.

And of course you can bring as much irony as you like to your work in the rehearsal room. Let irony rule there. Let no one be obliged to say what they mean or mean what they say if they don't feel like it. But never let the irony leech unwontedly into your performance. Learn to spot it when it happens. The symptoms are always the same. You will feel, as you rehearse a scene, that you are quite vividly in the presence of the actors but not of the characters, that the lines are all somehow being spoken with quotation marks around them. That the imaginary world of the play is being blocked off to you by wit or knowingness or smugness.

Some actors just can't help themselves. A little smile of knowledge, worn habitually just behind the eyes, can trigger off a bout of irony at the slightest hint of an opportunity.

Some directors just can't help themselves. They create a perfectly believable scene but then follow it with a clever piece of self-referential **business** that no actor, ironical or not, could play with any seriousness.

And it's contagious. A flash of irony from one actor can suddenly appear on the other side of the stage in another. In a minute it's all over the cast, like a rash.

The remedy is simple. As soon as you spot it, remark on it. Start the scene again and demand total belief. If any actor is unaware of what he is doing, or can't understand how to stop doing it, explain what's happening and find some real **motivation** to put in the place of the unwanted irony. Discuss the characters, the situation, the place of the scene in the overall story, the seriousness of the author's intention, anything that will help focus the actor's mind away from itself.

A subtle version of ironical playing can occur when actors allow their private relationships to get into their character relationships. The enjoyment that two fine actors can take in playing together can infect the scene they are playing with a kind of ironical distance, as if they are saying, 'This is a good play, and these are fine characters, but never before have they been played quite so beautifully as this,' or 'Our characters say they hate each other, but how deeply we take pleasure in expressing it.'

Any actors that play together in established partnerships should watch for this very carefully. It may creep up on them unawares. But good actors will respond immediately once they've had it pointed out to them.

Eradicating irony when it isn't wanted is not so hard. Instilling it where it doesn't naturally exist is quite impossible. Plays that require the ironical touch can only be played by actors that have it without trying for it. As Samuel Butler said, 'The most perfect humour and irony is generally quite unconscious.' If you want to create a production that has an inherently ironical tone, you must keep the nudgers and winkers at bay and cast only those with a truly ironical frame of mind.

J

Job Interviews

Theatre is a profession of occasional, seasonal and specialist employment, so throughout your career you will have to endure interviews as a test of your suitability for jobs as Assistant Director, Director and Artistic Director. Even the most secure and celebrated of directors may still find themselves having to face panels and boards of fearsome inquisition. Whatever your status, there are four simple rules for conducting yourself in interviews – be prepared, be relaxed, be yourself and listen.

BE PREPARED

Make sure you know exactly what the panel of interviewers is looking for and in what ways your particular profile fits or doesn't fit the ticket.

Know about the theatre company you are applying to be a part of. Research the successes and failures of recent years, the early history of the company, its place in the community and the way in which it is funded and governed. Ideally you should have seen productions in the theatre and have an opinion as to their merits, even if the politics of the interview require you to keep your opinion to yourself.

If the interview is being conducted solely by an Artistic Director, as is the case with most Assistant Director interviews, research that director's career so you can talk intelligently about his passions and predilections. There's no need to flatter or to demonstrate your honesty where diplomacy would be more appropriate, but a lively and informed conversation will give the interviewer the feeling that the discourse will continue in like manner if he gives you the job.

Don't prepare so elaborately that you find yourself on a rehearsed track, parroting your plans and views as if they were suitable for any panel at any time. For this reason you should avoid writing any-thing down that needs constant reference. A few short notes, if any, should be enough to remind you of the main points you want to make and springboard you into a fluent recital of them.

BE RELAXED

This is easier than it sounds, of course. Nervousness is the enemy here, and often the most imaginative people get the most nervous as they imagine themselves fouling up the interview long before it has happened to them.

Think up strategies to keep relaxed. Don't let this interview be the only one that matters to you. Give yourself a good talking-to before you go in about your value and talent. Make them need you as much as you need them.

Don't get dehydrated. You can't talk properly if your mouth is full of fluff. Ask for a glass of water and take sips from it whenev-er you feel the need.

Talk about your nervousness to your interviewers up front. They're human. They've been to job interviews themselves. They know how you're feeling or can well imagine it.

If you are the relaxed type and naturally brimming with confi-dence then a different risk appears – that of cockiness. No panel of interviewers likes to feel that they are being expected to give you the job and would be stupid if they didn't. They will tend to rebel from this expectation and may even warn you they are doing so in the course of the interview. Watch out for that.

BE YOURSELF

Don't pretend to be the person you think they are looking for. You don't know who they're looking for. Your best hope is that it's you. So your best tactic must be to show them who you are in your best light but without pretence.

Go into the interview with a real desire to know your interview-ers better and a determination to enjoy the conversation for its own sake, whether or not you end up getting the job. The contacts you make in an interview may do you good in the future, and if only one person on the panel really likes you and appreciates what you are saying, he may have some real power of employment in some later circumstance.

Above all, don't bullshit. If you don't know the answer to a question, don't make up a plausible-sounding response. Just admit your ignorance as gracefully as you can and move on. Nothing will be more destructive to an honest presentation of yourself than a squirming attempt to please the questioners with the answer you think they want to hear.

LISTEN

Interviews change the longer they go on, developing with the questions and the way you answer them. Listen to the questioners. Make silent judgements to yourself about the value and direction of their questions. A panel of interviewers will often be quite divided in its preconceptions about you and its opinion of itself. Ask questions yourself when you are not clear which way their questions are tending, and listen very carefully to the answers. An interview that starts badly can be turned around quite quickly by the feeling that the interviewee is receptive and attentive to atmosphere and argument.

Your ability to listen will also give the impression from time to time that your interviewers are the ones being interviewed and that you are keen to know whether they are up to the job of being your employers. This will help to put the boot on the right foot and stop you being kicked around whether you get the job or not.

Once the interview is finished you must inure yourself to rejection, and when it comes, as it probably will, you must never take it personally.

No interview should ever be the be-all and end-all of your life. The best you should expect for yourself is that the interview may have done you some good, that your time was well spent or at least not wasted, that you met some interesting people you didn't know before, and that you learnt a little more about how to conduct yourself in interviews.

K

Kitchen-Sink Drama

Before the theatre revolution of the 1950s and the emergence of socially realistic drama, indoor settings for naturalistic plays rarely broke away from the drawing-rooms, conservatories or studies of the upper and middle classes. The bedrooms and bathrooms were out of bounds for reasons of decency, and no middle-class playwright could imagine anything significant or interesting happening in a kitchen. Working-class characters were invariably villains or figures of fun, and if a kitchen was ever mentioned, it was decidedly below stairs. If a cook ever emerged from a kitchen she carried a rolling-pin and was either scatter-brained, big-hearted or drunk.

In the 1950s and 60s with the final disappearance of the servant class from normal British society, ordinary people started to live in their kitchens just as much as in the other rooms of their houses, and theatrical representations of their lives quickly followed suit. Much to the dismay of old-school critics and audiences.

The pejorative phrase 'kitchen-sink drama' was coined to describe plays that depicted what were still considered to be sordid or banal situations and behaviour.

Of course what was really happening here was part of a much wider class war, with plays by working-class authors about working-class life fighting for their place in the theatre repertoire. By the end of the 1960s the war was very largely won, audiences were just as likely to see a kitchen sink on stage as a chaise longue, and the phrase slowly went out of usage.

L

Language Coaches

In theatre a Dialect Coach is an indispensable collaborator if you are working in a **dialect** foreign to your actors, but you may also need a Language Coach if any part of your play is written in a foreign language. This is quite an unusual requirement in theatre but a very common one in **opera**, where singers must have a passing proficiency in many languages but actually be much better at some than others, or be in the awkward position of having learnt a role in one language and being obliged to sing it in another less familiar one.

In choosing a Language Coach, don't settle for someone who is merely a proficient speaker. Find someone for whom the language is their mother tongue and who has had some experience of acting or singing, someone that knows something of the dramatic process and can respond to the requirements of a scene or a character with expert advice on inflection, stress, style and meaning. The best language coaches are, or have been, actors or singers themselves.

Language Coaches should be encouraged to contribute freely in rehearsal so that any egregious errors can be nipped in the bud before becoming entrenched by repetition, and to take copious notes in run-throughs and dress rehearsals. They may also have to spend hours of patient time in private coaching sessions with the actors or singers that are having real difficulties with their text.

One word of warning. Whenever you add a collaborator to your creative team, you complicate the social and professional context of your rehearsals. Be aware that an overzealous or unsympathetic coach may be undermining the confidence of your performers. As you approach opening night, make sure your cast isn't being swamped with notes. Better a few inaccurate vowel sounds than a performer frightened to open his mouth for fear of the language police.

Latecomers

Latecomers are a pest. Just when your actors have established an atmosphere on stage, they come puffing down the aisles in the wake of flashlight-waving ushers, radiating their own peculiar atmosphere of apologetic guilt or acted frustration, and squeeze themselves down rows of grudging knees and feet into their vacant seats.

They then sit in sweaty regret, half involved with the play and half cursing the cause of their delay. A minute later they suddenly decide to wriggle out of their coats, check their phones are switched off, swap their glasses for the ones in the sharply clicking handbag or crush a stridulant plastic bag under their seat. Unaccustomed to the atmosphere around them, they remain blissfully unaware of the chaos they create. The rest of the audience rolls its eyes, glares, shushes and tries to regain its concentration. But it feels guilty too, or sympathetic, by association. It was that latecomer once, and will be again.

Some directors and managers are very fierce. No latecomers. If people arrive late, they wait for the interval. No interval, no play. Sorry, nothing we can do. People just have to learn. If they can't be bothered to turn up on time, they shouldn't be allowed to destroy everyone else's enjoyment.

Most theatres take a less proscriptive view. Latecomers are patrons, passionate theatregoers who have rushed to get there from their busy lives. They are thoroughly frustrated by the buses or the boss or the babysitter. They bought their tickets weeks or months ago. They've been looking forward to seeing their favourite author, actor or even, God save the mark, director. Give them a break.

Leniency requires a system, one that respects the latecomers' right to be admitted as soon as possible but also preserves the right to silence and comfort of those already assembled.

Find a place in the first ten or fifteen minutes of your show that feels like a natural hiatus in the action; the end of a scene, an applause moment, a highly populated entrance or exit. Find a second such moment ten or fifteen minutes later in case of very latecomers.

Latecomers

Your **front of house staff** will have to be trained to follow this system or something like it. They should start by calming the latecomers down. Get them to check their coats, bags and umbrellas so their progress through the auditorium is as smooth as possible. Make sure their cellphones are turned off. Provide a TV monitor in the foyer so the latecomers can watch and listen to the show while waiting. They won't pay much attention to it, but they will feel less excluded. A minute or so before the admittance point, the DSM, or whoever is calling the show, should give a warning to the ushers – a short blast in the FOH bells or a call through to the FOH Manager. The ushers should get everyone ready, check their tickets, know exactly where they are going. If possible, there should be one usher for each group of latecomers. Then, on a second blast of the bell, the latecomers are swiftly and silently ushered to their seats.

If there is standing-room space at the back of the auditorium, you might allow latecomers to congregate there as a halfway house. This is ideal, but only if there is sufficient space for the people sitting in the back row not to feel loomed over.

The final cue for admittance, wherever the latecomers are congregated, should be slightly anticipated by the DSM. It takes time for ushers to react to a cue. The DSM should try to coincide the most disruptive moment – when the latecomers are squeezing themselves down their rows – with the least important moment on stage.

Laughter

Laughter is one of the signifiers of recognition in the theatre, as are tears and thoughtful silence. An audience laughs or cries or falls silent when it recognises itself in the action or speech or thought of a good actor.

As director you must be ready to judge the quality and appropriateness of the laughter your actors inspire in the rehearsal room or theatre.

GOOD LAUGHS AND BAD LAUGHS

A good laugh is one intended by the author and achieved by the actor without strain. It arises from the surprise created by the dramatic tension of a particular moment. The surprise might be physical, social, intellectual or linguistic, but to be truly funny it should be necessary and the story should continue better with it than without it.

A bad laugh is one manufactured by actor or director in defiance of the author's intention or triggered off unintentionally by some incompetence.

In either case it disturbs the current stage **reality** and impedes the further development of the story. It draws attention to the actor who instigates it and away from whatever is the real centre of dramatic focus. At its worst it is contemptuous of the play or derisive of the talents of fellow performers.

The more serious a play the more destructive a bad laugh can be. Unwanted laughter in the final scenes of *Hamlet* or *King Lear*, whether manufactured or unintentional, can be as fatal as a poisoned sword or a hanged fool. Conversely, a series of manufactured 'gags' in a light farce is unlikely to impair the audience's enjoyment and may even serve to enhance it.

In the end, your own sense of humour is likely to be the final arbiter in deciding what is a good laugh and what a bad. If you find something genuinely funny yourself you can only trust the audience will share your taste. If humour is a short suit with you, you will not find such judgements easy. If you know yourself to be devoid of humour, you would be well advised to avoid comedy altogether and concentrate instead on plays of a darker complexion. There are plenty of humourless playwrights to choose from.

LAUGHTER IN REHEARSAL

Laughter is an essential part of **rehearsal**. It is a signifier of common ground and a necessary reliever of tension.

If a comedy is being rehearsed then laughter will tell the whole company how to proceed, from line to line and from scene to scene. But beware of the forced laughter that some show-off actors insist

357

on exacting from their impressionable colleagues. The laughter of 'look at how funny I'm being' will teach you nothing at all.

Dramas of unhappiness need as much rehearsal laughter as comedies, perhaps even more. Most actors cannot sustain deep emotion for very long without it becoming staled by familiarity. Laughter cleans the palate so that darker emotions can be better savoured.

A rehearsal room without laughter is a hopeless place.

THE LAUGHTER PARADOX

The longer and louder the laughter engendered in an audience by its recognition of an essential truth, the longer the actors on stage must wait before speaking their next lines. This creates an unreal hiatus in the action that is inimical to the truthful depiction of the characters and so destructive of further bouts of laughter.

Good comic actors devise ways of filling these strange gaps in reality with well-observed and silent **business** that can itself cause more laughter and increase the length of the reality gap. A good actor with a modicum of taste will know when enough is enough, but even tasteful actors are sometimes helpless victims of an audience's hilarity, and a good director must be ready to advise on the best exit strategy from a riot of laughter.

THE LAUGHTER RIPPLE EFFECT

This is noticeable in theatres where actors are not sufficiently projecting their performances into all parts of the house at the same time. A laugh line is delivered on stage and the laughter ripples back through the audience as the line is heard and understood, so those sitting at the very back of the theatre laugh slightly later than those at the front, creating a disunity in the audience's response. At its worst the ripple effect ends with those furthest away from the stage laughing at the laughter of those sitting nearest to it. If you notice this happening you must sort it out before it becomes a permanent feature of the rhythm of your production. It indicates a bigger problem – that the play is being perceived in different ways by people sitting in different parts of the house – an anathema to any self-respecting director.

The best solution to the problem is to run parts of the play with some of the actors sitting or standing on stage and others in different parts of the auditorium, especially in its furthest reaches where the **acoustics** are at their stingiest. Once a company has heard itself speaking its lines all over the auditorium they will be far more conscious at the next performance of how the laughter should follow the lines and the ripple effect should disappear without trace.

Legitimate Theatre

An old-fashioned and preposterous term used to describe theatre of a conventional form, including tragedies and comedies but excluding **music theatre** of any sort or television or film. As no one in those worlds refers to what they do as illegitimate it is difficult to see why the term itself should have any legitimacy.

Abbreviated to 'legit', the term is still current in America, but now increasingly used to differentiate all sorts of theatre from films and TV.

Libretto

The libretto of an **opera** is the text or book of words, whether the opera is partly spoken or entirely sung, as opposed to the **score**, which comprises the music.

In **musical theatre** the libretto is known as the **book**.

Lighting and Lighting Design

Ever since plays have been performed at night, lighting has been an integral part of the theatrical experience. Even in the most sophisticated of modern circumstances, the best theatre pieces are still redolent of ancient stories told around the fire, or of the arena lit by torchlight for a dance, song or ritual.

Of course, plays can be performed in broad daylight, but why are the best stories best told at night? From time immemorial members of the tribe have gathered after work and before sleep to spin their yarns to one another. Between work and sleep, or between waking and dreaming, is when stories have their greatest potency. Stories feed off work and life and in turn they feed sleep and dreams. But the storytellers are not just voices in the dark. Their faces and hands and bodies help them to tell their stories. Lighting design has its origin in this one simple fact – faces, hands and bodies must be lit. Lighting can do many other things, but if it isn't doing this first and fundamental job, it won't be doing anything else of much importance.

THE USES OF LIGHTING

1 To help tell the story.

2 To illuminate what you want the audience to see, whether it be the actors and their faces, the scenery against which they are acting or the audience to whom they are playing.

3 To darken or disguise that which you don't want the audience to see.

4 To draw the eye of the audience towards what you want them to see and away from what you want them to ignore. For each moment of a play there is an appropriate level and atmosphere of light – call it a lighting cue or state. You must decide, in collaboration with your **Set Designer** and **Lighting Designer**, what state of lighting is appropriate for each cue in the play.

5 To mark out the scenic structure of a play, as if to say to an audience, 'What you can see exists and what you cannot see does not exist or has ceased to exist.' A **blackout** or fading of the lights is a code for a particular block of time being finished.

6 As a coded message to the audience to behave in a certain way. They fall silent as the house lights fade. They pay attention as the stage lights come up. They leave the theatre when the house

lights restore. They applaud when there is a 'bump up' of lights at the end of a musical theatre number.

7 To impart scenic information.

a) To delineate night from day, using different intensities and colours of light.

b) To specify different times of day and night using direction and colour of light.

c) To create the illusion of exterior or interior settings.

d) To indicate different locations, using different sorts of patterning, fragmentation, direction or intensity of light.

e) To create, or supplement the effect of, natural light sources – candlelight, firelight, lamplight, starlight, moonlight.

f) As scenery – advertising neon, street lighting, flashing police lights, etc.

g) As a scenic device – e.g. strobe lights to create the effect of dislocated action.

h) For atmosphere – dark and sombre, mellow and romantic, bright and cheerful, etc.

10 SIMPLE LIGHTING RULES

1 Light the actor. No actor likes being in the dark for very long and certainly not when speaking. Light is oxygen to the actor.

2 It is easier to hear an actor's voice if you can see his face at the same time. If an actor's face is in darkness, he will struggle to be heard.

3 Comedy is funnier in the light than in the dark. Comedic plays need brighter states of light than others. If a very funny play is not getting sufficient laughter, look to the lighting or lack of it.

4 The lightest-coloured object on stage will attract the most light. White scenery reflects light back on itself and on the audience. If any piece of scenery, or costume or prop is lighter in tone than the actor's face, the audience's eye will tend to be drawn to it and away from the actor.

5 The bigger the space the more light you need. The further away the audience is from the action the more light it needs to see

what is going on. In a tiny space a candle can suffice – in a stadium, you need floodlights.

6 The greater the emotional and scenic detail in a play the more lighting cues you will need. There is an appropriate lighting state for every dramatic event and **stage picture**. Some plays change their events and pictures faster than others.

7 If the actors' faces were all to be equally well lit on every part of the stage throughout an entire performance then the stage would have to be flooded with bright white light all evening – a simulation of daylight as it were. The light must move as the actors move.

8 The actors are in charge of where they move, not the light or the Lighting Designer. That is why the follow-spot, manually operated by human agency, is such a sympathetic device. Its modern equivalent, the electronically programmed moving light – there are various companies making them – is a brilliant invention, but it mustn't be allowed to confine the actors to a set path of movement. The tail must not be allowed to wag the dog.

9 Beware of lighting the stage without the actors present. You may be creating very pretty pictures, but the audience want to see the actors – they have art galleries for pictures.

10 Inexperienced actors should be encouraged to 'find their light'. Experienced actors usually need no instruction. Their faces are as moths to the flame.

11 Some actors seem to be lightproof, while others practically glow in the dark. This is largely to do with skin texture rather than an intention to be seen or a need to hide. You must accommodate the level of light for different skin textures. Actors can't see themselves, so they rely on you to make them glow.

12 Light doesn't go round corners. However clever a Lighting Designer is, he can't make his lights go round a wall, or duck under the brim of a hat or a mass of unruly hair. If necessary, you must be ready to adapt costumes, wigs, props and scenery so that the light lands where it is most needed.

13 Light can't stop in mid-air. Once it has lit what you want it to light, it travels on and lights everything else in its path. The spill from a bright light will illuminate everything around it. A

sharp shadow from a brightly lit actor or piece of scenery can be just as eye-catching as the object itself.

14 Mirrors and other reflecting surfaces on stage, however small, reflect the stage light back into the audience's eyes, often in very small areas of the auditorium. Don't torture your audience. Check every part of the house for this problem and amend lighting angles or reflective surfaces accordingly.

MOVING LIGHTS

Moving lights are remotely controlled lighting instruments. They have the direction, focus and colour of their light programmed during the **technical rehearsal** from a desk at the back of the auditorium. They are expensive, as is the back-up equipment that controls them and the extra operators needed to programme them. But they can also constitute a saving in cutting down the number of lights required in the regular rig. They are quite a recent development in lighting design, so the technology is improving year by year – becoming easier to deploy and cheaper to install.

Moving lights are very useful things. At the touch of a button they can intensify the light in any part of the stage. They can be programmed to provide any number of different **gobo** patterns. They can provide specific local effects from one moment to the next and instantly reset themselves for their next cues.

There are drawbacks. They make a noise. If you have twenty or thirty of them they make a lot of noise. They need to be programmed with great accuracy to be truly effective, and the actors who are lit by them can feel they are being similarly programmed – that their moves are being defined by the moves of the lights. For this reason, it's worth pointing out that moving lights cannot be seen as an alternative to **follow-spots**, although devotees have started to make that claim for them. A follow-spot, controlled by a person on a perch, can follow wherever an actor goes, however wilfully he moves. And where would we be without wilful actors? A moving light has yet to be programmed to take account of an actor's sudden physical inspiration or improvisation. But maybe that technology is just around the corner.

Lighting Designers

The Lighting Designer is one of your most important artistic collaborators, and you must choose your man or woman with great care – care for a happy collaboration and for the technical and artistic demands of the work.

As a matter of courtesy and common sense, it is advisable to choose your Lighting Designer only after you have chosen your **Set Designer**. He may have a strong view about the way he wants his set lit, or an admiration for, or antipathy to, a particular Lighting Designer. You want your Set Designer to feel comfortable with this choice and incapable of being unhappy about it at a later date should anything go wrong. Set Designers are more passionate on this subject than almost anything else. How their sets are lit is how their work appears to their public and to other theatre professionals. In these circumstances grievances can easily be nursed if a set is not appearing at its best.

Good Lighting Designers are concerned not only with the lights, but with the whole production. They are there to help tell the story – with their technique certainly, but also with their intelligence, analysis and wit. The best Lighting Designers thoroughly read and understand the play, study the design in great detail, watch rehearsals like hawks, and engage with the actors as well as with the director and the other designers. A good lighting design needs to be accommodated within a set, so the lighting instruments are unobtrusive to the action. This requires considerable liaison with the Set Designer. The Lighting Designer's other crucial relationship is with the **Sound Designer**. They both have large amounts of bulky equipment to deploy. You can't hear sound that is blocked by lamps or see light that has been blocked by speakers. They have to talk – and be friends. In fact you all have to be friends. Otherwise nothing's worth lighting.

BOARD OPERATORS

The Board Operator is the member of the lighting department who controls the lighting cues during the performance. The lighting board – comprising the computerised command system for all the stage lights in the theatre – is usually situated somewhere at the back of the auditorium, giving the operator a clear view of the stage, but in some older theatres, the operator has to sit in one of the boxes adjacent to the proscenium with an inferior view of the stage and therefore less awareness if anything has gone amiss with lighting cues or lighting instruments. In some very ill-equipped theatres the board is on a perch on the onstage side of the proscenium and the operator has to use a monitor to see the stage, but this is now increasingly rare.

The Board Operator must be a sensitive and sympathetic collaborator with the **DSM** or whoever is **calling the show**. His vigilance and sense of timing will be called upon in keeping the show's lighting up to snuff, especially in a **long run**. Lighting Designers choose their Board Operators with great care. During the technical rehearsals they have to work with considerable mental agility on very complex equipment while constantly looking for short cuts or clever alternatives to the designer's technical plot. The best Board Operators become Lighting Designers themselves. Indeed, it is quite rare for a Lighting Designer not to have started out as a Board Operator.

Limelight

Limelight is now a word more used outside the theatrical profession than in it, people who 'enjoy the limelight' or who want to 'hog the limelight' being those who need to be at the centre of everyone else's attention, but the term has its origins in quite recent theatrical history. Limelight was the most intense form of gas-lighting in the theatre before electricity revolutionised theatre lighting for ever. Each gas-lamp was backed by a reflector and manually fed with a stick of 'lime' to intensify the brightness of the flame. Leading actors fell into the habit of stamping on the stage in front of the limed **footlights** just before they spoke, causing the lamps to flare up and illuminate their important speeches more brightly, some elderly leading actors continuing in the habit long after gas ceased to be used in the theatre.

Old-fashioned theatrical slang for **follow-spots**, the original follow-spots being the most intense and directional of the available 'lime-lights'.

Line Readings

A line reading is a spoken demonstration of how the speaker believes a line of dialogue should be correctly interpreted, inflected or timed. It includes no explanation of **motivation** or character background. It is a simply a demonstration that requires an accurate copy in response.

Directors should avoid using line readings when **rehearsing a play**. They can seem like a short cut when an actor is having trouble understanding the meaning of a line, but they are nearly always counter-productive, only serving to make the actor dependent on the director for a thought process he should be discovering for himself.

A rehearsal dominated by line readings becomes imaginatively dead, with the actors feeling under surveillance by the director, constantly wondering if they have said their lines 'correctly' and paying less and less attention to the important issues of **subtext**, motivation and character history.

Very few directors are good enough actors to have any real confidence that the way they say a line will be appropriate or properly motivated, although many directors think they are better actors than they are. In these cases the actors must be forgiven an exchange of looks when the director wheels out a line reading. But the case of a director who is a good actor, and is known to be one, is somehow worse. Here the actors can start to feel a sort of despair that they will ever be able to play their parts as well as the director could if he chose to.

In either case, what a line reading says is, 'If I was playing the character, this is how I would say the line,' to which the actor could quite properly reply, 'That's all very well, but you aren't playing the character, I am, and I don't hear the line like that at all.' Or worse still, 'All right, that's how you want the line. I can hear it sounds about right, but now it isn't my line any more, it's yours. So why don't you play the character?'

If line readings are character theft, they are a theft that makes the director-thief poorer, not richer. Once you have understood this simple truth, you will avoid using line readings if you possibly can, and when you find yourself resorting to one, out of forgetfulness or frustration, you will feel a little ashamed immediately afterwards. And so you should.

Perhaps even more lethal than director-to-actor line readings are actor-to-actor ones. It is perhaps the greatest of all rehearsal sins for one actor to give a line reading to another unbidden. If ever it happens, you will be aware of a silent intake of breath from everyone else in the cast, a freezing of everyone's blood. For a director to be guilty of character theft is one thing, but for an actor it is an inexcusable lapse of etiquette.

Line Run

A line run is a complete run-through of a play without physical movement, also known as a word run. Line runs are most often deployed when actors have been playing a production in **repertoire** and the play has been out of the rep for a while. A gap of anything more than a few days may give some actors a problem remembering their lines. The line run serves as a memory refresher, but also provides a good warm-up session for a company out of touch with itself.

If time is short, the run might be confined to a single act of the play or turned into a speed line run with the text being spoken intelligibly but at a brisk pace.

An actor playing a very large part might request a personal line run, even before the play has opened. Keeping all the text of parts like Hamlet or Richard III in your head can be a taxing proposition, and a quiet run-through in the dressing room or Green Room with a Stage Manager or Assistant Director can be a useful and timely remedy for an actor fretting over the accuracy of his text.

Literary Managers

See **Dramaturgs**.

Long Runs

If you work in the commercial theatre or **musical theatre,** or in a subsidised company that runs a **repertoire** system, you may have the good fortune to see one of your productions run for a considerable time. In the **West End** and on **Broadway** runs can last for many months, sometimes years, and in any repertoire system productions can recur in sporadic patches over a year or even two. Long runs require careful management.

Good productions don't stand still. They develop. If you have inspired your company, as you should, to be creative with their acting choices, they won't switch off their creativity after the first night. Nor should you want them to. If your production is to continue in creative vein, your actors must continue to explore new avenues of character and meaning in the text they routinely perform. This routine can be deadly. In the commercial theatre, eight performances a week is the norm, usually divided into six evenings and two **matinées.** Repeating the same moves, the same inflections, getting the same laughs, the same rounds of applause can drive actors crazy. They change things in order to keep themselves sane. Some of these changes will be healthy and artistically apt and some will be self-serving and tasteless. In order to separate the wheat from the chaff you, or your assistant, must keep a fairly constant watch, encouraging the healthy development that keeps a production fresh and discouraging the little pockets of unsavoury private enterprise that pull a production out of shape.

Actors also make unintentional changes. Plays have rhythms of their own and characters have lives of their own. The longer a production runs, the more these rhythms and authorial inner voices will assert themselves. Be prepared for your actors to discover things in a play you didn't know were there. It is natural that they should do so and a testimony to the way you have prepared them for the work.

In order to monitor a long run creatively, you must take great care over your choice of **Associate** or **Assistant Director**. Or, if you are an Assistant or Associate, your care must be to keep equally good relationships with your principal and with the cast. There is great opportunity in a long run for the exercise of petty tyranny and the duplicity that always accompanies tyranny by proxy. Most directors have little time for the maintenance of their own long runs. They are off directing other plays elsewhere. In their absence, acting companies change their social complexion. Leaders emerge and social structures develop. A good Assistant Director fits in with these changes and develops his own good relationships with the emerging leadership on and off stage. A bad one will fight them and assume a resentment of change on behalf of his absent principal. He will insist on absolute fidelity to the patterns of movement and speech established in the rehearsal room. He will choose favourites and attract enemies. He will upset favourites and enemies alike. And all this will be done in the name of directorial authority. For the absent principal this can be an agonising corruption of everything his production has sought to achieve. For the assistant, it bodes only bad blood and a reputation for duplicity. For principal and assistant alike, monitoring a long run is a test of character.

Good communication is the answer to all these problems. Over a long run, principal directors must keep in constant contact with their assistants, **Company Managers** and **producers**, and assistants must maintain good communications in the other direction, listen to the wise voices on all sides and scrupulously avoid the assumption of an authority they have not earned and therefore cannot own.

LX

The standard theatrical shorthand for **lighting** or the Lighting Department, being a contraction of the words 'Electrical' or 'Electrician'. Thus 'the LX Department' or 'the Guys in LX', or 'That's Ernie, he's the chief LX.'

Lyrics and Lyricists

Lyric is written to be sung, not spoken. Poetry, or **verse,** is written to be spoken, not sung. As a general rule, lyric without music is unspeakable and poetry set to music is unsingable. This is because lyric lines need music to complete them, while poetic lines, having their own music contained within them, seem overblown when other music is added to them.

Consider three passages from *As You Like It*. First, a lyric from Act V Scene 1:

> *It was a lover and his lass*
> *With a hey and a ho*
> *And a hey nonny no*
> *That o'er the green cornfields did pass*
> *In springtime*
> *In springtime*
> *The only pretty ring time*
> *When birds do sing*
> *Hey ding a ding ding*
> *Sweet lovers love the spring.*

Set to music, this stanza has enormous charm, whether sung by children, as intended, or by adults. As long as it is sympathetically arranged, it arrives in the story of *As You Like It* like the spring it describes. But try speaking the stanza and making any sense of it with its heys and nonnys and ding a dings. Compared with the poetic imagery in the verse and prose of the rest of the play, the lines will sound hollow, insistent and silly.

Now look at this piece of verse, spoken by Duke Senior in Act II Scene 1:

> *Now my co-mates and brothers in exile*
> *Hath not old custom made this life more sweet*
> *Than that of painted pomp? Are not these woods*
> *More free from peril than the envious court?*
> *Here feel we not the penalty of Adam,*

The season's difference, as the icy fang
And churlish chiding of the winter's wind,
Which when it bites and blows upon my body
Even till I shrink with cold, I smile, and say
This is no flattery. These are counsellors
That feelingly persuade me what I am.

Try singing it. Go on, no one's listening. Start from the first line and see how far you get. No good? Start again with a different tune and a different rhythm. Still no good? Give up.

However hard you try, the result will always be the same. 'Co-mates' doesn't sing. Neither do 'painted pomp', 'free from peril', 'season's difference' or 'bites and blows upon my body'. The sentences are too long to be sustained in sung phrases, the grammar and rhetoric too complex and the irony incommunicable. This is a great passage of dramatic verse, its words packed with meaning and music, but its music disappears when sung. Whatever melody you choose, whatever rhythm you force onto the innate metre of the verse, the result will be the same – an embarrassment of riches with one type of music cancelling out the power of the other.

Now look at another lyric from Act II Scene 7 of the same play. It is the second verse of a song sung by Amiens, one of Duke Senior's 'co-mates and brothers in exile'.

Freeze, freeze, thou bitter sky
Thou dost not bite so nigh
As benefits forgot.
Though thou the waters warp
Thy sting is not so sharp
As friend remembered not
Hey ho, sing hey ho, unto the green holly.
Most friendship is feigning, most loving mere folly
Then hey-ho the holly
This life is most jolly.

This is a serious lyric with the same theme as Duke Senior's passage of verse. The singer/songwriter has written a gloss on his master's philosophical belief, and it is tempting to think of Shakespeare deliberately lyricising the former passage in the latter. And look how he has done it, shortening the lines, intensifying the images in a few carefully chosen phrases and rhyming the ends of the lines to land them on a musical down-beat.

'The icy fang and churlish chiding of the winter's wind' has become 'Freeze, freeze, thou bitter sky'.

'Are not these woods more free from peril than the envious court?' is simplified into 'Thy sting is not so sharp as friend remembered not'.

'I smile and say, this is no flattery. These are counsellors that feelingly persuade me what I am' is innocently paraphrased in 'Hey-ho the holly. This life is most jolly.'

Both passages are serious. Both have great beauty. Both compare the beneficence of nature with the complacency of society. Both are expressed, we feel, by men who are feelingly persuaded by what they say, or sing. But the words of the former passage would be suffocated by music, while those of the latter need the oxygen of music to make them breathe. This is the difference between verse and lyric.

THE ART OF THE LYRICIST

Just as poetry does not make good lyric, so poets do not always make good lyricists. The two arts are very different. Poets who study to be good lyricists can, no doubt, learn to be as good as anyone else, but they must learn a set of skills that are in many ways alien to the art of poetry.

There is a warning in this. Many a director, working on a **new musical** or **opera**, has offered his services as lyricist when the existing lyrics have proved inadequate. He does this in the belief that his skills as a wordsmith will qualify him for the job. He has written a play or two in his youth, perhaps some poetry, and anyway, he reasons, his business is words and the analysis of language – how hard could it be to write a few lyrics? Well, if those around him let him take on the job, he will soon find out. It is fiendishly difficult.

Melody, to which lyric must be fitted, is comprised of a series of notes, some of them more stressed than others, some of them falling on the downbeat at the start of a bar, others on the unstressed upbeats, some of them in rising patterns, others falling, some at the top of the singer's range, others lower down, some of them with easily negotiable intervals between them, others with more challenging leaps, some in simple harmonic progression, others in complex chromatic phrases. For every lyrical phrase there is an appropriate melodic structure.

If the lyrics are written first, the composer must decide how to reflect the rhythm of the language in his musical phrase. A poorly written lyrical phrase will lack the rhythm and succinctness a good melody requires. It will be too long, or have too many polysyllabic words, colliding consonants or sibilance. Worst of all, it will contain words that don't 'sing' at all, words too packed with meaning, too technical, intellectual or abstruse. Then there are the vowels. The higher and longer the note, the harder it is for a singer to place a 'closed' vowel on it, especially an 'e' sound. Each vowel sound has its associated characteristics of colour and tone. Voices of different **tessituras** react to them in different ways, but they all prefer open vowels on the top notes of their ranges.

If the melody is written first, the lyricist's job is even more difficult. He must spend countless hours racking his brains for the phrase that will perfectly express the melody or the 'hook' that characterises the melody's most haunting phrase. If he is translating a lyric from a foreign language his task is a little easier, as he is constrained in his choice of content by the intention of the original text, but if he originates his own text, his range of choices can blind him with a snowstorm of words.

Assuming all the technical aspects of rhythm and structure have been mastered, the lyricist must also consider the characters he is writing for, how they would say or sing things, what they are feeling and thinking, what dialect they use, what class they are, what are their habitual turns of phrase. All this is made more difficult if a rhyming scheme is included. Landing rhymes at the end of lines is a notoriously difficult exercise, but without them many musical genres seem incomplete. Using internal rhymes complicates matters further. A complexity of rhymes will make the characters seem too clever for their own good, and over-simple rhymes will lurch the lyrics towards cliché. In comic writing, complexity can be entertaining, but in serious drama it easily becomes an irritant. Finding the right balance is always hard and avoiding cliché even harder.

Thus it is to be a lyricist. One well-known contemporary lyricist describes the job as being 'like doing your own root-canal work'.

It is easy to see from the above analysis why the composers of operas and musicals are often their own best lyricists, providing they have the wordsmithery required for the job. If they lack those skills, they can spend years looking for the right partner, hopping from lyricist to lyricist in a series of unsatisfactory liaisons and hanging on with grateful fidelity when they find a partner that suits them.

M

Make-up

See **Hair and Make-Up.**

Marking

In theatre, **musical theatre** and **opera** 'marking' is a rehearsal technique used by actors, singers or dancers as an alternative to playing, singing or dancing a part 'full out'. In dances, fights or heavily physical sequences of action, the performers walk through their moves, using rudimentary gestures to indicate their actual moves and to demonstrate the accuracy of their memories.

Marking is used to recall forgotten sequences or, during a repetitious rehearsal process, to conserve energy or emotion for a proper performance. It can also be used as a safety precaution. A preliminary 'marked' run-through of a realistic fight sequence can accustom the fighters to the split-second timing that separates the elegant-looking parry from the broken head.

There is a risk to marking. Some **technical rehearsals** can go on for days on end. If the actors mark their performances throughout they can easily get out of touch with the emotional reality of their characters. As director you must be sensitive to this and encourage the actors to play full out at least once while a scene is being visited, though you must also watch for any tiredness or lack of concentration in the air. Actors playing flat out when their hearts are not in it can get into equally bad habits.

You may at times have to be a referee over marking. If one actor clearly wants to go for a scene and give everything physically and emotionally, it can seem insensitive and rude if another actor continues to mark. For this reason the normal courtesy is for actors to agree beforehand that a scene is to be marked before they get started on it, and they should clear it with you before they do so. Some of your **collaborators,** too, may have a view about marking that they will expect you to take into account. A Sound Designer can't judge levels of **sound effects** or radio-mikes if voices are being marked. A Lighting Designer can't organise his follow-spot cues if none of the actors are standing in quite the right places. And a DSM can't call the end of a scene if the cue line is inaudible. Marking can cause an entire rehearsal to go flat. Don't be afraid to give everyone a kick and insist on a full-out rehearsal before a session ends.

In **opera,** marking means under-singing. No singer can sing flat out at all times and still have a voice left to perform with. By singing quietly, and down the octave for high passages, the voice can be kept in reserve, though singers should be encouraged to sing out at least once during a rehearsal or the role won't have a chance to play itself into the voice. If a singer is suffering from vocal strain, tiredness or a cold, then marking is essential.

The Mark-Out

The stage management team 'marks out' the floor of the **rehearsal room** with sticky tape of various colours to denote the limits of the stage area and the accurate position of any permanent scenic pieces, upper levels, staircases and so on, the different colours of tape representing different acts or scenes.

Stage Managers sometimes jump the gun by doing the mark-out before the director has seen the rehearsal room and approved the layout. Make sure you dissuade them from this in advance as the marking-out process is extremely time- and tape-consuming, and you and your Stage Manager will be jointly cursed by the rest of the team for insisting on a change. Wise Stage Managers will always check the layout with the director first, but where wisdom is in short supply or where you are the visitor to a well-established company with a rehearsal routine laid down by the preferences of others, you must make your instructions clear before anyone wastes a lot of time and money on your behalf. The safest way is to postpone the mark-out until the end of the first day of rehearsal, when you and the Stage Manager can have a quiet five minutes of bonding over the box of coloured tapes.

You will sometimes inherit a rehearsal room from a recently departed company and their mark-out will still be laid out on the floor, a ghostly memory of the hours of imaginative toil that have been spent by a company of actors believing in and then negotiating themselves around those thin coloured strips of scenic meaning. But at the end of most rehearsal periods the tape is lifted from the floor, leaving only ghost marks on the boards or cloth beneath, the best-loved rehearsal rooms having the most marks, an elaborate and honourable fretwork of theatrical history.

Marks

Not to be confused with the **mark-out,** marks are the little pieces of coloured tape the stage management team puts on the floor to indicate the furniture settings from one scene to the next, each mark corresponding to the leg of a chair or table or the corners of a solid piece or a carpet.

At the end of your rehearsal period, your SM team will measure the distance between all the marks and transfer them accurately to the surface of the stage. The mark-out will be torn up and thrown away.

The more furniture settings you have, the more little splashes of coloured tape you will accumulate on your stage floor, and they may not look too good. Once the **technical rehearsal** has finished and your cast and crew are thoroughly accustomed to finding their marks in the dark or half-light of scene changes, reduce the marks to tiny slivers of tape. Use fluorescent tape if necessary, but try not to make the surface of the stage look like a planetarium.

In the US, marks are called 'spikes' and marking-tape 'spiking-tape'.

Masking

Masking is theatrical shorthand for 'blocking from the sight of the audience'.

In acting parlance it refers to an actor blocking another actor from the audience's sight ('You're masking me!' 'Try not to mask each other in that scene'), but it can also be used to describe an actor being hidden by a piece of scenery or a large prop ('You're masked behind that tree, you know'), or even bits of costume or wig ('The hat's very pretty, darling, but it totally masks your face'), or an actor blocking from sight some piece of **business** he or another actor is engaged in ('You do know you're masking yourself, don't you?').

Experienced actors develop strong anti-masking instincts, but they will still need your help from time to time. Inexperienced actors will need much more attention. There is no sadder sight than a young actor doing something quite brilliant while masking himself from the audience in the process.

Masking also refers to the black drapes or tabs, usually made from heavy Bolton, velvet or other light-absorbing fabric, hung just off stage to mask the wings and the overhead lighting bars and flying pieces from the audience's view. At the start of every **technical rehearsal** you and your designer should visit every part of the auditorium and make a note of everything you can see in the offstage areas and hanging over the stage that you know you won't eventually want to see and that won't be obscured by simply switching off the **working lights**. Your Technical Director will then work out the most efficient and economical way of masking all around the stage.

In **opera**, soft fabric masking tends to absorb the singers' voices. This is particularly problematical when there are no other hard surfaces on the stage to reflect the vocal sound into the auditorium. For this reason, any masking you put close to your singers should be hard masking, not soft.

Masks

Many plays require masks of one sort or another, and many theatre traditions and production styles around the world depend on masks for their portrayal of human types.

From the classical theatre through **Commedia dell'Arte** to the **physical theatre** and **opera** productions of the modern day, masks have been used variously as amplification devices, character definers, alienation effects or conventional disguises. It is perhaps only in this last case that masks can be thought of as being absolutely necessary to the story and meaning of a play rather than to the outward trappings of its performance. When masks are called for in the text of a play, for characters attending a masked ball, for example, or in any circumstance where the wearing of masks allows for a conventional confusion of identities, it is difficult to see how, or why, one would want to do without them. In all other circumstances, masks represent either a requirement of tradition or a stylistic choice by author, director or designer. In either case the characters who wear them are unaware, as characters, that they are doing so and must incorporate the idea of the mask into their idea of themselves and each other. Modern productions of classical tragedy or Commedia plays might use masks, but it is perfectly possible, many would say preferable, that they should be performed without them.

Masks are not easy to use, and you should think long and hard before you incorporate them in a production. Even if your case for using them is a strong one, you will still have to take your actors and audience with you.

Actors hate wearing masks. Unless it can be proved to them that the case for them is unarguable, they may react strongly against them. Masks are uncomfortable. Edges cut into the face, ties bite at the back of the head and facial sweat gets trapped in every nook and cranny. Too tight and after a few minutes the discomfort becomes very irritating, too loose and the mask slides off with the sweat. Even when carefully fitted, masks constrict vision, speech and breathing. They stink of whatever they're made of – glue, paint, plastic, papier-mâché, varnish. More importantly, inside a mask the wearer hears his voice in a strange way. For singers this is especially difficult. The sounding chambers in the nose, sinuses and forehead reverberate weirdly on the ear. Most importantly, the mask reduces the actor's physical portrayal of his character to a facial stereotype. This is what actors hate most about them. Why should they put all that loving attention into exploring and motivating a character if all the evidence of their work is to be flattened, typified and suffocated?

That's the case against masks. The case *for* masks can still be a strong one. You may feel the characters you want to mask are anyway unremarkable for the complexity of their thought or motivation. Perhaps they have no complexity at all. You may wish to emphasise the stereotypical nature of their roles in the play, their goodness or evil, their experience or innocence, their victim-hood, obedience or complete absence of personality. In **opera**, designers are fond of masking entire choruses as a way of pointing up their essential lack of individualism, their herd instinct. You may be working in a broadly comic, Commedia-like style, where every character behaves according to a preordained type or 'humour' and masks are essential adjuncts to the physical life of the actors.

If, in spite of all the technical drawbacks, you decide masks are necessary to your production, you mustn't be complacent about the process. You have to take your actors with you. The best way to do this is to dedicate proper rehearsal time to exploring the relationship between actor and mask.

Because a mask cuts out the actor's normal means of facial expression, he is forced to use non-naturalistic acting techniques to create a character, including a greater dependence on physical movement and vocal effect. If the emotions cannot play across the face they must play all the more elsewhere – in the body and the voice. The mask itself still has a story to tell, but it can only speak if the actor feels it has become part of his being. This takes a lot of thought and a lot of practice.

The best masks are created by a partnership of actors and designers. Set aside proper amounts of rehearsal time for the designs to be proposed, discussed and agreed upon. When the prototype masks are ready, give each actor plenty of time to work on his own before introducing him to other masked, or unmasked, characters.

MASKS AND MIRRORS

Mask work is impossible without mirrors. Actors know their own faces intimately and they must become just as familiar with their masks if they are to use them with authority. Put mirrors all round your rehearsal room, enough so your actors can work independently of one another. A dance studio is a perfect venue for mask work.

Give the actors time to study the masks, on their faces and off. Then get them to create a personality for their character, one suggested by the mask. Tell them not to force a voice or a set of attitudes on the mask – but let the mask tell them what the voice should be like. Characters will slowly start to emerge.

Move on to a larger physical life for the characters. Full-length mirrors are essential here. Just as with the voice, let the mask suggest the character's movement. The more extreme the style of the mask, the further the actors can go in stylising their voices and movements.

Once everyone has found a strong character to suit their mask, mix the characters together and see how a relationship between them changes their behaviour. Adapt your favourite theatre **games** and **improvisations** to explore the life of the characters that emerge from the masks.

MASKS, MAKE-UP AND COSTUMES

As your mask work develops, keep refining the design of the masks. Actors should have individual consultations with the designer to make their masks more comfortable and effective. At this point, start introducing make-up and wig design so that the mask becomes more and more integrated into the overall look of the character. If the **Costume Designer** is not designing the masks, he must also be included in these discussions.

FULL MASKS AND HALF-MASKS

A full mask covers the whole face, including the mouth and chin. A half-mask stops just south of the nose, leaving the mouth free for speech.

Full masks are much harder to use than half-masks, unless the character is silent. Voices sound weird inside full masks, even when the mouth is made so wide that the mask becomes grotesque. Don't imagine you can solve this problem with a microphone. You'll just end up with amplified weirdness. Of course, if that's what you want, go for it.

Masque

Deriving from the French word for mask, masques were a form of usually amateur court entertainment popular in England in the late sixteenth and early seventeenth centuries. The actors, singers and dancers wore masks and often highly elaborate costumes, performing in extravagantly designed settings and culminating in a masked ball with performers and audience mingling together in joint celebration.

Ben Jonson was the most significant playwright to contribute to the form and the architect and designer Inigo Jones its presiding visual genius. The greatest masque, in purely literary terms, is undoubtedly *Comus*, written by the young John Milton in 1634, but as the genre developed, all pretensions to literary merit were slowly abandoned and it became an exercise in pure spectacle, perhaps the earliest precursor of the Las Vegas and Broadway-style musical extravaganzas of today.

The influence of masque on professional theatre was clearly discernible in Shakespeare's plays, particularly *As You like It*, *Cymbeline* and *The Tempest*, and continued into Restoration drama, where new standards of scenic and costume design clearly derive from the masque tradition.

Master Carpenter

The Master Carpenter is the chief stage technician in many theatres, especially in the West End playhouses and opera houses. He is responsible for the physical maintenance of the entire theatre – stage, backstage, **auditorium** and foyers. He supervises the **get-ins and get-outs** of shows, employs the stage crews for each production and provides technical support for the run of the show. He is the final arbiter in the theatre of what is technically possible or allowable and has to strike a careful balance between what a director or a designer may require of him and his staff and what his union will allow him to agree to. Master Carpenters vary enormously in temperament and ability, but a director and designer should always try to make friends with them. Their good will is gold dust. Their ill will can cause a lot of trouble.

Master-Classes

The master-class format was developed in the classical music world as a way of exposing young students to the talents and ideas of a master artist – a singer or pianist or violinist or whatever – masters who are not accessible to them because they do not normally teach or, if they do, they teach only the most accomplished of professional performers. A student plays a prepared piece, or part of it, and the master makes comments and asks for variations in the performance, sometimes illustrating what is required by a demonstration of his own skills. When the master has said all he has to say about the student's performance, another student steps up and the process repeats itself. The same format can be used for directorial master-classes.

Directorial master-classes can be very dull affairs, nothing more than question and answer sessions, unless they are carefully prepared for. They work best when the student directors have done some real work beforehand. Students should come prepared with examples of their work in the form of short scenes created around small groups of actors. It's never a good idea for young directors to appear in one another's pieces. They are rarely good enough actors and in any case they should be paying attention to the scenes being performed, not worrying about how embarrassing they're being. Out-of-work actors are only too keen to take part in such exercises, with or without payment. They get a chance to work with a young director and have their work seen by an established professional.

The scenes should be set up carefully by the student director, but with a minimum use of furniture and props. At the end of each scene the master director makes a critique of the work and may also redirect the actors or direct the student director in redirecting them. The other student directors, and indeed the actors, should be encouraged to contribute their own opinions and ideas.

Matinée

A matinée is a daytime, usually an afternoon, performance. Most professional theatre companies include matinées in their weekly schedule, usually one in midweek and one at the weekend, though they increasingly try to programme extra matinées at weekends when audience demand is at its height, especially when a show is proving popular with children.

For actors, matinées can be rather odd affairs, the make-up of the audience being quite different from that of evening shows. Block bookings for schools mixed up with large numbers of elderly and retired people can make for an unusual atmosphere – the hard of hearing struggling against the hard to control.

Whatever the make-up of an audience, never let your actors use it as an excuse for a lacklustre performance. There's no such thing as a bad audience, only a badly motivated cast. It's up to you to keep them up to snuff. Interestingly, the evening show on a two-performance day is often the best the actors do all week, but only if they've really given the matinée their best shot. As they start their second show they may be a little tired, but they are also relaxed and centred in their characters.

A two-performance day during a **preview** period can be a very good way of settling a show into a happy rhythm.

Memory

Memory is a crucial part of the actor's instrument, and control over it represents an important aspect of his technique.

There is an art to memory. In actors it expresses itself in two ways. They use memory to recall their experiences and observations. The accuracy of this recall and the taste with which they apply it to their acting defines them as artists. But they must also memorise their lines and the thoughts that underpin them. This is a different sort of memory and must be mastered in a different way. Emotions and experiences can be recalled from the long-term memory even after years of forgetfulness. Lines must be learnt in a matter of weeks and are often forgotten within days of the close of a run. Personal memory is permanent and life-defining. Character memory is temporary and ultimately inconsequential.

With good actors, these two streams of memory coalesce, the words and thoughts of the character mingling inextricably with the emotional and experiential recall of the actor. With less good actors, the two streams run on parallel lines, never touching each other and so never touching us.

You can help them. A failure to integrate the memory expresses itself, in its most extreme form, in **drying**. A dry is not merely a lapse of words, it is an inability to memorise the thoughts behind the words and a corresponding failure to infect the thoughts and feelings of the character with those of the actor. Encourage your actors to learn thoughts, not words. Steer them away from mnemonic tricks towards a real appreciation of the structure of the scene and their character's place within it. Talk to them about 'remembering' rather than 'memorising'. If they have true recall of their own experience or can imagine a character's experience as being truly like their own, if they can properly appreciate how like their characters they are, the memory of the bare lines will become a matter of much greater facility for them.

Method

The so-called 'Method' is the **Stanislavsky** theory of acting as taught in the Lee Strasberg School in New York and made famous by the likes of Marlon Brando, Marilyn Monroe and assorted other famous alumni, however briefly they may have followed or flirted with the school and its teachings.

The Method has had its passionate followers, especially in North America, and its equally passionate detractors, who see in its heavy reliance on techniques of emotional recall a perversion of Stanislavsky's original intention and meaning. Like all techniques, like all methods of acting, the Method can be effective in the hands of a talented and committed performer but deadly in the hands of a slavish devotee.

The director's relationship to all such techniques and practices must be finely judged. If you employ an actor who relies heavily on them, then you must learn how to talk to that actor in the language he is most comfortable with, or at least not be fazed when he expects you to understand it and work with him in using it. Equally you may have to protect other actors from being made to feel ignorant or insufficient by an actor who is exclusively wedded to a particular working method. If anyone's method of acting starts to get in someone else's way, then you will have to intervene and arbitrate. If all else fails then you must be ready to insist that your own method must prevail. In any event, good actors should always be ready to rise to the challenge of working alongside a new technique, however odd they find it at first, though there will always be some whose habits or cynicism prevent them from joining in. In such cases your own powers of persuasion, or self-deception, will be put to the test.

Metre

Metre is the rhythmic form of poetry, defined by the way words and phrases are broken up into their constituent stressed and unstressed syllables.

The study of metre is essential to the understanding of drama written in **verse**. If you seek to analyse a poetic play text, whether it be by Shakespeare or by one of his contemporaries or by any dramatic poet before or since, you must first acquaint yourself with the rules of metre and learn how to 'scan' each line.

SCANSION AND PROSODY

Scansion is the metrical analysis of a line of verse. If you scan a line correctly, you speak it with all its stresses on the correct syllables. The rules of scansion – or prosody – are by no means absolute, and within certain parameters a poetic line may be scanned in different ways and still retain its sense, though an alteration in scansion will usually change the meaning of a line.

Scansion is an essential exercise in the study of poetic texts and one you will have to perfect if you want to direct the plays of Shakespeare or his contemporaries. It is most useful when talking to actors about the meaning of a line of verse. If the sense of a line is proving obscure, as with Shakespeare it often is, or rhythmically awkward, the first thing you should do is scan it. Break it up into its constituent 'feet', decide where the stress in each foot lies and then put the line back together again, giving it the new stresses you have discovered. More often than not the correct scansion of the underlying rhythm of the line will make the meaning apparent.

METRICAL FEET

Every line of poetry can be scanned into a number of metrical 'feet'. A foot is a rhythmic parcel of two or three syllables. Each foot is spoken with a stress on one or two of its syllables.

The names of the feet are adapted from classical Greek and Roman poetic metres. The commonest feet used in English verse are the duo-syllabic iamb, trochee, spondee and pyrrhic and the tri-syllabic anapaest.

Poetic styles usually derive their names from the number of their governing metrical feet per line. Thus an iambic pentameter

Metre

(see below) is governed by five iambs to the line, a dactylic hexameter by six dactyls, a trochaic quatrameter by four trochees, and so on.

The principal feet used in English dramatic verse are:

Iamb: two syllables, non-stress + stress – as in 'suppóse' or 'depárt'

Trochee: two syllables, stress + non-stress – as in 'fáther' or 'háppy'

Spondee: two syllables, stress + stress – as in 'mán-chíld' or 'shé-wólf'

Anapaest: three syllables, non-stress + non-stress + stress – as in 'to despáir' or 'i' the níght'

Dactyl: three syllables, stress + non-stress + non-stress – as in 'énergy' or 'lóveliness'

Pyrrhic: two syllables, non-stress + non-stress – as in 'of the' or 'in the'

Tribrach: three syllables: non-stress + non-stress + non-stress – as in 'up in the' or 'out of the'

Iamb

Most of Shakespeare's blank verse has three or four iambs per line with other types of feet making up the balance, though there can be as few as one and as many as five iambs per line.

These lines from the Chorus's speech at the start of Act IV Scene 1 of *Henry V* are typical:

Nów én / tert'áin / conj'éc- / ture of / a tíme
When crée / ping múr / mur and / the pór / ing dárk
Fílls the / wíde vés- / sel of / the ún / i'vérse.
From cámp / to cámp / through the / fóul wómb / of níght
The húm / of éi- / ther ár- / my stíl- / ly sóunds
That the fíx- / ed sén- / ti néls / ál'most / rec'éive
The séc- / ret whís / pers of / each óth- / er's wátch.

To see how predominant the iamb is, look how these seven lines are scanned:

Spondee / Iamb / Iamb / Pyrrhic / Iamb
Iamb / Iamb / Pyrrhic / Iamb / Iamb
Trochee / Spondee / Pyrrhic / Iamb / Iamb
Iamb / Iamb / Pyrrhic / Spondee / Iamb
Iamb / Iamb / Iamb / Iamb / Iamb
Anapaest / Iamb / Iamb / Trochee / Iamb
Iamb / Iamb / Pyrrhic / Iamb / Iamb

Out of thirty-five feet, there are twenty-four iambs, five pyrrhics, three spondees, two trochees and one anapaest.

The iambs are therefore creating the regularity of the metre, with the five pyrrhics (non-stressed feet) there to stop it sounding *too* regular. The other types of feet are used for particular effects at particular moments.

The spondee (double stress) of the first line starts the whole speech on a strong note with the word 'Now', the rest of the line being regularly iambic with the neutral pyrrhic at the fourth foot. The second line is regular. The word 'Fills' is stressed in the trochee (stress + non-stress) at the beginning of the third line, with a spondee broadening the 'wide vessel' immediately after it and the rest of the line regular. The fourth line is regular until a startling image is created with a spondee for 'foul womb'. The fifth line is made up entirely of iambs, the repetitious rhythm mimicking the effect described by the words. The anapaest (two non-stresses and a stress) at the start of line six is necessary to break the rhythm sustained throughout the previous line, with the trochee on 'almost' nicely reflecting the meaning of the word and preparing the ear for the seventh line, which is regular.

Thus it is that iambs form the basis of blank verse, creating a rhythm from which irregularity springs and to which irregularity returns.

Trochee

A trochee is the 'opposite' of the iamb. Trochees are used in blank verse as a substitute for iambs, to break up the regularity of the iambic pentameter. They are most commonly used in the first, third or fourth feet of a five-foot iambic line. Thus from the first

Metre

scene of *A Midsummer Night's Dream* . . .

Fúll of / vexá- / tion cóme / I, with / comp'láint

. . . the first foot is a trochee, followed by two iambs, a pyrrhic and an iamb.

Later in the same speech . . .

With féign- / ing vóice / vérses / of féig- / ning lóve

. . . you have the trochee in the third foot with two iambs either side of it.

Two trochees often occur in the same line but rarely in consecutive feet and hardly ever in the fifth foot. In Act II Scene 1 of the same play . . .

Thére'fore / the wínds / píp'ing / to ús / in váin

. . . there are trochees in the first and third feet with the other three feet all iambs.

More than two trochees in a line would give trochees the majority and make the line trochaic rather than iambic. Rewrite the last line above as . . .

Thére'fore / wínds are / píp'ing / to ús / váin'ly

. . . and the point is clear. The line loses its iambic structure and becomes decidedly un-Shakespearean.

The most extreme example of trochaic pentameter comes from Act V Scene 3 of *King Lear*:

Néver / néver / néver / néver / néver

Spondee

Along with the trochee and the pyrrhic, spondees are used in blank verse to break up the regularity of the iambic line.

Because it has two equal stresses, the spondee is also used to give part of a line a stronger emphasis. In the Prologue to *Romeo and Juliet* we have . . .

A páir / of stár- / cróssed lóv- / ers táke / their lífe

390

. . . the spondee in the third foot with a pair of iambs on either side of it drawing strong attention to the central image of the line, the 'star-crossed lovers'.

A number of spondees used consecutively can create a solemn or passionate effect. In the first scene of *A Midsummer Night's Dream* Hermia has . . .

Só will / Í grów, / só líve, / só díe, / my lórd

. . . which consists of a trochee, followed by three spondees in a row and then a final iamb.

An iambic pentameter with only one iamb in it is a rarity, and Shakespeare only uses such a tactic when one of his characters has a very strong point to make. The last line of Jaques's 'All the world's a stage' speech from Act II Scene 7 of *As You Like It* is even more emphatic . . .

Sáns téeth, / sáns éyes, / sáns táste, / sáns év- / ery'thing.

. . . with four spondees in a row followed by a pyrrhic, though some actors might stress the last foot as an iamb.

Anapaest

Anapaests aren't commonly used in blank verse because the poetic line is so dominated by the duo-syllabic iamb.

Shakespeare uses the anapaest very sparingly in the early plays, but more frequently in the later ones. Thus from the second scene of *Macbeth* . . .

What a háste / looks thróugh / his éyes. / Só should / he lóok

. . . is an iambic pentameter, with the first foot an anapaest, the fourth a trochee and the other three all iambs.

Hamlet's second line has another good example in its final foot:

Not só, / my lórd, / Í am / too múch / i' th' sún

Dactyl

The dactyl is the 'opposite' of the anapaest. Much more common in French dramatic literature than in English, it is also the principal

foot of the classical Greek and Roman dactylic hexameter, just as
the iamb is the principal foot of the iambic pentameter.

Examples of dactyls in Shakespeare are extremely rare and in
any case can usually be scanned in some other way.

Thus from the first line of Sonnet 106:

Whén in / the chró- / ni'cle / of wás / ted tíme

The word 'chronicle' is a dactyl in itself, but here clearly scans as
the second half of an iamb and a pyrrhic. In order for 'chronicle' to
be a dactyl, you would have to rewrite the line:

Whén in / the óld / chró'ni'cle / of wás / ted tíme

Not a good idea.

PYRRHIC

Pyrrhics are used in blank verse to break up the regularity of the
iambic rhythm and thin out the richness of the imagery. Thus in the
penultimate scene of *Richard III* . . .

A hórse! / A hórse! / My kíng- / dom for / a hórse!

. . . is an iambic pentameter with three iambs, followed by a pyrrhic
and then another iamb in the final foot.

Shakespeare often uses a pyrrhic in the third foot of a line to
divide it into two equal parts, providing a rhythm perfect for the
use of **antithesis**. Thus Juliet on her balcony . . .

Den'ý / thy fáth- / er and / re'fúse / thy náme

. . . has a line of four iambs separated in the middle by a pyrrhic.

Tribrach

Tribrachs are rarely used within the iambic structure of blank
verse, but they do crop up from time to time. In Act V Scene 4 of
Macbeth, Old Siward has the line . . .

Thóughts spéc- / ulative / their ún- / sure hópes / re'láte

. . . which is made of a spondee and a tribrach followed by three iambs.

Caesura

In English blank verse, a caesura is the metrical break in the middle of a line occasioned by a fresh thought or by punctuation indicative of imagery or meaning.

In iambic pentameter, with its odd number of feet, the caesura will always fall either before or after the centre of the line. Thus in Sonnet 26 Shakespeare has:

To wítness dúty, / nót to shów my wít

The syllable count is equal on both sides of the caesura, but the stress count is two before and three after. In naturally resisting a balanced caesura, lines of pentameters maintain their forward drive.

A caesura affords the actor an opportunity for a change of thought or even a snatched breath, but rarely enough time for a pause. Thus from Act V Scene 1 of *Romeo and Juliet*, Romeo soliloquises:

> Well, Juliet, I will lie with thee tonight
> Let's see for means. / O mischief, thou art swift
> To enter in the thoughts of desperate men!
> I do remember an apothecary
> And hereabouts a dwells, / which late I noted
> In tattered weeds with overwhelming brows
> Culling of simples. / Meagre were his looks.
> Sharp misery had worn him to the bone
> And in his needy shop a tortoise hung
> An alligator stuffed, / and other skins
> Of ill-shaped fishes; / and about his shelves
> A beggarly account of empty boxes,
> Green earthen pots, bladders and musty seeds,
> Remnants of packthread and old cakes of roses
> Were thinly scattered to make up a show.

There are five observable caesuras (marked /) in the passage. The extent to which they are marked by the actor is a matter of interpretation, but the first one is clearly indicated by a change of thought and meaning. The second and fourth both represent slight changes of thought. The third is necessary for the sense of the words to be clear. Without it, 'simples' would run into 'meagre', making the line hard to follow. And the fifth marks a fresh thought and enough of a breath for the actor to be able to finish the sentence and the speech without further pause for thought or breath.

What cannot be emphasised enough is that caesuras are not **pauses**. If the actor makes a pause at each caesura he destroys the rhythm of the verse.

Elision and contraction

In blank verse, just as in modern conversational prose, the syllables of some words are contracted or unpronounced, two adjacent vowels may be elided or slurred together, as in 'I'm' or 'It's', and sometimes consonants may be omitted in the middle of words, causing the vowels on either side of them to coalesce, as in 'e'er' for 'ever' or 'o'er' for 'over'.

In the above passage from *Romeo and Juliet*, a most important elision occurs in the first line. 'Juliet' is a two-syllable, not a three-syllable word, her 'i' and 'e' being elided. If you hear someone saying he is about to do a production of 'Romeo and Juliette' you know he hasn't grasped the basic rules of scansion or even read the play properly. Juliet's name is mentioned some forty times in the play. Pronounced 'Juliette' that would make for forty mis-scanned lines.

The name Romeo must also be contracted to two syllables. If it isn't, then one of the most famous iambic pentameters in Shakespeare would end up with fourteen feet:

O Romeo, Romeo, wherefore art thou Romeo

In the third line of Romeo's speech above, the second syllable 'desperate' must be contracted, making 'desp'rate', or the line would have eleven feet and a bumpy rhythm. Similarly, in the next line 'apothecary' must be contracted to 'apothec'ry'.

The final -ed of past tense verbs is usually contracted, as in modern English. Thus in the speech above 'tattered' is 'tatter'd', 'stuffed' is stuff'd' and 'ill-shaped' 'ill-shap'd'. But you must always be on the lookout for the uncontracted form. In the passage from *Henry V* above, 'fixed' in the sixth line must be pronounced 'fixéd' for the line to scan.

In the scansion of blank verse, the final -ed problem causes more grief to actors than any other. To stress or not to stress, that is the question.

Untrained actors, even some trained ones, will sometimes sprinkle their text with stressed -ed endings, imagining they are thereby making it sound more 'Shakespearean', when what they are really doing is making it sound quaint and old-fashioned, the verse equivalent of a sign inscribed 'Ye Olde Tea Shoppe'.

Consider . . .

> An alligator stufféd, and other skins
> Of ill-shapéd fishes

. . . and you can hear what I mean.

On the other hand, there are professional actors who so dedicate themselves to making the verse sound acceptable to a modern ear that they feel a sense of failure if they have to observe a stressed -ed ending. They are usually the same actors who swallow the rhymes in rhyming couplets. But they should overcome their scruples and use a stressed ending when it is clearly indicated by the scansion. Consider these famous lines:

> Write loyal cantons of contemnéd love

or

> The good is oft interréd with their bones

or

> Accurséd be the tongue that tells me so

The scansion of these lines would be mangled by contracting the -ed endings, as would thousands of other lines in the works of Shakespeare and his contemporaries.

But there is no clear rule about -ed endings. You must judge each case on its own merits, even when the cases come fast upon one another as they do in Portia's courtroom speech from *The Merchant of Venice*:

> The quality of mercy is not strain'd.
> It droppeth as the gentle rain from heaven
> Upon the place beneath: it is twice bless'd:
> It blesseth him that gives and him that takes.
> 'Tis mightiest in the mightiest: it becomes
> The thronéd monarch better than his crown.
> His sceptre shows the force of temporal power,
> The attribute to awe and majesty,
> Wherein doth sit the dread and fear of kings;
> But mercy is above this sceptr'd sway
> It is enthronéd in the hearts of kings
> It is an attribute to God himself,
> And earthly power doth then show likest God's
> When mercy seasons justice.

Here 'strain'd' and 'bless'd' and 'sceptr'd' have contracted endings, 'thronéd' and 'enthronéd' uncontracted, 'droppeth' and 'blesseth' have archaic endings but are greatly preferable to 'drops' and 'blesses' for reasons of scansion and euphony, ''Tis' is a contraction of 'It is', and 'mightiest' must be stressed both times as a two-syllable word, as must 'temporal'.

And then there are the -tion words. By the time Shakespeare was writing, the duo-syllabic -ti'on or -si'on had more or less dropped out of everyday usage, but there are instances in his plays where the scansion demands it. They nearly always occur at the end of lines, where disruptions of scansion are hardest to disguise.

Hotspur has:

> And fellows, soldiers, friends,
> Better consider what you have to do
> Than I, that have not well the gift of tongue,
> Can lift your blood up with persuasion.

'Persuasion' here is clearly scanned as a four-syllable word. The actor has a choice. Either he ignores the scansion and leaves the line half a foot short, or he uses the context of the speech to over-enunciate all four syllables of 'per'sua'si'on' and suggest that Hotspur has little time for such fancy concepts, or he steers a middle course and slightly stretches the word to fill up the gap in the rhythm.

There are countless other examples. *King John* has:

> With dreadful pomp of stout invasion

Oberon in *A Midsummer Night's Dream* has:

> Such tricks hath strong imagination

Ulysses in *Troilus and Cressida* has:

> Of pale and bloodless emulation

The Duke of Austria, again from *King John*, has:

> For courage mounteth with occasion

In each case you and your actor must choose. Do you observe the correct scansion and disconcert the modern ear? Do you ignore the scansion and disrupt the rhythm of the line? Or do you stretch the word a little to fill up the space?

Masculine and feminine endings

A line of verse that has an extra, unstressed syllable in the last foot is said to have a feminine ending. The extra syllable is nearly always part of a two- or more syllable word. Only occasionally is it a monosyllabic word on its own at the end of the line.

Here are five consecutive masculine endings from *Love's Labour's Lost*:

> From women's eyes this doctrine I derive
> They sparkle still the right Promethean fire
> They are the books, the arts, the academes,
> That show, contain and nourish all the world
> Else none at all in aught proves excellent.

You can feel how the ends of these ten-syllable lines all land in the same way.

Metre

Compare them with these two balanced pairs of masculine and feminine endings from Romeo:

> A beggarly account of empty boxes,
> Green earthen pots, bladders and musty seeds,
> Remnants of packthread and old cakes of roses
> Were thinly scattered to make up a show.

Lines one and three both have eleven syllables with feminine endings on 'boxes' and 'roses'. The other two lines are regular pentameters with masculine endings on 'seeds' and 'show'.

Now look at these lines from Theseus in *A Midsummer Night's Dream*:

> The lunatic, the lover and the poet
> Are of imagination all compact
> One sees more devils than vast hell can hold:
> That is the madman. The lover, all as frantic,
> Sees Helen's beauty in a brow of Egypt.
> The poet's eye in a fine frenzy rolling,
> Doth glance from heaven to earth, from earth to heaven,
> And as imagination bodies forth
> The forms of things unknown, the poet's pen
> Turns them to shapes, and gives to airy nothing
> A local habitation and a name.

In a speech of eleven lines, there are five feminine endings – on 'poet', 'frantic', 'Egypt', 'rolling' and 'nothing'. The line that ends with 'heaven' is not a feminine ending – the word 'heaven' being elided both times in the line to 'heav'n', giving the line only ten syllables in all.

There is also a rare example of feminine rhythm in the middle of a line on:

> Thát is / the mád(man). / The ló / ver, áll / as frán (tic)

This is a twelve-syllable line, one of the extra syllables being accounted for by the feminine ending on 'frantic'. The only way it can scan is for the 'man' of 'mad'man' to sit unstressed in the second foot; 'man' cannot fall in the third foot to make up the first syllable of an anapaest because of the clearly indicated caesura after 'madman'. But two feminine rhythms in one line serve Shakespeare well here, the irregularity of the line perfectly reflecting its subject matter, as it continues to do throughout the speech. Both the poet's eye and his verse are 'in a fine frenzy rolling'.

Notice how, in every case, the first foot of a line immediately following a feminine ending is an iamb, the unstressed first syllable of the iamb making room for the extra syllable at the end of the previous line. This is generally the case in Shakespeare's verse, but you can see an exception in the first two lines of Romeo's speech immediately above.

Shakespeare uses a lot more feminine endings in his later plays than in his earlier ones, giving scholars a valuable clue as to their chronology.

End-stopped and run-on lines

An end-stopped line is one where the meaning finishes with the end of the line. A run-on line is where the meaning runs through the end of one line and into the next. This is also known as 'enjambment', taken from the French word for encroachment, the meaning of one line encroaching on the meaning of the following line.

A combination of end-stopped lines and run-on lines gives good poetry a variety of rhythm essential to the avoidance of monotony.

Here is Proteus from *Two Gentlemen of Verona* with six lines, only the fourth a run-on line, all the rest end-stopped:

> To leave my Julia shall I be forsworn.
> To love fair Silvia shall I be forsworn.
> To wrong my friend I shall be much forsworn.
> And e'en that power which gave me first my oath
> Provokes me to this threefold perjury.
> Love bade me swear, and love bids me forswear.

Here the character is taking short, quick thoughts, illustrating his confused state, the five sentences all finishing succinctly at the ends of the lines.

Metre

An actor speaking heavily end-stopped verse must be careful not to land too frequently or uniformly on the line endings or he will break up the overall rhythm of his text.

Rhyming couplets often feature end-stopped verse, it being easier for the poet to land the second rhyming word if the meaning finishes at the end of the line.

Thus Helena from *A Midsummer Night's Dream*:

> O, I am out of breath in this fond chase.
> The more my prayer the lesser is my grace.
> Happy is Hermia, wheresoe'er she lies
> For she hath blessed and attractive eyes.
> How came her eyes so bright? Not with salt tears.
> If so, my eyes are oftener washed than hers.
> No, no, I am as ugly as a bear,
> For beasts that meet me run away for fear.

In contrast, here are the opening lines of Jonson's *Volpone*, two end-stopped lines announcing the theme, then, as Volpone sees the gold in his treasure chest, Jonson gives him ten consecutive run-on lines of confident adoration before he comes to the next end-stopped period:

> Good morning to the day. And next my gold.
> Open the shrine that I may see my saint.
> Hail the world's soul, and mine. More glad than is
> The teeming earth to see the longed-for sun
> Peep through the horns of the celestial ram
> Am I, to view thy splendour, darkening his:
> That lying here, amongst my other hoards
> Show'st like a flame by night; or like the day
> Struck out of chaos, when all darkness fled
> Unto the centre. Oh thou son of Sol
> (But brighter than thy father) let me kiss,
> With adoration, thee, and every relic
> Of sacred treasure in this blessed room.

In heavily run-on verse such as this it is crucial for the actor to pitch up the line endings, using the last stressed syllable of each line as a springboard from which to bounce onto the first stressed syllable of the next.

A sure sign of an actor's inexperience in **verse speaking** is when he tails off the end of every line regardless of whether it is end-stopped or run-on, producing a monotonous rhythm and destroying the meaning of the text.

Rhyming couplets

Rhyming couplets are pairs of rhyming iambic pentameters, also called heroic couplets. Unrhymed iambic pentameters are known as blank verse (see below).

Shakespeare uses rhyming couplets very freely in his earlier lyrical plays, especially in *Love's Labour's Lost*, *A Midsummer Night's Dream*, *Richard II* and *Romeo and Juliet*. He gives the characters in these plays rhyming couplets when he wants them to talk in a deliberately measured or courtly way. The two pairs of lovers in *A Midsummer Night's Dream* talk almost exclusively in them, until they become too excited or too bewitched to keep it up. Friar Laurence in *Romeo and Juliet* similarly starts off in rhyming couplets, but as the plot develops and he loses control of the events, the couplets are replaced with blank verse.

In plays with a lot of rhyming couplets there are correspondingly fewer feminine endings, it being far easier to rhyme in English on a masculine ending than a feminine one. As Shakespeare's verse becomes more complex in his middle and later period plays, there are fewer and fewer couplets, though he still uses them to express aphorisms or to give a period to the final two lines of a scene and a good exit to the actor who speaks them.

Inexperienced actors are sometimes embarrassed when rhyming couplets crop up in their dialogue and try to speak them as if they weren't really there. This is usually caused by a misplaced sense of 'naturalism' and is always counter-productive, the attempt to swallow the rhymes making the whole couplet sound less natural, not more.

Rhyming couplets are not in the text as poetic decorations or conventions. They are pointers of meaning and character. If an actor swallows a rhyme he will never properly express the line in which it occurs. If he uses it, it will buoy him up and help him to reveal both the character and the moment in which the character is speaking. In any event, most rhymes are impossible to swallow. Try swallowing this one:

> I'll have grounds
> More relative than this. The play's the thing
> Wherein I'll catch the conscience of the King.

Or this:

> O time, thou must untangle this, not I.
> It is too hard a knot for me t'untie.

Now repeat them, landing on the rhyming words at the end of the line. These rhymes are a gift from the playwright to the actor and should be accepted as such with gratitude and pleasure.

Internal rhyme

A line of poetic text, or a lyric, is said to possess internal rhyme when a word or words within it rhyme with a word or words at the end of or in the middle of the same line or an adjacent line. Thus from *Henry V*:

> The country cocks do crow, the clocks do toll.

Or from *Henry IV Part 2*:

> Never, O never do his ghost the wrong
> To hold your honour more precise and nice
> With others than with him.

The general rule with internal rhyme in poetic drama or sung lyric is the same as with line-end rhyme; the actor or singer should observe the rhyme, high-lighting it with just enough stress for the audience to be aware of it.

If an actor ignores an internal rhyme or tries to swallow it out of a misplaced sense of naturalism, it has the curious effect of making the line sound poorly written, as if the writer had made a mistake in making the rhyme and didn't bother to correct it.

METRICAL FORMS

Iambic pentameter

As analysed above, the iambic pentameter, or decasyllable, is the governing poetic line of the Elizabethan and Jacobean verse drama, consisting of five iambs or iambic feet per metric line. Most English verse drama uses a basic rhythmic structure of five iambs, though other types of feet are almost invariably interspersed with the iambs.

The iambic pentameter is the fundamental pulse of Shakespeare's verse. As he wrote he must have had the iambic rhythm accompanying his thoughts at an unconscious level, with the line of five feet as the normal package of poetic meaning, however regularly or irregularly he observed it.

Pentameters serve the English language well as conveyers of thought, sound and meaning. English sentences can easily be rendered into iambs as a basic rhythm (the perfect metric foot for the French language is the dactyl), and the five-foot line is the perfect length to carry a set of complex images in a compacted form.

A line containing more than five feet starts to require too many thoughts for an audience to assimilate in one phrase and becomes just too long for an actor to speak in one breath. A line shorter than five feet is harder to fill with rhythmic variation, too short for thoughtful development or antithesis, and a series of them sounds bouncy and repetitive.

Blank verse

Unrhymed iambic pentameters are known as blank verse. Blank verse was first used by the Earl of Surrey in his translation of Virgil's *Aeneid*, then taken up by the writers of court tragedies and finally introduced into popular drama by Marlowe in *Tamburlaine*.

Most of Shakespeare's plays are written in a mixture of blank verse and prose, though the verse in the early plays is peppered with rhyming, or heroic, couplets and in the later plays the blank verse becomes so irregular that verse and prose are sometimes indistinguishable.

If you wish to direct Shakepeare's plays or those of his

contemporaries, you must learn the rules of **verse speaking** and
how the blank verse lines are structured according to their metre.

Alexandrines

An alexandrine is a line of poetry consisting of twelve syllables or
six iambic feet, also known as an iambic hexameter. It is used from
time to time in blank verse to extend the normal rhythm of the
iambic pentameter by an extra foot, especially at the ends of scenes
or to create elsewhere an effect of solemnity, strength or superfluity
of emotion.

Shakespeare uses alexandrines very sparingly in his early plays,
but more and more in his later ones. An early example from Act IV
Scene 1 of *A Midsummer Night's Dream* has Theseus calling to his
huntsmen to release his dogs:

Uncóu- / ple in / the wést- / ern váll- / ey lét / them gó

A later one, from Act V Scene 2 of *Othello*, has an alexandrine
nestling between two iambic pentameters, giving the double images
of *light* and *rose* a mounting and complementary emphasis:

I knów / not whére / is that / Promé- / thean héat
That cán / thy líght / relúme. / When I / have plúcked / thy róse
I cán- / not gíve / it vít- / al grówth / agáin.

In French poetry, alexandrines are lines of twelve and thirteen
syllables written in alternate couplets.

METRICAL VARIETY

Although a particular type of foot may govern a type of poetic
metre, poetry written with every foot stressed the same, as in a
nursery rhyme, is only useful for creating a deliberately comic,
childlike or sinister effect.

Thus in *A Midsummer Night's Dream*, Snug the joiner intro-
duces himself as a Lion in the play within a play:

You ládies, yóu whose géntle héarts do féar
The smállest mónstrous móuse that créeps on flóor

> May nów perchánce both quáke and trémble hére
> When líon róugh in wíldest ráge doth róar

This creates an atmosphere of gentle burlesque in perfect contrast to his role as a lion in a serious tragedy.

When we first meet the fairies in the same play, Shakespeare changes the pace of the language with a series of metrical flourishes. The First Fairy starts with two pairs of alternately rhyming anapaestic dimeters . . .

> Over híll, over dále,
> Thorough búsh, thorough bríer,
> Over párk, over pále,
> Thorough flóod, thorough fíre

. . . and then continues in rhyming trochaic tetrameters . . .

> Í do wánder éverywhére,
> Swífter thán the móonës sphére
> Ánd I sérve the fáiry quéen
> To déw her órbs upón the gréen.

. . . with four trochees to the line, the fourth one missing its final syllable. She finishes her verse with an iambic tetrameter and three iambic pentameters, all in rhyming couplets . . .

> Í must go séek some déwdrops hére
> And háng a péarl in évery cówslip's éar
> Farewéll, thou lób of spírits, Í'll be góne
> Our quéen and áll her élves come hére anón

As she bids farewell to Puck she creates an effective picture, but in obliging her to use such a range of metres, Shakespeare has created a sense of childishness and simplicity that tells us we are in a different world from the one in which the play started.

In *Macbeth*, the Weird Sisters' use of tetrameters has a similarly galvanising effect on the rhythm of the play, but in a much more sinister tone.

Good dramatic poetry is written with considerable rhythmic variety and even in the earliest plays of Shakespeare, which are mostly written in quite regular iambic pentameters, he still uses all the rest of the common metrical feet. His last plays are written with an astonishing variety of metre.

Every poet has a metrical style, a characteristic usage of metre that distinguishes his work from another's. At first glance all blank verse looks more or less the same, but by immersing yourself in the plays of the Elizabethan, Jacobean, Caroline or Restoration theatre, you will soon learn to distinguish between the metrical styles of Marlowe, Shakespeare, Jonson, Ford, Webster and Dryden, just as a classical music enthusiast can distinguish between the styles of Mozart, Beethoven, Brahms or Schubert.

Mezzanine

Mezzanine is an almost exclusively American term describing the upper tier of a two-tier **auditorium**, often abbreviated to 'the Mezz', the lower tier being the **orchestra**.

Most American theatres built after the turn of the twentieth century were constructed on the democratic principle that everyone in the audience should have an equal view of the stage, however far away they are seated. This laudable aspiration means that most American theatres are only built on two levels but have very wide stages and auditoria in order to fit in a commercially viable number of seats. If you have worked exclusively in British theatres you may find it hard to adapt your technique to such a broadly spaced audience, but no harder than if you are an American director trying to adapt to a British auditorium that rises to three, four or even five levels of giddily rising tiers on a very small site.

Mime

Mime is an integral part of the actor's craft. Few actors are expert mimes but most have rudimentary miming skills, learnt at drama school or picked up piecemeal in the course of their careers.

Pure mime, that is the art of wordless storytelling, is a form all

its own, and its specialist performers live in rarefied realms somewhere between theatre and dance. They are nonetheless our brothers and sisters in spirit, and some of them career between theatre
and mime just as others career between mime and modern dance.
If you plan a production that relies to any great extent on mime,
you would think yourself fortunate to have such an artist in your
cast.

Many productions use the miming of objects as a performance
technique. A play being performed in a **rough theatre** or **poor theatre** style can easily eschew **props** and furniture and require its
actors to work on the 'imaginary forces' of the audience. It is an
excellent discipline to say to a cast of actors, 'We will perform
without a single prop' – a discipline for actors, director and audience. In poor theatre companies it can also be a necessary discipline. If you can't afford the right props, better by far to have none
at all than to saddle yourself with inadequate rubbish.

If you decide to use a consistent mime convention you must insist
on your actors getting it right. If you can't demonstrate miming
skills yourself, get the cleverest mime in the company to do it for
you. Include miming **games** in your morning warm-ups. If you can
afford it, get a real mime artist in for a day or two and have him
watch the sequences that include mime and then let him loose on
your actors. They will appreciate it. Good actors have an admiration, even a fascination, for technical skills of this sort and will be
happy to emulate them as best they can.

If a door is to be solidly imagined, it must be solidly mimed. A
knock on it must stop at its surface and not go right through it. Its
handle must be firmly turned, not just twiddled in the air, and
some resistance felt in the turning. The next actor to come through
the door must turn the handle in the same place with the same
resistance. And the hinges of the door must be located on the same
side. As it closes, the sound of it must be imagined, the depth of
the sound depending on the weight of the door. And so on.

Even in productions that are essentially naturalistic in tone,
actors are often required to supplement their 'real' actions with
partially mimed ones. A tavernful of drinkers may be equipped
with bottles and glasses but have, by directorial decision, no liquid

to put in them. They seem to drink but in truth they are miming. In a poorly mimed production this will look unconvincing. Bottles will be swigged so quickly that no liquid could possibly be making its way from bottleneck to mouth or from mouth to gullet. Drink will be swigged but not savoured, or savoured but not swallowed. Glasses will be removed from lips at the same angle at which they were sipped, their imaginary contents emptying themselves down the actors' fronts. Bottles will be poured into glasses so roughly that real liquid would have splashed all over the room.

Eating, drinking, **fighting** and all manner of sexual activity are usually at least partly mimed in this way. The swatting of flies, the taking of snuff, the shedding of tears, the wiping of sweat will usually require imaginary flies, snuff, tears and sweat.

Whenever an actor is required to substitute a pretend object for a real one, or perform an action without the resistance of a real reaction, the arts of mimesis and acting become inextricably entwined.

THE SITTING PROBLEM

If you decide to have your actors mime all their props and do without furniture, you will have to address the sitting problem. In real life we sit down all the time. There are chairs, stools, benches, beds and all manner of perching places strewn around us in our everyday lives. Most of us don't habitually sit on the floor or stay standing up for hours at a time. We sit when we can.

So if you want your production to be like life, what do you do? Or even if you don't, what do you do?

1 Mime sitting. This looks daft. Only qualified contortionists can make convincing looking angles with their bodies. Even then it looks daft.
2 Create a chair-less world. If characters sit, they sit on the ground. A good solution if you can make the world work that way.
3 Do without all props and furniture *except* chairs, or boxes at chair height. A common compromise. Lightweight chairs or

boxes are scarcely noticeable if used as an apparently natural part of the actors' actions and moves.

Mimicry

The ability to imitate the physical and vocal characteristics of another person, usually for satirical purposes. Not to be confused with **acting**.

The Model

Once the director and **Set Designer** have had their initial creative discussions, the designer starts to make a scaled-down model of the set.

Many designers start with a rudimentary version of the model in black or white card before their ideas fully develop. This way they can easily start all over again if they, or the director, are unhappy with it. Once they are sure of the vision they want to create, they slowly build up an exact replica of the set as they wish it to be realised and they people it with miniature human figures to represent the characters of the play.

Models can be astonishingly detailed, and making them an extremely time-consuming craft in itself. Many young designers spend their apprenticeship years making models in their mentor designer's studios. But designers also recycle old elements from previous models drawn from a huge stock of doll's house-sized furniture and strangely clad figurines. Before a model is completely finished you do see some very bizarre combinations of these evidences of your designer's past career.

Most designers make their models to a scale of 1/25. Some work with 1/50, but unless your play is being mounted in a very small theatre these do lack detail and the human figures seem very tiny indeed, as if you were viewing the play from a vantage point outside the auditorium walls. They are also extremely fiddly to make. Working with 1/25 allows a designer to create real painterly detail where necessary and an apparent vantage point reasonably close to the stage.

Monologue

A monologue is a play or dramatic interlude performed by only one person, not to be confused with a **soliloquy**.

The term is also used to describe a long speech, or conflation of shorter speeches, extracted from a play for **auditioning** purposes. There are indeed many published collections of such monologues, but actors should beware of using them, unless they also consult the source of the monologue they choose. It is embarrassing for an actor to have to admit in an audition that he knows nothing of the play from which his monologue is drawn, and irritating for the director trying to draw a better performance out of him.

Motivation

Motivation is the word most commonly used by actors to describe the thought process of the character they are playing, what it is that makes their characters do what they do and say what they say. Interchangeable terms are 'intention', 'objective' and 'want', but they all describe the same thing.

Motivation is the active part of the **subtext** of a line. Thus an actor who doesn't know what his character's conscious or subconscious motivation is will make a gesture or deliver a line without the essential underpinning of thought, feeling or instinct required to make the gesture or the delivery seem real.

It is commonplace in rehearsal for an actor to say to a director, 'I don't know what my motivation is on this line,' meaning, in essence, 'I don't know what my character wants, or is thinking, when he says this line.'

It is the actor's job to have a sufficient motivation for every line or physical move in the text – the cleverer the actor the more complex, interesting and communicable the motivation.

It is the director's job to make sure that every actor is sufficiently motivating every line and move, to suggest suitable motivations for motivation-free zones of the production and to balance the motivations of all the characters so that they accord with one another.

Most acting methods in the Western theatre tradition are based on the investigation of motivation, or marrying the actor's investigation of himself with his ability to motivate the character he is playing.

All good naturalistic acting is based on the correct analysis of the motivation of character. One of the most characteristic features of bad naturalistic acting is that it appears to be, and usually is, **impersonation** without motivation.

The first great proponent of the theory of inner motive forces for actor and character was Konstantin **Stanislavsky,** and a study of his work is essential for the director of naturalistic dramas.

Movement Director

The role of the Movement Director is a comparatively recent development in the theatre, reflecting a modern preoccupation with more physical forms of theatre. Movement Directors may be permanently employed by large theatre companies to provide regular in-house training on all their productions. More often they work as freelance collaborators for any production that makes extraordinary physical demands on its actors but where an absence of dance or sequences of formalised movement makes it inappropriate to employ a **choreographer**.

The lines can be somewhat hazily drawn between the roles of choreographer and Movement Director, and the same people may work in both disciplines. In the end the **credit** accorded to both jobs is a matter of taste and degree. The more formalised the physical work and the more distinctive its style the more likely you will want to use a Choreographer credit, but where the physical work is completely subsumed into the acting style a Movement Director credit is more appropriate.

Movement Director

If you have the good fortune to work with a Movement Director, use him. Start each day with a movement session involving the whole cast. Work with him to find a physical language for your production that all your actors will be happy with and that plays to their physical strengths. Set him the task of loosening up your more physically constrained actors, helping them to integrate their intellectual, emotional and physical lives with their moves.

Whatever the historical period of your play, make sure your Movement Director bases his work on character rather than empty style. Include him in all your talks to the actors about their roles and what the story requires of their characters so that he supplements your work with his own.

In **musical theatre** and **opera**, a **Musical Stager** and a Movement Director are more or less interchangeable terms. Whatever they call themselves, encourage them to work with the singers on finding a character language that is appropriate to lyric and musical line. Get them to challenge the physical clichés that are so characteristic of acting in musicals and opera, but make sure they do it through character and the establishment of real situations or they will simply replace one set of clichés with another of their own devising.

Moving Lights

See **Lighting and Lighting Designers**.

Mugging

Mugging is the overuse of the face in order to milk a reaction from an audience. It is frequently engaged in by actors with unusually elastic features who take advantage of their gift as an easy way of scoring laughs.

The 'mug' might happen while the actor is speaking a line, or be a silent reaction to some other actor's line. Mugging can happen in isolated patches or in a more or less continuous stream, depending on how seriously the actor needs to mug and the audience feels obliged to enjoy it. Mugging ranges from the outrageous and shameless to the almost undetectable. It can break out in serious work as well as comic, but its natural home is the broad comedy or the **farce**, where it seems much less of a crime.

The cause of it is usually a lack of confidence in the actor, who believes that a more subtle method of communicating a thought will be less effective or less hilarious.

The effect of it with most audiences – and the more serious the play the more serious the effect – is that they stop believing in the **reality** of the character who is doing the mugging. Even while laughing uproariously at the effect they are quietly calculating that they no longer believe. But the accomplished recidivist mugger will never understand that point and will take the audience's laughter to be a licence for further excess.

Mugging, like many other aspects of mediocrity, is catching. If you diagnose one case of it, you must dose it quickly before it spreads to others.

Mugging is the enemy. Stamp it out.

Multiracial Casting

See **Casting**.

Music

The arts of music, dance and drama have been linked together since the dawn of time and are still so tangled up with one another that it is inadvisable to try to distinguish between them too definitely.

It is a rare production that has no music in it whatsoever. Most plays either call for music or may be enhanced by the addition of music. Characters play or sing, accompanying themselves or accompanied by others. Music plays in the distance, or from onstage electronic sources, live ensembles or bands play music on stage or in the wings or the **pit**, and all manner of recorded music supplements or underscores the spoken text.

All but one of Shakespeare's plays, *The Comedy of Errors* being the exception, require music. So do all of Chekhov's major plays and most of Strindberg's. Even Ibsen, who had a poor ear for music, works it into his plays. The real world is full of music, and any playwright who aspires to describe it must choose to include or exclude what he hears.

Leaving aside the theatre that defines itself by its music – **opera, musical theatre** or plays with songs – let us consider the various ways in which music can have an impact on the production of plays and the extent to which that usefulness is a matter for the artistic judgement of the director.

There are three basic applications of music in the dramatic theatre – integral music, atmospheric music and incidental music, but music being such a commonplace convention, perhaps one ought to add a fourth – absence of music, or silence.

INTEGRAL MUSIC

Integral music is music demanded or implied by the text and heard by the characters. It can be broken down into three basic categories:

1 *Music expressive of character*

The most common form of this is song. In real life people sing – they know songs, they make songs up and they share their songs with others. So it is on stage. There are countless plays in which characters are required to sing by their author. They sing to communicate feeling, to entertain others or to earn a living or some combination of all three. There are also plays in which characters play music, dance to music or simply listen to music as a way of expressing their thoughts or feelings to the audience. Music can also sound inside a character's head, unheard by the other characters. Whilst being integral to a particular character, this can also have a strongly atmospheric effect. For instance, a character obsessed with the music of

Bach and prone to soliloquy will provide a director with obvious opportunities for accompanying his thoughts with Bach's music. A character who used to be a famous instrumentalist but who can no longer play could motivate a director to use the music that used to fill his life – and still fills his ears. A character being driven mad by the clamour of modern life could take refuge in an inner landscape of musical sounds. And so on and so on.

2 *Music demanded by situation*

This might be music played live by a character or characters on stage, or come from a radio, gramophone or CD player that is part of the onstage environment, or it may be the feature of some off-stage event. This sort of music may not always be specifically mentioned in the text but may still be clearly indicated by the situation.

3 *Music in support of a storytelling device*

The **Chorus** in Greek drama, the **deus ex machina** of the Renaissance theatre and the Brechtian ballad could all fall into this category.

These three types of integral music may sometimes overlap. Integral music can also have a strongly atmospheric effect.

Chekhov, for example, was a master of the use of integral music. The sound of Andrei playing his violin in *Three Sisters* or the quiet hum of the spinning top or the offstage military band from the same play, the mysterious sound of the distant breaking string in the second act of *The Cherry Orchard*, Telegin's guitar in *Uncle Vanya* or the singing from across the lake in *The Seagull* – these sounds are all deeply necessary to the meaning of the scenes in which they occur, but they are also expressive of character and atmosphere. Such is the authority of Chekhov's musical ideas that it becomes problematical for a director to consider including further musical ideas of his own. But most playwrights are less specific in their musical demands, giving the director far more scope for invention.

Music

ATMOSPHERIC MUSIC

Atmospheric music is music played during the action of a scene but of which the characters of the play are unaware. This is the theatrical equivalent of film music and must be used with skill and selectivity if it is not to compete with the natural sonority of the words or the sense of the dramatic argument.

Music is a highly emotional tool, powerful in providing its listeners with pictures and feelings irrespective of anything else that might be happening on stage.

Some directors make the mistake of imagining they can use music in the theatre exactly as it is used in film, but the control that a film director or editor has over the volume and timing of a musical track, added after the film has been shot, is completely absent in the theatre, where good actors use their voices as instruments in themselves and the emotional content of a scene is created by a conspiracy between actor and audience, varying every night the play is performed. Unless the musical atmosphere is extraordinarily subtle, which it can be when a Sound Designer and composer collaborate to create a **soundscape** out of a mixture of **sound effects** and music, there will always be a risk that the audience will feel its emotions are being manipulated or that the feelings that should be communicated by the characters have been hijacked by the accompanying score.

Having said that, you may find that atmospheric music can support the actors rather than compete with them, especially in stretches of the play where no text is being spoken or where there is an ironic distance between the action on stage and the music accompanying it. For instance, the performance of a mundane task with gloriously heightened music in the background will serve either to elevate the meaning of the task itself or to reduce its value to comic meaninglessness, depending on the director's or the actor's intention.

Certain sorts of atmospheric music can easily be confused with music integral to the action. If you have a solo violin playing under the text of a scene, how is the audience to know whether it is an atmospheric effect or a naturalistic sound cue – a neighbour practising the violin, for instance? This confusion can, of course, become absurd. Who has not imagined, when a great orchestral music cue swells up around a pair of ecstatic lovers kissing on a balcony, that there really is an orchestra playing in the garden just below them? The risibility of such thoughts is reason enough to eschew atmospheric music unless you are absolutely sure of its appropriateness and integrity.

In *Three Sisters* the military band that plays stirring march music throughout the last few minutes of the final act serves as an ironic counterpoint to the plight of the three women left to grieve and hope for a better future in the wake of the departing troops. The power of this idea grows as the music grows, but only because the audience has been asked to imagine that there is a 'real' military band playing just out of their vision. If Chekhov himself had not set up this idea and made it integral to the scene it would be impossible to have the music playing at all – and a director who proposed that loud brass band music should be playing while the final moving speeches of the play were being delivered would be mocked from the rehearsal room. What is beautiful and poignant as music integral to the action would be preposterous if used merely for atmosphere.

INCIDENTAL MUSIC

Incidental music is music that is incidental to, rather than an essential part of, the dramatic structure of the play. It can be used in a variety of ways.

1 To define the overall architecture of a play, by the establishment of a musical background, the repetition of musical ideas throughout the course of the drama and the use of character or thematic leitmotifs.
2 To establish a sense of historical period or cultural location.
3 To help create a performance style – a musical tone of voice that underpins the authorial, directorial or acting style.
4 To support the flow of the play from one scene to the next – also known as scene change music. From the flourishes and

sennets of the Elizabethan theatre onwards, authors and directors have used music to mark the end of one scene and the start
of another and to cover any change of setting between the two.

5 As an **alienation** device, to create an ironical distance between
the feeling in the music and the thoughts of the characters or
the author.

6 To disguise any awkwardness of staging or drown out any
other undesirable noise.

ABSENCE OF MUSIC

The same audiences that go to theatre also go to concerts – classical, rock, pop and all the rest of it. Many of them will play music
themselves or sing or dance. Very few of them will not own a CD
player, a radio and a television. They hear music every hour of their
waking lives. Music plays in lifts, in shopping malls, in hairdressing
salons. It blares from loudspeakers on the streets, it busks to us on
the underground, it tells us to be patient on the telephone, it booms
past us out of flashy cars and sizzles from the earphones of passing
strangers. It is a constant accompaniment to television and radio
programmes, whether they concern themselves with music or not.
It pings from our computers, pongs on our dashboards, beeps from
our telephones and ding-dongs at our doors. Even in a silent theatre, where a thousand attentive pairs of ears are listening with rev-
erence to a perfectly uttered poetic phrase, the audience will
suddenly be assailed by the insistent, neurotic ring of a cellphone
burbling out 'Für Elise', thus simultaneously mocking the play,
Beethoven, and the audience's sanity.

Music has become one of the tyrannies of everyday life, and
many people seek an escape from it. You must think carefully
before you decide to add to the accumulated cacophony resound-
ing in their ears. People need some silence in their lives, whether
they realise it or not, and theatre is primarily a place of silence, for
silence is the ideal medium for thought, words and ideas. Music is
only useful if it helps us to understand the thoughts and listen better to the words and the ideas. At the very least it mustn't make
things harder to hear or to understand.

CHOOSING THE RIGHT MUSIC

Before choosing music for a production, you must address your own musical competence or lack thereof. You may have some musical proficiency – you may be an amateur instrumentalist of some sort, you may fancy yourself as a bit of a composer – but whatever your talents or vanities, you must be rigorously honest about your capacity to create music for a show at the same time as you are directing it. Most directors have good musical ears but little real musical creativity or originality. Unless you are quite exceptional musically, or the musical requirements of your play are absolutely minimal or can be supplied by the selection of a few tracks of already recorded music, you are going to need help from a **composer**, a **Musical Director**, a **Sound Designer**, or some combination of all three.

You and your collaborators, if any, should start by identifying all the examples of integral music in the play. If there is a song or songs, it or they will probably be the most significant musical feature. A character singing a song within a scene is usually an important event in the play, marking a moment of strong feeling or thought. If the song is sung well and the melody a good one, it will have a strong effect on the audience's attention and memory. Could the melody of the song be woven into the musical fabric of the play, making its impact as a song all the greater? If there are lots of songs, how do they relate to one another rhythmically and tonally? And how do the songs relate to the rest of the music in the play, if any? Can the incidental music derive its musical ideas from the songs?

If there is no integral music in your play, then start with the idea of silence. Ask yourself if music is necessary to the play at all. How will it help? Clear your mind of productions you have seen and enjoyed where music seems to have had an impact and look at the structure of your own play with clean ears. Is there any need for atmospheric music in the play? Listen to the music in the words themselves and decide whether music will support them or get in their way. Identify any periods of silence in the play and decide whether they would benefit from being accompanied by music or better left in real silence.

Music

If you decide that incidental music is important for your production, you and your collaborators must decide how to structure it. What is the first music the audience hears during the play? Is music playing when they enter the auditorium, thus setting up music as a basic currency for the whole entertainment? Does music precede the first spoken word? If so, how much music? Is there some sort of musical prelude or overture before the curtain rises or the first actors appear on stage? Is there music between the scenes? Is there music playing into the interval, or throughout the interval? How does the second act start? Is there music at the end of the play? Does it play on into the curtain call? Does it continue to play after the curtain call is over? Does it continue to play in the foyers?

You must decide what the musical idiom of the play should be. Should the music be drawn from the same historical period as the play? Should it deliberately conflict with it? Is there a cultural or social element to the choice of music? Some directors feel that the music in their plays must always be contemporary – the play is being directed, designed and acted in a contemporary style, so why should the music be any different? Others are addicted to historical authenticity – or some pastiche version of it. Others prefer a synthesis of historical and modern styles.

You must decide if music is to be specially composed for the play or drawn from existing sources. If the play is well known and often performed there will be a score or scores from which to choose. Some plays may have traditional melodies already strongly attached to them – the 'Willow Song' in *Othello* for example, or Feste's final song in *Twelfth Night*. Do you use such melodies or invent new ones?

If you decide to use an existing source of recorded music, then you must acquire the **performing rights** to be allowed to use it. This is not always plain sailing, so beware of falling in love with a musical idea that you can't afford or get the rights to use.

If you decide to create new music for a production then you and your composer will need to discuss the size of the band and the make-up of the instruments, according to the artistic needs of the play and the size of the overall budget. If you decide to record the music and have it played back mechanically during the show, you will have to make a deal with the **musicians** and their union. If they are to play live then they'll need somewhere to play from, and that will have an impact on the design of the show.

How visible do you want your musicians to be, or how involved with the action? Can your actors double as musicians, for artistic or economic reasons, or both?

Musical Director

In theatre and **musical theatre** the quality of the musical performance is controlled by the Musical Director, usually abbreviated to MD.

All musical decisions involve the MD in one way or another. He liaises between **composer, orchestrator** and copyists, participates in the auditioning of singers, works with the orchestral 'fixer' to appoint **pit** musicians, works with the singers in rehearsal and private coaching sessions, rehearses the band and usually conducts the performance. Where money is short he will also double as audition **accompanist**, copyist and rehearsal pianist.

If you direct a musical, the post of MD is one of your most important appointments. Choose very carefully. No other collaborator will have a more significant effect on the quality of the musical ingredient and the proficiency and morale of those that perform it.

An MD needs to be an unflappable optimist and pragmatist, constantly searching for ways to make individual performances better in sometimes very unpromising circumstances. He needs to have a true sense of the relative importance of the drama and the music, how the music can be harnessed to propel the story forward. He needs to be a good and subtle listener, juggling the musical demands and opinions of composer, **lyricist**, orchestrator, singers, musicians, director, producer and choreographer. He must listen with ego-less beneficence, try to oblige as many people as he can, but in the end come to his own conclusions and continue to exert a strong sense of musical authority over his cast and players. Above all, he must be truly devoted to the composer's score. An MD who feels the music is beneath him, or that he could have written it better himself, is a sorry sort of collaborator.

Musical Staging

A term used to describe the job of choreographing scenes in **opera** or **musical theatre** where conventional choreography, or 'steps', are not required.

The Musical Stager, just like his theatre equivalent the **Movement Director**, plies a trade that is a close kin to choreography. Indeed a Musical Stager can sometimes graduate to earn the title of choreographer if the quality of the work would strongly suggest it, though in America the difference in the two positions is also a technical and legal one, as they command two different scales of accreditation and pay.

If you find yourself working on an opera with a large **chorus**, a Musical Stager is an indispensable collaborator.

Musical Theatre

Musical theatre, for the purposes of this book, comprises all forms of **music theatre** not including **opera**, **operetta** or **oratorio**. (For more details on these see the relevant entries, and for a broader discussion on the differences between musical theatre and **opera** see **music theatre**.) Thus musical drama, musical comedy, dance musicals, **plays with songs** and rock operas are all covered by the term. For the sake of brevity, let's call them all musicals.

TERMINOLOGY

The word 'musical' started life as an adjective rather than a noun, and there are those who believe it should have stayed in its proper place. It works well, they argue, in qualifying musical comedy, musical drama or musical theatre, but is something of an abomination on its own. They have a point. In Britain especially the musical is still part of the cultural class system, regarded by many classical music-lovers as opera's poor but flashy cousin, just as opera may be regarded by lovers of musicals as overblown, dated and dull.

Those who dislike the perpetuation of these prejudices sometimes try to avoid them by redefining the terms of reference. They argue that because the term derives itself from 'musical comedy', there is a perception in the theatregoing and critical communities that musicals are, or should be, light-hearted affairs and that any pretensions they might have to seriousness are therefore misguided, that 'musicals' are like 'theatricals', to be got up in an amateur sort of way but not to be examined with any serious artistic scrutiny.

A number of writers of serious musical theatre have recently taken up the term 'musical drama' as a more apt description of their work. As time goes by, their sensitivity will probably prove to be unnecessary as more and more serious musicals are being written and readily accepted by public and critics alike as contributions to an ever-widening genre.

The following terms have a currency that does need defining:

1 Book musicals

A book musical is one that has a spoken libretto with songs and choral ensembles interspersed throughout the action.

2 Sung-through musicals

A sung-through musical is one that has few if any spoken words, the use of more or less continuous music helping to define its dramatic structure, its songs and ensembles growing out of, or giving rise to, its overriding musical themes.

3 Dance musicals

A dance musical is one in which dance is an integral means of expression for its characters. The characters in a dance musical are as likely to burst into dance as into song either because they are dancers showing off their skills in a show-business setting or because their authors have created a world in which dance is a natural mode of expression for ordinary people.

Musical Theatre

4 Compilation musicals

Compilation musicals are created by tacking a loosely structured story onto the back-catalogue songs of a famous pop group or singer/songwriter. There have been some notable recent successes in the genre that have bred a large number of feeble imitations. One can only pray the fashion passes swiftly.

Musicals, however they are defined, make special demands on a director, very different from the demands of 'legitimate' or 'straight' theatre on the one hand and opera on the other.

The casting, design and staging of musicals all call for specialist skills, but they are reasonably easily acquired. The elements that are harder to get used to can be summed up in two words – collaboration and cost.

COLLABORATION

In the theatre you have to collaborate with your cast, two or three designers of one sort or another, occasionally a **choreographer** or a **Fight Director**, and maybe a playwright if you're working on a new play. And that's about it. In such circumstances it is not so hard to maintain a strong sense of artistic vision, and your judgements can be made as part of a more or less private process. Not so in the musical theatre.

In the musical theatre your collaborators are legion. As in the theatre you have your usual slew of designers for set, costumes, wigs, lighting and sound, but if you're doing a **new musical** you probably won't be collaborating with a sole author but with two, three or even four different authors writing or co-writing the music, book and lyrics between them. Most composers of modern musicals don't write their own orchestrations, so you'll probably have an **orchestrator** in attendance. Most musicals contain dance or stylised movement and therefore require a choreographer or **Musical Stager**, and all musicals need a **Musical Director**, who may or may not also be the **conductor**.

In the theatre a **production meeting** towards the end of the

424

rehearsal period might include seven or eight people. In the musical theatre it will be closer to twenty or even thirty. For each of your collaborators there is an opinion, not just concerning their own departments but everyone else's, and for each opinion a counter-opinion in some other department. Each collaborator has an associate and a couple of assistants, all with their own passionately held opinions more or less contradictory with the opinions of everyone else. And that's before you take account of your cast of starring performers and ensemble, not to mention the stage management, all of them collaborators. The potential for chaos is extreme, and you are in charge of it all.

Just to complicate matters, last but not least of your major collaborators is your producer. In straight theatre, producers tend to occupy a back seat, leaving the art to the artists and only intervening on matters of business or budget. Because of the enormous costs involved in mounting a musical, the budgetary decisions taken by musical theatre producers will often involve them much more closely in artistic matters than is sometimes comfortable for the director and his creative team. Indeed, many producers feel, not unreasonably, that their ability to provide the creative team with a large budget entitles them to an artistic opinion on everything from casting to design to the quality of the performances on the stage, and they will not be shy at letting you know their opinion if they feel that the millions of pounds or dollars they have put together are at risk because of your faulty judgement.

To complicate matters even further, many modern musicals have more than one producer, a consortium being the only way to spread the financial load. For each producer there is an opinion – and each producer has a wife or a husband or a partner or a secretary or a child recently graduated from a very good university with a very good theatre arts degree – and they all have their opinions too. And you will get to hear them all whether you like it or not.

To be a successful director of musicals you must be a strategist. And a diplomat. With so many collaborators, the potential for disharmony and in-fighting is obvious. You must be the still centre of the storm, the person to whom everyone refers for clarity and certainty. To do this job well you must have impregnable individual relationships with every one of your creative team and be ready to listen to their ideas and problems without impatience or prejudice. You must also allow for them, even require them, to form strong relationships with one another, so that every little cross-department decision need not go through you. For example, your **composer**, orchestrator, **Musical Director** and **Sound Designer** must be a coherent team, able to make joint decisions about the music, decisions you may have an opinion about but which you need not be involved in until they are properly developed. Likewise with your **Set** and **Lighting Designers**. Or with your performers and the designers of their wigs and **costumes**. Learn when to take a back seat and to trust your teams, but be ready to spot where these relationships are threatening to turn sour.

You must keep certain of your most important relationships away from outside interference altogether. For example, you must insist that no artistic ideas are proposed to any member of your creative team over your head by anyone, including your producer or producers. Similarly, your performers must not be given acting notes by anyone save you, your choreographer or your designated associates and assistants under specific instruction from you.

But tread lightly. Even in the best-run musical you will have to cope with impertinence, ignorance, misguided enthusiasm and sheer bloody lunacy masquerading as passionate certainty. Don't bluster or insist or get in a state when your strategies or relationships are threatened. Quietly and kindly put the culprit right and then get back to business.

COST

If the extraordinary expense of mounting a musical gives the producers a greater sense of artistic ownership than in the straight theatre, it will affect all your judgements too. A sensitive and creative director cannot be immune from the sense of financial vertigo that is brought on by the contemplation of a budget twice or three times the size of a normal play budget. Even with chamber musicals, or 'micro-musicals', the cost will also be significantly greater than corresponding chamber-sized plays. When it comes to large-scale 'mega-musical' productions, with budgets running into millions of dollars or pounds, the vertigo can get very intense.

Such productions are not for the faint-hearted, but whatever the scale of the production, you mustn't ever imagine that a larger than normal budget means the right to unlimited artistic experiment. It means the opposite. The bigger the budget, the more likely you will end up exceeding it. The bigger the budget, the more your producers will look for ways to cut their costs and the more pressure they will put on you to justify even the smallest of expenses.

A wise director doesn't conspire with his designers to spend all the money he is offered. A wise director gets more than a little nervous at the prospect of spending money on things he suspects will be cut from the final show. A wise director saves as much of his producer's money as is artistically practicable.

Foolish directors overspend their budget by indulging a luxury, leaving no contingency for a crucial last-minute necessity. Foolish directors let their artistic judgements be hijacked by spendthrift members of their creative team. Foolish directors end up being hated by their producers and never work for them again.

However wisely you tend the purse strings, there's no escaping the fact that musicals are fundamentally expensive things to mount. If someone comes to you with the idea of doing a really simple, inexpensive chamber musical, allow yourself a wry smile but don't for a moment believe they, or you, are likely to get away with it.

Musicals cost, but it's the music in musicals that costs more than anything. Singers cost, but musicians cost a lot more than singers. And composers and orchestrators love to have lots of musicians. For every musician there is sheet music to be copied. For every small change in the music during previews, fresh copies of the music must be made by expensive copyists and distributed to the orchestra. Expensive extra rehearsal time must then be found for the changes to be rehearsed into the show before the next performance.

Sound systems cost the earth, even simple ones. Every little **radio-mike** is an expensive piece of micro-machinery, its little batteries having to be replaced on a regular basis.

Musical Theatre

Nothing costs nothing. In the commercial theatre even nothing costs a packet when it's a musical version of nothing.

GETTING THE RIGHTS

Before you definitely decide on the musical you want to direct, and certainly before you appoint your creative team, make careful enquiry about the **performing rights**. Because of the large number of collaborators involved in the authorship of musicals, there may be complications. There could be different versions of the piece available for licensing – sometimes with differently credited teams of authors – and the creative performing rights may be trammelled in some way.

REHEARSAL

Managing a musical theatre rehearsal is a curious business, a fascinating and rewarding one if you can learn to do it well, but frustrating and bewildering if not. So much of the time is taken up by other people's creative demands that whole days can go by when you seem to be deciding or controlling very little. In a musical requiring **choreography** you wonder at times if you've strayed into someone else's rehearsal by mistake. Directors used to being everywhere and deciding everything can get decidedly queasy until they figure out how to manage their time and focus their creative energies to suit the genre.

Music takes up a great deal of time, and in a dance musical the music and the steps between them take up most of it. The reason for this is that singing and dancing are both very technical crafts. Performers need to learn the notes or the steps, or both the notes and the steps, before they feel at all comfortable playing their parts. In the straight theatre, actors are usually quite happy to rehearse with script in hand, glancing at the words from time to time, trying things out, making notes on their scripts, slowly growing into their parts. Singers or dancers can't do this. They either know the tunes and the steps or they don't, and if they don't know them the rehearsal grinds to a halt.

428

Your Musical Director and your choreographer will both expect to be accorded a lot of quality rehearsal time. In a dance musical it's clever to start most rehearsal days with a physical warm-up or dance class followed by a refresher rehearsal of the most demanding of the dance routines. This will take at least an hour, more if the dance element of the musical is very heavy. It's best to do this sort of work at the start of the day when everyone is physically alert, but your choreographer will also need to refresh a particular dance routine if it forms part of a scene you are working on later in the day.

Similarly, your Musical Director will want a dedicated time for music learning sometime during the morning session, usually right after the dance class. Soloists can do their music learning in private sessions with the Musical Director or one of his associates, but the choral work with its attendant 'note-bashing', where the vocal parts are divided up amongst the ensemble singers, will always have to be done during the main rehearsal sessions.

This sort of work is extremely time-consuming, but you shouldn't leave your choreographer and Musical Director entirely to their own devices. Watch and listen carefully while your collaborators teach their notes and steps. Singers learning their notes and dancers their steps can easily forget that the learning is all part of a bigger process involving the building of characters and the interpretation of roles. Work as closely as you can with your creative partners as they make their interpretations plain. Be sensitive if they want to be left alone for a while to form strong relationships with the performers on their own accounts, but don't be shy if you think the work they are doing is inconsistent in content or tone with what you have been imagining as a final result. If you do have reservations, be careful how you communicate them. Don't undermine their authority in front of the cast. Wait for an appropriate break in rehearsal and have a quiet word. You may not have fully understood the drift of their work, in which case they can put you in the picture. But if they are on the wrong track they will be grateful that your pointing it out is done as discreetly as possible.

Always be aware that however well you collaborate with your choreographer and your Musical Director, exchanging ideas and interpretations in the very closest of artistic partnerships, they will always need time with the performers on their own to clean up the work you have done together. In fact, the more you affect the work of your collaborators in rehearsal, the more time they will need to put the finishing touches on the work you have achieved together. They have keen eyes and ears for the value of their own work and only they can fully approve the detail and the degree of finish that their work must attain. They are artists, too, and you must accord them their proper role as artists and not treat them as technical functionaries in your own more important grand design.

UNDERSCORE

In a book musical, the atmospheric music played under spoken text is called 'underscore', so termed because the musical 'score' is being played 'under' the spoken text, the melodic content usually deriving from the most frequently sung melodies or melodies that are thematically recurrent.

The underscore helps the composer get from tune to tune, softens the hard edges between the sung and the spoken words and keeps the musical ideas flowing through longer periods of spoken dialogue.

The starting and finishing points for underscore will often be marked clearly into the text as cue points, but playing music under text is a considerable skill. Your Musical Director and/or **accompanist** will need plenty of time to practise the timing and dynamics in order to make the underscore fit the mood and pace of the dialogue. If the performers speak faster or slower, louder or quieter, the music must follow.

If you work on a **new musical**, the underscore will probably be added by the composer and Musical Director as you work, and you will no doubt be involved in the choices they make. In applying underscore to a scene, there is a tendency to over-lard the pudding. Don't be over-eager to fill every spoken scene with music. Don't be afraid of silence. Your audience may be quite grateful for a chance to clean their ears so they can listen afresh when the music starts up again.

ACTING, SINGING AND DANCING

When you work on a play you cast your actors because they are talented and right for the part. The assumption is that all the members of your cast will at least be proficient in their acting skills. In the musical theatre you cannot make the same assumption. Some performers have thrilling voices or are brilliant dancers but are unblessed with much acting talent. You need these people. They can change an ordinary evening into an extraordinary one with a soaring song or a dazzling routine of steps, but they will need your help. Work patiently with them. Some will need to be animated out of their native woodenness. Others will need to be saved from bouts of conventional histrionics or sudden lapses of taste. Make them your special project. Help them to blend in with the rest of the company. Teach them about eye contact and fluid movement, where to place their focus when active and where in repose. Your patience will be rewarded when you sit in the theatre at the first preview surrounded by an audience thrilled by the artistry of your non-actor stars, not caring a whit that they are not as entirely submerged in their characters as you would want them to be.

You have two main tasks in a musical rehearsal period: making sure your creative collaborators feel creative at all times and ensuring that the disparate elements of the work end up forming a cohesive artistic whole. This is harder than it sounds. Musical theatre is a highly artificial form. People in real life do not soliloquise their feelings in rapturous or tragic ballad or break into complex dance steps on the receipt of good news. People in real life do not rely on a concealed orchestra to accompany their thoughts or communicate with thousands of other people with the help of minute microphones cleverly threaded into their wigs. People in real life are capable of maintaining a rhythm to their lives without constantly glancing at a partly concealed man beating time with a little white stick. Your job is to make all the strange behaviour on stage seem like the most natural thing in the world, a version of real life with such a powerful internal logic that it seems to be as real as life itself.

Musical Theatre

LIGHT AND SOUND DESIGN

The relationship between the Lighting and Sound Designers can be a source of friction in musical theatre. To start with, they are in competition for rigging space, the favoured positions for side and top lights often coinciding with favoured speaker positions. Once the rig has been agreed, lighting and sound equipment must sit in close proximity on it and be accessible for maintenance and adjustment. Sloppy or selfish rigging from one department can cause animosity in the other. The difficulty here is that the two departments have little in common artistically other than a stake in the overall success of the show, so if the relationship is bad between them, it is easy for both to imagine that the other is being favoured in terms of budget or artistic profile, especially if one of them has been denied the purchase or hire of a piece of equipment they think is vital to their plan. The best way to address such friction is to keep both designers very close to you individually but also to have frequent meetings at which the overall artistic goals are kept in sight. This will appeal to their sense of artistic community – and they may even end up helping each other.

STAGING AND AMPLIFICATION

Staging for musical theatre is not so different from straight theatre. You have to keep your **stage pictures** fluid and interesting, give a central focus to your main characters – moving other characters downstage of them to give them someone to talk to – and make sure that the movement of all the characters is conducive to good storytelling.

One difficulty peculiar to musical theatre is a direct consequence of the use of amplification. Because the voices are miked and transmitted through speakers in a mix with the orchestral sound, the audience doesn't hear them acoustically. In a small theatre with light amplification they will probably hear a mix of the acoustic voice and the amplified sound and therefore be more able to locate the voice to the singer. In bigger theatres, only the audience in the front few rows will hear anything of the acoustic voice. Everyone else will be hearing an amplified mix of voice and orchestra that they locate to the singer partly by visual means and partly by virtue of good sound design, which balances the vocal mix in the speakers so that the sound seems to be coming from the singer himself. But even the best sound designs can't deliver a perfectly balanced mix to the audience's ears. Some of the audience will be sitting nearer to the side speakers than others; some will be sitting under an **overhang** a long way from any speaker; some will have less acute hearing than others.

This gives the performer and the director a problem. If the audience can't see the singer's face they will have no idea he's singing. This will worry them and they will search the stage until they locate the source of the sound they are hearing, but different members of the audience will search in different places, creating a split focus for as long as the confusion continues. The problem becomes extreme when there is a quick-fire exchange of sung lines between several different characters, especially if they are grouped tightly together on the stage.

There is no easy solution to this difficulty. You can tell your cast that they must always be facing downstage when they sing, but that can make for entirely predictable staging. You can tell them to make sure they are physically active whenever they sing a solo line, but if everyone does that you end up with a strange relay of jerky eye-catching movement unlike anything in real life. You can avoid creating tight groups during complex vocal ensembles, but sometimes an intimate and populated scene will demand a degree of closeness. You can appeal to the Lighting Designer to focus the face of whoever is singing throughout the show, but this can make for an impossibly complex lighting plot and a straitjacket for the singers, who must thereafter comply with it for the run of the show.

The answer lies in a subtle application of all of these techniques at appropriate times but without overusing any of them. You can also help matters enormously by keeping the general level of amplification down to a bare minimum. The louder the orchestra is the louder the voices have to be, and the louder the general level of the voices the greater the risk of the audience not being able to identify a particular voice with its owner. When the amplification is very loud character identification becomes next to impossible.

FEEDBACK AND FOLDBACK

Feedback is the nasty whistling sound you hear when a singer or speaker stands too close to a speaker, when a microphone is turned up too high or when two or more microphones get too close to one another.

Foldback is the mixture of orchestral and vocal music that is played back to the singers through onstage speakers so that they can hear their own voices above the general level of the music and pick out salient features of the orchestral accompaniment for cueing of entries or to provide rhythmic and tonal security.

Without foldback a singer won't hear his **accompaniment** or the sound of his own voice and will run the risk of singing out of tune or out of rhythm or both, but if the foldback is turned up too high it can itself become a cause of feedback.

However cleverly the Sound Designer positions the foldback speakers, he can never provide a constant level of coverage to all parts of the stage. And even if he could, the levels would still be more appropriate for some singers' ears than others. Thus different scenes and different singers will always require different foldback plots. Indeed, two singers standing close to each other in the same scene may have conflicting requirements. What seems a perfect level to one will seem too loud or too soft to the other. A singer moving across the stage will move out of range of one speaker and have to adjust to the volume and direction of another.

Because of this complexity, foldback can become a real bone of contention during **technical rehearsals**. With time running out and fears running high, singers can become intolerant if the foldback isn't exactly as they want it. Furious signals are made from stage to sound desk, voices are raised and solutions loudly demanded, Sound Designers and their assistants run up and down the aisles in a panic, expert opinions are given by ignorant bystanders and bad blood breaks out everywhere.

In a well-ordered technical rehearsal this should never be allowed to happen, and the solution is in your hands. Before the technical begins, you and your Sound Designer should spend five or ten quiet and concentrated minutes initiating the cast into the mysteries of sound design and the perils of feedback and foldback. Show them where the speakers are and explain why they have been put there rather than somewhere else. Be very clear that the only way foldback problems are ever solved is if the singers quietly and methodically let the sound department know what they require, when they require it and when the system is failing them. There is no catch-all solution to the problem, only a long series of correct plots from one moment of the show to the next, and the company's 'feedback' is essential in establishing how the plot should be written. Encourage your soloists especially to have a good one-on-one relationship with Sound Designer and Operator so that the foldback plot can be a continuous work in progress throughout the run.

Music Director

Not to be confused with **Musical Director,** this is an **opera** house appointment. The Music Director, who may or may not also be the resident **conductor,** is in ultimate control of **repertoire, orchestra, chorus** and choice of solo singers.

Music Drama

Not to be confused with **music theatre,** this term refers to the operas of Wagner (see **Gesamtkunstwerk**) and his ilk. It was coined in support of the idea that the dramatic action of an opera should always create the need for the music without unnecessary halts for extended arias or any other repetitious ensembles.

The ideas behind music drama have now been so successfully subsumed into the mainstream of modern **opera** that the term defining it has become rather redundant, but some devotees persist in using it.

Musicians

If your production requires **music**, the first thing to decide is whether you use an existing source or commission a living **composer** to write a new score.

Either way, your next step will be to decide how the music is to be delivered in performance. Here you have three choices. Use an existent recording or recordings played over a sound system. Record the music afresh with live musicians and play the subsequent recording over a system. Have the music played live.

EXISTENT RECORDINGS

Start by making sure there are no intractable **performing rights** issues with your choice of recording. You probably won't have a problem, but do check first.

SPECIALLY RECORDED MUSIC

If you are working with a new score but decide, for artistic or financial reasons, not to have it played by live musicians, you will obviously need to get it recorded. The best advice here is to leave the recording until as late as possible in the rehearsal process. Your composer should be in rehearsal as much as possible and the precise quality and duration of the music cues discussed between you as work develops. He will have decided quite early on which instruments he wants to write for and will have contracted the musicians he needs for the recording sessions, but the later you leave the finalisation of the score, the more the composer can take account of the tempo of the scenes and the stage atmosphere that relates to each cue. It's a good idea to invite the musicians to a run-through so they can get a feel for the quality and style of the work they are contributing to.

The best time to record the music is in the last few days of rehearsal before the **technical rehearsals** begin, though you may need to start earlier if the music is to be integrated into a complicated **sound design**. Your Sound Designer can advise on a timetable.

LIVE MUSIC

When considering the artistic advantages and disadvantages of using live musicians in the theatre, you must weigh up the relative importance of three factors: cost, usefulness and location.

Live musicians are always more expensive than recorded sound, the more musicians the greater the cost. If you're sure you want them, work out how many you can afford before you decide on anything else. However few you have, one of them must be your **Musical Director**, unless you're very flush and can afford a non-playing MD. If the sounds you require exceed the number of musicians you can afford, think how different combinations of instruments could be doubled by a small group of players. Most clarinettists can play the saxophone, flutes may double with oboes and recorders, violinists can play mandolins, synthesisers can sound like anything, though they sound most convincing when surrounded by real live instruments. You may have particular musicians in mind that can double unusual combinations of instruments. Cost is always a factor. Producers and administrators will always try to convince you to have as few musicians as possible. You must be ready to address their concerns.

The expense of live musicians will force you to justify their artistic usefulness. How important will they really be to the success of your production? With **musical theatre** or **plays with songs** or indeed with any play that has an accompanied song in it, the case for live music is incontrovertible. When an actor sings on stage he needs a live **accompaniment**. It is unfair to ask anyone to put life into a song if it has to be done to a pre-recorded soundtrack. There's no give in the music. The phrasing has to be the same every night, with no room for any variety of expression. As the performance develops the song will always stay the same. This rigidity will come to infuriate the actor. The effect will also seem artificial to the audience. If the accompaniment is recorded, why not have the singer mime to the tape? The most unpleasant examples of this sort of false economy are the grim cut-price touring musicals where a pre-recorded soundtrack splurges its mechanical noise into the theatre and the performers sing and dance along with it like so many manic puppets.

437

Musicians

If cost is to be the deciding factor, better by far to have a single pianist, or a tiny band, playing at the side of the stage.

Usefulness is harder to justify when the music is purely atmospheric or incidental. Here you must decide for yourself what live performance gives you in artistic terms. How does your production benefit from the presence of the musicians? Are they important to the atmosphere of the play or to the larger environment of the theatre? Would their presence affect the context of the story in social or stylistic terms? Is the interplay between music and text so crucial that it needs to be mirrored in a similar interplay between actors and musicians?

This brings us to location. Where are you going to put your musicians? Do you have room for them? Is there an **orchestra pit**? If so, do you want to use it or would the gap between stage and auditorium be a drawback? Is there anywhere they can sit on stage? Should you ask your designer to build their position into the set design? If he does, should they be visible at all times or just when they play? Will you need to screen them, or put a **scrim** in front of them? If you're in a **playhouse**, could you put them in a box on one side of the stage, or with a bigger band, split into two on both sides of the stage? If the only place to put them is out of the audience's view, do you really need them? If the audience is unaware throughout the performance that live musicians are playing, what justification remains for having them at all?

Many of these questions will answer themselves if you decide to incorporate your musicians into the action of the play, but be careful if you do. Professional musicians are not good actors, and the ones that think they're good are often the worst. They don't know where to focus or how to listen or walk. Even after careful instruction they will never be completely comfortable. Actors train for three or four years to be able to do these things. Musicians won't pick up the same skills in three or four weeks, and in fact you won't even have three or four hours to spend on them. Worse still, if you put musicians on stage, you have to costume them. Musicians don't wear costumes well. They feel stupid in them. Their trousers get twisted, their hats fall off, they wear their own socks or forget to take their glasses off, and everything about them screams 'I'm not an actor. Get me out of here.'

438

If you have strong artistic reasons for having your musicians on stage then cast them very carefully and limit their physical involvement as much as you can. Or cast actor musicians.

ACTOR MUSICIANS

Many actors are talented musicians. In any ensemble of, say, twenty actors you will commonly find a pianist or two, a sax player, a cellist and three or four guitarists, perhaps a singer/songwriter amongst them. Their proficiency will vary a great deal but the same artistic bent that made them passionate about acting will at some time in their pasts have made them just as passionate about music. They may have let their talents slip, but a surprising number keep practising and are keen to show off their skills if the opportunity arises.

In the big national companies and in commercial theatre such opportunities for actors are rare, actors and musicians being very selectively employed for their specialised skills. Union agreements, too, militate against the use of actor/musicians, the amalgamation of two talents in one person being seen as an erosion of someone else's opportunity. But there are occasions when a play demands a musical talent from one or several of its characters, or when a director decides that a production would benefit in atmosphere, authenticity or excitement by having its music played live by the characters of the drama.

There are potential hazards in relying entirely on actor musicians, and a director who takes this course would be well advised to secrete a couple of genuine musicians in the company disguised as actors, one of them a Musical Director and another a seriously good player whose performance skills will bring everyone else up to the same snuff. Without a competent core of musical experience at the heart of the company, tempo, tuning and technique can all become variable commodities with the possibility of cacophony lurking round every corner. In fact, if you want to make the best of this type of show, your actor-cum-Musical Director should perhaps be employed very early on and then help you to cast the play, auditioning the actors' musical skills as you assess their acting.

Musicians

While working with actor musicians, be careful to give them musical material well within their capabilities. An actor struggling to play or remember his notes will not be able to stay in character at the same time, and an actor who spends all his free time away from rehearsal madly practising his instrument will not be giving enough thought to the character he is supposed to become. Where a character is written to sing to his own accompaniment but the actor has no aptitude for playing the instrument in question, don't torture him, let another actor accompany him. Or let him sing a cappella.

If you're involved in running a small and/or poor theatre company and you want to include musicals or **plays with music** in your repertoire, you would be well advised to have an actor/musician as one of the permanent members of your ensemble.

Music Theatre

Music theatre I take to be a catch-all term describing any theatrical piece using music as a central part of its structure, the musical component usually, though not necessarily, taking the form of singing. Music theatre can thus comprise **opera**, **operetta**, and **musical theatre** in all its forms – including musical comedy, musicals of all descriptions, rock operas and so-called **plays with songs**, even **oratorios** and passions, when enterprising directors take the trouble to stage them.

Having defined the term as I perceive it, it does have other subtler applications, depending on the partial view of the user. In opera companies, music theatre describes any piece playing in the repertoire that can't quite be called an opera, like the Brecht/Weill *Seven Deadly Sins*, Schönberg's 'monodrama' *Ewartung* or Stravinsky's *Soldier's Tale*. It can also be used as a term of admiration. I recently read a review of a production of Verdi's *Falstaff* in which the critic referred to it as 'great music theatre', giving a nod, no doubt, to the Shakespearean genesis of the work but implying too that the best opera should always aspire to be as dramatic as the term implies.

Categorisation of the various branches of music theatre, to revert to my terminology, will always be problematical, though perhaps more of a practical problem for librarians, publishers and writers of Theatre Companions than for anyone else. Consider, for example, *The Beggar's Opera*, John Gay's satirical masterpiece. It has been called an opera, a folk opera, a play with songs and a musical – indeed, it has been claimed by some as the first ever musical. Whatever you call it, it will continue to defy categorisation, wherever it is performed. What about Brecht's *Threepenny Opera*, or his *Rise and Fall of the City of Mahagonny*? Are they operas or musicals or plays with songs? Is there really any difference between operetta and musical comedy? If so, how would you define it?

In wrestling to define some of these hybrids, it is perhaps instructive to ask more generally if there is any fundamental artistic difference between the various forms of music theatre. In the simplest terms, how does an opera differ from a musical and is there anything important to be learnt from defining the difference?

OPERAS AND MUSICALS – TELLING THEM APART

In terms of subject matter and basic dramaturgy, there is no great difference. Both forms can be comic or serious, long or short, 'sung through' or partly spoken. Both may or may not contain dance, choral singing, an overture or other purely musical interludes, and both may have rhymed or unrhymed lyrics.

The musical form of operas and musicals is often rather different – operas tending to be written in classical 'long form', with a strong sense of overall thematic unity, and musical scores tending to be written as a succession of 'short-form' songs – but there are plenty of operas and operettas that do not boast any 'long-form' qualities and an ever-increasing number of musicals that do.

The musical idiom in the orchestral writing and the use of the voice is often quite different between the two forms, but is it a defining difference? Not really. The presence in the pit of electric guitars, synthesisers and a drum-kit does not constitute an exclusively musical theatre sound, modern operas often deploying such forces as part of their orchestral colour, and modern musicals increasingly eschewing them.

Opera singers nearly always use a highly developed head voice when they sing, while musical performers tend to sing more on the chest, but again not exclusively so. Plenty of opera singers sing in musicals without any great change to their vocal style. In any event, we can't define an entire theatrical form by the way in which certain singers happen to perform it.

Is there a difference in the way words are used in the two forms? An impartial observer might be led to think so. In musical theatre, if the 'book' and the lyrics are not completely audible in every part of the house, audiences register their strong disapproval, but one rarely hears all the words of the libretto when one attends an opera, especially in the larger houses. Operas, of course, are often performed in languages not one's own, adding to the feeling that the words are of secondary importance to the music. But most opera houses now use the device of **surtitles** to help the audience understand what's going on, thus confirming that they do indeed care very much that the words on stage are clearly understood, if not always clearly articulated.

Again, the voices in most musicals are amplified, but this is more for commercial reasons than artistic ones. Musical theatre performers are usually required to sing eight shows a week, and they could not possibly sustain that number of performances without some electronic help, especially when they are competing with electronic instruments in the pit. Opera singers rarely sing their roles more than twice or three times a week, almost always without amplification, but even this is starting to change, with many opera houses sneaking in subtle forms of 'voice enhancement'.

Some devotees of opera would assert that the difference is quite simply one of artistic quality, but this won't do at all. There are plenty of bad operas and plenty of good musicals, depending on your musical and dramatic taste. Puccini's *Turandot*, a work of great musical value, has a libretto which any modern producer or director of musicals would want to have fixed. There are similarly countless musicals and operas with watertight books or libretti that are musically dull, derivative or trivial.

These inconsistent and often insignificant differences between the two forms are more associated with the way the works are perceived by their audiences than with any fundamental artistic qualities they might possess. In other words, most of the differences between the forms are traditional and social rather than artistic.

It can be hard for people trained only to listen to classical music to hear music written in a popular idiom. The presence in the pit of popular modern instruments makes the very content of the work seem less valuable to them. And the reverse is true too. Opera can seem overblown and pretentious to ears not trained to appreciate its worth. There is a strong correlation here between tradition and class, especially in Britain, where opera is largely a middle- and upper-class pursuit, whereas a West End musical will draw a more socially diverse crowd.

If there are differences between operas and musicals, they are more to do with the manner in which the two forms are written and brought to the stage than anything fundamental to do with their form or content.

Operas are written by composers. The composer is in charge of the creative process from start to finish. He may employ a librettist or he may write, or adapt, the libretto himself. However the story is treated, the finished article is regarded as a more or less unalterable musical work. Whatever the quality of its libretto, it will ultimately be judged on the quality of its music. In all publicity material and in critical reviews the composer will be primarily credited with its authorship. The composer will also take the lion's share of the commissioning fee and the subsequent royalties. We know that Mozart could not have written his greatest masterpieces without the help of Lorenzo da Ponte and that the *Rake's Progress* would have been impossible without the collaboration of Chester Kallman and W. H. Auden, but we still refer to Mozart's *Don Giovanni* and Stravinsky's *Rake's Progress*.

Musicals are written by equal partnerships of composer, book writer and lyricist – or rather they consist of equal components of music, book and lyrics, in that the three components may be written by one, two, three or more collaborators. It is unusual for one author to write in all three disciplines, but not unheard of. It is

443

common for two authors to share the three disciplines between them, one of them writing music and lyrics while the other writes the book, or one of them writing book and lyrics while the other writes the music. Co-authorship is also quite common, though more usually on the book than the music or lyrics. In contractual terms, it is generally assumed that the authors of the three disciplines will be accorded equal fees and royalty shares of a third each for music, book and lyrics, and that no one's contribution is regarded as more important than another's. Thus if someone writes music and lyrics, he would get two-thirds of the fee and royalties, and the book writer one-third. In practice, when two long-standing partners write musicals together, they might agree to go fifty-fifty, especially when one of them is acting as composer/lyricist, as he stands to earn much more than the book writer on the publication of the songs and the score.

If an opera is credited to a composer, a musical is more usually credited to a partnership of authors, the partnership often being such an equal one that many theatregoers would be hard-pressed to tell you which author was responsible for which discipline. Did Rogers or Hammerstein write the music? Lerner or Loew? Boublil or Schönberg? Surprisingly few people could tell you for sure.

Once an opera is written, it is handed over to a **conductor**, who assumes primary artistic control of it thereafter. Once a musical is written, and often before it has been finished, it is handed over to a director, who supervises any further development it might need before it goes into rehearsal.

As a director you will rarely, if ever, be involved in primary creative work on an opera – and if you do you will certainly not thereafter be credited or remunerated for your work. In the musical theatre, the work is so collaborative that you could easily find yourself involved in authorship in one way or another. As in film, the director of a musical has to be such an artistic linchpin that work on the staging often becomes work on the book.

The only other difference between the two forms is perhaps the most significant one. Operas are nearly always performed by subsidised companies or in some other circumstances of financial dependency or patronage. In other words, they don't make

444

money, nor do they need to. Musicals are nearly always produced by commercial entities, or if they start out in a subsidised theatre, they still have the capacity to make money in the commercial arena. They usually have to make money or they close, and close for good.

Opera runs are short, with very few performances, and the most ambitious opera entrepreneurs have no ambition to make the runs much longer or the number of performances much greater. Musicals run for as long as the producer can profitably keep them going. To this end they perform a minimum of eight times a week. If an opera fails, it's an artistic disappointment. If a musical fails, it's a financial disaster.

Because of the extreme commercial pressures on most musical productions, the producer tends to have much more power than his counterpart in the opera world. Because he has to raise the money, and stands to lose it too, along with his financial credibility, he will often take a far greater interest, even a significant degree of artistic control, than he would ever be accorded, or get away with, in the opera house.

Having outlined the differences between the forms of opera and musical theatre, it must be said there are many areas of both where the work for a director is more or less identical, and many other areas where they are both similar to the directing of straight plays. Any significantly different directorial challenges are outlined in the different entries on **Opera** and **Musical Theatre**.

For the purposes of this companion, if you are in any doubt as to how you should classify a piece of music theatre, please refer to the entry on **Musical Theatre** for anything that isn't an **Opera** and vice versa.

N

Narrators and Narration

From the Greeks onwards, playwrights have relied on narrators or other narrative devices to help them tell the stories of their plays.

Narrators are usually characters who exist outside the imagined reality of the stage events. They describe the action that happens between the staged scenes, as it were the offstage action, and provide narrative short cuts and objective commentary within scenes. They are also used to provide an authorial tone of voice, a moral, political or intellectual spin on the action that cannot be subsumed within the lives of the characters.

Narrators are a challenge for the director, the biggest problem being how to integrate them with the rest of the stage action. For example, how do you costume a narrator? Do you apply the same period and design aesthetic to him as to the rest of the cast, or do you deliberately differentiate him? Is he assimilated in the physical action or kept separate from it? If a cast appears both as characters and narrators, how do you indicate when they are being one thing and not the other? And how do the characters themselves behave when they are partly in the story and partly out of it?

These questions will be all the more pertinent if you ever find yourself working on an **adaptation** of some sort. Adaptations are often from story-laden sources that would be greatly helped by the use of a narrative device. You and your collaborators must consider your options carefully. There are plenty of theatrical precedents to draw on, from the Greek **Chorus** to the present day, but different devices are useful for different narrative tasks. Look at this list and decide how best your story and your cast of characters might accord with it.

GREEK CHORUS

In the Greek theatre, a group of twelve or fifteen performers. In the modern theatre, often a lot fewer. They are representatives of the people and therefore also of the audience. They tell the story but also react to it as if they were indeed members of the audience, voicing concern for the characters, warning, judging and consoling. They can speak or sing in unison as they did in the Greek theatre or their material can be broken up into individual speeches, making the Chorus a group of characters rather than a characterful group. Members of the chorus can also cover small roles in the play. See also **Chorus**.

SOLO CHORUS

Third-person narrator or author's representative, as in Shakespeare's *Henry V*: 'Permit me chorus to this great accompt.' He outlines the story so far, pushes the action forward when there is a jump in time and describes scenes that are un-stageable through lack of theatrical resource. He can also delineate the characters and manipulate the audience's perception of their motives. But he remains anonymous and uninvolved with the stage action. The characters in the play are never aware of him. In many Elizabethan, Jacobean and Restoration plays he speaks only the prologue and the epilogue of the play.

SOLO STORYTELLER

A charismatic and authoritative figure, like the Narrator in Dylan Thomas's *Under Milk Wood* or the Storyteller in Brecht's *Caucasian Chalk Circle*. Not an actor given a part by the writer, but someone who seems to have written the story himself. He personifies the writer and the writer's attitude towards his characters. A deadly form of this sort of narration is the Lectern or Rocking-Chair Storyteller, the narrator dressed up as Dickens or Charlotte Brontë reading at the side of the stage from a leather-bound edition of the adapted novel.

447

Narrators and Narration

STORYTELLER PROTAGONIST

First-person narrator who also plays a leading role, as Salieri in Schaffer's *Amadeus*. The storyteller drops in and out of his role throughout the performance, maintaining the right to re-establish direct contact with the audience at any moment.

STORYTELLER ACTOR

Third-person narrator who also plays another role or roles, as the Common Man in Bolt's *Man for All Seasons* or Voltaire/Pangloss in the Voltaire/Bernstein *Candide*. The Common Man plays all the working-class characters, emphasising the role that ordinary people play in the workings of history. Similarly, a storyteller actor could play all the female roles in a play otherwise dominated by men, or all the authority figures or all the fathers.

ENSEMBLE STORYTELLER

The whole ensemble tells the story in third-person narrative, as in the Edgar/Nunn/Caird *Nicholas Nickleby*. Any member of the acting ensemble can take up the story at any moment, making for swift, economical and unprejudiced storytelling. A character can even narrate his own actions in the third person.

FIRST-PERSON ENSEMBLE STORYTELLER

The whole ensemble takes up the first-person story – the collective 'I'. Here the ensemble shares the responsibility for telling the story with the storyteller protagonist. This enables the protagonist to narrate some scenes but to immerse himself fully in others, especially those where an objective storyteller's point of view would alienate him from his own experience. This idea can be developed to exclude the protagonist from narrating any of his own first-person narrative.

CHORAL BALLAD

A choral ensemble sings a recurring storytelling ballad, as in Brecht's *Galileo* or Sondheim's *Sweeney Todd*. This could be a choral group attached to the **orchestra** but uninvolved with the action, as with the Eisler score for *Galileo*, or a fully integrated chorus as with *Sweeney Todd*.

SCENIC STORYTELLING DEVICE

Narration can also be communicated without human agency. Short, informative headlines, dates, times or locations are often better communicated with a scenic device than by an actor storyteller. You can use banners, projections, scene drops, electronic **surtitles** or anything else that communicates the information clearly and succinctly.

Casting a narrator

When casting a solo narrator character, look for an actor with charismatic storytelling skills, someone who is interesting in his own right. He should have a resonant voice, a strong and relaxed personality and some natural warmth. If in doubt, ask yourself – will the audience trust this person? Without trust the story will not be believed.

Naturalism

Naturalism is a term, or a concept, much bandied about in the professional theatre. It most commonly crops up in phrases like 'naturalistic design' or 'naturalistic acting', but, despite many theatre practitioners imagining they know what they mean by it, it has no universally agreeable definition. Indeed, like 'realism', it seems prey to so many different interpretations that defining it may be next to meaningless. But let us try.

At its root, naturalism would seem to imply a close following of nature without the adulteration of idealism or any of the stylisations that idealism might foster. The term was used in the middle of the nineteenth century, first in the world of art by Rossetti and others and later in literature by Zola. In an article in *The Daily News* of June 1881, a correspondent refers to 'that unnecessarily faithful portrayal of offensive incidents for which M. Zola has found the new name of "Naturalism"'. This one phrase well illustrates the essential subjectivity of the concept. For those who like their art to be full of artifice or idealism, naturalism can be offensive or at least 'unnecessarily faithful'. For others, nothing that is true to nature could ever cause offence and no fidelity could ever be described as unnecessary. Rather artifice and idealism are the things that cause offence.

Of course the ideas behind naturalism go back much further than the nineteenth century. Look at Hamlet's advice to the players.

Suit the action to the word, the word to the action, with this special observance, that you o'erstep not the modesty of nature. For anything so o'erdone is from the purpose of playing, whose end, both at the first and now, was and is to hold as 'twere the mirror up to nature; to show virtue her feature, scorn her own image, and the very age and body of the time his form and pressure.

Shakespeare is talking about acting or, more broadly, the art of theatre. In doing so he refers to nature as being 'modest', but here too we are in the presence of subjective values. If the 'purpose of playing' is to hold the mirror up to nature, it is the audience that must be looking into the mirror. How else would virtue and scorn be able to see their features, or the age and body of the time their true images? And there's the rub. No two members of an audience ever perceive their own images in quite the same way. What to some seems natural, to others is overdone. Where some see truth, others see falsehood. Most commonly, people see their neighbours as more accurately portrayed than ever they see themselves. Indeed, audiences leaving a theatre often describe their experiences so differently as to make one wonder if they have been watching the same play. Based on their personalities and experiences, different people often have diametrically different views about the precise shape of nature, or how their own natures fit into the 'age and body of the time'.

Naturalism also seems to have a shelf life. What one generation thinks natural, the next sees as artificial. Perhaps the body of the time ages like our own bodies. As we grow older we perceive our reflections more and more as we remember them and less and less as they truly are. And we do the same thing with our perceptions of artistic reality. An older theatregoer may see naturalism in painted canvas flats and a gently glowing **cyclorama**, where a younger one would see only a stylised and dated convention.

Perhaps naturalism can only ever be defined in terms of aspiration. If the purpose of author, director, designer or actor is to imitate everyday life as each perceives it to be, and an audience agrees with the perception, the resulting work deserves to be called naturalistic. Aspirations that do not include an attempt at faithful imitation must perforce be stylisations of one sort or another.

The task for the stylist is to find a coherent enough theatrical form to stand for a version of real life. The task for the naturalist is to find sufficient form in real life to make it stand up as theatre.

Nerves

Nerves are endemic in the theatre. We go from play to play, from first night to first night, from judgement to judgement, from success to failure and back again. We are obliged to lose ourselves in our stories, our productions, our characters, but fear of failure or over-consciousness of self can make the task seem impossible. We look at the tightrope stretched out in front of us and lose our nerve.

ACTORS' NERVES

Actors habitually stand in front of audiences of a thousand people or more pretending to be people they are not. Being imaginative, they can easily see themselves forgetting or **fluffing** their lines, or publicly disgracing themselves in one way or another. Nervousness is the natural response to the imaginative process. Or rather it is part of it.

A good actor will seek to harness his nervousness rather than eradicate it. He will take advantage of the way his nerves heighten his awareness and put his emotions and responses on a higher level. A completely nerveless actor is usually a dull one, as unable to imagine the true nature of the character he is playing as the possibility of his failure to play it well.

The deleterious effects of nervousness are usually reduced by experience, or at least they become more manageable, different actors creating different strategies for coping. But in the worst cases your intervention and understanding will be necessary. Be ready to talk to a chronically nervous actor – a few reassuring words and a sympathetic ear are often enough to restore a realistic balance in his mind. Take him outside himself. Give him, or the character that speaks through him, an external focus. Florizel's advice to a nervous Perdita in *The Winter's Tale* is most apposite:

> *Strangle such thoughts as these with anything*
> *That you behold the while.*

Give the actor a stimulus to make him forget his self-consciousness and fear. Put him in touch with another character. Give him stepping-stones of eye contact from one character to another. Distract him from imagining his failure by concentrating on his character's view of the world around him.

The effects of nervousness may be impossible to eradicate altogether, and the worst sufferers will sometimes seek to relieve their discomfort with the use of various anaesthetics – most commonly alcohol or drugs. You, and your Stage or Company Manager, must be ready to spot any such act of desperation or laziness and take instant action to address it. There is nothing more destructive to the collective art of theatre than individual reliance on stimulants or narcotics. Drugs and alcohol numb the true human response, reducing the actor's ability to speak, hear and react to his fellow actors. Serious professional actors are unforgiving when their colleagues destroy their talents and the play in this way, and so must you be.

DIRECTORS' NERVES

Directors suffer from nerves too. This will most often happen to you at the beginning of your career, especially when you're about to go into rehearsal with a company of actors more experienced than yourself. Don't fret. Work your way through your nervousness. It will disappear as you apply yourself and your actors to the job in hand. If it persists, talk to your actors about it. You will find them sympathetic. They know all about nerves.

If you are prone to first-night nerves, be careful not to infect others with your complaint. Actors get nervous enough on their own without you twittering about making them more so. Try to enjoy your first nights. Sit next to a loved one in the middle of the auditorium and watch your show with pride. Don't slink about at the back of the stalls or slouch in the bar with a large scotch. What have you got to be nervous about? If you're not proud of your work the way it is then why did you direct it like that?

STAGE CREW NERVES

It is easy to forget in the manic preparations for a first night, that the **stage management** and crew are just as prone to nerves as the actors. That's why mistakes happen on first nights that never happened during previews.

Make the rounds of all the departments before the first-night curtain goes up and check that everyone is calm and sure of what they are doing. Pay special attention to your Stage Manager or whoever is calling the show from the **prompt corner**. If he is nervous, everyone that takes a cue from him will pick up the tension and be more likely to make a fudge of something.

New Musicals

If you work in the **musical theatre** you will almost inevitably find yourself working on new musicals – or at least be obliged to read and listen to new musicals and be ready to give your dramaturgical advice for their further development. If you become known as a director interested in musicals it will be impossible to stem the tide of new work flowing your way. New musicals will flop through your letterbox at an alarming rate and on a bewildering variety of subjects. Musicals based on novels, plays, films and poems. Historical musicals, biographical musicals, political musicals, rock musicals. Historical-biographical-political-rock musicals. And they come along in groups, like herds of buses. In a period of only a few months you might receive three Picasso musicals, two Wuthering Heights, four Hunchback of Notre-Dames and a dozen or so Vampires.

The modern commercial musical theatre has become a massively popular form, inspiring countless thousands to try their hands at authorship. Perhaps because the form is such a collaborative one, the individual writers of book, music and lyrics often derive more comfort than they should from exposure to one another's talents. In any event, the vast majority of their attempts fall well below the standard necessary for professional exploitation. However, the pursuit of fame and fortune by their authors, or by commercial producers on their authors' behalves, can sometimes create such a whirlwind of spin and overconfidence that many a wretched musical makes it through to a catastrophically expensive production, losing millions in the process before returning its authors to a well-deserved obscurity. In the end, it isn't the waste of money that rankles. Most theatrical investors are gambling with money they can afford to lose or they wouldn't do it. It is the horrible waste of time and talent lavished on these projects by creative people who should have known better, should have chosen better. If you can possibly avoid being part of one of these monstrous debacles, you should. But in the blizzard of new musical ventures, how do you choose? How do you tell the good from the bad, the talented from the untalented, a worthy project from a waste of time?

If you are considering involving yourself with a new musical, consider the following rules of engagement and judge the work accordingly. If you are unsure of your powers of analysis in any of the disciplines involved, ask an appropriately qualified friend to give you a second opinion.

QUESTIONS TO ASK AS YOU READ A NEW MUSICAL

1 Is it dramatic?

The story of a musical should be as engaging as the story of a good play or a good novel. However exciting the music and the lyrics are, if the story is feeble, the musical will be feeble.

2 Is it suitable?

The story must lend itself to musical treatment. In other words, there must be emotional, psychological or intellectual elements to the story that are made more expressive by having music added to them.

3 Is it natural?

It must seem natural for the characters to 'sing', and if they are to sing solo ballads direct to the audience, they must have inner lives that make such soliloquising necessary to their development. If a character has no such inner life, lyrical cleverness will never compensate for it.

4 Is it original?

The composer of the music should have a distinct voice. New musicals are judged largely on the quality of their music. If a score is drab or derivative, tinkering is unlikely to improve it. Even when a score is intentionally written in a pastiche style, the pastiche must be witty and well observed and not merely a slavish copy of some other composer's style.

5 Is it hackneyed?

The lyrics should be characterful, elegant and free of cliché. Cast your eye down the list of songs on the demo CD. If the titles of the songs are clichés in themselves, the lyrics will probably follow suit.

6 Is it generic?

The songs should not be standstill emotional outbursts but should further the story in some way or reveal the complexity of a character,

455

or both. If the lyric of any song is so general that it could just as well be in some other musical, it isn't doing its job properly.

7 Is it pretentious?

Be on the lookout for pretentiousness, the abiding flaw of the modern musical theatre. If the music is too grand for the characters or the message unearned by the plot, if the lyrics are too poetic for the music or the music too rhapsodic for the words, then the piece will be pretending to something it hasn't the power to deliver. That is the meaning of pretentiousness.

8 Is it finished?

If the musical is unfinished, which will often be the case, first clarify what the authors or producer require of you before committing yourself to working on it. Some musicals are sent out to work when they are a mere collection of songs in search of a plot, or a set of characters in search of a tune. In these cases you may be courted not just for your dramaturgical advice but also for your authorial participation. If so, be very careful how you proceed.

HOW TO RESPOND TO AN UNFINISHED MUSICAL

If the piece is not to your taste or is so unfinished as to be un-assessable, then a polite decline is your best option. But if your curiosity is aroused by the subject matter, or by a particular excellence in music or lyrics, or by the reputation of one of the authors, then you should proceed, but with caution.

First find out why the piece is incomplete and how long it has been in this state. A lot of musicals stay in the idea stage for years and years, because the authors have been unable to decide how to proceed, or because the authorial team has been 'developing' the piece through a series of **workshops** and has lost any sense of objectivity about their creation or indeed any feeling of personal ownership over it. Many are the musicals that have been 'workshopped' out of existence, all the life sucked out of them by endless rounds of producorial tampering and well-meaning advice.

New musicals are often instigated by songwriters – sometimes a composer/lyricist working alone, sometimes a team of two or three working together. They start with a story of one sort or another – from a novel or a film or a historical event – and write a series of songs for the protagonist characters to sing at the most climactic moments in the story. They then go in search of a dramatist to help them flesh out the story behind the songs. This is a lethal way of writing a musical, but unfortunately one of the most common; lethal, because it is almost impossible to write a coherently dramatic story to fit a prescribed series of emotional climaxes.

The best way to write a musical is precisely the other way around. Start with the story. If the story is an original one, talk to the author about intentions, motives and aspirations. If you are making an **adaptation** from an original source, make a rigorous examination of the source material. Sort out the structure of scenes and acts. Let the characters react one with another. Decide if the piece is to be sung through or if spoken scenes will be included. If the latter, decide which scenes will be musicalised and what the musical structure will be. As this work patiently proceeds, it will become clear where the songs proper must fall, which characters deserve an emotional ballad and which do not, where the reprises if any will occur and how the songs will emerge from, or be worked into, the overall musical structure.

The writers of unfinished musicals are often in a vulnerable state of mind. However strong a conviction they may have about the ultimate worth of their work, they are usually in a muddle about how to proceed with it. Because the form is such a collaborative one, the director's position is thus made all the more powerful, the conflicting pressures of artistry and commercialism requiring a strong and knowledgeable arbiter to stop the whole project from tearing itself to pieces. Indeed, the writers may have been told by their producers or by their host theatre that without a director 'aboard', their work will have little chance of ever seeing the light of day. This puts you in a flattering but dangerous position, and before you decide to come to their rescue you must be sure that you have the right qualifications for the job. Are you really the dramatist they are looking for? Are your directorial skills really relevant to the work in hand? And even if they are, are you really prepared to spend hours and hours, weeks and weeks, months and months, locked into a development process on a musical project that may never get produced? Remember, most of them don't. How much do you want to know these guys? And know them you must. If you co-write a musical you are bound to spend a great deal of social as well as writing time with your collaborators. You will need to get to know them intimately in order to write well in their company. Do you really want that? If you have doubts on any of these matters then it would be better to send the writers off in pursuit of a real dramatist, perhaps a playwright you admire, one that is a little blocked and in need of a new challenge in a fresh form. If you think the piece has real promise then you can declare your long-term interest in it and look forward to the time when a finished and much better version lands on your desk ready for a production. And if the dramatist that you introduce to the project has proved to be a good match, your claim to be the director of the finished piece will be more or less assured.

If after consideration you decide you do have the skills and the will necessary to become an authorial partner in the unfinished work, then again you must proceed with caution. Many producers, and indeed many authorial teams, believe that we directors should give dramaturgical advice free of charge, that even if we make serious structural changes to a musical work we shouldn't expect a penny in recompense or credit. It is up to us to disabuse them of this pernicious view. But we have to do so before we embark on the work, or our position becomes weaker and weaker the more of the writing we do for free. Of course, if the work is all but finished and only minor changes are necessary, it would be churlish to withhold our advice or unreasonably charge for it – a better musical will make our work on it shine the brighter. But if the changes are major we should be unembarrassed to demand authorial credit and financial recompense. You may meet considerable resistance to this idea, especially if the team you are joining has a catalogue of successful work behind it or feels it has a sacrosanct partnership to protect. If this is the case they may be more happy to give you an authorial royalty for your work than the credit that should go with it, which is why many directors are credited for their writing work in a roundabout or mealy-mouthed way, as 'adaptors' or suppliers of 'additional material'. Be prepared for your involvement with the work to fall at this stage. If you cannot work out a satisfactory business arrangement that properly reflects your involvement, you should probably withdraw from the project before you get taken for a ride on it. If you continue and the work scores a great success, it will be very hard for you to see the authors earning large sums in royalty from future exploitation of a work that includes significant slices of your own authorship. The fact that you were the director of the original production will seem scant recompense as the royalties and accolades pile up for subsequent productions.

If you do decide to involve yourself as an author, be quite certain that the work is one that will satisfy you intellectually and artistically. The musical theatre has a nasty habit of trivialising its subject matter. It doesn't mean to, but it does. There is nothing more depressing than finding out after months of hard labour on a new musical that you have been trying to attach meaning to an inherently meaningless story. It can't be done. Meaninglessness is a black hole, sucking all well-intentioned ideas into it. And you never see them again.

LYRICAL WARNING

Most new musicals have wretchedly poor lyrics – cliché-ridden, falsely rhymed, starved of imagery and impossible to sing. But if you get involved with a musical that is otherwise interesting, don't imagine that fixing the lyrics is an easy matter. Above all, don't fall into the even nastier trap of imagining that you could write better lyrics yourself. See further under Lyrics and Lyricists.

New Plays

New plays are the lifeblood of the theatre. A theatre community that has no new writing in it will quickly become moribund. Companies that only ever perform classical plays tend to turn themselves into theatre museums, theatrical equivalents of Madame Tussaud's. Or they try so hard to make their ancient plays relevant for today that their productions fall into modishness or pointless conceptualism. A healthy theatre company has relationships with new writers, a Literary Manager or **dramaturg** commissioning new works and actors that are just as happy in new plays as they are in Shakespeare, Chekhov or the Greeks.

Similarly, directors that only work on classic texts can become fusty-minded. If you feed yourself an uninterrupted diet of Shakespeare, you will end up thinking in antithetical structures and walking down the street in iambic rhythm, one foot falling slightly heavier than the other. You will also slip into the heresy of believing that the director is the fountainhead of all artistic authority in the theatre. With only dead playwrights to talk to, the echo of your own opinion will start sounding very loudly in study and rehearsal room. If you want to keep your mind fresh and test your opinions and beliefs against a worthy and argumentative opposition, then get into a rehearsal room with a living writer and a lively group of actors and sink your teeth into a freshly baked play.

Be on the lookout for a good new play or for a good new playwright to write you a good new play. You will see enough of them, no doubt, good or bad. And read enough of them. But how do you tell good from bad, talented from untalented, important from unimportant, true from untrue? Have a look at the following list of questions and apply them to any play you happen to be reading to see how it measures up.

QUESTIONS TO ASK AS YOU READ A NEW PLAY

1 Is it necessary?

Is there anything in the story or in the central ideas of the play to make what it says important for a modern audience to hear? Is the playwright making a contribution, large or small, to the intellectual, social or political debate of the nation?

2 *Is it original?*

Does the writer have an original voice? In storyline, character delineation, prose style or imagery does the play feel original? Do you get the feeling you have read the play before, that it's a poor man's version of some other, better writer's work?

3 *Is it ambitious?*

Is the writer tackling a story, or wrestling with an issue, or creating a world that is out of the ordinary scale of conventional theatre? If so, how successful has he been?

4 *Is it honest?*

Does the writing seem to represent the true feelings of its author? In other words, does the writer have a passion for his subject and the characters with which the subject is explored? Or does the play feel cynical, written to someone else's order, or purely for commercial profit?

5 *Is it true?*

However well intentioned the writer's motives, do the story and characters represent a truthful account of the subject matter?

6 *Is it coherent?*

Do the events of the play seem to grow out of the characters or does the story seem to be forced on them? Does the plot rely in any way on coincidence? Does the **dénouement** seem to be a natural climax to the events of the play?

7 *Is it natural?*

Does the moral, political or social message of the play, if any, grow naturally out of its events, or does one or other of the characters have to spell it out in the last few pages?

8 *Is it psychologically apt?*

Are the characters believable? Does every character have a strongly differentiated personality? Do their ages, genders and cultural attitudes really belong to them?

9 Is the dialogue authentic?

If the play is written in naturalistic style, is the dialogue well observed? Do the characters speak as they would speak in real life?

10 Is it poetic?

If the play is written in **heightened language**, does the poetic imagery sound right in the voices of the characters? If all the characters sound the same, is the style of the writing strong enough to make this an acceptable stylistic device?

11 Is it funny?

If the play is a comedy, are the situations truly funny, or does the writer strain to make the audience laugh? Does the comic dialogue grow naturally from the situations or are you aware of jokes being tacked artificially onto the characters? Are you laughing aloud as you read the play? If not, why not?

12 Does the writer need it?

How badly does the writer need this play to be produced? Sometimes a play may not be brilliant, but if it isn't produced the playwright could lose heart and never write another. Sometimes a fledgling playwright needs to have a first play produced to be given the courage to continue as a writer. Is this play one of those?

13 Do you need it?

Are you the right director for this play? Do you have sufficient talent and experience and desire to do the play justice, or would it be handled better by another director? Are you the only option the writer has? Is the writer a personal friend, or relation? If you directed the play, would it be for the right reasons?

14 *Does the theatre need it?*

Is the play really suitable for the theatre? Would it make a better film, or television drama, or radio play, or even novel? Does the writing demand a theatrical setting?

15 *Does the audience need it?*

In view, or in spite, of all the above, do you like the play and, by extension, think audiences would enjoy it? Does it speak to you? If you weren't directing it, would you be happy to buy a ticket for it and think your money well spent?

If the play you are reading registers more positive than negative answers to these questions, it may be worth producing, though an overwhelmingly negative answer to any one of them might prove fatal. You must be the judge.

In any event, you may be looking for a particular sort of play for a particular reason and therefore the answers to some of these questions may be academic or weigh more heavily in your judgement than others.

If you read enough plays you may occasionally be rewarded with one that is necessary, original, ambitious, honest, true and all the rest of it. But usually you will have to make a series of tactical judgements about the value of what you are reading, the value to the writer, the value to a prospective audience and the value to your career as a director.

Do not be misled in your judgement by the way in which writers sometimes choose to package or present their work. Glossy folders, multicoloured inks and arresting fonts usually mean the work itself will be dull and colourless in comparison, but not always so.

Do not be too irritated, either, by over-explanatory stage directions or character descriptions. There is nothing more annoying than a play that starts with 'A shaft of light picks out a lone figure in the darkness . . .' or 'The stage is divided into three distinct areas. The first is George's study, the second a bit of desert outside Baghdad, the third a hospital waiting-room.' Writers try too hard sometimes to protect themselves from the unimaginative reader and leave no room for you to imagine things for yourself. Look beneath these self-protective measures. There may be some good writing lurking underneath.

DIRECTING NEW PLAYS

The great joy of working on a new play is that you are not alone. All those days when you wished you could ask Shakespeare what he meant by such and such a line, or wondered what Strindberg would make of a rearrangement of text to make a translation more comprehensible, or how O'Neill would feel about your cutting a whole scene – those days are behind you. Instead you have at your disposal a living, breathing playwright who knows, or can be inspired to know, the answers to all the questions you or your designers or actors want to ask.

Involve the writer in every step of the creative process, or as much of it as he is happy to collude in. The writer knows his characters and he will also probably know his actors, though maybe not as many as you know. He will be a theatregoer, an interested onlooker to the contemporary scene. He will know the designers he admires and dislikes. It would be a mistake in the first production of a play to appoint a designer or cast an actor to whom your writer has an aversion.

Form a conspiracy of mutual interest with your writer and be faithful to it from first meeting to first night – and beyond.

Only if you are pusillanimous or paranoid should you consider working without your **playwright** in rehearsal.

NEW PLAYS AND YOUR CAREER

Do not be surprised or upset when a new play that you direct is reviewed and your name is scarcely mentioned as the midwife-director. Directors are rarely the stars when a play is premiered, nor should they want to be. Indeed, if you have done your job well, the playwright will be the star and you must be content to bask in the reflected glory. If a famous actor is in the first cast of a new play you will be completely overlooked and must study how to bask in two sets of reflected glory at the same time.

Some directors get upset by being thus overlooked and calculate that their careers will be glossier if they concentrate solely on the reinterpretation of classic plays where directors can achieve a glamorous pre-eminence with no other living creative artists around to nudge them out of the reviews. If this notion was shared by everyone, the theatre would become as narrow as the minds that perceive it so. The more new work you direct, the less tempted you will be to become an **auteur director**, with all the attendant perils of voguishness and pretension, the better your sense of proportion about your own career and the broader your understanding of the literary traditions of the theatre, past, present and future.

Notes and Note Sessions

Once a play is up and running, from the final run-through in the rehearsal room and onwards to the **technical rehearsals, dress rehearsal** and **previews**, note-taking is an essential part of your craft.

You will need: 1. A notebook. 2. A pen.

If you are taking notes in close proximity to members of the audience, make sure your pen writes silently. Pencils tend to be scratchy. You might think you're writing quietly but the annoyed looks around you will tell you otherwise.

You may think you also need: 3. A light.

You would be better advised to perfect the art of writing in the dark. The use of a little penlight, or something similar, can be very annoying for people sitting near you. Writing in the dark is not so hard. You will tend to write bigger, and stragglier, and you'll occasionally write one note on top of the other, making both indecipherable, but they'll be clear enough for you to work out what they mean when you look at them later.

Whatever you do, try to avoid the awful habit of whispering notes to an assistant. This drives other members of the audience crazy and anyway is a lazy, self-aggrandising and inefficient method. If you don't write your notes yourself you'll be far less able to recall what you meant by them later. Your assistant may not know exactly what your whisper means and will write down a mis-interpretation of it that you will have to unscramble at a later date. Anyway, your assistant should be taking his own notes, notes that can be shared with you later, not waiting dog-like for scraps from your table. If you can't watch a play and write notes at the same time, you must be feeble.

Undoubtedly the most comfortable location for taking notes is a **Director's Box**, but there are disadvantages that you should consider before pitching camp there permanently.

If you are taking notes at a series of previews, sit in a different part of the house on each occasion. A close position will give you a better view of the detail in your actors' performances and any flaws or exaggerations in their make-up, costumes and wigs. More dis-tant positions will tell you all you need to know about audibility, **sightlines** and how well your actors are projecting their perform-ances into all parts of the **auditorium**.

NOTE SESSIONS

A note session is a meeting of director and cast at which the direc-tor goes through all the notes he has taken during a run, preview or performance. A well-taken note session can make or mar company morale. Your notes must create a positive atmosphere, one that makes every member of the company feel he can do better at the next performance. Some useful tips:

1 *Timing*

Try to avoid having note sessions immediately after performan-ces. Actors respond better to notes after a good night's sleep. What they need after a performance is encouragement and a hint or two as to how things will be made better on the morrow. What they don't need is an exhausting hour of ill-considered critique. Schedule your note session for as early on the next day as will fit in with whatever other work needs to be done. Your mind, too, will work better after a night's rest. Everything looks better in the morning.

2 Method

Work through your notes in advance of the session. Put a box round each one of the technical notes. They will have to be given to the **creative team** and **stage management** at a separate session either before or after your note session with the actors, but don't obliterate them once they've been given. You may need to advise the actors of any changes the technical notes propose in lights, sound, music or costume.

3 Structure

Before your note session begins, consider your notes carefully. Do any patterns emerge? Are there recurrent issues of audibility, clarity, pace or audience reaction? Are there simple solutions you can propose that will solve many small notes with a single general instruction?

4 Location

Talk to your Stage Manager about where the note session should take place. You need a quiet, calm atmosphere for giving notes. If you use the auditorium or the stage, make sure you can police an absolute quiet. If technical work is going on around you, the actors will be distracted and you will struggle to get their attention. If you can't ensure that the crew are on a break while you give your notes, drop the **iron** to seal off the auditorium, or give notes in a rehearsal room or the foyer and only go into the theatre for notes that require rehearsal.

5 Dialogue

Start each note session with a dialogue. How did the actors feel they performed? What surprised them in the reaction of the audience? How well did they think they told the story of the play? What pleased them about their own individual performances, and what frustrated them? Once you've got a feel of the company's mood, you will know much better how to pitch your notes.

6 *Big notes*

Don't pitch straight in with niggling little notes to particular actors. Talk about the big picture. Talk about your own reactions – what pleased you, surprised you, frustrated you. Share with your cast any plans you are considering for big changes of direction and explain your reasoning. If the **storytelling** is at fault, explain how you plan to address the problem. If the play is too long, talk about **cuts** or **pace** or both.

This dialogue will make the giving of notes a mutually instructive exercise. The actors must continue into the run of the play without your intervention, so you need them to be self-reliant. The more constructively self-critical your actors learn to be, the shorter your notes will get – and the more effective.

7 *Sensitivity*

As you go on to the individual notes, be careful how you proceed. Actors are never more sensitive than when they are being criticised in the presence of their peers. In a permanent ensemble of like-minded players, most notes can be given publicly, but in ad hoc companies there will be things that are best communicated privately, especially when you know the note could create embarrassment or contention. The higher the status of the actor and the more fragile the ego the more a private note may be preferable to a public one.

8 *Privacy*

Use a private note for any major change of direction you require from an actor. Actors don't take kindly to having weeks of rehearsal overturned in a couple of sentences. A big change, especially at the last minute, will need careful explanation and a considered plan of action. Circle a note that requires a private conversation and waylay the actor after the session or beard him in his dressing room later. But remember that the change, once agreed, may affect other actors with whom you will have to share the plan.

9 *Rehearsing notes*

As you work through your notes, some of them will require changes that cannot be made without proper rehearsal. Any note that affects more than two actors or that requires a change in the physical staging will have to be rehearsed rather than just noted. Mark these places in your notes and rehearse them immediately after the session. Or, if most of your notes require rehearsal, have a working note session on stage and give all the smaller notes as you work through the play or at the end of the session.

10 *Encouragement*

Don't give actors negative notes – or notes you know will be received negatively. Even the most critical points can be made with a light touch and with the intention to inspire a better performance. Laughter is an important ingredient of a good note session, or a spirit of gentle raillery, but never mock, never belittle, even with actors who seem not to mind. They might join in the public laughter but they will smart inside. Let the self-mocking actor mock himself but let no one else instigate the mockery against him.

11 *Kindness*

Never single out someone for special condemnation. If an actor's performance is insufficient, it will be made more so by an unkind or dismissive word. Notes are for making things better Directors that tyrannise at note sessions are simply expressing their own incompetence. If the mistakes the actors make are so flagrant, so risible, why did the director not fix them in rehearsal? If the actors are so bad, who but the director cast them in the first place?

12 *Inspiration*

Actors should be inspired and excited after a note session. If they are depressed, or angry or bewildered, you have given your notes in the wrong way and must study to do your job better.

Notes and Note Sessions

THE ACTOR AND THE NOTED MOMENT

Be aware that whenever you give a note to an actor, you set up a chain reaction that continues through to the next performance and beyond.

Actors set up patterns of thought and motivation in their characterisations. A note disturbs this pattern; you hope for the better, but a disturbance it is nonetheless. The actor thinks about the note, practises the new pattern in private and prepares to try it out on stage, but until he has actually performed it he won't have proved it to himself and to his character. Watch him in performance. Half a page or so before the noted line, you will see the shadow of the note flit across his mind. This shadow will disturb all the other patterns he has set up and cause a ripple effect in the characters around him. If you've given dozens of these little notes, you will create dozens of associated ripples. Again, you hope this will be all for the best, but you can't know until they have been proved in performance.

For this reason you should be very careful about giving little notes just before an opening. The last thing you want to see on an opening night is an entire cast madly considering the notes you gave them that afternoon.

If you have important notes at a late stage, rehearse them properly on stage and repeat the noted moment three or four times so the actors get the new pattern into their systems.

TECHNICAL NOTES

'Tech notes' are often given at the end of a performance, so that members of the creative team can include them in their work schedule first thing in the morning, but try not to keep your team waiting longer than absolutely necessary. Just like the actors they will be tired and in need of a drink, or a smoke, or a good night's rest, so if there are notes that can wait 'til the morrow, let them wait.

If there are serious problems to be discussed in the wake of a performance, go to a restaurant and include a bottle of wine or a few beers in the discussion. Everything will be easier to solve with a little good fellowship thrown into the mix.

Not-For-Profit Theatre

See **Subsidised Theatre**.

Nubbing

Nubbing is a most arcane and curious phenomenon.

A 'nub' is an actor's improvised line, created to cover for an onstage lapse of memory and communicate the predicament to fellow actors. Having made his nub, the nubber leaves the stage to refresh his memory at the prompt copy. The remaining actors, having been warned of the lapse, improvise their way forward until the nubber returns with the correct text in his head.

Nubbing derives from the seventeenth century, when the word was popular as a slang term for hanging. It is used in Fielding's *Jonathan Wild* – Mrs Wild visits her husband in prison and says

> *Damn me, I am committed for the filing-lay [pick-pocketing], man and we shall be both nubbed together. I'faith, my dear, it almost makes me amends for being nubbed myself, to have the pleasure of seeing thee nubbed too.*

The term must have been purloined for theatrical use sometime thereafter.

An elaborate 'nub' of recent memory was coined by the actor Peter O'Toole. I only have this on hearsay, though from a very good source: Nat Brenner, the late principal of the Bristol Old Vic Theatre School and friend of O'Toole. Like most of these supposed practices, it's more likely to be a story he told about himself than anything he actually ever did on stage – but you never know, he may have had recourse to it during a particularly hung-over matinée, or used it to spice up a dull evening, just for the devilry of it.

O'Toole's nub is only good for Shakespeare and requires the actor to carry a purse with him at all times. On **drying**, he claps the actor standing next to him on the back, looks sharply into the wings and says:

> Here come the lords of Ross and Willoughby
> Bloody with spurring and fiery-red with haste.
> Take thou this purse of gold, thou naughty knave
> And meet me straightway in the market-place.

You then hand him your purse and stride off into the prompt corner to reacquaint yourself with the text.

The great benefit of this nub is that it has a universal Shakespearean application. Drawing, as it does, from *Macbeth*, *Richard II* and *Twelfth Night*, it can be used for almost any tragedy, history or comedy regardless of situation. If more than one actor is on stage with you, you just stress the 'thou' in line 3 as you hand over the purse. The only circumstance in which this nub is useless is during a soliloquy.

Some 'nubbing' authorities, notably the great historian of comedy, Ken Campbell, assert that the nubber must work the word 'nub' into the first line or two in order to alert his fellow actors and the prompter to his predicament, a second mention of 'nub' indicating the end of the inserted passage. If the words 'Milford Haven' are included in the last line then the actor has managed to get back on course without any further assistance.

With the passing of weekly and fortnightly 'rep' the curious craft of nubbing seems to have faded further and further into obscurity.

Nudity

Nudity on stage is rarely a good idea. Even when the dramatic justification is ever so great, the actor ever so willing and the nakedness ever so compelling, you will struggle to maintain the same control over your audience's reaction as you do with almost any other effect.

Being unaccustomed to public nakedness, or perhaps to nakedness of any sort, audiences become fixated by the precise form of the parts on unaccustomed view. They can't help themselves. Nor should you expect them to. There is a natural curiosity, even prurience, about nakedness that only dedicated naturists manage to overcome – and then only in themselves rather than others.

When an actor takes off all his clothes on stage, a mental hush falls on the audience. Hundreds of pairs of eyes are all focused, or purposely not focused, on the same thing – or things. Hundreds of minds are assessing, comparing, sympathising; or striving not to assess, compare or sympathise.

Audiences can grow uncomfortable, even angry, if they feel the nudity they are being obliged to witness is gratuitous or exploitative. This comes from a natural sense of empathy. Dreams, or nightmares, involving shameful public nakedness are commonplace. It is all too easy to imagine oneself in the vulnerable persona of a naked performer.

Because the effect of nudity is so marked, it often succeeds where it is most intended to shock, where the audience's natural surprise, curiosity or embarrassment is reflected in the feelings of the characters on stage. If a character's nakedness is brought about by madness or cruelty or blatant exhibitionism, the audience and the other characters all become equal co-witnesses – even co-voyeurs. A feeling equally shared by a whole theatre becomes the only available context for reaction and disables both embarrassment and prurience.

Conversely, nakedness can also work when it constitutes a uniform reality.

A recent all-male production of *Macbeth* in Germany had its whole cast performing naked from start to finish, actors old and young, fat and thin, hairy and smooth, inhabiting a world where to be clothed would be abnormal. The performance was electrifying, the vulnerability of the actors' bodies telling an evocative story about the frightening vulnerability of mankind. After a slight opening frisson, the audience quickly accepted a naked Scotland as the only observable reality and became deeply empathetic with the plight of the performer-characters.

Even when the justification for nudity seems overwhelming, you must still contrive to take the actors with you. Many will not consider stripping off in public, whatever the circumstances. They may agree the play requires it, they may be ashamed of themselves for refusing, but refuse they will. Some actors are too embarrassed by their bodies, too ashamed of their lumps and bumps, their bags and sags, too aware of the difference between how their bodies look and how they would wish them to look. You may try to persuade them, but in the end you must take their decision as final.

Other braver, or more complacent, souls may agree in certain circumstances but not in others. The lighting must be right; a back view would be fine but not a front; upstage behind a **scrim**, maybe, but not downstage centre. Once you get into this sort of negotiation, you're dead in the water. Nakedness isn't nakedness if it's dressed in body stocking and voluminous wig and subtly lit behind a screen. Give it up as a bad job.

If you feel a nude scene is crucial to your production, square it with the actor or actors as early as you can. To be absolutely safe, get it agreed at the casting stage. Explain the dramatic necessity, the duration of the scene and the environment of design and lighting. Once you have your agreement, you must still handle the actor with privacy and respect in rehearsal. Ironically, actors can derive a sort of comforting anonymity from onstage nakedness, whereas the familiar intimacy of the rehearsal room can cause real embarrassment. Let the actor decide how quickly he wants to proceed. Start with the greatest possible privacy. Banish everyone else from the room except yourself and the naked actor or actors. Some directors have broken the ice by having everyone stripping off for the first rehearsal, themselves included.

As rehearsals develop, consider the way your actors are coping with the experience. Make sure they are happy with all you ask them to do. Don't push them into physical moves that will compound their embarrassment. Robert Helpmann, the dancer and choreographer, put it well when he said, 'The trouble with nude dancing is that not everything stops when the music does.'

Once you get to the stage of run-throughs and **technical rehearsals**, a lot more pairs of curious eyes will be on the ogle. Don't get complacent about your naked actors. Protect them. Surround them with dressing gowns and sensitive scheduling.

When you get to **previews** and performances you must look anew at the effect on both actors and audience. Watch your actors carefully for any signs of discomfort. This could come in the form of mental blankness – 'Please let this be over so I can get my clothes back on again' – or as brazen self-confidence – 'Yeah, it's a penis, what's the big deal? Haven't you seen one before?' Either way, the actor is no longer playing the character, he is simply trying to survive. Talk to him. Reassure him. Get him to focus outside himself on the predicament of his character, or subsume his embarrassment into that of his character.

Your actors' behaviour will affect the reaction of the audience and vice versa. Watch the audience for signs of embarrassment or irritation. If the nakedness is having the effect you imagined, fine. If it isn't, you should question the wisdom of continuing with it. Even then, move carefully. Your actors will have gone through a lot at your behest. Don't chuck in your hand lightly, as if their courage was worth nothing to you and your artistic arguments a lot of hot air. Share your observations with them and come to a conclusion you can all support.

O

Observation

Acting and directing skills all begin with observation. Your ability to observe accurately what you see in the world and then faithfully reproduce it on stage is at the heart of what you do. It follows that what you observe will define the content if not the form of your work. How accurately you observe it will define the truth of your work. How faithfully you are able to reproduce what you see will be defined by your technique.

If you want your work to reflect people's real lives, you must keep your eyes open to the way real people behave in real situations. People who work in the theatre don't always do this. The more successful they become the more time they spend in rehearsal rooms and theatres, the more their acquaintanceship excludes all but theatre folk. Theatre folk are all very well, entirely real, of course, in their way. But theatrical society is unrepresentative of the rest of the world, and highly successful theatrical society highly unrepresentative.

The more you work in the theatre the more careful you have to be to stay in touch with life as it really is. If all you are aware of is who's running which theatre, who got cast as what, who got the best and worst reviews, who's up for the next set of awards, you will no longer be seeing what you should be seeing. You will be keeping observances rather than making observations.

Observers

If you achieve even a moderate success as a director you will be asked to let people into your rehearsals as observers. They might be academics researching a thesis about the play you are directing, journalists wishing to see a particular actor or writer at work or, far more often, inexperienced directors desperate for a glimpse inside the rehearsal room.

Actors, Stage Managers and designers all get to work with a variety of directors, but other young directors have no points of access to rehearsal unless they are employed as assistants. Their only other chance of widening their knowledge of rehearsal practice is to observe another director at work.

Some directors find the very idea of observers an anathema. They believe the rehearsal room is a sacred place where actors and director must be able to communicate with absolute discretion and privacy. Others of a more down-to-earth disposition try to accommodate an observer or two whenever possible. They remember the days when they were on the outside looking in and the rehearsal room seemed impossibly out of reach.

The director cannot always be the final authority in this matter. The actors should be consulted, and if any one of them has a deeply felt objection to an observer being present, their vote should count the most.

Objections to the presence of observers can usually be countered with the establishment of some simple guidelines, which the observers are expected to observe:

1 An observer must follow the entire rehearsal period from the first day to the opening night. Actors are disturbed if observers come and go whenever they please, or appear halfway through the rehearsal period.
2 Observers must be quiet and respectful, never participating in rehearsal discussions or social activity involving the cast unless specifically invited to do so.
3 Observers are allowed to take written notes, but all other recording devices are banned. The use of tape recorders or video cameras is inimical to the privacy of the rehearsal process. The odd photo may be taken, but never casually – director's and actors' permission must first be sought.
4 Observers must not seek to profit from their privileged position by publishing or broadcasting what they have witnessed in rehearsals, unless authorised to do so by prior agreement.

Observers

Observers can be a positive influence on a company of actors, both professionally and socially. A rehearsal can sometimes become a rather inward-looking process, and a quiet but enthusiastic student or two can help to remind everyone that there is another world outside that must shortly be allowed inside.

Obstructed View Seats

The obstructed, or restricted, view seats in an **auditorium** are those seats that have only a partial view of the stage or which require a spectator to make constant physical adjustments in order to achieve a satisfactory view of the stage. In most theatres these seats are discounted at rates that reflect the degree of obstruction involved.

The commonest areas of obstructed view are the seats at the extreme edges of the auditorium where the **sightlines** are at their least favourable, the very worst being the seats that are both peripheral and high up.

Theatres also have particular local difficulties, especially where pillars or posts have been used to support the upper balconies, obscuring the view of the stage for the seats behind them.

The design of a production may affect the view of seats near the stage. For this reason the Box Office Manager and producer will usually visit the auditorium as soon as the set has been installed in order to decide which seats are compromised and how steeply they need to be discounted.

In **opera** and **musical theatre** the three or four seats immediately behind the **conductor** are sometimes designated as obstructed view, though there are maestro-groupies who would pay double for the privilege of sitting in them.

One-Man and One-Woman Shows

This is a genre that has become quite popular in recent years, though artistic success is rare and audiences are in danger of becoming allergic to it. This is because most one-man or one-woman shows are sorely constrained by the motives and methods behind their genesis, the most obvious and venal of which is the commercial prospect of having a successful show and only one actor's wage to pay. Even where the profit motive is not the overriding one, the genre can still present considerable problems. Most one-man shows are trying their best to be plays. They fall short of the mark because they are nearly always written not by playwrights but by thwarted actors.

The story generally goes like this: an actor or actress is having a tough time getting work and so decides to take a positive step to ameliorate the problem. They need to find a project that will use all their talent and enthusiasm and experience, that can be performed with the smallest possible financial and logistical risk and that can also be easily slotted into future working schedules if things look up in other areas of their careers. Of course – a one-man show – perfect! They start by choosing a famous person from History or Art with whom they have a physical similarity, or whom they think they resemble in some more emotional or psychological way, or with whom they flatter themselves they share a life story. They research the famous person's history, work and life and, being actors and therefore expert at identification, the more they read the more they seem to resemble the object of their research. The quest for a performable theatre piece then gets lost in the romance of the personification. The result is nearly always the same – an evening in which the performer seems to be having a wonderful time and everyone else in the theatre can't quite work out why they are there.

The problems are twofold. The performers are nearly always much less like their subject than they would like to believe, so the search for identification becomes more than a little tinged with vanity – the vanity of needing to be thought like the subject in spite of all evidence to the contrary. This is especially so when the performer does the writing himself and ends up making all the artistic decisions unfettered by any objectivity. If a writer is involved, he is given the one-man format as a fait accompli, and has no chance to decide for himself if the genre is indeed the best way to address the material at hand. In other words, there is always a risk of the cart being put before the horse and then the horse turning out to be a donkey all along.

There are noble exceptions, of course. One-man shows have worked brilliantly, but it is a mark of how unloved the genre has become that the minute they are perceived as successful the tag of one-man show falls away and they start qualifying as plays. Or they never pretend to be plays in the first place and are happy to occupy a less lofty place as evenings of stand-up or cabaret.

The best advice to give an actor/writer or an actor and writer team who announce that they are developing a one-man show is to research the material first and decide on the suitability of the form later. After all, one woman could perform *King Lear* all on her own – let's say the story of Lear as told by Cordelia in the split second before she dies in her father's arms – a glorious flashback of the whole tragedy. That would be a one-woman show – and it might be a good one. But if Shakespeare had been given the task of writing a one-woman play about the life of Cordelia he wouldn't have ended up writing *King Lear*. And that would have been a pity.

Onstage and Offstage

Commonly used directorial **stage directions**.

Open-Air Theatre

Directing plays in the open air presents both challenges and rewards.

First the rewards. Wherever you are, in ancient amphitheatre, ruined castle, urban wasteland, walled orchard or remote cliff-side, the natural setting defines the atmosphere of the production.

The naturalness of the environment defines the design. You fight it at your peril. To build a conventional theatrical set against a real backdrop would look absurd, not to say ungrateful. In open-air theatre, you use what you have, you take advantage of everything around you and celebrate your freedom from the prison of theatrical architecture.

The horizon is especially important – the relationship between sky, earth and the actors in the landscape. Real sunlight, moonlight and starlight shining down on the protagonists. A breeze blowing across the stage. Clouds scudding across the sky. Thunder, lightning, rain, tempest. These are the natural effects you can only dream of reproducing accurately in the theatre. And here you have them for free.

The challenges are obvious. None of the natural effects are dependable. You hope for sunshine and you get rain. Where most you want a thunderstorm you get dazzling sunlight. The breeze blows across the stage and takes all the actors' words with it. The moon rises after the show is over. The hero prays to the stars and sees only clouds. Worse still, the natural world is surrounded by the unnatural. Planes thunder overhead, traffic roars in the distance, people chatter just beyond the trees, someone practises the trumpet in a nearby apartment. In opera and musicals, none of the instruments stays in tune for more than five minutes. And so on, and so on. The problems are legion. But if you dedicate yourself to an open-air production you must conspire to solve them. Your task is made easier by your audience's willingness to be co-conspirators. They know what they're in for. They know you don't control the weather or the ambience beyond the theatre. They forgive you in advance. But you can still do a lot to head off the worst disasters.

Start by making sure your stage is correctly aligned. If you play in daylight, make sure the sun isn't going to be shining into the eyes of your audience. If the sun shines directly onto the theatre, let it shine on the stage. It doesn't matter if the actors are a little blinded. They're used to it. You wouldn't shine the stage lights into the audience's faces in a closed theatre, so why do it in an open? This would seem to be the simplest and most obvious measure, but one that some permanent open-air theatres have failed to observe. Don't make the same mistake.

If you're performing in the evening, work out when the sun sets on your performance days. Can you take advantage of the gathering darkness? Many plays written before the advent of closed playhouses and artificial light are written to end in darkness. As the story resolves itself the characters gather in torch-, lamp- or candlelight. There is something very ancient and evocative about starting a play in daylight and ending it in the dark. But you have to get the timing right.

Be ready for rain. In an unpredictable country like England, most of your audience will come prepared, but be ready to help the foolish virgins. Have a secret supply of plastic macs with hoods. Umbrellas aren't any good: they obscure the view of people sitting behind them. The basic rule with rain is a doubly honoured contract. From the actors' point of view, if the audience are enduring the rain, they must go on playing in it. From the audience's point of view, if the actors keep stoically playing, the audience must bite the bullet and be stoical too. If the rain becomes truly torrential but seems like it might let up, take a pause or bring your interval forward. If there isn't a let-up in sight and everyone gets thoroughly miserable and would rather be having a drink or be home in bed, give it up as a bad job.

You must provide cover for musicians. Their instruments are too precious to risk getting soaked.

Let the text of your play, and the way it is received, be affected by the natural environment. Don't perform it *in vacuo*, as if you weren't really where you are. The audience will have a keen sense of propriety about its participation and irony about local conditions, especially where its comfort is concerned. In an open-air production of *A Midsummer Night's Dream* the biggest laugh of the evening might come in the very first scene with Hermia's line 'belike for want of rain'. Let the audience laugh. They will have earned the right.

Opening Night

The opening night of a play used to be the first public performance, when the doors of the theatre were opened to paying customers for the first time, and it still is in theatres that only do very short runs or are therefore not dependent upon critical approbation for their box office sales. For most professional theatres, the opening night is the first evening performance that is deemed to be completely ready for public enjoyment and critical judgement.

This sometimes involves wishful thinking, of course. Some shows are never ready and will never be much enjoyed, whatever their critical reception. But the principle remains. There must be a moment in the life of every production when the work stops, the actors take control of the stage and the audience the auditorium. Some directors cannot bear this simple truth and continue to work their productions throughout the run of the play, never allowing the actors their sovereignty. But even they have to allow their shows to be visited by the **critics**, for there to be a moment when the theatre's publicity machine goes into top gear so that the general public is fully aware that tickets are on sale.

In most theatres the opening night and the **press night** are the selfsame event, but some theatre companies now separate the two nights or even, especially in the commercial theatre, spread the critics over a series of nights prior to the opening.

In **opera** companies, where only a very few performances are ever scheduled, the opening night is nearly always the actual first performance to a paying public. Indeed, in most opera companies, if the opening was delayed for a few days it would have to happen on the closing night.

The best opening nights are true celebrations – nothing to do with critics, nothing to do with judgement or approval, everything to do with a joyful community celebrating an artistic creation. Here is a play that has never been seen before. Here is a play you have loved all your life, but in a production that has brought it to life in a new way. Here is a great actor in a role that is perfect for him. Here is another in a role you would never have thought he could play. Here is an evocative stage design, a beautiful set of costumes, a ravishing musical score. Here is a world, created for you out of artistry, cunning and intelligence. It will only be here for a few days, or a few weeks, or a few months and then it will be gone for good, to be replaced with some other wilful act of theatre. We open our doors to you. How clever we are. Celebrate with us.

Opera

I will not attempt in this entry a complete description of the craft of opera direction – another whole book would be required to do that. In the entry under **Music Theatre** I have outlined what I believe are the essential characteristics of opera and how it differs from other types of **musical theatre**, but there are also fundamental differences between the disciplines of opera directing and theatre directing.

This entry will serve as a brief outline of the challenges, opportunities and pitfalls lying in wait for the theatre director unused to the special demands of the opera house.

ARTISTIC AUTHORITY

It is significant that in the world of opera the director is still often known as the producer, as indeed he used to be known in the theatre, though in this entry I shall use 'director' to stand for both terms. The continuation of the term 'producer' in many opera houses is not merely the result of old-fashioned thinking but rather a response to the problem of artistic authority. The term 'director', originating as it does from the film industry, implies someone in overall charge. Directors of films or stage plays have grown accustomed to a more or less absolute artistic authority. In opera houses nothing is absolute, but the artistic authority tends to reside more with the music than with the drama, more with the score than the libretto, more with the sound than the pictures, and the person best placed to 'direct' this authority is the conductor rather than the 'producer' or 'director'. Even when an opera house employs a General Director or 'Intendant' to supervise the overall artistic plan and the choice of repertoire, a resident conductor will still call the musical shots.

The primacy of music in opera is not just a matter of internal governance and tradition. There are strong external pressures, too. Opera audiences also attend classical concerts. They may have no interest in the spoken theatre at all, though many do. Opera critics

484

are critics of classical music rather than drama. Their judgements are based primarily on the quality of the music. In fact, all judgements in the opera world are based more on the quality of the music than on anything else. Audiences and critics would assert that the best opera productions are those where the music, the singing, the acting and the staging all do equal honour to the work. But they will more readily forgive a bad production than they will forgive bad singing. They may pour scorn on a ropy bit of staging or design and still be able to lavish extravagant praise on the music that comes from pit and stage. But the opposite is never the case. No production, however brilliantly conceived, is regarded as redeemable if the singers have substandard voices, the strings play out of tune or the brass section cracks its notes. Musical excellence is the starting point for opera just as it is in the concert hall. In both places the conductor rules and the best conductors often rule in both.

THE CONDUCTOR

If you want to direct opera you must accept the primacy of the music and the conductor's authority over it. You may have the good fortune to strike up a partnership with a conductor that allows both of you full and uncompromised artistic expression. But if you work consistently in opera you will also have to adapt your working methods to a wide variety of conductorial styles, and some of the conductors you meet will be more talented than others at adapting to a variety of directorial styles, your own included. A good relationship between conductor and director is essential for a happy rehearsal period and an artistically cohesive production. A bad one is often the cause of the most explosive and damaging battles of ego to be found anywhere in the performing arts. The problem is always one of authority. As a production gets closer and closer to its opening night there are more and more opportunities for clashes of authority. Rehearsal time gets increasingly scarce and has to be fought for. Conflicts of interest crop up over staging, audibility of singers, disposition of sets and even musical tempi. If conductor and director can keep their egos in check then none of these things need become major problems, but fiery temperament and thwarted artistry can combine to make a volatile mix. When this happens, the whole opera house quakes and nothing will serve but that one of the egos backs down or that both parties agree to be friends, which is what they should have been in the first place. And there's the point. If you work in opera as director or conductor you must learn to thrive on artistic challenge and be happy to share the highs and lows of artistic authority. If your ego is too big or too brittle to allow you to do this you should leave opera well alone and return to the theatre or the concert hall where you can tyrannise to your heart's content.

CASTING

You will have far less control over the casting in opera than you do in the theatre. There is a premium on the best opera singers, as in the world of football there is a premium on the best players. All the top opera houses want to sign the same handful of singers and they outdo one another in contracting them years in advance. Lower down the scale, smaller opera houses compete for the next best singers and so on down to the tiniest little summer festivals.

Attracting the right voice to the right part at the right time is the name of the game. Indeed, in many houses the appointment of the director for a production is considered secondary to the appointment of the singers – or at least not more important – and if you are asked to direct an opera you may very well find that at least some of the casting has already been done or is at least being very strongly proposed to you.

If you are appointed prior to the engagement of the singers you will generally be accorded some input into the casting process, and more if you take care to demand it and your demands can be backed up by clear musical and dramaturgical argument. You may even be able to exercise a veto over certain bits of casting you consider hopelessly inappropriate, but you will by no means be able to hold the absolute sway in casting matters that you will be used to in the theatre. Nor should you want to. The characters in opera can only be brought to life by a combination of acting and singing skills in the performer, together with an inherent 'rightness' for the part and the purely technical skill of being able to hit all the notes, high and low, that the score requires. If the highest or lowest notes in a part are just outside the singer's range, his neurosis about hitting them will become an overwhelmingly negative influence.

In the matter of 'rightness' there is no great difference between the theatre and opera – the same judgements about age and weight and sexuality and so on apply in just the same way, with the one caveat that opera voices tend to develop more slowly than theatre voices, making it difficult to cast really young parts with really young singers. But in matters of singing and acting and how they relate to 'rightness', you and your conductor must be ready to negotiate. Or, more commonly, you must be ready to negotiate with yourself. If the singer with the perfect voice walks into an audition and sings thrillingly but is too old or too fat or too short to be a serious candidate, you will nevertheless have to spend some serious time considering how to make the casting work to fit the voice. You must imagine how that singer would fit in with the other singers, how the audience would respond to the singer in the role, how to encourage the singer to invent a character that would make sense of his age or physique.

You must never forget that certain voices belong to certain roles – and that you are not casting a film. In this respect, the singer's acting ability can be a great help. The better the actor, the more compellingly the character will be inhabited and the more likely the audience will be to overlook any inherent 'wrongness' of the singer in the role.

ROLE FAMILIARITY

In the theatre it is rare to be in rehearsal with an actor who has played the same role in a previous production. In opera it is commonplace. Certain voices are perfect for certain roles, so the owners of those voices get asked to perform the most popular roles in a variety of different productions. When you talk to such a singer about his character, you may perceive an inner tussling as he tries to reconcile your ideas with what he has previously found or been obliged to find in a role. Experienced singers are used to this, and you mustn't be offended if they take time to assimilate your ideas or argue against them based on their previous experiences. They need to inhabit a role wholeheartedly, and it takes time to wipe the slate clean, especially if their previous experience of the role was a positive one. If they had a bad time in another production it won't take them long to forget it, provided, of course, you are replacing a bad idea with a better one.

Role familiarity in its most extreme form can create a feeling in the singer that the rehearsal process is pointless or at least a hopelessly ephemeral stage in the journey from one performance to another. This occurs most commonly with internationally successful singers who jet around the world repeatedly performing a small repertoire of roles. They bring a sense of 'Let's just get it on,' into rehearsal, of 'Just show me where you want me to stand,' or 'Oh, you want me to do it like that – fine.' You can best treat this malaise by slowing things down, discussing the role and the scene in detail with all the singers in it and then creating real specificity in the relationship between the characters. Most singers, however celebrated, respond well to the feeling that a particular colleague expects a particular stimulus from them in a particular scene. Singers, like actors, are social creatures and respond well to the social pressures of a creative rehearsal period.

THE CHORUS

The chorus is a strange and hungry beast, strange because it exists in a unique form in the world of opera and hungry because it consumes a disproportionate amount of time, energy and money in relation to the limited time it spends actually performing on stage. But it is also a necessary beast. An opera house without a chorus would be a soulless place indeed and would have a very small repertoire of works on which to draw. Ever since opera's emergence from oratorio, composers have continued the tradition of using large choral forces to make big musical statements and to paint rich human backdrops to the foreground events. Some opera composers create individual detail in the use of the chorus, but most choruses sing and act with a collective voice, all its characters thinking and communicating the same material in the same way. This is the main reason why theatre directors have such trouble with them, but there are others.

Most theatre directors work in a fundamentally naturalistic style, even if some like to pretend they don't. Choruses are very tricky to weave into a naturalistic production style. You can spend hours encouraging different members of a chorus to do physically different things on stage, but they will never have the real differences of thought and motivation present in a real crowd of people, so the result will always seem a little artificial unless the work is very cleverly done. Experienced chorus members are aware of the tension in their work between the individual and the choral and will have learnt the necessary 'double think' required to perform it. But choruses can also be cynical and even obstructive if they feel they are being thoughtlessly required to jump through physical hoops that are at complete odds with the sense or feeling of what they are singing. And who can blame them?

Choruses also have a significant influence on the design of opera. When the chorus is on stage it must be heard, and so that it may be heard it must be seen. A chorus member standing immediately behind another will be largely inaudible to the audience. So designers are set the task of creating spaces that are chorus-friendly. This is why so many opera sets rise steeply as they go upstage, or are multi-levelled. The chorus must have somewhere to stand, sometimes for long periods, where it doesn't obstruct the soloists or pull attention away from the downstage action of the opera. In other words it must be present but not dominant, except when it is required to be so. But if a structure is built into the design of the opera, it must be done in such a way that it doesn't itself dominate or obstruct anything else that needs to happen on the stage. It's a perennial problem for directors and designers and one they must resolve again and again with each opera they produce.

The chorus beast also eats schedules. Because chorus time is so expensive – every time you call the chorus you have forty or so people to pay for a minimum session of three hours or so – and because a chorus in a busy opera house might be rehearsing or performing three or four other operas in the repertoire at the same time and because the chorus is comprised of people who need to know what they're doing from day to day and have lives to lead, you will be told by the Chorus Master or his office when the chorus is available to you and when it isn't. Rehearsing an opera chronologically is therefore practically impossible, the chorus availability rarely if ever coinciding with the order of the scenes to be rehearsed. The problem is compounded if you work at an opera house that employs an amateur chorus. Here what you gain in enthusiasm you lose in convenience, chorus rehearsals only being possible in the evenings or at weekends. The members of the chorus arrive raring to go from their surgeries and classrooms and offices just at the moment when you've finished a full day's work with the soloists and want to go home. So you have to learn to pace yourself, and them, and the soloists, so that everyone stays at the top of their game whatever time of day they're rehearsing.

Whether your chorus is professional or amateur, you will always be short of chorus rehearsal time. You may get only one shot at creating a chorus scene and if you bungle it you might not get another chance. So be prepared, and if possible use the services of a **choreographer**, **Movement Director** or **Musical Stager** to help you map out the movement of bodies in the scenes the chorus is in. You will probably not have time to imagine it all, teach it to the chorus, and then record what you have taught all by yourself.

THE CHORUS MASTER

Chorus Masters are a potential source of disharmony for the director. They may be quite delightful collaborators, but they can also be strange beasts in themselves. They are often ex-singers who have graduated to their mastership through the ranks, but they may also be *soi-disant* or aspirant conductors. Whatever their origins, they will have a strong view about how their choruses should sound, responsible as they are for rehearsing them musically. But their view might not coincide with that of the conductor. Beware, therefore, of being caught in a struggle of musical egos between conductor and Chorus Master, or being made the scapegoat for a failure of musical authority in either of them.

In terms of rehearsal etiquette, you should never give a musical note to a chorus member without first consulting the Chorus

Master. If you have a strong musical view about the chorus material it's a better idea to put it to the Chorus Master first and then let him, if he agrees with it, communicate it to the chorus himself. Or better still, talk to conductor and Chorus Master at the same time. That way your idea stands much less chance of being reversed by a higher, or alternative, authority at a later date.

THE ORCHESTRA

The orchestra is an even stranger beast than the chorus, though only strange in the sense of remote. As a director you will have very little to do with the orchestra. Even singers and orchestral players rarely mix, professionally or socially. It's a rather sad aspect of the opera house that there are two separate worlds on the stage and in the pit. Only the conductor and the répétiteurs live in both worlds, though even they spend more time with the singers in the rehearsal room than they do in the pit with the musicians. Some musicians take an interest in what happens on stage and make an effort to mix socially with the singers, but it tends to be one-way traffic. Singers inhabit a world of their own, especially the soloists. They belong to an itinerant breed, here today gone tomorrow. Pit musicians can play in the same orchestra for years. They watch the singers come and go, but spend their entire creative lives playing in a place from which the stage is largely, or entirely, invisible. Of course they have highly tuned ears and can appreciate a great voice when they hear it, but the lack of social and artistic ensemble slowly gets into the bloodstream, and it's quite normal for there to be two completely separate societies in an opera house. Like some tired old married couples, singers and players can live in the same house without ever exchanging a word or taking the trouble to recognise each other's existence.

THE ORCHESTRA PIT

There is one shock you must prepare yourself for when you direct an opera for the first time: the size of the orchestra pit and the effect it has on your perception of the stage from the auditorium. In the theatre you will be used to the front row of the audience being more or less in the same position, relatively, as the one you have been occupying in the rehearsal room. Even then you can experience something of a shock when you first move from your rehearsal space into the theatre. The height of the stage can seem forbidding, or its relationship to the galleries, or to the back of the stalls. But nothing you will have experienced in the theatre will prepare you for the moment when you go from rehearsal room into the opera house and contemplate the yawning gap between the front row of the stalls and the stage. It seems an insurmountable abyss and becomes even greater in your mind when you first see the conductor standing in full view of the audience, brightly lit even in the darkest scenes on stage. Don't worry. There's nothing you can do about it, and opera audiences are thoroughly used to the convention. The conductor needs to be strongly lit in order to be clearly visible to the singers and the musicians. He's a star too. Opera audiences like watching conductors. It's part of the buzz of going to the opera. Wagner tried to change it all when he built Bayreuth, with the pit buried in the bowels of the earth and the orchestra completely invisible, conductor included. But it didn't catch on. There's something about a visible orchestra that makes the blood of opera fans run warmer in their veins. And the music sounds better when the orchestra is exposed – including in Wagner. You get the full blast of the brass and the luscious warmth of the strings and the sense of danger that the music must be played well and seen to be played well for the opera to succeed. If the production is truly awful and you're sitting in an upper circle, the orchestra gives you something interesting to watch.

REHEARSALS AND VOICES

In the theatre you rehearse more intensively the closer you get to opening night. In opera it's the other way around. Because opera singers can't sing large roles more than two or three times a week at the very most, the lead-up to the opening night is a dangerous time for them. If they rehearse too much and even slightly strain their chords the first night will be thrown into jeopardy. If a voice gives out, the singer can't just 'soldier on' as an actor is often obliged to do in the theatre. The voice is either there or it isn't, and singers live in mortal fear of singing when not on form, or permanently damaging their voices by overusing them.

As opening night approaches, whole days are set aside for 'vocal rest', and the sort of last-minute tinkering over detail that you will be used to doing with your actors in the theatre is out of the question in the opera house. This drives some theatre directors crazy, especially the ones who control their own nervousness or lack of confidence by working everyone else to death or who reserve the right to make radical changes to a production right up to the last minute. Experienced opera directors plan their productions very carefully and use the rehearsal room to put in as much detail as they can, knowing that it might be their last chance to do so.

If vocal rest is a crucial part of opera planning and scheduling, it also affects every part of the rehearsal process. If singers 'sang out' all the time, giving their parts full vocal and emotional force whenever they rehearsed, they would be hoarse by the end of every week. Singers do vary in this respect, some being equipped with seemingly undamageable larynxes while others have to take much more care, but all singers are taught how to 'mark' their parts as a fundamental part of their training.

MARKING

'Marking' means under-singing, or producing just enough sound to give a sense of the lyric and the musical line but not enough to tax the voice. Marking is especially used for passages of high notes, with the singer pitching everything down the octave, it being harder to sing quietly in a higher register and more of a strain on the chords, and is therefore more prevalent in morning rehearsals when voices are still warming up to the day.

Towards the end of a day's rehearsal singers will often want to sing out a whole scene at least once in order to get the role sung into their voices and to know that they have the vocal stamina for a whole scene or act. When singers are singing out, you must be careful to keep your own interventions to a minimum. Do your detailed work on character, motivation and physical movement while they are marking, but stand back and look at the big picture while they are singing out. A singer in full flight can get very testy if stopped by a pernickety director desperate to impart an insignificant piece of acting advice.

The problem with vocal marking is that it tends to make the singers mark everything else they do – the acting, the thinking and the feeling. The best way to get over this is to insist on fully articulated consonants at all times, obliging the singers to invest in the meaning of the words and the thoughts and feelings behind them. This is especially useful when the language is not the singer's mother tongue – as is often the case in opera.

STAGE REHEARSALS

Once the production goes from rehearsal room to stage, time is further constrained and controlled by various new pressures. In the theatre it's far easier to find extra time for solving unforeseen problems as a production goes into its last few days. In the opera house the advance schedule makes extra time all but impossible to find and in any case prohibitively expensive. But the biggest difference between theatre and opera is how the **technical rehearsals** are accomplished. In the theatre the 'tech' is a work-through of the play involving all of the technical departments in order to prove the efficacy of the design, costumes, lighting and stage machinery. It might take a day in a poor theatre or a couple of weeks for a big Broadway musical, but it is dedicated time and tends to be accomplished at the pace dictated by the technical requirements of the play, leaving sufficient time to solve any problems on the way. In the opera house the technical period is divided between 'stage and piano' rehearsals and 'stage and orchestra' rehearsals.

Stage and piano rehearsals are the nearest equivalent to the 'tech' in the theatre, but they only constitute half of the allotted technical time. When you get to the stage and orchestra rehearsals, the stage is still firing on all technical cylinders, but the pace of the rehearsal is dictated solely by musical requirements and the man in charge is the conductor. This means that any change you or any member of your creative team wants to make must be done silently and invisibly. Some opera directors actually leave the theatre while the stage and orchestra rehearsals are happening, unable to cope with the frustration of watching the same mistakes being endlessly repeated without any hope of a cure. But this is a mistake. You can achieve a great deal as you sit in the darkness with your collaborators – the lighting especially can be refined in a way that you often don't have time for during theatre techs. And you can send your choreographer onto the stage with surreptitious notes for the chorus – or even flit about yourself making unobtrusive changes of positioning or motivation while the conductor is busy with the woodwind sound or the placing of the offstage chorus. You can even take time to listen to the music. Listening to the orchestral colours and to the balance between singers and orchestra can often give you a fresh insight into the staging, an insight you couldn't have had listening to the rehearsal room piano tonking away in the corner. And you can listen to the conductor. His insights into the music, his rehearsal process, his desire to make things better may require your help. Don't get thrown by not being in charge of things. Listen, evaluate and collaborate.

STAGING

In most respects staging an opera is like staging a play. You must keep the leading performers in focus, maintain a fluidity of movement in the active characters, avoid repetition in the creation of your scenic pictures and, depending on the style of your production, create a stage environment in which the performers can behave in a natural and unaffected way. There are, however, two considerations that will take up far more of your time in the opera house than in the theatre: audibility and breathing.

Of course, actors in the theatre need to be audible, but the nature of the spoken text is such that there are many more possibilities of interpretation in a play than in an opera. The spoken text is usually projected into a silent space, while the sung line is almost always accompanied, often by considerable musical forces. Very few playwrights give strict indications in the text as to the volume or phrasing of a line. Most composers give clear dynamic markings to the singer or provide an atmosphere in the accompaniment that a singer must reflect or a challenge to which he must rise.

It is therefore more or less axiomatic in the opera house that when a singer is singing his face must be angled downstage most of the time, his voice unimpeded by the scenery, furniture or props, or by his costume or his wig, or by any other singer's body, costume or wig.

If a singer turns his back on the audience while singing, his voice becomes relatively inaudible to the audience – and the conductor, whose ears represent all the ears in the house, will be suspicious of the move, if not outright hostile.

Good singing requires good breathing. In order to produce long legato phrases in their arias, singers need a huge reservoir of breath, the lower and longer the notes the more breath required. Anything other than singing that causes a singer to lose his breath is therefore to be avoided. Most singers will object if a director asks them to run across the stage or climb a ladder just before they sing. If they are about to sing a long phrase or a whole aria, they will object strenuously, and with good cause. If a singer is overweight, the problem can become more extreme, with even small moves on stage causing obvious shortness of breath.

Because the leading performers in an opera often enjoy extended periods of solo singing, there is a tendency for them to want to stay as still as possible while they are doing it. In duets, trios, quartets and larger ensembles, the problem is obviously intensified. The larger the ensemble, the more inventive a director must be to avoid a complete stasis in the movement of the leading characters on stage.

Of course, no two singers are the same. While some are hopelessly lardy and need extraordinary encouragement to move around at all, others pride themselves on their athleticism and sometimes have to be stopped from compromising the quality of their singing by engaging in wilful bouts of strenuous movement.

You must get to know your singers. Their reservoirs of sustainable breath will all be different. You must also study the score. Look for gaps in the sung lines of an aria. A few bars will generally afford enough space to let you move an actor across the stage without any damage to the sung line. In larger ensembles, look for places where the soloists have less active vocal lines and give them moves accordingly. But don't limit yourself unduly. Many singers like their strong moves to coincide with their more emphatic phrases, thus giving their more dramatic moments a stronger impact. Experimentation is essential, and while experimenting you must have great sensitivity to the needs of the singers and the conductor on the one hand while gently maintaining your right to keep the stage picture fluid, emotionally appropriate and engaging.

Opera rehearsals that are dominated by a desire in the singers to stand in one place for the sake of their vocal line, to the exclusion of all other dramatic considerations, will inevitably result in static and lifeless productions. The resulting performance style, known derisively in the profession as 'park and bark', is the bane of live opera all over the world. It is partly caused by singers, abetted by critics and audiences alike, comparing their own live performances with the best available recordings and believing that they can only achieve similar results by behaving on stage as if they were in a recording studio. This misplaced perfectionism is becoming increasingly prevalent, but it is pointless to argue that your singers shouldn't try to emulate the recorded sound that their greatest heroes have created on disc. They will not hear you. Rather you should argue that it is quite possible to sing the perfect aria while acting with feeling, movement, and conviction, and that a balance of the two disciplines is what makes opera worth attending. Then help them find performances that will make good your words.

ACTING

There is good acting and bad acting in opera just as there is in the theatre, but your evaluation of what is good and bad involves a more complicated process in the former than the latter. A few great singers are also great actors, but most have limited acting talent and skills. Some average singers make up for their lack of vocal power or skill with better than average acting. Many good singers are physically wooden, confining their acting powers to their vocal chords. Others will have picked up a histrionic style of acting by observation or emulation and will be unhappy to relinquish it unless provided with a set of better options. You must be the equaliser, reconciling the differences in each singer between their vocal and acting skills, balancing one singer's acting style with another's, creating an atmosphere and a style in which all the performers seem equally happy and equally real.

Talk to your singers about acting just as you would talk to actors. Discuss the motivation of their characters, their ages, sexuality, intellectual capacity and sense of humour. The more you give them to think about, the more complex their responses can afford to be and the less likely they are to take refuge in conventional techniques or received ideas.

Your equalising skills will be most challenged when directing a comic opera. Here a lack of talent, skill, taste and unity in a cast can be quite perplexing, the most prevailing problem being the idea that comedy requires a different kind of acting from more serious work. The commonest symptoms of this heresy are the flexed-knee walk, the silly voice and the overworked eyebrows. Your job will be to calm everyone down, examine each scene for what is truly funny in it, and then inspire your cast to play the situation rather than the comedy. As in the theatre singers must learn to examine their material with intelligence and taste and not bludgeon it to death with comic clubs.

In more serious work, don't imagine you have to confine the singers to purely naturalistic movement. When they are singing up a storm in a highly charged aria, they need to have some physical freedom to produce the huge sounds demanded by the music. Too much freedom can express itself in tasteless histrionics, but you can use your own taste and judgement to arrive at a happy compromise.

EYE CONTACT

A common problem with opera singers is that they don't know where to look. Whenever they are singing they must keep at least one eye on the conductor or they risk losing the beat and incurring the conductor's wrath. They are often very careful where they place what is left of their focus. Role familiarity and musical perfectionism can make them more attentive to their inner thoughts than to their fellow performers, resulting in a sort of mental glaze and a lack of awareness of anything else on the stage around them. It is by no means unusual in the opera house to see two singers performing an entire love scene together without once looking each other in the eye. Their voices tell you they are desperately in love but their eyes tell you they are in love with the idea of each other rather than with the flesh and blood person standing in front of them. This is a state in which singers will never vary their performances, from one night to another, from one year to another. It is also a perfect breeding ground for bad acting. Two or more singers performing in their mutual vacuums will produce exclusive realities, exclusive styles of acting. The more unrelated these worlds become, the less likely they are to resemble anything like real life. Singers that are allowed to perpetuate this hermetically sealed style eventually become caricatures of themselves. They make strange faces when they sing and move around the stage in unaccountable ways, becoming irritated with anyone or anything that interferes with their private world. And those who are being cut out by them become irritated in return, adding angry little demonstrations of annoyance to their performances.

Eye contact between singers is the only antidote to this illness. Indeed, it is as profoundly necessary to the art of opera as it is to theatre. The stimulus of one singer's mind working on another's and being stimulated in return is what makes the stage a living environment. Without it opera becomes like an animated musical version of Madame Tussaud's – you marvel at the expertise that has been lavished on each dummy but you remain unmoved by the dummies themselves.

You must insist that your singers make eye contact with one another, that they seek out places where eye contact can restore their sense of reality and give them opportunities for creating their performances afresh to take account of the people around them. For every moment of eye contact a whole new series of responses and counter responses is created. Within seconds a performance starts to go live and can subsequently be shaped and controlled by conductor and singers alike before a new live stimulus starts up the process again.

You may meet considerable resistance to demands for eye contact, as well as all sorts of excuses and avoidance tactics, and you may have to persist beyond the patience of some recidivist dummies. But persist you must, as much for their sakes as your own. With a little luck and some gentle persuasion you will soon wake everyone up to the joys of a living performance.

ARTICULATION AND COMMUNICATION

Because singers are cast more for the quality of their voices than their acting talent or their nationality or their skill with the spoken word, they often have problems of articulation or communication of meaning that would be considered hopeless handicaps in a theatre actor.

If you are having trouble hearing a singer's words, first diagnose the problem correctly. It might be a language issue, a Russian singer struggling with French, or an Italian struggling with German, or anyone struggling with Czech. Unless you are extremely well-versed in the language yourself, you will require here the services of a **Language Coach**. If this is indeed the problem, only a complete familiarity with the meaning and inflection of the language will give the singer the confidence to lean heavily on his words.

Your singer might be fudging the words in order to disguise a speech impediment of one kind or another, a lisp, a lazy 'r' or a sibilant 's'. In this case, get him to sing distinctly wherever he can and help him fudge in an undetectable way, but only when the impediment really begs to be fudged.

Lack of articulation in most singers is not owing to difficulties of language or technical flaws but rather a failure to understand the importance of the words, the meaning of the words or the opportunity the words might give for characterisation and emotional expression. A singer half using his words is only half expressing the part he plays, however well he sings it. Or put it another way, a singer half singing his words is not properly singing his part at all.

Before you start rehearsing a scene, make sure your singers

understand all the words they are singing – their meaning, their emotional impact and what they carry in the way of character, feeling, comedy or irony. Take your singers carefully through the score and explore how the weight of the accompaniment underpins the weight of the words, where the two diverge and where the climaxes occur in music and meaning. This should be done in the company of your conductor who will no doubt have his own readings to express. Once the singers have fully assimilated the text and all the opportunities it affords them, show them where the meaning of their words might overlap or thematically connect with the words of the other characters so that their discoveries can be shared wherever appropriate.

Once you start rehearsing, keep the pressure up. Help your singers 'land' the important words in their text, by connecting them with another character, or communicating them to the audience or feeling them within themselves. Never let the text get 'fluffy'. Every consonant is an aid to meaning, just as every vowel is a chance to sing.

Problems of articulation and communication of meaning have been compounded in recent years by the widespread use of **surtitles**. Because the audience can read the singer's words with a quick glance at a screen, it seems the singer can afford to bear less of the responsibility to be distinctly heard. This is a nonsense, of course, and must be fought strenuously by anyone who values the spoken word, the endless hours of labour put in by generations of librettists and the very meaning of the works themselves.

Operetta

'Operetta' is a diminutive form of the Italian word **opera**, and operettas are indeed operas in diminutive. They are diminutive musically, intellectually and emotionally, generally deriving their content from light-hearted and unpretentious stories of a sentimental or farcical nature.

In historical terms, operetta developed into musical comedy and musical comedy developed into the musical. But operetta is still a very popular form, and many opera houses still programme the most popular ones on a regular basis.

Operetta may also be referred to as 'light opera' or, more unkindly in some circles, as 'opera-lite'.

Oratorio

Oratorios are large-scale dramatic works, usually based on biblical themes, with solo singers, **chorus** and full **orchestra**, written to be performed in church, cathedral or concert hall without action, scenery, costumes or props.

Based on the form of the medieval mystery play, they grew out of the musical services in the Oratory of St Philip Neri in Rome in the second half of the sixteenth century, hence their name.

They are now performed in concert halls more often than anywhere else, but in recent years some **opera** companies have successfully explored the oratorio repertoire, fully dramatising them with scenery and costumes.

There is certainly something rather depressing about concert performances of oratorios, passions or requiems, with their stiff line-ups of formally clad soloists not knowing where to look or how to place their performances, the audience's attention uneasily balanced between faith and art.

Oratorios and passions play best in beautiful old cathedrals where the very stones speak of faith, the soloists effortlessly become a sort of temporary musical priesthood, and the audience can let its imagination wander in and around the narrative. But perhaps in a secular and sceptical age, opera house dramatisations are useful in introducing these great works to people who can only enjoy their musical stories if they come with pictures.

Orchestra

In the ancient Greek theatre, the orchestra was the semicircular area at the front of the stage where the **Chorus** danced, the word deriving from the Greek word for dancer.

In the modern age, the term came to mean the space where the musicians play their instruments, and now describes the instruments themselves and by association their players.

The orchestra stalls are the seats on the ground floor of the **auditorium**, abbreviated in America to the orchestra and in Britain to the stalls.

If you work in **opera**, the orchestra and the **pit** in which it sits will have a significant effect on the way you direct and design your productions.

Orchestra Pit

The orchestra pit is the sunken space between stage and auditorium where the pit musicians play in **opera** and **musical theatre**.

Most pits are built at the same level as the **understage** from which they are easily accessible, allowing members of the **orchestra** to assemble and tune their instruments in relative peace and privacy.

Pits come in many different shapes and sizes. In modern, or modernised, theatres they are often quite adaptable, allowing director, designer and **Musical Director** or **conductor** to choose the most suitable dimensions of pit for the show in hand. Hydraulic lifts can change the level of the floor in relation to the floor of the stalls, and the whole pit may even be dividable into different blocks to allow for various sizes of orchestra. This is done for both economic and artistic reasons. If you have a small band, you don't want them swimming around in a huge pit. You close down the floor to a smaller size and put an extra row or two of stalls seats over the resulting void.

In opera houses with variable pit floors, there is often some debate between conductors, directors and singers about the height at which the musicians should play. In baroque opera the orchestra originally played on the same level as the stalls seats, and it is now fashionable, for the sake of an 'authentic' sound balance, to see them creeping back to the same level once more. Singers hate this. They struggle to be seen and heard with the musicians playing so visibly, and never quietly enough, in front of them. Directors, too, are never happy when the stage realities they have carefully established are compromised by a conductor acting out his own little dramas in front of the orchestra and in full view of the audience.

In musical theatre, whenever it is a commercially motivated enterprise, which it usually is, you will find yourself under considerable pressure from producers and theatre owners to maximise the number of stalls seats and so minimise the size of the pit. From the stage side of the pit comes a different sort of pressure. Directors and designers like to get their sets as close as they can to the auditorium to create the greatest possible intimacy between performers and audience, so they build **thrusts** and **aprons** out over the **forestage**. The orchestra pit becomes squashed between these two imperatives, and it is not uncommon to see a musical theatre band reduced to playing through a mean little letterbox of remainder space. This is always a pity. If there isn't room for the real acoustic sound to get out, the instruments have to be amplified to be audible, and the resulting sound becomes so artificial it might as well be recorded and played back over the auditorium speakers.

If you use an orchestra pit for a musical, it should always be open enough to allow the real sound of the instruments to be heard by the audience. Don't let anyone tell you the sound is amplified anyway so it doesn't matter. It does matter. The musicians are part of the show. Their contribution is vital to the atmosphere of a live performance. It is demoralising for them to be shut away out of sight, out of mind and a shame for the audience to leave the theatre unaware they've been listening to a live band.

Orchestrators and Orchestrations

Orchestration is the craft of arranging music for orchestral instruments. Orchestrators are the artisans of orchestral sound. They may also be **composers** in their own right, as indeed most of them are, but here we consider them in their capacity as musical enablers.

A good orchestrator knows all about instruments. He knows

their ranges, that is the highest and lowest notes they can play, the quality of sound they produce at various pitches, their technical capacities, how they are fingered, blown, scraped, plucked or struck, what clef their notation is written in and, if they are transposing instruments, how the music as written differs from the music as heard.

It goes without saying that they must also be completely musically literate, happy to write in any key or time signature and fully conversant with the mysteries of modulation, harmony and counterpoint.

When composers write their music, they generally start by sketching out their melodies and harmonies on one or two staves only, usually working at a keyboard or some other harmonic instrument, like a guitar. If musically literate, they will then write out a fully harmonised keyboard version on two staves with a **lyric** written under the melody if the music is to be sung. This is known as a piano/vocal score. If they are a little less than musically literate they may write a single stave melodic line with coded chords written under the melody and lyric. If musically illiterate, they will play and/or sing their music into a recording device and get someone else to transcribe it into musical notation.

There are composers who write out their music in full score form, exactly as it will eventually be played, with every instrument separately designated, but they are in a very small minority. In **musical theatre**, and increasingly even in **opera**, composers take the writing of their music to the piano/vocal stage and then rely on orchestrators to express the work in its final, playable form.

The dependency of composers on orchestrators accounts for enormous additional expense in the production of musicals, but the artistic benefits can be significant provided care is taken when arranging the marriage. A good orchestrator will write to a composer's strengths and fill in for his weaknesses, but he must have a genuine admiration for the music he is arranging. An unsympathetic orchestrator, who thinks he could have written the music better himself and has taken on the job just for the money, will tend to over-elaborate and bury the score under an avalanche of his own invention. Both parties should work harmoniously together to agree on key relationships, rhythmic patterns and orchestral colours, and the orchestrator should be happy to offer up ideas for counter-melodies, reprises and additional instrumental material.

Orchestrating can be a thankless task. In the musical theatre, where opinions are two a penny but competent knowledge a rare and precious metal, the orchestrator can bear the brunt of any artistic disagreement about the score. When composers get anxious and lose their objectivity about the value of their work, Musical Directors, lyricists, book writers, choreographers, directors, singers, even producers, weigh in with their opinions. Songs are cut or shoved into some other part of the show, or have their keys or tempi changed, a dance gets shortened or a scene change lengthened and everyone seems to have a strongly conflicting opinion about the rightness and wrongness of each measure. At the end of the discussion, the poor orchestrator is left with the problem, often horribly uncertain what he is required to do. He has a day, or perhaps only a night, to come up with a new arrangement that will satisfy all parties and not completely alienate his composer.

Truly happy orchestrators are a rare breed. They can be content for a day or two but then they get that faraway look about their eyes that says, 'What am I doing here? I'm an artist, not a mechanic. Please let me go and write my own music.' As their director, you must protect them from such feelings. The best way to do this is to insist on the supremacy of the composer–orchestrator relationship. When everyone else has had his say, yourself included, leave the two of them together to agree on exactly what they want to do. Trust them to do what is right for the score and abide by the wisdom of their decisions.

Overhangs

In any multi-tiered theatre the ceilings of the upper tiers will overhang the lower. The more tiers there are in a theatre the more extreme the overhangs are likely to be, causing obvious difficulties with both **sightlines** and **acoustics**. Clever theatre architects manage to avoid these problems, but there are many theatres where shoddy design or managerial greed or both have crammed so many seats into a small space that the resulting overhang makes things very uncomfortable for audiences and actors alike.

The most difficult problems arise at the very back of the stalls or circle in very deep **auditoria,** the overhang from the tier above giving the audience a sort of letterbox view of the stage. From such seats, Juliet will be invisible on her balcony, projected effects on a **cyclorama** will be completely obscured, and the heads of the audience members in front will blot out any view of the actors from below the waist. These seats are sometimes sold cheap as having an **obstructed view,** but you will still have the problem of making your show tolerable for members of the audience sitting in them. If a theatre has a very serious overhang problem then you and your designer must be careful not to compound it with a design that continuously raises the action above stage level, but you shouldn't let yourselves be completely tyrannised by a bad theatre design. Just be aware that in such circumstances you can't have long and important scenes taking place on an upper level of the stage. Audiences watching a play from under an overhang will forgive you as long as the actors aren't stuck in an invisible position for too long. Keep the actors on the move, most of the action on the level and all the words clearly audible and you won't get too many complaints. And don't try to do *Romeo and Juliet* in such a space. If you have to make Juliet's balcony so low that Romeo could vault niftily onto it with a short run-up then the Nurse wouldn't have to supply them with a ladder.

P

Pace and Rhythm

Pace is the term most commonly used in the theatre to describe the tempo of a performance. This is defined by the rate at which the actors deliver their lines, the extent to which they come in on cue or **pause** between lines and speeches, and the overall energy and drive of their performances. Pace can also be affected by the efficiency of **scene changes** and the tempo of any accompanying **music** cues and **sound effects**.

The rhythm of a production is defined by the relative tempi of its constituent speeches and scenes. Each scene, each encounter between characters, has an appropriate rhythm, just like the rhythm in a piece of music, slow or quick, considered or headlong, jagged or smooth, grave or carefree. Rhythm and pace are thus intimately related. A production that has uniform pace, fast or slow, will lack the sense of rhythm required to make each scene interesting and true.

In **opera** and **musical theatre**, the pace of a performance will largely be defined by the tempi and drive of the musical numbers. Here the director must collaborate with the **conductor** or **Musical Director** to find an appropriate pace and rhythm for every part of the **score** and, if there are spoken scenes, a melding from speech to music and back again that honours the value of both forms of expression.

In a play, the director must mine the text for evidence of rhythm. Good playwrights create patterns of rhythm in the events of their plots and in the characters that animate them. Look at every scene and sense the rhythm in its language and in the relationship between the characters. Decide which characters have a quick tempo and which a slow. Whatever tempo you choose for individual characters, remember that each scene has a rhythm that the characters must contribute towards and so does the play as a whole. You must be ready to take the lead here. Pace and rhythm are extremely subjective matters. Some actors have a feel for the common good, but some can't hear anything beyond their own deliveries and will need to be told they are dawdling or rushing.

Some actors are 'pace makers'; 'pace dictators' might be an more apt term. Others are 'pace followers' or 'pace mimickers'. Pace-dictating can have positive and negative impact. An actor forcing too much speed into a performance can cause everyone else to hurtle accordingly, at the expense of meaning and understanding. An actor with a ponderous delivery can grind a scene to a complete halt. The pace mimickers will follow wherever they are led. If you want to affect the overall pace of a production or change the rhythm of particular scenes, enlist the help of the pace dictators in your cast. Persuade them of the sense of injecting a higher tempo or slowing things down and the rest of the cast will follow.

In the case of a chronically slow actor, don't just tell him to speed up the delivery of his lines. Talk to him about the tempo of his character in terms of how quickly he thinks. Get him to speed up his thought processes, or make his character more volatile and less predictable, so his thoughts come as a surprise even to himself.

When the **running time** of a show has unaccountably lengthened, use a **speed run** to inject more pace but always remember, the overall rhythm of a production should be defined by a contrast of appropriate rhythms for each scene and each character. Speed is not pace.

Pace and rhythm can also be affected by the speed of thought in the audience on any one night. Some audiences think more quickly than others. Experienced actors feel this and play the pace they sense an audience requires of them. In a stale production, where the actors have fallen into established **patterns** of behaviour, this never happens. The pace will be the same every night, with the audience getting ahead or falling behind and the actors taking no account of them.

If you have a problem of pace or rhythm in a production, make it the headline of your next **note session**, so the whole cast can be made aware of the problem and address it at the next performance.

Papering

The mass issuing of slips of paper (free) in lieu of theatre tickets (expensive) in order to bulk up audience numbers.

See **Complimentary Tickets**.

Pass Door

The door leading directly from the foyer to the stage or backstage, only accessible to actors crew and creative team.

See **Front of House**.

Passerelle

Passerelle is a French term describing a walkway extending from both sides of the stage around the front of the **orchestra pit** to enable the singers in **musical theatre** and cabaret to promenade within flirting distance of the audience without losing touch with the **conductor** or **accompanist**. Some passerelles have three access points, one on either side of the stage and one in the middle, the conductor's podium having to shift to one side of the pit or the other.

Patterns and Patterning

When actors have been performing a play for many weeks, their performances can start falling into predictable patterns of physical and vocal behaviour and inflection. As the weeks go by, the patterning can become more and more extreme, resulting in stilted and over-stylised characterisations that defy comparison with any known human behaviour. The cause of patterning is physical repetition in the absence of a creative thought process.

The antidote is simple and easily addressed with a sympathetic **note session**. Most ensembles will respond well to having the problem pointed out, but be careful not to make your examples invidious. Spread the notes around, so that the whole company feels jointly responsible for the problem, even if there are clear pockets of guilt that need a more private touch after the session is over.

However serious the problem has become, don't be negative about it. Don't forbid the actors their patterned moves or inflections. Rather suggest that they find ways of refreshing their performances by trying new interpretations on the most patterned areas. New thoughts will generate fresh moves. Unmotivated new moves will just become new patterns.

Make everybody in the ensemble more aware of their fellow actors' performances. It is far harder to maintain a non-human performance if an actor is in eye contact with one of his fellows. One actor's humanity is instantly reflected back to the other, causing an equally instant change in behaviour. Show how potent a force this is by running little sections of the play with and without eye contact between the actors and their characters. Sometimes the tiniest sidelong glance can change the emotional temperature of a scene and revive a badly patterned piece of text. Encourage the actors to make further eye contact experiments while performing.

Patterning is a more or less constant threat to the spontaneity that makes a live theatre experience worth anything, and in a **long run** it will need constant monitoring.

Pauses and Pausing

Pauses are brief intermissions of silence in the spoken text of a play. They may be indicated by the author in a stage direction, suggested by the rhythm of a text, discovered in rehearsal by actor and director, or interpolated by an actor extempore. They may occur wherever author, director or actor believes the unbroken spoken text cannot sufficiently communicate a character's intention, thought or feeling. This belief may be erroneous but it is generally the originating factor.

How do you decide when a pause is appropriate? How do you

know when an actor is using a pause for essential effect and when he is merely being self-indulgent? How do you interpret a pause indicated in the text in the absence of any obvious motive for it?

In **verse** plays you should try to do without pauses altogether. Nothing breaks up the natural rhythm and impetus of a poetic text more than unwarrantable pausing. Ideally you shouldn't even pause between scenes. Occasionally you will see evidence for a pause in a broken line of verse. Where this happens, the actor should pause only as long as the missing syllables in the **metre** allow. In all other cases, when actors argue for their right to a pause you should require them to prove the pause has been 'earned'.

An 'earned pause' is payment, as it were, for extraordinary intensity of thought, speed of delivery or power of dramatic effect. In other words, the earner of the pause must be able to fill the wordless moment with something not communicable in the surrounding text. The pause must be so full of thought or feeling that the words spoken immediately before or after it are strengthened rather than weakened by it.

This will rarely be the case. A pause usually kills the effect of the words that follow it because the actor wastes it in generating the thought that motivates the words. If the thought is communicated to the audience in the 'unearned' silence, the subsequent words are made redundant. Thus actors can rarely justify pauses in a poetic text. Whatever the thought or feeling, there will almost invariably be a way of expressing it on the text rather than off it.

Even in naturalistic plays written in realistic prose style, the rule of the earned pause is still a useful one. Some actors feel that by peppering their dialogue with pauses they somehow make it sound more real. People pause all the time in real life, they reason, so constant pausing in a text is simply a reflection of that reality. One can have some sympathy with this technique if it is used very sparingly, but in practice serial pausing becomes like a nervous tic, an irritating habit that breaks up the natural rhythm of the text without adding an iota of meaning or dramatic tension.

Where an author has indicated pauses in a text, you and your actors must fill them with something. You can't just stop and observe an empty silence. Pauses should always be full of something. They can be used to generate the thought that inspires the next line, or to think unspoken or unspeakable thoughts, to hesitate out of fear, respect or shyness and so on. The important thing is to find an idea to put in the pause that is dramatically necessary to the development of the character and/or the scene. If the necessity cannot be proved, the pause has not been earned, whether required by the writer or not.

Pausing can be addictive and contagious. An actor can grow to love the power he gets from having the complete attention of audience and fellow actors while he obliges them to wait for the next line. The more self-regarding the actor, the more addicted he will get to the feeling. As with all serious addicts, his justification will involve a special plea for the sanctioning of his dependency, irrespective of the feelings of those around him. Pausing becomes contagious when one actor so breaks up the rhythm of a play that the broken rhythm becomes the accepted norm, with no actor feeling the need to keep the text on the move.

Pausing can even become competitive. If a leading actor gets addicted to the thrill of the unearned pause, a fellow actor can decide to beat him at his own game. One pause begets another, each pause getting longer and longer and more and more filled with phoney significance. Night by night, whole extra minutes can be added to the **running time** until the director or his associate comes in and calls a halt.

If pausing gets out of hand in your production, call a **note session**. Talk to the actors about the problem. Show them the last few days or weeks of **playing times** so they can see how the production is being pulled out of shape and which bits of it are coming off worst. Explain to them how dead these unearned pauses are. Nothing new has been added to the play and yet the audience must sit in the theatre for say an extra seven or ten minutes. Try a little experiment. Ask the actors to sit in complete silence for a whole minute. Once the minute is up, ask them to multiply the boredom they have just felt by seven or ten or however many extra minutes they've added to the show. That is the equivalent amount of boredom they are subjecting their audiences to! As a final exercise, do **speed runs** on bits of the text, especially the pausiest bits. Speed runs are the business.

In some modern play texts, a longer-than-usual pause is called a 'silence' and a shorter-than-usual pause a '**beat**'.

Per Diems

A per diem payment is a daily living allowance payable to an artist working away from his home base, also known as a subsistence allowance. Touring actors and crew are generally paid per diems, the rate usually based on **union** minima. Directors, however, are not necessarily included in such arrangements, so check your contract carefully before agreeing to work far from home: you don't want to spend your entire directing fee on your living expenses. In fact, as a rule of thumb, you should be able to live on your per diems and take your whole fee home with you. Few theatre managements will see it that way. You, or better still your agent, may need to be strong in negotiating this point. Never be embarrassed in demanding that you earn a proper living from plying your trade. Just because a theatre company is poor doesn't mean you should be obliged to subsidise it.

In calculating an appropriate per diem rate, look at the going rate for actors or other union members in that territory. If no such rate applies, tot up everything that will cost you more than if you were living at home – rent or hotel bills, food (you'll have to eat out a lot more than you normally do), laundry, transport, internet access, phoning home. Once you've arrived at a daily total, double it and then start negotiating.

Performing Rights

As a general rule, if the play you want to direct was written by an author who died more than seventy years ago, the work will be in the 'public domain' and you will not need permission to perform it or be obliged to pay a fee for the rights or a royalty out of the box office receipts.

If the author is alive, or died within the last seventy years, you will have to acquire the rights to perform his play, from him or his agent or, if dead, from his estate, and then pay whatever fee and/or royalty you manage to negotiate.

Never embark on planning a production unless you have first clarified the availability of the rights. Never assume a play is in the public domain just because an author is famous and died before you were born. Seventy years is a long time.

It is heartbreaking to spend weeks planning a production, imagining the set, dreaming up the perfect cast, talking up the idea to all your friends, only to find weeks or months later that the rights are unavailable, that another production is in the offing that will knock yours off the map, or that there are hideous artistic constraints on the play that make what you want to do with it quite impossible. Save yourself the heartache and check the rights out first.

Most published plays that require licences have the details of how to acquire them on the back of the title page. If there is no agent's name and address listed and you have any doubts about the rights, then you should contact the publishers and they will tell you what you need to know.

If you are working for a theatre company of any substance, you won't have to negotiate on your own behalf for the rights to a play. Indeed, if you can possibly avoid doing so, you should. Producers, and administrators or their literary managers, will be much better qualified than you to get the best possible deal for the theatre, and you will only be concerned if there are special performance stipulations involved with the rights being awarded to you.

If you have to negotiate on your own behalf, you may have to gird your loins a bit when you contact some writers' agents. Most of them are quite friendly and helpful, only too happy that you are taking an interest in one of their clients' works, just as they should be. But you will run into some very snotty behaviour on occasion, especially if your production is a small one and unlikely to earn much money for author or agent. Agents can be frightful bullies, especially the ones that have themselves been bullied by their unreasonable or disappointed clients. But take a deep breath, keep your temper, and try to get the best deal you can for your production, though on many occasions there will be little negotiation involved, you will just be told what the fee and royalty are and be obliged to pay up.

Negotiating amounts of money for option payments or percentages for royalty is never really very complicated. The agent tries to get as much money for the client as he can and you, or your manager, try to get the rights as cheaply as possible, and you settle somewhere in between depending on the relative strengths and weaknesses of your positions, which generally comes down to the celebrity of the author and his play as against the authority and status of the theatre in which it is to be performed. The greater the potential profit, the hotter the arguments become, but also the more both sides will need to reach an agreement for the mutual profit of both. If there is a feeling that the author needs the play to be performed more than the theatre really needs to perform it, the theatre will tend to get the better of the deal, and vice versa.

The rights issue that often makes for the greatest contention is that of the option period. When you license a play you have the right to perform it for a certain period only. No agent is going to give a theatre the indefinite right to perform a play. You buy the option for a year, or eighteen months or two years, and if you don't produce the play within that time, your option lapses and the money you have spent on it is forfeit to the author. An option usually has the right to an extension attached to it, at which point a further sum of money will be payable to the author, but you won't be able to go on extending your rights indefinitely if you show no evidence of your production getting off the ground. Fights between agents and producers often break out when a final option period is nearing its end. Some other interest may have emerged for the play, and the agent will want to award the rights to the director or the company most likely to produce it. The author, too, may have got tired of waiting and started up a conversation with some other director. But the producer will try to make the agent feel that the considerable sum of money he has already spent on the rights gives him a moral hold over them. He won't have much of a legal case, but on the other hand the agent and the author might not want to make an enemy of him.

The lessons here are simple. Don't buy the rights for a play unless you have a concrete timetable for producing it and know that you can make it stick. If possible, form a relationship with the writer so that your rights in the play are also protected by his interest in your production happening. If you don't know the author or if the author is dead, try to be on friendly terms with his agent or the agent for the estate. Most good agents are genuinely interested in their clients' work being well performed and will treat you with respect if you treat them likewise.

MUSIC PERFORMING RIGHTS

Music played live follows the same rules as play texts. If the composer died over seventy years ago, the rights are in the public domain. If not, you must negotiate for permission and remuneration with the composer, his agent or his estate.

In the case of recorded music, different countries have different rights laws. In the UK you must apply to the Performing Rights Society (PRS), in the US to the American Society of Composers, Authors and Publishers (ASCAP).

The PRS has a simple system of charges. For music that is heard by the audience and not by the characters in the play – that is, for **scene changes, exits and entrances, intervals, curtain calls** and pre- and post-show foyer and auditorium music, there is a flat annual fee of around £100 per theatre space. And you can choose whatever music you like from any existing recordings. If the music is heard by the characters in the play and thus forms part of the action, the situation is more complicated. The PRS must ask the publishers who in turn may consult with the authors or performers of the music before permission is granted. This is because some authors or performers might be offended by the dramatic circumstances in which their music is played. The music might be mocked, for example, or associated with a character or an idea that the rights owners find politically or morally abhorrent. In practice, permission is very rarely withheld, but you will nonetheless have to fill in the forms and submit your production ideas to the judgement of the PRS and their relevant clients. Music of this sort is charged for over and above the annual PRS fee. You pay per performance and the rates rise incrementally with the duration of all the music played.

MUSICAL THEATRE RIGHTS

Musicals are often written by a team of two, three or even more co-authors. This can complicate the acquisition of rights. When a musical is first performed, the authorial rights 'merge', giving the co-authors permanent contractual slices of the authorial pie in terms of credit and royalty. In some cases, musicals are subsequently rewritten and the rights reworked to include shares for the new authors. You may have to choose between versions and in doing so give up some of your own creative rights.

The original director or choreographer may also have continuing rights in some types of production. For example, if you are doing a 'first-class' production in the **West End** or for **Broadway**, or have an aspiration to end up there, you might be obliged to use the original West End or Broadway choreography, even if it is now hopelessly dated or familiar to the point of cliché. However much you admire the musical in question, in these cases you may decide that your hands will be too tied for you to create anything really original.

If you're a writer of musicals, please think twice before ceding any of your authorial rights to your temporary creative collaborators. You will make your work impossible for future talents to interpret with any freedom. The famous musicals that can only be done in first-class productions with their 'original' choreography have effectively been killed off for two or three generations of creative teams and audiences alike. Don't add to their number.

Period

When embarking on a production of a classic play you will often be asked, 'What period are you setting it in?' What this question usually means is, 'Will your actors be wearing costumes from the period in which the play was written?', and in that simple sense it may be an easy enough question to answer. But it's a question that begs a lot more questions, all well worth talking about.

Let's start by trying to define 'period'. It's a vague enough term. The Roman period in Britain lasted nearly five hundred years. The Tudor period lasted for 118 years, the Elizabethan period covering the last forty-five of them. The Restoration period lasted from 1660 to somewhere around 1720, or was it a little later? The 60s of the twentieth century were a mere decade. And what does anyone mean by 'modern'? How far back 'modern' goes depends on how old you are.

'Period' and 'modern' can also have different applications depending on the play and the author. A play may be written in one age about the events of an earlier one – Shakespeare's *Julius Caesar* and *Troilus and Cressida* for instance, or Jonson's *Sejanus*. Such plays may be set in an ancient or mythical age but constantly refer to the manners and thought of the age in which they were written. If you play *Julius Caesar* in its period, do you play it in Roman times or Elizabethan times? Or should you be faithful to Shakespeare's idea of modernity? The one drawing we have of Shakespeare's actors in costume depicts them in Elizabethan dress with Roman accessories. Should you not follow suit and set the play in the modern dress of today, with or without Roman accessories? In such a case you certainly wouldn't include Elizabethan accessories. Or would you?

A play may be set in an imaginary period in the notional past or future and therefore have no clear historical bearings at all – Shaw's *Back to Methuselah*, for example, or Wilder's *Skin of Our Teeth*. Here you must invent your own version of the author's imagined period.

Plays may be adapted from an earlier period to suit a later one, as in the French neo-classical tradition of Racine and Corneille or the historical plays of Schiller or Brecht. In these cases, you must decide what 'period' really means in relation to the text, and what your 'fidelity' to period is worth, to you and to your audience. Take Schiller's *Don Carlos*. Schiller was writing at the end of the eighteenth century about sixteenth-century events. Part of his motive in writing the play was to express his anger and frustration at the tyranny and injustice inherent in his own contemporary society. You are directing the play in the twenty-first century. Do you remain 'faithful' to Schiller's choice of a sixteenth-century tale, or unravel the 'code' he was writing in and set it in the eighteenth century, or directly address the tyranny and injustice in your own society and set it now? If you direct Verdi's opera version of *Don Carlos* and you want to honour his keen awareness of the tyranny and injustice of the mid-nineteenth century, you must add another period to the mix.

Plays that are written in a realistic style about a moment in history contemporaneous with the playwright's life are of course quite common, but playing them in a faithful period style may not be doing them any favours. The manners and mores of the period in which they are set may be so alien to a modern audience that 'fidelity' will make museum pieces out of them. By bringing them closer to the events of contemporary society, you may be able to clarify the social, political or moral motives that inspired their authors. To a twenty-first-century audience, the nineteenth or early twentieth centuries might prove more accessible than the sixteenth. By setting *The Merchant of Venice* in the Berlin of the 1930s, you make a statement about anti-Semitism that is hard for a modern audience to miss. You thus overcome a natural modern distaste for the apparent Christian absolutism of Shakespeare's Venetian society, but you give yourself other problems. Venice isn't Berlin. The wealth of local reference in the play must be moved wholesale across three and a half centuries and into an entirely different European cultural setting. But maybe it's worth the imaginative effort. Or maybe some other period speaks even more vividly to you.

Translation and **adaptation** can also affect your choice of period. Chekhov done in Russia, Ibsen in Norway or Shaw in England will all be performed in the original language, language that exerts some pressure on the director to stay within the historical parameters defined by it. Plays are usually translated into a modern idiom of the translated language, an idiom that may also serve to distance them further from the original period. This effect can be even more marked if the translator is a playwright and the translation a version. If the liberties taken with the original text are imaginative, there may be a commensurate 'infidelity' in relation to the period in which the play was written.

Thus the 'period' of a production is often a matter not for fidelity but rather for negotiation, a search for an imaginative amalgamation of the year in which the play was written, the age in which it was set, the theatrical tastes of then and now, and the potential evocations, social, moral, political or emotional, of any period of history subsequent to the period in which the play was written and on into the future.

If, after considering all your options, you decide to go for a 'faithful' period setting, your fidelity must be carefully studied if it is to have any real value. Of course you have to get the **costumes** right and all the accessories that go with them – the weapons, jewellery, spectacles, handbags, watches and so on. And the **hair** has to be right, with or without the aid of wigs. And the **make-up** has to be right, with a distinction made between the apparent 'realness' of the faces and any period cosmetics they might be wearing. And you will have to **research** all other aspects of your production so that the behaviour of the characters chimes with the period. This is no small task. Music, movement, gesture, dance, textual delivery, props, furniture, all must be right if you are to have a truly period production. And more importantly than any of these, your actors must learn to think in a period way. This will require them to get involved in the research process and read around the characters they are to play. Get this right and everything else will be much easier to achieve.

Most period productions are nothing of the kind. The costumes are period, vaguely, but nothing else really matches. The haircuts, make-up, body language and cultural behaviour are all modern and the inner lives of the characters are motivated by entirely modern thoughts.

Period

However hard you work on getting period production right, there will still be tensions. The lighting design will not be period, nor probably the musical instruments and the sound system that amplifies them. The **sound effects** will be drawn from modern libraries, the food and drink made from modern recipes with modern ingredients and so on. Accuracy and artifice will conflict and combine to achieve a semblance of period. The craftier you are the more convincing the semblance will be.

Persistence

If you are to sustain a directing career, persistence must be your constant ally. There are countless thousands of aspirant young directors in the world, and most of them will fall by the wayside as rejection, failure, poverty or self-doubt take their toll. If you are not to be one of the fallers you must of course have talent, intelligence, skill and diplomacy, but these will not be enough on their own. However cleverly you play your hand, you will still spend your first few years being controlled by the will of others more powerful and successful than you are. You will be rejected for the most arbitrary of reasons, unfairly criticised, driven into soul-destroying jobs to keep body and soul together, and made to feel insignificant when what you crave is to be in control and in demand. In this climate of competition only the most resilient survive, and the most persistent. Persistence is hard when everything seems to be stacked against you, and you will need a lot of self-confidence for your persistence to mean much.

Never take rejection as a personal rebuke: there will be many reasons you are not being favoured, some of them within your power to correct and some not, but either way you are unlikely to be told the whole truth of them. Your prospective employers may already have made up their minds on another candidate long before you walk into the room. Your experience and skills may not be the ones they are seeking. They may already have decided, consciously or subconsciously, on a particular type of candidate and you are not the right gender, age, class or culture. You may have performed poorly in interview but even then you won't know for sure why you haven't been favoured. Don't let your failures haunt you. Don't assume it's because you're no good. Persist. Apply for more jobs. Get more interviews. Get better at it. Don't fold up into yourself. Persist. Insist.

When you have succeeded and you find yourself sitting in a circle of actors on the first day of rehearsal, look round the faces in your ensemble. They will all have some talent, but some will have a lot more than others and some very little at all. The one thing they will all have is persistence. They wouldn't otherwise be there, and you won't be there with them if you don't have plenty of it yourself. So it is with any group of artists. Look round the orchestras of this world, and the art studios and the dance companies. You will find the same thing everywhere. Persistence is the great motivator and the great unifier.

Photographs and Photographers

Theatre and photography are allied trades. It isn't so hard to imagine what theatre was like before photography, but quite impossible to imagine the modern theatre doing without it. In the last century and a half photographs have come to form an important element of almost every stage of the production process.

Leave aside the photographs that inspire design, communicate imagery or facilitate research. Many modern professions use photography in ways such as these. It is the relationship between photography and the actor that creates the alliance that is so special to theatre.

Actors need photographs to sell themselves. They choose their photographers with great care. They, their families and their friends spend countless hours poring over contact sheets trying to identify the elusive images that will convince an employer to match their faces to a part. The choices they make are reproduced as the 'headshots' that appear in **casting directories** and, stapled to their biographies, in work letters and on audition-room tables. Directors and **Casting Directors** learn to interpret these images and make allowances for them. The winsome smile, the intense glare, the cheeky grin, the sullen pout are all carefully chosen for effect. They may be accurate reflections of the talent that chose them or maybe not. Never judge a book by its cover. Actors, so good at being other people, are often not so relaxed when being themselves. Look beyond the glossy sheen at the person underneath. Compare the image with the parts the actor has played and the company he has kept. Look in the face for intelligence, humour and kindness. If you can't see clearly what you seek, divide the face in two. Put your hand over one half of the face so that a single eye looks back at you. What does that eye tell you? Now change sides. What does the other eye tell you? How great is the difference between the two? What does the difference teach you? In either eye, is there fear or watchfulness, reproach or bitterness, laughter or mischief? This is not an exact science, but a little scrutiny goes a long way.

PRODUCTION PHOTOGRAPHS

Theatre is ephemeral. That is one of its most enduring and endearing features. We preserve it most perfectly in our memories. Nevertheless, something in us rebels against this lack of permanent physical evidence. We can't trust our memories, and those of our audiences, quite as much as that. So we photograph our rehearsals and performances and fill our programmes and archives with still images of moving events. Very few of these images have any real usefulness in the production or publicity process, but we treasure them nonetheless.

Take care when choosing your production photographer. There are specialists in the field and they really know their stuff. But they're not all equally good at the same stuff. Consider your play and consider photographers who would best suit the material. Look at examples of past work, old theatre programmes, photos outside theatres. Ask advice of your producers or administrators. Choose a photographer whose work you really admire.

Rehearsal photos are usually taken in the last week before the **tech** begins or sometimes a few days earlier. Some photographers like to come earlier, but early rehearsals can be a little static.

As a courtesy, you should warn the actors in advance that a photographer is coming, but ask them not to glam themselves up. For this reason it's a good idea to warn them a few days in advance so they forget all about it by the time it happens. You don't want a lot of heavily made-up faces or self-consciously sexy garb in your rehearsal shots.

When the photographer comes, give him plenty of freedom to roam around. You'll get the best shots that way. A good theatre photographer is very sensitive in the rehearsal room and the actors will soon forget he's there.

Always use the same photographer for rehearsal and performance shots. His experience in the rehearsal room will tell him where the best shots are in performance and stop him stumbling around in the empty auditorium trying to catch up with swiftly moving action on the stage.

Performance shots are usually taken at the **dress rehearsal**. This can cause problems. Costumes and set are rarely completely finished by this time, and it's quite common to see evidence of this in the first set of photos. You may sometimes have to have a separate shoot in order to get production stills that will satisfy all eyes. **Designers** especially are very sensitive about having their work memorialised in an unfinished state. You can also arrange to have your photographer return to take shots during a performance – from the back of the auditorium or from a side box – but if they do this they must use a completely silent camera. The repeated clattering of a shutter right behind their heads will drive an audience crazy.

The best of the production photographs may be blown up and mounted outside the theatre and in foyers. Take great care when selecting these shots and consult the actors before making a final choice. Also, try to include a shot of everyone who expects to be included. It costs little to be kind in this respect and makes a huge difference to those involved.

PRESS PHOTOGRAPHS

Most newspapers insist on using their own photographs when reporting on or reviewing a show. This is largely a matter of economy, in that they employ their own photographers and object to paying a separate fee for any other shots. Thus you must learn to endure a 'press call' just before you open, usually on the day of the final **preview** but sometimes even on the day of **press night**.

Press calls can be monstrous affairs. The better known the actors, the more photographers turn up. With real stars you can have thirty or forty of them turning up and vying for the best shots, but even very small-scale productions may have to accommodate a handful of them.

Don't be blasé about press calls, and don't leave them to be managed by others. A badly run press call can make for an extremely frustrating couple of hours for your actors. Well managed by you, most calls can be done and dusted in half an hour. So close to an opening, you owe it to your actors to keep the pain of a press call to the minimum.

You will have agreed in advance which scenes, or bits of scenes, will be run. Take care here that no actor is offended by being excluded. Even if you reckon it unlikely their pictures will turn up in the press, a concentration on only your leading actors can seem invidious to the others.

Once the call starts, don't insist that the actors play the scenes exactly as they do in performance. Voices don't show up on photos. Have the actors play with some animation but not full out, unless there is a particular physical effect you want captured that can only be shot at full tilt. Get them to improvise a restaged version of intimate scenes so that their faces are closer together than they would be in performance. This is why you should run the call yourself rather than leave it to a Stage Manager or Assistant Director. They will feel awkward about changing your work. You can chuck it about with impunity.

Have a lighting man on call so you can adjust the lights to suit the shoot. The lighting cues you use for an actual scene are often too dim for the sort of cameras they use. Once you've run through a scene, be responsive to demands that the scene be run again. Let the photographers rearrange themselves, or re-angle a scene so those shooting from the side of the stage have as fair a chance as those hogging the middle. Do a scene as often as you need to, but keep an eye out for actors getting frustrated and for photographers calling the shots too cockily.

You'll know when you've lined a shot up right. The shutters will all clack at the same time. Press photographers are always looking for the same sort of shots, heads close together, one head right behind the other, two silhouettes face to face, a kiss, an embrace, a moment of close physical action, and a dark background so the faces stand out strongly in relief.

Don't let the actors be forced into anything unrepresentative of the production, or vulgar or sentimental. But don't be precious either. The point of a press call is to get a photo into the press and the photographers know what the Arts Editors will go for.

Physical Theatre

'Physical theatre' is a subjective term describing a style of performance in which actors use their bodies with an unusual degree of imagination, skill and freedom.

The term has gained some currency in Britain amongst a new generation of actors and directors, many of whom feel that a reaction against traditional 'text-based theatre', which they regard as the enemy, is long overdue. They have a point. The traditional theatre scene in Britain and throughout the English-speaking world is heavily dependent on the great plays of the past, many of them written in a **heightened language** that requires a degree of linguistic skill for its interpretation. It could be argued that a concentration on problems of text can make actors and directors ignore the fundamental physical elements of drama, those born of **dance**, acrobatics, clowning and ritual.

In truth, all good theatre is physical to some extent, and the best so-called physical theatre still has a strong intellectual, narrative or imagistic basis. Some modern theatre troupes have created very exciting work, with and without language, inhabiting a new region somewhere between drama, dance and circus, and largely relying on visual image for dramatic impact. Physical theatre is perhaps a good description of what they do.

But for many, the term is no more than a synonym for **rough theatre** or **poor theatre** and, like those terms, is bandied about with no intention that it should have a definitive meaning.

Pit

In the modern theatre, pit means **orchestra pit**. The term derives from the Elizabethan theatre, where the lowest level of the **auditorium,** dug into the ground in front of the stage, was called the pit, based on the cockpit where cockfighting took place.

A 'pit player' or 'pit musician' is a musician who plays habitually in musical theatre orchestra pits. **Opera** musicians are never 'pit players', they are members of the **orchestra**.

'Pit lights' are music-stand lights, one for each pit player. **Designers** and **Lighting Designers** like these to be kept at such a low level that the players can't see a note of their music. Pit players like them so bright they drench the whole theatre in ambient light. Directors negotiate.

Platform Stages

See **Thrust Stages.**

Playbills

Playbills are American **programmes**. In the commercial theatre, they are usually given away free, unlike their expensive European counterparts. This is because the companies that print them derive their income from advertising rather than sales.

Thus playbills may be free but they are also badly designed, sparsely worded and deadly dull.

Playhouse

A playhouse is a theatre with an **auditorium** possessed of a good enough **acoustic** for the comfortable performance of spoken dialogue without **amplification,** as opposed to a 'musical house' that can be as big as it likes.

In practical terms, a good playhouse usually has fewer than a thousand seats. Any larger than that and its acoustic has to be particularly fine.

An auditorium with fewer than three or four hundred seats is usually called something else – studio, **Black Box, courtyard, in-the-round** or whatever.

Playing Time

The playing time is the time it takes for a play to be performed not counting the time taken up by **intervals** or delays.

The playing time is a very important indicator for a director. There is often nothing you can do about the overall **running time** of a show – the audience or the front of house staff or both can hold up the start of the play or the return after the interval – but the playing time is entirely controlled by what happens on stage.

Whether your play is running at an hour or five hours, there should be some consistency in the time it takes to perform it, though there are bound to be minor changes of **pace and rhythm** from one night to the next. Alarm bells should ring, however, if there are major unplanned fluctuations in playing times.

If a play starts running much faster than rehearsed, the actors may be short-changing the audience emotionally, skimming over the surface of the relationships between the characters in a rush to reach the end of the play. The reason for this may be an individual or collective unhappiness with the material being performed – or a collective decision that certain performances, an ill-attended matinée for instance, are less worthy of their attention than others.

Playing Time

If a play runs much slower than rehearsed, the most likely cause is self-indulgence in one or more of the actors. Especially in a **long run** of a play, and especially in a serious drama, actors can start prolonging their **pauses** for thought in the belief that by doing so they are extracting more meaning out of the text. If more than one actor starts to behave in this way, the pausing can become competitive and will have a noticeable effect on the overall length of the evening. The best way to address this is to call a rehearsal and talk out the issue with the actors involved. A particular actor may be unaware that he is slowing down the show, or aware but unconcerned. Indeed, most actors are intensely aware when a colleague is dawdling and unaware, or unwilling to be aware, when they are dawdling themselves.

To keep a cast aware of time fluctuations, it's a good idea to have the playing times posted at the stage door or announced over the tannoy after each performance – with a breakdown of the times for each act and the starting and interval times.

Play Readings

Play readings are useful for a variety of reasons. Some directors are more talented than others at reading plays and knowing from their private study when a play has a particular resonance for them. This is a skill you must cultivate if you are to succeed as a director – and the more successful you become the more plays you will be obliged to read. A single private reading should be enough for you to assess the worth of a play, but there are often complicating circumstances, especially when you are making a judgement about a **new play**.

New plays are the lifeblood of the theatre but new **playwrights**, however talented, are often strangers to the everyday life of the theatre and to the actors who define that life. A play reading is the best way to introduce a new writer to one of the most basic tools of his profession – the actor. Thought he can accomplish on his own, and argument and structure, but only through his characters can any of these elements come to life, and a new playwright often has more trouble with delineation of character than with any other part of his craft. The characters of a play affect its structure just as the structure affects the characters. But the actors themselves will also affect the way the characters behave. An experienced playwright, or a playwright who has been an actor, will naturally allow for this chemistry while the play is being written, but an inexperienced one can only learn it by exposure to the actors themselves. A play reading is the easiest way of opening up this process to the budding writer.

Even experienced and successful writers can learn a lot from listening to a reading of their work, especially if they are stuck in any way – with character or structure. Hearing a play being read in unpressured circumstances by a small group of sympathetic actors can relieve even the most pernicious case of writer's block.

Play readings can also be useful to explore old plays by dead writers. Some authors are much easier to read than others, and the **heightened language** of old plays becomes vivid in the mouths of a group of actors where it may have seemed dry, uninspiring or archaic on the page.

Because readings can be so influential for writers and directors they must be cast with care. A writer will learn next to nothing about his play if he hears it performed by unsympathetic or inappropriately cast actors. Cast a reading as carefully as you would a production, and cast it with analytical actors – the sort of actors who will enjoy debating the merits of the script and making suggestions for the enrichment of the characters in it. The best play readings become seminars, and all who attend them leave them a little wiser for the experience.

Readings can also be useful as part of the **casting** process for a subsequent production. Sometimes a leading actor can't decide if a role would be a suitable vehicle for his talent. The play might be hard to understand in content or form, the central role might be off the actor's beaten track or have technical difficulties that frighten him, or he might have a worry about the relative importance of the role in relation to the other major roles in the play. A reading should help to separate real from imagined difficulties and allow the actor to feel what it would be like to play the part. To speak a role is to act it – to act it is to know it.

Play Readings

UNREHEARSED READINGS

The most private reading can sometimes be the most useful – just you, the writer and the actors. No one rehearses the play in advance. The actors may not even have read it. You read the play quietly, not performing it, just letting the actors be the characters. The writer or the director reads the stage directions. No fuss.

If you want, you can have a few guests – the writer's agent, a **dramaturg** or Literary Manager – but keep it small, no pressure and the lowest of expectations. Let the writer learn what he can learn, then maybe have a little discussion afterwards. Actors can be eloquent about their own and one another's parts.

After the reading, take the writer out to dinner and discuss first impressions. Have another meeting a few days later to exchange more mature thoughts and talk about the next step. After rewrites, do you go on to a full production or have another, fuller, perhaps more public reading?

REHEARSED READINGS

Take a whole day, if necessary, or two. Work through the play, with actors talking to director and writer about the parts, both giving and receiving directions. Involve a dramaturg if you have one.

Discover a good **pace and rhythm** for the play and its constituent scenes. If appropriate, discuss and implement **cuts** and any easily achievable restructuring, but don't oblige the writer to write new material in front of everyone. If he has to do that, the play isn't ready for a reading. Work on the play as it is, warts and all.

A well-rehearsed reading will cry out to be performed. Get a good audience together – the writer's and actors' agents, friends and relations. If you're working in a theatre company, invite any interested and informed members of staff. Make a show of it. A sense of occasion will tell you a lot about how the play would be received by a paying audience.

A rehearsed reading may be proposed to you by a producer as a way of soliciting support from theatre owners and investors, or **angels**. Such readings are quite common in the commercial arena, especially for **new musicals**. They are sometimes called **presentations,** or workshop presentations if they've been preceded by a **workshop** period.

In some countries there are **union** regulations controlling the use of actors and stage management in rehearsed readings and presentations. These rules are often quite strictly observed and define the number of hours you can work and the extent to which the actors are allowed to perform off the book and the minimum payments they must receive. Figure out the rules before you promise your writer or your actors anything.

Plays with Songs

Plays with songs are a subspecies of the **musical theatre** genre. They have too many songs to be thought of as regular plays, but their songs don't add up to a sufficiently coherent musical structure for them to be described as musicals.

Works that fall into this class are Brecht's *Caucasian Chalk Circle*, Pam Gems's *Piaf* and, arguably, John Gay's *Beggar's Opera*. As a general rule, plays with songs are best cast with actors who can sing rather than with singers who can act.

Play Texts

Theatre publishers are always interested in good new plays. If the play is by an established **playwright** then a publisher will probably already be attached. If it's a new play by a new writer, the fact that it's being produced at all will be enough to spark the interest of a publisher. Once the interest has been confirmed and the author put under contract, the publishing of the text can start to have an influence on your role as director of the play. The main reason for this is commercial. A publisher will sell a lot more plays if he can have the text on sale in the foyer by the opening night. Indeed, in the case of a poorly received play that disappears from view after its initial run, the foyer sales may be the only way to recoup any part of the publisher's initial investment. So there is pressure on the playwright to deliver a finished text several weeks before the opening night, in other words in the middle of the **rehearsal** period.

Most writers are still making changes in the text right up to the first preview and often beyond and are being encouraged by the director and the actors so to do. But they are also very conscious of posterity. They want the published version of their play to be as close as possible to the performance text. As the publisher's deadline approaches, inexperienced writers can become more and more anxious about changing the text, an anxiety that can destroy their appetite for constructive work. Similarly, once the play has been handed over to the publisher, some writers can become resistant to any further change and even deafen themselves to their own best inspirations, thereby stunting their play's further growth.

Tension in rehearsal is always a bad thing, and a tense writer can be one of the most powerful sources of it, so you must relieve the writer of the cause of his anxiety. Argue thus: 'It doesn't matter if the published text has minor differences to the text as performed, or even major ones. No one in the audience is going to read and watch the play at the same time. Very few people will remember the performed text so accurately that they will be upset to find it differs from the published one. If the play succeeds there will be opportunities for later reprints of the published version that can involve as many of the changes as the writer wishes and more. Give the publisher what you have so far – a disclaimer can be inserted at the front of the book along the lines of "the playscript that follows was correct at the time of going to press but may have changed during rehearsals" or some such flannel. It's a very fine play. Hand it over and farewell it. And now let's get back to work and make it even better.'

Playwrights

If you want to grow as a director you must nurture your relationship with the lives and minds of the playwrights with whom you are working, be they alive or dead.

DEAD PLAYWRIGHTS

When you direct a play by a dead writer, try to bring the writer back to life in your imagination in any way you can. Read around the play. Read biographies, an autobiography if one exists, other plays by the same writer and anything else he may have written in the way of essays, or novels or short stories. Try to build up a complete picture of the artist, his life, his relationships, his preoccupations and his influences. Examine his work in the context of the writers that preceded him and those he may have later influenced. Understand his motives for writing, the society that engendered his thinking and his work, and the way his work changed and developed throughout his life.

The more of a dead playwright's work you direct, the more he will come to life for you. Some writers are more elusive in this respect than others. Shakespeare never quite manifests himself, however much one immerses oneself in his work. But Bernard Shaw strides around the rehearsal room demanding to be heard and admired, while Ben Jonson sits at the back of the room, a mischievous and enlightened spirit, delighted that his work is being re-explored. These are my fancies, but you will no doubt create your own or have them created for you.

LIVING PLAYWRIGHTS

Directing a new play is a great privilege. There is nothing more satisfying than opening a newly published play text and seeing your name printed under the original cast list, along with the rest of the creative team. These were the people that brought this play to life for the first time, who worked with the writer and the actors in the rehearsal room, shaping the final structure of the play, adding the details of **staging** and **motivation** that allowed an audience to appreciate the true value of the work. The main accolade goes to the author, of course, but the play could not have happened without you, and after it has closed and the scenery has been destroyed and the audience dispersed and the reviews written and read and recycled, what will remain will be the play text for future generations to read, your name still there, the last remaining evidence of your career.

Your little line of credit may be a touching, even a humbling, reminder of your involvement in a new play, but your true reward lies in your relationship with the writer. Writers do what you cannot do. They start with a blank sheet of paper and conjure up a world of their own. They react to events, to people, to history, and they turn their reactions into a play. You then react to the play and bring it to life as best you can. You appoint designers, you cast actors and you create a physical life for the imagined world on the page. But to do this well you must try to coordinate your reactions with the reactions of the writer. Know why he has written his world the way he has. Know his characters as well as he knows them. Know why they say what they say, do what they do, think what they think. Know the structure of the play, its tempo, its rhythms and its climaxes. Know its strengths and its flaws. In other words, you must know the mind of the writer. You must think like the writer. And what better way to achieve this than to know the writer himself? Talk to him, debate with him, break bread with him. Learn what makes him think and feel and laugh. The writer's mind is the key to the play.

If you do this well, during the course of rehearsals you will find yourself becoming a little like the writer, your own thoughts and rhythms and feelings subsumed in the life of the play and the mind of the man or woman who wrote it. In exchange, your work should enrich the writer's process, broadening his vision and refining his technique.

Good relationships between writers and directors can be nourishing for both parties and may even develop into lasting artistic partnerships or friendships. If you seek such nourishment and take pleasure in rubbing shoulders with the best minds in your business, then find common cause with playwrights and make them your friends. Nothing will sustain you better in your career as a director.

PLAYWRIGHTS IN REHEARSAL

If you direct a new play or the revival of a play by a living play-wright, you must be happy to rehearse with the author present. It is one of the most preposterous aspects of modern theatre practice that some directors feel they have the right to ban authors from the rehearsals of their own plays. The excuse given is always the same, that the actors will be confused if they are given a conflicting vision of the play from two separate artistic sources, but this is egregious nonsense. The real reason is that the director is frightened that any insufficiency in his understanding of the play will be exposed by the author and he will be made to look foolish in front of the actors. Or the director is just jealous. He knows he couldn't write a play himself and can't bear someone cleverer and more interesting than him being allowed to have access to 'his' actors.

Refusal to allow the author into rehearsal is therefore a tacit admission either of incompetence or pusillanimity, and should be treated as such.

Of course, some playwrights can be awkward, disputative, nerv-ous or unreasonable – or all of those things. There is a fundamen-tal perversity built into the working life of a playwright. Writing is a private process, requiring a great deal of solitariness and reflec-tion, but ultimately it must also involve considerable public expo-sure, first to director and actors and then to audience and critics. Most playwrights have some difficulty handling this paradox in their lives. Some have stronger nerves than others. Some are posi-tively neurotic in moving between private and public, their one touchstone being their child – the play – of which they are fiercely protective. Others relish the companionship of the rehearsal room so much they are dismayed to have to return to the study when the play has finally opened.

It is part of your job as a director to address the fears and feel-ings of inadequacy in your playwrights just as you address them in your other collaborators. In any event, by treating the playwright as an equal partner in the rehearsal process, you will remove the feeling of powerlessness that is often the root cause of any difficul-ties he might be having. You will also give yourself access to his imagination, intelligence and sense of humour. He is, after all, the final authority on the meaning of his own work.

If treated with respect, a playwright will become your best ally in rehearsal. If an actor has a question about a line or a thought or a relationship and you are hazy about the answer, the authority is sitting in the room with you. If you are doubtful about the efficacy of a scene or a moment within a scene, a discussion with actors and writer will flush out whether the weakness is in the acting, the writing or the direction. How could such a debate threaten your authority if it ends up improving the play or the production?

By creatively involving the writer in rehearsal you will also be according him the opportunity to make the play better. Most playwrights do not sit dumbly at the back of rehearsal resenting the power of the director and plotting his downfall. They ponder the efficacy of their own work and often discover significant improvements in the text that they could not possibly have imagined outside the rehearsal room.

If a writer has been banned from the rehearsal room you will find him very defensive in discussions about any changes you want in the text – and understandably so, as he won't have experienced the problem in rehearsal that has given rise to the need for a change. Having thought deeply about the text for months or even years, he will suspect that a few minutes of discussion in rehearsal will be an inadequate reason for a change of any sort. And after a long day of rehearsal you may lack the patience to make your points clearly and conclusively. Save yourself and him a lot of grief and share the rehearsal room with him.

If you cannot overcome your fear or your jealousy of playwrights in rehearsal – don't do new plays. Confine yourself to dead writers, whose plays you can dominate without any argument. Alternatively, get over yourself, let the author in and study to be a better director.

Poor Theatre

Poor theatre is a term derived from the visionary Polish director Jerzy Grotowski's experimental study of acting and actor training, set out in his book *Towards a Poor Theatre*.

Grotowski, in his *Teatr Laboratorium*, explored a theatre that was rich in the skills and psychological acuity of a small group of dedicated performers but poor in the sense that it eschewed the use of conventional production values. In doing so, he pushed the acting methods of **Stanislavsky** to new limits and inspired a generation of directors, teachers and actors.

By training his actors to an exceptional level of physical, mental and emotional awareness and stripping away all the trappings of set, costume, lighting and sound, he created a performance style that more resembled the monastery than the laboratory and plays that were more remarkable for ritual intensity than narrative cohesion.

He also experimented with a wide variety of audience–actor relationships with a view to breaking down the barrier between the actors' and the audience's perception of the theatre experience.

His idea of poor theatre has gained such currency that the term is now used to describe any rehearsal or performance technique that favours the expressiveness of the actor over all other considerations. 'Poor theatre techniques' have become more or less synonymous with those of **rough theatre**.

Posters and Poster Design

If your production is promoted with the use of posters or flyers, you should take an active interest in their design. In a well-run theatre company you will be consulted as a matter of course, but there are companies and producers that don't afford a director this courtesy. They are wrong not to do so. As the originator of the ideas behind your production you are best placed to advise about the graphic imagery chosen to represent it. If you choose not to involve yourself, you must not be surprised to see a finished poster design that misinterprets your work, or worse, vulgarises it. There is nothing more galling than seeing your work being advertised with an image you despise.

Make it clear when you embark on a production that you expect to have a say in the matter. You need not demand a contractual right to be involved. Such a right would be unusual. The expression of a strong interest should be enough to guarantee your participation.

Arrange a meeting with the graphic designer and explain your production ideas. Show him the **model** of the set and the **costume** designs and any graphic images that may have inspired you or your designers. Bring him into the body of the church. However he interprets your ideas, he should be a welcome part of the **creative team**. Talk about the style and content of the poster – whether to go for a graphic or a photographic treatment, to involve images of the actors, characters or author and so on. If you have a strong idea, argue it strongly but be ready to hear a better idea. You are not a graphic designer.

Your designer's first efforts may not please you, or may please you and displease your producer. If there is any continuing disagreement, a foundation of artistic understanding can only be helpful in bringing all parties to an agreement.

Pre-Performance Chat

ANNOUNCEMENTS

Announcements over the auditorium speakers have become a common feature of the modern theatre. It's a shame, but it's sometimes hard to argue against them. Thoughtless people will leave their cellphones switched on. Stupid people will try to take flash photographs. Crafty people will try to record a performance with video cameras or sound recorders.

If your production is in a small theatre, such announcements are daft. Much better for the ushers to give a quiet reminder as the audience takes its seats. The personal touch is always better if it can do the trick. Good, too, are notices in the foyer and clear warnings in the programme.

If you, or your producers, feel you have to have them, make them as personal-sounding as you can. Get an actor to record a polite but friendly message. Or have a Stage Manager speak the message live. Avoid the bing-bong chimes and the mechanical voice. And don't get too cute. Jokey cellphone rings played over the speakers have become a bore.

SPEECHES

It is sometimes necessary for the audience to be addressed from the stage before the performance in order to announce a deviation from routine, explain a technical failure or apologise for a delay. This most commonly occurs at the first **preview** of a show when, because of a delay in technical rehearsals or some other complication to do with staging or safety, things are deemed likely to go wrong during the course of the performance. As the director and the person most responsible, culpable or capable of public utterance, you will very likely be elected to speak.

Start by introducing yourself. You may not think much of your status, but the audience rarely meets a live director and will be interested in making your acquaintance. Adopt a relaxed tone, engaging whatever wit you are possessed of, but don't tell any elaborately prepared jokes. You are the bearer of bad tidings to people who have paid for their tickets, sometimes more than they can really afford. Explain politely what the problem is and crave their patience without being syrupy or sycophantic. If there is a technical problem, be as specific as you can about it but don't blind them with science. If they are given an understanding of the difficulty they are more likely to maintain an interest in its solution. Reassure them that in the event of a hiatus the performance will continue as soon as it possibly can. And then get off the stage. Make sure in advance that the performance starts the minute you are in the wings. You don't want the first hiatus to occur on your exit.

Pre-Performance Chat

Speeches of this sort may be sprung on you at the last minute because of some unforeseen emergency, but they will more likely be planned for a few hours in advance. They are sometimes a useful tactic in appeasing disaffection in your cast or giving them comfort when they feel unprepared or wrong-footed by something outside their control. It certainly isn't fair for your cast to be obliged to appear on stage when they know they are on a crash course for some technical failing that will make them look or feel unprofessional. If you tell them in advance that you will personally speak to the audience before the start of the performance their worries will be diminished.

By breaking the normal barrier between stage and auditorium before the performance has begun, you set up a conspiracy of hope in the audience that the evening will proceed without a hitch. A hitch, if it happens, will seem less of a problem and the solution to it more interesting.

Don't get addicted to the pre-performance speech. It should only be used when absolutely necessary and not as a means of buttering up the audience on a regular basis. Audiences are canny beasts and can smell when they're being stalked.

APPEALS

Some **not-for-profit theatre** companies, especially in America, have fallen into the habit of making appeals for financial support before each public performance. These are deadly and should be avoided if at all possible. However strapped for cash a company is, it cannot help the cause to destroy the atmosphere in the auditorium by thrusting a begging bowl in the audience's face just when you most want them to engage with the art for which they have already paid their dues.

If you have to make a direct appeal for funds, much better to do it at the end of the show than at the beginning. If the audience have hated the show, your task will be the harder, but have a little faith.

Presentations

Sometimes called 'workshop-presentations' or 'backers' auditions', these are the rehearsed **play readings**, or **musical theatre** readings, specially prepared for producers, investors and/or theatre owners in the commercial arena as a way of touting for investment money or theatre space.

Presentations may come at the end of a **workshop** rehearsal period, or they may be more hastily thrown together, simply as a means to a financial end. Either way, don't confuse the presentation with the work process and don't think of presenting anything to your professional peers that you aren't completely confident about.

In preparing a presentation you must rehearse your actors or singers really thoroughly. Their confidence will set off the play or musical to the best advantage. If the presentation comes out of a workshop, leave a couple of days clear of cutting, rewriting and restructuring to work on the performance for its own sake.

Make the presentation a relaxed affair. Have a run-through with the actors in the precise audience format you will use for the performance so they get used to the **acoustics** and **sightline**.

Welcome the audience as they arrive. Chat to them and let them chat to one another. Have a printed cast list so everyone knows who's who, in the play and out of it. Talk to the audience before the performance. Introduce the writer or writers and any other members of the **creative team**, even if their work will not be manifest in the performance. Introduce the actors and the characters they will play. Tell the audience everything they need to know about the story that won't be apparent from the presentation. Fill them in on any production or design ideas that will help them understand what the proposed production will be like. Professional audiences are generally pretty imaginative, but they need plenty of cud to chew on. Don't hold anything back that could prove useful to them.

Give the audience the feeling they're getting a sneak preview of something important. Make the performance special. If possible, persuade one of the authors to read the stage directions, or read

them yourself. You will do this job much better than an anonymous Stage Manager. A Stage Manager will never feel free to
extemporise or fill out a stage direction, as a writer or director will.
The more personal you can make the presentation the better.
Producers and investors will feel more inclined to give you money
if they feel it would be good to spend time with you. No one wants
to spend time with a bunch of nervous, sweating, anxious geeks,
desperate to please and fearful of failure. Be cool.

Press Night

Press night is the night the **critics** come and review your play.
Theatre is news and the more famous your author and your actors
are, the more newsworthy your play is deemed to be.

Readers of newspapers like to know what's going on, how good
it is, who's in it and how good or bad they are being. One of the
reasons they buy their papers is to find out. Newspaper proprietors
supply their curiosity by employing theatre critics. The critics see
the play and make judgements on behalf of their readers.

Theatre reviews are publicity. The people that run theatres and
produce plays need the public to know their shows are up and
running. They woo the Arts Editors of newspapers to send their
critics in the hope, or faith, that the subsequent reviews will be
favourable and the public will believe them enough to buy tickets
for the show.

That's the deal. Theatres and critics need one other. They are in
a co-dependent relationship, not always happy but bound together
by a mutual need to protect their livelihoods.

The press night and the **opening night** don't always happen on
the same evening. This is often because, in a small theatre, the critics, en masse, take up too much space, forcing out the people who
really have to be at an opening night: the friends and family of the
cast and the sponsors and long-term supporters of the company.
Others feel it is impossible to celebrate anything in the presence of
critics, that their natural feelings of pride and achievement are
undermined by anxiety over how they will be judged. In these cases

the critics are invited to one of the performances immediately preceding the opening, with an agreed embargo on their reviews appearing until the morning after.

This makes some critics unhappy. For all their vaunted objectivity, many of them like to be at the theatre on the same night as the celebrations – and the celebrities – and they have a point. The more socially alert of them are not just critics of the drama but reporters of the theatre scene. They are not just reviewing the play, but also the atmosphere surrounding the play. Part of that atmosphere consists in how the theatre company sees itself. Others are only too content to see the play on a more ordinary night. Opening nights can become rather hysterical occasions, with the family, friends and supporters of the cast determined to enjoy every last minute to the hilt, over-laughing at the comedy, over-crying at the moving bits and over-ovating at the end. The more enthusiasm whipped up by the supporters of the show, the sourer some critics will feel towards it, especially if it isn't very good. Any residual sense that they should be giving the show the benefit of the doubt gets drowned out by the premature celebrating of All Rabbit's Friends and Relations.

Even if everyone stays calm and behaves themselves, press nights can be strange evenings. Most theatres do their best to put the critics in the best seats so that they see the show to its best advantage. Many critics request to sit on the aisles where they can get away in a rush at the end to file their reviews. They often end up sitting together within a few seats of one another in the middle of the stalls, forming a clump of non-responsiveness. This isn't because they are unresponsive people, or that they are determined to dislike the show until it proves itself worthy of their attention. It's because they are not just watching the show, they are also deciding what to write about it. This makes it very difficult for them to be spontaneous in their reactions, other than on paper. While the rest of the audience can afford to be completely involved in the world that is presented to them, the critic is jotting down the phrase that perfectly describes the experience.

The critics' relationship to the show on press night is therefore subject to Heisenberg's uncertainty principle: the very fact of their presence disturbs the integrity of the piece they are watching. For this reason, it is a very good idea to spread the critics across a series of nights. This also spreads the risk of all the critics being present at your one bad performance.

Sometimes a critic will make a special plea to be allowed to attend an early preview, because of a clash with another show or because he is writing for a paper that has a deadline immediately before your press night. Unless you have a particular reason for denying such a request, you should accede to it, even if the critic has said harsh things about you in the past. The show might not be completely ready, but a good critic will take account of that and may even cut you more slack because of it. And you never know, the performance that night might be the best you ever do. Spread the risk.

PREPARING THE CAST FOR PRESS NIGHT

The main thing you have to avoid on press night is the cast being adversely affected by the presence of the critics. This is an important part of your job. You have dreamed of your production for months, even years, and planned for many months more. You have rehearsed for weeks and finally the show is ready. You mustn't let the presence of a few critics throw everything you have done out of kilter. They will say what they will say, but let them say it about what you mean them to see, not some botched version of it. It's still all in your control.

The calmer and more experienced members of your cast may have their own strategies for dealing with first-night nerves, but the cast as a whole may not be so balanced, and you shouldn't leave anything to chance.

Always have a cast get-together as late as possible on the afternoon of a press night. However well prepared the show is, the cast will need a moment of quiet focus to get in the right state of mind for a performance. The call should be late in the day to give them the maximum time to do their own preparations. First-night guests have to be organised, agents' tickets sorted out, overnight beds arranged for visiting relations, flowers received and put into water, first-night cards and presents bought or manufactured, and any other important rituals observed.

After a day of mad preparation, the cast is likely to turn up to the call in a state of chaotic excitement. Look around their faces. You will see a mixture of elation, dread, overexcitement, panic and pretended indifference. Not a group of people likely to perform the play with any finesse. Your job is to harness the elation and allay the panic. How to do it?

Don't give **notes**. If you have a lot of notes in your book from the night before, cross all of them out except the ones which are absolutely essential or completely harmless. Detailed notes are lethal on a nervous night. Your actors will end up playing the notes and not the show, thus adding to their nervousness. Big general notes are a sign of panic and should be avoided at all costs. Never tell a cast to be quicker, or slower, or louder on a press night. Later that evening you will be sitting in the theatre while the actors are speeding, or crawling, or shouting their way through the play and you will fold up with remorse.

If you really have to give a note to a particular actor, give it personally, not in front of the whole cast. No one should be singled out on a night of collective endeavour.

Talk to them about the critics. Explain to them that the audience response might be a little different from what they have learnt to expect in the previews, that the presence of friends and supporters might make for an artificially heightened atmosphere and that the presence of the critics might deaden everything.

Tell them not to be thrown if a laugh they usually get is not there, if an atmosphere feels strange, or a silence empty. The audience may be less responsive in their audible reactions, but extremely attentive to the meaning of the play.

In comedies, the cast mustn't panic if laughs are muted. They must keep playing the situation and the truth of the characters and trust that the laughs will gather as the evening continues. If they overreact to the unwonted silences, by trying too hard for laughs, they will run the risk of killing the laughter off altogether.

Advise the cast how to cope with the critical reaction to the show in the days ahead. As an ensemble of artists they must try to be impervious to critical opinion. If they must read the reviews, they must respect the feelings of those who never do. No critical opinion, positive or negative, must be allowed to destroy the integrity of all that has been achieved. Never commiserate with someone who has been picked out for his inadequacy – he may be hearing it from you for the first time. Never congratulate someone on a good review – you may be reminding him it was the only good review he got. Never inveigh against a particular critic – he may have praised the person to whom you are doing the inveighing. Avoid talking about the reviews altogether.

Avoid even thinking about the reviews. No member of the cast should change his opinion of himself, or of any of his colleagues, because of a critic's opinion of him, or of them. If an actor walks through the stage door on the night after the reviews with an inflated view of himself because of something a critic has said, he will be a poorer artist for it, and certainly a poorer colleague. If an actor has a lower opinion of a colleague because of a bad review, he betrays the fundamental compact implicit in a theatre company, the conspiracy of belief that binds everyone together. Every cast member must believe in the worth of every other member, their rightness for their parts, the fact that the character has become subsumed in the actor. Without this belief, a company cannot function as a company. It splits into a number of individual careers, each man acting on his own behalf, heedless of the conspiracy that gives the imagined world of the play its reality. It's hard enough maintaining this belief night after night, week after week, but to let a critic steal it from you would be shamefully careless.

Tell the Stage Manager that no review must be posted backstage, however glowing. The producers will probably insist on advertising the most favourable critical quotes in the foyers and outside the theatre, but backstage must be a critic-free zone, an actors' space free of impertinent opinion.

A note you can give the whole cast is a note about spontaneity. Ask them to think of the press night not as any sort of an end in itself, but as the first night of a continuing run of performances that only ends when the run ends. To keep the whole run live and interesting, every performance they do must be different from every other performance, so how will tonight's performance be new for each one of them? Put the actors under an instruction to create two or three new things for that night only – a motivation, a physical move, a change of focus – something for their fellow actors to notice and play with. This will sharpen everyone's wits for the rest of the evening. To field one another's little changes, they will have to be very aware of one another, eye contact between them at a premium. Novelty, invention and a sense of company are the three best antidotes to nervousness.

Don't talk too much. Spend at least half the session warming the company up physically, vocally and mentally. If there are dances or fights, run through them. If there are company songs, have a vocal warm-up with the Musical Director. Spend the last ten or fifteen minutes doing something physically and mentally energetic. A jumping speed run serves very well, or some other company-inclusive **game** to shake out everyone's tension with a bit of quick-thinking merriment.

PREPARING YOURSELF FOR PRESS NIGHT

The best way to inoculate yourself against reviews is to be well advanced in the planning of your next project. As the previews proceed and the actors make the production more and more their own, start making the phone calls and personal contacts that will inform your future work. If you carry all your artistic eggs in one basket, you must be ready for a smashing. The more you see your present production as part of a bigger body of work, the less vulnerable you will be.

On the press night itself, concentrate on how you get everyone else through the evening unscathed and then be proud of what you have achieved. Don't skulk at the back of the auditorium or wear holes in the foyer carpet. Sit in the middle of the auditorium with your family and friends and enjoy the work of your actors. Show them how proud of them you are and how much you trust them to play the work as you have agreed it should be played. Bugger the critics, whatever they think. The play's the thing.

Preview Performances

Previews are performances that are played to a paying audience in advance of the **press night** or official **opening night**.

Previews are designed to give the director, the **creative team** and the cast a chance to perfect the production before the critics descend on it and make their judgements. The first performance of any play is usually lacking in confidence and technical finesse. In every department, practice makes perfect.

For the actors the transition between rehearsal room and stage is often a difficult one. They must adapt themselves to a new **acoustic** and a new set of physical relationships with **set, costumes** and **props.** Most importantly, they are meeting the **audience** for the first time. The presence of a large number of strangers scrutinising their work makes them listen to themselves and their fellow actors in a different way. In comedy **laughter** changes the rhythm of every scene, and in any play, signs of restlessness or lack of attention in the audience will cause unease.

Nerves, too, are at their rawest, the unfamiliarity of it all making some actors incapable of performing with their usual naturalness and confidence. And they're not the only ones. The stage management and crew will all be getting used to new rhythms, the flying cues, the **follow-spot** pick-ups, the lighting and sound plots, all will have their teething problems.

LEARNING FROM PREVIEWS

Previews are a learning time for everyone. But for you especially they give an overview of your whole production. However well you have imagined the piece in performance, an auditorium full of paying customers is likely to make you feel very differently from how you felt in the rehearsal room. Having a live audience listen and watch and attend to your play will make you perceive it in a new way yourself. This new perception can make an inexperienced director quite panicky and even doubt the value of the work. But you mustn't give in to such negative feelings. Rather you must harness the new energy the audience is bringing to the work and make full use of it, listening with their ears, watching with their eyes, attending with their minds. Get a feel for when they are completely with you or when their attention may be wandering, for when the pace of the play is right for them or when it is going too fast or lagging behind their apprehension of it. Sit in different parts of the house at different preview performances so that you can make informed judgements about any audibility or **sightline** problems. Use the previews to the full for your own advantage and for the advantage of everyone else in your production.

Previews are where every element of the production can be improved, but only if every element receives detailed and loving attention. Take copious notes, notes about the acting, the staging, the music, the lighting and the sound. If you are doing your job properly, you will be writing continually throughout the performance. In every department, your colleagues will want to have detailed and supportive notes at the end of the show or at the next day's rehearsal. Generalisations will be unhelpful. Never say to the actors or to the sound and lighting departments, 'It was all too slow/too loud/too dark.' Where was it slow? Where loud? Where dark? And in every case, why did you feel the way you did and how do you think you should collectively put matters right?

PREPARING FOR PREVIEWS

Before the first preview, make sure that everyone understands that the performance represents work in progress. That no one is expected to be perfect. Try to create an atmosphere of calm in the middle of all the excitement of an audience joining you for the first time. Tell the actors to hold back 10 or 15 per cent of their performances in order to watch and listen to themselves performing and to be aware of the way in which the audience is watching and listening to them. If they get too carried away with their performances, the whole evening will pass them by too quickly, scenes will rush towards them, be hurriedly despatched and then left behind in a wash of uncritical emotion. Tell the actors that in the **note session** following the performance or on the next day, you will want to hear from them what they thought. The first preview is the beginning of the actors making the show their own. The notes must therefore start to come both ways, not just from you to them.

DEBRIEFING AFTER PREVIEWS

In your post-preview note session, treat all your collaborators with respect. Let everyone start to feel what it will be like when you are gone, when they must be solely responsible for the value of their contributions. When you discuss the show, let your actors, composer, choreographer, and designers of set, costume, light and sound have their views about what went right, what went wrong and how things could be made better. Don't drown out their ideas with a flood of your own opinions. Listen to what they propose. You employed them for their skill and artistic judgement, so take advantage of that and as far as possible let them mend their broken bits in their own way.

PREVIEW AUDIENCES

Preview audiences can be strange beasts, unrepresentative of the normal, everyday theatregoing public. Some people love previews. They love being present at the first outing of a new production. They love being able to say 'I was there,' before everyone else discovered it, before the critics praised it or damned it, before the second act was cut or the interval changed to a different place. They are the preview vultures, picking over the carcass of the first performance 'kill'. At celebrity productions in the West End and on Broadway they also behave like critics, not just attending to the show but wondering throughout how they will blog it on the internet that night. There may even be some simultaneously writing blogs from their seats.

There will also be a fair sprinkling of personal and professional friends of the cast. Many actors like to have an early critical judgement from an agent or a loved one. If the previews have been poorly booked by the general public, your producers may also have 'papered' the house with free tickets, the recipients being friends of the cast and crew or groups of students from local colleges, or nursing staff from hospitals and homes, people who wouldn't otherwise have been able to afford a ticket.

This mixture of hypercritical or over-grateful people can make for an entirely unrepresentative response on a preview night, although a full house is better than an empty one, however it is comprised.

FROM PREVIEW TO OPENING

The pace of the work you do after the first preview will be defined by how many more previews you have before the opening. The shorter the run of a play, or the poorer the theatre company, the less likely you are to have more than one or two previews, three at the most. In some theatres, previews are unheard of. The first night is the first night and that's the end of it, especially in companies where the stage has been available for technical rehearsals for weeks and weeks prior to the first performance, or in theatre communities where the judgement of critics is considered to have little commercial impact. But where there are to be many weeks of subsequent performances and where the critics wield power over the public's decision whether or not to attend those performances, directors and producers will always fight for as many previews as are practically possible to schedule, in order that the work may be presented to its best possible artistic advantage.

You can have too many previews. In the commercial theatre, producers sometimes try to insure themselves against failure by scheduling weeks and weeks of previews. They reason that the longer they can keep the critics at bay, the longer the creative team will have to fix the show. Of course, this implies that the show needs fixing, which makes one wonder how much trust the producers have in the director and his creative team. What they really want to be able to do is to make what they call 'radical changes' to the show once an audience has reacted to it, the popular audience being the ultimate test of what works and what doesn't work. Indeed, some producers aren't really sure what they think of their own show until a popular audience has responded to it. A similar thing happens in the film industry, where a movie can be re-edited or even re-shot at enormous expense in order to align its story or its message more closely with the wishes and prejudices of a preview audience.

Of course, the ploy of endlessly prolonging the previews only works if you have a considerable advance at your box office and performances are well sold out with curious or trusting punters – but most productions are not in this position. Even if this is the case, the benefits of it are very doubtful. The trust issue is important. If you know you have to fill weeks and weeks of previews with endless rounds of tinkering, it makes for a restless rehearsal period. No one makes up his mind about anything, because you can always fix things later. People can be fired and replaced with 'better' people – there's always plenty of time, no need to worry. This causes everyone, from the director and producer down, to make sloppy decisions. If everything can be second-guessed, the first guess becomes an arbitrary choice. This sort of thinking trickles down into every department. 'Don't bother making that prop carefully, it'll get cut anyway.' 'I know you said you wanted that song by today, but I thought you'd change your mind.' People never do their best work when there's a strong chance it might be cut, or changed beyond any sense of their ownership of it.

A very long preview period is nearly always agonising for everyone. By the time the show finally opens, the endless bouts of tinkering will have shorn it of all spontaneity and originality, the cast will be exhausted from rehearsing and performing at the same time and the director and producer will be at each other's throats. If anyone offers you a lot of previews, think of them as candy offered to a child by a stranger. Be polite but say 'No, thank you,' and go straight home.

However many previews you end up with, the work you do after the first performance will expand to fill all the available time allotted to it. Every day you will rehearse on stage and every day you will knock off a list of the most serious faults in your production. As you work, other departments too will be mending their contributions. If you work well, and calmly, the second preview will be better than the first and the third better than the second and so on. You will take fewer and fewer notes as each preview goes by and become more and more satisfied with the work you have done to fix all the mistakes. Your goal, of course, is to watch the opening-night performance without being tempted to take a single note, to sit in the audience with a sense of unalloyed pleasure and pride at the sheer splendour and perfection of it all.

And so you will, if the work is good and you have used every moment of the preview period to improve it as best you can.

Producers

Producers are the businessmen of theatre. You do the art. They do the business.

In the subsidised sector, the administrators, **Artistic Directors**, General Managers or General Directors look after the business end of things, but in the commercial theatre where nothing comes for free, and no one is permanently salaried, the producer is king.

Directors rely on producers. At the very beginning of your career you may, to some extent, have to be your own producer, but as soon as you possibly can you should seek out producorial partnerships. You can't do everything in the theatre, nor should you try. If you want to be an artist, you will need the mental space to develop as an artist, and a good producer will give you that space by relieving you of quotidian producorial worries.

Good producers are good at all the things that good directors do least well. They put productions on their feet. They marry plays with directors and directors with actors, raise money for productions, drum up sponsorship and investment and supervise publicity, marketing and merchandising. They contract Production Managers, stage management, creative team and actors and do deals with **unions** and theatre owners. They book the audition spaces and rehearsal rooms. They balance the books. Against all the odds, they create employment and provide an environment in which creative work can happen creatively.

If the best producers are genuinely creative people, their creativity is not the same as yours. There will always be tensions between you and your producer. You may both want the same final product but you won't achieve it in the same way. The greatest tensions arise when you try to do each other's jobs. Some producers used to be directors or actors and have a good artistic eye, but they aren't you and you mustn't let them try to be. Listen to your producer on artistic matters and expect to be listened to in return on business matters, but don't dictate or be dictated to. Trust.

If, for whatever reason, you can't trust your producer, be very careful not to overreact. The more you try to compensate for producorial dysfunction, the more you risk compromising the integrity of your work. If a good producer enables you and provides you with protection, a bad one disables and exposes you. If this happens to you, keep the dysfunction out of the rehearsal room. Protect your actors from any hint of instability or panic.

Producers can get more and more unstable the closer you get to **opening night**. Head off the panic by staying in close touch. Go out to dinner together. Discuss your concerns openly. Be generous, realistic and pragmatic. For good or bad, success or failure, you're in this thing together. Stay solid.

Production Managers

The Production Manager is the senior technical administrator of a theatre company. He manages the construction and integration of all the 'physical' elements of a production – the sets, costumes, lighting, sound, wigs and make-up. He also controls the **budgets** for these elements and liaises between the Financial Controller and the **creative team**.

Production Meetings

If productions were created solely in the rehearsal room there would be no need for production meetings. As it is, there may be as many as a dozen or more different places where production work goes on – scenery, costume and prop shops, lighting and sound departments, music studios, press and publicity offices and so on. Based on initial meetings with director and designers these departments will all have been given their briefs, but as rehearsals progress, there will be inevitable changes of direction. **Stage management** makes notes and passes on the changes to the relevant departments in written form, but detailed clarifications may also be required. The departments, too, will have encountered problems they must communicate to director and designers – unavailable equipment, technical impracticality, time limitations, budgetary constraint. Thus the production meeting.

Meetings are generally held once a week during the rehearsal period and every day during **technical rehearsals**. All heads of department attend, the meetings being chaired by the **Production Manager**.

Production meetings can be frustrating and time-consuming but they are very necessary. All the demands you have made in the previous week will be revisited on you in detailed form. Many of the issues that arise will require agreement between you and your designers, whom you may not have seen since the last meeting. Where money is short, economies will be proposed and you will have to fight your corner for things you think are indispensable, or negotiate between departments for reallocation of funds to suit the changing demands.

Don't try to run the meeting yourself. It's important that you're not in charge. Be happy to be an item on the agenda. The Production Manager will speak first and then the heads of each department will take it in turns to air their concerns, other colleagues joining in when they feel they can help or when one item sparks off another in their minds.

If the key to good collaboration is communication, the production meeting is the essential village pump where you and your colleagues can talk away the problems of the day.

Programmes

Programmes – **playbills** (or programs) in America – are part of the public face of theatre companies.

They provide the only significant means of communication,

other than what happens on stage, between those who produce a show and those who attend it.

They list the characters and the actors that play them and credit the **creative team**.

They help tell the story of the play and how a director or a company intends an audience to receive it.

They are souvenirs. Devoted theatregoers hoard them, sometimes all their lives. Programmes continue to exist long after the scenery has been trashed and the props recycled. They may very well become the only palpable record of your production, and even if you have no wish to acquire a personal archive, someone else somewhere will be doing it for you.

They represent you and the work you have so carefully prepared, so you would be foolish not to take an interest in their contents.

CREDITS

The audience likes to know, deserves to know, and is often contractually obliged to be told who is responsible for the creation of the play and the production and the identities of the actors performing it, so the most important information in any programme comprises the names of author, director, designer, actors, composer and all the rest of the **creative team**, and indeed anyone else who has helped in any way with the mounting of the play. These are the credits, the term being derived from the Latin *credere*, to believe. Credits should tell the truth about who has done what for the benefit of the audience.

In many theatre companies the order in which credits appear in the programme, and their relative prominence, is laid down by an in-house tradition that never wavers. In the commercial theatre it is more often defined by a negotiation between the producer and the creative artists and their agents, resulting in a system of accreditation that may have more to do with contractual expedience than truth.

While the creative team and the actors have a contractual right to be clearly credited in the programme, the names of the technical and administrative staff are often hidden away in the small print at the back, even though their contributions to the production may be just as relevant to its success. Some theatre companies are more generous in this respect than others, crediting every last usher and cleaner. Others consider that credit should only be given where there is a manifest connection to the particular production, but this seems mean to me. Inclusiveness is always good for general morale, and good morale finds its way back to the stage very quickly.

Every credit has a meaning to the credited person and very often a value in career terms. They cost nothing but a little care and attention to detail, while the omission or misspelling of a name or the mistitling of a job can cause real distress. When considering the credits, be as generous as you can, and as accurate and as inclusive. Above all, make them a truthful description of who has done what.

FREE CAST LISTS

If you work for a small or poor theatre company you may not be able to afford a published programme for your play. Instead you can supply your audience with a free 'cast list' printed on a single sheet of paper. You can put the actors' photos and biographies and credit for any sponsorship you may have received on a wall in the foyer.

Some larger companies, out of consideration for their poorer patrons, may also provide a free cast list as an alternative to an expensive glossy programme. A very commendable practice, theatre tickets being the price they are.

LIST OF CHARACTERS AND ACTORS

Audiences like to know who's playing what. The identification of actors' names against their characters' names helps an audience to understand the story.

The commonest and often the best order for the character list is the order of their appearance, giving the audience an easy method of identification, but in plays with a few very large roles and a scattering of smaller ones, you might decide to put the big roles first regardless of their order of appearance.

Programmes

In large-cast plays with a great variety of big and small roles, a blizzard of character names in the programme can be confusing. You can convert such a list into a useful storytelling tool, helping the audience to understand the structure of the story and the way the characters fit into it. You can separate characters into families: Montagues and Capulets, Fairies and Mortals and so on.

You can also divide the list chronologically into scenes, with characters only mentioned in the scenes in which they first appear.

Arrange the list to make identification and comprehension easiest for your audience.

SOCIAL INFORMATION

Audiences with buses to catch or babysitters to relieve or restaurant bookings to honour are going to be very interested in the **running times**. You will be badgered by the editor of the programme to supply this information before you know it yourself or are willing to admit it to yourself. In the first print run of the programme you may have to settle for an approximation, but try to be as accurate as you can. Audiences are unforgiving if their plans are disrupted by shoddy estimations.

They are also interested in the number and timing of intervals, if any. Bladders come in a variety of different sizes, and most people can accurately forecast their need for a break if given the right information beforehand.

ESSENTIAL EXPLANATORY MATERIAL

Traditionally programmes described the geographical setting of the play and the historical period in which the action occurs, though this information is often redundant. You may feel that if you can't make such things clear from the stage then a few words in the programme will scarcely help matters.

There are occasions when an audience might be grateful for some assistance – when a story ranges to and fro across a broad range of places and dates or dips in and out of different realities.

THE STORYLINE

In **opera** or **musical theatre** or in plays with **heightened language**, audiences will expect a précis of the story in the programme. This is especially necessary where a **libretto** is in a foreign language or where the storyline is so swift or sketchy that the audience is in danger of getting lost.

Make sure the précis is one you are happy with. Someone else will probably draft it for you and it may not coincide with your view of the play at all, or be drawn from the programme of a previous production with an entirely different tone from yours. Make the final draft your own, so that the emphases in your production are suitably reflected.

In any theatre that relies on a tourist audience, the storyline is particularly important. If you cruise the foyers of any West End theatre before the show or during the interval you will see ample evidence of this in little groups of foreign theatregoers poring gratefully over their storylines.

INTERESTING ADDITIONAL MATERIAL

The more serious and thought-provoking a play, the more audiences appreciate programme material in support of its arguments and themes.

Notes from the author of a play can often illuminate the work or the originating ideas behind it. A critical essay by an accessible academic can help to put a historical play into its social or intellectual context. A director's rehearsal notes or a conversation between author and director or translator and author can all provide unique and fascinating insights for an audience.

A play based on real events or people can be supported by accounts of its subjects' lives or a chronology of relevant contemporary events – anything that will broaden the audience's view of the play or give them landmarks based on what they might already know.

A play based on complex political, social or scientific ideas can benefit from a concise analysis of the issues in the programme for later consumption and digestion.

Programmes

Beware of padding a programme with arbitrary guff. There is a line of thinking that goes thus: *As You Like It* is a play about marriage. Marriage is an interesting theme. Lots of really famous and interesting people said something about marriage. Let's include a few quotations from them. The audience is then obliged to trawl through a lot of clever snippets about marriage from Freud to Rilke to Walter Raleigh. This is lazy stuff.

GRAPHIC DESIGN

A programme that has had the attention of a decent graphic designer is always much the better for it, but your attention will also be necessary. Before the programme copy has been finalised you may already have approved the image for a **poster** and whatever your designer has created may make an appearance here too.

Make sure the background colours and typefaces are complementary and clear. Auditorium lights can be dim and audiences' eyes not of uniform strength. If you see your audience straining to read the names of the actors, you know the inks are too pale or the backgrounds too busy or the fonts too fancy.

BIOGRAPHIES

These are usually confined to the creative team and actors, though in the commercial theatre, producers or their offices may be included.

Most theatres have a formula for programme biographies in order to avoid divergences of length or style. Most commonly this includes a headshot of the artist together with his name, role or credit, followed by a list of past professional engagements.

A programme editor may write the biographies from material provided by the artists, or the artists may have to write them themselves. Whatever the process, some editing will always be required, to weed out long-windedness, grandiosity or feeble attempts at humour.

If in doubt about appropriateness of content or tone, remember that biographies are there to provide information for the audience, not to massage the egos of the artists. Audiences like to remember where else they may have seen an actor's work in theatre, film or television, and to notice the way a career has developed. They will be far less interested to know that the choreographer has just had twins or the leading actress is an Aquarius. They can buy glossy magazines for that sort of rubbish.

DEDICATIONS

In recent years a rather mawkish tradition has developed, largely in America, for actors to dedicate their performances in the last sentence of their biographies. Dedications are made to 'my beautiful wife Nancy', or 'my lover Eric', or 'my Lord and Saviour' or 'my dog Bonzo'.

There should be no place for such sentimental stuff in a theatre programme, however well meaning or deeply felt. It smacks of the self-aggrandising drivel spouted by prize-winners at award ceremonies and breaks the essential contract between actor, author and audience.

An actor's performance is dedicated to the play and its author, to the event and to the people watching the event. At the **curtain call** the audience has an opportunity to express its gratitude and pleasure that the contract has been honoured. They should not be demoted to second place in the professional affection of the performer and the performer should not wish them to be. Serious professional actors should be seriously embarrassed to have their private lives devalued in such a way, as if they were no better than politicians. Where the tradition has taken a grip, it has quickly become competitive, actors feeling obliged to dream up more and more genuine-sounding dedications or they blackmail themselves into including a cherished loved one they dare not omit. If you have any influence on what appears in your programme you should help stamp out this sentimental practice.

REHEARSAL PHOTOGRAPHS

If you only have one print run of a programme, these may be the only **photographs** you can include. In choosing the shots, make sure you include everyone at least once. If you get a set of really good pictures, you can use them instead of biography headshots. Put the names of the actors next to their shots so the audience can cross-reference them against the biographies.

An audience only sees the actors as they appear on stage and takes real delight in comparing rehearsal shots with finished performances. A good set of rehearsal photographs can reveal a lot about the personalities behind the characters and also include shots of people the audience never sees – director, designers, stage management and other members of staff.

PERFORMANCE PHOTOGRAPHS

These are in many ways less interesting to the audience than rehearsal shots, so even if you have a second print run of your programme you should think twice about replacing all your rehearsal shots with performance shots.

Choosing the shots may cause you difficulty. The editor of the programme will want a finished set of photos before you or your actors, and especially your scenic and Costume Designers, are happy they should be taken. The programme is their archive too, and a photo of an unfinished hat or a badly tacked-up pair of trousers will make the Costume Designer look bad for ever.

DRAWINGS

As an alternative to rehearsal shots, think about employing a graphic artist to make drawings of the actors. They are often more relaxing to have in rehearsal than a photographer, especially one who crouches all around the room looking for sexy angles and making everyone feel self-conscious. An artist sits in the corner quietly sketching away and can bring a freshness of wit and artistry to the business of capturing the actors at work.

If you are directing a comedy or satire, a caricaturist can add his own pinch of salt to the stew. If you seek such a graphic talent, you may not have to look far. Many an actor is a talented draughtsman or caricaturist. Check out the margins of the actors' scripts and you'll often get a nice surprise. For a small fee or a little gentle cajoling these inspirations can provide very good programme copy.

PLAY TEXT PROGRAMMES

Many new play theatre companies like to publish a combined **play text** and programme. This has the advantage of ensuring publication of a new play when the writer is not celebrated enough to have acquired a publisher and/or the shortness of the run would make a separate publication an un-commercial proposition. When this happens you will be put under pressure to agree a final version of the script before you or the writer are quite ready, but you mustn't let that put either of you off your stride. The script will look after itself, however many changes it endures. Look at *Hamlet*.

ADVERTISING

At least half of any programme consists of ads. They often look awful and may even jar with the intellectual or moral content of your play. But there's little you can do about it. The theatre needs the money and that's the end of it.

Projection

Projection is the technique that theatre actors use to amplify their voices in order to be audible in every part of an **auditorium** - nothing to do with **projections**, below.

Properly mastered, projection should be an undetectable technique, the best actors filling the theatre space with their voices while seeming to speak quite naturally. Used unskilfully, projection can become mere shouting, the need for volume overwhelming any sense of meaning or naturalness.

Well-trained actors learn to support their lungs on a strong diaphragm so their voices seem to be dredged up from their bowels or their boots to resonate all around the theatre. Actors with less fruity voices find projection more difficult, but even the thinnest voice will grow stronger and more resonant with constant practice in a well-voiced company.

For both strong- and weak-voiced actors, the most important element of projection is **diction**, or enunciation, rather than volume. An actor who works the consonants as powerfully as he works the vowels will be much better heard than a lazy-consonanted vowel-barker.

Different theatres and different theatrical sets have different **acoustics**, so the amount of projection needed will vary from one production to another and from one theatre to another. This is nowhere more apparent than on tour when a company playing the same show week after week will have to make constant adjustments to their levels of projection to suit their new surroundings.

The term 'projection' is usually used to mean vocal projection, but it rarely comprises only vocal considerations. A properly projected voice will also involve a projected character and a projected acting personality – voice, body, thoughts and all.

You will become most aware of the need for projection when you move a company from rehearsal room to theatre. Encourage your actors to use the **technical rehearsal** period to bring their performances up to an appropriately projected level.

Projections

Projections, or projected images, are widely used in the theatre as a feature of lighting or **set design**. When **Lighting Designers** talk about projections they mean images produced with a projector. Images can also be created by adding **gobos** to the lenses of standard lighting instruments, but these aren't called projections.

Front projections have their light sources hanging **FOH** or on stage, their images appearing on the scenic walls or floor by reflection or absorption. Back projections have light sources upstage of the translucent surfaces upon which their images appear.

As a general rule, back projections appear brighter and more distinct than front projections. This is because the surfaces on which they appear are specially made to receive light. The material of a BP

(Back Projection) screen is made up of thousands of tiny lenses that refract and intensify the light as it passes through. Images projected onto the same screen from the front appear with nowhere near the same intensity. **Cycloramas** are usually made of BP material of one sort or another, often combined with **scrims** to soften or deepen the resulting images.

Projections have a variety of uses but they are much better at conveying atmosphere than specific scenic location. When considering the use of projection, you and your scenic and Lighting Designers should also consider the competition. Cinema creates vivid photographic imagery with absolute clarity by using very powerful projectors in completely darkened theatres. Theatre cannot compete with these conditions. Actors must stand between the images and the audience and they, together with the scenic elements around them, must be lit. Anything strongly lit downstage of a projected image will serve to wash it out. For example, if you project the image of a room on an upstage screen and light real furniture downstage of it, the image will turn grey, lifeless and two-dimensional in relation to the real objects. Even a strongly projected scenic image will pale in comparison with a single well-lit actor standing downstage of it.

This difficulty has become more pronounced in recent years with the advent of computer-generated design. Many Set Designers have taken to using computers to design their shows, and in the process they get used to seeing vividly luminous images on their screens, images they want to see reproduced on stage in the form of projections. But they will never be completely happy with the results. In **technical rehearsals** they will seek your help in dimming down the light on the actors to the point where the images behind them are sharpened by contrast. You will find yourself swithering between the devil and the deep blue sea, the devil being the projections and the deep blue sea being the audience's right to see the actors' faces clearly. You will not find this a pleasant experience and you will, like many before you, struggle to keep your feet dry.

Promenade Performances

These are performances that oblige all or part of the audience to stand for all or part of the play and/or to promenade from one point of interest to another in a production with flexible locations.

The most common form of promenade is to be found in replica Elizabethan theatres where the 'groundling' audience stands in the 'pit' and the tiered levels above are fully seated.

There may be financial advantages to promenade performances. You can fit more people into a theatre standing than sitting, but then again you probably shouldn't charge them so much for the privilege.

A more significant advantage can be a heightened sense of participation. A standing audience seems more physically connected to the actors on the stage than a sitting one. It becomes a crowd, a living, many-headed organism with an ebb and flow of its own. Excellent for plays with a public social context – like *Julius Caesar*, *Coriolanus* or *Candide*.

In modern theatre spaces promenade performances work best when there is some element of **environmental design** in the production.

Prompt Copy

Also known as the prompt book, or **book** for short, the prompt copy is the text of the play annotated by the Stage Manager or **Deputy Stage Manager** for **cueing** a performance.

It may also be the text from which a **prompt** is made on the rare occasions when an actor needs one – hence its name.

There are many different ways of preparing a prompt book, and DSMs all have their peculiar methods, but the end result should be more or less the same. The pages of the text are generally cut up so that each page is faced with a blank page where notes can be written and the timings of the cues can be delineated for easy reference in performance.

The blank pages contain sketches of the actors' moves together with the lighting, sound, flying and any other cues, all tabulated to be triggered by a word in the text or a physical action. These cues are all preceded in the text by 'warns' or warning cues.

If actors make textual errors in run-throughs or performances, the DSM underlines them in the text for future correction.

A well-maintained book is a joy to behold, with its coloured inks and ruled lines and tiny sketches of actor, furniture and prop moves, and it augurs well for a clockwork performance. A shoddily made book will make for a shoddily called show.

The prompt copy should be usable by any competent Stage Manager or Deputy, but only its creator will know exactly how the cues relate to their relevant entries. When another DSM takes over a show it is usual for him to shadow the original DSM for two or three performances so that all the rhythmic nuances of the show can be properly observed.

The prompt copy is the bible of the show – no bible, no show.

Prompt Corner

The prompt corner is situated in the wings of a theatre, usually in one or other of the extreme downstage wings just behind the **proscenium** arch, where the **DSM** sits to 'call the cues' of the show and hopes never to have to make a **prompt**.

Prompts and Prompters

A prompt is a word or phrase fed to an actor when he forgets his lines. The essence of a good prompt is that it should be clearly audible to the actor but inaudible to the audience. The prompter should therefore sit as close to the action as possible, though obviously hidden from the audience's view.

A good prompter follows the text like a hawk, knows all the actors' moves and the accompanying rhythm of the lines with their little breaths, hiatuses and pauses. He can sense when an actor is getting into trouble, or when a new inflection from one actor has thrown another. When a prompt is required, he makes an instant diagnosis of the problem. Has the actor had a tiny lapse of memory or has he gone completely blank, unaware even of which scene he is in? Do the other actors know where they are? Can they help? When he gives a prompt he speaks softly but distinctly the exact words that will put the actor back on course. He then stays especially vigilant until the actor gets his confidence back. An actor can get badly thrown by having to take a prompt and may need further help to get to safer ground. Prompting is a sensitive craft.

Eighteenth- and nineteenth-century theatres had prompt boxes built into the forestage, the prompter sitting below stage level with his head just visible to the actors. From this position a prompt could be whispered without any chance of the audience hearing it. In many theatres, the prompter whispered the entire performance a split second before the actors spoke their lines. In France the prompter is still called *le souffleur*, the whisperer. This practice continues in some continental theatres today, though the downstage centre prompt box has now almost entirely disappeared.

In most modern professional theatres a prompt is actually quite a rare occurrence. In the days when theatre companies carried a large **repertoire** of constantly revolving productions or performed a weekly repertoire of one play after another, actors were far more prone to forget their hastily learnt lines and far less capable of helping one another out with a muttered onstage prompt. With the advent of long rehearsal periods and **long runs**, the prompter has become a far less important figure. But actors are not infallible. They are all capable of **drying**. There is scarcely an actor living who cannot regale you with some awful story about a famous dry or an embarrassingly taken prompt.

In most British and American theatres, the prompter is a member of the **stage management** team, usually the **DSM**, who prompts as part of his duties in 'calling' the show. This is never quite satisfactory. The caller of the show has so much to do, so many calls to make and cues to give, that his attention cannot but wander from the text. It's bad enough when an actor dries, but if he has to wait for his prompt, or worse, gets the wrong line when it finally arrives, his embarrassment is compounded.

In theatres where the caller of the show sits in a box at the back of the auditorium, prompting cannot be done with any finesse. A prompt given over the auditorium speakers always sounds like an embarrassing public rebuke and completely destroys the credibility and atmosphere of a production.

In many continental theatres prompters have no other duties than following the text in rehearsals, hearing the actors through their lines outside rehearsal and prompting during performances. The prompter's department can serve as a most valuable support system for an acting ensemble. Good prompters can be to actors what good dramaturgs are to directors, artistic helpmeets and therapists. Nonetheless, they can still be intrusive in performance. They sit at the front of the auditorium, sometimes semi-obscured, sometimes in full view of actors and audience, whispering the lines in the time-honoured way, or at least so obviously available to help that the actors almost feel obliged to rely on them. If you work in a theatre of this sort, you need to find a balance. Move the prompter a little further away, to the side of the stage or into a proscenium box. Make the actors rely on one another rather than the prompter. It is an undeniable fact that the more invisible a prompter is the less his services will be required.

Prompt Side and Opposite Prompt Side

Commonly used and rather confusing directorial **stage directions**.

Props

Props are 'properties', the onstage objects that may be considered the personal property of the characters.

There is often some confusion as to exactly what constitutes a prop, as opposed to a piece of furniture or scenery, especially when it comes to deciding who should build or find the object and continue to be responsible for it during the run of the play. Different theatres have different ways of delineating these responsibilities. Some have prop shops manned by dedicated staff. In others, **stage management** must supply and maintain the smaller props while the designer and his team find the furniture. In the commercial theatre props and furniture are generally hired from professional prop stores or specially made by a freelance prop-maker. In theatre communities that are controlled by **unions** there may be quite strict rules controlling the making and handling of props, furniture and scenic pieces. As a general rule, anything bigger than a prop is furniture and anything bigger than furniture is scenery.

If there are disputes about responsibility, your designer and Production Manager should address them at the very first production meeting. Have your Stage Manager or DSM make out a comprehensive prop list and allocate every item on it to one department or another. Your designer will then be able to control the way the list develops and ensure an artistic cohesion between props, furniture and scenery. As rehearsals continue, the prop list will change. Things will get cut. New props will be added. At the end of each rehearsal day a list of changes should be mailed round all relevant departments so no one wastes time working on things that are no longer required.

The props that often cause most trouble are the ones requiring electrical wiring. For safety reasons, often reinforced by strict union rules, anything electrical must be made and/or maintained by the lighting department. But lighting departments are generally pretty hopeless about making props and may even resent having to do so. Your Production Manager and designer may have to negotiate carefully to get the electrical props looking and working as they should.

HAND PROPS

Hand props are props that are handled by the actors as part of the action. They may be preset on the stage or carried by the actors from wings to stage. In the latter case they are set out on prop tables in the wings. A well-ordered prop table has a taped-off area for each prop and is carefully checked by stage management before each performance.

PERSONAL PROPS

Personal props are hand props that become the personal responsibility of the actors, things like watches, spectacles, cigarettes and matches. Stage management places them on the actors' dressing-room make-up tables before the half (see **Calls**) and then checks they haven't been forgotten when the actor reaches the wings.

REHEARSAL PROPS

A good stage management team will have a complete set of props for you to work with in rehearsal. You won't start with all the props being perfect, but there should be something on the rehearsal prop table to represent every performance prop that will eventually make an appearance.

A good set of rehearsal props will form the basis for the ones you use in performance. Make sure the actors know which is a rehearsal prop and which is an 'actual' prop. If an actor asks, 'Is this the actual?' he may be expressing a negative reaction, as in 'This had better not be the actual,' or he may be curious to know how seriously he should be getting used to it. Talk to your designer on a regular basis about the appropriateness of the rehearsal props and encourage your stage management and/or prop department to keep improving the stock with a steady flow of 'actuals'.

Above all, keep the actors onside. The longer they use the rehearsal props the fonder they can become of them. When the actual props arrive, they may be so despised in comparison that the actors conceive a real objection to using them. This will not please your designer, but he may have to take a deep breath and make cosmetic changes to a rehearsal prop rather than enforce the use of the actual.

Proscenium

In the ancient theatre the proscenium was the area between the scene, or background, and the **orchestra**, where the action of the play took place.

Proscenium

In the Restoration theatre it came to mean the area between the main curtain drop and the orchestra, what we would now call the **forestage**.

In modern terminology the proscenium, 'prosc' for short, describes the arch or opening that separates the stage from the auditorium in a proscenium or 'prosc arch' theatre.

FALSE PROSCENIUM

A 'false' proscenium is a scenic piece specially built as part of a set design to give a theatre a proscenium arch when it doesn't have one of its own, or to conceal or change the dimensions of an existing proscenium opening.

Prosody

See **Metre**.

Pub Theatres

Most pub theatres started up as part of the huge expansion in small **fringe** theatre venues from the 1960s onwards. Many public houses were originally built with function rooms attached to them. These were used for wedding parties, union meetings and clubs of one sort or another, at a time when the local pub was the social hub of its community. With the advent of television and the subsequent changing patterns of social behaviour, thousands of these rooms in pubs all across the country fell into disuse and disrepair. They became the perfect venues for struggling, financially strapped theatre companies wanting to put on shows at very low cost in a socially inclusive atmosphere. So an old relationship was re-forged – that of tavern and stage, barrels and boards, wine and song.

Some of the most celebrated of contemporary playwrights had their first plays produced in pub theatres, and they are still an ideal finishing school for inexperienced theatre writers or directors or actors to hone their skills. Because they are places of low expectation they can also be places of unexpected delight. The intimacy of their playing areas, involving the audience in a very close relationship with the stage, reduces the need in actors and directors for sophisticated large-theatre technique, but creates an equally important demand for complete truthfulness of playing and naturalness of invention.

In recent years, as pub theatres have become more and more part of the theatrical infrastructure, young producers and directors increasingly find them a rather expensive option. With rent pegged at £1,000 a week or more, the minimum rental period three weeks and a projected nightly audience of, say, twenty at the most, it is easy to see how aspiring directors, or more often their supportive parents, can lose a packet.

Whether affordable or not, one of the best features of pub theatre is the social setting of the pub itself. Whatever happens during the performance, the bar provides a natural haven for celebration or despair, a relaxed debating chamber for critical and uncritical opinion, and a few quiet corners for writing, rewriting or starting all over again.

Puppets and Puppetry

If you decide to use puppets in a production you will almost certainly need help from an expert. Whatever sort of puppet you use – glove or hand puppets, rod puppets, marionettes or giant processional figures – they need to be cleverly made and elegantly manipulated.

They are not a simple answer to anything. Beware anyone telling you, 'We can always use a puppet,' as if it was an easy solution to an otherwise intractable problem. It's like saying 'We can always use projections,' when you can't think of a decent design solution. Puppets can be useful and effective, but they need an enormous amount of work to make them so.

If you think puppets are a good idea for your play, they must be worked into your design from the outset. Your production must allow for them stylistically, making an onstage world that is equally good for human figures and their puppet equivalents.

Puppets and Puppetry

For example, if you're doing a production of Ibsen's *Doll's House* and you can't afford or don't want the bother of having children appear with Nora at the end of Act I, puppets are only a good idea if your production has prepared the audience for the use of them. If you are working in an otherwise completely naturalistic style and Nora comes on with three puppet children, the audience will simply think she is mad and likes pretending she has children. Hardly the point of the play.

Similarly, there are many plays where characters are required to carry pet dogs or cats. **Animals** on stage are always a worry, but not as disturbing as a badly manipulated puppet. Either use a real animal or get someone to help you make a puppet look absolutely real. What you don't want is an audience wondering whether an animal is real or not when they should be attending to the story.

WORKING WITH PUPPETS

If puppets make up a significant aspect of your design, get your actors working on them from the get-go. It's just like working with **masks.** You need to get your designer in rehearsal together with your puppet-maker and you need to allocate proper slices of rehearsal time for the actors to get used to manipulating and characterising their puppets. Each puppet needs to be given a life of its own, a way of moving, a tempo and a rhythm, a voice and a personality.

You, your designers and your actors will need to agree between you what the puppet is helping you to achieve. How is the puppet helping to tell the story? How can you animate its movement so the audience can fully appreciate it? Do you need one operator per puppet or more? In the Bunraku tradition of Japan, each puppet has three manipulators – one for the body, head and right hand, one for the left hand and one for the legs. How many do *you* need? Should you try to conceal your manipulators from the audience's view or does their appearance add to the effect of what you are doing? Are your puppets silent or voiced? If the latter, do the manipulators supply the voice as well as the action or does the voice come from elsewhere? Do you need music to accompany the movements? Do the puppets sing?

As with mask work, have plenty of mirrors in rehearsal so the actors can appreciate the effects they and their puppets are making. In the case of human-shaped puppets, as their characters develop, let them interact with one another. Play theatre **games** with them and involve them in **improvisations**. Treat them almost as if they were living actors in the play. Make them your friends. It might sound silly, but the more they become humanised, the more they will seem to think like real people and take on distinct personalities of their own. Puppets that have been fully brought to life seem to control their puppeteers rather than the other way round. When this starts to happen you know you've got it right.

Q

Quick Changes

Quick changes are changes of costume made in very short time. They might be occasioned by a character having to change costume between scenes or by an actor exiting as one character and entering as another shortly afterwards.

Quick changes usually happen in the wings unless the dressing rooms are very close to the stage. In most theatres, if an actor has time to go back to his dressing room for a change, it can't be called quick.

The first principle to establish with quick changes is that there's no such thing as an impossible change. In **technical rehearsals** you may be told by wardrobe staff or by an actor that a change cannot possibly be achieved. Don't believe them. Changes can always be achieved. Indeed, changes are often proposed as quick changes that are no such thing. The speed of a quick change obviously depends on how many elements of costume, wig and make-up are involved and on the dexterity of the actor and his dresser or dressers, but as a general rule, anything longer than a minute can't really be called a quick change. A complete change of costume in half a minute is nearly always perfectly achievable. Total changes of appearance can be made in a matter of seconds if there's a will to achieve them.

You and your **Costume Designer** and **wardrobe** department should prepare yourselves well in advance. If a change looks like it might be a problem, costumes can be specially designed for speedy doffing and donning. Anything needing laces can be permanently laced up and fastened instead with hooks or Velcro. The sides of shoes and boots can be elasticated. Wigs and facial hair can be ready-prepared with toupee tape or glue at just the right degree of tackiness. And so on.

Costumes can also be over- or under-dressed, that is the costume for one scene or character can be worn over or under another costume. The top layer is ripped off and hey presto, the next appearance is revealed. But under-dressing cannot be the answer to every quick change. The more layers of clothes an actor wears, the fatter he will look. A pair of pyjamas worn over a three-piece suit makes an actor look like he's had a very lumpy night.

Don't make your actors do their quick changes in the open wings. Some changes require actors to strip to practically nothing and even quite subtle changes may involve some loss of modesty. Get your crew to make quick-change booths in the wings. Put mirrors in them and make-up tables or shelves.

When you rehearse quick changes in the tech, don't move on if a change hasn't been achieved. Rehearse it as often as is required to get it right. Make amendments to costume and dressing technique each time and let your actors and dressers get a rhythm going. Practice will do the trick. A change that seemed hectic and impossible at the start of a tech will be a doddle by opening night.

R

Radio-Mikes

Radio-mikes are wireless microphones commonly used for the amplification of performers' voices in **musical theatre**. Singers and stand-up comedians use the hand-held or stand-mounted variety, the mike often doubling as a prop or performance tool. In musical theatre where singers have to perform eight shows a week against a loud, often electronic, accompaniment, they are kitted out with a miniature version, the mike attaching to the head or the chest and the transmitter and battery worn in an elastic belt somewhere under the costume.

Radio-mikes are delicate little instruments, sensitive to moisture in the form of sweat and susceptible to feedback when operated too close to onstage speakers or other radio-mikes (see **Musical Theatre**). They must be monitored throughout every performance and a 'runner', usually the most junior member of the sound department, makes running repairs to them and replaces their fading batteries when required.

In contemporary pop and rock musicals radio-mikes are usually worn undisguised on little armatures that look like external cheek-bones.

In traditional musical dramas where a more naturalistic effect is desired, mikes are cleverly concealed in the hair or wig of the performer as close as possible to the resonating chambers in the head, but total concealment is difficult to achieve and battles often break out between the music and sound departments on the one hand and the director and **Costume Designer** on the other.

The **Sound Designer**, instructed by the composer or the conductor, will try to creep the microphone further and further down the performer's forehead, while the Costume Designer, instructed by the director, will try to creep it back up again so as to make it disappear into the hair or under the wig. Performers, caught in the middle, try not to resent being used as mike-stands. Solutions can be found that will almost satisfy all parties, with mikes being coloured to suit the complexion of the performer and the make-up and wig departments using their subtlest forms of camouflage, but there will usually be a grumble left hanging in the air somewhere. Short of giving all musical theatre performers a microphone implant in the head, a complete solution is difficult to imagine.

The less an actor wears, the harder it is to conceal the mike and its connective wiring and battery-pack. This is most apparent when an actor strips off his shirt on stage to reveal a sweaty back with a wire taped to it, nape to arse, giving the impression that his actions are all being remotely controlled from the sound desk.

Radio-mikes are increasingly being used in **sound enhancement** systems in the non-musical theatre as a way of combating bad acoustics, overlarge theatre buildings, noisy stage technology and poor vocal training, but few self-respecting actors will agree to wear them without a nagging sense of failure.

Raked Stages

A raked stage is one that slopes upwards away from the audience. Some stages, mostly old-fashioned **proscenium playhouses**, are permanently raked in this way, usually quite gently at a ratio of between 1:24 to 1:30. By tilting the whole surface of the stage towards the audience a rake serves to project the stage action into the auditorium. Most auditoria are also raked, some very steeply, so a raked stage can be seen as a reflection of a raked auditorium, bringing actors and audience closer together.

Many directors and designers like using rakes in big theatres, though anything much steeper than 1:18 becomes impossible to walk on naturally or even safely, not to say worrying for the audience to look at. In the US there are union laws forbidding steep rakes.

Whatever the artistic arguments for the use of a steeply raked stage, director and designer must first consider all the possible consequences before subjecting the actors to it.

Raked Stages

For designers

A designer working on a permanent rake must bring the angle of the rake into all his calculations. On a raked stage every bit of standing scenery has to be 'anti-raked' so that its vertical features remain vertical. Depending on the steepness of the rake, even tables and chairs must sometimes be anti-raked, making them impossible to use in any other than their set alignments.

If a designer wishes to put a rake of his own on an existing rake, the calculations become even more tortuous. Most perplexing of all is when a **revolve** is mounted onto a raked stage – unless the whole revolve is anti-raked then everything you place on it will change its relationship to everything else as the stage revolves – verticals that are true on one part of the stage are un-vertical elsewhere, doors that are set to open upstage will slam shut downstage, and furniture that is carefully anti-raked for one locality looks drunken in another.

Designers are of course trained to cope with these problems, incorporating the angle of a rake into the general perspective of the set so that the audience perceives the setting as artistically harmonious.

For actors

A very gently raked stage is unlikely to be a problem for most actors, but steep rakes can be enormously troublesome. Actors cannot stand naturally on a rake. The steeper the rake the more they must adapt their stance to accommodate it. An actor standing on a rake presenting his profile to the audience will automatically put more of his weight on his downstage foot than on his upstage. In other words he will be using his downstage leg to prop himself up. If he walks across the stage, turning as he goes, he must shift all his weight onto his other leg. If he stands with his back to the audience he puts strain on his Achilles tendons. If he stands facing the audience he must thrust his hips forward in order to stay upright, like a woman wearing high heels. An actress obliged to wear high heels on a rake is in the worst situation of all – and if she has to dance she's in real trouble.

When you remember that a cast will be spending upwards of two or three hours a night in these unnatural positions – or twenty-four hours a week – you can imagine the resulting strain on tendons, ligaments and muscles unused to such patterns of movement. Back problems become quite common – the steeper the rake and the longer the run, the bigger the problem. If you do decide that despite all the risks, a steep rake is essential for artistic reasons, you must be ready to foot the physiotherapy and insurance bills when they arrive, as arrive they will.

For directors

The laws of physics apply to raked stages just as they apply elsewhere on earth. A round object dropped on the stage will roll into the auditorium. A bottle or a cup accidentally knocked off a table will very likely end up in the lap of the lady sitting in the front row, mesmerising the audience on its way. Anything with wheels will tend to roll downstage unless braked, whether it be Mother Courage's cart or an old invalid in a bath chair. Movable objects placed on a steeply raked stage tend to get laughs.

For audiences

In most theatres the rake, if there is one, is so slight that an audience is unaware of it, but as soon as a rake is steep enough for an audience to notice, it becomes part of their perception of the piece they are watching. A steep rake creates a sort of neurosis in the audience as they notice the actors and the props behaving strangely and they start to worry, whether consciously or not. An audience empathises very easily with a cast of actors. You want them to empathise in all other ways and so they will in this. They feel instinctively what it would be like to move around on a very steep rake and something in them rebels on the actors' behalf.

REHEARSAL RAKES

If a raked stage is essential to your design, try to get a version of it installed in the rehearsal room for at least the last week of rehearsals, if not longer. Your actors will need to acclimatise to the rake, and it isn't fair to expect them, or their muscles, to do so at the last minute during the technical rehearsals when they will have so much else to think about.

The Read-Through

The read-through is the customary first reading of a play by the actors on the first day of **rehearsal**, and unless you have a strong alternative method of work that obviates the need for a read-through, there is no good reason not to follow the custom. The actors will certainly expect to read the play unless they are informed otherwise in advance, and if the play is a new one, the author will be disappointed not to hear his characters animated by a cast he may be meeting for the first time.

Some directors are dead against a cold reading of the play on the first day. They argue that it does no good at all for the actors to be obliged to read their characters before they have had a chance to explore them in rehearsal, that an uninterrupted reading merely serves to emphasise the misconceptions about character and motive that the actors have jumped to in private study, and seems prematurely to enshrine the reading of the play as an interpretation of it. Such directors react to these misgivings by dispensing with the read-through altogether and going straight to rehearsals proper, or in some cases having a read-through but with the actors reading one another's parts. Most actors hate this. Their part is theirs, and no one else is going to tell them how to read it.

A read-through can be a little difficult for a director. Your **casting** choices are being proved for the first time, to the author, to the cast and to yourself. Any obvious deficiencies in an actor, of skill or rightness for a part, can be exacerbated by the roughness of it all and the lack of control you have over what is a very raw process.

ACTORS AND READ-THROUGHS

Different actors respond to the pressures of a read-through in many different ways. To start with, some actors are far better at reading than others. Don't be deceived by this. The best readers are not always the best actors. The actor that stumbles haltingly through the text making a hash of all the long words and mangling the grammar could well turn out to be the best actor in the show.

Some actors react to their fear of failure at the read-through by **mugging** up their parts in advance and giving a completely finished performance at the reading, playing to the gallery of actors around them and milking every moment for all it's worth. This can be more than a little embarrassing and may betoken a rough ride in rehearsal as you try to shift the actor away from inappropriate preconceptions.

Others are so fearful of appearing to be well prepared that they adopt a studied monotone, as if to say, 'I'm not the sort of actor that jumps to conclusions about his character. It will take me weeks to understand a word of any of this,' but this is a minor vanity that usually disappears as the read-through continues and the actor gets involved in the story.

Despite these curious drawbacks, a read-through can be an exciting and instructive way of kick-starting a rehearsal process. The first day is nervous anyway, and you have to start somewhere. Members of the cast may not know one another very well; and a reading is a nicely neutral ground on which actors can make one another's acquaintance personally and professionally.

Many of your actors won't have read the whole play with any scrutiny, or if they have they will have concentrated more on their own parts than on the piece as a whole. And you yourself may not have studied the play as well as you think you have. Hearing it read by actors for the first time allows you to make important discoveries about its rhythms, the relationships between the characters and the overall impact of the story. You will also learn a lot about the work you have to do with the actors, which of them seem to be close to an understanding of their characters and which have a long way to go. You will hear the mix of the actors' voices for the first time and how they sound as an ensemble. You will sense how the company will comprise itself in terms of humour, intelligence and awareness of one another. Listen, watch and learn, but don't jump to any conclusions.

READ-THROUGH GUIDELINES

You can turn the read-through into a positive experience for everyone by giving clear guidelines about how you want it to proceed. Tell the actors that no points will be awarded for finished performances and that all misreading and fumbling over grammar and pronunciation are forgiven in advance. Ask everyone to listen carefully to the story as it proceeds. If it's a well-known play, ask them to listen with unprejudiced ears, untainted by any productions they may have seen previously, discovering in one another how this production will be unlike any other version of the play.

Once you have explained the rules of engagement, you may opt to read the play through without any interruption in order to gain the best possible understanding of how the story stands up as a drama. If you do this, you must decide what to do about the **stage directions**. In Shakespeare's plays, and those of his contemporaries, there are no stage directions to speak of, but many modern plays are peppered with them. If you stop to read every little detail, you will break up the rhythm of the text and frustrate the actor whose text you are interrupting. A good rule is to read the major stage directions, the ones that describe actions and events, but ignore the ones that are interpolated in the text as clues to the actor. Read the stage directions yourself. This will serve to involve you in the reading and also give the actors a clue as to how you feel about their content.

STAGGER-THROUGH READINGS

You may decide that an uninterrupted reading is unlikely to teach you or the actors very much and opt instead for a **stagger-through** approach, reading the play a scene at a time and stopping on the way to discuss content, characterisation and meaning. This is a good solution for a play with **heightened language** or a mystifying structure. To read such a play without analysis or discussion can be quite depressing for a cast. Actors easily get bogged down if they lose track of the story, becoming less and less sure of how their individual parts fit into the big picture.

A read-through of this sort can last a whole day, or run into two or even three days, the whole cast slowly becoming experts on the text, the background of the play and the author's intentions in writing it.

Or you may decide to do both sorts of read-through, reading the play straight through on the first day and then going back to study it in much greater detail in the two or three days following.

NEW PLAYS

With a new play, the read-through is an important occasion for the author. He may have been writing the play for months, even years, and this may be the first time he hears the characters brought to life.

A writer can be vulnerable at a first reading and may need to be looked after. Some of the characters may not sound as he intended them, the rhythm of the play is often fudged at a reading, and none of the jokes will be as funny as he wanted them to be. As the read-through continues, don't pay all your attention to the cast. If there are obvious misinterpretations of text or character, stop and let the author talk about what he intended.

He will be particularly anxious to know that the actors are enjoying playing the parts he has written for them. Encourage the actors and the author to talk to one another about the play and how he has imagined the individual characters within it. Actors love to hear about the genesis of their characters, how the author conceived them and to what extent he drew them from life or purely from his imagination.

Don't be threatened by the necessary bond between author and actor. Take advantage of it.

AUTHOR'S READINGS

There was a tradition in the early years of the Moscow Arts Theatre of the author reading his new play to the cast so that they could all be instructed by his tone of voice, imbibing the meaning of the play by attending to every nuance of the author's reading. There are photographs of Chekhov doing just this, though the set-up looks suspiciously staged for the camera. There may be a good case for deploying this method in the reading of any new play, provided of course that the author is happy to comply. Perhaps what you should consider is asking the author if he would like to read his play to the cast. If he jumps at the idea, it may be a good one. Otherwise probably not.

Reality

Reality in the theatre is a deeply subjective concept. Those things we perceive as being real or unreal are, undoubtedly, more appropriately defined by broader and more useful notions of **belief and believability**, but the term has a wide theatrical usage, so it needs some attention.

Let us leave aside those forms of theatre that create their own realities. The subjectively perceived worlds of Kabuki theatre or classical ballet can only be judged by those familiar with the codes of performance associated with their traditions.

Unless you work in a highly stylised form such as these, you will not have to invent your own performance reality or subscribe to a concept of reality you have inherited from others. Your touchstones for reality will rather be the world around you, how things are and the way people behave in real life.

There's the rub. Different people perceive real life differently. No two actors in your rehearsals will see the world in exactly the same way, even when they are working in a so-called **naturalistic** style. You must therefore be the discriminator. If your productions are to have any artistic cohesion, the characters created by the actors in them must all seem to belong to the same world, the same reality.

You will often hear actors describing their rehearsal experiences and processes in terms of reality or truth. 'This moment doesn't seem real.' 'I'm finding it very hard to be truthful here.' 'Can we talk about the reality of this situation?' As you watch rehearsals you will have similar reactions. An actor will make an entrance and the carefully crafted reality around him will suddenly fall to bits. He has come in at the wrong pace, or in a faulty rhythm; he has misunderstood an atmosphere or is playing in a more heightened style than his fellow actors. Whatever it is, you will be thinking, 'That just isn't real.' But it might not be any good saying so. Or you might say so and not be believed, or provoke disagreement or offence.

Whenever you find yourself in difficulties like these, explain to the actor, or actors, how you think the reality or truth of the scene ought to be reflected on stage. Talk about the character **motivation** or 'need' that you think they are overlooking. Refer them to a real-life situation that would be exactly commensurate with the scene. Ask them to imagine how they would react in that real place, at that real time with other real people around them. Their performances in rehearsal and on stage should be as much like the real-life version as possible.

A good test of reality is to challenge the actors to take their performances into the street, or at least to imagine doing so. Could their performances pass unnoticed on the tube, in the pub, in the supermarket, in church? If they are noticed, would passers-by, neutral observers, believe in the truth of the performance or would they assume the actors were just having a laugh? This is the acid test. Merely making the challenge is often enough to put your actors back on the right track. Imagination is a great thing in actors, and imagining their characters being true to life in real situations will help them to discover real behaviour to put in place of the unreal, truthful acting in place of untruthful.

Rehearsal Calls

The rehearsal call is the daily schedule detailing which actors are required to rehearse which scenes at what time. The call is published by the Stage Manager but is really the responsibility of the director. You can make yourself very popular with an acting company by taking this responsibility seriously and discharging it thoughtfully.

Rehearsal Calls

Nothing in theatre is more frustrating for actors than being kept waiting for long hours in rehearsal by a director who lacks the discipline to keep to the times of an existing call or is too lazy to make an accurate call in the first place.

The creation of a good call is an art in itself. The bigger the acting company and the more complex the play, the harder the call will be to create and subsequently adhere to, but a well-made call accurately observed will help you use everyone's talents to the full.

PARAMETERS AND LIMITATIONS

Before making your call consider the following points:

1 *The availability of your actors*

Not all actors are available at all times. Some will already be performing in another play and therefore be unavailable during evening and matinée performances. Others may have prior professional commitments of a minor nature – adverts, voice-overs, radio plays and the like. Or your own production may involve them in **costume** or wig fittings, publicity interviews or work sessions of one sort or another to help them with **dialect** or **choreography** or singing or the playing of instruments. Actors also have medical and dental appointments, crises with children, and births, marriages and deaths in the family. An awful lot of things can turn out to be a little more important than Act III Scene 2 happening on a Wednesday afternoon.

2 *The order of scenes*

You may have decided in advance that you can only rehearse the play in the order in which the scenes are written, especially on your first trawl through the play. The less strictly you need to observe this point, the easier will be your task in making up a coherent daily call.

3 *The availability of your other collaborators*

If scenes require a **Dialect Coach, choreographer, Fight Director** or

Musical Director, they will have their own non-availabilities to throw into the pot.

4 The availability of the space

Your rehearsal room may be unavailable to you at particular times, forcing you to shift to a space that can only accommodate small groups of people and therefore small scenes.

5 The distribution of parts

Most large parts have recurrent appearances throughout a play, but some quite important ones are only present at the beginning or the end. If you want all your actors to be working productively all the time you may have to jump around the play a little in order to keep them all on the boil.

6 The state of mind of the actors

Some actors need more attention than others. Some become nervous and frustrated if they are away from rehearsal too long. Others get overtired if they are required at all times. Ignoring a worried actor is never a good idea. Neither is overworking an exhausted one.

7 The frequency or recentness of previous rehearsals

When did you last rehearse that scene? When did you last rehearse that actor?

8 The need for repetition

Is there a particular actor or group of actors who would benefit from repetition rehearsal to help them commit a scene to memory? Complex movement, physically dangerous stunts, difficult choreography or anything outside the actors' normal expertise – dance scenes, singing scenes or fight scenes – all require more repetition than scenes involving simple spoken dialogue.

Rehearsal Calls

9 *Your own need to explore*

You may decide you need to revisit a particular scene because you directed it badly the first time. Or you may want to re-examine a relationship between characters in an early scene because of something discovered in a later. Or throw light for yourself on any aspect of the play or the production.

10 *The need to demonstrate to others*

A collaborator – a Musical Director or choreographer, a Costume Designer or Lighting Designer – might need to see a previously rehearsed scene in order to assess the appropriateness of their contribution.

MAKING A CALL

Once you have weighed your limitations, proceed to make the call – but make it coherently and realistically:

1 Divide the play into sensible rehearsal sections, chosen to reflect the scene structure and the presence of the actors within it. Don't call an actor for a whole rehearsal if he only arrives at the very end of a scene.
2 Don't cut the play up into tiny fragments. Give the actors and yourself the chance to work at decent-sized bites.
3 Leave sufficient time for long or difficult scenes. There's nothing worse than having to guillotine a crucial rehearsal just because it's lunchtime.
4 Don't schedule more than you can handle in one day because you 'must get through it all'. These are wishful-thinking calls: you want to get through it all, knowing if you're honest that you don't stand a chance, but you schedule the scenes anyway. Sure enough, you finish the day an hour or two behind schedule with a room full of frustrated actors and the feeling that you've let everybody down. The same actors will have to come back in the morning – and they will have a leery look in their eyes.

5 Actors always like to know as far as possible in advance when they will be needed for rehearsal, but they won't bully you about it. They will bully the Stage Manager, who will bully you. As far as possible, give your actors some idea of how their week is going to look and try to keep to the basic outline.

6 If you are working towards a rehearsal **run-through** (see **Running a Play**), warn the actors a few days in advance so they have a chance to get used to the idea.

Rehearsal Discipline

Rehearsal procedures will always differ, according to the methods of the director, the nature of the cast and the needs of the play, but there are some fundamental disciplines of rehearsal behaviour that should never vary, and anyone who sets foot in a rehearsal room should be aware of them and respect them.

PUNCTUALITY

There is nothing more destructive to a good atmosphere in rehearsal than an actor who is habitually late. 'The traffic was terrible,' 'My train was late,' 'I didn't get the call.' One of these in a week is annoying, with a whole cast kept waiting for an hour with nothing to do. Two is maddening. Three is grounds for dismissal. The lack of respect implicit in chronic lateness will inevitably express itself in performance. An actor who is constantly late for rehearsal is an actor who will be late for an entrance or late for curtain up.

SILENCE

The basic atmosphere of a rehearsal room should be one of respectful **silence**. Of course, the silence will be continually broken, by pre- and post-rehearsal gossip and laughter, by necessary breaks in concentration for jokes, anecdotes and irrelevant remarks, by the rehearsal text itself being spoken, shouted, whispered or sung, and by the ensuing discussions, debates and arguments about the meaning of the play and the motivation of the characters.

Nothing else should make any noise. Extraneous noise can be deeply disruptive to concentration and mood. Rehearsals are largely about finding order and meaning in an imagined world. Arbitrary and unwanted noise from outside that world can pull everyone out of it, sometimes quite destructively. So: all cellphones and beepers must be turned off, no whispering at the sides of the room or talking in the corridor just outside, no searching in noisy plastic bags. As soon as the room hits a concentrated state, everyone within it must observe the rule of the silence.

LINE LEARNING

At some point between the first day of rehearsal and the first performance all the lines in a play must be learnt, but not all actors learn their lines at the same pace. This can cause a great deal of grief. If by the last week of rehearsal all the actors but one are 'off the book', and that one still has a script in hand or is stumbling from line to line with constant prompts, the actors who have taken the trouble to learn their lines will lose patience very quickly. It is more than a courtesy for an actor to learn his lines at the same pace as the rest of the cast. It is a basic discipline.

Of course some actors have better **memories** than others, some find it very difficult to learn lines, some assert they have to learn their lines slowly as a necessary part of their character-building process. But in the end there isn't any excuse. They all have to know their lines by the first night, and leaving it to the last minute constitutes bad behaviour and may even result in an actor not being considered for a job in the future.

As the director, you may have to decide on a day of reckoning – an all-lines-to-be-learnt-by day – but a well-disciplined company of professionals won't need to be given a timetable.

Some directors solve this problem by demanding that all lines are learnt before the first day of rehearsal. While this might seem unnecessarily prescriptive and certainly foreign to many an actor's natural process, it has the virtue of even-handedness. Perhaps more importantly, it allows director and actors to use the time they would have spent groping around for the words far more productively in examining the meaning of the text and the **motivation** behind it. But then again, many actors would argue that groping is part of the process. Groping for words allows them to grope for meaning and motivation.

ALCOHOL

If you employ an alcoholic actor, there isn't much you can do to enforce discipline on him. You just have to hope that his need to be well thought of by his fellow actors will outweigh his reliance on the booze. The stable alcoholic, who knows his limits and has learnt to manage his habit, isn't much of a problem; it's the neurotic alcoholic, who uses drink as a way of allaying panic or unhappiness, who can cause serious disruption. In these cases, the drinking nearly always gets worse as the opening night gets closer.

The best way to react is to talk to the actor about his problem, or have the Stage Manager talk to him. Let him know that his drinking isn't a secret and that he has to control it. If he can't, then you must consider replacing him. An actor that comes back to rehearsal drunk in the wake of a liquid lunch is an actor that will walk on stage drunk in the wake of a liquid intermission.

SMOKING

The days of actors rehearsing with a script in one hand and a cigarette in the other are now officially over. Health and safety regulations all around the world are dictating a smoke-free environment for all, and quite right too. If you are one of those directors who can't think without a deep draw of nicotine, you must find some other form of intellectual stimulation. No one will put up with it any more.

Be aware, though, that long periods of nicotine-free rehearsal can play havoc with the attention spans of the seriously addicted. Know who your smokers are. They'll be the ones standing on the fire escape outside the rehearsal room puffing away, even in sub-zero temperatures. They will need more frequent breaks than the non-addicted. A serious smoker finds it very hard to go on concentrating for more than an hour without a nicotine break. And there's nothing you can do about that.

Rehearsal Periods

For every play there is a suitable period of rehearsal. Too short a rehearsal period will leave the actors unprepared when they first meet an audience. Too long a period will result in the actors being bored and frustrated and the rehearsal process turning in on itself and becoming over-analytical and artistically destructive.

Of course, there is a financial issue here. Rehearsals cost a lot of money before the play has earned a penny in revenue. Most producers, responsible for raising the money, have a strong financial interest in keeping the rehearsal period as short as possible without actually damaging the production's chance of success. Most, though not all, directors would rehearse for longer than is financially possible if given the chance.

10 QUESTIONS TO HELP YOU DETERMINE THE LENGTH OF A REHEARSAL PERIOD

1 How much money have you got?

That's how many weeks you can afford.

2 How long is the play?

The longer the play, the longer you will need.

3 How finished is the play?

Does your rehearsal period need to allow time for restructuring of scenes, rewriting of dialogue or **adaptation**?

4 How many hours a day will you rehearse?

In most Western countries there are strict **union** rules governing the hours that can be worked and the minimum periods of rest in between.

5 Is there a massive leading role in the play?

If so, then rehearsals can only proceed at the pace of the leading actor. Hamlet, Iago and Mother Courage have to learn their lines and moves at a pace they can manage.

6 How many actors are there in the play?

A large cast doesn't necessarily mean a long rehearsal period or a small cast a short one. In an 'ensemble play' with a large number of equal-sized roles, no one actor has to have a long development time because of the size of his part. In a play with only two or three characters, the opposite is the case.

7 What is the distribution of characters across the play?

In some plays the characters in the main plot overlap very little with those in the subplots. You can rehearse the different parts of the play at different times of the day without exhausting any one actor in the process. *You* may get exhausted but the rehearsal period will be shorter.

8 How difficult is the text to understand?

Do you need to allow time for the actors collectively to study the text before putting the rehearsal 'on its feet'?

9 How complicated is the action?

Are there fights or dances or complex bits of choreography or staging? It all takes time.

10 Are you doing a musical?

Before you can start rehearsing a musical drama, the singers must learn the score or you won't have anything to rehearse. Add an extra week.

Some directors insist on a long rehearsal period whatever the answers to the above questions might be. They may have a work process that requires a long and complicated **improvisation** process to create characters or story. They may be using the rehearsal process to discover whether there is a play to be performed at all. They may so hate the pressured world of deadlines and openings they can only be creative with an open-ended rehearsal schedule. But such directors can only work in this way by being heavily subsidised and backed by a strong artistic policy. Most directors will be happy, or be obliged to be happy, with a rehearsal period that is just long enough to achieve the following:

1 A reading and discussion of the play that gives the whole cast an understanding of its meaning.
2 A rough first staging of the whole play.
3 A rough stagger-through run of the play – optional though certainly advisable.
4 A second, more detailed work-through.
5 One or two runs in the rehearsal room.

And how long will that be? Only you can tell – by answering the ten questions above and then, equipped with the answers, deciding how quickly or how slowly you can or must work.

Rehearsal Rooms

A good rehearsal room has four essential elements: space, light, air and quiet.

SPACE

The floor area of a rehearsal room should be at least half as big again as the stage area which the show will eventually occupy. This will allow for a **mark-out** of the acting area with a good space in front of it where the director and stage management will sit to observe rehearsals, and where the actors can imagine an audience, and some space on either side of it to correspond with the 'wings' or offstage areas.

If the rehearsal space is cramped then some part of this balance will be compromised: either the director and stage management will have to sit on what will be the forestage, or the acting area will have to be crushed into a scaled-down version of itself. Cramping is dangerous, as actors get used to the dimensions of a space and are thrown when the stage space turns out to be on a very different scale. A small rehearsal room will encourage you and your actors to scale down your work to a correspondingly intimate scale, making subsequent projection into a large auditorium more difficult.

You may occasionally find yourself working in a space that is much too big for your play. Huge tracts of unused floor can look daunting in a rehearsal room and can create a feeling of unreality, especially with a very small company of actors. The **acoustic** can seem strange in such a space too, even when everything is reasonably audible. Try screening off the rehearsal area from the rest of the space and create a little tent of creativity in the surrounding desert.

LIGHT

Actors necessarily spend considerable periods of their working life in the darkness of theatres under strong beams of artificial light. To make them spend their daylight hours rehearsing in dark spaces under artificial light is cruel and unusual punishment indeed.

Some new theatres, built in the last few decades by architects whose sense of natural human life and scale would seem to have been removed at birth or bred out of them by the dehumanising strictures of their Brutalist training, have been specially provided with rehearsal rooms buried deep in the earth beyond the sounding of any plummet. Do not ever be tempted to rehearse in such a space. You will be forced to work under fluorescent light of one sort or another, specially designed to oscillate at a rate guaranteed to drive you and the actors blind-mad and make coherent thought impossible after two or three hours of continuous concentration. If you have no option but to work in one of these architectural dungeons then you must reckon on having a maximum of three hours' productive work a day before your entire team is rendered stupid by its surroundings.

Rehearsal Rooms

Of course, the architect who designed such a space would never dream of working in these conditions himself. He would regard natural light as a prerequisite for a natural creative process, and so must you. You and the actors are holding a mirror up to nature, and if there is no natural environment you will probably end up with nothing to show in your mirror.

If your space has some natural light but supplementary overhead fluorescent lighting, there is still a danger of daily concentration burn-out. Fluorescent light also flattens everything out visually, turning all in its path to a uniform grey. A good antidote to this is to place a few incandescent stage lights around the rehearsal space, not necessarily pointing at the actors as this will make them feel they are prematurely on stage, but directed at the walls or up to the ceiling. These extra sources of light will give the space a much more rounded and relaxing feel and will considerably lengthen everyone's daily concentration span.

But of course daylight is what you need, and lots of it. The best rehearsal rooms have windows on at least one wall, but preferably two or even three, flooding the space with strong sources of natural light. Skylights are also a good source, though on their own they tend to provide a rather flat light.

AIR

When rehearsal spaces are built without natural light they are invariably airless too, or rely on air-conditioning systems that pump you God knows what recycled rubbish. The same mental health warnings apply to airlessness as to lightlessness, and a plague on the architects who design them so.

But a well-lit rehearsal space with an abundance of windows can, especially in a modern plate-glass building, be as airless as a tomb, as the windows are often sealed shut. Try to avoid rehearsing in such spaces if you can, or find a way of cracking open the windows. If you want good, clear thoughts running through your and your actors' heads then good, clean air is an essential ingredient to the atmosphere in which you work.

QUIET

A rehearsal room may be airy and light and spacious and still be an impossible place to work because of a noisy local environment or a lousy acoustic. It's no use being able to open a window if there's a main-line railway track running just outside it. Luckily most noisy social activity happens outside normal rehearsal hours, but if you plan evening rehearsals then raucous local pubs and clubs, jubilant choir practice from the upstairs room or the roar of the local foot-ball stadium can be serious noisemakers. Check out the neighbour-hood for obvious problems before you sign up to a particular space.

Whatever the local environment, noise from outside the rehears-al space can be less disrupting than noise from within. If the acoustic in the room is highly resonant and echo-y it will be diffi-cult enough for you to hear the actors' words, but they will be fur-ther plagued by having to compete with every other noise in the room, however slight. A cough or a whispered comment or the noise of a quietly opened door will bounce around the room, mak-ing onlookers feel they are sitting at the centre of the action. You can sometimes address such a difficulty by erecting acoustic baffles of one sort or another. Thick velour curtains hung from the walls or, in a room with a vaulted ceiling, canopied over the space, will often improve the acoustic quite radically, but some rooms are pretty much impossible whatever you do to them. In such spaces you have to have a rigorous discipline about extraneous noise, only those utterly attentive to the rehearsal being allowed to sit in the room and the stage management communicating entirely by sign language and written notes, a silent craft they should have at their fingertips anyway.

MAKING THE BEST OF IT

In reality, of course, you may have no choice whatever about the rehearsal space in which you have to work. Repertory theatres often have their own rehearsal rooms attached, or ones they habit-ually use nearby, and are unable or unwilling to afford the expense of hiring an alternative space. Commercial producers sometimes have long-standing deals with particular rehearsal studios from which they are unwilling to deviate. So you must get used to the idea of making the best of whatever space you find yourself in. If any of the four essential conditions above are seriously lacking, then you must make whatever adjustments you can to make things better. In spaces without natural air or light you should take more frequent breaks than you would normally consider necessary, so that you and your actors can be regularly sprung from your dungeon. And for spaces that are too big or too small or where there are unhelpful acoustics, don't feel embarrassed about asking your producer or your stage management team for help in solving the problems. The quality of your time in rehearsals is crucial to the success of the whole enterprise and a good supporting team will be sympathetic to any reasonable requests for a betterment of conditions.

LAYING OUT THE REHEARSAL ROOM

Once your rehearsal room has been chosen, whether by you or for you, there are still some important decisions for you to make concerning the layout of the room and how you work within it, the most important being the direction in which the actors will play. There are two considerations here: the direction of the light source in the room and the position of the access door or doors.

If there is a dominant light source, it should shine onto the acting space from the direction of the audience, or from one side of the stage. You should be watching the action with the strong light source coming from behind or from one side, never with it shining in your face. You will find it a terrible strain directing a play with more of the light shining towards you than on the actors' faces.

If there are mirrors in the room, as there often are in professional rehearsal spaces, cover them up. Some actors can't resist looking at themselves, and mirrors are too great a temptation. Unless you are doing a dance musical where mirrors are necessary for the 'spotting' of moves, you want your performers to concentrate on one another, not on the image of their own developing performances.

The access doors into the rehearsal space should not lead directly onto the acting area, or into any part of the room that would create a distraction during rehearsals. If there is more than one access door, it is a good idea to use only one, making any others out of bounds, so that a routine is established for entering and leaving the room. It's also a good idea to put a screen in front of the access door a few feet inside the rehearsal room, creating a sort of visual airlock for anyone coming in and out and baffling any noise the door itself might make.

Once the orientation of the room has been decided, you must also allocate how much of the room will be used for the acting area or **mark-out** of the stage and how much for yourself and the stage management team and the observing actors and other creative staff.

You will often have to fit a large stage playing area into a small rehearsal space. Be careful how you do this. Even if it means losing a lot of the upstage area, make sure there is plenty of space between the notional edge of the stage and where you will be sitting. You don't want to be sitting squeezed up against a wall with the actors playing two or three feet in front of you. You need distance to see what you and they are doing, and they need space in front of them to act into, a space in which they can imagine an audience. You can make your spatial economies in the upstage areas and at the sides of the stage where it is easy for actors to imagine that a few square feet is half an acre of space.

Make yourself happy with the layout of your rehearsal room and make everyone else happy to be in it with you. Don't compromise on this. If anything feels wrong in the way you have laid out the room, then change it. You must wear your rehearsal room like a familiar suit of clothes. Nothing must be allowed to itch or scratch or flap around the ankles. If you're uncomfortable, everyone else will feel it.

REHEARSING ON STAGE

You will on occasion be offered a stage to rehearse on, usually the stage for which your show is bound. Indeed, in some theatre companies rehearsal is conducted on stage as a matter of routine. Beware of this. A stage is not the best space for the quiet dissection of the meaning of a play or experimentation with its physical or emotional landscape. An auditorium of empty seats acts as a kind of rebuke. It seems to be saying, 'Talk all you like, experiment as you will, you don't have much time do you? These seats are waiting for an audience and they can't hear you, they don't think you're funny and the last time they saw this play they liked it much better.'

Actors rarely rehearse well on stage. Their performing instincts click into action and they start playing everything out towards the empty seats, ignoring the essential investigations of character and motive that make rehearsing a play such a pleasure. If you cut off the auditorium from the stage by lowering the **iron**, you create a claustrophobic space dominated by a threatening blank wall where an audience ought to be. Stay in the rehearsal room for as long as you can. And fear the producer Greeks bearing the gift of free time on stage.

Occasionally, in the middle of a rehearsal process, you may start to be concerned about the eventual audibility of your actors when they finally get on stage, especially when the rehearsal room is small and the theatre large and the actors' performances show signs of being introverted and exclusive. An hour on stage at such a point can prove very helpful, reminding the actors of the size of the space they must eventually inhabit and the vocal and emotional energy required to reach every seat in the house. But don't overdo it. Return to the rehearsal room as soon as the point has been practically made and use the experience as a reference point thereafter.

Rehearsal Technique

The preparations for a production start long before rehearsals begin and the run of a play continues, you hope, long after they have finished, but the rehearsal room is where your work will have its greatest value. This is the proving ground for the quality of your ideas, choices and skills. Whoever you have chosen to work with, whatever the piece you are working on, however clever you are, or well prepared or confident, you are now at the helm of the creative ship and your job is to sail it safely into harbour.

Every department of the theatre will look to you for guidance and you must be ready to meet every expectation thrown at you, but your most important charges in rehearsal are the actors, and their expectations will monopolise most of your time and energy.

14 THINGS THE ACTORS HAVE A RIGHT TO EXPECT FROM YOU

1 An understanding of the meaning of the play and why the author wrote it.
2 An explanation of the appropriateness of your production of the play and its design.
3 A description of the historical and social background of the play.
4 An insight into each one of the characters they are playing.
5 An analysis of the relationship between the characters.
6 A respect for each actor's personality and method, even when you require them to adopt a directorial method of your own.
7 An atmosphere of creativity, friendship and good humour.
8 An individual care that inspires confidence and daring.
9 A right to experiment and fail without censure or embarrassment.
10 A schedule of rehearsal calls that minimises the frustration of wasted time.
11 Sufficient rehearsal time for the practice and repetition of all that has been achieved.
12 Adequate free time to assimilate and consider all that is being achieved.
13 Protection from arbitrary or pointless decisions involving staging or design.
14 The power to take over control of the play from you by the time it opens.

Rehearsal Technique

As well as your own duty towards the actors you will also be ultimately responsible for the way they are supported by the **stage management** team. A good Stage Manager will usually protect you from any direct involvement with these issues, but you had better be prepared all the same in case anything goes wrong. If you have a good relationship with your actors they will tend to appeal to you for help with any grievance they might have or for any shortcomings they perceive in other departments.

10 THINGS THE ACTORS HAVE A RIGHT TO EXPECT FROM STAGE MANAGEMENT

1 Clear and efficient rehearsal calls with as much detail and notice as possible. Actors have lives as well as jobs.
2 The proper observance of statutory rehearsal hours and breaks.
3 Protection from any infringement by the director, whether witting or not, of the statutory rehearsal times.
4 A clearly marked-out floor indicating the stage layout, the position of all major scenic pieces, and the furniture settings for individual scenes.
5 An adequate supply of rehearsal scenery, furniture and **props**. Everything that will eventually appear on stage must be represented by a version of itself in rehearsal.
6 Access to the use of rehearsal **costumes** when necessary or requested.
7 An accurate record of previous rehearsal positions and moves for easy reference at subsequent rehearsals.
8 A discreet but firm indication when the text has been mis-learnt or is being incorrectly spoken.
9 Clearly audible **prompts** when required.
10 A sympathetic understanding of the personal circumstances and foibles of each actor.

No two directors work in quite the same way, but there are still some general rules of engagement for directors in rehearsal that you would do well to acknowledge before deciding to infringe.

8 RULES OF ENGAGEMENT FOR DIRECTORS IN REHEARSAL

1 *Avoid the first person singular*

A director who constantly refers to 'I' and 'Me' is likely to create resentment. Learn to say 'We' instead of 'I' wherever possible. Don't say 'That's not what I want.' Say 'What I think we should try is . . .'

2 *Never raise your voice*

If an unruly rehearsal room needs to be quietened, or attention demanded, ask a member of stage management to call order for you. You can't skip lightly from the role of screaming slave-driver to that of quiet philosopher without losing your authority as both.

3 *Be sensitive to the actors as people*

Actors feel and think as private people. They are not automata. What is happening in their lives will have a significant effect on how they behave in rehearsal and on stage.

4 *Treat the actors as themselves*

In other words, not as their characters. Never, never, never call an actor by the name of his character nor let anyone else do so. It sounds and is lazy and betrays a lack of interest in the actor as an artist.

5 *Be collaborative, not dismissive*

Never dismiss an actor's questions or refuse to respond to his view. An actor will hear 'It's just the way I see it' as 'Just do as you're told.' Actors are your co-conspirators. Whether you agree with their views or disagree, their opinions about the characters and the play are part of the raw material of rehearsal.

6 *Listen before you instruct*

React to what an actor gives you in his performance before demanding something else from him. An actor who has been frustrated in making a point or demonstrating a wish will be unlikely to treat a contrary direction with any sympathy.

7 'No' is not enough

If you disagree with an actor's view or choice, don't be frightened to say so, but give a full explanation of why. Don't say 'No' when you can say 'Yes, but . . .' If you have to say 'No', say 'No, because . . .'

8 Wear your authority lightly

Don't feel you have to control every moment of time in the rehearsal room. Dare to be silent. There is no better creative sound than the silence of actors thinking. But they will never be able to think creatively in the rehearsal room if the air is dominated by your talk. A constant stream of controlling talk is a sign of creative and intellectual weakness. Properly motivated, the actors will do some of your most creative thinking for you. Don't be so noisy and assertive that you can't hear and appreciate their contribution. A creative silence is never empty. If a silence in the rehearsal room causes you panic and embarrassment, then you've been talking too much up to that moment.

Rehearsing a Play

There is no prescription for how to rehearse a play. One can only talk about what is customary, or appropriate or preferred. Directors have their different methods and theatre companies their different traditions. Every play makes different demands and every group of actors is idiosyncratic. You must decide how to proceed with your rehearsals based on your own instincts for what is right and on how you use your **rehearsal technique**.

The following description of a rehearsal period is therefore an indication, a rough plan of action that you must feel free to adopt, or adapt or reject as you see fit. It is, inevitably, based on my own experience, technique and temperament. If it doesn't suit you, or if any of it proves impossible to put into practice, you must invent your own solutions as you go.

DAY ONE

To say you do such and such a thing on day one, and something else on day two, and then move on to this, that or the other by the end of the week, would be presumptuous. No two professional directors would ever agree on a single minute of any of it. I will only describe what is customary in certain conventional circumstances, so you can decide for yourself whether to abide by the custom, diverge from it, or that it doesn't in any event apply to you.

It is customary in some theatre companies to invite all the departments of the theatre to a 'meet and greet' on the first day of rehearsal, so that the cast and the **creative team** can be introduced to the rest of the theatre staff and be able to identify them thereafter – but you might not have other 'departments' to introduce your cast to, or you might be rehearsing miles away from their workplaces, making it impractical for them to join you, or you might decide this isn't the way you want to start your first day of rehearsal.

It is customary for you and your designer or designers to show the **model** of the set and the **costume designs** to the cast and the rest of the creative team, so that everyone in the company is up to speed on what the production will look like when it gets into the theatre. If you choose to do this, it might be appropriate to take half an hour to explain what led you and your designers to make the decisions that are manifest in the model and the costume drawings. Even if you decide not to do this on the first day, don't leave it too long before you share with your cast as much of your pre-production thinking as you can. They are the ones who have to play on the set and wear the costumes, and if your design ideas are in any way unconventional, you really do owe them an explanation and perhaps even some reassurance.

It is customary to have a **read-through** of the play on the first day, but this is not always appropriate, many directors preferring to start their rehearsals with theatre **games** or **improvisations** or research, leaving the read-through until later in the week, or spreading it over more than one day as a sort of extended seminar on the play, or not having one at all.

NAMES

Actors' professional names are not necessarily the names they go by in private. Some actors will have changed their names to comply with Equity's quite sensible rule that no two actors should trade under the same name. Some may have chosen a stage name too grand for daily use. Some may like to be called by a nickname. Others will be irritated by a nickname unbidden.

Unless you work for a permanent ensemble of actors, your rehearsals for a new production will generally start with a room full of nervous strangers with no one actor knowing everyone else's name. In a big production you may not even know all the names yourself.

Sometime in the first couple of days of rehearsal, once the initial hysteria has died down, ask your company what names they prefer to be called by. Once actors have overcome their nervousness they start to get curious about their colleagues and annoyed with themselves that they can't remember all the names in the room. Most actors enjoy talking about themselves and will relish the opportunity to tell the story of their name if there is one. A name described by the face that owns it is hard to forget.

If someone doesn't know what he wants to be called, find out what his mother calls him and use that.

WEEK ONE

Once you have got the first day of rehearsal out of the way, how you proceed with the next few days greatly depends on the sort of play you are doing. If you are working in a performance style that requires a lot of imaginative input from your cast, this is the best time to set up improvisations to help them on their way. For instance, you might have an adult cast all playing children, or a play set in an insane asylum, or a huge sprawling story in which only a few actors have to play dozens of characters, or any play that is set in a world very distant from the actors' own experience. In all these cases, the improvisations that will inform the way the text is finally performed are best done before the actors start to make specific acting choices. With improvisation, the cleaner the slate the more vivid the final picture will be.

In a play with a large population of subsidiary characters, you may even decide to use improvisation and **workshop** techniques in the **casting** process. If you do this, try to keep things as democratic as you can. Actors don't like to feel they are being auditioned within the rehearsal process. It's hard enough getting cast in the first place.

Improvisation might not be part of your plan at all. If it isn't and you see no use for it in your production, you are not obliged to do it. Improvisation is not a virtue, it is a means to an end.

You may decide that you want your entire cast to analyse the whole play together. This is especially appropriate if you are working on a text that contains complex **heightened language** governed by the rules of **metre,** or one that has a tangle of difficult ideas.

In order for the whole cast to understand the author's meaning they must learn to speak his 'language', and many of the linguistic or intellectual devices he uses in writing one character will be deployed in exactly the same way on all the others. By having the cast come to a collective understanding of the author's style your production will gain in intellectual rigour and emotional depth. On a practical note, you will also save yourself having to repeat the same set of instructions about the language or the ideas and themes in the play to different actors on different days of your subsequent rehearsals.

This 'extended seminar' method of reading a play is best done with the cast sitting at tables arranged in a square or circle so that the actors can take notes in comfort, and there is no pretence that the process will be a quick one. The tables say, 'We're going to be sitting here for a couple of days at least, so get used to it.' Go through the play with a fine-tooth comb, the actors reading their parts slowly and thoroughly. Stop if anyone in the company has a question about anything in the text. Let your maxim be: 'There is no such thing as a stupid question.' When a question arises about a character, let the actor who is playing the character lead with the answer before letting others speak, or pronouncing on it yourself. The actor's instinct about the answer to a question is often very important, whether it is right or wrong. Sometimes a misconception about the text will be instructive when looking at other similar places in the play. Again, let the process be as democratic as possible. The whole cast must understand the play, so the whole cast is responsible for finding out the answers to all its questions.

This is the time when devotees of **actioning** will also want to deploy their skills, though if you don't know what you're doing in this most pernickety of analytical methods, you should tread warily. Actors can be short of patience if they think you don't know what you're doing. Being trained in the analysis of human behaviour, they are acute detectors of bullshit.

The seminar approach is greatly helped by the introduction of back-up material in the form of research books, maps, fine art, photographs, social histories, biographies and anything else that seems relevant to the study of the play, or its period, or the life and thinking of its author. Build up a library from whatever sources you can, your own books or any the cast might have, local libraries or the internet. Books can be studied by the actors in rehearsal or taken home and read at greater leisure. Maps and illustrations can adorn the walls. Surround yourselves with the world of the author so that everyone can breathe in as much of it as they can.

You can also use the company itself to **research the play**. Give members of the company research projects, with a deadline for reporting their discoveries and a time limit for their subsequent talks.

The seminar process may also reveal areas of ignorance that can only be illuminated by a real expert in the field. Think about whom you might call in to supply the need. Are you doing a play about nuclear physics, or senile dementia or the Russian revolution? Get a nuclear physicist or a psychiatrist or a historian to talk to you about it. And the same for any subject that is beyond your powers of understanding or area of expertise.

In plays that require a special physical life from the actors, an outside expert can bring in the exercises and disciplines they will need in performance; a sergeant major to drill a cast of soldiers or a coach for footballers or a mountaineer for an Everest play. Whatever you need to know, there is usually an expert only too pleased to help, for a little cash in hand, for tickets to the first night or for the acquaintanceship of actors.

However long the study process takes, don't let it dominate the whole of the first week or the actors will start to be restless. Have an end in sight and stick to your deadlines for completing this part of the work. If you are still sitting round a table at the end of the first week, you're a college not a theatre company.

It will help to know that you don't have to answer all questions definitively. Many answers will only present themselves empirically as you clash the interests of one character with another on the rehearsal floor.

This is also a good moment to decide on any major **cuts** in the text. If the play is a very long one, or you have cuts to make for structural reasons, they are best put in early, before the actors start learning the text. Late cutting drives actors crazy. If you know you have to make cuts, but are unsure where they should go, it is sensible to involve the actors in the cutting process and there is no better time to do this than when you are slowly working through the play, analysing the language and examining the structure of the story.

PUTTING THE PLAY ON ITS FEET

Unless you are blessed, or cursed, with an extremely long **rehearsal period**, it is unwise to finish your first week's work without at least starting to put the play on its feet. If you go into your first weekend without having done any physical work at all, the actors will start to get anxious, some of them perhaps mutinously so.

The transition from reading and discussion to outright rehearsal is always an awkward one, but the longer you leave it the more awkward it gets. You can discuss the play for ever and create the perfect production in everyone's imagination but the problems you will encounter on the floor of the **rehearsal room** with the actors engaging their bodies and faces and voices as well as their minds are in many ways undiscussable, only to be solved with practical and pragmatic techniques, informed by the intellectual process but not defined by it.

Dive straight in. The water is never as cold as you think. Clear away the tables and chairs and start to inhabit the whole room. You will already have instructed the stage management how you want the room oriented and how much of a **mark-out** is necessary. There may be rostra set up to indicate raised areas of the stage, or ladders for higher vantage points. There may be a rehearsal **rake** or **sprung floor** if your production demands them. There may be racks of rehearsal **costumes** and tables of rehearsal **props**.

Explain the mark-out to the actors and how the dimensions of the rehearsal room accord to the shape of the stage they will play on. You will often be rehearsing in a room that is significantly smaller than the stage set. If this is the case, show the actors how you have economised on space, where they are notionally 'in the wings' and where all the entrances and exits are. Pay special attention to the relationship between the marked-out front of the stage and the first row of the **auditorium** and to any associated **sightline** problems.

Unless you have a compelling reason for not doing so, you should start at the top of the play and work through the scenes in order. The characters of a play gain their knowledge of themselves and one another as the events of their lives unfold, just as we do in real life. Investigating these events out of their natural chronological order can be confusing for the actors in terms of **motivation** and character development.

Set the scene for the actors. Talk about where the characters are, the time of day or night and the weather conditions. Describe the architecture if any, its age, style and atmosphere. Discuss with the actors where their characters have just come from – physically, emotionally and spiritually – in their lives generally and on that day in particular. Talk about any prior relationships between the characters. How long have they known one another and in what circumstances? As far as possible base your suppositions on textual evidence, but be ready to supply imaginative supplements where the text is vague.

Place any furniture or other temporary features there might be in the first scene, but don't be too fussy about it. You'll probably want to change the positions later, or add different elements, or get rid of things altogether.

Decide whether the characters are to be discovered on stage as the play begins or if the audience is to see the setting first without any characters on it. If the latter, then where will the characters enter from? These opening images of a play are very important and the impact they make should stay with the audience all through the evening. You need to get them right. If you don't have a strong idea about what your opening image should be, don't waste a lot of time looking for one at this stage. An opening image, or sequence of images, could very well occur to you as you are working through the rest of the play. Sometimes the most enduring images succeed so well because they are thematically linked with images that recur elsewhere.

Once the actors start working through the scene itself, it is often a good idea to run the whole scene without interruption, warts and all. This will give you and the actors a sense of the task to be accomplished and stop you getting too bogged down in detail before you've properly begun. It can be a little painful watching the actors stumbling through without any practice or supervision, but it's nearly always worth it, and if everybody knows it's just a means to an end, they won't be too embarrassed by their insufficiencies.

Once you've run through the scene, start from the top again, this time working slowly and thoroughly. Unless you are bound by tradition or lack of imagination to the constricting technique known as **blocking**, you should not feel obliged to tell the actors exactly where they have to move or stand or sit. You, and they, must take account of the basic rules of **staging** that govern the physical disposition of the actors on the stage and their relationship to one another and to the audience, but you will alienate the actors and disable their judgements if you try to dictate how those rules should be applied.

Let the discovery of appropriate moves and staging positions come out of a dialogue between you and your cast. You might propose an idea for a move or a position; you might even insist that your idea is so good it must be tried. If it succeeds it might well become a permanent feature of the production, but don't let it be the only idea. Try others, and let your first thought give way to a better one if it proposes itself. If an actor has a strong antipathy to a move, understand what it might be based on. If the antipathy is groundless, argue against it, but if reasonable, accommodate it into your thinking. If an actor has an idea that is born of a strong acting instinct, try it out. See how it accords with the feelings and ideas of the other actors.

If an actor raises an important question about his character or any other character, take time to discuss it. If the question raises other questions of even greater importance, it means you haven't yet discussed the scene thoroughly enough. If this is the case, don't brush the issue under the carpet. Sit down and talk it through. The more unanswered questions there are, the less likely you will be to find a positive staging solution to the scene. Actors are always looking for certainty. A lack of certainty in the background and motivation of their characters makes it difficult for them to function properly as actors. Without it, they will flounder about or resort to generalisation. Once they are certain, they can relax and make their certainties seem like natural and spontaneous character choices. But if you, or they, can't answer all questions about character immediately, don't jump to unwarrantable conclusions in the search for instant answers. Know that if you go on working through the play calmly and thoroughly, answers will present themselves, or your imaginations will supply answers for the empty spaces that remain.

Some actors are great talkers. They would rather theorise about a scene than actually rehearse it. Don't let their curiosity or verbosity control the rehearsal. Be ready to guillotine a discussion that seems to be going round in circles. And don't talk too much yourself. A director that talks and talks and never gets the rehearsal under way will soon have the actors rolling their eyes at one another in frustration. Develop an instinct for knowing when enough discussion is enough. An apparent Gordian knot of rehearsal discussion can often be sliced through quite easily by running the scene once more or by applying a bit of gentle improvisation to it.

Try to create an atmosphere where everyone has an equal right to express an opinion or to try an option. Let there be a pool or well of imagination that everyone feels free to draw from. Let there be no ego involved in the adoption or rejection of staging ideas, especially your own.

As you progress through the scene it will become more and more apparent to you whether or not you have chosen the correct environment for the action and the correct staging to fit the environment. The more experienced you are the more you will be able to sense this as a natural 'rightness' of the choices you have made. If they are right it will be because they feel right. A less experienced director should monitor his choices against the general rules of staging that apply to most scenes in most plays.

Be constantly aware of the **stage pictures** you are creating as you proceed with the scene, the overall picture of the scene and the moment-to-moment changes you are making to the basic image. Think how the actors will appear to the audience when they finally get onto the stage. Have further back in your mind how the Lighting Designer will light them and the stage around them, and which parts of the stage will be comparatively dark.

As you watch the scene develop, ask yourself some questions. Is everyone visible who should be visible? Is anyone **upstaged** at a vital moment of the scene? Is anyone hogging the focus of the scene who should be more peripheral, or anyone peripheral who should be better focused? Is the movement in the scene taking good account of its rhythm? And so on. Let the scene tell you how to direct it.

If things don't go as you expected and the scene proves intractable or the actors feel uncomfortable within it, be ready to acknowledge that what you thought was a good initial set-up has been proved by rehearsal to be less than ideal. When this happens, you have to make a quick decision. Is what you have noticed an easy fix? Can you make instant changes to the set pieces or the furniture settings and ask the actors to map through the scene from the start, taking account of the changes? Or does what you have discovered mean a complete rethink of the scene? If so, would it not be better to carry on with the staging as it is, all the way to the end of the scene, and have a think about alternative solutions when you have more time? You can always come back to the scene on another day with a fresh solution that takes account of everything you have learnt. Never try to fix something in a panic. You'll probably end up with an even worse solution than the one you are in the process of rejecting.

Once you have finished working through the scene, don't move on until you have run it through once more without a break, even if the actors are tired and you really should be breaking for lunch or for the end of the day. This will make it much easier for them to recall the moves of the scene when you come back to it in a week or so's time. Without a run to cement the work done, the moves and the positions can easily slip out of their minds. A run will also give you an overview of the value of the work you have done and tell you how much more will need to be achieved. Sometimes a scene you thought was going very well looks thin when it is run. Conversely, a scene that gave you a lot of trouble as you were working it through can suddenly play itself out very nicely.

Learn when it is time to move on from a scene, even when it is quite clear that you haven't solved everything in it. Nothing will be perfect at first, and you should be suspicious if it is. The easiest solutions are often the ones that make least demands on the actors' imaginations. Actors take time to mature into their characters and all the other scenes in the play will eventually inform the scene you have been working on.

ACTORS AND THE TEXT

A great deal of your work-through time will be taken up with explaining to the actors what you think their text means, or negotiating with them a meaning you can both agree on. In other words, every line of the play has to be interpreted, or 'read' in a way that seems appropriate to the scene in which it occurs.

The 'reading' of a line is comprised of a variety of different and sometimes conflicting ingredients. The line was written by an author who means something by it, and is spoken by a character who also means something by it. You would expect these two intentions to tend towards the same conclusion but they don't always do so. The actor might have a strong interpretation of his character that seems to you to be at odds with what the author or his character is trying to say, or you yourself might have an interpretation of the line that the actor feels is at odds with the author's meaning or with the actor's interpretation of it. On top of this the character has a motive for saying the line that is informed by a set of needs engendered by the story of the play. He also has an attitude of mind that informs the motivation, and a character history that informs his attitude of mind. There is a great deal here that has to be agreed upon before the interpretation of a line can be settled between director and actor. And once the reading of a line seems to be settled, it then has to be spoken to another character, played by another actor, who will in turn interpret how to hear the line in order to respond to it, adding another interpretation to the mix.

Some lines are spoken incorrectly because the actor has simply misunderstood the meaning of the line or the way the line should be inflected to make it sound sensible. This is an easy fix. Much harder is when the actor has chosen a motivation for his character that doesn't make sense in terms of the other characters or the basic **reality** of the scene. Here you will have to argue the logic of your position, why you think your interpretation of the line is the right one and what impact his interpretation and yours will have on the other characters and the scene at large. Ego may come into play here. Some actors become defensive if they feel they are being made to look foolish in front of the rest of the cast and will dig their heels in over an interpretation rather than back down.

However you choose to communicate your feelings about the text to the actors you should try as far as possible to avoid using **line readings**. This is lazy directing. It can also be extremely counter-productive. There are dozens of ways of delivering any one line of dialogue even when the motivation behind the line is broadly the same for each delivery. The way an actor chooses to deliver a line will nearly always be more inventive and more right for that actor than the director's delivery. But if the actor has the director's inflection ringing in his ears he will find it all the harder to invent one for himself.

If an actor struggles with a line, be patient. Find the words to explain what you think are the thoughts or feelings within the line, or what is the **subtext** of the line, the fundamental **motivation** or 'want' of the character at that moment in the scene. If you give the actor enough background, the line should end up saying itself, for both of you.

ACTORS' MOVES

The physical equivalent of the line reading is the demonstration. Try to explain the physical moves you think might be appropriate without stepping into the actors' shoes and demonstrating them yourself. Actors get very uneasy when directors do this. It feels like you're trying to steal their character from them. If you do it well, the actor will feel intimidated, unhappy about looking incompetent in comparison with you. If, as is far more likely, you do it badly, you will disable the actor's own physical judgement and make yourself look foolish into the bargain.

Let the actor find the move by trying his own different solutions. You can help him by thinking as his character is thinking. Directors who have been actors will find this a quite natural process. Let the characters tell you how the actors should be moving on their behalf. Feel the moves in your body but don't then demonstrate them physically. Use your kinetic knowledge to inform the discussions you have with the actor who owns the role.

Moves are an expression of character and must therefore develop as the character develops. Keep experimenting with the moves until they seem equally natural to characters and actors alike.

THE ACTOR'S PROCESS

If it is nearly always a bad idea to read a line to an actor or to demonstrate a move, it is because by doing so you interfere with his process. The actor is becoming his character and he must be allowed to do it in his own way. A simple rule to follow in your relationship to this process is the 'What and Why but never How' rule.

You can talk to the actors as much as you like about the What, that is, what you think their character might be feeling or thinking, and the Why, why they might be feeling or thinking it. These are a proper part of your process as director, as interpreter of the author's intention to the actor. What you should avoid is the How, how a feeling or a thought ought to manifest itself in the actor's performance. By concerning yourself with the How, you are pre-empting the actor's process, perhaps even disempowering him from exercising it.

Thus it is quite proper for you to say that you think a character would be restless at a certain point in a scene, or angry or regretful or sad. This is the What.

Quite proper too to explain the Why. Why is the character restless, angry, regretful or sad?

What is improper is to take the next step for the actor, to say the restless character should be pacing up and down the room or biting his nails, the angry one slamming his fist on the table or banging the door as he leaves the stage, the regretful one glancing anxiously at one of the other characters, the sad one crying. This is not part of your process. It belongs to the actors and to them alone. There are dozens, hundreds, thousands of ways to express restlessness, anger, regret and sadness and all other manifestations of human behaviour. Each actor has a well of these behaviours that he draws on, the better the actor the deeper the well. And for each character the actor plays there are appropriate behaviours, manifestations of feeling and thought that suit the character and the scene, the place and time that the character finds himself in. However good you are as a director, you will never be able to guess in advance what will be the most appropriate and exciting choices for your actors to make, far less be able to demonstrate to them what those choices should be. Once they have chosen for themselves, drawn from their wells of experience and skill, then you can help them select the best choice, edit, arrange, control and focus. But the original choice, the How, must be theirs and not yours.

If you follow this rule, investigating the What and the Why to their fullest extent, but leaving the How to the actor, you will see restlessness, anger, regret and sadness and all the rest of it painted in ways you could never have conceived of. You will honour your actors and their process and with the best actors, you will be rewarded by witnessing the human mind and heart being played with all their myriad subtleties intact.

SCRIPTS IN HAND

One thing that will stop you and your actors getting ahead of yourselves is the fact that most of them will be holding scripts in their hands as they work through the play for the first time.

Some directors find it hard to work with actors that are physically constrained in this way. They insist that actors are 'off the book' from day one, as a basic **rehearsal discipline**. But this isn't always practical. Your busiest actors may be coming directly from previous jobs and have no time for learning lines in advance, or no aptitude for learning a new part while the old one is still taking up so much of their concentration.

Some actors find it hard to work without scripts in hand, relying on them as aids to thinking, making notes in the margins as they work, underlining words and drawing circles and arrows all over the text to explain the grammar and the imagery to themselves and indicate what their moves and positions are.

Many actors also find it hard to learn their lines when out of the rehearsal context. They rely on marrying their moves and positions with their lines for the lines to mean anything to them. Of course some actors are just lazy, but some really do have problems with cold line learning.

Whatever their preference, get the actors to abandon their scripts as soon as they possibly can. A held script stops the actor from using his hands as the character would use them. The sooner the character can be freed to use his hands naturally, the better.

A correlative problem is that many actors need glasses to read their scripts, adding another temporary prop for their character to deal with. Glasses can also give the actor a focus problem. When not looking at the script, does he look at his fellow actors with glasses on or off? If it's an older actor and the glasses are only for reading, can he even see the other actors with his glasses on? If he can't, then his glasses have to be constantly transferred from nose to pocket and back, or perch on top of his head, or dangle from a chain around his neck. With a script in one hand, glasses in the other and a pencil behind his ear, an actor can become a veritable twitch of mannerisms before he's even begun to understand his role.

Learning lines apart, myopic actors must still decide at what point in rehearsal to abandon their glasses or replace them with contact lenses. You should encourage them to do this early on in the rehearsal process. Actors used to very strong lenses often look rather weird without them, their eyes seeming blank and a little fuzzy as they search around the stage for some semblance of eye contact with their fellow actors. Contact lenses can help this, but they need getting used to. If an actor switches to contacts at the last minute, the character he is playing can look completely different from the one he created in rehearsal. With very myopic actors it is often appropriate to let the character wear glasses just as the actor does. Talk to the Costume Designer and the prop department about finding some suitable frames and having the actors prescription lenses put into them.

WEEK TWO AND BEYOND

It will probably take you the whole of the second week and even some of the third to complete your first work-through of the play. But even if you are working on a long and complex play, you should try to push on to the end before you get to the halfway mark in your **rehearsal period**.

The longer you take over your first work-through, the longer it will be before you return to the first scenes of the play and the more likely the cast will be to forget everything that was achieved in them. By the time you finish the first work-through you ought to have half your rehearsal period left for further work-throughs and runs.

As you reach the end of the play, don't worry too much if the last scene is very difficult to direct. This is often the case if there are significant unresolved character issues in the play leading up to it. Don't fret. Go back to the beginning of the play and put all the other problems right. If you get the main body of the play right, the last scene doesn't exactly direct itself, but it becomes much easier.

Rehearsing a Play

The end of the first work-through is your first opportunity for an early run of the play. Running is an excellent test of the work done. It allows the actors to practise what they have achieved in the work-through and feel how their characters respond to the story when it's in full flow. Most importantly, it is an opportunity for you to see the work as a whole and make judgements about tempo, rhythm and structure before you go back to the top of the play and start taking it all to pieces again. Early runs are very informative. Nobody will be 'ready' to do one, but they won't need to be. However many mistakes are made, everyone will benefit from what they find out in the process of making them. An early run is also a great motivator. It reminds everyone that there is a stage to be inhabited at the end of the rehearsal process, and an audience to be entertained.

If you do decide to run early, the rehearsal room doors should be closed to anyone other than you, the stage management, the cast and any close creative colleagues that have had a hand in the rehearsals thus far. There should be no one in the room likely to frighten the actors or make them feel they have to deliver performances before they are ready. Your designers of set, costumes, lighting and sound are the exceptions. They will learn a lot from a run, and the presence of these few close artistic friends will give the actors a friendly and unthreatening audience to play to. No strangers. No agents. No friends. No parents if there are children in the play. Above all, no Artistic Directors, administrators, producers, investors or angels.

Make it clear to the actors that no one is to feel under pressure. If scripts need to be held, they should hold them. If **prompts** need to be taken, they should ask for them clearly and without embarrassment. When they make mistakes, which they will, they must let them go and sail on regardless. No one is allowed to get angry with himself or anyone else for **fluffing** a line, or forgetting a move, or taking a prompt, or dropping a prop. Neurosis is not allowed. Anxiety is banned. Curiosity is the order of the day, and belief, and understanding.

When they are not performing their characters, the actors should sit at the front of the rehearsal room with you and the stage management. Ask them to watch the play very carefully, to follow every detail of the story, to pay special attention to the atmosphere of a scene they are about to join, or have just left. The more the company can get a sympathetic collective feel for the work they are doing, the more cohesive a reality they will be able to create within their own personal character contributions. Ask them to prepare for their entrances at the last possible minute, and then move quietly and unobtrusively to where they need to be just before they enter. Don't let anyone go off into a corner or a corridor to obsess about his part, and make himself and everyone else nervous in the process.

Don't take notes. There is nothing more nerve-racking for the actors than a director who keeps diving into his notebook, scribbling furiously and muttering to himself, or whispering his notes to a dumbly nodding assistant. Whenever a note is taken, every actor on the stage will assume he is the cause, and an important part of his focus will disappear along with the assumption. And every time you take a note, you're not concentrating on the play.

Anyway, notes are completely unnecessary. What are you going to do with them? Study them at home? Keep the actors sitting in an exhausted circle listening to you droning on for an hour or two after the run is over? Forget it. You don't need notes. Use your mind instead. Watch the play. Feel how the pace and the atmosphere and the stage pictures are relating to one another. Monitor the journeys of the characters and how they develop as the action develops. Make yourself a member of the audience and hear the story being told as if for the first time. If mistakes happen, or staging ideas occur to you, or thoughts about how to change the emphasis of the characters or the relationships between them, take a mental note. You should be capable of keeping a couple of hundred consecutive thoughts in your head. Don't forget you're going to be working through the play in great detail all over again. As you do so, you don't want to be jumping in and out of your notebook trying to remember what you felt at a run the week before. If you watch well and think clearly, you'll remember every detail of your thoughts as you get to them in your subsequent rehearsals. Notes are for obsessives. They will cause you to close down the creative process far too early.

When the run is over, get the company together and have a brief discussion about what was achieved. Don't make judgements about particular things, unless an obvious new tactic for staging or structuring occurs to you that you feel sure you can share with your company right away. Let the actors react to what they have done. Ask them what they discovered about the story and about playing the characters. Were there any surprises, nice or nasty? How did they feel the characters developed? Were there any *longueurs*, moments when the play seemed to be standing still? Or times when the action seemed to be moving too fast for the story to be properly appreciated? Let them know you have mental notes for all of them and new ideas for work within the scenes, but that you'll get to those details as you work through the play for the second time.

At this stage, don't give personal notes to any actor in front of all the other actors, positive or negative. If you assure the actors before the run that mistakes are allowable and understandable, you can't then berate them when the run is over, and particular bits of praise will always be invidious. Talk to the company as a company. If individual actors seem worried by what they have done and are exhibiting signs of unhappiness or lack of confidence, have private conversations with them once the company has broken for the day. Talk about how to remedy their problems and reassure them that there is plenty of time to do it. Send everyone away with a positive sense of what has been achieved so far and an excitement about making everything even better.

THE SECOND WORK-THROUGH

As you start your second work-through, it won't be so important to follow the scene order of the play, especially if you've done an early run and the shape of the whole play is fresh in everyone's mind.

You should probably go back to the start of the play before too long or it will start to seem like foreign territory to the actors, but once you are into the body of the play you can afford to jump around a bit more. In any event, you will tend to go more quickly through the material having already worked it once and so find yourself re-rehearsing scenes that are more familiar because they've been done more recently.

You may, anyway, have to rehearse the play out of order for reasons beyond your control. If you are working in a **repertoire** company some of your actors may be performing in other plays and therefore be unavailable to you in the evenings or during their matinées. Your actors might be called to **costume** fittings that can only happen at set times because of the availability of cutters and fitters.

Whatever unavailabilities you have to deal with, make your **rehearsal calls** carefully. Don't let any one scene lag too far behind the rest of the play or any one character lag behind the rest of the cast.

Some scenes will demand to be rehearsed more than others: scenes you or the actors are having problems with or scenes that contain technically difficult things like **dances** or **fights** or comic routines. Any scene that requires a lot of diligent practice should be given short bursts of rehearsal on a regular basis. **Repetition** is important in these cases, but actors' minds can quickly tire once they have repeated the same routine for more than half an hour or so. Don't try to get a fight or a dance right in one session. Little and often is the key.

As you work through the play, you will encounter a whole new set of challenges as well as the familiar ones you didn't solve during the first work-through. Most of them will be to do with adding depth and detail to the work you have already done, but you mustn't lose sight of the big picture in the process. Start each rehearsal by running the scene you are working on, at least once. This will remind the actors of what has been achieved so far and will also give them a chance to get comfortable with their moves and try out new motivations and emphases. You should do this even if you intend to change the scene quite radically. There is nothing more unsettling for actors at this stage than the feeling that everything is up in the air, that the work they have achieved so far is all wrong and the first rehearsal of the scene was wasted time. Run first, to familiarise and reassure, then make your changes.

Rehearsing a Play

If the actors are trying to get 'off the book' a run of the scene will also serve as a line run, making them far more fluid with their text in the rehearsal proper. If actors are not off the book by now, they should be. If any actor is still glued to his script at this stage, you should be concerned and perhaps suggest a private line coaching with the Assistant Director, the Prompter or one of the Stage Managers. The bare suggestion will usually shame the actor into getting his act together, but if he has a chronic problem with line learning he'll be grateful for the help.

More than ever, at this stage you must work by agreement and consent. The actors will have made significant discoveries about their characters by now, and will even have started to think like their characters. As actors or characters they will have developed strong views about what feels right and what feels uncomfortable. Listen to them. Engage with their ideas. Let them discuss their relationships with one another. The more they start to think independently from you, the more they are testifying to the value of the work so far.

Your main responsibility at this point in rehearsals is to ensure that each actor becomes his character and that he does so convincingly and cohesively with all the other actors. The best acting is a sort of becoming. Each actor makes a journey towards his character until he feels he can play him convincingly. At the same time, the character is making an unseen journey towards the actor, the playwright's original creature changing subtly to accommodate the personality of the actor. As actor and character meet, somewhere in no-man's land, the actor becomes the character.

At its best, this is the most magical and mysterious part of the rehearsal process and witnessing this coalescence of actors and characters can be very exciting. All good actors know when it starts to happen, and you must cultivate the ability to know it as the actors know it. It has nothing to do with physical transformation, though that might be a small part of it. The actor might not have to change physically at all. Becoming a character requires an inner change, a psychological, emotional and intellectual melding of the actor's mind with the character's mind. If you know how the characters of the play think and feel and you know how the actors in your company think and feel, you won't miss it.

The more sensitive you are to the chemistry of becoming, the less you will want to get in the way of it. At this stage, don't bombard the actors with detailed notes of your own. As much as possible let them find their journeys through the scene for themselves. Only intervene if you think a wrong choice is taking an actor up a blind alley, or making life difficult for one of the other actor/characters.

Keep checking the scene for all the usual practical issues – the balance of the stage, the stage picture, rhythm, tempo, sightlines, upstaging – but don't let those things predominate in your thinking. If the characters are starting to take off, and the story is being animated by them, all other considerations are details to be fixed sometime before opening night.

Finish each session by running the scene again. Repetition is very important for the actors. This might be the last time they work the scene before the next run-through and the moves should start becoming second nature to them.

ACTING AND STAGING PROBLEMS

In spite of all your best-laid plans you may, of course, encounter seemingly insoluble difficulties with your actors or with your own staging plans.

An actor may prove incapable of playing his character as it seems to you to be written. An irritating habit in an actor may seem ineradicable. A relationship between two actors may have come to an impasse, neither of them able to develop their characters beyond it. A false emotional note may be marring the climax of a scene or of the whole play, an actor obviously faking his emotion or overindulging it beyond **belief**. Actors might be marring their performances with inappropriate levels of **irony** or comic indulgence.

Whatever it is, you try to solve the problem with a note, or a discussion, but it does no good. What do you do?

In some cases, there is very little you can do, especially if you find, to your disappointment, that the actor you have cast is 'wrong' in the role, or is simply not a good enough actor to play the part as written. In extreme cases, all you will be able to do is limit the damage, by cutting the actor's text, severely controlling his moves or refocusing the scene so that his most egregious errors are less apparent. In cases where the actor's incompetence is destroying the production you may even have to consider replacing him with another actor. But none of these solutions are really solutions at all. They constitute failure, not the actor's failure but your own. To fire an actor, or put him in a straitjacket on stage, is an admission of your own incompetence as a director, your incompetence in casting or rehearsing, or both.

More commonly, acting problems are specific to particular moments in the play and cause particular and local frustration that is hard to diagnose. You can see that something's wrong, but not why it's wrong.

Ask yourself some diagnostic questions. Is it a problem with the actor, or with the relationship between two actors, or three, or between one actor and the rest of the ensemble? Is it an attitude problem, an ego problem, a style problem or a skill problem? Is your own staging at fault? Are you asking the actor to do something that he can't hear as being right for his text, or that he is physically embarrassed to attempt? Have you made a mistake, or a miscalculation, in the way you have staged the scene? Share these questions with your key collaborators, your Assistant Director, designers, and any actors you can trust to take an objective view, but be careful not to involve actors in public judgements about their colleagues' work.

One possible solution, when you encounter these puzzling or seemingly intractable problems, may be **improvisation**. Even if you have used improvisation earlier in the rehearsal period as a means of opening up the play or finding a performance style for the actors, it can also be used as a problem solver. Some problems are beyond intellectual discussion and can only be solved by physical experiment. Sometimes the physical set-up of the scene you are rehearsing becomes stuck in a rut, with the actors doomed to repeat the same errors over and over again, their moves and actions becoming less and less natural the more they repeat them. By putting the scene in a completely different physical environment, you can jump-start the scene into an interesting new direction. A completely new physical or emotional impetus can sometimes be far more powerful than words in showing an actor where he's been missing the point. And watching the actors make their new discoveries can tell you where your staging may have been limiting their opportunities for expression.

THE FINAL WEEK – LETTING GO

As you enter the final week of rehearsal, you should have a clear schedule for the time you have left, and you should share it with your actors. For example, if you are working Monday to Saturday on a three-act play, you could plan to rehearse an act a day on Monday, Tuesday and Wednesday and **run** the play on Thursday, then spend Friday working on the scenes that need it most, and run again on the Saturday. However you plan it, make sure that you rehearse everything at least once at some point during the week and make sure you have at least one run, though two will serve you better for most plays and most companies.

On your rehearsal days, work in big chunks. Let the actors have a good run at whole scenes or acts. It's important for the protagonist actors to appreciate the juxtaposition of the scenes in which they appear, how long they must wait between one scene and another and how changed their characters become in the interim. There are always surprises here. For you, watching the play, the scenes will seem to have a natural rhythm, but for the actor, immersed in his part, a particular scene will suddenly loom up much faster than he expected, or a long hiatus between scenes will require him to create a strategy for surviving a long absence from the action. Every actor in the company must learn to navigate his journey through the play, and no two journeys will be quite the same, the bigger and more complicated the role the more potentially confusing the journey. Actors playing **doubles** will have two or more journeys to interweave, one character-map to be laid on top of another. Some actors may have physically demanding, even exhausting roles, and must start building up their stamina for playing eight times a week. Some characters may be emotionally draining and require a different sort of stamina from their players.

Rehearsing a Play

Whatever the character journey, and however experienced the actor making it, working through the play in large swathes will help everyone get a better view of the big picture, you included.

Interrupt as little as you can and don't make long speeches when you do. Say what you have to say succinctly and then let the actors have another go at it. This is the week when they must take over the play from you. Don't talk them, or yourself, out of it.

If you give them the time and authority to do it, the characters created by the actors will start to speak to one another. The relationship between the characters, rather than the actors, will start to have a momentum of its own. This is a relationship that must exclude you in order to function, but you mustn't be jealous. The director will always be a wallflower at a party of characters. The more you fight the inevitability of this, the more awkward you will look. Be happy that the characters can have a life of their own. Be happier still that you have rehearsed the actors to the point when they no longer need you.

Letting go is part of the director's job, and the part that many directors do least well. As the enabler of everything in the rehearsal room, as the person who cast the play, chose the design team, researched the text, motivated and cherished the actors and acted as midwife to the characters, you will feel understandably proprietorial about everything and everybody. But you must learn to convert feelings of ownership into feelings of parental pride. Don't be a clingy parent. Don't be one of those directors who can't bear to see the actors happy and independent. And some actors will make it hard for you to let them go. If you don't cling to them, they will cling to you. But you must gently prise their fingers off, whisper encouraging words and send them on their way.

LAST RUN IN THE REHEARSAL ROOM

Schedule your last run in the rehearsal room for the last full day of rehearsals. If you're working a six-day week, run on the Friday and keep the Saturday free as a stand-by day. If the run goes well and everyone is happy, you can all have two days off before the exhausting **technical rehearsals** begin. If there are problems with one or two scenes, then you can give them special attention on the Saturday. If the run goes haltingly and the actors are unhappy at the end of it, you can run again on the Saturday. If you leave a run until the very last minute of rehearsals and it goes badly, you will have left yourself no time in which to fix the problems or to run again.

The atmosphere for this run should be absolutely the same as for the first run, as described above. No neurosis allowed. Remind everyone that they still have a week to go. The fact that you will shortly be leaving the rehearsal room doesn't mean that the creative work will grind to a halt. There is still plenty of time for reappraisal, repetition and refinement. Remind them that in the technical rehearsals they will have to repeat sections of the play again and again so that the lighting and sound plots can be built around them, and they must use the repetition as primary creative time. They mustn't stop growing in their roles, and thinking about the play, and exploring new ways of expressing the relationships between the characters.

Insist, as far as you can, that the actors watch the run when they are not involved in the action, for all the same reasons as before. They will be involved, more than ever, in the lives of their own particular characters, but they mustn't lose sight of the play as a whole and how their fellow actors are performing it.

There will be much more external pressure at this run than at previous ones, and so there should be. Don't try to replicate the conditions of any previous run you may have had, especially if it was a positive experience for everyone. You will be performing the play to a paying audience in a few days' time, so you need to start opening it out a bit. Try to get a small, non-threatening audience into the rehearsal room as a way of bridging the gap from rehearsal to performance.

You will anyway have to accommodate some of your colleagues from other departments. In small theatre companies this will be only a handful of extra folk, but in bigger companies it can turn into an invasion. All your artistic collaborators will need to be there – your designers of set, costumes, lighting and sound and any of their attendant associates, runners, dressers and operators, your choreographer, composer and Musical Director and all their assistants, and perhaps a musician or two, your prop master, your senior stage technicians. They will all have a professional interest in the show and they will all do their jobs better after watching a run. If you are working in a permanent subsidised company, the **Artistic Director** may want to inspect your work (and take you out to dinner afterwards to tell you how to fix it), and he may be accompanied by an administrator or two and a Literary Manager or **dramaturg**. In the commercial theatre, this will be the point when a bevy of producers and investors turns up, overexcited and potentially volatile. None of these people should be there without your prior knowledge. You will have had the opportunity to vet every one of them, but the accumulated number may seem a little threatening at first. Don't let it be. Welcome the invaders and make sure the actors know who everyone is and that they are all there as friends, not foes.

Don't let the actors get too excited by the presence of an audience. This is a fine balancing act. They are performers so they will have smelt the blood of a fresh audience, but don't let them go over the top. They must keep working and thinking and developing, and they won't do this if they are over-anxious to please. Keep the integrity, the intimacy of your bond with them. You will do this best by behaving normally yourself. If the director starts to get jumpy, or defensive, or uncharacteristically jolly because there are a lot of important people in the room, his behaviour will spread to the actors and they will mimic it, or react against it, or lose their faith in his judgement, or transfer their focus away from the play onto pleasing the people the director seems so keen to please.

Arrange the audience seats carefully so that the actor/audience relationship in the theatre is simulated as accurately as possible. Explain this to the actors and ask them to play the rehearsal room audience as it is, to focus their performances on the real people in the room and not on some larger imaginary audience outside the rehearsal room walls. Everyone should behave as if the rehearsal room were a small studio theatre and the invited audience a real audience of paying customers. By doing this, you and the actors will start to get a feel for how the finished production will come across when you get into the theatre space itself.

Give a little talk to the audience and actors before you start. Explain anything you think they need to know about the way the play will sit in the theatre, how the set works, why some of the scene changes are shorter or longer than they will be eventually, whatever seems appropriate. If there is anything significantly unfinished, point that out too, so that the actors aren't embarrassed by lack of rehearsal or technical support.

Once again, if you can possibly avoid it, don't take notes. Or take as few as you can. You still have the technical rehearsals to work through. Every moment of the play has still to be examined when you get it onto the stage. You should be able to make a mental list of all the little changes you want to make in the scenes and pass them on to the actors as you work through the play. There will also be new challenges and opportunities during the technical rehearsals that cannot be anticipated. You must be ready to recognise these and react to them with pragmatic creativity. If your nose is in your notebook trying to fix all the little problems from the last run in the rehearsal room, you'll never be up to the challenges and opportunities a good tech will afford you.

Once the run is over, reassert the integrity of the rehearsal room. Get the audience to leave within a few minutes. Don't take whispered notes from producers, administrators or Artistic Directors. If the run has been enjoyed, don't let the room turn into a party, or a post mortem if not so enjoyed. The first night is still a week away, more or less. Never party prematurely, and never let your producers write reviews for you, good or bad.

Once the room has been restored to calmness, get the actors together in a quiet circle. Once again, talk to them about the run and listen to their thoughts. Don't give a generalised pep talk or bombard them with screeds of notes. Keep everything specific and concentrated on solving the remaining problems thrown up by the run and the new problems they will meet in the theatre as the technicals begin.

Talk to them about the tech, how you intend to run it and how you expect them to react to the pressures between now and the first preview. Give them a really accurate map of the week to come so they can pace themselves to the work as it happens. Reassure them that the lights, sound, set, costumes and props won't take over the play and force the actors into the background of your attention. The challenge for everyone is to make sure that the creative atmosphere and human feeling of the rehearsal room survive the move to the stage, that nothing is lost, or damaged or contorted because of a change of scale and location. This is especially problematic if you are moving into a large auditorium. Studio theatres are never much of a problem, but in a space that is significantly larger than your rehearsal room, your actors may struggle to retain the truthfulness and detail of their rehearsal work. While recognising this as a possible worry, you must conspire with the actors to fight it as best you can. Voices may have to be more projected in a large space, but it doesn't follow that performances must become cruder or physically telegraphed or lacking in emotional detail. You can retain everything you've achieved in the rehearsal room as long as you all continue to be adaptable, pragmatic and creative.

GETTING INTO THE THEATRE

If all has gone to plan, you and your actors will be leaving the rehearsal room with a sense of achievement about the work done and excitement about the work ahead, tinged, perhaps, with a little sentimental regret about leaving the cradle of your creative endeavours. Certain rehearsal rooms cast something of a spell and can be quite hard to leave.

In most production schedules, this is the point when the actors will get a day or even two days off so that the physical production can move from rehearsal room to theatre. Stage management must uproot their rehearsal apparatus and transfer it to the stage. Furniture, props, sound equipment and all the rest of it will have to be shifted into the wings and technical booths of the theatre. In most theatres, the set for the previous show will still be on stage on the Saturday night, sometimes right up to Sunday afternoon. Before your technical rehearsals can start the previous show must be got out of the theatre and your set loaded in. Your crew will then have to build the set on stage, the lighting department will have to rig and focus all their lamps and the sound department set up their systems. With musicals, the musicians will need a special session to get themselves 'sat' in the pit, and the sound department will need to balance the orchestral and vocal sound.

In a small theatre with a simple set, all this might take no more than a day, a day that coincides with your actors' day off, but with a more complex set-up in a larger theatre it could take two, three or even four days. A hiatus of more than two days will be very hard for your actors to endure, and you have to be careful that your whole production doesn't go off the boil at this point. If you rehearse on the Saturday and have the Sunday off, you could have a call for the actors to get into their dressing rooms on the Monday afternoon or evening ready to start a technical on Tuesday morning, but if the delay is any longer than that you must think of how to fill the time. If you still have access to your rehearsal room, and some productions will rent the room for an extra day or two in case of technical delays, then you could do another run, or a **speed run**. Running the play without props or furniture or any elements of costume can be very informative and exciting. You could even consider changing the audience/actor relationship in order to keep everything fresh, by doing the whole play in-the-round, for instance. If you all feel particularly adventurous, the actors could play the text as it stands while improvising a completely new set of physical situations for each scene.

If you only have the spaces at the theatre available to you, you could get the actors together in the largest of the foyer spaces for a **line run** or a speed run. Or you could dedicate a day, or half a day, to sorting out the problems of a particular department. In productions with a lot of **doubling** or with difficult **quick changes**, you could do a costume run in the rehearsal room, or a costume parade in the foyer. Your Musical Director or choreographer or Fight Director could use the time to refine their work. Or you could make specific scene calls to sort out any last glitches in staging or characterisation.

Whatever you do, you mustn't let your production drift or your actors feel they've been abandoned while your attention is focused elsewhere. The technical rehearsals can be the most creative and inspiring days you have in the whole rehearsal process, but only if the company spirit and energy you have created in the rehearsal room remains intact when you get into the theatre.

Rehearsing a Musical

Most of the **rehearsal disciplines** and **rehearsal techniques** for musicals are exactly as they are for **rehearsing a play**. **Research** can be done in the same way, and so can **adaptation, games** and **improvisation**. But there are considerable differences in the way rehearsals are scheduled and how your collaborators work with you and around you. For a full account of these, see the entry under **Musical Theatre**.

Repertory and Repertoire

The words 'repertory' and 'repertoire' have a variety of subtly conflicting meanings, all of which are more or less current in professional theatre terminology (where both terms are commonly abbreviated to 'rep'), causing confusion to professional and layman alike.

A repertory theatre is a theatre company that mounts a succession of productions, usually at regular intervals. A three-weekly 'rep' company changes from one play to another every three weeks, a four-weekly rep every four weeks and so on. Once a production has closed, it doesn't return. Repertory theatres commonly employ a more or less permanent ensemble of actors, but they may have a fresh cast for each play.

A repertoire company is a company that can keep two or more productions running over a scheduled **season** of performances, allowing audiences to see different plays in the same theatre over a defined period of time.

Thus the terms can be used to describe forms of theatrical management. 'The RSC and the National are both repertoire companies' means they are companies that are able to run two or more plays in the same theatres in the same week. 'The Bristol Old Vic has just announced its new repertory season' means it has published its list of upcoming productions, each play to have its own short and unextendable run of performances.

Both terms can also be used to describe the type of plays that a theatre puts on. Thus 'The repertoire of the National Theatre

638

includes both English and foreign-language plays,' or 'The Royal Shakespeare Company will always have three or four Shakespeare plays in its repertory.'

Note the way in which a distinction between the two terms is signified by their shared abbreviation. If you say, 'I spent two years in rep,' you mean you worked in repertory theatres for two years. If you say 'My production was in the rep for two years,' you mean it was scheduled in the theatre's calendar of performances, along with other productions, over a two-year period.

Répétiteur

The répétiteur is the rehearsal pianist in **opera**, from the French word for rehearsal – *répétition*. He may also be responsible for teaching the singers their parts. Opera conductors often begin their careers as répétiteurs, the job being an education in itself as it exposes them to a great variety of singers, scores and styles.

In ballet the répétiteur is the person who supervises rehearsals and teaches the dancers their steps.

Repetition

The French call rehearsal *répétition*, and for a very good reason. Repetition is the method used by most actors to get their thoughts and moves and lines thoroughly into their systems. Many directors underestimate the value of repetition when **rehearsing a play**, largely because it requires their silence as well as their attention. Actors can get dazed or fretful if more time is allocated for analysis and debate than for the practice of their craft. Repetition allows them to discover how to apply their craft empirically, without a self-conscious intellectual process.

As a general rule, you should try to repeat a scene at least twice during the time set aside to rehearse it, and make sure that the final repetition is done at the end of the session so that actors can leave the rehearsal with a sense of something having been practically achieved.

Replica Theatres

A replica theatre is a theatre built in imitation, or imaginative reconstruction, of a theatre from the past. The commonest attempts are theatres built in imitation of one or other of the Elizabethan stages – the Swan, the Globe, the Rose and so on – though the evidence for their precise construction is somewhere between slim and non-existent.

If you work in a replica theatre, don't get caught up in the phoney pursuit of 'authentic performance'. Enjoy the theatre for what it can offer in terms of intimacy, audience/actor relationship and atmosphere, but direct your play as you would direct any play anywhere, with strict regard for truthfulness of performance and clarity of storytelling.

Most replica theatres were built in a flurry of historical interest in the 1960s and 70s and have now been standing for much longer than their originals ever did or were ever intended to do. The social and cultural contexts in which they existed have also changed beyond recognition, so there is little point in pretending that actors and audience are stepping through a magical door when they enter these buildings. They are doing nothing of the kind. And those who persist in the dream of authenticity do so by blinding themselves to the emergency exit doors, the disabled access points, the sophisticated lighting rigs, the glossy programmes, the lavishly appointed toilets and the cellphone-brandishing audiences.

Theatre is a living, ever-changing artistic organism. You cannot recreate the theatre of the past any more than you can breathe life into a dinosaur fossil. So use these replicas in a spirit of creativity rather than re-creativity. Let the spirits of past authors and actors inspire you to create visions of your own and not copies of theirs.

Researching a Play

All plays need researching, even ones that have only just been written. There are always aspects of a play that the author will know more about than you and as far as possible you should try to close that gap. You need to know what the characters of the play are thinking about, why they do what they do, say what they say, but you also need to know to what extent their thoughts and actions are conditioned by their social, political and religious background and beliefs.

With a **new play**, the problem is easily solved. The answers to most of your questions will lie in the society around you, a society with which you are very familiar. But if a character is behaving in an unaccountable way or the story takes a turn you can't understand, ask the author why and he will tell you. Even if the author cannot rationalise the behaviour of one of his characters, a conversation with him can easily lead to an instinctive understanding of your own that you can then pass on to your actors.

With a new play written in another language or from a culture quite alien to your own experience, your research may give you more problems, but you will still be dealing with a contemporary society, one that you can understand in apposition to the way you understand your own. Here your author might not be available to you, but your **translator** may be, or you can find an expert witness, someone who has first-hand experience of the culture in which the play is set, and quiz him about the characters' motives and their social milieu.

With the plays of the past, research becomes more important and more difficult. Dead playwrights are infuriatingly silent. The behaviour of their characters relates to social customs and historical events that you can read about but not know as they knew them or as you know your own society. The author is assuming an understanding and a set of attitudes in his contemporary audience that helped them fill in every aspect of his characters' behaviour. Everything is topical: the state of the nation, the power of the Church, the beliefs of the people, the food, the drink and the jokes. The more you know about the author and his world the more your apprehension will come to resemble that of a member of his contemporary audience and the closer you will get to the true meaning and intention of the play.

Depending on the nature of the story and the predilections of its

Researching a Play

characters, there may be particular topics you want to pay special attention to, but here is a basic research list suitable for most plays.

TOPICS FOR RESEARCH

1 *The social hierarchy*

From head of state to lowliest-born, what does the social beehive look like? If there is a monarchy, how absolute is it? What is the nation's attitude to its ruling class? How many classes are there and how much mobility is there between classes?

2 *Political institutions*

What are the main engines of government? How are the people represented in the political process, if at all?

3 *Foreign affairs*

How does the country relate to the countries around it and to the world at large? Is there a war going on? What are the most recent conflicts? How much of the world is known? What is the relationship of the country to its colonies, if any?

4 *The Law*

Who appoints the judges and how respected are they? What sort of justice do the courts dispense and what are the prevailing forms of punishment? What are the prisons like?

5 *Religion and the Church*

Is it a religious society? What do people believe in? Is the Church respected? How much political power does the Church wield? Are the priests part of the ruling class or antagonistic towards it? To what extent is the Church in conflict with science?

6 *Education*

What proportion of the population is educated? If children go to school, how old are they when they leave? How organised are the

642

schools? Is there a universal system of education or is it piecemeal? What is taught? Is religion involved in education?

7 Money

What is the currency? Who issues it? Whose picture is on it? Who runs the banks? How much does money buy? What are the relative incomes of different classes of society? Does money have a different meaning for different sorts of people? Is it legal to lend money at interest? Where do people store their surplus?

8 Science

What is known? What are the latest discoveries and inventions? What do we know and have today that they didn't know or have then?

9 Doctors and medicine

What is the extent of the medical knowledge of the day? Are doctors trusted? Do their cures work? What are the commonest diseases, in childhood and maturity? What is the average life expectancy? How many women die in childbirth? What is the rate of infant mortality?

10 Food and drink

What do people eat and drink? How well fed are they? Is there starvation at any level of society? Or surfeit? Do different classes eat and drink different things? Is this an alcoholic society? Is alcohol used as a social anaesthetic? What are the effects of diet on health?

11 Clothes and fashion

What do people wear? How do people's clothes relate to the social class they are in? Is there a social or religious aspect to the clothes any one class is expected to wear? What are the fashions of the time, for women and for men? How important is fashion in the ruling class or the middle class? From where is the fashion derived?

12 *Men and women*

How deep is the social divide between men and women? What are the social functions of men and women in society? To what extent are women bought and sold by men? What age are men and women when they marry? Is divorce possible? How rife is prostitution and across how many social classes? What is the life of a prostitute like?

13 *Families and children*

What is the family unit like? What is the relationship between adults and children and between older children and younger children? How big is the average family? What sort of life do children lead? How soon are they put to work? Is there any child slavery? How are children punished?

14 *Culture*

What are the prevailing artistic forms? What is happening in theatre, literature, music and fine art? How exclusive is the appreciation of the arts? Is there an intelligentsia? What are the folk traditions and how alive are they?

15 *Sports and pastimes*

What do people do to entertain themselves? What are the prevailing sports for the different social classes? What games are played at home or in social gatherings? Is gambling a feature of sport?

16 *The life of the author*

When was he born, how long did he live and when did he die? What was he like? Did he have a family? Who were his friends? What was his relationship with his artistic peers? Did he admire them and they him? Other than writing what did he do? What did he believe in? How typical of his society was he? Where does this play fall in his life and in the greater body of his work? Is he writing about his own time or a time in the past?

COMPANY RESEARCH

If you set a play accurately in its period, your whole cast should know as much as possible about the daily lives of the characters they are playing. All the people in the play would know some of the answers to the questions posed in the above list. Whatever the characters would know, the actors playing them should know.

A company research exercise is an excellent way of putting your actors in touch with their characters' world.

Call the company together and read through a list of research projects. The one above is a good general guide, but you might want to add your own categories to suit the play you are doing. Each actor should choose a category to research. If possible, their choices should relate in some way to the particular characters they are playing. If two or three actors want to research the same category, let them share the task. Some actors like to work alone, others much prefer to work in pairs or groups.

Once the categories have all been allocated, make sure everyone has access to research material of one sort or another and give a deadline for the work to be completed. Within a couple of days, the quickest actors will be ready to make their reports. You can do two or three reports a day; just after lunch is a good time, or at the end of the day, or whenever an appropriate moment presents itself. Ask the actors to limit their reports to five or ten minutes, leaving five minutes or so for further questions and discussion. Some actors will find it hard keeping to this brief, but if you don't have a limit, reports can ramble on, natural enthusiasm turning into long-windedness.

You and your company should come away from these sessions with a broader view of the work you are exploring and a greater ability to challenge the conventional wisdom about the world in which it is set. You will also have learnt a lot more about one another, the unusual demands of the work causing the actors to reveal themselves in ways they might never do in a normal rehearsal period and allowing the more junior members a brief experience of equality. However old your actors are, in study they will all tend to revert to the behaviour of their schooldays and be as studious or humorous, as serious or mocking as they were in childhood.

Restricted View

See **Obstructed View.**

Revival Director

This is a term used mostly in **opera,** where productions of past triumphs can go on being revived for decades and the original director, if still alive, is unwilling or unable to revive the production himself.

If you work as a Revival Director you can enjoy a fair amount of autonomy within the obvious constraints of rehearsing with the original set and costume designs. You may even be able to make quite radical changes if the opera management thinks the production has dated or when the demands of a new set of starring singers require a major rethink. This will all depend on how much the original director wishes to remain involved, whether he plans on attending any of the final rehearsals or checking up on the production in performance.

Paradoxically, a production that has been completely abandoned by its original director may stay more faithful to its original shape but may also suffer from staleness and unoriginality – the singers all being obliged to perform exactly as their predecessors did. Your job here will be to shake things up a bit, but you may find yourself in an invidious position. If some of the singers are repeating past roles they may be unwilling to change their performances to suit your new ideas. Your stage management team might be protective of the original production and find you guilty of directorial *lèsemajesté*. There will be deeply subjective memories of particular moments in the original production that those around you will wish to see recreated.

Your best route through this minefield is to have the original director as your ally and guide. By having a lively artistic relationship with your principal, by having attended the original rehearsals, by studying the production in performance or by conferring in detail with your principal before the rehearsal period starts you will get ahead of the game and be able to head off any conflicts of artistic interest or authority.

If you have no access to your principal and no first-hand knowledge of the original production you must do the best you can, but try not to paint yourself into a corner by being too assertive before making yourself thoroughly familiar with the material and with those who already feel they have a stake in it.

Some young directors see the post of Revival Director as a rung on the directing ladder and use their experience to inform and develop their own directing style before branching out on their own original productions. Others are career Revival Directors, only too happy to avoid the creative pressures that attend originality.

A Revival Director permanently employed by a single opera company is usually called a **Staff Director**.

Revivals

A revival is generally a remounting of any play that has been seen before by the theatre community for whom it is to be staged. Thus most productions, if they aren't premieres of one sort or another, are revivals.

In practice though, you rarely hear someone saying he is off to see a revival of *Hamlet* or *Three Sisters*. He will more likely say he is going to see a new production of those plays.

The term is more frequently used to describe a new production of a play written within living memory that hasn't been seen for a while, or since it first opened.

In subsidised **repertoire** companies, a revival is the remounting of a production of a play that has been out of the repertoire for a significant time.

In **opera** companies, revivals are the constantly recycled productions that are in the staple repertoire, usually remounted by **Revival Directors**.

Revolve

Revolve is short for 'revolve stage' or 'revolving stage'. Revolves are large circular discs set into or built on top of stage surfaces for moving actors and scenery round in circles. They are driven by internal winches, manual or electric, and often these days computerised.

Large stages with revolves permanently built into their surfaces can cause problems for designs that don't use them. The super-structure under a revolve is usually impermeable, so **traps** are often out of the question, and the stage surface covered by the revolve can be a little shaky when large numbers of actors walk across it at the same time. Brand new revolves can be speedy and efficient, but old-fashioned ones can be cumbersome.

The problems become more complicated with 'drum revolves'. These are revolves that are as deep as they are wide, making them drum-shaped if you could see all of them, and that go up and down as well as round and round. They may also have independently inbuilt lifts to take scenery up and down from stage to **understage**. Be very wary of using one of these contraptions in a show. The more mechanical options there are in the kit the more things can go wrong in performance. As a basic rule of thumb, if you use a revolve you should add an extra day to your **technical rehearsal period**. Two for a drum revolve.

If you and your designer decide to use a revolve and your theatre doesn't have one built in, you will encounter some difficulties. First of all cost. They're expensive to hire and even more expensive to build, unless you can recoup the cost of a build over a long run and you have to be very confident to be sure of that. They raise the level of your stage by as much as a foot, so there may be **sightline** implications for people sitting in the front few rows. The stage all around them has to be built up to the same level all the way into the wings. This is a costly and time-consuming business. And revolves go wrong. A production that relies on accurate revolve cues grinds to a halt when the revolve unexpectedly stops. And you wait while the revolve is fixed. And the audience waits.

And if the revolve can't be fixed, the audience goes home. Or the actors have to soldier on making up the show as they go along.

Revolves can be extremely useful and effective. There are some plays and productions that cry out for them: a story that includes a continuous journey or that visits multiple locations in very quick time, or a play that continually alternates between two or three different locations, or a permanent installation that can be viewed interestingly from many different angles.

If your production makes constant use of a revolve, you would be well advised to get one installed in your rehearsal room, at least for the last week of rehearsal. Actors need time to acclimatise to moving around on an unstable floor and stage management and crew need time to sort out their cues and timings. If you can't afford a rehearsal revolve, tape out the round shape on the floor, fix any permanent scenic pieces or furniture to it, and revolve your position (the audience's point of view) around it. This will mean you will sit in different parts of the **rehearsal room** for different scenes in the play. This will be particularly necessary when you run the play. If you stay in the same place your stage management will spend the whole run chasing the action round and round in circles and the play will judder to a halt every time a revolve cue happens.

Rhubarb

See **Crowd Scenes.**

Rough Theatre

'Rough theatre' is a much-quoted term, coined by Peter Brook in his formative book *The Empty Space*, that describes a type of theatre characterised by 'Salt, sweat, noise, smell: the theatre that's not in a theatre, the theatre on carts, on wagons, on trestles, audiences standing, sitting round tables, audiences joining in, answering back; theatre in back rooms, upstairs rooms, barns; the one-night-stands, the torn sheet pinned up across the hall, the battered screen to conceal the quick changes . . .'

The term is now used, more loosely, to describe a rough design or performance style regardless of the surrounding theatre architecture. Directors talk about using 'rough theatre techniques' when doing productions at the National Theatre or in the West End or on Broadway. What they mean is that they hope the powers of **improvisation** and imagination will be more evident in their finished work than the production values. In this usage the term is more or less synonymous with **poor theatre**.

Royal Box

Many Victorian and Edwardian theatres are equipped with a royal box where members of the royal family would sit when attending plays. As most royal families in Europe have been utterly philistine for the last hundred years or so, these boxes were seldom if ever used and are now never used at all. Theatres in some countries still refuse to use the royal box for anyone other than a member of their royal family, but most are happy to sell the seats to common theatregoers and risk the pollution of the royal atmosphere in and around the box.

All royal boxes suffer from the same ironical drawback: they look beautiful and people look impressive sitting in them, whether royal or not, but they are actually the worst seats in the house as they have a better view of the wings than they do of the stage. This, of course, is the point of them. They were built to display royalty to the audience rather than show the play to royalty. Perhaps, then, we should forgive royalty for preferring a day at the races, where they are afforded the very best seats for the very best view of their very own horses.

Behind many of the royal boxes are royal retiring rooms that are now used by producers and theatre owners for entertaining their investors and friends, though most royal rooms are poky little affairs and not in the least sumptuous or romantic. There are some gems though, if you know where to find them, as well as the occasional royal loo with fabulously ornate painted porcelain-ware and mahogany seat. You should use these luxurious appointments as often as you can, as they might otherwise fall into disuse and neglect.

Royal Circle

Many multi-tiered **proscenium** arch theatres built in the eighteenth, nineteenth or early twentieth centuries have a royal circle in their auditoria, usually the tier immediately above the stalls, on the same level as the **royal box**.

Of course, there is nothing remotely royal about the royal circle. The name was coined by Theatre Managers as a way of getting people to pay more for the best tickets on the assumption that people sitting in the royal circle would feel more royal than the people sitting below them in the stalls and grander than the people sitting above them in the grand circle.

RP (Received Pronunciation)

See **Dialect**.

Running a Play

A run, or run-through, of a play is a complete performance in the rehearsal room or on stage, without stopping and without an audience.

Runs are important staging posts in **rehearsing a play**. Some directors like to run very early in a rehearsal period, others like to leave it late. Some like to run often, some seldom. Actors likewise.

A dress run is a **dress rehearsal**. A **line run** or word run is a sit-down rehearsal of text without moves. A **speed run** is a run-through at double- or triple-quick time with or without moves to wake up or speed up a show by obliging the actors to get on with it.

Running Times

The running time is the time it takes to perform the play. It can be expressed either as a total time including intervals or as a **playing time** without intervals or delays. Running times are usually posted in the **programme** as a courtesy to patrons, broken down into times for each act and an interval time.

One of the most galling aspects of modern critical reaction is in the reviewers' misreading of opening-night running times. On a **press night**, a play that normally takes two hours and twenty-five minutes to perform, including interval, will go up ten minutes late to allow for all the 'hello darlings' in the foyer and last-minute re-allocations of tickets. Then intervals get stretched by another five or ten minutes and, before you know it, your show is two and three-quarter hours long and being written up by the critics as 'long at nearly three hours'. Beware. If you think your show is going to try anyone's patience, ring the foyer bells early and bully the audience into their seats in good time.

The Run of a Play

The run of a play is its total number of performances from opening to closing nights or the period in which all the performances are played.

In the subsidised theatre the length of the run is usually known in advance. In commercial theatre the producers are nearly always hoping to extend the run for as long as possible, the ultimate length of the run being defined by pressure at the box office on the one hand and the continuing availability of actors on the other.

Most plays run for a very short time. In **repertory** theatres, your run will be no more than three or four weeks, with your production having to make way for the next scheduled show. In a **repertoire** system, you might get the same number of performances over a much longer period of time.

S

Safety Curtain

The impermeable fire-wall that can be lowered to separate the stage from the auditorium in case of fire, known to theatre practitioners as the **iron** and in the US as the 'fire curtain'.

Scansion

See **Metre**.

Scene Changes

Scene changes and the ability to manage them with sensitivity and skill will always loom large in a director's working life. How do you get from palace to wood, from Verona to Mantua, from café to hospital, from ship to shore?

A lot depends on your **set design**. Generally, the more naturalistic the design, the more stuff you will need to haul on and off the stage. If you and your designer insist on depicting everything the text suggests, those depictions will have to be moved around. With an 'environmental' set, the same basic setting serves as an environment for the whole play, making big changes unnecessary, though there may still be token bits of scenery and large props to manage as the play moves from scene to scene.

Whatever your design style, scene changes should take as little time as possible and be as undetectable as possible unless they are designed to be an effective part of the way your production presents itself.

The time element is crucial. Nothing is more destructive to the atmosphere of a production than the audience having to wait in semi-darkness for two minutes while the stage crew manages a clunky scene change behind a set of front **tabs**. This is most common at the **opera**. The audience gets a magical first act; love, grief, heroism and sacrifice, all wrapped up in heart-stopping arias and choruses. Then five minutes of invisible elephants moving furniture, the conductor standing in the pit shuffling his baton from hand to hand, before the curtain finally rises for another dose of magic. After such an interlude, it takes a long time for the magic to be restored, and the longer the audience have to wait, the more they will expect from the set when it finally appears – nearly always a recipe for disappointment.

And it's the same for all productions. If you let an audience off the hook for more than a few seconds, all the labour you have put into the drama up until that point is frittered away. And what are the audience to think while the scene change is happening? Certainly not what you want them to think. They can't go on contemplating the fates of the protagonist characters for more than a few seconds without drifting off onto something else or, worse still, thinking too hard about what they've seen. 'Why didn't Juliet just climb down off the balcony and run away with him?' 'Could any man really be as credulous as Othello?' 'Those supposedly identical twins wouldn't fool me.' More likely they will lose their concentration on the plot entirely, leafing through the programme to check which TV programme they saw the leading actress in, or discussing with their partner where to go for dinner afterwards.

The poor actors or singers who have to restart a play or an opera after a long scene change will not enjoy the ensuing ten minutes as they struggle to reassert the energy of the drama over the energy of the extraneous thoughts in the auditorium. And it will be many minutes before the atmosphere in the theatre is unified once more, minutes during which the events of the story will be ignored and later only hazily remembered.

If you can't keep a scene change short, you should consider making it into a proper interval. Then if you end up with too many intervals, rethink your design.

Many theatres today don't have the option of long scene changes behind curtains because they don't have curtains. They use the convention of the **blackout** instead. But this can be a lazy, unnecessary and irritating convention. If the hiatus between two scenes is as brief as it should be, a complete blackout of the lights is pointless. Much better to have one lighting cue fade out and another take its place in an overlapping movement. If changes need to be made to the stage between two scenes involving the use of stage management or crew, a blackout is particularly unhelpful to everyone, especially the audience. The stage crew have to wear 'blacks' to make themselves as invisible as they can. They then grope around in the dark looking for barely discernible **marks** on the floor, bumping into the actors, the furniture and one another. If the marks on the floor are bright enough to be seen in the dark they become clearly visible during brightly lit scenes, covering the floor like confetti. More importantly, if a stage is blacked out for more than a few seconds, the audience's eyes grow accustomed to the dark and can easily make out the shapes of black-clad stagehands moving around in the glow of the surrounding light spill. Nothing is more interesting to an audience than something they think they are not supposed to be looking at. If actors have to set themselves in the semi-darkness, the audience's interest grows all the greater while the actors are left in a half world, partly visible and therefore only partly in character and understandably wrong-footed when the lights finally come up on them.

Think of blackout scene changes as a last resource. If you have to use them, try to link the scenes on either side of them by keeping some part of the stage or one or two of the characters visible throughout the change. Lead the audience's eyes away from what you don't want them to see by providing them with something worth watching. Or you can put the stage into a half-light and make the movement of actors and crew interesting or thematically relevant in some way. But be careful not to over-ice the cake in this respect. A long, elaborately choreographed scene change will still be a scene change, whatever extra meaning you think you've attached to it. Audiences know when their time is being wasted.

If your set has to be significantly changed between scenes, encourage your designer to make its movement simple, fluid and a pleasure to watch. **Revolves, flying** pieces and **trucks** can all look good if their movements are well timed and their machinery is silent. If the design is a good one, the way it moves from one setting to another will help you tell the story of the play.

If small changes need to be made to the settings, let them be made by members of the crew masked from the audience's view while the actors are continuing to perform the next scene. It is never advisable to expose members of the stage crew or stage management in scene changes if you can possibly avoid it. They always look awkward on stage, and especially so if they know they are being watched. Their self-consciousness increases all the more if they are obliged to wear any elements of costume. They lurch on and off stage in ill-fitting gear, hats perilously perched on heads, with their hairstyles, watches, glasses and shoes all looking wrong. And in many theatre communities you will have to pay them considerable extra sums in appearance money. Much better to create a style for your production where it is quite acceptable for the actors to work the scene changes for themselves. If every character in a play adopts the same convention, an audience will accept the naturalness of them moving their own furniture on and off. Unlike stage crew or stage management, actors are trained in the graceful handling of props and minor scenic pieces, and provided they are working in a style that allows for it, they can easily maintain the integrity of their characters in the process.

Music can be an important component of scene changes. The tailoring of specific music cues to the movement of actors, props and scenic pieces helps to give scene changes a form. The structure of the music makes the audience feel that the change has a clearly defined time scale and is therefore a necessary part of the story structure, while the sound fills the void left by the actors' voices and picks up on the atmosphere of the story, propelling it forward into the next scene.

Score

The score of an **opera** or **musical** is the sung and instrumental music in printed form.

An orchestral or full score has staves for every instrument and is generally only used by **composer, orchestrator, conductor** and **Musical Director.**

A piano-vocal score is a reduction of the full score for keyboard and vocal parts only and is used in rehearsal by singers, **répétiteurs** and **accompanists.**

Scrims

A scrim is a cloth made from light-permeable material, also known as a gauze.

Scrims are usually flown, and most commonly hang the full height and width of the stage just upstage of the **proscenium** opening. They can also be hung at mid-stage, or in front of a **cyclorama,** or cut to a specific shape to cover any opening.

The theory is, if you focus a light on the audience side of a scrim, everything upstage of it goes into darkness and if you light objects on the stage side of it, it seems to disappear. In practice, light shone on the front of a scrim bleeds through to the other side of it, so if you want to project an intense image on a scrim, you have to fly a 'black' behind it, unless you don't mind seeing the stage space behind it. If you then want to reveal an image behind the scrim, you must first fade the **projection,** then fly the black out in darkness, then reveal the upstage image. It's all in the timing.

Scrims are very good for sudden revelations or for slow, atmospheric reveals. By keeping some light on the surface of the scrim while lighting objects on the other side of it, you can create interesting perspective effects. They are also very useful if you want some part of the stage to appear and disappear on a regular basis – if you have an orchestra on stage, for example, and only want to see it for specific cues.

You have to be very careful when lighting and cueing scrims. If a scrim flies out too early or too late, it can pick up light from neighbouring lighting cues. So you can't change the cue point of a scrim without changing the lighting cues to suit. A scrim should be flown in a comparative blackout, or when something is brightly lit downstage of it. If you can see an image beyond it, the bottom edge of the scrim will make a hard line against the light as it flies out.

A scrim hung in front of a cyclorama gives the cyc the appearance of more depth and stops it looking quite so much like a cinema screen.

Seasons

A season is a period of time in which a **repertoire** of plays is performed by a theatre or group of theatres. Thus, 'The Broadway season is looking pretty thin this year,' or 'The RSC has just announced its 2009–2010 season,' or 'The Fleabite Theatre Company will play a season of little-known Icelandic comedies during the third week of March.'

See also **Repertory and Repertoire**.

Second Nightishness

The performance on the night after a **press night** or **opening night** is notoriously dodgy. Actors forget lines and moves, props are dropped, playing times are longer, laughs shorter and technical gremlins run amok. It's not always like this, but it happens often enough that you must be ready to safeguard against it.

Second nightishness has five basic ingredients:

1 Tiredness

Actors, stage management and crew work very hard up to and including opening night. The next day they can feel completely knackered, especially if they've over-partied the night before.

2 Lack of adrenalin

When a show is under-rehearsed or badly learnt, adrenalin can see the actors through the first night. Without it they revert to what they really know, or don't know.

3 *Complacency*

The first night went so well. Everybody was brilliant. The critics loved it. My mum loved it. We're a hit. We can do the show standing on our heads. Instead we fall flat on our faces.

4 *Delusion*

Actually the first night was just as bad, but the combination of adrenalin and triumph has fooled the cast into believing everything went well. Without adrenalin and triumph the second night comes as a dose of corrective reality.

5 *Depression*

People have been silly enough to read the reviews. Word has got around. One actor in particular has been victimised and nobody thinks it's fair. Or the director has been mocked and everybody thinks it's fair. Whatever. Carefully cherished expectations have been dashed.

The best antidote to all these conditions is for the director to go into pastoral mode. Be in the theatre long before the half. Meet people in the dressing rooms and **Green Room**. Cheer the downtrodden and sober the triumphant. Give a few **notes**. Give the actors something to think about, new things to achieve, old things to chew over. Have a warm-up session on stage before the show starts. Do a bit of a **speed run**. Get the energy levels back up to snuff. Remind everyone what the show's about. The second-night audience deserves a first-rate show.

Set Design and Designers

There are many different terms to describe the art of designing the stage environment and none of them has a precise or universally agreed meaning.

Some designers dislike the term 'set design' as being too limiting a description of what they do in transforming the stage for a performance. Set design, they argue, implies the use of conventional, and therefore despisable, naturalistic scenery. Thus designers are credited in programmes in many different ways according to their individual taste or the tradition of the theatre in which they are working. You will read, variously, 'Designs by . . .', 'Designed by . . .', and 'Designer' to describe someone who designs both set and costumes, and 'Set by . . .', 'Sets by . . .', and 'Settings by . . .' to describe someone who only does the stage work and leaves the costuming to others. More recently, 'Scenographer . . .' or 'Scenography by . . .' has started creeping in from the Continent.

Whatever you call him, this entry describes the work of the scenic artist as opposed to the Costume or Lighting Designer. I shall call him the Set Designer.

CHOOSING A DESIGNER

While first reading your play you will have started to imagine its physical life in terms of people, locations, atmosphere and any other visual demands made explicitly or implicitly by the author. Once you have fully digested the needs of the play's physical life and started to imagine how it might be realised in theatrical terms, you are ready to choose a designer with whom you can further develop your visual ideas, or to whom you can entirely entrust the visual world of the play.

Some directors have a close relationship with a particular designer with whom they habitually work, or even an exclusive life-long director/designer partnership, but most directors will want to choose, or be forced through the unavailability of other alternatives to choose, a particular designer for a particular play.

Whether you employ your designer after a great deal of prior thought, or develop all your design ideas in partnership with your designer, you will discover that there are countless different ways of designing any one play, that there are no absolute rules governing the appropriateness of any set of design ideas, and that over the course of your directorial career your choice of designers and your tastes and instincts with regard to their designs will help to define you as a director.

CHOOSING A DESIGN

Having chosen a designer, you must decide between you what is the appropriate style of design for the play, for the theatre or theatres in which the play is to be mounted, for the actors who are to appear in the play, and for your own preferred directorial method. There are countless styles of theatre design, the ones most commonly referred to in modern theatre parlance being **naturalistic**, **abstract** (or **conceptual**) and **environmental**, though design also comes in packages labelled 'constructivist', 'minimalist', 'decorative', 'expressionistic', 'epic', 'rococo', 'post-modern' and so on.

Most designers are happy to work in a number of different design styles and many designs use a mixture of different styles. It is commonplace, for instance, to find elements of naturalism cropping up in otherwise abstract design concepts, and vice versa. It would therefore be foolish to try to define the appropriateness of any design 'concept' for any particular play based on traditional or conventional aesthetic ideas of any sort.

Suffice it to say that there are important considerations in the selection of any design, some of which may be crucial for one play, director or designer and less important for others, but all of which are worth rehearsing at some point during the design process. In no particular order of significance, here they are:

15 QUESTIONS THE DIRECTOR AND DESIGNER
SHOULD ASK THEMSELVES WHEN DESIGNING A PLAY

1. How did the author or authors envisage the physical life of the work when it was originally created? Would it be valuable to honour this vision? Or would it be valuable to ignore it, or transgress it? Whatever importance you accord this question, it can never be completely irrelevant, and answering it may give you a deeper understanding of the physical structure underlying the topography of the drama.

2. Is there an appropriate design style for the style of writing? If your play is written in an intensely naturalistic style, do you have good reason for not designing the play in similar wise? Or if the

play is written in an abstract or absurdist style, would an abstract or absurd design be a necessary, useful or interesting response to it? Should you design *with* the style of the writing or against it? Or go with some elements of it and ignore others?

3. How many scenes does your play have and how many disparate locations? If the play is written in an epic style with multiple locations, how well will your design accommodate the swift and elegant movement of your production from one scene to the next?

4. Does your play evoke a particular historical period? How accurately do you want to portray that period, if at all? Or do you want to set the play in a different historical period from the one in which it was written, or bring it up to date, or project it into the future, or none of these, or some mixture of these?

5. Are you going to be directing the play in a particular performance style? If you are fond of working with '**poor theatre**' or '**rough theatre**' techniques, how will your design accommodate this? For instance, if the actors are to use **mime** instead of actual props, what impact does that choice have on the scenery or furniture, if any?

6. What are the central imagistic themes of the play and should your design physically reflect them in some way? If so, should these references be literal, allusive or abstracted?

7. What do your actors need in order to feel comfortable and real in the physical lives of their characters? How will the style of the design marry with the acting style and avoid irreconcilable contradictions between the two? What are the rules, if any, governing the use of furniture and props? Will the actors be happy with them? If you want to dispense with furniture entirely, how do you solve the 'sitting problem' inherent in the art of mime?

8. Will your design be physically and acoustically friendly to the actors? Are you unwittingly providing them with hazards of any sort? Will your design impede their movements, endanger their health, compromise their safety, or soak up the sound of their natural voices? Have you done everything you can to help them? In **opera**, is your set enough of a sounding board for the singers' voices?

9. Does the play present any specific physical problems in terms of its scenic demands? In *Romeo and Juliet*, Act I Scene 2, Juliet requires a balcony. Or does she? In *Antony and Cleopatra*, Act IV

Scene 15, Cleopatra drags the dying Antony up into her tomb. How? In *Macbeth*, Act IV Scene 1, a cauldron appears, apparitions come out of it, and then it disappears again. Or does it? How do you *do* a cauldron? What *are* apparitions? It's all up to you.

10. How will your design fit into the particular theatre or theatres you've chosen or had chosen for you? Are there any intrinsic problems of visibility or audibility that your design can help to address? If Juliet is on her balcony, will the **sightlines** allow her to be visible to everyone in the audience as well as to Romeo?

11. What is the most dynamic relationship your design can promote between stage and auditorium, between actors and audience? Do you want to change the theatre's normal set-up? Is a **forestage** useful to your production or a **thrust** stage, or a **hanamichi**? Will your actors need access from the stage into any part of the auditorium via stairs, ladders or platforms?

12. Should your design encroach into areas of the theatre not normally affected by design considerations? How far out into the auditorium should your design **environment** reach? Should your design have an impact on the auditorium, or on the foyers and bars, or on the outside of the theatre building?

13. Will your play be performed in more than one theatre? If your production starts in one theatre and ends up in another, should your design be more appropriate for one than the other, or equal to both? If your first theatre is merely a try-out venue, are there commercial considerations involved in this decision? If your play is to tour many theatres, how can it do so with a minimum of technical pain and stay within the time constraints of **get-ins and get-outs**?

14. Are you intending to use stage machinery of any sort and if so, have you considered the implications of cost, reliability, safety and noise? Things electrical, hydraulic, mechanical or computerised can cause problems far beyond any artistic benefit they might provide. Are you sure you have real control over your machinery?

15. What is your **budget**? Can you afford any of what you want to do? Will you have to cut some of your ideas in order to retain others? What are your priorities? Is there any element that is obviously so expensive that a righteous producer would be mad to give you the money for it?

Set Design and Designers

WORKING WITH SET DESIGNERS

If you can, you should always try to meet your designer in his studio, especially for the first two or three meetings. You will have much better ideas when you discuss your show in the designer's environment, surrounded by drawings and models from other shows and with ready access to the research and art books that are the designer's staple sources.

At your first meeting spend plenty of time talking about the play. Don't jump straight into design solutions. Talk about the meaning of the play, what you want it to say to the audience, how you think the story works and what the central themes are. Talk all around the play, about the period in which it is set and about the life and mind of the writer.

Share everything you've thought of in your reading of the text so far. If you have visual images you think are important, bring them along. Don't force them on your designer but do get them out of your system. Once you've shared your first visual ideas with a designer, they may not seem quite so clever.

Be careful with inexperienced designers. They can easily be over-influenced by a director's ideas, wanting to please the director so much that they lose track of what they think themselves.

As your meetings continue and your designer starts making a **model** of the set, keep your head clear. Don't fall in love with a visual world at the expense of a practical environment for your actors. Keep referring back to the play and what the scenes require. Whatever you and your designer decide will have an impact on every minute of your rehearsals.

Try to solve the basic staging problems of the play. Use the designer's little human figures on the model to get a sense of scale, image and action. Don't go into rehearsal with any major problems left unresolved. When you reveal the model on the first day of rehearsal, you and your designer must be confident you have provided an appropriate environment for everything that happens in the play. You don't have to work everything out in minute detail in advance, but you must be sure there are no nasty surprises lying in wait for you.

If your Set Designer is also your **Costume Designer**, don't leave the costumes until last. Incorporate your costume ideas in your talks about the set. Everything must be of a piece.

If you are using a separate Costume Designer, make sure he is on board at an early stage of the design process. Share images of the model with him as soon as you can. The style of the costumes must meld with the style of the set to create a unified world. If you oblige the costume designer to work in a void, the costumes will always look more like costumes and less like clothes.

Similarly with the **Lighting Designer**. Share your design ideas as soon as you can so he can start designing a rig that will complement the set, technically and artistically.

Sightlines

The sightlines of a theatre are the imaginary lines drawn between the eyes of the spectators and the edges of those parts of the stage they are able to see.

A theatre with perfect sightlines is one in which every spectator has an uninterrupted view of every part of the stage.

A theatre with good sightlines is one in which most of the spectators have a good view of all of the stage with only a few spectators, sitting at the extreme edges of the **auditorium**, unable to see the edges of the stage.

A theatre with poor sightlines is one in which only the spectators sitting in the middle of the auditorium or on the front edges of the balconies have a good view of all the stage.

To a certain extent, there is little a director, designer or actor can do about the basic sightlines of any given theatre. Theatre architects must bear the responsibility for the way the auditorium is put together, the rake of the seats, the depth of the balcony **overhangs**, the number of permanently **obstructed view seats**, and the fundamental relationship of auditorium to stage. Whatever problems the architects have left us to wrestle with, wrestle with them we must, and the awareness of a theatre's sightlines and their effect on an audience remains one of our most fundamental duties. A lack of awareness, resulting in sightlines being consistently obscured throughout a performance, can cause an audience to feel cheated.

There are seven main sightline questions to answer:

1 When you are sitting in a seat on the extreme left of the auditorium, how much of the left-hand side of the stage can you see (stage right)?
2 When you are sitting in a seat on the extreme right of the auditorium, how much of the stage-left area can you see?
3 When you are sitting in one of the uppermost seats of the auditorium, how good are your views of the very back and the very front of the stage?
4 When you are sitting at the very back of any section of the auditorium, how good is your view of the stage floor and how far over the actors' heads can you see? Does the overhang above your head cut off your view?
5 Are any elements of production design obscuring your view of the stage, including lighting or sound apparatus?
6 At any point during the play, are any actors on the stage consistently obscuring your view of their fellow actors?
7 When the actors are standing off stage or in the wings, are they visible to the audience or is the audience visible to them?

Some of these problems will be endemic to your theatre building, some will be caused by the design of your production and some by the way the actors behave on stage. You must therefore check the sightlines in your theatre on a regular basis throughout the **technical** and **dress rehearsals**.

On your first visit to the theatre, before you and your designer have decided how to set your play, you should both make an analysis of the sightlines. Visit the worst seats in the house. Imagine what it would be like for spectators sitting there and think of ways to make their experience of your production as rich as it can be.

In the rehearsal room, have your Stage Manager mark out the sightlines on the floor at the downstage edge of your **mark-out**, so that you and the actors are constantly reminded of the true parameters of the stage/auditorium relationship. If you suffer any doubts in rehearsal as to the visibility of what you and the actors are devising, take them on a brief 'field-trip' to the theatre to prepare yourself and them for the real environment of the production.

When you arrive in the theatre for the technical rehearsals, make sure the actors visit every part of the house and watch at least some of the technical rehearsals from the seats with the biggest sightline problems.

As the technical rehearsals continue, make constant trips to the very edges of the auditorium to check the sightlines on every level of the house for every scene of the play. This is a very good job to share with an assistant, especially one that might benefit from the exercise of trudging up to the gods and back on a regular basis.

Be aware throughout the technical and dress rehearsals of any new equipment that your Lighting or Sound Designers might decide to hang from the theatre walls or the edges of the balconies. A sound or lighting instrument may create better technical opportunities on stage but may also be hanging directly in the eye-line of an audience member. Audience members take priority.

Have your Stage Manager mark out clear white lines on the stage surface at the point where an actor walking out of the wings first becomes visible to the audience. Make every member of the cast and offstage crew aware of them.

Silence

Silence is one of the absolute prerequisites for good theatre but astonishingly difficult to achieve. Absolute silence is unattainable in a theatre, unless you fancy doing plays all on your own in an airless **Black Box** or a windless desert waste. The silence required for theatre is the comparative quiet that occurs when an entire audience and cast all seem to be listening at the same time and with the same intensity to what an actor is about to say. Comparative because there may be many perceivable extraneous noises happening at such a time that are drowned out by the sound of the listening – the sound of the silence. How do you achieve this balance of

Silence

what must be heard as opposed to what must be ignored? Only by vigilance – or whatever the aural equivalent is – aurilance?

You must first eliminate all the possible sources of extraneous noise you can, some of which may be within your power and some not.

NOISEMAKERS IN THE THEATRE

Exterior noise

Theatre owners and producers depend on passing trade and most theatres are built in the middle of towns, often in the busiest areas of the middle of towns.

Even in a well-soundproofed theatre with thick walls, an auditorium surrounded by corridors and a stage surrounded by dressing rooms, the sounds of the outside world are still clearly audible. The revving of car engines, the wail of police sirens, the rumble of underground trains or the tuneless bellowing of aggressive drunks are all familiar features of the soundscape of the average West End or Broadway play.

There is very little, if anything, that a director can do about this, and in any case, these are the sorts of noise to which most members of an urban audience will already be quite inured. It's the people up from the country who are more likely to be disturbed by them. Just as a townie visiting the country can be kept awake all night by unaccustomed silence, so a rustic visitor can be deafened by the unaccustomed roar of the city.

You can solve some of the very local human noise by having the **front of house** management patrol the outside of the theatre pleading for silence from the worst offenders, but it's none too easy breaking up a drunken brawl or a blazing domestic argument without adding to the noise yourself – and calling the police will just add a siren or two to the mix.

Pub theatres or theatres built in close proximity to pubs or bars have a particular cross to bear. A pub full of drinkers makes a good racket on Friday and Saturday nights even at normal levels of enjoyment, but if you add to that an amplified sound system or a nice loud DJ or karaoke machine, you have a recipe for cacophony. Breweries and other owners of pub and bar chains have come to believe that they sell more booze when the music levels are well cranked up and are unsurprisingly unsympathetic when asked to keep the noise down to Chekhov level or below. The best thing to do is get a really good relationship with the local manager and hope that a few complimentary tickets will do the trick – or the chance to spend time with the cast. The social allure of the acting profession is an amazingly effective bribe on occasion.

Interior noise: machines

All machines in the theatre have the capacity to make some noise, however carefully they are operated.

In recent years theatre has become more and more dependent on technical effects in lighting and sound. This has added more and more complex machinery backstage and in the auditorium. Every one of these machines makes some noise, and collectively they add up to a persistent low-grade electronic hum, present now in every theatre equipped with the latest technology. Most of the noise is made by the fans that cool the equipment so it doesn't overheat and blow up. Even the smallest of moving lights in the rig above the stage is equipped with a little fan, inaudible on its own but deafening when multiplied by fifty or a hundred. The LX racks have big cooler fans and are hardly ever screened off from the stage. These make a dull roaring sound, adding a tenor range to the overall noise. But the bass line is usually supplied by the worst noisemaker of all – the air-conditioning plant. Audiences expect to be kept warm in winter and cool in summer – not an unreasonable demand – and the machines that do the work have the biggest fans of all, rumbling and roaring as they push currents of air all around the theatre. Sometimes the air-conditioning plant is attached to the walls of the fly tower or auditorium and makes the whole super-structure of the building gently vibrate.

The accumulated effect of all this noise is to make the background atmosphere inside the theatre highly unsuitable for the spoken word. Before the play has begun the actors are already working at a terrible disadvantage, and the more intimate and sensitive the writing the harder it is for an actor to achieve a real moment of human-scale emotion. But the audience rarely knows this is happening. Their ears quickly adjust to the constant background of ambient noise, and if they have trouble hearing the actors they assume that the actors are incompetently mumbling their lines.

Actors respond to background noise by raising their voices, over-projecting their lines, biting off their consonants and singing their vowels, their battle with the surrounding machinery making them sound less and less human and more and more like machines themselves.

There is a real danger that the roar of technology is slowly but surely drowning out the art of the spoken word. But what can you do about it? Well, you mustn't do nothing. You have to join in the war against noise. For the sake of your actors and the integrity of your own work, you must try to eliminate as much of the noise as you can and finds ways of living with the noises that are irremediable.

So what to do?

You can rely on technology to defeat technology, but you shouldn't do so as a first line of defence. All problems of actor audibility can easily be solved by giving everyone a body-mike or by putting pick-up microphones all around the stage and amplifying the voices through the auditorium speakers. But this way lie the perils of noise inflation. The technology gets louder, so you crank up the microphones. Ah, the actors' voices are clear as a bell now, we don't need to worry about the background noise, so let's get some more noisy technology into the theatre. Oops, the actors are inaudible again. Crank up the microphones! And so on and on until visiting the theatre will be like attending a spoken rock concert. Technology then cannot be the easy answer, even though it might become your last resort.

There is a simpler and cheaper route to take that will be far more effective in the long run. Start by identifying the noises that your theatre makes. This isn't as easy as it sounds, as a lot of the noise is subtle and ambient in nature. Stand in the middle of the auditorium with your Sound and Lighting Designers and your Chief

Technician and ask for complete silence from everyone in the theatre. After a few seconds you will start to hear the level of background noise in its true colours. Make a judgement about where
you think the worst noises are coming from. As you identify them,
switch off the piece of machinery that is making the noise and listen again. Keep going in this way until you have identified every
major noisemaker in the theatre. The air conditioning will probably be a major contributor. The lighting racks will also figure, but
there will be other sources you couldn't have known about without
tracking them down. Eventually you will have switched everything
off that is contributing to the noise and you will hear the traffic in
the street outside and people's voices and a plane passing overhead.
At that point your investigation is over. Now make a list of all the
noisemakers in the theatre in order of seriousness and allocate various members of your team to finding appropriate solutions for
each problem. Something can usually be done to diminish the
sound of each culpable machine.

When air conditioners are regularly and properly serviced they
make a lot less noise. They can also be turned off just as a performance begins or at the quietest moments of a performance and
turned on again during the interval. Most theatres don't heat up
or cool down so quickly that the air conditioning can't be
switched off for an hour at a time without making the audience
suffer unduly. Nuts and bolts can be tightened to cut out noisy
vibrations. LX racks can be muffled by soundproofing. Doors to
machine rooms can be soundproofed and kept shut during performance hours. Some lighting instruments make much more
noise than others, the oldest often being the worst. Get your LX
department to identify the culprits and have them properly serviced. Ice-cream refrigerators in the front of house area or domestic fridges in the Green Room or crew room are often humming
away very successfully and can be screened off or switched off,
soundproofed or serviced.

The auditorium itself can also be a sort of noisy machine. Doors
from foyer to auditorium can squeak. Oil them. Auditorium seats
can creak and clunk. Oil them or fix them or shut them up somehow.

Silence

Any serious noisemaking machine that can't be muffled in some way or another should have its rights read to it and be chucked out of service. There's no room for sentiment. The war must be won.

Interior noise: people

Machine noise is sometimes infuriatingly insoluble. People in the theatre can be silenced much more easily, but not without care and discipline. Backstage and front of house chatter can be cut out altogether simply by making people aware where they can be heard on the stage and where not. The simplest rule is: If you can hear the actors on the stage, they can hear you.

Actors and crew must be made aware that even a whisper can cut through a silence and that everyone on or near the stage must be mute as a general rule, only speaking in an absolute whisper when absolutely necessary.

Members of the crew engaged in **scene-change** duties must also be able to work in absolute silence. No chair or table must be clattered, no flying piece should hit the deck suddenly and noisily and no rostrum set down with a hollow clunk. Anything that makes a noise when it scrapes across the stage should be padded with felt or leather, even the legs of chairs and tables. The wheels on moving stage pieces should be made of silent material, rubber or nylon, and their axles and rotating joints greased, oiled or graphited to the nines.

Shoes, too, are prime noisemakers. Actors' shoes should be rubber-soled or felted, and the crew's trainers or work-boots should be treated or trained to be silent. Nothing on stage or backstage that makes a noise through human agency should be allowed to get away with it.

Audience noise is sometimes far harder to address, but there are solutions there, too. All experienced actors know what it's like to play to an audience of barking bronchials, though audiences do tend to cough more when they're bored or when the tension on stage has lifted for a while. But audiences can be disciplined, too. Some theatres put notices in the foyer or notes in the programme asking for people to lessen the effects of their coughing by using a handkerchief. Some theatres have jars of readily accessible and free sweets with silent wrappers for coughers to pick up on their way into the auditorium. People being made aware of what is expected of them can make a huge difference, though theatres do sometimes shoot themselves in the foot by selling sweets and candy bars in the foyer with crackly wrappers specially designed to drive everyone in the audience frantic with annoyance.

The only two audience noises that are entirely acceptable are **laughter** and **applause**.

Sitzprobe

The sitzprobe ('sitz' for short and in opera pronounced 'zitz', the German way) is one of the most exciting events in the schedule of an **opera** or **musical theatre** production.

The word comes from the German 'seated trial' or 'sitting test'. Throughout rehearsals the singers will have been performing to a piano **accompaniment**, unaware of the colours of the **orchestra** that will eventually accompany them. Towards the end of the rehearsal period, the orchestra or band will rehearse with the conductor or Musical Director in a separate space, the sung lines they will eventually be accompanying more or less a mystery to them, or at best groaned out to them by the **conductor** as they play. The sitzprobe is the day when the singers first hear the orchestra and vice versa. Everyone sits in the same space and the score is probed.

This is a rehearsal that belongs to the **conductor** and/or **Musical Director** and not to you, but you must have your ears open all the same, ready to be surprised or challenged by the sounds you and the singers are hearing for the first time. Be especially mindful of places in the **score** where the orchestration seems to be drowning out the words, because of volume or the texture of a particular passage. If the score is a new one and there is still some leeway in the way it has been orchestrated, take careful notes throughout the day and talk to the composer and **orchestrator** afterwards about your concerns.

Sitzprobe

Above all, the sitzprobe should be a day of celebration, a big shot of musical vitamins for everyone concerned. Try to schedule the day of the sitzprobe as late in the rehearsal process as you possibly can. It is difficult for the singers to go back to the rehearsal room with the piano in the corner after they've heard the full orchestra. The sitzprobe should serve as a springboard onto the stage and help to mitigate the inevitable slog of the **technical rehearsal**.

Smoke

Smoke, also known as 'haze' or 'mist', is a scenic effect much loved by directors and designers but disliked by actors and positively hated by singers. There are various types of smoke machine, some oil-based, some water-based, creating effects of various intensity, from dense cloud to wispy mist.

The last twenty years have seen smoke effects become more and more fashionable, so much so they've become something of a design cliché. They are used to create mysterious or dreamy atmospheres and weather conditions, making naturalistic exteriors look somehow more authentic and romantic. They also serve to make set and lighting designs look better than they really are. A little smoke in the air breaks up the light before it hits the stage and catches shafts of light in mid-air. This can be extremely effective, and many Lighting Designers are unhappy if they're not allowed to use smoke of some sort. A belief has taken hold that if you don't use smoke, your lighting design will never win an award. 'No smoke, no Tony' as they say in New York.

There are problems with the use of smoke. The makers of smoke machines assure us they have no effect whatsoever on throats and voices, that if people cough when shrouded by stage smoke, they are doing so psychosomatically. The coughers don't agree with them, in the auditorium and on stage. There are actors and singers who are so convinced the smoke does them harm, they won't share a stage with it. In some theatre communities, there are now **union** rules governing the use of smoke, and some individual opera houses and theatre companies have unilaterally banned it.

If you are allowed to use smoke, be aware it can have a life of its own. Smoke behaves differently in different atmospheric conditions and with different numbers of people in the auditorium. Depending on whether FOH or backstage doors are left open or air conditioners are turned on and off, smoke can be blown up the fly tower or billow out into the auditorium, and you never know which way it's going to go. If in doubt, take it easy on the smoke cues.

DRY ICE

Dry ice isn't smoke. Dry-ice effects are produced by putting solid carbon dioxide into water and then pumping the resulting clouds onto the stage. Because the gas is heavier than air it stays close to the ground. If it drifts into the auditorium it tends to drop off the front of the stage and disappear. Theatre companies that hate smoke won't be so severe on the use of dry ice, but it's still a pretty hackneyed effect – and quite expensive too.

Soliloquy

A soliloquy is a speech made by a single actor in direct address to the audience, from the Latin *solus*, alone, and *loqui*, to speak.

Soliloquy is often used as a synonym for **monologue**, but the distinction between them is a necessary one. A monologue is a play or an extract from a play, to be performed by one person only. A soliloquy is a speech within a play where the character seems to be speaking or thinking to himself. Herein lies the most common misconception about how soliloquies should be performed. It is all in the 'seeming'.

Most soliloquies emerge from scenes. A character is in a scene with another character, or a number of other characters, and for one reason or another the other characters leave the stage. At that point, the remaining character's relationship with the audience changes. The **fourth wall** that separates actors from audience threatens to disappear. The actor has no other human contact on the stage around him. So what is his reason for remaining there?

675

Soliloquy

He cannot sit or stand in silence for very long before the audience will start to wonder what he is thinking about. If he starts to talk to himself, how does he do it? In a monotone, under his breath? Or loud enough for the audience to hear? Either way, unless he acknowledges the audience, he will be doing a very unnatural thing.

Very few people in real life talk to themselves out loud. When they think, they do so silently, their words only sounding in their own minds. If they talk in coherent sentences out loud to themselves they generally only do so when they are addressing an imaginary interlocutor – but most stage soliloquies are not written in this manner. They are clearly supposed to represent the most intimate thoughts of the soliloquiser – and in a purely naturalistic copy of real life those thoughts would only be expressed inwardly, in silence.

Thus in a film, soliloquies are nearly always done as 'voice-overs'. While the camera plays on the face of the actor, his voice tells you what he is thinking. You could try the same technique on stage but to little effect. Most audience members sit too far away for the facial features of the player to express a sufficiently interesting or entertaining emotional reading of the spoken words. And the words themselves will always seem dislocated and mechanical when coming from a loudspeaker somewhere else in the auditorium. You can try this technique for a few lines or for a special local effect, but an audience would soon tire of it in a long, psychologically complex speech.

A soliloquy offers the actor the chance to share his character's inner thought processes with the audience. If there are soliloquies in your play, don't let the actors get into the habit of playing them to themselves as if they were all alone in an empty universe. Some actors find the idea of direct address awkward, but you must help them out of their embarrassment. An actor speaking a soliloquy to himself will always come across as paranoid and furtive, unable to trust the audience with his thoughts and awkward about expressing them to himself.

The first moment of every soliloquy must include an awareness of the audience. The actor alone on stage is not really alone. The audience is part of the soliloquy. It represents his thoughts and is ready to start thinking with him as long as it is given the attention and the information it needs to complete its side of the bargain.

Sharing a soliloquy is difficult in rehearsal with so few people properly attending to the scene. Nonetheless, you can still get the actor to play to the people in the room, to you, to the stage management and the other actors. They can also play to an imaginary audience beyond the people in the room, but they should keep referring back to the real people.

A soliloquising actor should think of changing the focus of his speech to a different member of the audience every time his character has a new thought, his individual thoughts being shared with individual members of the audience. Or he should think of his mind, his intelligence, as encompassing the whole auditorium, each member of the audience representing a potential thought. By grazing through the audience for his thoughts he creates an authentic image of thinking and, more importantly, he takes the audience with him as he thinks. He makes them feel they are thinking his thoughts with him.

In this way the soliloquising actor creates an empathy with his audience. By sharing his thought process, the audience fully imagines the intellectual and emotional journey of the character. If the thoughts are vividly evoked, imagination soon becomes identification and the magic circle of soliloquy is made complete. It makes no difference how sympathetic or unsympathetic a character's actions or motives might be. If a soliloquy is genuinely shared, Richard III and Iago can become as persuasive and attractive as Hamlet or Viola.

Sonnets and Sonnet Classes

Shakespeare's Sonnets can be used as a teaching tool in the study of his plays. (See under **Verse and Verse Speaking**.)

Sound Design and Designers

The sound design of a show comprises all sounds electronically composed, reproduced, modified or enhanced. A Sound Designer creates the most efficient and artistically appropriate means by which these sounds are transmitted to the audience's ears.

Although a Sound Designer is often in the business of mixing natural or acoustic sound with electronically produced sound, a completely natural sound plot, involving human voice, manually produced sound effects and unamplified music, does not require the attention of a Sound Designer. The craft of sound design is essentially a feature of the electronic age.

THEATRE SOUND DESIGN

If you use a Sound Designer for a theatre piece you need to start talking to him as early as possible in the rehearsal process. He should have read the play and made a note of all the places where **sound effects** or **music** are mentioned in the text or could be appropriately interpolated. But he will need to know how you are 'hearing' the show. If music is involved, is it live or recorded? If the former, how many instruments will be used and where, on or off the stage, have you and your designer decided to put them? If the latter, what recordings are you proposing to use – or are you expecting him to search for them?

By the end of your first meeting he should have a good idea what you want and will go away with a shopping list of sounds to find. He will also be able to start designing his 'rig'. This is the arrangement of strategically placed speakers and microphones, on and off stage and FOH, all connected up to a sound desk. The desk is usually placed at the back of the auditorium where the Sound Operator, who may or may not be the designer himself, can make canny judgements about the volume and balance of the sound cues.

The design of the rig will involve liaison with Set and Lighting Designers. Speakers can be quite large and may have to compete for space in wings and on flying bars.

Your Sound Designer should be at all **production meetings**, but you may need additional meetings to discuss new ideas that come up in rehearsal. Better still, the Sound Designer should attend rehearsals after, say, the second week or at least two weeks before technical rehearsals start. That way he can play you the cues as he has imagined them and you can start working them into the scenes as they're being rehearsed. If you do this, you'll need a rudimentary sound rig in rehearsal.

If you're using specially composed music, your composer will also be in rehearsal. He and your Sound Designer can discuss between them how the instruments should be amplified, if necessary, and the balance of live sound to recorded effects.

Sound Designers must also take responsibility for the 'show relay' that transmits the sound of the show to the dressing rooms and backstage corridors so the offstage actors and crew know where they are in the show, the short-wave radio circuit used by the technical departments to communicate with the Stage Manager and DSM and any video monitors that might be required for blind cueing. They will also provide you with a **'god-mike'** for use in **technical rehearsals**.

MUSICAL THEATRE SOUND DESIGN

Sound design for **musical theatre** is far more complex than for 'straight' theatre. The designer must amplify the orchestral instruments and the voices, a separate microphone for each instrument and a **radio-mike** for each performer, mix the sound at a desk in the auditorium and transmit a carefully balanced result to all parts of the theatre. He may also have to mix in sound effects for good measure.

Mikes and speakers are positioned all around the stage, float-mikes on the edge of the stage, 'rifle'-mikes pointing at inaccessible places or at singers without radio-mikes, 'FX'-mikes hanging in the air to create echo effects and the like, **foldback** speakers in the wings or buried in the stage surface so the singers can hear their own voices, and so on.

The average musical has hundreds of cues, each microphone

having to be turned on just before the singer sings and off immediately afterwards. The contiguity of mikes and speakers can cause feedback (see **Musical Theatre**), so each moment of the show must have a corresponding state, or cue, that delivers a pleasing sound, changing as the characters move around on stage and the instrumentation changes in the pit.

The sound plot for a musical can be unbelievably complicated and entirely reliant on computers, which is why most Sound Designers are serious computer geeks.

THE SOUND OPERATOR

A good Sound Operator is like an instrumentalist in his own right. He plays his sound desk like a church organ. He must be dextrous, sensitive and alive to every little change coming from stage or pit. He must learn to operate the show as the Sound Designer hears it, but must also trust his own ears when the atmosphere in the theatre changes or a singer's voice fails or the staging unexpectedly changes, and adapt his plot accordingly.

In musical theatre, Sound Designers and their operators must be diplomats. From the sitzprobe onwards they must take conflicting instructions from a variety of sources without losing their temper or compromising the integrity of the design. They must maintain amicable and creative relationships with director, composer, orchestrator and Musical Director, often in the teeth of the most unreasonable demands.

The pressure on them is made all the greater when a show starts previewing by dint of their location in the auditorium. The sound desk usually stands at the back of the stalls, which also happens to be the place that neurotic or frustrated composers, orchestrators, producers and directors congregate to watch **previews**. These poor souls, neurotic about relinquishing control of their beloved show to the performers and crew, will take out their frustration on the only employee within earshot. Experienced Sound Designers know to expect this and curtain themselves off, ostensibly to keep their working light out of the eyes of the surrounding audience members, but actually to stop the composer leaning over the back wall of the sound desk and twiddling the faders up and down as the fancy takes him.

Sound Effects

Sound effects are artificially produced sounds substituting for real ones. The artifice may involve human agency, vocal or manual, or be mechanical or electronic, and the sounds may be reproductions of real sounds or crafty imitations.

At the simplest level, sound effects can be produced by actors. The effect of a slap on the face can be made by a clap of hands. The slapping or the slapped actor, or another actor standing near them, simply claps his hands as the slap seems to land on the receiving face.

Some actors are extraordinarily clever at creating sound effects with their voices and bodies – liquid being poured from a bottle, telephones ringing, doors creaking, birds calling, dogs barking – all so well produced you would take them for real sounds. These talents can be very useful if you are working in a **rough theatre** style. Large groups of actors can also produce remarkably evocative sounds – wind, water, fire and whole environments of sound can be made out of dozens of carefully mimicked noises.

The simplest manually operated instruments can also be quite effective. Coconut shells for horses' hooves. Rain-sticks or old-fashioned drum-and-canvas wind machines and metal thunder sheets. Offstage door-slams. Crash boxes full of broken china. Slapsticks. Before the advent of recorded sound, theatres equipped themselves with a battery of noisemakers such as these. Some even had wooden 'thunder-runs' built into their roofs. A cannonball rolling slowly down a wooden trough sounds remarkably like, well, a cannonball rolling down a wooden trough. But the attempt was all-important – and the audience knew what the sound meant.

The age of recording has brought with it a limitless menu of sound effects. We can, if we wish, fill our plays with a continuous **sound-scape** of recorded sound. But we should be careful how much we wish it. However naturalistically our plays are written, the characters within them do not speak exactly as they do in real life. They come in on cue, take turns to speak and use **heightened language** of one sort or another. They do not exist in a real aural landscape, so if you surround them with one, they may not survive the experience.

When deciding what sound effects to use, and how they should be produced or reproduced, consider first how much you really need them. Just as with your **music** cues, so it is with sound effects.

INTEGRAL EFFECTS

A sound effect is integral to your play if it is mentioned in the text, heard and/or commented on by the characters or deemed necessary for **storytelling** purposes. Comb through your play and make a list of the integral effects. Then decide how the effects should be delivered.

If you decide to use recorded sound and you have a long list of effects, you'll need some help from a **Sound Designer**. Go through the list with him and decide on the quality of the effect you want. For any one effect there may be hundreds, even thousands, of alternatives. Be as specific as you can and get your designer to offer up a selection. A good designer will have a huge library of effects to choose from. Some of them will be poached from sound-effect tapes and CDs, some will be his own recordings, others he may have to record specifically for your play.

If you're using music, you may need to consult with your composer or Musical Director about the use of the sounds and how they are to be mixed with the music cues.

ATMOSPHERIC EFFECTS

These are effects that are not strictly necessary to the plot, but may help you with your storytelling or add a useful ambience to a scene.

In choosing these effects, you must decide how present you want them to be and how continuous. This isn't just a matter of volume. A sound effect is only loud or soft in relation to the other sounds around it. This in turn is affected by the relative **silence** of the theatre in which you are working.

In real life we tune out the perpetual noises around us. This is harder to do in the theatre. It also requires a certain amount of sympathetic selectivity from the audience. You can play recorded birdsong for a scene set in the country, but it must compete with the real sound of traffic in the street outside the theatre.

Long and unvarying sound effects in the theatre can become grating. The sound of waves on a beach or wind in the trees can become just another irritating noise once they have made their first dramatic impact. Sound Designers make plots for these continuous cues that vary the volume and impact of the sound, starting and finishing loud and fading out completely in the middle of the scene, or playing at a subliminal level with little rises for effect at appropriate moments in the text.

Sound effects can be used to great emotional effect. The distant barking of a dog, seagulls calling from a cliff or rooks from a copse, a baby crying in a neighbouring house, a clock ticking on a mantelpiece, a bell tolling from across the fields, can be tokens of happiness or loneliness, despair or joy, security or fear, depending on the context. A well-designed sound rig can deliver an astonishingly evocative array of subtle effects.

IMAGINING A SOUND PLOT

When you think about sound effects, think about the total effect of all the sound in the show – the actors' voices, the meaning and music in their words, any singing there might be, or incidental and atmospheric music. How do all these sounds mix together to make a coherent whole?

Ask yourself how necessary sound effects are to the telling of your story. What will they add? Could they detract? Are they duplicated in the actors' voices or obviated by the text? If you choose to have an effect, how do you deliver it? What style are you working in? What are you hearing?

Let's take a well-known scene as an example, the storm scene from *King Lear*, Act III Scene 2 of the Folio text. Lear enters at the top of the scene and speaks these lines:

Sound Effects

Blow, winds, and crack your cheeks! Rage, blow,
You cataracts and hurricanoes, spout
Till you have drenched our steeples, drowned the cocks!
You sulph'rous and thought-executing fires.
Vaunt-couriers of oak-cleaving thunderbolts,
Singe my white head; and thou, all shaking thunder,
Strike flat the thick rotundity o'th' world,
Crack nature's moulds, all germens spill at once
That makes ingrateful man.

How would you imagine this passage in performance? Do you let the actor play in silence? You might think his words contain all the storm you need. Any sound you add will fight with them. Is that why Shakespeare used such evocative words, so you could imagine the storm rather than hear it? Or do you follow Shakespeare's stage direction at the top of the scene – *Storm still*? If he didn't write the stage direction someone in his theatre company did. If they didn't have a storm in the original production, why does the text ask for one?

If you decide against the silence option, what sort of storm do you have? Are you working in a rough-theatre style with a company of actors making all the sound effects? How good a storm can they conjure up? Do they just use their voices or do you give them thunder sheets, rain-sticks and a wind machine?

Or do you choose the music option? A percussionist or two can blow up a terrific storm. Big drums, timpani, gongs, tam-tams and cymbals can create a cacophony of thunder and lightning. Do the actors do this? Or musicians?

Do you use a different sort of music, more formalised? Let the words do the storytelling, while the music tells a different subtextual story. Do you use stormy music? Beethoven, Wagner, Mussorgsky. Or the opposite? Music that plays gently in ironical counterpoint to the storm as described.

Or do you go the naturalistic route and play real storm effects throughout the scene? If so, what effects? How close is the lightning overhead? When you mix in your lighting cues, how long are the pauses between lightning and thunder? How distant is the thunder? Is it rolling or crashing? How much wind do you want in the mix? And how much rain? Is the rain steadily torrential or does it come in bursts? From a technical point of view, do you use over-head speakers or wing speakers? Or do you wrap the storm all round the auditorium so the audience hears what Lear hears? Where in the text do you put your lightning strikes? On the two exclamation marks? Or somewhere else? How many do you want? And do you put a clap of thunder just before 'and thou, all shaking thunder'? How literal do you want to be?

However you deliver your storm, think too about the actor. What sounds are going to help the actor? He may appreciate a bit of competition here, but you don't want to drown him out. He has to play the part again tomorrow and he needs his voice. Work it out with him. How much is helpful and how much is too much?

And so it goes with every sound effect you ever consider. How do you deliver it? What's your style? Do you really need it?

SOUND EFFECTS AND ACTORS

Whether you are working with a Sound Designer or not, get your effects into rehearsal well before you start your **tech**. Don't surprise your actors with sound effects at the last minute. They won't thank you for it. But don't start playing them before they've had a chance to work on their text and characters. They won't thank you for that either.

Sound Enhancement

Sound enhancement is a system of **amplification** built into some modern theatres to allay bad **acoustics**.

Soundscape

'Soundscape' is a recently coined term used to describe the way atmospheric and incidental **music** can be mixed with real or

685

synthesised **sound effects** to create a more or less continuous accompaniment to a production, in the same way a film score accompanies a film.

Soundscapes may be created by **composers** or **Sound Designers** or by a partnership of both.

Spear-Carriers

'Spear-carrier' is a pejorative term describing an extinct function. In the days when actors were the least expensive components of a production, classical theatre companies performing large-scale tragedies and histories would use junior members of the ensemble to populate the stage in public scenes and battles, create a sense of pomp in throne-rooms and generally add status to the entrances and exits of important leading actors. Typically they would enter before the king or queen and their nobles, and then stand on guard either side of a doorway with legs planted firmly apart and spear at the ready.

In reality spear-carriers were little more than stage dressing and had as great a capacity to destroy the grandeur of the scenes they were in as to enhance them. The slightest untoward movement or earnest attempt to react to a principal performer's speech could result in egregious upstaging. Bored, resentful or jealous spear-carriers could create considerable comic mayhem if they so wished with nothing more complicated than a back-to-front helmet or a barely audible simultaneous critique of a star's best efforts.

The economy of the modern theatre has extinguished spear-carriers. Even in plays of great historical sweep, the fashion is now to agree with the Chorus in *Henry V* that 'a crooked figure may attest in little place a million'. Every character on stage must be central to the action or be unworthy of his hire. And so it should be.

The term is still used by lazy commentators to describe the junior members of a theatre company, especially if they have qualified for distinction later in their careers. By saying that such-and-such an actor started at the RSC or the National Theatre as a spear-carrier, implying his true talents were overlooked by his myopic employers, a journalist or biographer spins a double falsehood. The actor in question will have played small parts and understudied larger ones from the first rehearsal onwards and will have been chosen by a discerning Casting Director from amongst dozens of other less talented candidates. But rags-to-riches stories are always more interesting than stories of quiet and deserving endeavour so there will always be mendacious reports of spear-carriers rocketing to stardom in spite of being held back by the very people who actually spotted their talent and helped them to develop it in the first place.

Speed Run

A speed run is a complete run-through of the play with the actors performing their lines and their actions as fast as they can without gabbling or skimming. In the US a speed run is called an 'Italian' run, and by some a 'Russian' run.

Speed runs can be extremely useful in a number of different circumstances, but especially if you're concerned that a play is overlong, or being performed at a sluggish pace, or beset by overindulgent acting.

The rules of speed running are simple:

1 Actors must speak as fast as they can without swallowing or **fluffing** any of their words.
2 Actors must do all their moves at the same heightened speed but without the use of props and furniture.
3 All of the actors must attend all of the run, their entrances and exits being made from and to wherever they are observing the run.
4 Nothing must be allowed to slow up the action. Complicated emotions must be sketched, bits of physical business speed-mimed and interplay between the characters played like a particularly sparky game of squash or tennis.
5 Any actor thought to be slowing things up or falling into a

normal performance pattern must be goaded to go faster. Some actors are much better at this exercise than others, so allowances must always be made for old brains and dull wits. Let's say everyone must be going as fast as possible without anyone being made to feel inadequate.

The effect of a speed run can be quite extraordinary. Actors' wits are sharpened, their tongues, lips and teeth are made to work over-time, benefiting their diction, and the playing of a whole company is enlivened.

The performance immediately following a speed run is usually several minutes shorter than the one preceding it. That's several minutes of unearned and wearisome **pauses** you are much better to have shed.

Comedies are nearly always funnier after a speed run, tragedies more intense and naturalistic plays less self-indulgent. The actors explore new rhythms in the language and the audience is energised by new vitality coming from the stage.

There are two slight modifications of the speed run. One is mere-ly a fast **line run**, following the same rules as the speed run but without the physical movement, usually performed in a rehearsal room or Green Room after a lay-off in performances. The other is a 'jumping speed run', done when there isn't the time or the energy for a whole run or when there are particular parts of the play that are going too slowly. The rules are the same as the speed-run rules, but with a director or one of the actors controlling the action by jumping from one selected line in the play to another.

The controller calls out a line from the play. The actor whose line it is immediately repeats the line at speed-run pace while getting into position on the stage and the action continues from that moment with the other actors joining in as in a normal speed run.

At a suitable moment in the action the controller shouts out another line and the process repeats itself from wherever in the play the line is derived. The jumps can be made in play order or dotted to and fro in the action, and they can be pre-chosen by the con-troller or selected at random, but care should be taken that every actor gets a chance to perform, even those with very few lines.

A jumping speed run is a good wit-sharpener, less exhausting than a complete speed run, and can have the effect of speeding up the whole play, even those bits that weren't involved in the run, the energy derived from the selected passages spreading itself throughout the action. It's also an excellent company relaxer for the last afternoon of rehearsal before a **press night**; useful, fun and not too time-consuming when a cast is worrying about the critics, where their families will be sitting, and how many good luck cards they still have to write.

Spikes

'Spikes', or 'spike-marks', are the US equivalent of British **marks**, the taped indications of where stage furniture is to be placed from one scene to the next. 'Spiking-tape' is marking-tape.

Spotlight

Spotlight is the layman's term for a stage-lighting instrument, usually implying a finely focused beam of light on a particular actor. A **follow-spot** is a manually operated spotlight.

Spotlight is also the best known of the British **casting directories**.

Sprung Floors

A sprung floor is a wooden floor so constructed that it gives a little under the weight of actors' and dancers' feet. Most good **rehearsal rooms** are equipped with sprung floors, but if you come across one that isn't you should think twice before you agree to work in it, especially if your show contains a lot of **dance** or strenuous physical movement.

If you are doing a dance musical, your choreographer will demand a rehearsal room with a sprung floor. Without it, the dancers will be far more likely to injure themselves and will be unable to move or leap about with any flair or confidence.

Sprung Floors

Even in a show without dance, a sprung floor is much nicer for actors to work on. They get less physically tired than they do if they are working on thinly covered concrete.

If you can't get or afford a room with a sprung floor, then warm floors are much better than cold ones. Check out your rehearsal room in advance, and if you have any doubt about it, let your choreographer decide. He will know what is endurable for his dancers and what not.

Staff Directors

Not to be confused with **Associate Directors**, Staff Directors work in permanent theatre and **opera** companies reviving other directors' productions or assisting principal directors on new productions with a view to reviving them in the future. Their permanent employment is an economic measure, as they can be seconded to any production the management needs them to work on without the cost of **per diem** and travel payments.

If you work in a large theatre or opera company as a **Visiting Director**, you will need to rely heavily on your Staff Director, so a good relationship is essential. He will know all the customs of the country, the **union** rules, the in-house traditions, and the personal histories and animosities of the major players, artistic and administrative. In the opera house he will save you hours of brain-numbing torture in devising the weekly schedule and steer you expertly between the Scylla and Charybdis of Chorus Master and Conductor.

If you work as a Staff Director yourself, you must be practised at adapting your thinking to a wide variety of directorial styles and egos, and jumping from the demands of one principal director to another, sometimes in a matter of days. If you're a young or inexperienced director this can constitute a great training, as you learn your craft at the feet of a number of different masters. But if you have ambitions to be a director in your own right, be careful not to stay a Staff Director for too long. It may be a secure job, but if you do it well your artistic judgement will slowly become subsumed by the judgements of your principal directors and you will stunt your ability to imagine a production for yourself. If you're happy to remain a staff director that's fine, but don't kid yourself that there will be a perfect time to move on from the job at some unspecified future date. There won't be. And the longer you do the job, the harder it will be to move away from it.

You should be aware, too, that theatre and opera companies peg people at the level of their present experience. If you work as a Staff Director you will be thought of as having a Staff Director's mentality because that is how the management of the company treats with you on a daily basis. Unless they are peculiarly imaginative they will always think of you as someone else's second. If you want to work for the same company as a principal director you will probably have to move away from it first, get a job as a director in some other company and return at a later date when your old status has been rinsed out of the system.

Stage Directions

There are two sorts of stage direction – let's call them authorial and directorial.

Authorial stage directions are instructions to the actors in printed play texts, interpolated between the speeches of the characters.

Directorial stage directions are a shorthand form used by all theatre practitioners in application or interpretation of the authorial stage directions or simply to describe the delineations of any stage.

DIRECTORIAL STAGE DIRECTIONS

Whether you are sitting in the auditorium or at the head of your rehearsal room, you must be able to articulate, swiftly and clearly, where you want your actors to move in relation to one other and to the environment around them.

In order to apply stage directions to your rehearsals you must first have a clear map of the stage in your mind. This map will change from play to play, theatre to theatre and production to production, but the imaginary delineations of the stage that are implicit in conventional stage directions will serve for most of them. An obvious exception is theatre-in-the-round, where normal stage directions must be adapted for a circular or four-sided format.

In Britain and America and some other countries, stage directions are imagined from the actors' point of view – stage left being the actors' left and stage right the actors' right. This is as it should be, not just as a courtesy to the actors but as positive inspiration to the director to think like the actors and not like the audience, who shouldn't be thinking of such things at all.

Many other countries have different systems, some of them imagining the stage from the audience's point of view and others using methods of their own that have no correlative elsewhere in the world. In Japan, for example, what we would call stage left in Britain is known as *kami-te* (upstage) and stage right is *shimo-te* (downstage). In France, stage left is *Cour* and stage right *Jardin* (dating from the time of Molière, whose Théâtre du Palais-Royal was situated between the Royal Court and the Tuileries Garden). When working abroad, you will have to learn the local system or risk being sadly misunderstood by your stage management and design teams.

The following descriptions and abbreviations are the ones most commonly used in Britain. The directions are always relative to an audience's perception of them on the one hand and the position of the actors on the other.

Centre Stage (CS)

The central area of the stage, however far from the audience. The precise line dividing stage left from stage right is usually marked out on the rehearsal floor as the Centre Line (CL).

Upstage (US)

That part of the stage that is furthest from the audience or further away from the audience than where the actor happens to be standing.

Downstage (DS)

That part of the stage that is nearest to the audience, or nearer to the audience than where the actor is standing.

Stage Left (SL)

That part of the stage that is to the actor's left when he is standing stage centre facing the audience.

Stage Right (SR)

That part of the stage that is to the actor's right when he is standing stage centre facing the audience.

These five basic directions are made more particular by amalgamation. Downstage can be left, right or centre (DSL, DSR and DSC), as can upstage (USL, USR, USC).

Two more descriptions commonly used in rehearsal but rarely in printed texts are:

Onstage (On)

When you ask an actor to move from either side of the stage towards the centre, you ask him to move 'onstage' or 'further onstage'.

Offstage (Off)

When an actor moves from the centre of the stage towards either side of the stage he moves 'offstage' or 'further offstage'.

'Moving offstage' should not be confused with 'going offstage' which means leaving it altogether, or going into the wings.

Prompt Side and Opposite Prompt Side (PS and OP)

Prompt side and OP are old-fashioned designations for stage left and stage right respectively, old-fashioned and a little confusing in that the **prompter** is often obliged for technical reasons to sit on the OP side of the stage. Thus you can go to the prompt desk and ask the prompter for something only to be told that whatever you want is over on prompt side.

Stage Directions

To make matters more confusing, prompt side in the US is on stage right, though the prompter often sits on stage left.

There should be an international treaty drawn up to decree that prompt side is wherever the prompter is sitting, regardless of what theatre you're in or which side of the Atlantic you're on. Or abolish the term altogether and rely on stage left and stage right, terms which cause quite enough confusion as it is.

AUTHORIAL STAGE DIRECTIONS

The older the play the fewer the stage directions. Up until the nineteenth century playwrights use them very sparingly. They observe where the beginnings and ends of scenes are and where the characters enter and exit. Everything else is implicit in the text. The actors and director must devise movements for the characters and settings for the scenes from what the characters say.

With the advent of more naturalistic forms of drama a new sort of theatrical language appeared. Playwrights stopped requiring their characters to locate the scenes in which they appear by describing their surroundings. Stage directions became a necessary adjunct to this development. How else would designers, directors and actors know how to set the plays?

Compare two passages. Here is Friar Laurence's speech at the start of Act II Scene 2 of *Romeo and Juliet*:

> *The grey-eyed morn smiles on the frowning night*
> *Chequ-ring the eastern clouds with streaks of light*
> *And fleckled darkness like a drunkard reels*
> *From forth day's path and Titan's fiery wheels.*
> *Now e'er the sun advance his burning eye*
> *The day to cheer and night's dank dew to dry*
> *I must up-fill this osier cage of ours*
> *With baleful weeds and precious-juicéd flowers.*

And here is the opening stage direction from Act I of *The Cherry Orchard*:

(A room that used to be the children's bedroom and is still referred to as the 'nursery'. There are several doors, one of them leading to ANYA's room. It is early morning. The sun is just coming up. The windows of the room are shut but through them the cherry trees can be seen in blossom. It is May but in the orchard there is morning frost.)

Shakespeare uses Friar Laurence's first eight lines to tell his audience all it needs to know. It is dawn and the clouds in the eastern sky are patterned with light. The ground is still wet with dew and Laurence is gathering medicinal herbs from his garden. He is holding a basket, which is not 'his' but 'ours', implying the order to which he belongs. The scene is vividly set and Laurence has established a relationship with the audience in setting it. Directors and designers may wish to add touches of their own to the setting but they may also choose to do nothing. The eight lines are enough.

Chekhov uses his opening stage direction to tell the director, designer, Lighting and Sound Designers and actors all they need to know to create an appropriate setting for the scene. Even though the actors within the scene go on to talk about the time of day, the blossom in the orchard and the untimely frost, Chekhov's vision of the physical production of his play is contained in the stage direction. Directors and designers may follow his instructions or choose to ignore them, but there they are.

Wherever you find stage directions, it is up to you to decide how strictly they must be observed. Some directions are easier to ignore than others, and in many cases you must separate the wheat from the chaff. Take this one from the opening scene of Shaw's *Misalliance*:

(Hypatia rushes in through the inner door . . . she is a typical English girl of a sort never called typical: that is she has an opaque white skin, black hair, large dark eyes with black brows and lashes, curved lips, swift glances and movements that flash out of a waiting stillness, boundless energy and audacity held in leash.)

Stage Directions

This direction is useful as a guide to Hypatia's character, but no sensible director would feel bound to follow it slavishly when casting the play. If an actress was right for the part you wouldn't care if her eyes, brows, lashes and lips conformed to the description, but the 'swift glances' and the 'audacity held in leash' are valuable pointers and shouldn't be ignored.

With some stage directions, you may have to consider the circumstances in which they were written or the author's motive for writing them.

Some writers fear for the future lives of their plays and try to make them actor- and director-proof by peppering their texts with protective instructions. But these instructions are often drawn from the rehearsal period of the first production where the writer has observed the actors 'creating' the roles. You can usually tell from the context where this has happened, especially when you find bracketed instructions inserted between the character name and the speech, as in

Laura (with a light laugh)

or

Alec (glancing round furiously)

As a general rule you can tell your actors to disregard such directions, or to treat them as clues rather than instructions.

ACTING EDITIONS

Acting editions are texts that have been specially prepared for amateur companies that are short on staging and acting experience and have limited rehearsal time. Editors of acting editions record the moves of the first productions of plays so that the companies that use them feel they are reproducing them at their authentic best. Avoid using these editions if you possibly can. They may provide a foolproof production for the amateur director but they are a recipe for complacency and convention for the professional.

SPECIALISED AUTHORIAL DIRECTIONS

There are writers whose stage directions cannot be ignored. These are the ones for whom the physical gesture is as important as the speech, and the **pause** or the **silence** as informative of character as the words surrounding it. The most commonly cited example is Harold Pinter, but there are countless others and they all have more or less idiosyncratic ways of communicating their wishes. Some of them, recently deceased, reach out from beyond the grave to enforce their stage directions by legal writ. If you are considering acquiring the **performing rights** for a play by one of these writers, ask yourself first if you can bear to have their stage directions policed by an ignorant band of lawyers and self-aggrandising executors from the writer's estate.

Some writers have refined the directions within their characters' speeches to an extraordinary degree, completely subsuming them within the lines of dialogue. Thus . . . (three dots) may mean a pause for thought, - (hyphen) a broken thought, and — (dash) an incomplete sentence. **Beat** is shorter than pause, and pause shorter than silence, and so on. When studying the texts of these plays, you must acquaint yourself with the method each writer is using and what he is trying to achieve by it. Often they are seeking to establish a rhythm to the language that mimics the way people talk to one another in real life – in incomplete sentences and half-baked thoughts. Again, you must decide what is important and what isn't, but whatever you do, don't slavishly follow these directions without knowing why they are there. Actors act thoughts, not pauses, and they can only play a rhythm if it seems natural to them. The more indications there are in the text, the more detailed work you and your actors will have to do before they become familiar and comfortable with the writer's intention.

Stage Door

The stage door is the entrance into the theatre used by everyone concerned with the performance of the play. Actors, crew, stage management, technical staff and creative team all check in and out at the stage door at the beginning and end of rehearsals and performances. It is also the place where members of the audience congregate in order to meet the actors once the play is over.

The job of stage doorman is an important one. He is the guardian of the gate, the keeper of lists, the holder of dressing-room keys and the distributor of fan mail and bouquets. If he's a good one, he learns the names of all the actors and stage management and makes everyone feel welcome as they step into the theatre every night. At the end of each show, he politely keeps out the more loony of the fans and lets through the actors' friends and family. If he's a bad one he sits in a surly nicotine silence gawping at a tiny television, occasionally grunting at the more important actors as they hurry past him and rudely refusing access to anyone whose name isn't on one of his lists.

Stage Left and Stage Right

Commonly used directorial **stage directions**.

Stage Management

Stage management is both the craft and collectively the craftsmen and -women who ply it.

Stage Managers and their deputies and assistants are responsible for the artistic and logistical administration of a production in rehearsal and performance. They manage the stage on behalf of actors, directors, designers and technicians. They are the go-betweens, the fixers, the callers and schedulers, the list-makers and record-keepers, the prompters, prompt-book makers and cue-givers, the prop and furniture finders, the markers-out and whippers-in, the actor-wranglers, the tea and biscuit providers, the travel arrangers, the rule-enforcers and rule-benders, the lookers after everything that isn't looked after by somebody else.

The smaller and poorer your company, the fewer Stage Managers you get. In **fringe theatre** you'll be lucky to have one. At different levels of subsidised and commercial theatre there are **union** rules governing the number of stage management per production. However many SMs you have on your team, your relationship with them is a crucial one. In larger teams you must have a particular sort of closeness to each member.

For a full account of what you and your actors should expect in rehearsal from your stage management team, see the entry under **Rehearsal Technique**.

The main stage managerial posts are as follows:

STAGE MANAGER

The SM in the British theatre is the most senior member of the team, unless a **Company Stage Manager** is employed, in which case the former's job is subsumed within the latter's.

In America the Stage Manager **calls** the show (like the British DSM below) until such time as one of his ASMs can take over. From that moment he takes on a more supervisory and managerial role, rehearsing the **understudies** and coordinating the rehearsal and production schedules. For **billing** purposes he is called the Production Stage Manager.

DEPUTY STAGE MANAGER

The DSM is responsible for the maintenance of the **book** in rehearsal, and **cueing** or 'calling' the show in performance. Your relationship with your DSM is important. A poor DSM with a bad sense of rhythm, lackadaisical attitude to cueing or short attention span can destroy in one evening all the work you have dreamt up over months of preparation. A good DSM is your prop, your hand on the tiller and your artistic friend for every performance that your show runs in the theatre. Note well.

ASSISTANT STAGE MANAGERS

The ASM is the most junior member of the team, usually responsible for the dispensation of props, furniture and set-dressing in the rehearsal room and for the run of the play. On a big show more than one ASM may be employed and rehearsal duties divided, one being responsible for props and one for the running of the stage and liaison with actors and wardrobe staff. In performance, one of them may manage stage right and the other stage left.

You should be on the friendliest of terms with your ASMs. As well as being the prop-setters and the furniture-luggers, they are the message-runners and the tea-makers. They do all the things for you that you should never ask your Assistant Director to do. Treat them kindly and they will treat you so in return.

ACTING ASMS

An Acting ASM is a junior member of the acting ensemble whose duties also include the most menial of stage management tasks, or vice versa. At one time actors commonly entered the profession as Acting ASMs, and those whose first jobs did not include some ASM-ing duties considered themselves lucky. The post is now all but extinct, many companies having union agreements that preclude the employment of Acting ASMs. Stage Managers generally dislike having one of their employees discharging a dual responsibility. There can indeed be problems of divided concentration and split loyalty.

Acting ASMs still exist in some small commercial productions, especially where a young actor has to be employed to make a single insignificant appearance on stage and would otherwise be sitting in the dressing room for the rest of the evening, but the notion that setting out the props and making tea is good for a young actor's soul has now largely expired.

DIRECTOR STAGE MANAGERS

This is not a post but a process. A spell in stage management can be an excellent **education** for a director. The post of DSM is particularly instructive. By making the book and calling the cues you get a real insight into the pace and rhythm of plays, how actors think and what an extraordinary variety of directorial options there are. Watch your DSM carefully. He may be a trainee director in disguise.

Stage Picture

The 'stage picture' is how the stage looks at any given moment in a production from the point of view of the audience – a snapshot, if you like, of the characters within their environment.

Part of your craft as a director is to make stage pictures that are pleasing to the eye, appropriate to the action, emotionally engaging, meaningful in terms of image or design and natural for the actors to inhabit.

The making of stage pictures starts with **set design**. It continues in **rehearsal** with the director and actor finding positions and movement for the characters that accord with the design around them. It is finished in the **technical rehearsals** when the Lighting Designer and the director use light, darkness and colour to complete the images.

There is no time limit for the duration of an individual stage picture. You might sit in the same vivid image for five minutes or get through fifty images in the space of one minute. There is also no prescription for how many images you use in any one production. A very still and tense production could be very sparing with the use of its pictures, while a busy one could get through hundreds of them. In a still production, a minor physical change in the position of a single actor can make a big impact. In a production busy with pictures, a moment of surprising stillness can make a similarly strong impression.

However successful a stage picture seems to be, don't try to hold on to it for longer than it is worth. As you watch it inhabiting its moment, feel the point at which it has achieved its full impact and think how you can intensify it further by changing it or abandoning it in favour of a new image. A good production makes its moves from one picture to another so fluidly that the audience is unaware of having seen a picture at all.

You should avoid repeating a stage picture that you have used earlier in a production, unless for thematic reasons you want to make a deliberate connection between the two moments. Images have a **storytelling** value, and if you unintentionally reuse a stage picture you run the risk of confusing one part of the story with another. Repeated reuse makes a production seem to stand still, the characters locked in a frozen frame of directorial dullness. Let your characters and your story suggest pictures of their own. Don't trap them. Trapped actors are like trapped animals – they lose the capacity to behave in a natural way. If one of your pictures becomes a prison, then break the frame and let your actors roam free until a better, freer picture appears.

Stage to Screen

Theatre productions are increasingly being recorded on DVD for archive purposes or for transmission on television. You have to take account of this development. You can't just let other people manage it for you. The recording companies don't necessarily know best or have your best interests at heart. They are indeed quite capable of exploiting your work commercially without giving a single thought to its artistic merits.

Some see in these recordings a serious threat to the uniqueness of theatre. Others see a serious opportunity for theatre to make itself more accessible. It all depends on your point of view. Either way you must take them seriously. Your work is being recorded. For ever and ever. Long after the live production has been forgotten, the recording will remain.

There are various types of recording.

ARCHIVE RECORDINGS

These are made by play-producing companies, or by professional archives working in tandem with them. They are strictly for library purposes, and the actors agree to the recording on that basis. They are never to be sold commercially and can only be viewed by appointment in secure circumstances at the archive site.

Traditionally these recordings are made with a single camera set up at the back of the auditorium and with minimal camera work, but methods are now becoming increasingly sophisticated.

The accessibility of these recordings has become something of a hot topic in recent years, with some companies and organisations wanting to put their archives on the internet so productions can be studied all over the world. Despite the obvious commercial opportunities, these attempts are being blocked by actors and directors. Understandably. The artistic standard of the recordings is poor, and it would be next to impossible to solicit permission from every artist and then work out an equitable method of remunerating them.

RECORDINGS FOR TRANSMISSION AND DVD

Some television companies are always on the lookout for great pieces of recordable theatre. If you have a hit in the theatre, especially if it involves a bankable star or two, a transmission of your play makes for a reasonably inexpensive TV programme. If a deal can be made for subsequent DVD sales, the whole enterprise can pay for itself and even make a profit for all concerned.

The TV company makes a deal with the theatre company for the rights and with individual artists – playwright, composer, director, actors and so on – for their contributions.

You will have to decide how involved you want to be. If you have experience of working in television, you may want to direct the recording yourself. More likely you will find yourself collaborating with a specialist TV director.

Get a good contract. Have your agent, or lawyer, negotiate upfront with the TV company and/or your theatre company so nothing falls through the cracks. You need to keep control over your work.

These are the things you have to watch out for:

1 *Where will the recording take place?*

In the theatre? Or in a studio once the play has finished its run? If the former, will the performance be screened as live, with obvious evidence of a live audience? Do you think this is a good idea? Do you want the feeling of a live event, or would you be better with a studio format? Will audience reactions – **laughter** and **applause** and so on – feature in the recording? Will a **curtain call** be part of the event? If the recording is to take place in a studio, or in the empty theatre converted into a studio but with no audience present, how do you treat the **fourth wall**? Do the actors ever play to camera instead of to the audience?

2 *How many cameras will you need?*

TV companies have budgets and will tell you what they can afford, but you must counter with an artistic bottom line. You will be used to seeing every little reaction between the characters. How many cameras do you need to pick up all that detail? To make a theatre piece work on TV you need to get much closer with the cameras than a live audience gets with its eyes. At least two-thirds of your shots will need to be close-ups or mid-shots. Wide shots must be used very sparingly because the actors look so tiny in them. If you want to use tracking shots, where will your tracks go? How many seats will you need to remove to accommodate them? Make sure any onstage cameras you might have are not in shot from the FOH cameras' point of view.

3 *How many recording machines will you have?*

If you have twelve cameras and only six machines, the TV director will have to make instant judgements about which camera is recording and which isn't. He'll have to know the show very well to be able to do that. The last thing you want is to go into the edit and find the close-up shot you most need was on one of the non-recording cameras. To be safe, try to have all your cameras recording all the time. Keep your options open.

4 *Is there a live audience?*

If so, how do you integrate the audience with the shoot? The cameras must not impair the enjoyment of the live audience but they still need to get their shots. Do you need to talk to the audience beforehand – or even have a special performance for the shoot?

5 Do you need to make changes to the moves or lighting?

You may need to do this in order to accommodate the cameras. Some scenes may not be bright enough to pick up on tape, some effects invisible to the cameras.

6 How do the actors look when they appear on screen?

Theatrical wigs and make-up are much rougher than their TV counterparts. You will have to tone everything down for the cameras. Have camera tests for all the actors before the recorded performance.

7 How big do the actors' performances have to be?

The actors that project their performances on a big scale risk looking preposterous on screen. Tone down performances accordingly.

8 Will you be in control of the editing process?

You need to be. You can't let somebody do it for you. You know the production, its pace and rhythms. You know where the camera should be looking. Where the reaction shots are. Where the emotional highs and lows. If your TV director is diligent he will see the production many times before the recording. But he may not be diligent – or even artistically qualified. He may be coming straight from shooting a sporting event. And your editor may not have seen the show at all. You must have the contractual right to be present in the editing suite at all times.

9 How long is the TV programme to be?

TV producers always want cuts. If your play runs for three hours, they will want the two-hour version. If it runs two and half, they will want the ninety-minute version. If it's for commercial TV cut another five or ten minutes an hour for the commercials. The producers will blind you with science. These are the only slots available. We'll never sell the show overseas if it's too long. You must decide what can and can't be done. How much can you cut without entirely destroying the piece. Be helpful but know when to hold the line.

10 *What do you show when the credits are rolling?*

This applies to the beginning and end of the programme. Think about this before the shoot. Will you need footage of the audience coming into the theatre, or applauding at the end? Do you need backstage footage?

LIVE TRANSMISSIONS

These can be very exciting. For these your TV director will have to call all the cuts live. This is a nerve-racking business. One little slip and he's on the wrong camera looking at the wrong actor, or no actor at all. He won't want you breathing down his neck. In fact you'll probably be banished from the recording van for the night. This makes it all the more important for you to be involved in the preparation period. Look at the shooting script very carefully. Make sure the cameras will always be looking at what you want them to look at.

Live transmissions are often recorded for later reuse or DVD issue and may be re-edited with greater consideration after their first transmission. In which case you'll still need to answer all the points raised for recorded transmissions above.

Stagger-Through

A stagger-through is the first run-through of a play in the **rehearsal room** after all the scenes in the play have been rehearsed at least once but before the actors are capable of running the whole play without a stop. The actors 'stagger' through the play stopping whenever they or you wish, making quick-fix amendments to any outstanding problems that crop up but not stopping for any serious investigation, discussion or re-rehearsal.

Staging

The staging of a play is the disposition of the actors on the stage in relation to one another, to the environment of the **set design** surrounding them and to the audience.

The old-fashioned and restrictive term **blocking** is often used as a synonym for staging, but most good directors don't start their rehearsals by blocking out the physical moves of a play regardless of other considerations. Staging is a more inclusive term, better describing the totality of the physical relationships that occur on stage between all the elements within the director's control.

A whole book could be written on this most subjective of subjects, and many have been. This entry will serve only as a brief set of guidelines against which directors can measure their methods and preferences when **rehearsing a play**.

For every stage and every play there are appropriate forms of staging. For every **acoustic** and every size of **auditorium**, for every **set design** and every **company** of actors there are appropriate forms of staging.

The experienced director will know instinctively what is appropriate in each circumstance, but then the experienced director will also have a style of staging that is only really appropriate for his own temperament and taste.

All that is attempted here is a set of basic rules that may be kept or broken according to craft, taste and circumstance. The neophyte director should beware of breaking them, the experienced director may sometimes need to be reminded of them, and the wilful *auteur* will delight in breaking them whatever anyone thinks.

14 GENERAL RULES FOR STAGING

1. Try to vary the **stage picture** throughout the performance as far as the requirements of the play will allow. Unless the text specifically requires it, an audience's eye will tire of a monotonous setting or repetitive movement. A variety of stage pictures will help an audience to locate a scene visually within the process of a story and

707

recall it vividly at a later date. In a play with multiple settings, do not exactly repeat any staging, even if the play returns to the same location more than once with the same group of characters.

2. Use the best parts of the stage for the most important parts of the action. In most theatres, the area of constantly usable acting space is only a small fraction of the entire stage space available. It is the area downstage centre area immediately in front of the audience and extending upstage and offstage for as far as the **sightlines** and **acoustics** allow. This is usually an area of no more than three or four yards deep and four or five yards wide.

3. Keep the actors moving. While avoiding pointless activity or physical fussiness, the relationship between audience and actors works best when there is a flow of physical action. Movement is a useful **storytelling** tool. Stillness can be a good quality in an actor, but inactivity is generally more appropriate for an audience than for actors.

4. The actor who is speaking, or on whom the action is focused, should be clearly visible to all parts of the auditorium.

5. As a general rule, the faces of all the protagonist actors should be continually visible to the audience, especially when they are speaking, but also when the manner of their listening may give the audience an important clue to character or motive.

6. Audibility and visibility are connected. It is easier for the audience to hear the voice of an actor when his face is visible. Faces turned away from the audience make for inaudible voices.

7. When a character is speaking to other characters on stage, the listening characters should be positioned so that the speaker can address them in a physically natural manner. In most theatres this means that at least one listening character should be placed downstage of the speaking actor without obscuring him for more than a few seconds from any part of the auditorium. Without a listener in a downstage position, the speaking actor must either play everything out front or crane his neck from side to side in search of interlocutors. Not a recipe for naturalness.

8. Characters should avoid making moves when they are not in command of the focus. It is usually safe for characters to move when they are speaking and usually inadvisable for them to move when another character is speaking. However well characterised a

move may be, it can be a distraction if it isn't contributing to the central focus. If a non-speaking character makes a move during someone else's speech, he must listen to the speaker in such a way as to make his move a positive contribution to the audience's focus on the speaking actor.

9. Try to avoid one actor getting stuck in the same position for too long. The key here is relaxation. An unrelaxed actor will transfer his tension to the character and freeze in one position, unable to risk a move for fear of drawing attention to himself. Talk to the actor about how the character is listening, what matters to him in what is being said by the other characters, and how to manifest his attention with a move, or an adjustment in his position.

10. In long duologue scenes, don't let the two actors get stuck in the same face-to-face profile position for too long. Move them around each other so that the audience gets a complete view of both of them. The more the audience sees of the actors' faces the more they can read the complexity going on in both characters' minds.

11. In **crowd scenes** or any other highly populated scenes, keep the characters moving. The more characters there are on stage, the more they will look like a static extension of the audience. Characterise all of them and give them reasons for being active.

12. Position the scenery in such a way that actors can easily navigate their way through it, across it or around it. Avoid putting insurmountable pieces of scenery in the most usable parts of the stage.

13. In settings that require furniture, arrange the pieces so that the actors have a number of possible routes around them. Actors and audience will tire of the physical life of a play if the furniture settings force the actors into repetitious movement.

14. Beware of placing scenery or objects of any kind between the actors and the audience. An actor even partially obscured by furniture is less watchable than an actor unimpeded. If furniture at the downstage edge of the stage is necessary, make it as skeletal and as low as possible. If an audience can see through or over something they can forget it's there.

These rules apply to all theatres, however they are configured. You can find more specific guidance on particular theatre structures

Staging

under **In-the-Round**, **Rehearsing a Play**, **Stage Pictures** and **Thrust Stages**.

Stalls

The stalls are the seats at the lowest level of the **auditorium**. The front seats of the stalls are usually several feet below the level of the stage and rise in a gradual rake to level or above level with the stage at the back of the stalls.

The stalls seats are nearly always the most highly priced as they tend to get the best view of the stage and command the best **acoustic**. The prices tend to go down towards the back of the stalls as audibility and **sightline** problems increase.

Most of your work in **proscenium** arch theatres will be done from the stalls, as they provide you with the easiest access to the actors on stage during **technical rehearsals**. Because of this you must beware of having a stalls-only view of the stage. In most theatres, most of the seats are in the upper tiers, so when you have a full house that's where most of your audience will be. If you direct only from the stalls you will only ever represent the view of the stalls audience. This may comprise the most affluent members of the audience and, nearly always, the critics, but sometimes the most passionate theatregoers are in the poorest seats and just as worthy of your attention. Learn to direct from every part of the house. Represent your whole audience.

In America the stalls are called the **orchestra**. Both terms are abbreviations of the term orchestra stalls, describing the seats that are immediately adjacent to the orchestra pit, whether or not there is an orchestra playing in it. 'Orchestra stalls' is also a colourful example of cockney rhyming slang, as in 'He kicked me right in the orchestra.'

Stanislavsky

You must read Stanislavsky. If you take yourself seriously as a director and want your actors to take you seriously, you need to read *An Actor Prepares*, *Building a Character* and *Creating a Role*, especially the first of these.

Stanislavsky was the first person to articulate a proper system of actor training and was the *fons et origo* of **improvisation** as a rehearsal technique. He was actor, director, Artistic Director, teacher and producer and a wise, broad-minded and endlessly inventive intelligence.

His theories and exercises have become such an accepted part of Western theatre practice that you are very unlikely to meet a professional actor who hasn't to some extent been trained in them. Whether you are conscious of it or not, a great deal of the terminology and analytical method you and your actors use in rehearsal originates in Stanislavsky's teachings. Better to know where it all comes from than to spout it in ignorance.

Because he was an actor first and a director second, he has a naturally sympathetic understanding of the actor's craft. He knows it all inside out – that is from the inside to the outside. He talks about consciousness and unconsciousness and the power of the creative subconscious, the inner life of the human spirit in contrast to the moribund artifice of theatrical convention, **improvisation** and the enablement of the actor's imaginative forces, the danger of cliché and the limitations of technique, the importance of 'living' the part, text and **subtext**, objectives and super-objectives, the relationship between the life of the actor and the life of his character and the perils of arbitrary directorial and designer 'vision'. He demands a regime of physical, mental and vocal exercise and encourages the idea of actors playing as children play. He describes all manner of different exercises and techniques to improve the actors' powers of concentration, observation and impersonation. He demands what we should all demand, that the actor and the director be accurate observers of humanity and conscientious purveyors of truth.

There have, of course, been many good books about acting and directing written since Stanislavsky, but they all depend on him in one way or another. Read him first and then the others in relation to him and you won't go far wrong.

Stars

Commonplace theatrical, cinematic and sporting slang for the most celebrated and bankable performers, but such an overused and subjective term that it has no universally applicable meaning.

In the commercial theatre a producer will define a star as an actor whose name alone will help to sell enough tickets to ensure some sort of a run, whatever the part in whatever the play. Thus you will hear producers saying of an actor, 'The woman's a star. I could sell tickets for her reading the phone directory,' or of a play, 'Without a couple of stars it's a complete no-no.'

Whenever you are **casting** a commercial production you will have to live through the inevitable and incredibly time-consuming process of trying to persuade starring performers into your leading roles.

Of course, actors can still be called stars without having any pull at the box office whatsoever. Thus a different definition might be 'any actor whose name appears above the title'. Whether you've heard of the actor or not is irrelevant – if his name is in lights he's the star of the show. This might seem daft, but it can have a significant effect on the careers of actors and their chances of winning prizes or even simply making a living.

Some producers in recent years have asserted their own star status by making their shows un-dependent on a star's pulling power. This is the concept of 'the show is the star'. The title of the show becomes the bankable commodity.

Stardom will always be a hopelessly subjective and relative concept, as befits a term derived from the relativist universe, where every star's brightness is variable depending on where the beholder is standing. Thus one man's star is another's jobbing actor or actress. A star in the theatre may be completely unknown in the world of television and a star in television unknown in the world of film. The leading actress in a provincial **repertory** theatre may have star status in the absence of any suitable competition, but will return to lowlier public perception when back in the capital.

In the end we must allow the term to be defined by whoever is using it and all we should expect of stars is that they twinkle now and again.

Storytelling

Think of plays as stories. Audiences love to be told stories. When you read a play, old or new, or when you watch your play in rehearsal, scene by scene or in a run-through, ask yourself 'What's the story?', 'Is the story being told?', 'How clear is the story?'

To tell a story well you need clarity at every step. Of course, stories can have mysteries and ambiguities, but only when you want them to. At all other times your audience should know everything the characters know. But you have to be able to work out how well they are being told it.

Start with the characters. What are their names? Are they mentioned in the text? Who has the first mention of each character's name? Are the actors who speak the names attributing them clearly to the named character?

Go on to the scenes. Where are we? How important is it to the story that we know our exact location? What time of day is it? How long have we been here? Where have we come from? Where are we going?

Does anything happen between the scenes that needs to be clarified in the scene before or the scene after? Has the playwright made a shortcut that sends the audience off in a different direction? How can you get them back on the right track?

What's going on between the characters in each scene? How clear are the intentions, animosities, attachments, familial relationships and so on? What's the human story of the scene? Try to put it into one sentence. Are you telling that story?

Think of each character as having a separate story. Is each of those stories clear? Put each character's story into one sentence. Are those the stories you're telling? How do they fit in with the stories of each scene?

Once you've analysed all the little stories, how do they add up?

Do they all contribute to telling the big story? What is the big story? Put it into two or three sentences. Are you telling that story?

As you sit in the audience at your **dress rehearsal** or your first **preview**, tune in to the audience's awareness of the story. Are there lapses in the storytelling? Does the audience lose its way? What can you do to help them? What have you missed? There's always something. Conversely, has the audience got ahead of you? Are they twiddling their thumbs waiting for the action to catch up with what they already know? Have you told them too much? Have you spelt it all out too crudely? Or are you just going too slowly? Be ready to adjust the **pace and rhythm** for the next performance. Talk to your actors about storytelling at the next **note session**. Remind them what the big story is and all the little stories contained within it.

Straight Plays

'Straight plays', 'straight drama' or 'straight theatre' are all more or less current terms used to describe spoken plays as opposed to sung ones. In a professional theatre in which the same artists work in both types of drama, some sort of differentiation is necessary and useful, and though 'straight' for theatre implies that musical theatre is crooked, it's a better term than **'legitimate'**.

Straight Run

A play is said to have a straight run when it has been programmed to play in a particular theatre for a finite length of time. If a play is running in **repertoire** it cannot be said to have a straight run even if the number of performances is known in advance. When a play in a subsidised theatre has done particularly well running in repertoire, the company may decide to revive it. When they do so, they often reschedule the **revival** as a straight run in order to capitalise on the limited time the cast will be willing to play it for.

In the commercial theatre most runs are straight runs, the hope being that they will run straight on for ever. When producers are forced to keep a run short, usually because of the unwillingness of their starring actors to play for a long time, the straight run is known as a limited run.

Stress

Stress is the emphasis given to a word within a line of text. Not to be confused with **accent**. See **Accent** for a full definition and comparison of these terms.

Subscription Seasons

The subscription season is almost unheard of in Britain but is the staple of the American **not-for-profit** repertory system. Unlike in Europe, the American theatre enjoys little or no government subsidy, so it has to look for other ways of stabilising its economy. This can involve prodigious feats of fund-raising from dedicated supporters. The loyalty of this audience is ensured by selling tickets a long way in advance for a whole season of plays. Theatregoers buy tickets for four, five or six consecutive productions, or for some proportion of them, four out of six shows or three out of five or whatever. A theatre company might sell tickets to thirty or forty thousand subscribers before a season has begun. That still leaves a lot of tickets to shift, but it gives the company a massive head start, not to say a welcome injection of cash before any money has been spent.

Actors and directors have mixed feelings about subscription audiences. Long-term subscribers come to the theatre whatever is showing. They sit in the same seats. They meet the same people sitting in adjacent seats. They have dinner with the same people before the show. It's a social ritual. Like going to church. The play isn't necessarily the main thing on their minds. The majority of subscribers are middle-aged or older and middle-class and reasonably affluent, and they overwhelmingly define the social atmosphere. As one American director of my acquaintance caustically remarked of a subscription company he had just worked for, 'There are two theatres on the same site. The big one sleeps six hundred, the small one sleeps two hundred.'

Subscription theatres must programme their seasons to cater to the tastes of this quite narrow demographic. Adventurous Artistic Directors have a fight on their hands to be allowed to direct the plays and musicals that really excite them and to keep their seasons vibrant enough to attract younger audiences.

What actors and directors really miss is the uncertainty, the excitement of a word-of-mouth hit, that sense that a successful show can connect with something in society at large that drives people to the theatre to witness the discovery. Fans of subscription have little patience with this view. What if you don't have a hit? What if you haven't connected with anything much? At least you don't close. At least you get reasonably good audiences. Be grateful. Oh, and here's your cheque.

Subsidised Theatre

Subsidised theatres are theatres that receive government subsidy as opposed to, or as well as, corporate and private sponsorship.

If you work for a subsidised theatre, you work in public trust. The money you spend on productions and salaries comes from a source that could easily decide to take it away and give it to some other, arguably worthier, recipient. Part of your job, therefore, is to prove your worth. In everything you do. The best way to do this is to ensure that your work is a necessary part of the lives of the people who are giving you the money. Not the government but the people who give the government the money in the first place, the taxpayers. Whether you are funded locally or centrally, taxpayers and their dependants are your target audience. They pay for you. You must strive to please them. If you can't please them or if you waste their money, you mustn't be surprised if their elected representatives decide to spend it elsewhere. You can see their point. You're a taxpayer too.

It's easy to make an argument in support of the necessity of theatre, or of art in general. What would our lives be without access to art? What's the point of being human if we can't aspire to great thoughts and the beautifully crafted expression of those thoughts? Without art we are less human, less thoughtful, less civilised. It is the mark of a cultured society to have a vibrant artistic community. And so on.

It's easy to assert that all great art has been sponsored in the past, that artists require patrons, that government subsidy is just like the enlightened patronage of Renaissance dukes and princes, that the creation of art will never give a financial return and should never strive to do so.

It's easy to point out the connection between a thriving artistic community and a healthy tourist industry, that a town with culture attracts people who spend their money in all sorts of other places, shops, hotels, restaurants and so on.

As artists we argue these things to ourselves very successfully, but we are not always believed. The only thoroughly clinching argument is supplied by full houses, strong popular appeal and the advocacy that comes with the approbation of our peers.

Politicians and funding bodies are nearly always impressed by success. They like to be associated with popularity. If you are too successful, they also like to pretend you can manage on your own without their help, but they can never argue this point too vehemently when the people who vote for them are all going to your theatre.

If success brings financial reward and financial reward allows you to build for more success, many smaller and less popular theatre companies get left out in the cold. The new, the young and the experimental will always have a struggle to persuade the funding bodies they are worthy of subsidy. If you are one of these – and if you aren't now you must have been once – don't waste a minute of your time bellyaching about how all the money goes to the large established companies. Of course you should lobby the funding bodies and demand to be noticed, you should network and scheme and cajole, but envy is not an attractive trait and never goes down well as an appeal strategy. All theatre companies are hard up and all believe they deserve more support than they get. Funders are besieged by large and small, rich and poor, popular and unpopular. Strive to be as good and successful as the companies whose budgets you envy. It's a matter of belief. If you believe in your work you must want as many people as possible to share your enthusiasm, however experimental it is, or difficult or apparently marginal. A full house of inspired theatregoers is the best advocate you will ever have.

NOT-FOR-PROFIT

This is the American term for subsidised theatre. It is theatre that relies for its economic survival on a mixture of public demand, private patronage and corporate sponsorship. There may also be some small contribution from federal or local government arts funding bodies, but nothing like the sums that European governments are willing to spend.

If not-for-profit companies do well and find themselves with an unaccustomed surplus they feed it back into the core operation. But this rarely occurs. They are usually operated on shoestring budgets and survive against a background of constant financial crisis. The most successful companies do well because they inspire support from a local community of passionate theatregoers, people who cannot imagine their town without a theatre or opera house.

The wealthiest patrons are also encouraged to be the most generous. In exchange for their support they have their names carved in granite in the foyers or façades of the theatre together with the names of similarly generous local companies and arts charities. If they outspend all their other competitors they may even get a theatre named after them.

Despite their dependency on private and corporate sponsorship, most not-for-profit theatres also rely on selling seasons of plays on **subscription**, a tactic that can prove something of a two-edged sword.

Subtext

The subtext contains the unwritten but implied thoughts that motivate the text and inform the actor how to play his character. If an actor takes his text at face value, he assumes his character always means what he says or says what he means. In plays, as in real life, this is rarely the case. By delving down beneath the text the actor can find the objectives, needs and desires that are the true driving forces of his character's behaviour.

Subtext is an invention of **Stanislavsky**, who describes it as 'the inwardly felt expression of the characters, which flows uninterruptedly beneath the words of the text, giving them a life and a reason for existing'.

In other words, without the subtext the text can have no meaning. When **rehearsing a play**, you will be constantly helping your actors search for the subtext that gives their words a sense of truth and reality. You may not always call it the subtext, but you'll be looking for it nonetheless.

SHAKESPEARE AND SUBTEXT

When directing the plays of Shakespeare or his contemporaries you may need to steer your actors away from searching too keenly for subtext. Indeed, there is a case for saying there is no subtext in Shakespeare – that his characters always mean what they say and, unless intentionally trying to deceive one another, always say what they mean. This might seem an over-prescriptive view, and you might find it hard to nurse your actors away from their carefully acquired Stanislavsky-based training, but what you can assert is that no actor in a Shakespeare play should be allowed to substitute a subtextual hunch for a textual certainty – and that a subtextual idea should only be applied if the text itself has failed to yield the necessary information for the building of a character. This may provide a useful discipline in the search for meaning in a **heightened language** play.

Superstitions

Theatrical superstitions are a terrible bore – calling *Macbeth* the Scottish play, not saying the last line of a play, not whistling backstage and all the rest of it.

Superstitions

It's a complete myth that *Macbeth* is more plagued by misfortune than other plays. There's no evidence whatsoever to support the idea. And actors aren't any more superstitious than sailors or tailors or snailers and a lot less so than football or baseball players or any other sport where the vicissitudes of chance drive participants into believing they can change their luck by the way they re-strap their gloves or refuse to launder their underwear. It's all just a lot of nonsense, like astrology or UFOs or any of the same sort of mindless guff people cram their lazy brains with.

Accidents happen in the theatre, of course, and previews are cancelled, but when they happen in *Macbeth* people say 'Ah, you see, the curse has struck,' and they remember the incident, however slight, for years after. But if a production of *Macbeth* goes off without a hitch it has no effect on its mythic status as a plagued play. And if some other play suffers a really terrible series of misfortunes, no new superstitious myth originates around the events. *Macbeth*'s grim reputation will never be supplanted in the minds of the credulous.

In a busy career, you are bound to come across some mild cases of actor superstition, and maybe even a few serious ones, nearly always amongst the mildly rather than seriously talented actors. Perhaps a lack in them of any real belief in the power of their art has had to be replaced by something else. Belief in theatrical superstition is a way of creating a comfortable little club that only 'we actors' can belong to. 'You wouldn't understand, you poor mortals, but these superstitions are terribly important to us thorough-going old pros.' And then they bully the young pros into observing their daft routines. Real professionals, of course, have no time for the gobbledygook of theatrical clubbery. They have quite enough to do reading their plays, learning their parts and earning their livings.

Call the play *Macbeth*. Or go for broke and call *Twelfth Night* the Illyrian play and *Hamlet* the Danish.

Surtitles

If you work in **opera**, or if ever your theatre productions are toured abroad to non-English-speaking countries, you will have to deal with the problem of surtitles.

These are the electronically generated simultaneous translations of the onstage dialogue or lyrics that appear in light boxes, usually suspended over the front of the stage, but sometimes placed strategically, or not so strategically, in other parts of the auditorium. They are cued live at every performance, by a member of the literary department from a booth at the back of the **stalls** or the dress **circle**.

Surtitles have become more or less ubiquitous in the opera world, both as translation devices and as aids to hearing. Many opera singers are incapable of articulating their words clearly, especially in the larger houses, and they rely on the surtitles to come to their rescue. Audiences, in turn, have come to rely more and more on surtitles as a supplement to meaning and hearing. This co-reliance has recently become so extreme that most opera companies now use them for works performed in the audience's native tongue.

Surtitles have enemies, on both sides of the footlights. People argue that the constant flicking of the audience's eyes from stage to surtitle and back constitutes a betrayal of the author's and the performers' right to a unity of response. While the eyes are looking at the surtitle, they can easily miss a crucial look or gesture coming from the stage. They also see surtitles as a slippery slope – the more they are used the less the singers will feel obliged to make their words audible. In the end, singers will become singers of vowels, the consonants mere vestigial appendages to the words so lovingly crafted by their librettists.

What singers hate most about surtitles is that they disable the intimacy of their relationship with the audience. In a comedy, the audience laughs at the line as it's flashed up on the screen rather than while the singer is delivering it – or in a more serious work they are moved by a revelation or shocked by a **dénouement** as it appears in print rather than in the singer's voice.

Surtitles

There are technical objections, too. Surtitles cannot appear word by word. They must be cued in the form of sentences or half-sentences, but there is never a perfect word in the libretto for them to be cued on. The audience either gets the line pre-emptively before it has been sung, disruptively while it is being sung or redundantly once it has been completed. The machines that transmit them can also emit a lot of light. In a darkened scene on stage, the surtitles can become the brightest focus in the theatre. And the machines can break down, or get out of sync with the singers' voices, causing all manner of confusion.

But surtitles have powerful friends, too. They argue that the very future of opera is in its ability to popularise itself and that a crucial part of this process is the audience's right to understand in plain language what is happening on stage. They believe that surtitles can be made unobtrusive and that audiences have learnt to use them without any significant harm being done to artistic quality.

The best modern systems involve each seat having its own tiny screen only visible to the person sitting in the seat. With some systems the individual screen can also be folded away if not required. But these sophistications do little to convince the passionate anti-surtitlers, who see in them a further diminution of the unity in an audience's response.

You will be obliged to make up your own mind in this battle of wills. You may even decide to take a stand. Many directors have refused to countenance surtitles in their productions, successfully arguing the artistic case with the house that has engaged them. But beware. When surtitles are withdrawn from an audience that has come to rely on them, there is an inevitable fall-out to be dealt with by the public relations department – and the person who has demanded their suspension will be the focus of opprobrium.

Many opera houses will not accord you the option and you will have to work with surtitles whether you like them or not. When this happens, you would be well advised to take an active interest in their preparation. Don't leave it to others to decide how the audience will read your work. The first draft of the surtitles will have been done by someone who has no clear idea about the nature of your production and certainly will lack any knowledge of the way in which the characters relate to one another in your staging of the work. They will probably be using a version that has been borrowed from some other production or pinched from the sleeve notes of an established recording. The translation might be inaccurate or pedantic, the comedy unfunny, the style old-fashioned or the phrasing over-poetic. The language might feel archaic in a modern-dress production or overly colloquial in a period piece.

Audiences will not make allowances for inadequate or risible translation. They will associate your production with it, believing in the words they are reading as the true voices of the characters. Critics read the surtitles too, even if they pretend they don't need them, and if there's a real howler somewhere in the surtitles it could easily turn up in a review.

Work through the surtitles with whoever has been responsible for preparing them. Start early, in rehearsal, so that the work isn't all left to the last minute. Refine the words until they perfectly represent what you think their author intended and/or what you want your audience to 'hear'. Check them all over again when you get into the stage and piano rehearsals in the theatre. Some of them may be too long, too short, or mistimed. Whenever you find yourself distracted by a surtitle, make a note of it and see if you can find a better cueing point for the line, or a change of emphasis in the text. And don't translate everything. Leave out repetitions, unnecessary character names and obvious monosyllables.

Swings

See **Understudies**.

T

Tabs

'The Tabs' is theatrical slang for the main curtain dividing the stage from the auditorium, more specifically called 'The Front Tabs', obsolete in many modern theatres.

Without the definite article, the term also describes any curtains hanging anywhere on stage, used in **masking** or as **acoustic** baffles – thus 'a set of tabs', or 'a pair of tabs'.

Take-Overs

An actor 'takes over' a role when he replaces another actor after the play has opened, a common occurrence in a **long run**.

Faced with recasting an important leading role, directors and producers spend a lot of time trying to persuade leading actors into take-overs they have no intention of accepting. For many actors, a 'take-over' is beneath their dignity or perceived status. They argue that a take-over automatically pegs them on a level below the actor they are replacing and devalues their casting and earning power in all subsequent negotiations. It is hard to argue with this assessment, though many actors thereby deny themselves the opportunity to play really great roles in which they would not otherwise be cast.

Take-over actors do get a bit of a raw deal. They get very little rehearsal time. They generally have to rehearse on the set rather than in a rehearsal room and are required to fit into an established set of moves and character **motivations**. They rarely get the attention of the original director, who has usually moved on to another job, and must rely instead on an **Assistant Director** when there is one, or on the Stage Manager or CSM when there isn't. They may also have to cope with a resentful cast, aggrieved at being pulled in for rehearsal every day while continuing to play eight shows a week. This can be a real test of a **company**'s character.

For director or assistant, rehearsing take-overs entails a bit of a balancing act. You must give the new actor the freedom to explore the role afresh but not allow the resulting changes to compromise the production or throw the existing cast members off their stride. This is reasonably easy to do if you're the original director, but harder if you're the assistant. An original director can change his own production and inspire change in the rest of the cast, making the experience a refresher for all. An assistant will get caught between the demands of the new actor and loyalty to the original director.

Diplomacy may be required, especially if the new actor starts changing everything in order to impress the director and the rest of the cast with his independence. Whether you are director or assistant, try to remove this element of ego from the mix. Talk the new actor and the rest of the cast through the text and re-rehearse the arguments that led to your original decisions. Take the time to listen to the new actor's ideas and get everyone excited by the changes they entail. Inspire the old cast to rise to the challenge of playing the 'old' show every night while rehearsing the 'new' show during the day. The new actor will probably have seen the show before agreeing to be in it, but don't insist he watches it again. Most actors will feel constrained by having to watch the original actor playing a part they are trying make their own and it will encourage them to feel they have to be different.

In long-running shows, a whole cast may get to the end of a contractual period and have to be replaced. In this case the 'take-over cast' may rehearse on stage but may also go back to the rehearsal room where the work can continue during performance times. If a rump of actors remains from the old show, don't hesitate to use them as proxy assistants. Their goodwill and knowledge of the play in performance can be a valuable asset.

Tears

Just as **laughter** is the most obvious way an audience expresses its recognition of the absurdity of human dilemmas, tears are the signifier of an audience's sympathy or empathy.

They are also a good test of the efficacy of rehearsal. An engaged objectivity is the most useful state of mind in rehearsal, but don't feel you have to suppress your natural sympathetic feelings. Your own tears, and those of your cast, are often the most reliable test of the accuracy of an actor's emotion or the true humanity of a scene.

Tech

'Tech' is theatrical slang for **technical rehearsal**. A 'techy' is a technician or crew member in any of the stage departments.

Technical Gallery

The space over a **Black Box** or similar theatre, correlative to the grid and fly floors of a **proscenium** arch stage, from which technical departments can gain access to lighting instruments and other technical equipment without the use of ladders from below.

Technical Rehearsals

The technical rehearsal is the last stage of the rehearsal process before **dress rehearsals** and **preview performances** begin.

The 'technical', or 'tech', should start as soon as the set has been erected on stage and all the technical departments have made themselves ready for the fray, but there may be a conflict between the technical departments and the director about the proper time for starting the tech.

On the one hand the departments want to be as prepared as possible, with the **get-in** completely finished, the set made safe for the actors, the lights fully rigged and focused with a sketch of lighting cues ready for the whole play and the sound rig installed and balanced. On the other hand the director and cast want to get from rehearsal room to stage with as short a hiatus as possible in order to keep the momentum of their work going.

This conflict is caused by the pressure of time. Time is at an absolute premium during the tech. This is because producers, administrators and theatre owners want to have as few **dark** days in their theatres as possible. Most theatre companies will be fitting their shows into a narrow schedule of possible performance nights and are always unhappy about giving up an entire week of revenue and public access. They will usually insist you get to a performance by the end of the technical week, and the poorer the company the earlier in the week they will want the first performance to be. You should be sympathetic to this view. You too want your show to get as many performances as it can. But you must also defend your right to make it as flawless a show as you have dreamed it to be.

THE TECH SCHEDULE

Planning is everything. From the very first **production meetings** onwards, you must insist on a realistic amount of technical time, but you may have to insist in the teeth of stiff opposition. The first draft schedules are likely to short-change you. Examine them closely. Count how many tech 'sessions' there are. A session might be anything from three to five hours long and you might get two or three of them on each tech day, depending on the working practices of the theatre company and the prevailing **union** agreements. Plan how to tech your show within the available sessions. How many sessions will it take to get to the interval? Are there scenes of great technical complexity that you know in advance are going to slow you down?

If you're planning a lot of lighting or sound cues, don't forget each cue takes time to get right, and some **Lighting** and **Sound Designers** are quicker than others.

If you can see from the schedule that there isn't going to be enough time, argue for more. There is often room for negotiation. Look carefully at the start of the schedule. Could you not start earlier than suggested? The drafter of the schedule, usually your

Technical Rehearsals

Production Manager in consultation with your Stage Manager, will have been under pressure from the technical departments to give them adequate time before the actors and director are allowed on stage. But will this time be well used? Some Lighting Designers like to have a complete plot of cues in the computer before the tech starts, but how useful will those cues prove to be? Will not everything look very different once the actors get on stage? Try to push the tech forward to the earliest possible starting time. Reassure your collaborators that you will give them adequate time to work on their cues as the tech progresses, that you won't motor on and leave them flailing in your wake. The sooner you start the tech the sooner every department in the theatre will be actively working towards the same goal at the same time.

If there is no slack at the start of the schedule and you feel you are bound to run out of time, you must look at the dress rehearsal and performance end. How many **dress rehearsals** have been scheduled? If more than one, would one be enough? What would happen if you never got to a dress rehearsal and had to do your first run in front of a paying public? This happens in the professional theatre much more often than you would imagine. And it isn't a pleasant experience – for audience or cast.

If it looks like the technical schedule has been drafted more by wishful thinking than by sensible planning, you must press for previews to start a day later than scheduled. Much better to plan the loss of one night's revenue than be forced to cancel a preview at the last minute. Cancelled performances are always a disaster, with angry audiences, resentful box office staff and a general pall of disappointment and failure descending over the whole theatre.

PREPARING FOR THE TECH

Techs are usually well organised in permanent theatre companies equipped with their own workshops and storage facilities. They will have a system for building the set and moving it from workshop to stage and then storing it if the play is to run in **repertoire**. But in the commercial theatre, and in theatres without workshops on the premises, the tech can cause considerable chaos. Every available space gets filled with apparatus of one sort or another and the auditorium gets turned into a building site. You must insist the mess doesn't get out of hand. Make a tour of inspection with your Stage Manager and arrange for a clean-up before the tech begins. Make sure there are plenty of access routes through the auditorium with whole rows of seats kept clear so you and your staff can visit every part of the auditorium to check for audibility and **sightlines**.

Pay special attention to dust. The technical departments work right up to the moment when the actors go on stage and in every subsequent available moment. The dust they raise gets into the actors' throats and can cause them to lose their voices. Arrange for the stage to be regularly mopped. In particularly dusty environments, your stage management team should have an industrial-sized water spray they can use to slake the dust five or ten minutes before the actors go on stage. This can make a real difference to the quality of the air in the theatre.

You should have a desk in the auditorium with a dimmable light and a comfortable padded board laid across the armrests of the auditorium seats. The seats themselves are usually too low for a desk to be fitted in front of them, and if you perch on an upturned seat you will soon be suffering severe arse-ache. Make sure your position is in front of the Lighting and Sound Designers' desks. If you sit behind them, your view of the stage will be obscured by their consoles and computer screens. But don't sit immediately in front of your Lighting Designer or every time you stand up you'll drive him crazy. His view of the stage is just as important as yours.

In theatres with raised stages, insist there are sets of access treads leading directly from auditorium to stage. You will be making countless trips from your desk to the stage and back and you will get out of touch with what's going on if you have to use the **pass door** every time.

Be ready to be lonely and unloved. The rehearsal room surrounds you with friends and helpers, everyone in the room more or less in your eye-line, most of them highly attuned to your moods and needs, with cups of tea and sympathy arriving at regular intervals from a solicitous stage management. But the social atmosphere of rehearsals disappears in the tech. Every member of your support team will now have a job elsewhere, most of them on stage, and all of them doing more important things than keeping you happy. In the darkness of the theatre you become a king without a court.

Be ready to feel abandoned. Respond by creating new structures of support and communication for yourself.

DRY TECHING

A dry tech is a technical rehearsal without actors present. This is necessary when you have a set that makes complicated or potentially hazardous moves. Indeed, any **scene change** that needs more than one or two practice runs should be dry teched in advance by your Stage Manager and crew. Actors get twitchy if they have to go through endless repeats of the same scene change through no fault of their own and twitchier still if their safety is being compromised.

In the commercial **musical theatre**, where it is not uncommon for the set to go into the theatre a week or so before the end of rehearsals, designers and Stage Managers may dry tech entire shows before the director and actors get on stage.

COMMUNICATION

Having negotiated adequate time for your tech, you must be careful that you keep control of it. Your biggest problem is communication. Poor communication wastes a lot of time and causes frustration in all departments. Good communication saves time and keeps tempers, your own included, on an even keel.

Throughout the tech you must be in constant communication with three different groups of people: your stage management, your creative team and your performers. Each group will have different and sometimes conflicting interests, so your method of communication cannot be the same for all.

Your Stage Manager will run the tech for you. Be grateful and don't disable him by trying to do it yourself. You will only come to grief. Talk to him before the tech begins and let him know that you expect him to drive the tech along at as quick a pace as is commensurate with the work that needs to be done. He will be in constant communication with his deputy, who will be **calling the show**. In some countries he may be calling the show himself. The deputy may be sitting in the **prompt corner**, or in a booth at the back of the theatre, or, as a temporary measure, right next to the Lighting Designer in the auditorium – different theatres and designers have different methods. Your Stage Manager will be on 'cans' talking to the crew, the wardrobe, the dressers, and everyone else. He will always know what's going on, why there's a hold-up with a scene change, which actor is in his dressing room when he should be on stage, who just hurt himself in the darkness of the wings. If you want to know the answer to anything technical, don't bellow your question into the darkness, ask your Stage Manager. And don't be tempted to wear a set of 'cans' yourself. All you will hear are your own instructions being implemented and any further interventions you make will annoy everyone else on the circuit. You will also clog up your ears with unnecessary technical chat when they should be listening to the play.

In a big theatre, what you will need is a **god-mike**. This is a microphone that carries your voice to the stage and auditorium speakers. The sound department will equip you with one. Nothing is more stressful and damaging to the atmosphere of a tech than a director shouting his instructions to the Stage Manager and cast. Shouting makes everyone nervous and bad-tempered. And it's catching. If a director shouts, everyone starts shouting. And everything slows down as all departments take time out to curse the director under their breaths. Talk quietly into the god-mike so your Stage Manager, and everyone else, can calmly follow your instructions. Use the god-mike for all easily communicable instructions regarding staging or timing. Don't use it for debate or discussion. If anything complicated or sensitive crops up, go to the stage and talk to your Stage Manager or actors in person.

Your Lighting and Sound Designers will be sitting right behind you. If you have an instruction for either one of them, go and talk to them, but choose your time carefully. Don't interrupt a Lighting Designer when he's building a cue. And wait for him to explain what he's doing before you instruct him to do something else. He may already be working on a solution to the problem you have spotted.

Technical Rehearsals

If you have anything urgent to say to your Set or Costume Designers, ask the Stage Manager to call them to the stage or auditorium, but be patient if they're not instantly available. They may be doing something crucial somewhere else in the building. And don't call them for trifles. They may have to hoof down four flights of stairs to get to the stage. When they do arrive, talk to them privately about your concerns, not in front of actors and crew. They are your collaborators, not your servants.

When talking to the actors, only use the god-mike for notes of a general nature. If you have a note for a particular actor, go to the stage and talk to him there. Giving personal acting notes over the microphone is demeaning for the actor and a betrayal of your prior work in rehearsals.

If you have an **Assistant Director**, this is where a good one will come into his own. Use him unashamedly. Send him on errands, as messenger and peace envoy. Get him to police the more inaccessible parts of the auditorium for audibility and sightline problems. If the tech throws up unresolved acting or staging problems, get him to take the actors into the foyer or back to the rehearsal room for top-up rehearsals or line bashing.

TECH ETIQUETTE FOR ACTORS

Make sure all your actors understand how to behave in the tech. Inexperienced ones may need to be told.

Whenever the tech comes to a halt, actors involved in the scene or scene change on which you are working should remain on or near the stage until they are told they are no longer required. A lot of time can be wasted by maverick actors assuming that the tech has moved on when it hasn't.

Actors should only make costume changes when instructed to do so by the Stage Manager. This is especially true of **quick changes**, which have to be carefully choreographed by the wardrobe department and timed to coincide with onstage events. A scene change may have to be tech'd ten times in a row, a costume change only once or twice.

If any part of the tech is being done without costume, actors should wear dark clothing, or colours that approximate to those in their costumes. Inappropriately bright or colourful clothing makes it difficult for the Lighting Designer to choose the right levels and tones of light.

As a general rule actors should play full out during the tech and only **mark** their performances when their voices get tired or when a sequence has to be repeated many times. Physical or vocal marking makes it impossible for lighting, sound and Costume Designers to assess the value of their work. Marked performances also tend to be slower than full-out ones, upsetting the timing of cues. More importantly, if an actor repeatedly marks his performance, the repetition gets into his system and is likely to be reproduced in performance. The constant repetitions of the tech are a gift to the actor. They allow him to work his performance into his body and voice, adapt his acting to the size of the theatre and anticipate the way the audience will respond to it.

Throughout the tech, actors should be encouraged to sit in the auditorium as often as they can find the time. They will learn a lot from watching their colleagues from the audience's point of view. By taking the trouble to watch the tech from the most distant seats, they will return to the stage with a practical understanding of how far and at what angles their performances have to be projected.

LIGHTING THE ACTORS' FACES

As you work through the tech, your Lighting Designer will be following every move in the play, creating an atmosphere for each scene, and adding new cues whenever the **stage picture** changes in any significant way. The plot he will be working to will be one that you and he and your Set Designer have agreed in advance, but there are two aspects of the lighting that will still require your constant attention:

1 The actors' faces must be lit at all times.
2 Nothing else on the stage must be lit more brightly than the actors' faces.

You owe this to your actors. Most Lighting Designers would agree with these two premises, but some may be better at implementing

733

them than others or take a different view as to the levels of light required. You must be the final arbiter here.

TECH TEMPERAMENT FOR DIRECTORS

You need to be physically and mentally fit to run a tech.

If you're doing your work properly you will go from auditorium to stage and back twenty or thirty times an hour. You will walk to and fro across the auditorium a further ten or twenty times an hour, checking for sightlines and audibility. You will shift from your seat to the Lighting Designer's position ten or twelve times an hour. This is a necessary part of your job. An armchair director runs a tech very poorly. He sits in isolated gloom at the centre of the auditorium, sending out emissaries to do jobs he should be doing himself and getting more and more frustrated that his instructions are being misinterpreted or getting lost in translation. His tone on the god-mike becomes correspondingly edgy and unforgiving, as if everyone in the building is being stupid and he is the only intelligent and artistic person present. This at a time when, in reality, the actors are starting to take control of the production and the director's views become increasingly irrelevant. 'Why are you being so rude?' the actors will think. 'You directed us like this in the first place. It's not our fault you don't like what you're looking at.'

A tech is the ultimate test of the **director's temperament**. If you are unconfident, small-minded, impatient or lacking in self-control, the tech will find you out. You will shout at someone, or make someone cry. You will destroy a confidence and make someone feel small. You will cut a costume or a piece of scenery or a wig or a music cue without considering the feelings of the person who spent hours designing it or making it. You will throw away all the good humour and intelligence you have deployed in rehearsal and be remembered as a bad-tempered bully. And it will show in the work. It always does.

Don't be that sort of director. There's no need. Maintain your relationships throughout the tech as you would in the rehearsal room, or in production meetings, or in your home. Find time for everyone. Listen to their worries with real interest. Their concerns are your concerns. They're not stupid, so don't make them feel stupid. Visit the offstage departments before each tech session begins. Calm everyone down. And stay calm yourself. Calm and creative.

STAYING CREATIVE

If you run a tech well, and keep yourself and everyone around you in a creative frame of mind, you can radically improve your production as you do so. Don't let the shortage of time pressure you into drying up creatively. The tech should be as creative as any other time in the rehearsal period but in order to stay creative you must be able to adapt to your new environment.

Nothing ever looks quite as you imagined it would when you were sitting in the rehearsal room or poring over the **model** with your designer. Don't be dismayed by this. Rearrange your vision to accommodate what you have. Don't waste time mourning for what seems to be missing.

The secret of good teching can be summarised in two related rallying cries. Creativity for all. Idleness for none. Make sure all your collaborators are as happily creative as you are and that they are all working flat out at all times. The two greatest enemies to creativity in a tech are tension and inactivity.

If the tech becomes frustratingly slow, find out why. The cause will usually be a bottleneck point. Someone or some department has too much to do and everyone else is waiting for them. It may be the costume department has too few dressers, or the sound department has only one runner to replace batteries on twenty-four microphones, or a new light has to be rigged before the next LX cue can be programmed. Most commonly, your Stage Manager has too much to do. Everything is going through his desk and he can't keep up with all the demands on his time and attention. Wherever the problem is, cut the Gordian knot. Reallocate a responsibility. Rearrange the personnel. Or simply make your staff aware of the problem and let them solve it in their own way. Whatever you do, crack open the bottleneck and get the tech flowing again.

Technical Rehearsals

If your show is long and complicated and you have more than one day for your tech you may decide to run sections you have already achieved before carrying on to the end. This is a good idea, for instance, if you get to the end of an act or scene and have only an hour or less to go before the end of the day's work. Rather than pushing on into the next scene at a late hour with everyone tired and longing for the day to wind down, go back to the top of the show or the act or the day's work and run everything achieved so far. Or if you have no time at the end of the day, start the next day with such a run. In a long tech, actors and crew tend to forget what they have done unless they have the chance to repeat it, and there may be days to go before a dress rehearsal. Quick changes, follow-spot cues and flying cues all rely on individuals getting things right and they all take practice.

Running a section of the show at its proper tempo also gives everyone a chance to assess the work as it will eventually be seen by the audience and make adjustments accordingly. Periodic runs of this sort give everyone a lift.

FINISHING THE TECH

If all goes to plan you should finish the tech on time or even with half an hour or so to spare, but techs rarely go exactly to plan. If you haven't finished the tech before your first dress rehearsal, you'll have a decision to make. If you have more than one dress rehearsal you should probably cancel the first one and carry on teching. If you have only one, you mustn't cancel it unless you are so far behind with the tech that you're also considering cancelling a preview or delaying the opening.

If the end of the tech is in sight but not quite finished, do your dress rehearsal anyway.

When you get to the un-teched bit of the show, keep running on to the end whatever happens. It won't matter if the lights aren't right or the scenery is in the wrong place, just keep running. The actors will get a real sense of achievement from finishing the show and a welcome run at performing the entirety of their characters' journeys. But warn everyone beforehand what the plan is.

Go back and finish the tech once the dress run is over. This could be on the same day but will more likely be the following morning. Then do another dress rehearsal if you have time for it, or a first preview if you don't.

If you've been a wise virgin and finished your tech with a little time to spare, you can most usefully use the remaining time staging the **curtain call**. Curtain calls are best rehearsed in tranquillity rather than thrown on at the last minute. The last half-hour of the tech is often the aptest time.

Tessitura

Tessitura, the Italian word for texture, is a term commonly used in **opera** to describe the prevailing range of notes in which a voice can comfortably sing, or in which a piece of vocal music is written. This is quite different from the total 'range' of a voice, which might include high and low notes that a singer has to strain to achieve. A singer might have a range of two and half octaves but a comfortable tessitura of only an octave and a third.

The basic delineations of vocal pitch – soprano, mezzo, contralto, tenor, baritone and bass – are only approximations of range. Roles written for any of those voices also have their tessituras. These gradations become extremely important when you are casting an opera. A baritone role written in a very high tessitura will only be suitable for a singer whose voice lies in a similarly high place. And so with all roles and all voices.

Theatre Manager

The Theatre Manager is in charge of running the theatre building. He employs and manages the **front of house** staff, including ushers, box office, cleaners and bar staff. In a commercial theatre he may also employ the permanently engaged stage crew. In small theatre operations he may double as Box Office Manager, or manager of everything that isn't to do with the mounting of the play.

During performance times, he also becomes the smartly dressed maître d' of the foyers, interacting with the audience, discreetly dispensing complimentary tickets and keeping everything front of house on an even keel.

Theatrical conventions

Theatre relies on convention. The conspiracy of **belief** between actors and audience that what is happening on stage is a version of reality is the most comprehensive of conventions and in a way subsumes all others. It is instructive nonetheless to examine the way the most fundamental tools of our trade work. How else can we appreciate the difference between invention and convention, our inventiveness and our conventionality?

Has anyone ever written a comprehensive history of theatrical conventions? I've never read one, or heard of one. It would make a fascinating study – and particularly so for directors and designers imagining new productions. How many of the traditional rules of theatre do they wish to follow and how many to break or reinvent? We take so much for granted when we imagine our productions. We borrow without knowing it. We rely on conventions that we have no idea we are using.

One may think of theatrical conventions as being a sort of shorthand created by the profession in order to find some consistency in a fundamentally inconsistent form. But the unquestioning use of convention inevitably leads to derivativeness and cliché. If you write exclusively in shorthand you mustn't expect to be understood. Squiggles on page or stage can only be read by experts.

You will never be able to dispense entirely with theatrical conventions, nor should you try. They are an indispensable part of theatre craft – but you should know when you are using them and as far as possible exercise your judgement whether to use them or not, and certainly to define consistent ways of using them that are aesthetically pleasing.

Consider the following list. I'm sure it isn't exhaustive, but a few moments in its company when you are dreaming up your next production might trigger off an inventive response to your material in place of a conventional one.

1 The identity convention

That the characters are who they say they are or who the author says they are. That the author knows what is to happen to the characters and the audience is right to trust him.

What happens to the identity convention when an actor **doubles** a role – i.e. when he plays two or more parts in a single story? Is the actor's identity more or less present in one of his roles than the other?

2 The convention of authorial control

That the author controls his characters rather than vice versa. In Pirandello's plays the characters seem to rebel against the authority of their playwright. How much control does an author really have over his characters? In Alan Ayckbourn's Intimate Exchanges, the audience votes on the direction of the plot. Is this a relegation of the author's control or an intensification of it? As in the story of *Rashomon*, the author calculates what all the possible stories are and controls them.

3 Timescale conventions

That the reality of the play starts only after the audience has been seated and the theatre prepared for the start of the play. That when the lights go down or the curtain falls at the end of a scene or act, the reality within that scene is suspended. That when the **curtain call** starts, the reality of the play is replaced by the reality of celebrating its performance. That the time taken to perform the play is a representation of the time experienced by the characters within it.

4 The fourth wall convention

That there is an imaginary wall that separates the reality of the play from the reality of the spectators watching it and that the two realities cannot overlap.

Theatrical Conventions

5 *The exit and entrance convention*

That a border between two realities exists between onstage and off, a border the actors cross when they go from wings to stage and back again. That the audience believes in the onstage reality and ignores the off. In most productions, this convention is scrupulously observed, but directors and designers sometimes like to blur the borders, making the world of dressing rooms and costume changes an onstage reality. Actually the borders remain, whatever the directors and designers decree. Actors still have to leave the theatre at the end of the performance, go through the stage door, meet their friends or accidentally bump into members of the audience.

6 *The soliloquy or aside convention*

Breaking the fourth wall. That when an actor is left alone on stage, or we are asked to imagine he cannot be heard by the other characters, the barrier between auditorium and stage disappears.

7 *The disguise convention*

That the identity of someone wearing a **mask** is impossible to confirm, however skimpy the mask. That an actor playing a member of the opposite sex really resembles the part he or she plays. The conspiracy to ignore the true age, shape or size of any actor. That the audience judges the success of any such disguise by the way the other characters are taken in by it.

8 *The laughter convention*

That an audience's laughter cannot be heard by the onstage characters. This in spite of the fact that the sound of the laughter affects the rhythm of the dialogue.

9 *The visibility convention*

That the characters in a scene should be visible at all times with helpful spaces between them so an audience doesn't get confused about who's who. That the face of a speaking character should be visible for as long as he speaks.

10 *The audibility convention*

That everything the characters say on stage should be audible to all of the audience. That a whisper from one character to another should be audible to the audience but not to other characters sitting closer than the audience are sitting.

11 *The **applause** convention*

That the clapping together of hands represents an appropriate way for an audience to register its approval. That the actors only hear applause during the curtain call and not during the performance.

12 *The **chorus** convention*

That a group of anonymous onlookers, broadly representative of the audience's point of view, are able to inhabit the same imaginative world as the characters of the drama and comment on the action without affecting its outcome.

13 *Lighting conventions*

That a **blackout** is a token of completed time. That leading characters shine a little more brightly than the characters around them. That blue light means night. And so on.

14 *Design conventions*

That token pieces of scenery may stand for entire realities. That a hat can change an actor from one character to another. And so on.

The list could go on at greater length, though some conventions can easily be contained in others, and no set of conventions is equally applicable for all styles and traditions of theatre. The important thing is to be aware of them. Know how you're playing them and when you're breaking them. Think how far you can rely on an audience accepting an established one and how much help they need if you introduce them to a new one.

Thrust Stages

A thrust stage, also known as a platform stage, is one where the stage surface thrusts out beyond the **proscenium** arch into the auditorium, requiring the audience sitting near the stage to be configured on three sides. The term started to be used during the 1960s and 70s when old theatres were being adapted or new ones built in deliberate contravention of the proscenium tradition, the very word 'thrust' implying a dynamic new relationship with the audience. Of course there is nothing new in the 'thrust' idea, harking back as it does to the stages of the Elizabethan and Jacobean theatre. Some element of 'thrust' is now a common design feature of productions mounted in traditional proscenium arch theatres.

If you work in a thrust theatre you will have to solve the **staging** problems that attend it. These problems are similar in most respects to those you find in **arena** and **in-the-round** theatres, but with some interesting local variations.

Because the audience is sitting on three sides, an actor standing downstage will tend to obscure one or other of his fellow actors further upstage. If he has an important speech to make, you must figure out how to get him into pole position upstage in a natural way and get other actors downstage of him so he has someone to speak to. This requires a fluid form of staging that keeps the actors constantly on the move, but an audience will become irritated by this technique if there is no variation in it. You can vary your stage pictures and the overall amount of movement with a little cunning use of the downstage edge of the thrust.

The downstage corners are particularly useful in this respect. Make sure there are exit **treads** on the corners. This may involve removing an 'aisle seat' or two from the front two or three rows. In a theatre with a central aisle you can also put treads leading from the stage to the middle of the auditorium, or have your designer incorporate a complete run of treads across the front of the stage. If the stage is very high, the treads will have to be steep in order not to take up too much playing space or lose too many seats. With a low stage you can afford to broaden the treads and make them more useful as part of the acting space.

With downstage entrance and exit points you radically improve your staging possibilities. Actors can enter from upstage into the space and exit downstage making room for the next entrances. You can 'park' actors on the downstage treads at a level that doesn't impede **sightlines** but creates interlocutors for the actors with most to say. These positions are also not so bad for short speeches and responses.

For interior scenes, you can create a more dynamic thrust space by placing low pieces of furniture – benches and stools – at the downstage corners or, if the stage is not too high, in the downstage centre position. Actors sitting in those positions provide a natural focus for upstage speakers and can be comfortably engaged in the action even when they do have dialogue. But be careful in using this device. No member of the audience should be obliged to stare at an actor's back for more than a minute at the most. You don't have to be too sensitive about this – backs are part of theatre too – but make the actor aware that he is an obstacle as well as a point of interest so he can shift his position from time to time.

Downstage entrances and exits will naturally involve the actors moving through the audience on their way to the stage, thus involving the audience more than is usual in the action of the play. Don't be embarrassed by this. A stage that thrusts out into the audience is already doing half the work for you. Go the rest of the way by mixing the actors up with the audience whenever it seems appropriate to do so. A brief entrance of a character with a message can be usefully made from further back in the auditorium or from the edge of an upper tier. A **crowd scene** allows you to imagine the audience as part of the crowd. Don't force the actors on the audience if either side seems resistant to the project, and don't single out one member of the audience for special attention unless the action is so comic and good-natured you know you will create delight rather than offence. Be sensitive to the atmosphere of the moment and adapt accordingly.

If your production has some elements of **environmental design** spilling into the auditorium you will want to exploit opportunities like these to the full.

Tongue Twisters

Tongue twisters are a useful and enjoyable supplement to regular vocal and textual training and exercise. As part of a warm-up exercise before the start of rehearsals or as an antidote to outbreaks of **fluffing** in an acting company, they have an immediate and noticeable effect on articulation and projection.

Most actors have their favourite twisters, and **voice and text** coaches have an inexhaustible supply for every possible failure of tongue, lips and palate.

Tongue twisters are only efficacious if they are spoken as rapidly as possible without error. They lose their point if you garble them. The more mistakes you make, the slower you need to go and the more repetition you will require to perfect them and get them up to speed. If you have serious trouble getting your tongue round them, you're probably not imagining them properly. Don't just make the sound of the words, think of their sense. Even when repeating the short ones dozens of times, make sense of the words on every reiteration.

When used by large groups of actors, tongue twisters should be spoken in strict unison rhythm, starting slow and getting quicker as the group gains confidence.

Here are a few examples, starting with some old favourites:

> She sells seashells by the seashore
> The shells she sells are surely seashells
> So if she sells shells on the seashore
> I'm sure she sells seashore shells

> Swan swam over the sea
> Swim, swan, swim!
> Swan swam back again
> Well swum swan!

> Moses supposes his toeses are roses
> But Moses supposes erroneously
> For nobody's toeses are posies of roses
> As Moses supposes his toeses to be

Betty Botter had some butter
But, she said, this butter's bitter
If I bake it in my batter
It will make my batter bitter
But a bit of better butter
That would make my batter better
So she bought a bit of butter
Better than her bitter butter
And she baked it in her batter
And the batter wasn't bitter
So 'twas better Betty Botter
Bought a bit of better butter

Hetty is hoping to hop to Tahiti
To hack a hibiscus to hang on her hat
But Hetty has so many hats on her hat-rack
How can a hop to Tahiti help that?

Peter Piper picked a peck of pickled peppers
A peck of pickled peppers Peter Piper picked
If Peter Piper picked a peck of pickled peppers
Where's the peck of pickled peppers Peter Piper picked?

And here are a few that have to be repeated three, four or ten times
to be effective . . .

Sister Susie sewing shirts for sailors

Red lorry, yellow lorry
Red lorry, yellow lorry, blue lorry

Toy boat. Toy boat. Toy boat.

Pretty Peggy Babcock

Unique New York

This bloke's back brake-block broke

Many an anemone sees an enemy anemone

Popocatepetl
Copper-plated kettle

Tongue Twisters

. . . and here are some difficult ones . . .

> She stood on the balcony
> Inexplicably mimicking him hiccupping
> And amicably welcoming him in

> The Leith police dismisseth us
> The sea ceaseth and sufficeth us

. . . and some dangerous ones . . .

> One smart fellow, he felt smart
> Two smart fellows, they felt smart
> Three smart fellows, they all felt smart

> Mother Puddy-Wuddy
> Had a rough-cut punt
> Not a punt-cut ruff
> But a rough-cut punt
> It was square at the back
> And round at the front
> Yes, Mother Puddy-Wuddy
> Had a rough-cut punt

> I'm not the pheasant-plucker
> I'm the pheasant-plucker's mate
> I'm only plucking pheasants
> 'Cos the pheasant-plucker's late

> Plain bun
> Plum bun
> Plain plum bun

. . . or make up your own. There are blank pages in the back of this book for your own inventions and discoveries.

Touring

If your production is to tour, you and your designer will be required to make your set as simple, light and easy to turn around as possible. Touring is a percentage business. The set weighs this much and is this bulky. It will take this many lorries at this much cost per driver per mile. The **get-ins and get-outs** will take so many hours. Stage management and actors will have this much time on the set before their first show. Each venue will get this number of performances at this much maximum box office revenue.

When setting up your tour, you and your producer should conspire to appoint a stage management team and a cast that travel well. Your **Company Manager** must be particularly unflappable, fair, efficient and kind. Look for some of the same qualities in your cast. Actors that behave badly at home will be worse when away. Constantly changing locations, horrible accommodation, irregular hours and strange audiences can be stressful for those who depend for their sanity on the routines of their home life.

Touring throws people together in unaccustomed closeness. A company of well-balanced actors will cope with this well, forming little clubs of friendship and working out how to function as a group. A single neurotic actor can throw this balance out of kilter and drive everybody nuts. Nothing is ever right. The hotel room is dirty, the dressing room is small, the fellow actors are disrespectful, I'm ill, I left my pills at home, I need to see a special sort of doctor, my cat misses me. Travel broadens the mind in some but narrows it in others. Bad behaviour of this sort is just a way of saying, 'I hate it here, I want to go home.' Do them and yourself a favour. Leave them at home.

Tragedy

Tragedies are not merely plays that end unhappily. They are plays that *must* end unhappily. It is in this 'must' that most of the problems of directing tragedy reside.

Unless your audience is exceptionally ill-read or naïve, it will know from the beginning of a tragedy that the outcome of the plot will be unhappy. Indeed some tragedies, like *Romeo and Juliet*, have prologues that foretell the unhappy outcome. In such instances the audience is being instructed, as it were, to witness the process of the tragedy rather than worry about the happiness or unhappiness of its outcome. But even in the absence of such guidance, sensitive audiences know from the tone of a tragedy that an unhappy outcome is inevitable and, in aesthetic terms, desirable. What is this tone? And what do you need to do as a director to help your actors play it?

In his *Poetics* Aristotle defines tragedy as being 'a representation of an action that is serious, complete and of a certain size . . . with incidents arousing pity and fear with which the drama accomplishes a *catharsis* of these emotions'. The catharsis, felt by the audience, is a purification of the emotions by vicarious experience. They fear the events of the tragedy on behalf of the principal characters and pity them their sufferings by empathising with them.

Most tragedies are written in **heightened language**. Your actors must be thoroughly at home using this elevated, poetic style of speech. Don't let them adopt an acting style they think is suitably 'tragic' or 'serious' in tone. A tragedy will not be more moving to an audience because of the actors' feeling that it should be so or by moving themselves with their own depth of feeling. Quite the opposite. The more truthful the acting and the more real the people of the play the more an audience will be able to recognise itself in their behaviour. Recognition allows for empathy and empathy for the vicarious experience of fear and pity. By playing the characters of a tragedy with the same human understanding, intelligence, humour and wit as with any other play, your actors will open emotional doors for the audience into the tragic world of the play. If the characters are played with a bombastic, solemn delivery or with self-indulgent emotionalism, all the doors will close, and the audience will be shut out of the tragic events, observing everything but feeling nothing.

As director, you must ride the inevitability of the tragic events very carefully. This is all in the **storytelling**. The audience may know that the events will end unhappily, they will often know exactly how the dénouement will occur, but they mustn't get ahead of you. You must play with the possibility that the inevitable is not inevitable at all. Hamlet need not die. Juliet will wake up just in time. Othello will see through Iago's deception. Right up until the last second, the characters could choose fates other than those laid down for them. You must play very cleverly with your audience's emotions. Never let them off the hook. Never let your actors feel more than your audience is feeling. Never let your characters know everything their author knows. The fear and the pity reside in happiness denied, hope cherished and snuffed out, the brightness of future life darkened by present experience. If all is denial and darkness, there can be no journey. For a tragedy to bite deep it must portray a world that could be happy and hopeful, a future that could be bright, people that have the capacity for goodness, mercy, pity and sympathy.

In order to understand the history of tragedy and how the form relates to previous ages much more easily than it does to our own, read George Steiner's great book *The Death of Tragedy*. His findings are fascinating, his reasoning exemplary and his terms of reference very broad, so much so that the book also serves as a sort of compendium of tragedies. Trawl through it and learn.

CASTING FOR TRAGEDY

To play one of the principal roles in a tragedy, an actor must have easy access to his emotions. Just as the best comic actors are people who are funny in themselves, so the best tragedians are those that naturally feel things deeply. You don't want an actor to have to dig too hard to come up with an emotional result. Tragic heroes and their antagonists are characters caught up in extraordinary events that require extraordinary reactions. Some actors are much happier than others at playing on the darker side of their emotions. They are emotionally skilful. They seem to have fewer layers of protective skin than others, their feelings playing on their faces and in their movements without any seeming effort. They may not live their real feelings so close to the surface, but as soon as they are faced with a fictional tragic predicament, their natural empathy kicks in and they become the characters they are playing, their more dangerous emotions ready to erupt from just under the surface. Cast one or two actors like these in any tragedy you direct and you'll get a massive head start in the catharsis stakes.

Translators and Translations

If you decide to direct a play translated from a foreign language, you have a lot of work to do before you get text and actors into rehearsal.

If you are fluent in the original language of the play, you start with an obvious advantage. You can study it as originally written, compare existing translations, even decide to make a translation of your own.

If you're an English-speaking director, you probably won't have this skill in more than one language, if at all. It's one of the drawbacks of having the dominant world language as your mother tongue. Continental European and Scandinavian directors are used to switching to and fro between different languages, but Brits and Americans are notoriously bad at it. Europe has a vibrant tradition of doing the latest new plays from other countries. In Britain and America we do each other's plays and maybe a few from Australia and Canada to leaven the lump, but we are by and large blissfully ignorant of the new work coming from countries whose languages we do not speak.

We are far more conversant with the foreign plays that have had time to emigrate into our cultures. The works of Ibsen, Chekhov and Strindberg are as well or better known to us as those of their British and Irish contemporaries Pinero, Wilde and Shaw. *Hedda Gabler*, *Uncle Vanya* and *Miss Julie* have become far more important elements of our repertoire than *Trelawney of the Wells*, *Lady Windermere's Fan* or *The Devil's Disciple*. But how well do we know them really? We know their plots and characters, but the language they were written in is a mystery to those of us who don't speak Norwegian, Russian or Swedish. We only know them through a constantly changing tradition of translation. If we decide to direct them, we must first decide where in that tradition we wish to meet them.

You would think, on the face of it, that the best translation of any play would be the original one, or the one closest in time to the period in which the play was written. With Greek and Roman plays, a few hundred years here or there obviously don't make much difference, but in plays written in the modern age the original translator would seem to have the advantage. He knows the manners and mores of the time and uses the contemporary language of his own country to mirror the language of the original. He is aware of the impact the play had at its first performance in its mother tongue. He may even have met the writer and spent time with him working on the translation. Surely his claims to have written an authentic text should be pretty strong. But this is rarely the case. Whatever the dramaturgical skills of the pioneer translator, translations date.

Translators can only translate into the idiomatic language of their own day, and idiom changes very swiftly. The idiom of the original language changes at the same rate in the host country, but historical idiom is always easier to interpret in one's own tongue. We don't update Shakespearean language because his idioms have stayed with us and developed as our language has developed. We can understand his language by hearing it back through our own daily usages, the natural rhythms and patterns in his speech and in ours. For the same reason, Russians don't update Chekhov. But we must. Chekhov's language translated into an English idiom of 1910 remains locked in its own linguistic backwater. It isn't the language of Chekhov and it isn't the English we speak now. So what is it? And what use is it? Nineteenth-century translations of Shakespeare into Russian are similarly moribund. They may be written in beautiful Russian, full of poetic conceit, packed with meaning, imagery and music, but they cannot be easily understood by a contemporary Russian audience. They are two and a half centuries away from Shakespeare and a century and a half away from today. They are lost in the wilderness.

When selecting a translation, if there is a choice, look at all the available options. Even the dated ones may help you to delineate the characters and place them in their social milieu. Read them all carefully and compare the different texts. Each one will shed light on some aspect of the original play, and taken together they should illuminate it very clearly for you. In making your final choice, ask the following questions:

Translators and Translations

1. Is the translator thoroughly in tune with the author? Do author and translator seem to think alike, have similar values, share a sense of humour? Would they have enjoyed each other's company?
2. Has the translator found useful rhythms in the text? Does the language flow? Does the style of the translation suit the style of the original?
3. How faithfully have the words been translated? Have creative liberties been taken? Are these productive or counter-productive?
4. How has the translator coped with the social or regional context of the play? Are there **dialects** in the original? Has he found good correlatives for them?
5. Does the dialogue give the characters ease of expression? Do they sound natural? Can you imagine the characters as real people? Can you find correlatives for them in your own contemporary society?
6. Will your actors enjoy speaking the text? Have all the acting opportunities in the original made their way into the translation?

You may find you like different bits of different translations, but don't be tempted to cobble together a bastard translation from various sources. This is always a mistake. A good translator has a style of his own. If you continually interrupt his flow with bits of someone else's work, you will destroy all sense of rhythm in the play. You will also be infringing the copyrights of all the translators involved. Translators and their agents can be very fierce about this. They know their own texts very well. They turn up at performances and notice that their work has been changed or thieved.

Choose a single translation and keep faith with it. Treat it as you would a new play. If you have a problem with bits of it, try contacting the translator through his agent or publisher. Many translators like to get involved with productions of their work. They will be flattered that you chose their version and may be happy to help you. Best of all is to get them involved in **rehearsal**. Let them make the changes they think advisable in the creative heat of the rehearsal room.

Whatever you do, don't use the pick 'n' mix, chop and choose method. The text will be a muddle and you will have a horrible time in rehearsal. Your actors will be constantly trawling through different options looking for 'better' version of their lines. For every change you allow, another actor's text will be affected. A sort of company neurosis will develop with actors vying with one another to improve the 'speakability' of their lines. This is a trap. The most easily speakable lines are not necessarily the best expressions of character. You will find yourself in an endless process of arbitration and advocacy. It will drive you crazy.

COMMISSIONING A TRANSLATION

If you decide to commission a new translation, take great care in choosing the right person for the job. Your first decision must be whether or not to use a speaker of the original language. This is much easier with some languages than others. With languages that are obscure to your own culture, you may not have much choice. Don't settle for someone with no theatrical experience. There is something of the playwright in all the best translators.

You may indeed decide to ask a playwright to do the job. If he doesn't speak the original language you will have to commission a literal translation from which he can work. When commissioning a literal translation, make it absolutely clear to the translator what the deal is. His work will not be spoken by the actors but serve as a template for the work of the playwright. Ask him to make notes in the margins of his text explaining any ambiguities, alternative meanings or idiosyncratic usages in the original language.

A translation made using this method is often called a version, in order to make it clear that the 'translating' playwright has no actual first-hand knowledge of the original text. The term can be used, perhaps more accurately, to describe a play that has been significantly altered in translation. By including elements of his own dramaturgy or by writing in a strongly individualistic style a playwright may pull an original play so far off its moorings that the work cannot be described as a translation.

When an original text merely provides the framework for a completely new piece of theatre, **adaptation** is a more appropriate term to use. Or call the work a new play 'based on' the original text.

Trap Doors

The 'trappable' area of a stage is that part of it that can be dismantled and adapted to give access to the **understage** by way of trap doors. The 'trapped' area of a stage is that part of it that has trap doors already fitted.

Trap doors, 'traps' for short, can be very useful design features, allowing you to break through the stage surface to another dimension underneath. Traps come in all shapes and sizes. You can open up large swathes of the stage as part of your overall design environment or use smaller openings for more local effects.

By emerging through a trap door, an actor can be coming from the lower floor of a house into an upper floor or attic, from a dungeon, or a manhole, or from hell. Because the audience can't see much through the trap, the space they imagine can be a very evocative one. Filled with smoke or light or sound, the understage can tell a vivid story.

Traps are also great for fast or surprise entrances and exits. The normal and expected routes to and from the stage are lateral. A sudden use of the vertical by going down a trap, or up a ladder to the flies, can be very effective.

ACCESS TO TRAPS

Unless you use a mechanical lift with your trap door, you will need **treads** for your actors to ascend from and descend to the understage. These take up much more room than you would at first imagine. A small opening in the stage will make for impossibly steep steps and an uncomfortable, even dangerous, climb for the actors. Your technical director and designer must discuss how to make the access safe and comfortable.

TRAP SAFETY

Never forget, for as long as your trap door is open there will be a gaping hole on stage. During **technical rehearsals** your Stage Manager must have such holes policed by the crew or someone is bound to fall through it. The sickening crash of an actor backing down a trap is not a happy sound two days before you open.

STAR TRAPS

Not a method for forcing a leading actor to accept a role – though such a device would make its inventor a fortune – a star trap is a small trap door with star-shaped cuts fitted into the stage surface and operated from below. It allows an agile and slender actor to appear or disappear with extraordinary speed.

Traverse

A traverse theatre is one where the audience seats are laid out in two opposing banks, like the House of Commons. The actors play in the space between the seats, usually a wide oblong strip but sometimes quite a narrow one.

Some theatres are permanently laid out in traverse shape, but most plays performed in this format are played in **Black Box theatres** that have had their seats appropriately adapted.

The traverse shape is really just an interesting variation of **in-the-round** or **thrust** theatre, but with two distinct access points at both ends of the space that also provide the actors with places where they can remain static observers of the action without masking their fellow actors from the audience.

Travesty Roles

A travesty role is a male role written to be played by a female performer or vice versa. The word derives from the same root as transvestite, from the Latin *trans* across and *vestire* to clothe, thus 'cross-dressing'.

A role in which a character disguises him or herself as a member of the opposite sex is not a travesty role, though the term is often used to include such parts.

Travesty Roles

A male character disguised as a female, like Babberly in *Charlie's Aunt*, is a petticoat role. A female character disguised as a male, like Viola in *Twelfth Night*, is a breeches part.

A travesty role is not played *en travesti* for any integral dramatic reason but solely because the author wishes it or tradition demands it. Thus Cherubino in Mozart's *Le Nozze di Figaro*, Octavian in Strauss's *Der Rosenkavalier* or the Dame in any British pantomime all qualify.

Treads

Treads are short flights of portable stairs, most commonly used in the theatre for getting from one level of a designed stage to another, or from stage to wings off a **raked stage**, or from stage to auditorium in technical rehearsals.

Most theatres have a small selection of sets of various sized treads that can be quickly adapted to different heights and widths.

Trucks

Trucks are pieces of scenery on wheels, in America called 'wagons'.

Scenic pieces are 'trucked' in order to get them on and off stage quickly and safely. Light trucks can be pushed and pulled manually but heavy ones need winches, either manually or electrically operated. A winched truck usually has a keel under it to stop it moving from side to side. This is a steel plate that runs through a groove, or 'track', on the stage surface. When the truck reaches its 'dead' or resting position, it is temporarily bolted to the stage surface to stop it moving around when being used by actors.

If you do a show with a lot of trucks in it, be careful how the tracks are laid down. They can be quite dangerous to walk on. Dancers hate them. Ask your designer and Technical Director to keep groove-gaps to a minimum and have your Stage Manager make a regular check that steel edges and screw-heads remain flush with the stage.

U

Underscore

In **musical theatre**, 'underscore' is the atmospheric music played under scenes of spoken dialogue.

The Understage

The understage is the void area underneath the stage, whether or not it is accessible to the stage by traps. If **trap doors** are featured in a design, the understage provides the access point.

In theatres with a lack of backstage space, the understage may be put to use as a technical or wardrobe store, a crew room or a 'Green Room' for the actors. In highly populated shows it can also serve as a **quick-change** space or a temporary changing room for musicians or stage staff.

The understage may be a **crossover** route, providing actors with a swift passage from one side of the stage to the other in the absence of an onstage alternative.

Understudies

Understudies are substitute performers, also known as 'covers'. They study to perform a role and go on if the principal performer is injured, ill or absent for some other reason. If there is more than one actor understudying the same role the 'first cover' will be the first choice to take over if the principal performer is off, the 'second cover' the second choice and so on.

An understudy may appear in a smaller role in the same production. If he goes on for his principal, his part will be taken by someone playing an even smaller role and so on down the acting

Underststudies

hierarchy. An understudy who doesn't have a regular role in the play is called a 'walking understudy'. He must be at the theatre for the half-hour call but sits in the dressing room or Green Room for the entire performance or at least until there is no danger his principal won't finish the show. Walking understudies are often allowed to go home at the interval.

In the US, 'standbys' are understudies for particular leading performers. They check in at the half-hour **call**, but if their principals are fit and well they need not sit in attendance for the rest of the performance.

SWINGS

Swings are the understudies of the understudies. The term is almost exclusively used in **musical theatre** to denote a member of the company who does not normally appear in the show but can fill in for any one of a series of smaller characters as required. Thus swings are expected to 'swing' from one part to another across a wide variety of roles. Though there are generally both male swings and female swings they should even be able to pinch-swing for one another – in a pinch.

Swings are often deployed when a principal character is off and his understudy takes over, leaving a hole in the ensemble. Shows involving dance use swings a great deal as even quite small injuries can keep a dancer out of a performance at short notice.

The perfect swing is a versatile quick learner who enjoys the challenge of a large number of different characters and is unfazed by sudden changes of routine. In a physically challenging and energetic show, swings are usually kept very busy and, unlike understudies in the straight theatre, they spend very little time in their dressing rooms.

TO UNDERSTUDY OR NOT TO UNDERSTUDY

Many theatres don't employ understudies or swings. Small theatres can rarely afford them. Runs of plays are short and money even shorter, so they just have to cast healthy actors and hope for the best.

If an actor is off, another actor must 'read in' the role. He might be an actor playing a smaller role that can be covered by someone else or he might have to be brought in specially. He plays the character with book in hand. If the principal is off for more than a day or two, the reading actor learns the role as quickly as he can. If the part is a leading one or the performance deemed inimitable, the show must be cancelled and the audience given its money back.

Without question, a company that doesn't employ understudies has far fewer occasions when actors are off through illness or injury. If an actor can't be ill, he won't be ill. Or at least not so ill he can't perform. If there is no alternative, he must perform – in a high fever, in plaster, in a wheelchair – the show must go on. But this stoical ethic does put a great deal of physical and emotional pressure on actors. Bravery is all very well. Most actors will enjoy the kudos they receive for soldiering on in physical adversity. Emotional demands are far harder to manage. What do you do about a death in the family? Or a birth? Or an unexpected illness? How do you decide what is more important than the play? When such an emergency occurs, making the actor responsible for the decision is really unfair. If you take the risk of having no understudies, you must also take the responsibility for cancelling the performance when compassion demands it.

Some large, well-established ensembles on the Continent don't use understudies on principle. It isn't that they can't afford them; they object to the very idea of them. They think of a role, especially a leading one, as being the property of the actor that plays it. No one else should have the temerity to think he could duplicate a leading actor's performance. It would amount to a sort of *lèse-majesté*. Better to cancel a performance than force an audience to watch a second-rate actor in a first-rate role. There are all sorts of things wrong with this way of thinking. First of all, the audience is not consulted. Of course it's disappointing when a leading actor is off, but more disappointing, surely, not to see the play at all. Members of the audience may have come from miles away or be celebrating a special occasion. Rescheduling for another night may be out of the question for them, and in any case the run may already be sold out. From the theatre's point of view, the loss of revenue and public confidence can be disastrous and, in a sub-sidised theatre using public money, more than a little scandalous.

A theatre without understudies cedes a great deal of its authority to its actors. An unscrupulous or badly behaved actor can hold a theatre hostage by blowing hot and cold with his performance. A dispute with another actor, a disagreement with a director, a mild illness, a bad hangover or a rampant ego can all turn into cancelled performances.

In the best-run subsidised companies and in commercial theatre, where cancellation is regarded as an absolute last resort, under-studies are the order of the day. Quite apart from financial impera-tives, there are positive artistic advantages to an understudy system. Actors get to study parts they would never otherwise be considered for and **Assistant Directors** get valuable experience rehearsing them into their roles. Most importantly, the whole the-atre, audience included, develops a healthy attitude to the perform-ance process. No one is indispensable. A part can be played in dozens of different ways. Change and variety are essential features of theatrical craft.

CASTING UNDERSTUDIES

In a play with a massive leading role – like *Hamlet* or *Hedda Gabler* – you should consider who you want to cover it when cast-ing your supporting roles. You can even attract a better actor into a minor role by offering him the cover of the lead.

In casting the other roles you will have to choose from amongst the actors contractually obliged to understudy.

Don't choose someone with a large role to understudy a slightly bigger one. It isn't worth it. If he has to go on for his principal, he too will have to be replaced by someone lower down the order, leaving two gaping holes in your normal line-up.

If you're casting from within a company rather than using walking understudies, have an eye out for the domino effect that will be created when a leading actor is off. For example, if Benvolio is covering Romeo, Gregory is covering Benvolio and Peter is cov-ering Gregory as well as playing his own part, you have three major changes to make if Romeo is off. Also, as far as possible, try to have your actors cover parts in scenes they are not already in. It's unwise, for example, to have Horatio covering Hamlet, with whom he shares nearly all his scenes. The cover for Hamlet, if he goes on, will rely heavily on the actor who plays Horatio. On a night when Hamlet and Horatio are both played by covers, there will be little security for either of them.

Don't overload a single actor with too many covers. In a large-cast play, one large cover and two or three small ones is about the limit. As you allocate the parts, consider what it will be like rehearsing them. Don't oblige any of your actors to cover two large parts appearing in the same scenes.

Above all, choose actors you know will enjoy playing the roles and/or will learn something from playing them. When an under-study goes on there should be excitement all around the theatre, not dread.

In musical theatre, where singers can easily be off with bad throats, you may have to cast two or three covers for each role. You may decide to nominate the covers in order of precedence, first cover, second cover and so on. This is usually a good idea, though a company management will often like to have the right to decide which cover should play on any given night. If you leave the prece-dence too fluid, bad feeling can grow between the different covers. Let them all know they will be given a chance to play the part if at all possible and get your Company Manager to play as fair as he can.

REHEARSING UNDERSTUDIES

Understudies should always be called to rehearsals of the scenes they are covering. By watching their principals rehearse, they will learn by absorption most of what they need to know. Give them as much access to the rehearsal process as you can. Don't banish them to the back of the room out of earshot of the discussions about **motivation** and background. Some principal actors are sensitive about having understudies too close to the process, so you may have to tread carefully. Covering actors certainly shouldn't be vocal in discussion, but try to involve them as much as you can without upsetting anyone. As rehearsals develop, the relationship between principals and covers should become increasingly cordial, but if a cover gets too pushy or if your principal is allergic to your cover, you may have to intervene.

Understudy rehearsals should start as soon as reasonably possible after rehearsals proper begin. Some of your actors may have more concern about their understudy commitments than they do about playing their small supporting roles and they will need to get started on them.

In most companies the **Assistant Director** will rehearse the understudies, though in some commercial productions the job is done by the Stage Manager. If you have any influence one way or the other, try to ensure this doesn't happen. Stage Managers can be rigid and unimaginative in rehearsal. If your play is intellectually and emotionally complicated, your covers will feel short-changed if they don't have the opportunity to discuss their roles with a proper director. A bright but callow assistant is far preferable to an experienced but jaded Stage Manager. Understudy rehearsals should be driven by enthusiasm, good humour and patience, not just by professional duty.

If you are the assistant, start rehearsing in the evenings of the second week or even at the end of the first week. Stay for an hour or two after the end of normal rehearsals so you can rehearse on the same set-up as the principal actors. Pay most attention to the covers with the biggest roles. They will obviously need the most work and the more they work the easier it will be for them to learn their roles. Give them as much freedom as you can. Don't insist on them exactly duplicating their principal's performances. On the other hand don't waste time inventing wildly different moves or interpretations. If the covers go on they will have to fit in seamlessly with the other actors. Try to develop exciting acting relationships within your understudy company. Draw the best talents out of everyone and mix them together as inventively as you can. Don't forget, though, these actors will probably never play their roles with one another. If they ever go on, it will be one at a time and not as a group. Don't refine their relationships so much that they'll have difficulty playing with someone else.

Covers should be off the book and ready to go on by the time the first **preview performance** happens. They may not be completely ready but they should be able to go on in a pinch. Pinches happen.

If you're the director, take a real interest in how the understudy rehearsals are developing. Give your assistant and your covers some of your time so they can discuss their concerns. Be sensitive to demands for rehearsal time. In the last week of rehearsals, let your leading covers go off and rehearse with your assistant rather than hanging around doing nothing in principal rehearsals.

UNDERSTUDY RUNS

An understudy run is a dress rehearsal of the play with all of the parts being performed by the understudies rather than the principal performers. It is usually scheduled within a week of the opening of the play and serves two very useful purposes. It provides a goal for the understudy company, a date by which they really must know the roles they are covering, and an opportunity for them to run the play from start to finish without interruption and so experience the way their roles develop throughout the play.

If you're the assistant you will have rehearsed the understudies yourself and the run will allow you to see how well you've achieved your task. It will also consolidate your relationship with the understudy company who will rely on you for feedback and continuing support.

If you're the director you should try to attend the understudy run. It is an occasion of great pride and accomplishment for the covers and you will grow in the esteem of your company if you take them seriously. It will also give you the opportunity to assess the true talents of actors you have only seen in subsidiary roles. An understudy run always provides pleasant surprises and will feed you with useful **casting** ideas for the future. It also provides an opportunity for discussing the career and ambitions of your assistant, who will feel that his talents, if not fully exploited, have at least had an airing worthy of your attention.

When only a few understudies cover a great variety of roles, the run can be a little problematical, not to say hilarious, with actors playing scenes with themselves or changing from one character to another in the blink of an eye. The fun will turn to frustration if an actor covering a leading role has also been required to chuck in a few minor ones. In this case you should allow the actor to play the whole play in the major role and let others read in the smaller parts.

In the best-regulated companies with the most generous leading actors, the principal players will attend the understudy run and help out wherever required. You should encourage them to do this, though no principal actor should be forced to attend. Some of them may find the sight of another actor playing their part too frightening to contemplate.

Everyone in the company should at least be invited, not just the actors but the staff as well, the backstage crew, wardrobe and wigs – even the box office staff. The more of an occasion it becomes the higher the stakes will be and the more like a proper performance, giving the covers a real sense of what it would be like to perform to a paying public.

Understudy runs can serve to bind an ensemble more tightly together. The best of them are talked of years later, especially when they have involved an embryonic star in his first major leading role.

Unions

In Britain, Europe and America, the theatre industry is comprehensively unionised. The working hours and pay levels of actors, stage management, musicians and crew are contractually defined by agreements between unions, Theatre Managers and producers. Some very small or semi-professional companies may manage to fly beneath union radar, but they are few and far between. If you work as a director you have to accept that your working conditions are regulated by union agreement.

Union rules can be extremely complicated. Different rules apply to different classes of theatre. There are rules for different sorts of **workshop**, for readings, for **technical rehearsals**, for **touring**.

Different classes of performer get different treatment, and any of the rules might change from one year to the next to take account of changing practice. You need to be a real expert to understand them fully and unless you're a total sucker for punishment, you'll leave the detail to others. They are one of the main reasons why directors need producers, administrators and general managers.

Union rules can drive you crazy. You have to break for lunch before two, you can't go on past six, you have to have an eleven-hour break at night, you're not allowed to move that chair or touch that light, you need a minimum of eight musicians in that pit, your show runs more than three hours so everyone gets double overtime, and so on and on. But however crazy they make you, don't fight the unions. It's a complete waste of time. You can spend hours arguing the toss about some rule you don't like and it will make no difference. Much better to know what's expected of you, work the rules to your best advantage and gracefully toe the line.

EQUITY DEPS

In Britain and America, a company of actors will elect an Equity (the actors' and Stage Managers' union) Deputy at the beginning of the rehearsal period. This is an Equity member, usually an actor, deputed to represent his colleagues in union matters and communicate with the union office in the event of any problems. Equity 'deps' can be mild or militant depending on the personality, but you shouldn't have any need to discuss the rules or working conditions with them directly. If they have a problem they will go to the Stage Manager in the first instance and the Stage Manager will come to you.

FOLLOWING THE RULES

Stage Managers know the rules. It's part of their job. They will know how to protect you from unreasonable militancy but they will also be firm in applying the rules. Enlist their help in understanding them and, where possible, gently reinterpreting them. If a minor rule is completely daft and no one likes it, you might get away with bending it a little but even with silly rules, be prepared for a backlash if you infringe them consistently.

Don't try to enlist your actors' sympathy in breaking a rule you don't like or imagine you've got it when you haven't. They may pretend to agree with you in finding something frustrating but will privately think otherwise. Actors don't like disagreeing with directors publicly and object to being put in the position of having their loyalties tested.

In most cases union rules exist to protect members from exploitation or abusive practice and to safeguard the jobs of other, unemployed, members. Theatre is an irregular, unpredictable and often emotional business. Without rules of employment, theatre workers would be constantly overstretched and exploited – all in the name of art, or the perfectionism that art inspires in its practitioners. With them, theatre workers are able to command decent, or at least not indecent, levels of pay and reasonable conditions of employment including a safe working environment, time to spend with their families and even holidays.

In the application of union rules, you will be perceived as part of the problem. In the minds of union members, directors count as bosses along with producers and administrators, even if they belong to unions themselves.

Directors can behave badly. They beg for extra hours and, wittingly or not, try to blackmail their casts into breaking the rules. Don't be one of these. Have some respect for the agreements that give your fellow workers some dignity of employment.

Join a union yourself. In any case, you may be obliged to. In some territories, your employment will depend on union membership and some small proportion of your fee or royalties will be payable to the union in exchange for employment protection and insurance and pension benefits. But you should join without being obliged. Directors' unions were founded by erstwhile colleagues who fought hard for the agreements and benefits from which you now derive your living. Honour their efforts on your behalf and gladly join their ranks.

Upstage

A common directorial **stage direction**. Also the site of a common acting crime, for a description of which see **Upstaging** below.

Upstaging

Upstaging occurs when an actor, either deliberately or accidentally, moves upstage of a fellow actor or actors, forcing them to play with their backs to the audience, to the detriment of the speaking actor's performance and the focus of the established **staging**.

Accidental upstaging is caused by incompetence or carelessness and is easily remedied by gently pointing out the infringement to the culprit. Deliberate upstaging is a much trickier problem, as it can be tactically deployed by an actor intent on hogging the audience's attention or stealing it from a fellow actor. Flagrant examples are easy enough to spot, but a skilful perpetrator can be very subtle and thereby all the more infuriating to a colleague.

Dealing with upstaging problems can be ticklish as no actor likes to be accused of professional incompetence or discourtesy, let alone wilful self-aggrandisement. You must therefore be diplomatic, whatever the circumstances, though some chronic upstagers will prove intractable, especially those who believe it is their right to be centre stage surrounded by a cast of 'supporting' actors.

Most upstaging problems are caused by over-static positioning of characters on the stage. If a group of actors stay in the same relative positions for a long period of time then one or other of them is bound to feel upstaged at some point in the action. The best solutions are usually found in greater fluency of character movement within the general staging. If no actor is allowed to settle for too long in any one position, he will become far more aware of the importance of the other actors around him.

In a naturalistic play the solution to an upstaging problem may not be with the actors but with the furniture. Sometimes the slight adjustment of a bench or the re-angling of a chair will release an actor into a new position previously unavailable to him and bring another actor's face into focus.

The most potent antidote to upstaging is generosity. A company of actors who have been inspired to care for one another and for the play they are performing will be all too aware if one of them is being disadvantaged or overlooked on stage and will reform themselves accordingly.

V

Verbatim Plays

A verbatim play is a play entirely made up from the accurately recorded dialogue, observations or memories of real people. The authors of verbatim plays use their own artistic judgements to select, edit and interweave the material they collect from their subjects, but they never make up material of their own to suit a preconceived artistic idea.

Verbatim plays often start with a political or social issue – childhood poverty for instance, or the effects of Alzheimer's disease or war in the Middle East. Having researched the subject, the writer will then go to the human subjects affected by the issue and garner the dialogue or views of the possible protagonists, weaving the resulting material into a coherent drama.

Verfremdungseffekt

The verfremdungseffekt is the 'distancing' or **alienation** effect proposed by Bertolt Brecht and deployed in a variety of ways in his Epic Theatre.

Verse and Verse Speaking

Verse is language arranged in measured lines, in contrast to prose, which is the ordinary form of written or spoken language. The writing of verse is governed by the rules of prosody, which define how the verse is structured according to its length of line and rhythm, or **metre**.

From the Greek theatre onwards playwrights have written their tragedies in verse and their comedies in prose, but by no means exclusively so. In English drama from the Middle Ages through to the Restoration there are plenty of comedies written wholly or partly in verse and some tragedies written partly in prose, though very few entirely in prose. Many of the most popular writers from that period, Shakespeare included, use a mixture of verse and prose in their work. In tragedies verse tends to dominate, prose being used for the more comic or domestic scenes, while in comedies prose tends to dominate, verse being used for when the characters are being romantic or fanciful or where the rhythm of the verse helps to delineate the comic invention or propel the onward drive of the story. From the eighteenth century onwards verse started to disappear as a vehicle for both comedy and tragedy, and though there have been valiant attempts since then to revive it for dramatic usage, the overwhelmingly predominant form for plays of all descriptions is now prose.

The writers of verse plays knew the rules of prosody governing their craft, so you must learn them too if you are to understand how the verse is structured and therefore how your actors should speak it.

15 BASIC RULES FOR SPEAKING VERSE

1. Every line of verse has a rhythmic structure or **metre**. When the scansion of the line is correctly observed, it will sound right and it will yield up its meaning.
2. In iambic pentameters, or blank verse, there are five feet to a line but usually only four possible stresses. If the actor evenly stresses all five feet, the verse becomes monotonous. If he stresses fewer than four, he's probably missing something.
3. The actor should maintain his vocal energy through each line of verse, not dropping in pitch or volume at the end of the line.
4. The last word of each line of verse is nearly always important in terms of rhythm and meaning. Give it full value and use it as a springboard for the first word in the next line.
5. There are no **pauses** in verse drama unless they are clearly indicated by the structure of the metre. Pausing breaks up the rhythm and clouds the meaning of the line.

6. Just as one line feeds rhythmically into the next, so it is with speeches. At the beginning of a new speech the actor should come in on cue, with no pause for thought. His thought should be generated as the previous character is speaking or in the split second before his speech begins.

7. There should be a minimal pause between one scene and the next if there is to be a pause at all. Think of the verse play as a single poem with its scenes as different stanzas. The overall rhythm of the poem is crucial to its effect. This will be damaged if you break it up with long **scene changes** or other interpolated business.

8. If there are prose scenes in your verse play, don't let the freedom of the rhythm in those scenes interfere with the rhythm of the rest of the play.

9. Think of the verse as having no **subtext**. All the thoughts the actors need for the motivation of their characters are to be found on the text. If the thought isn't on the text it probably isn't worth exploring.

10. Actors should use the full complexity of the verse for the exploration of their characters. They should think of the poetic devices in the text as being invented by the characters as they are speaking. In other words, in verse drama all the characters are poets.

11. Actors must not generalise their emotions. They must look for the particular word or series of words that evoke the emotion and express the emotion with the word. Generalised emotion is an enemy to meaning and therefore also to comprehension.

12. Verse is not naturalistic dialogue and cannot be spoken as such. The inflections of modern naturalistic speech do not make the verse more accessible, they make it sound like the actor is apologising for the verse.

13. Verse is not spoken **lyric**. Declaiming or singing the verse is as bad as mumbling it. The more euphonious the verse, the more the actors will have to be dissuaded from elevating its sound over its meaning.

14. Rhymes and internal rhymes should be fully observed as part of the characters' expressiveness. Actors who swallow their rhymes are missing an opportunity for the communication of meaning and feeling.

15. Actors must listen to themselves and to their fellow actors as they speak their verse. Listening is a crucial part of verse speaking. A musician who cannot listen cannot play in tune. So it is with a speaker of verse. If he hears the meaning and the music in his words as he speaks them, the audience will hear them too.

In order fully to understand the importance of these rules, you and your actors must study the rules of scansion (see **Metre**), which govern the technique or craft of the poet, and you must acquaint yourselves with the particular modes of expression and inventiveness that govern your poet's choice of words, images and form.

THE POET'S MIND

The language in a verse play should sound like the natural mode of expression for its characters. To make this possible, your actors must learn to think as their characters speak. But in a verse play the characters speak in **heightened language**, using images, similes, metaphors and other poetic devices not associated with normal everyday conversation, so the actors must learn to think in those same images. To help them understand how to do this, encourage them to examine every line, every image, in their text before they commit to an interpretation and its accompanying inflections.

Why has the author chosen those particular words and not others to express what his characters are thinking? Why has he chosen to structure the speech of a character the way he has? What has inspired his choice of metre? How does metre affect meaning, feeling and atmosphere? What are the prevailing images and how do they relate to the images in the rest of the play?

If we examine a short passage in some detail you will get a good idea of how the poet's mind works and therefore how complex the thoughts of the character and the actor must be.

Take these three lines from Juliet's speech at the beginning of Act III Scene 2 of *Romeo and Juliet*:

Come night, come Romeo, come thou day in night
For thou wilt lie upon the wings of night

Whiter than new snow on a raven's back.

Start by scanning them. The terms referred to here are fully explained in the **Metre** entry.

Cóme níght, / cóme Ró- / meo, cóme / thou dáy / in níght
For thóu / wilt líe / up'on / the wíngs / of níght
Whít'er / than néw / snów on / a ráv- / en's báck.

They scan as:

Spondee / Spondee / Iamb / Spondee / Iamb
Iamb / Iamb / Pyrrhic / Iamb / Iamb
Trochee / Iamb / Trochee / Iamb / Iamb

The three spondees in the first line are very unusual. Seven stresses in a single line give it a highly emphatic and commanding tone.

The second line is a regular iambic pentameter, with a neutral pyrrhic at the third foot to give it shape.

The pair of trochees balanced either side of an iamb in the third line helps the actor to observe the five stresses on 'white', 'new', 'snow', 'raven' and 'back' without the line becoming jerky, as it would be if it were written:

As whíte / as néw / snów on / a ráv- / en's báck

Having scanned the lines, you can go on to analyse their meaning and notice how the scansion helps the character say what she wants to say.

The speech is a **soliloquy** that starts sixteen lines earlier with Juliet talking to the sun, urging it to move across the sky quickly so that night will come to take the place of day. Having secretly married Romeo earlier that day, the coming night will be her wedding night.

In the first of our three lines she now talks to the night, commanding it, or willing it, to arrive and commanding, or willing, Romeo to arrive with it. She then personifies Romeo as the day, coming to her in the night.

In the second line she creates an image drawn from the idea of Romeo being the day. As night flies towards her, Romeo will be lying on its wings.

Verse and Verse Speaking

In the third line she intensifies her own invention. Romeo, bringing with him the light of day, will be white in contrast to the darkness of the night upon whose wings he rides. But how white will he be? Not just whiter than snow, which is white enough, one might think. No, he will be whiter than *new* snow. And to intensify the whiteness of the new snow even further, Juliet changes her image. The wings of night become the wings, or the back, of a great black bird, the raven. Nothing could be purer and whiter than new snow, nor anything more black and ominous than the raven.

In the fever of her excitement, Juliet doesn't consider that no self-respecting raven would let snow, new or otherwise, settle on its back. And an audience won't consider it either if the actress playing Juliet has woven her spell over their imaginations. What we understand her to mean is that she thinks Romeo is the personification of light and goodness in contrast to the darkness and danger of the night to come.

But these three lines also hold for Juliet a terrible dramatic irony. Her marriage to Romeo does prove to be ominous for both of them and we, the audience, already know what Juliet has yet to discover. Indeed, every other character in the play knows it before Juliet knows it. Romeo has killed her cousin Tybalt and has been banished for his crime. If she sees him tonight it could be for the last time.

The actress playing Juliet must understand all this and more about these three lines. She must also discover how the words and images in them relate to her other speeches and to the speeches of the other characters in the rest of play.

Later in the same scene the Nurse tells her that Romeo has killed Tybalt. In her grief, anger and confusion she calls Romeo

> Beautiful tyrant, fiend angelical!
> Dove-feather'd raven, wolvish-ravening lamb!

There's the raven again, but this time Romeo is the raven, dove-feathered because she loves him, but a raven all the same.

There are five other 'wing' references in the play. Cupid's wings are mentioned twice, once by Mercutio and once by Juliet. Mercutio also tells us that the cover of Queen Mab's coach is made of the wings of grasshoppers. And Romeo compares Juliet to an angel, or 'wingèd messenger of heaven', before telling her that he flew over her orchard wall with 'love's light wings'.

'Night' is mentioned three times in Juliet's three lines above and eight more times in the soliloquy as a whole. Eleven mentions of the same word in a speech of only thirty-one lines is an evocative statistic. And there are some sixty other references to 'night' in *Romeo and Juliet*, more than in any other Shakespeare play. Compare that, for instance, with five in *As You Like It* and seven in *The Tempest*.

The play is riddled with references to day and night and to images that connect with them: light and dark, sun, moon and stars, fire and torches, heaven and hell. If Shakespeare was preoccupied with these images while he was writing the play, his characters must also be preoccupied with them while living in it and so you and your actors preoccupied with them in rehearsal and performance.

The three lines analysed above are by no means exceptional for Shakespeare. Almost every line he wrote comes in the form of a dense package of rhythm, sound and meaning.

And so it is with all good writers of verse drama. Marlowe, Jonson, Webster, Ford, Middleton, Massinger, Marston, Beaumont and Fletcher, Tourneur, Dryden, Eliot, Auden, all in their own styles, the great and the not so great, deliver their characters to the actor in like poetic form. And if your actors are fully aware of the linguistic complexity of the verse they are performing and manage to convey it through their characters, your audiences will hear these plays in all their poetic richness.

ANTITHESIS

Antithesis is one of the principal forms of Shakespeare's linguistic structure and certainly the one most useful for actors to exploit.

An antithesis occurs when two or more opposing or contrasting words or ideas are used in the same sentence or in contiguous sentences.

Verse and Verse Speaking

Shakespeare relied on antithesis more than he did on any other poetic device; indeed, his very thoughts must have been antithetical for him to have so depended on it, so if you want to direct one of his plays you must learn to spot antithesis wherever it occurs. If you allow your actors to ignore the antithetical structure of the language, the lines they speak will be unintelligible to the audience – but if they use the antitheses for all they are worth, the language springs off the page and an audience responds with a commensurate understanding.

Examples are everywhere in Shakespeare's text – stick a pin into any page of the complete works and you won't be more than a line or two from an example of antithetical writing.

Here is a classic example, actually in prose rather than verse, from Act III Scene 2 of *Julius Caesar*. It is a formal antithesis perfectly balanced and rhetorically contradictory:

Not that I loved Caesar less, but that I loved Rome more.

'Caesar' is balanced with 'Rome', 'less' with 'more', and 'Not that I loved' with 'but that I loved.'

Wherever you find a word balanced with or contrasted against another word in the same line or an adjacent line, there you will find antithetical thinking at work. Look at this from the Prologue of *Romeo and Juliet*:

> From forth the fatal loins of these two foes
> A pair of star-crossed lovers take their life

'Fatal' is contrasted with 'life', 'lovers' with 'foes', and 'two' with 'a pair'.

Or this more complicated set from *Twelfth Night*:

> Make me a willow cabin at your gate
> And call upon my soul within the house
> Write loyal cantons of contemnéd love
> And sing them loud even in the dead of night.

Here Viola contrasts 'willow cabin' with 'house', 'loyal' with 'contemnéd' and 'sing them loud' with 'dead of night'. The vocative verbs at the beginning of each line: 'make', 'call', 'write' and 'sing' are contrasted with each other but also balanced with the end words of each line: 'gate', 'house', 'love' and 'night'. Thus: 'make ... gate', 'call ... house', 'write ... love', 'sing ... night'.

Awareness of antithesis is essential for an understanding of how Shakespeare's characters think, and your ability to communicate its importance to your actors will largely define their success in speaking his verse.

SONNETS AND SONNET CLASSES

If you are directing a Shakespeare play and there are actors in your cast with limited experience of verse speaking, the Sonnets can be used as an excellent teaching resource.

There are 153 of them, all rich in imagery and full of the poetic device and metric variety characteristic of the verse in his earlier plays. Nearly all of them are about love, and the joy, pain, frustration and confusion that attend it. Some of them are addressed to a man and some to a woman but most could be addressed to either, and despite all of them being written by a man, they can all be spoken just as well by a woman as by a man, making them perfect exercises for mixed companies or classes of actors or students.

Each sonnet consists of fourteen lines, made up of three quatrains and a couplet with the rhyming scheme a-b-a-b, c-d-c-d, e-f-e-f, g-g. Generally, the first quatrain sets up the situation, the second develops it, and the third concludes the story, with the final couplet forming a surprise twist or an encapsulation of the poem's motive or meaning.

The reason they make for such good teaching exercises is that you can think of each sonnet as being like a little monologue, and the actor speaking it playing a character in a one-person Shakespeare play. And the Sonnets are amazingly responsive to different emotional and intellectual interpretations. Packed with feeling, they give the actor any number of choices at the turn of every line, but unlike speeches and soliloquies taken from the plays, they are untrammelled by traditional associations of plot and character, so they can be approached without preconception.

Verse and Verse Speaking

Let's look at an example. This is Sonnet No. 2:

When forty winters shall besiege thy brow
And dig deep trenches in thy beauty's field,
Thy youth's proud livery, so gazed on now,
Will be a tattered weed of small worth held.
Then being asked where all thy beauty lies
Where all the treasure of thy lusty days,
To say within thine own deep-sunken eyes
Were an all-eating shame and thriftless praise.
How much more praise deserved thy beauty's use
If thou could'st answer 'This fair child of mine
Shall sum my count, and make my old excuse',
Proving his beauty by succession thine.
This were to be new made when thou art old,
And see thy blood warm when thou feel'st it cold.

It is clear what this sonnet is about. It seeks to persuade the person to whom it is addressed that he, or she, should get over his, or her, personal vanity and have a child, that being the only way to insure against the physical depredations of old age.

But what is the context of the poem? Who is talking to whom? This is where you have considerable latitude.

Once you forget it was written by a man in his late twenties or early thirties, probably to another man, it can be spoken by almost anyone. It could be a man talking to a man, a woman to a woman, a man to a woman or a woman to a man. It could be an older person talking to a younger or vice versa, or young to young, or old to old.

It could be delivered as a seduction speech, or a cool personal appraisal or a bitter recrimination or in a dozen other ways, angry, persuasive, passionate or amused.

Let the actor choose.

Involve the whole company in the exercise, whatever their different levels of experience with verse speaking. Print out twenty or thirty of the Sonnets, several copies of each. Give the actors fifteen minutes or so to look through them and decide which one they want to work on. It doesn't matter if two actors choose the same one. Their different interpretations will help you when it comes to analysing the verse. Some actors may know the Sonnets well. If this is the case, encourage them to choose one they don't know at all, so that every member of the company is covering some new ground.

Give your actors half an hour or so to prepare their sonnets on their own; to scan them as best they can, understand their meaning and decide how to deliver them. But patrol the room dispensing advice where necessary. Then get the whole company sitting in a circle and have the actors read their sonnets one by one. After each reading, the other actors should contribute to analysing the sonnet they have just heard. Let them do as much of the work as possible, talking about the meaning of the poem, where the scansion seems problematical or the imagery obscure.

Leave no stone unturned as you analyse the verse. Here's a checklist of things to cover. Details refer to Sonnet 2 above.

1 Structure

Look at the fourteen-line structure and see how the poem and its meaning break up into three fours and a two.

2 Metre

Scan the poem. Notice how the iambic rhythm predominates and where the irregular feet fall. In Sonnet 2 you have a strong spondee in the second foot of the second line, making 'dig deep trenches' a powerful image, an unusual first foot pyrrhic in line eight followed by a strong spondee for 'all-eating', and an unusual number of lines with five necessary stresses in them at lines 2, 3, 4, 7, 8, 10 and 14.

3 Rhyming scheme

See how the last words of each line define the poem as a whole. Get the reader of the sonnet to speak the last words slowly, one by one. In this case: 'brow', 'field', 'now', 'held'; 'lies', 'days', 'eyes', 'praise'; 'use', 'mine', 'excuse', 'thine'; 'old', 'cold'. These words are the poem in miniature. And a perfect illustration of how rhyme and meaning are connected.

Verse and Verse Speaking

4 Internal rhyme

There isn't so much in this sonnet – perhaps 'brow', 'proud' and 'now', 'days' and 'say'. Some of the sonnets have a lot of internal rhyme.

5 Repetition

Look for repetitions of important words or phrases and how they relate to one another. In this poem 'beauty' is repeated four times, 'praise' and 'old' twice, and you have 'deep' and 'deep-sunken'.

6 Association

Look for words and phrases that are associated in meaning. There are the old-age images: 'forty winters', 'old', 'tattered', 'deep-sunken', 'thriftless', 'cold'. And the youth and beauty images: 'beauty', 'youth', 'lusty', 'fair', 'child', 'succession', 'new'. There are words associated with warfare: 'besiege' and 'trenches'. With worth or value: 'livery', 'small worth', 'treasure', 'thriftless', 'sum', 'count'. There are winter images: 'forty winters', 'cold', 'deep trenches' in a 'field', and there are words associated with sight: 'gazed on', 'eyes', 'see'. And so on.

7 Imagery

Look for the larger images that are suggested by the imagistic words: the once youthful brow furrowed with deep trenches, the treasure of youthful beauty deeply buried in the eye sockets, the warmth and pleasure enjoyed by an old person observing a child. And so on.

8 Alliteration

Here there is 'besiege thy brow', 'dig deep trenches', and 'will', 'weed' and 'worth' all in the same line.

9 Antithesis

Look for instances of the poet placing a word against another word of contrary meaning. Here you have 'forty winters' and 'youth', 'proud livery' and 'tattered weed', and so on through the poem right up to the last line where you have 'see' and 'warm' put against 'feel' and 'cold'.

10 Motive and tone

Why did the poet write the poem the way he did? To whom was it addressed and what might be the poet's relationship to him or to her? What might be the reader's relationship to the listener? What does the emotional temperature of the poem seem to be? What other interpretations could you bring to it?

Once the poem has been thoroughly discussed, the actor should read it again before you move on to the next sonnet so that the rest of the company can listen with fresh ears to the verse they have helped to analyse.

If you are working in this sort of detail, you won't have time to analyse more than three or four sonnets in a session unless your class takes up a whole day. Better anyway to spread sonnet classes over a number of days, or even weeks, so that the actors' understanding can develop alongside any other work you may be doing.

If sonnet classes are part of your rehearsal process for a Shakespeare play, they are a very good way of starting the day, or kick-starting rehearsals after a lunch break.

There are other ways you can play with the Sonnets. Get two or three actors to perform a sonnet together, breaking the lines up into speeches by individual characters, making a little play. Or get two or three actors to make a play out of two or three different sonnets, each actor using a complete sonnet to create a character in conflict with the other sonnet-characters. Or have the actors speak a sonnet, line by line in a circle, each actor responsible for passing on the rhythm and the meaning to the next actor.

However you use them, the more your actors immerse themselves in the complex language and imagery of the Sonnets the better prepared they will be to use the same language in the plays.

Versions

See **Translations**.

Visiting Directors

A Visiting Director is one employed to direct a play for a permanently established, usually subsidised, theatre company. The company may have an **Artistic Director** and **Associate Directors** but still be in need of the occasional Visiting Director to supplement the permanent staff. Visiting Directors are paid on a single-fee basis.

Voice and Text

Actors are taught to use their voices at drama school. They are trained in breathing, **diction** and **projection**. They sing. They learn to connect their vocal technique to the texts they speak and the characters they play. But the quality of drama-school training is variable, as is the aptitude and talent of actors. Whenever you gather a group of actors together to rehearse a play you will find some of them have greater vocal gifts than others, and some of them will be more proficient or more in practice than others when it comes to speaking text. If your play uses **heightened language** this disparity will seem especially marked. Part of your job as director is to unify your company's approach to text and demand the highest possible level of vocal proficiency from all of them. This takes practice.

Start your rehearsal day with a physical and vocal **warm-up**. Give your actors breathing and vocal exercises to improve their diction and fluency. Play vocal and word **games**. Use **tongue twisters**. If you're not good at leading such exercises, nominate someone in the company to lead, or rotate the leadership to keep the exercises fresh and engaging. Your company will soon decide what suits them best.

You may be working for a company that has a voice and text expert on tap. If so, take full advantage of the luxury. If your company doesn't employ such a person and you really think your production would benefit from some in-depth voice and text work, persuade your producers to bring someone in. If your play is a poetic text and your actors not quite up to snuff with the language, voice and text work is not a luxury but a necessity.

Vomitorium

Vomitoria are the concealed passageways under the seats of an **arena** theatre from which the audience is spewed at the end of a performance. They may also be places where actors stand feeling queasy just before they make an entrance into an arena theatre, but they derive their name from the former rather than the latter usage.

Wardrobe

Wardrobe Masters and Mistresses, or Supervisors as they are now sometimes called, are important folk in the theatre, and grow more important the longer a run continues and the **Costume Designer** makes fewer and fewer visits to the actors.

Good Wardrobe Supervisors have a talent for psychotherapy as well as stitching. Actors' insecurities are nowhere more evident than when they are worrying about their costumes, wigs or make-up. An undiplomatic Supervisor can undermine an actor's confidence in the run-up to an opening. A sympathetic one will calm everyone down and be a source of stability.

You may at times find yourself in a tricky dialogue over an actor or actress's appearance, with actor and Costume Designer in conflict. A calm word from the Wardrobe Supervisor can help to defuse an explosive mixture of artistic temperaments.

Make friends with them. Along with the **Company Manager** they are often the most reliable source of backstage gossip. Actors will discuss things with the wardrobe or wig staff that they wouldn't tell one another, and the Wardrobe Mistress gets told everything in the long periods of idle time during the run of a show.

Warm-Ups

Actors need to be in shape, physically, vocally and mentally, to do their jobs well. Some will always be in better shape than others. Warm-ups are equalisers. At the start of a rehearsal session or before a performance they get everyone ticking over at the same rate, blood flowing faster, breathing deeper and minds more alert. You can use them as a daily routine and/or in combination with theatre **games** and **improvisation**.

Warm-ups are a good idea anyway, but if your production makes unusual physical or vocal demands on your actors, they are essential. Any play that has dances, fights or choreographed physical movement needs a physical warm-up. Any play that has songs or **heightened language** needs a vocal warm-up. They are an essential feature of most **musical theatre** rehearsals.

Use the first half-hour of your day. Don't lead the warm-ups yourself unless you're a real expert. If you're doing a musical, your choreographer and Musical Director will take the lead or have assistants do it for them. If they don't like doing them, choose someone in your company. Someone physically fit and motivated should lead the physical warm-up. If one of your actors is good at it, let him lead, but make sure the other actors are enjoying the experience. Or you can rotate the leadership, using different actors for different days. Different leaders will have different routines, using music tapes, or based on yoga, ballet or Pilates. If you have a **voice and text** person attached to your theatre, get him to take your vocal warm-ups. He can then assess the actors for any further private work they might need.

Once your play is up and running, talk to the actors about keeping warm-ups going as a pre-show routine. You can make them obligatory – and you may have to for fights, dances and close choral work – or voluntary. Either way, you'll have to arrange with stage management and crew to have the stage available half an hour or so before the half.

West End

The historic West End of London is the central area of the city west of Charing Cross and Regent Street, including Mayfair and Knightsbridge but stopping short at Pimlico and Chelsea. By inference it comprises the theatres of the area, although most of them are actually not in the West End at all, but rather to the east of it.

There are some forty-five West End theatres, varying in size from 300 to 2,500 seats and in age from two hundred years old to a mere thirty-five. They include the National Theatre with its three houses and the two opera houses, Covent Garden and the London Coliseum. Most of them were built in the late nineteenth or early twentieth centuries and comprise some of the most beautiful and actor-friendly theatres in the world.

The term West End also denotes, somewhat pejoratively perhaps, a type of play and the sort of audience that might want to go and see it. When people talk about a play being a 'West End play', they mean it has been written to please an audience without involving too much of an intellectual challenge and therefore, supposedly, having a good chance of commercial success. By implication this definition excludes any play that is dark, troublesome or that deals with difficult ideas. In fact, this type of play is just as likely to succeed in the West End as any other, so the definition has lost most of its meaning.

The West End is the theatrical Mecca of the English-speaking world. You could spend a month going to the theatre there every day and still not see everything it has to offer. Throw in the fringe and the work would be impossible to keep up with. So much so that the major national newspapers need more than one critic each in order to cover all the openings. If ever you need your artistic batteries recharging, spend a week in the West End. The range of work, if you include the fringe and the outer London theatres, is quite astounding. Shakespeare, classic plays, new plays, translations, musicals, opera, ballet, physical theatre, mime, circus and children's theatre all coexist in a thriving, competitive and endlessly imaginative community with some new surprise waiting round every corner. People come from all over the world to warm their hands, hearts and minds at it. If you're lucky enough to live near it, never take it for granted. If you live far away from it, visit as often as you can.

Wigs

See **Hair and Make-up.**

Word Run

See **Line Readings**.

Working Lights

The working lights ('workers' for short, 'worklights' in the US) are the stage lights used by the technical departments during the normal theatre working day. They usually consist of small white floodlights over the stage area and neon light on the fly floors and in the grid. They provide just enough light for technical work but rarely enough for rehearsal or audition.

If you find yourself rehearsing or auditioning on stage, you should always remember to request supplementary light from whatever instruments are hanging on stage or front of house. Rehearsing in working light can get very depressing as the low intensity light tends to grey everything out and after a couple of hours concentration levels start to fall.

Working lights must always be switched off for **technical rehearsals** and performances as they will otherwise illuminate all the parts of the stage you least want to see. At this point the Stage Manager will call out the rather disconcerting command, 'Stand by to kill the workers.' The warning is necessary because some member of the crew might be working in a dangerous place on fly floor or grid and will need to get safe before being plunged into darkness, but if no protests are heard, the Stage Manager shouts, 'Workers going out,' and out they go. The offstage working lights are replaced at this point by low-level incandescent light, usually masked with blue gel, but only in places where light is absolutely essential for the efficient running of the show – the **prompt corner**, the **prop** tables and anywhere else where pitch darkness in the wings might be a danger to the performers. Spill from these lights is the **Lighting Designer's** bête noire – the equivalent of splashing inappropriate colours across an otherwise sombre canvas – so your Stage Manager and board operator between them will need to police any infringements. In some very dark backstage areas the stage management themselves can become the problem as they sometimes use small flashlights to light up **quick changes** or other necessary bits of offstage **business**. The spillage from these will also have to be policed but not by the Stage Manager, who will rarely be in a position to see them – this is rather a job for you or your assistant, if you have one.

Workshops

The word 'workshop' crops up all the time in the theatre world, as it does in many other art forms. It has no precise definition but three common usages. It appears in the titles of theatre companies that pride themselves on the experimental nature of their work; it is used to describe a type of educational seminar that concentrates more on practical participation than academic discourse; and it defines a process whereby a piece of theatre may be created, extensively rehearsed or otherwise worked on in order to prove its artistic worth or commercial value without resulting in a public performance.

As a director you may work in any or all of these categories of workshop during your career. Even if you don't involve yourself in the management of a workshop-style company, they are often good employers of outside directorial talent and you could find yourself attached to one for a while. As a student you will probably have taken part in educational workshops, and the more experience you get as a director the more likely it is you'll be asked to lead them. And it would be an extraordinary, or very unsuccessful, directorial career that never exposed you to the excitements and frustrations of a workshop rehearsal of one sort or another.

WORKSHOP COMPANIES

A theatre company may sport the word 'workshop' in its title and not be in the least bit innovative. To that extent the word may have lost some of the currency it had when Vladimir Mayakowsky, Max

Reinhardt or Joan Littlewood first used it to describe their struggles against the conventional, the privileged and the second-rate. One ought to be able to assume that any company choosing to call itself a workshop has somehow enshrined its artistic aspirations in the simple, practical world of the factory floor or the machine-shop, where plays, operas, musicals, actors and singers can all be examined and broken down and built up again as a way of revealing their fundamental structures and usefulness. In many ways this is a noble ideal, stemming as it does from an irritation with the arty pretensions of the avant-garde or the crass presumption of commercialism. In practice, however, the workers in the shop must beware of becoming the very thing they have rebelled against. Truly innovative work is very hard to create and even harder to sustain, and the attempt to create it will often end up in fruitless self-regard or introspection. If the work is successful and popular, the commercial vultures will soon start circling over it. Then the creators must decide what their 'workshop' is worth to them, how much they should charge for their wares, and whether copies of their works can ever be as valuable as the originals.

EDUCATIONAL WORKSHOPS

If the defining word in workshop companies is 'innovation', in educational workshops it should be 'participation'. Whatever the educational environment or the subject matter, a workshop should differ from a lecture, seminar or even **master-class** in this one regard.

People who attend workshops expect to become practically involved as well as intellectually stimulated, but in the hands of a thoughtless, verbose or lazy leader there is often little difference between a workshop and a lecture, with the participants obliged to become passive listeners. If you agree to lead a workshop you must arrive with a clear idea of what you want the participants to learn and a well-thought-out plan for letting them learn it empirically.

As far as subject matter goes, there are limitless possibilities, depending on the needs of the participants and your expertise as a director, but whether you are leading a Shakespeare workshop, or

Workshops

a Chekhov one, or a workshop on acting or directing or voice and text or musical theatre, there are some basic rules of engagement that will be common to most of them.

The best workshops are the best prepared for and the most specifically targeted for their participants. So:

1 State the aim

Make sure that the workshop is accurately described in its prior publicity. You don't want the participants to be in any confusion as to why they are there or how they are expected to behave.

2 Encourage preparation

If possible or relevant, ask the participants to prepare their own material in advance. They will arrive better focused for the day, week or fortnight, if they have something to offer and know they will get a chance to perform it or otherwise share it. If you are doing physical work, make sure the participants are suitably clothed in workout clothes and soft shoes.

3 Prepare materials

If you are using texts of any sort, have them carefully prepared in advance and make sure there are enough copies for all participants. If you want to leave your choice of texts open until the last minute, make sure you have ready access to copy machines and a willing gofer or two to gofer them. One of the most dispiriting phrases you will ever hear in a workshop is 'So – what shall we do while we're waiting for the copies to arrive?'

4 Make acquaintance

Introduce all the participants to one another – or better still, let them do it themselves. Nametags may be useful for ease of identification, but you learn a lot from hearing people identify themselves, however briefly. For workshops of a week or longer, you can let people describe themselves more fully, but always have a time limit. Some people are a little too fascinated by their own stories.

5 Use games

Whenever possible use theatre **games** and acting exercises to involve and stimulate the participants, to break down any barriers of class, age, gender or attitude, and to get people reacting physically and emotionally as well as intellectually.

6 Create groups

Encourage the participants to learn from one another as well as from you. Break up a large group into smaller ones and let them discover their own solutions and create their own social and artistic hierarchies without your intervention. There is nothing more exciting in a workshop than the concentrated atmosphere created by self-defining and highly motivated huddles.

7 Monitor yourself

Develop a keen ear for the sound of your own voice so you can sense when you're overdoing the chat. The tell-tale signs are the same as in a distracted theatre audience – shifting in seats, coughing, whispering, eye-rolling and surreptitious visits to the toilet. When you've been going on too long, remark on the fact and then shut up.

8 Keep it moving

Don't flog dead horses. If any subject seems fruitless or beyond the capacity of the participants, move on and start something new. Joyful abandonment is always preferable to barren resolution.

9 Listen to the participants

Their feedback will give you a good idea of how the workshop is going and may tell you how to develop it further. Establish the rule that there's no such thing as a stupid question. By answering one person's apparently naïve question, you may be answering the same silent question in other minds.

Workshops

10 Take breaks

The better and more concentrated the workshop, the more necessary the breaks – for mental rest, onward planning, food, drink and flirtation.

11 Be constructive

Avoid harsh or subjective judgements, from yourself or others. Participants of varying talents and temperament should all derive benefit from the workshop. No one should go away feeling small, got at or undervalued.

12 Be democratic

Don't let the workshop get hijacked by the vainest, loudest or most entertaining participants. Be ready to contain the wayward egotist and encourage the shy, humble and unassuming.

13 Be sociable

End with a social event, preferably away from the workshop space, or in the workshop space transformed. A trip to the pub, a meal or a party can help to seal what has been achieved and provide a good opportunity for networking. Even if nothing much has been achieved, then forging of friendships or partnerships may be achievements in themselves.

WORKSHOP REHEARSALS

There are many different forms of practical theatre workshop. Some types of theatre, such as **devised plays**, **verbatim plays** or **adaptations**, use workshops to initiate a writing or rehearsal process, deriving the characters of the drama from work done by the actors and then building a storyline to fit them.

Some playwrights derive their scripts from real political, social or historical events and work with a director and actors to explore the issues involved before starting on the writing process. Some already written plays have problems of structure or staging to which the author cannot find a solution in the privacy of his study.

In this case, a **play reading** may be a useful diagnostic device before the writer returns his wit to the grindstone, but sometimes a reading isn't enough.

The method of workshopping the material will differ widely depending on the artistic needs of the show, but the basic ingredients of a workshop are always more or less the same: an author or authors, a director, a group of actors, singers or dancers, a script or an idea for a script, and a large empty room. Other ingredients may be added to taste: specialist performers, expert advisers, artists from other disciplines and any technical equipment, costumes, props or other clobber necessary to your particular process.

There may be constraints on your time or working methods laid down by **union** legislation of one sort or another, and you should make yourself thoroughly conversant with them before you get going. Your producer or Stage Manager should be able to steer you through the small print.

Particularly in the field of **musical theatre** and particularly in America there are quite rigid rules governing workshops and readings, even to the extent of granting the participating actors in a workshop an ongoing authorial royalty for the work they do, should the piece go on to have a successful commercial life. But musical theatre workshops are also fraught with other dangers. Owing to the massive cost involved in mounting a musical, producers would rather spend a few thousand dollars or pounds on a workshop to prove the stage-worthiness of a show than millions on an ill-considered production that only manages to run a week. It's a perfectly understandable view – and any director who wants to get involved with musical theatre must first learn how to control the workshop process – but it brings with it the possibility of considerable artistic compromise. Decision-making in the musical theatre is in any event a complex business owing to the large number of **collaborators** involved. The workshop process adds an extra layer of artistic interest as **producers**, potential investors or **angels**, and theatre owners will all attend the workshop **presentations** and will all have a view about the strengths and weaknesses of the material. If you then conflate every view

Workshops

you receive from every interested party you end up with a daft hotchpotch of contradictory advice, passion and prejudice informed by a rich mixture of traditional and fashionable ignorance. Thus it is that a perfectly good musical theatre idea can get itself locked into 'workshop hell', endlessly recreating itself in a more and more fruitless process until the project is abandoned by its authors or its paymasters, or both, or until someone says, infuriatingly, 'You know, I really liked the original script. The show seems to have lost its way.' At which point, all the authors and director can do is to laugh hollowly and exit to pursue alternative employment.

Workshop rehearsals are too various in their demands and usefulness to be defined by a set of strict rules and there will always be a great deal of scope in them for individual directorial inspiration, enthusiasm and style. It may, however, be useful to précis the most obvious pitfalls.

So, when setting up a workshop, bear in mind the following:

1 Have an aim

Agree with your partners what you want your workshop to achieve and how to monitor your progress. Stay on the tracks you have laid for yourselves. Don't get derailed or diverted onto another track. If you do you'll probably end up in a siding.

2 Check restrictions

Research any union agreements binding you to a particular schedule or method of working. Are you sure that your work will thrive within the restrictions imposed on you?

3 Keep it relevant

Don't let the workshop become an end in itself. However pleasurable the work is, it must continue to relate to your long-term aims. The atmosphere of workshops can be exciting, peopled as they often are with quick, funny and gifted performers. Take what you want from your cast, but don't let them become the show, unless that was your intention in the first place.

4 *Don't rewrite*

Don't use the workshop period itself to write or rewrite the show. You will only do shoddy and ill-considered work that way. Once the workshop is over, do the writing or rewriting in tranquillity. And never allow writing by committee, or the author's voice will be drowned out by a Babel of conflicting attitudes and styles.

5 *Don't not write*

Don't use a workshop as an excuse for not writing the show in the first place. If a play is unfinished or badly thought out, then go away and write it, don't workshop it.

6 *Don't let it become a presentation*

Let the work be the most important thing you do, not the presentation of the work to others. Workshops should never be confused with **presentations**. A presentation often happens at the end of a workshop period, but preparing for it is rarely germane to the workshop process itself and is often harmful to its development or directly contradictory to its purpose.

7 *No sublimation*

Don't use a workshop to resolve a crisis of artistic partnership. You'll just be wasting everybody else's time. If you have artistic or personal problems with your co-authors, sort them out in private first, then finish the writing, then do the workshop.

8 *Don't get addicted*

Don't become a workshopaholic. Not all shows need workshops. Some just need to be rehearsed and performed and may be dis-improved by the inevitable collective bargaining of the workshop process.

ACTUAL WORKSHOPS

There are, of course, real, practical workshops in all theatre

companies. I mean the kind of workshop where wood is sawn, costumes sewn, steel welded, props made and paint applied to canvas.
The workers in these workshops should be forgiven a slight curl of
the lip when contemplating the efforts of the workshops described
above.

If you work in a permanent theatre company with workshops
like these attached to it, you should make it your business to visit
them on a regular basis. The workshop buildings are often some
distance from the theatre, and the people who work in them can
feel isolated. Your designer will be no stranger to them and neither
should you be. A friend or two in those quarters can be valuable
when you run into problems during the technical period.

See also **Adaptation**.

Work-Through

A work-through is a slow and thorough investigation of an entire
play in rehearsal, as opposed to a run-through, which is a non-stop
run of all the work that has been achieved, or a **stagger-through**,
which is a stopping run-through.

In working through a play the director and actors examine the
meaning of the text, motivate the characters and find appropriate
solutions for the **staging**.

X Y Z

I couldn't think of any entries for these letters.

The Xerox machine undoubtedly had a crucial influence on the development of fringe theatre in the 1960s but history has now passed it by. Youth Theatre is a fascinating subject but one about which I know too little to risk an entry. And there must be dozens of really good Zoroastrian theatre companies but I've never seen their work.

Instead I leave the following pages blank for you, my fellow directors, to make your own notes, your observations about the preceding entries or perhaps the outline of new and better ideas of your own.

If you fill them well, they could become the most important pages in the book.